꽃 Borders in East and West 꽃

MAKING SENSE OF HISTORY
Studies in Historical Cultures
General Editor: Stefan Berger
Founding Editor: Jörn Rüsen

Bridging the gap between historical theory and the study of historical memory, this series crosses the boundaries between both academic disciplines and cultural, social, political and historical contexts. In an age of rapid globalization, which tends to manifest itself on an economic and political level, locating the cultural practices involved in generating its underlying historical sense is an increasingly urgent task.

Recent volumes:

Volume 45
Borders in East and West: Transnational and Comparative Perspectives
Edited by Stefan Berger and Nobuya Hashimoto

Volume 44
Historical Reenactment: New Ways of Experiencing History
Edited by Mario Carretero, Brady Wagoner and Everardo Perez-Manjarrez

Volume 43
Dynamics of Emigration: Émigré Scholars and the Production of Historical Knowledge in the 20th Century
Edited by Stefan Berger and Philipp Müller

Volume 42
Transcending the Nostalgic: Landscapes of Postindustrial Europe beyond Representation
Edited by George S. Jaramillo and Juliane Tomann

Volume 41
Territory, State and Nation: The Geopolitics of Rudolf Kjellén
Edited by Ragnar Björk and Thomas Lundén

Volume 40
Analysing Historical Narratives: On Academic, Popular and Educational Framings of the Past
Edited by Stefan Berger, Nicola Brauch and Chris Lorenz

Volume 39
Postwar Soldiers: Historical Controversies and West German Democratization, 1945–1955
Jörg Echternkamp

Volume 38
Constructing Industrial Pasts: Heritage, Historical Culture and Identity in Regions Undergoing Structural Economic Transformation
Edited by Stefan Berger

Volume 37
The Engaged Historian: Perspectives on the Intersections of Politics, Activism and the Historical Profession
Edited by Stefan Berger

Volume 36
Contemplating Historical Consciousness: Notes from the Field
Edited by Anna Clark and Carla L. Peck

For a full volume listing, please see the series page on our website:
http://www.berghahnbooks.com/series/making-sense-of-history

BORDERS IN EAST AND WEST

Transnational and Comparative Perspectives

Edited by Stefan Berger and Nobuya Hashimoto

berghahn
NEW YORK • OXFORD
www.berghahnbooks.com

First published in 2022 by
Berghahn Books
www.berghahnbooks.com

© 2022, 2025 Stefan Berger and Nobuya Hashimoto
First paperback edition published in 2025

All rights reserved. Except for the quotation of short passages
for the purposes of criticism and review, no part of this book
may be reproduced in any form or by any means, electronic or
mechanical, including photocopying, recording, or any information
storage and retrieval system now known or to be invented,
without written permission of the publisher.

Library of Congress Cataloging-in-Publication Data
Names: Berger, Stefan, editor. | Hashimoto, Nobuya, 1959- editor.
Title: Borders in East and West : transnational and comparative
  perspectives / edited by Stefan Berger and Nobuya Hashimoto.
Description: [New York] : Berghahn Books, [2022] | Series: Making sense of
  history | Includes bibliographical references and index.
Identifiers: LCCN 2022019376 (print) | LCCN 2022019377 (ebook) | ISBN
  9781800736238 (hardback) | ISBN 9781800736245 (ebook)
Subjects: LCSH: Borderlands--Europe. | Borderlands--East Asia. | East and
  West. | Europe--Boundaries. | East Asia--Boundaries.
Classification: LCC JC323 .B646 2022 (print) | LCC JC323 (ebook) | DDC
  320.1/2--dc23/eng/20220727
LC record available at https://lccn.loc.gov/2022019376
LC ebook record available at https://lccn.loc.gov/2022019377

British Library Cataloguing in Publication Data
A catalogue record for this book is available from the British Library

ISBN 978-1-80073-623-8 hardback
ISBN 978-1-83695-050-9 paperback
ISBN 978-1-83695-165-0 epub
ISBN 978-1-80073-624-5 web pdf

https://doi.org/10.3167/9781800736238

Contents

List of Illustrations	viii
Preface *Nobuya Hashimoto*	x
Introduction. Border Experiences in East Asia and Europe: Some Theoretical and Conceptual Thoughts *Stefan Berger*	1
Part I. Economic Borders in the Chinese and Habsburg Empires during the Eighteenth and Nineteenth Centuries *Andrea Komlosy and Kwangmin Kim*	21
Chapter 1. Xinjiang and the Peripheral Pattern of Economic Development in Qing China *Kwangmin Kim*	31
Chapter 2. Habsburg Borderlands: A Comparative Perspective *Andrea Komlosy*	49
Part II. Tourism and Borderlands *Shizue Osa and Małgorzata Głowacka-Grajper*	69
Chapter 3. Travelling *Jokoshi* Students: Construction of the 'Imperial Gaze' through Colonial Tourism during War *Shizue Osa*	73
Chapter 4. Borderlands Tourism as a Memory Practice: A Case Study of the 'Kresy' (The Former Polish Eastern Borderlands) *Małgorzata Głowacka-Grajper*	95

Part III. Borders and Migration: A Comparison between Water and Land   123
Nobuya Hashimoto

Chapter 5. Crossing the Water Border: Migrations and the Japanese Imperial Seaway between Taiwan and the Yaeyama Islands   127
Hiroko Matsuda

Chapter 6. A Border Town and Migration: The Case of Narva and Russian Speakers in Estonia   142
Nobuya Hashimoto and Hiromi Komori

Part IV. Borders and Food Classification   169
Loretta Kim and Ilaria Porciani

Chapter 7. The Way We Eat: Evolving Taxonomies of Non-Han Food Customs in North-Eastern China   171
Loretta Kim

Glossary   186

Chapter 8. Imagined Communities and Communities of Practice: Participation, Territory and the Making of Food Heritage in Istria   196
Ilaria Porciani

Part V. Gazing at and Defining People in the Borderland   217
Takahiro Yamamoto and Takehiro Okabe

Chapter 9. The Japanese Gaze and the Memory of the Kuril Ainu   219
Takahiro Yamamoto

Chapter 10. From Finnic to Soviet Family: Finnic Kinship and Borders in the Soviet–Finnish Controversy over the *Kalevala* from the Mid-Nineteenth Century to the 1940s   242
Takehiro Okabe

Part VI. Migration and Interethnic Conflict at China's Edge   263
Seonmin Kim and Balázs Szalontai

Chapter 11. Environmental Relations in the Yalu River Region in the Nineteenth Century   267
Seonmin Kim

Glossary   279

Chapter 12. Smallfolk in a Clash of Empires: Sino-Mongolian Relations and the Ethnic Chinese Community in the Tsedenbal Era, 1960–84 283
Balázs Szalontai

Part VII. Geopolitical Rivalries in Russia's Far North and Far East 319
Elena I. Campbell and Zhao Xin

Chapter 13. Russia's Expansions towards the Amur River and Westerners' Corresponding Explorations in Early Modern Times 325
Zhao Xin

Chapter 14. 'Land of Bounty': Constructing the Russian North as a National Treasure 347
Elena I. Campbell

Conclusion. The Horizon of Border Studies: US Military Bases as a Network of Exclaves 373
Shinji Kawana, Keisuke Mori and Minori Takahashi

Index 389

Illustrations

Figures

3.1.	Routes of Two Jokoshis' Travel (1939).	75
5.1.	The Ryukyu Islands and Taiwan.	129
9.1.	Kuril Ainu hunters on a hunting ship, c.1882.	222
9.2.	Konkamakuru in Hakodate.	223
9.3.	The Kuril Ainu in Shikotan.	224
9.4.	'The Chishima Province, Shikotan Island villagers'.	225
9.5.	Five Kuril Ainu.	226
9.6.	'Jacob, Ainu Chief, Seen from the Front and the Side.'	227
9.7.	'Mr. Yakov Strov, Mayor of the Kuril Ainu.'	227
9.8.	'The Party of Shikotan Native Yakov, taken in June 1900.'	228
9.9.	'Shakotan Island Chief Strozev Yakov and the Author.'	229
11.1.	The Qing–Chosŏn borderland.	269

Tables

1.1. Revenue duties of the Muslim governor of Kashgar District, Zuhur al-Din, 1835.   36

1.2. The amount of cotton collected from Yarkand and Khotan and sent to northern Xinjiang (1779, 1784, 1792, 1797, 1821 and 1822).   39

6.1. Population in 2000, 2011 and 2017 (Estonia, Ida-Virumaa, Narva).   157

7.1. 2010 comprehensive official census figures of principal ethnic groups in north-eastern China.   180

Preface

Nobuya Hashimoto

Borders in East and West: Transnational and Comparative Perspectives started its long period of gestation at the international conference 'Border History', organized by the research project 'Interdisciplinary Research on the Function of National Histories and Collective Memories for the Democracy in the Globalized Society (NHCM)'[1] in cooperation with the Eurasia Unit for Border Research (Japan) at the Slavic–Eurasian Research Center at Hokkaido University (Sapporo, Japan)[2] and the Japanese–Korean Forum of Western History. The conference was held at Hokkaido University on 3–4 August 2017, and more than fifty scholars and graduate students from about ten countries and areas of Asia, Oceania and Europe participated in it. With great enthusiasm, speakers and participants listened to and discussed miscellaneous topics of border history and border studies, ranging from ancient Roman borderlands to the islanders' daily lives at the southern and northern sea borders around Japan. The purpose of this publication is to share the meaningful insights acquired at the conference with wider audiences and to elaborate and deepen our thinking on borders, inviting eminent scholars as additional contributors. Between 2017 and 2020 we built teams of two scholars who each worked on similar themes to do with border research – one with expertise on East Asia and one with expertise on Europe. We also asked them to connect their articles through 'bridging texts', bringing out the comparative perspectives and angles. In this way, we aim to refine our comparative analyses between Asia and Europe and to facilitate future collaboration among scholars from the East and the West.

The NHCM Project: Agenda, Organization, Activities

The NHCM project was conducted from February 2017 to September 2019 under the commission and sponsorship of the Japan Society for the Promotion of Science (JSPS: a governmental funding agency for scholarly and scientific research in Japan) as part of its 'Topic-Setting Program to Advance Cutting-Edge Humanities and Social Sciences Research, Global Initiatives, 2016–2019'.[3] This programme sought a 'dialogue and interaction between Japanese and overseas researchers' and aimed at 'the generation of globally significant results through the advancement of international joint researches across diverse fields of the humanities and social sciences and the building of robust international networks'. When the programme was proposed, JSPS assigned to us an incredibly difficult agenda that required developing interdisciplinary research on ... exclusivism and democracy in the globalized society through the formation of global networks of researchers dedicated to investigating relevant topics. This mission was apparently designed following concerns about the 'diffusion of ethnic, racial, religious and cultural exclusivism, and hatred against "others" under globalization and the crises of democracy in the contemporary world'.

Burdened with this significant assignment, we organized a research network consisting of Japanese, Korean, German, Polish, Australian, American and Canadian scholars from various fields of the humanities and social sciences, while establishing the major themes that the project should tackle:

- How have different histories and memories been constructed in the national framework?
- How have complex past events been mobilized for political or diplomatic usage within and between nations?
- What is the mechanism through which histories and memories function as dividing forces and exclude artificially constructed 'others'?
- What are the roles and responsibilities of history and historians confronting an endangered democracy?
- What kind of common experiences have Asia and Europe had concerning these problems, and how do they differ from each other?

At the same time, the NHCM developed institutional cooperation between four universities in Poland (University of Warsaw), Germany (Ruhr University Bochum), South Korea (Sogang University) and Japan (Kwansei Gakuin University), based on our previous international scholarly dialogues among historians. When we recalled the experiences of the Second World War and the post-Cold War management of war memories in East Asia and Central and Eastern Europe from a comparative perspective, the composition seemed very provocative, enabling us to reconsider the East–West scheme in historiographical terms.

East and West as Challenges

Professor Jie-Hyun Lim of Sogang University in South Korea made several provocative points regarding the East–West scheme in his keynote address for the Annual Congress of the Japan Society for Western History, held in 2014 at Kyoto University:

- Making national histories in East Asia was not conceivable without referring to a world history based on the dichotomy of 'normative' Western history and a 'deviated' Eastern variation.
- Conscripted to modernity at large, willingly or unwillingly, 'Easterners' rendered themselves the objects and agents of Western modernity, which was thought to have become global over time.
- Writing national history in East Asia was a voluntary act of inscribing Eurocentrism on its own past.[4]

These phrases may apply not only to East Asia but also to Eastern Europe, and these two regions seem interchangeable in this context, which suggests multiple layers of the East–West scheme. As Lim suggested, the contrast between Germany and England in the *Sonderweg* discourses was the first step to differentiating East and West hierarchically (deviant versus normative). When we glance further east than Germany, we can acknowledge that Europe itself has been split into two parts along the geographical East–West axis, and that Eastern Europe and Western Europe have been placed in hierarchical order. Lim's assertion that 'European history as a model had nothing to do with Eastern Europe'[5] resonates with the impressive representation of Eastern Europe as the 'opposite bank' for the West, coined by a Japanese historian of the former Habsburg lands – the late Professor Chikara Rachi[6] – and with Norman Davies's condemnation of 'the complacent confrontation of superior west and inferior east.'[7] These scholars impressively sought to understand Eastern Europe as *non-European* Europe.[8] Under the impact of the Cold War, this dichotomy was converted into the ideological formula of 'Communism in the East' versus 'Liberal Democracy in the West', and, therefore, the political slogan for the Eastern Europeans under the regime transition to democracy in 1980–90s was 'Becoming European'.[9] Furthermore, Central and Eastern Europe, which had been humbled by Western Eurocentrism, consequently assumed a haughty attitude towards the lands even further to the east, which, caught in the trap of Orientalism,[10] they deemed to be non-European. While the historiography of Eastern European countries endeavoured to exemplify their Europeanness, emphasizing national awakening (resurgence) and the growth of a mature civil society in the nineteenth century, it cast insulting gazes towards the 'backward' Russian and 'alien' Ottoman Empires, accepting the Western standard as its own internalized norm. The Russians, in turn, took both the Orientalist and Eurasianist attitudes towards neighbouring Asian lands and peoples, maintaining their long-inherited ambivalence between the East and the West, while some Russian historians tried to assert Russia's Europeanness from the age of Enlightenment onward.[11] Finally, the modernizing Japanese defined their civilization agenda as 'Out of Asia, Into Europe' at the end of the nineteenth century, which became a prerequisite for Japanese colonialism.

Professor Naoki Odanaka of Tohoku University (Japan), in his comment to Professor Lim's keynote address, discussed above, noted the ambition in national histories to differentiate, which, he argued, should be distinguished from the ambition to rank national histories.[12] According to Odanaka, different trends of 'postcolonial history' that derived from world-system theory, neo-Marxist dependency theory and Edward Said's 'Orientalism' commonly condemned the Eurocentric national histories of European countries, which took Western standards as the universal norm in order to legitimize their (post)colonial dominations and exploitation in the East and South. Postcolonial historians claimed to revise and invert history from Southern (or Eastern) viewpoints. However, Odanaka argued that advocates of global history, who assumed themselves to be heirs of postcolonial histories, did not always escape the 'ambition for hierarchical ranking', resulting only in reversing the South (or East) and the North (or West). Kenneth Pomeranz's *The Great Divergence* covertly exemplified the inverted Eurocentrism (East Asia-centrism?) that failed to overcome this 'ambition for hierarchical ranking' between the East and the West. According to Odanaka, therefore, practices of differentiating and sorting out the East and the West are inevitable and indispensable in historiography, even though advocates of global history declared the intention 'not to sort out'. In fact, we cannot ensure the accuracy of scientific research, including history, without comparisons on the basis of the well-organized method of 'differentiating'. Odanaka called for efforts to explore good ways of 'differentiating' without hierarchical ranking and sought to develop a 'globalized/decentralized' history. The NHCM and this book's methodological challenge to connect and compare experiences in the East and the West derived from his appeal to facilitate such historical perspectives.

Acknowledgements

We received great financial aid from the Japan Society for the Promotion of Sciences, which sponsored the NHCM project, and obtained moral and logistical support from many colleagues and institutions in Poland, Germany, South Korea and Japan, which enabled us to organize conferences and publish this volume. I sincerely appreciate their cooperation with the NHCM's activities.

The colleagues and staff of the Slavic–Eurasian Research Center (SRC) at Hokkaido University kindly allowed us to use their assembly hall for the Sapporo conference and supported our operations in the venue. It was our great pleasure to hold the conference at SRC, since it is the most eminent research institute that carries out Eastern European, Russian and Eurasian studies in Japan. In particular, I would like to express my thanks to Professor Akihiro Iwashita from SRC, who is the leading scholar of border studies in Japan and kindly gave an excellent keynote address about islanders of the sea borders of Japan to the conference.

Chairpersons and commentators for four sessions of the Sapporo conference – Professor Takahiro Hasegawa (Hokkaido University), Professor Toshie Awaya (Tokyo University of Foreign Studies), Professor Norihiro Naganawa (SRC), Professor Eisuke Kaminaga (Niigata University of International and Information Studies), Professor Yu Hashimoto (Hokkaido University), Professor Satoshi Koyama (Kyoto University), Professor Tessa-Morris Suzuki (Australian National University), Professor Chris Lorenz (Ruhr University Bochum) and Professor Jie-Hyun Lim – provided important suggestions for speakers and led fruitful discussions impeccably. Thank you very much.

Finally, I express my many thanks to all contributors to this volume. Thanks to their collaboration, we can now contribute, through this volume, to a challenging dialogue between the East and the West.

Nobuya Hashimoto is Professor of Russian and Baltic History at Kwansei Gakuin University in Japan. His fields of interests are the sociocultural history of education in the Russian Empire, Baltic area studies and history and memory politics in Russia and in Central and Eastern European countries. Among other works, he is the author of *Memory Politics: History Conflicts in Europe* (2016, in Japanese) and 'Maneuvering Memories of Dictatorship and Conflicts: The Baltic States, Central and Eastern Europe, and Russia', in Paul Corner and Jie-Hyun Lim (eds), *The Palgrave Handbook of Mass Dictatorship* (2016). He has edited many books in the fields of comparative social history of education and memory and history politics.

Notes

1. About the project, see http://history-memory.kwansei.ac.jp/en/index.html (accessed 17 February 2022).
2. About the Unit, see http://src-h.slav.hokudai.ac.jp/ubrj/eng/index.html (accessed 17 February 2022).
3. See https://www.jsps.go.jp/english/e-kadai/ (accessed 17 February 2022).
4. Lim, 'World History as a National Rationale', 10–11; Lim, 'Historicizing the World in Northeast Asia', 418–419.
5. Ibid.
6. Rachi, *A World History from the Opposite Bank*.
7. Davies, *Europe East & West*, 16.
8. Wolff, *Inventing Eastern Europe*.
9. Cf. Mälksoo, *The Politics of Becoming European*.
10. Cf. Zarycki, *Ideologies of Eastness in Central and Eastern Europe*.
11. Karp et al., *Century of the Enlightenment*.
12. Odanaka, 'Western History in East Asia and "Global History"'.

Bibliography

Davies, Norman. *Europe East & West*. London: Pimlico, 2007.
Karp, Sergei et al. (eds). *Century of the Enlightenment* [in Russian], 6 vols. Moscow: Nauka, 2006–18.
Lim, Jie-Hyun. 'Historicizing the World in NorthEast Asia', in Douglas Northrop (ed.), *A Companion to World History* (Hoboken, NJ: Wiley-Blackwell, 2012), pp. 418–32.
———. 'World History as a National Rationale: On "Patriotic World History" and its Consequential Euro-Centrism in Japan and Korea' [in Japanese]. *Shiso* 1091 (2015), 6–32.
Mälksoo, Maria. *The Politics of Becoming European: A Study of Polish and Baltic Post-Cold War Security Imaginaries*. London: Routledge, 2010.
Odanaka, Naoki. 'Western History in East Asia and "Global History"' (in Japanese), *Shiso*, no. 1091 (2015), pp. 2–5.
Pomeranz, Kenneth. *The Great Divergence: China, Europe, and the Making of the Modern World Economy*. Princeton, NJ: Princeton University Press, 2000.
Rachi, Chikara. *A World History from the Opposite Bank: The 1848 European Revolution* [in Japanese]. Tokyo: Miraisha Publishing, 1978.
Wolff, Larry. *Inventing Eastern Europe: The Map of Civilization on the Mind of the Enlightenment*. Stanford, CA: Stanford University Press, 1994.
Zarycki, Tomasz. *Ideologies of Eastness in Central and Eastern Europe*. London: Routledge, 2014.

Introduction

Border Experiences in East Asia and Europe
Some Theoretical and Conceptual Thoughts

Stefan Berger

Introduction

This is a book that seeks to compare border experiences in East Asia and Europe in a number of thematic clusters, ranging from economics, tourism and food production to ethnicity, migration and conquest. It thus seems appropriate to start with a chapter that reflects on the meaning of borders more generally. For many years now the discipline of border studies has been developing in highly transdisciplinary and interesting ways, and there are now a number of introductions, handbooks and encyclopaedias that provide excellent overviews of the wealth of theoretical approaches, disciplinary perspectives and empirical research that has been carried out in this field of study.[1] Research centres have been appearing, such as the Centre for International Border Research at Queens University in Belfast,[2] the Center for Inter-American and Border Studies at the University of Texas in El Paso,[3] the Centre for Border Research in Nijmwegen[4] and the Eurasia Unit for Border Research at Hokkaido University in Sapporo.[5] Journals such as the *Journal of Borderland Studies* have been established and linked to associations, in this case the Association of Borderland Studies.[6] In a brief chapter, I cannot possibly discuss all aspects in which diverse bodies of research have illuminated border experiences in recent years.

However, I would like to start with some reflections on definitions, demarcations and agendas that have been influential in border studies and that should be of interest to historians, to whom this volume is, above all, addressed. As this volume underlines, historians have much to learn from border studies, and as the articles in this collection show, they benefit enormously from taking into account the multi-, inter- and transdisciplinary nature of border studies.[7] Many articles in our volume are about state borders, which is why I want to discuss briefly the role of borders in state-centred territorial orders. Here, I highlight the necessarily peripheral nature of border regions and the development of border identities that are often different from state identities. In trans-state conglomerations, such as the European Union (EU), border regions often play an influential role in underpinning their legitimacy, as is clear from the EU's 'Europe of the regions' concept. Finally, I would like to draw attention to the importance of exclaves and enclaves for border experiences. Overall, the chapter is supposed to work as a very short introduction to the study of borders in historical perspective, which will contextualize the field more generally before we embark on a series of detailed case studies comparing East Asian and European borders over a wide thematic spectrum.

What Is in a Border?

While in everyday usage it might be perfectly clear to people using the term 'border' what they mean in conversation,[8] scholarly definitions of what a border actually is are highly contested. One of the leading theorists in the field of border studies, Anssi Paasi, has described political borders as processes and institutions that are moulded over time by boundary-creating practices and discourses. They are often the result of political contestation, conflict and negotiation. To what extent competing practices and discourses materialized and were symbolized differed from place to place, and also changed over time.[9] Material borders, such as the Cold War border between East and West Germany, can be differentiated from conceptual or symbolical borders, such as the 'white sausage border' that demarcates southern from northern Germany.[10] Hard borders can turn into soft borders and vice versa. The Franco-German border in the nineteenth and the first half of the twentieth century was one of the most contested in Europe. Yet in the second half of the twentieth century it became, in the context of the development of the European Union, one of the softest borders – to the extent that the border region of Alsace, once at the heart of three wars between the two countries within a seventy-year time period, now prides itself on being an in-between space.[11] The fluidity of borders is emphasized by the relational quality of territories that are often bounded by specific borders only for a limited amount of time.[12] Much research has emphasized the performative nature of borders, which draws attention to various agents who perform the border in very different ways.[13] The very fluidity of borders has led some researchers to talk about the 'territorial trap' in relation to desires to draw firm borders around territories.[14] Others have referred to 'cartographic anxieties' in relation to the same fixation with making borders stable and less porous.[15] Given the impossibility of fixing borders, Paasi has suggested to abandon any attempts to develop an overarching theory of borders. Instead he champions a multiplicity of perspectives, borrowing from diverse bodies of theory depending on what aspects of borders are being studied.[16]

Yet we can differentiate between different types of borders.[17] For a start, borders of nation states remain the most studied borders. However, next to them, there are cultural borders that may divide nation states or cut across them.[18] The same is true for ethnic and religious borders. Constructions of a 'Christian Europe',[19] for example, are made for exclusionary practices, denying belonging to non-Christian groups, or they could be made to push a bordered Europe in the direction of adopting particular values and norms. Borderlands that contain different ethnicities from the dominant ethnicity in the nation state have drawn particular attention.[20] We have linguistic borders – within nation states and transcending them.[21] The old saying that a language is just another dialect, but with an army, also points to linguistic diversity even within the same language group, and to the power that constitutes what might develop into a language. Then there are social borders – between different classes or groups of people constructed as being somehow socially different.[22] And, of course, we also have economic borders: customs unions and free trade zones are all about getting rid of borders.[23] Nation states sometimes create special economic zones in order to promote economic development. In all of these bordering processes, spatial and non-spatial alike, questions of power are very much to the fore in explaining why some constructions of borders are more successful than others. Mechanisms of inclusion and exclusion are vital in the construction of borders. These may have repercussions in law or they may operate at a more social level. What should be clear by now is that borders are multiscalar: they have not only different qualities but different spatial scales; indeed, they create spatialities and territorialities.[24]

Researchers have paid special attention to the gendering of borders. They have shown how gender ideologies have shaped lived experiences in borderlands, but they have also underlined that borderlands could play a vital role in contesting dominant gender ideologies. Borderlands have often been places of empowerment and opportunities for women, who have been powerful border creators but also important in facilitating contacts and communication across borders. As economic migrants have crossed borders, gender research on borderlands has focused on gendered labour markets on both sides of the border. Migration and assimilation theory has been put to good use in understanding how travelling gender ideologies on both sides of the border have influenced gender regimes at the border. Women have been highly symbolic border guards. They have been seen, through their role as mothers, educators and 'homemakers', as safeguarding the border against perceived enemies on the other side. At the same time, they have been represented as being particularly vulnerable to aggressions coming from the other side of the border and in need of special protection. Researchers have been particularly interested in exploring the diverse ways in which gender has intersected with class, race, ethnicity, religion and other constructions of identity at the border.[25]

Borders are constructed and implemented to demarcate and separate, yet in practice border regions often become contact zones where people on both sides of the border collaborate, cooperate and interact in manifold ways. The tensions created by interlinking processes of separation and interaction at the border lead to manifold ambiguities and practices.[26] The specific constellations that we find at the border depend to a large extent on the management of borders though a variety of state and non-state actors. In other words: what kind of border crossings are possible depends considerably on the ways in which the border in question is managed.[27] Scholars in border studies have therefore been moving the discipline away from a 'line in the sand' approach. Instead, they have successfully decentred studies on borders from being transfixed by lines on maps.[28] Studying alternative border imaginaries highlights the extent to which borders have been and continue to be contested. Rather than talking about 'the border', scholars are increasingly referring to 'bordering practices', as this allows them to focus on activities that constitute, sustain and modify borders. These bordering practices are moving targets, highly dynamic and fluid, strongly choreographed and often to be understood as a theatre spectacle. Given the labour that goes into constructing, maintaining and imaging borders, some scholars have also talked about 'borderwork'.[29]

Glocalization and Trans-Border Experiences

It is by no means a coincidence that border studies have been a booming field since the last decade of the twentieth century, as they benefitted from accelerated processes of globalization that have been a characteristic of the post-Cold War world emerging in the 1990s. The migration of tens of millions of people worldwide fleeing across a variety of different borders, as well as phenomena such as war, violence and economic misery, smuggling across borders, security concerns at the border and questions of assimilation policies vis-à-vis minorities in borderlands, are just some of the issues that have had strong contemporary relevance over recent decades, thereby contributing to the popularity of border studies.[30] All of these developments have highlighted the increasing porosity of the borders of nation states, where more and more decisions are no longer taken at the nation-state level. This is particularly true for the European Union, where a trans-nation-state level of decision-making is at the heart of efforts of closer integration of policy processes across the Union – a process not without its problems and resistances, as the exit of the United Kingdom from the EU underlines. Not only are decisions no longer taken exclusively at the level of the nation state, it has also been increasingly difficult for nation states to control their borders – in terms of movement of people as well as goods. In Europe but also globally, transnational organizations and institutions are becoming more important: Free Trade Agreement zones, the International Monetary Fund, the World Trade Organization and Mercosur are just some examples of trans-nation-state institutions that have come more and more to the fore over recent decades. At the same time, however, we should not underestimate the resilience of the nation state as a category of identification and a meaningful reference point for many people in a rapidly globalizing world. The recent rise of right-wing populisms around the globe – from the US to India, and from Brazil to France – is directly related to the strength of national feeling in most parts of the world. Worldwide we have more than two hundred nation states with more than three hundred land borders. Furthermore, there are, according to different estimates, between six hundred and eight hundred nations that are still struggling to establish statehood – a clear indication that it would be premature to see the nation state as a thing of the past. For many decades now, not only in border studies but also in memory studies and various other transdisciplinary fields, the emphasis has been on transnational networks and links and on avoiding 'methodological nationalism'.[31] This has had many beneficial effects on the disciplines in question, yet one has to be careful not to throw out the baby with the bathwater. Only 3 per cent of the world's population in the early 2000s were living outside the borders of the states into which they were born.[32] For many of them, the nation state still represents an anchor in a deep and dangerous sea represented by globalization.

In this complex process of globalization and national resilience that has often been described in terms of 'glocalization', where do border regions stand? Historically, it is interesting to observe that many nationalists emerged from border areas.³³ At the border, nationalism, both state-promoted and arising from the midst of civil society, has often been particularly strong, as it has seemed necessary to fight an alleged or real threat to national belonging that was located just on the other side of the border. One of the chief ideologues of National Socialist Germany, Alfred Rosenberg, was a Baltic German. In his espousal of German nationalism he drew heavily from his experiences in the multicultural and multi-ethnic borderland territories of the Baltic.³⁴ Under conditions of glocalization since the 1990s, processes of deterritorialization are intricately bound up with processes of reterritorialization, leading to contested imaginaries of borders. Thus, for example, the language of Brexit in the UK was intricately bound up with reimagining the borders of the UK. The Channel was constructed as a firmer border – with Britain appearing as a global power with a global past, and a global future that allegedly could build on that past. Thus, in a lead editorial published by the *Daily Telegraph* on the day the British exit letter was delivered to Brussels, Boris Johnson outlined this future vision.³⁵

The Multidisciplinary Nature of Border Studies

It should be clear by now that the study of borders and borderlands necessitates at the very least a multidisciplinary approach. As we often find strong geopolitical tensions around borders, for instance around struggles for natural resources in sea waters claimed by Russia, China and Japan in the Far East, an international relations perspective on borders is often invaluable.³⁶ As wars have frequently been fought in and about borderlands, a military and strategic perspective is necessary to understand this.³⁷ The contestedness of borderlands has frequently led to strenuous attempts to integrate these borderlands firmly into the economic structures of the state to which they belong. At the same time, the borderlands themselves have had a strong interest in retaining beneficial economic links with regions that lay on the other side of the state border, and this could conflict with the political wishes of the state government. Hence, complex negotiations between borderland regions and central or regional forms of governments often followed. Economic expertise in one way or another has been central to issues relevant to the development of borderlands. Where the latter were underdeveloped, states have looked to economic means to support the borderlands economically in order to tie them closer to the state. Understanding how borderland societies have been working necessitates the skills of social scientists, who can tell us about how diverse social groups in borderlands interact and how they are represented by various social actors.³⁸ Given that borderlands have often been meeting points of different cultures, religions and ethnicities, producing both multiple synergies and tensions, cultural studies perspectives are also extremely useful in border studies. Postcolonial studies are often concerned with the borderlines between colonial and postcolonial societies and between the colonizers and the colonized. As at least some borderlands have been semi-colonial spaces, the theoretical arsenal of postcolonialism is invaluable to understanding those borderland societies. In particular, Homi Bhabha's notion of 'mimicry' as a technique employed by the colonized to mark out a space of their own vis-à-vis the colonizers has been very useful in understanding the relationship between borderlands and centres.[39] As several borderlands have been home to minority languages, linguistics has been a very important discipline in understanding the strong interplay between language and identity in many borderlands.[40] Finally, to avoid the curse of presentism, historians have been vital in presenting a longer-term perspective on borderlands, their existence and workings in previous times and their longer-term development, including the manifold changes that borders and borderlands have undergone over the course of time. Arguably, the field of border studies would benefit from being less present-centred and more historically minded, in order to understand the importance of historical path trajectories for explaining the workings of present-day borders and borderlands.[41] It would be easy to go on, as in particular geographers, ethnologists, anthropologists, archaeologists and literary scholars have all been working very productively in the field of border studies.

The various disciplines have studied borders and borderlands in a variety of different ways. One of the most central concerns in this multitude of themes has been the place of borders and borderlands for the principle of territorial integrity of nation states. This principle has been the backbone of the territorial order in Europe from the Peace of Westphalia that ended the Thirty Years War in 1648 until today. Borderlands were a challenge for the desire of the modern post-1648 state to homogenize its territories. The states, in their fixation on territorial integrity, implemented policies that attempted to fix and essentialize as well as naturalize borders, so as to hide their constructive, arbitrary and fluid nature. From the perspective of central state agencies, borderlands have been dangerous peripheries in need of tight supervision and integration. However, from the perspective of the borderlands, their function was not restricted to being barriers against possible enemies or filters of foreign influences. Borderlands were contact zones and meeting points, zones of cultural exchanges and transfers. The relational nature of borderlands on each side of the border creates multiple disjunctures, affective, identificatory, structural, organizational and territorial.[42] This complex positioning of borderlands has led researchers to call for examining 'border landscapes'[43] and their fluidity over time – with peripheral regions becoming more central and, vice versa, central regions becoming peripheral.[44]

Arguably no border has been studied more than the Mexican–US border, where processes of migration and economic asymmetries on both sides have attracted particular attention.[45] For various themes it is often seen as a paradigmatic case and a benchmark for other studies on borders elsewhere in the world. Thus, at one level, it is a border at which a nation state, the US, seeks to defend its territorial integrity against unwanted in-migration. Therefore, a national 'us' is 'defending' itself against another 'them', here in the form of Mexican or Latin American migrants. Borders have played a crucial role in establishing the modern 'regimes of territoriality'.[46] Yet the identity constructs at the border are not easily contained within such 'us' versus 'them' dichotomies. Instead we find complex layers of local, regional, national and transnational identifications that interact with diverse social, religious, linguistic, cultural, ethnic and gender identities – many of which cannot be contained or restricted to one side of the border. Identity politics at the border are thus particularly contested and hot issues. If we take the example of the Chinese–Russian border, we see on the Chinese side a very uneasy construction of the border.[47] On the one hand we have museums celebrating the Russian–Chinese alliance in defeating Imperial Japan in the Second World War. On the other hand we have museums, such as the Aihui Historical Museum dedicated to Russian imperialism vis-à-vis China in the nineteenth and early twentieth century, where Russians appear as a highly antagonistic enemy. In this museum, there are also lessons to be learned for contemporary China from this traumatic border history: 'Building strong national strength, consolidating national defense, and strong military is to guarantee the dignity of the state's sovereignty, territorial integrity and the security of life and property.'[48] Given the central role of the Communist state in all expression of history politics in China, the views represented in museums tend to be, in most cases, very much in line with the Communist Party perspective, so we do not know to what extent such representations coincide with sentiments on the ground in the borderland, where Russian consumer items in shops appear to be very popular with Chinese consumers.[49]

The study of border identities is today very widely based on a constructivist consensus that space is socially and culturally constructed. The drawing of territorial boundaries has been and continues to be connected to the construction of those social and cultural identities.[50] This construction takes place both from above and from below. More recently there has been a definite shift to studying the agents that are active on the level of civil society, with many scholars focusing on the everyday life and culture in borderlands. Ethnographic approaches have been particularly prominent here.[51] Actor-centred approaches to borderland studies have increased our understanding of how meaning has been given to specific territories. The interaction of different actors, both in discursive processes and in social practices, ultimately defines forever unstable and shifting understandings of borders and borderlands. The importance of narratives for collective memory has been usefully applied to the memory landscapes in borderlands. The cultural productions of the meanings of memory through various media and other genres of memory production are relational and hardly ever unitary or consensual.[52] The contested nature of 'mindscapes'[53] and memorial landscapes at the border raises the question of what kind of memory regimes dominate in borderlands. Here the differentiation between antagonistic, cosmopolitan and agonistic memory, introduced by Anna Cento Bull and Hans Lauge Hansen, might be an interesting tool with which to analyse these memory-scapes.[54] Studying how borderland memories have been meaningfully connected to the present will reveal the extent to which such memory work is not so much about acts of reliving the past or of resuscitating or reproducing experiences of it, but rather about analysing the acts of construction, reworking, reconfiguring and reinterpreting of that past.[55] Such memorial processes actively construct bordering processes.[56] In doing so, they also have, at times, the capability to challenge hegemonic discourses within the wider nation states.

Antagonism and Cosmopolitanism and Their Impact on Border Experiences

One of the big differences between the two regions of the world that are the focus of this volume is that in East Asia we have highly antagonistic national memorial cultures, which have a huge impact on perceptions of borders and borderland. In contrast, the formation of the European Union after the Second World War and its remarkable development since then has been accompanied by the development of cosmopolitan memory frames that seek to overcome previous antagonisms between the different nation states in Europe. In this context, borders within the EU are de-emphasized, and borderlands become areas where memory discourses are keen to underline contact zones and cooperation rather than hostilities.[57] In particular, the popular idea of a 'Europe of the regions' seeks to deflect from the importance of nation states and instead highlight a level below that of the nation state, partly as such emphasis on regional identities will avoid the question of national antagonisms of the past. The EU has thus encouraged borderlands to celebrate their existence as meeting points of diverse cultures and ethnicities, thereby contributing to the diffusion and travelling of national ideas from one national space to another in an attempt to move towards a meaningful Europeanization of culture. The plurality of identities at the border thus almost foreshadows the 'unity in diversity' idea underpinning the dominant rationale of the EU today.[58] It is interesting that such conceptualizations of contemporary Europe almost seek to revive the spectre of a lost Europe, where, in the nineteenth century, especially in East Central and Eastern Europe, many regions were highly multicultural, multi-ethnic and multilingual in outlook. Much of this was lost in the 'bloodlands' of the twentieth century.[59] If we look, for example, at the presentation of the history of Europe in the House of European History in Brussels, we encounter a master narrative that presents the first half of the twentieth century as the dark foil against which a brighter future develops, first in Western Europe after 1945, and, after the fall of Communism around 1990, also in Eastern Europe. While the musealization of Europe has been based on diverse attempts to forge master narratives, it has often failed to go beyond the 'Europe of the regions' and the 'unity of diversity' narratives.[60] These are the ones that seek to provide a future perspective in which 'ever closer integration' is combined with notions of multiculturalism, in which borderland regions play a special role. It is part and parcel of the making of a new, complex geosociology of political identities, where local, regional, national and transnational overlap and form unstable and manifold identities across time and space, with varying political connotations.[61]

This political vision of Europe, promoted above all by the EU, has resulted, among other things, in a range of EU-funded projects on the border that have been, generally speaking, in line with the ideas of promoting the Europe of the regions, in which borderlands have played a special role as mediators and agents of political and cultural transfer. Scientific research was to underpin the construction of these new European identities. The vision of a post-national Europe overcoming the past antagonisms of European nation states could be strengthened through highlighting the positive contribution of borderlands to such a post-national future.[62] At the same time, projects have also paid attention to the EU's external borders, seeking to avoid the construction of hard exterior borders and instead promoting cross-border contacts with Europe's neighbours.[63] Yet those more fluent and cosmopolitan identities that have been in the making in the EU have recently been challenged by Eurosceptic and vernacular nationalist voices.[64] Borderlands have within those discourses re-emerged as zones of conflict, highlighting once again how borders are processes rather than products. Europe has not been the only place where transnational institutions and organizations have been studied in order to assess their potential for overcoming antagonistic forms of nationalism. In South America, the Mercosur has received considerable attention.[65] Similarly, the North American Free Trade Agreement area has been studied.[66] In East Asia there have been few internal attempts to move to transnational alliances. Everywhere where they have come into being, these transnational institutions have provoked, like in Europe, a vernacular nationalist backlash.

Enclaves/Exclaves as Borderlands

Caught in between the conflicting desires of reducing the importance of borders as dividing lines and keeping those divisions as an important anchor of identity are the enclaves and exclaves that we can find around the world today. Scholars have distinguished between different types of enclaves and exclaves: first, independent enclaves such as the Vatican state or San Marino; secondly, hard territorial enclaves with firm physical borders; thirdly, non-territorial 'soft' enclaves, such as language, economic, cultural, ethnic or religious enclaves; and, fourthly, semi-enclaves that share at least one border, which may be a sea border, with the 'motherland'. These different types of enclaves and exclaves face different types of conflict. Some are about sovereignty, often involving the surrounding 'foreign' state and the 'motherland'. There are also many specific issues concerning enclaves and exclaves that can result in conflict between the enclave or exclave and the surrounding territory, but also sometimes the 'motherland'. These include issues of migration, access, smuggling and the actual fixing of the border. Finally, there are substituting conflicts, where the enclave or exclave is just a pawn in a wider conflict between the surrounding state and the state to which the enclave or exclave belongs.[67] Enclaves and exclaves have been particularly prone to these types of conflict, as they violate the principle of the territorial integrity of nation states and are thus a source of potential instability to them – both those that have to look after the exclave and those that have to deal with an enclave in their midst. They often represent challenges to administrative hierarchies and territorial jurisdictions working within states. This is also why in Europe in the period of nationalism and hyper-nationalism during the second half of the nineteenth and first half of the twentieth century, most of the hard enclaves and exclaves disappeared from the map. War, annexation, sales, territory swaps – they all contributed to the demise of hard enclaves and exclaves in Europe. Today they are an exception, but in other parts of the world, they are far more common. In the global perspective, colonialism and imperialism had a major impact on the formation of enclaves and exclaves, such as Gibraltar, Hong Kong, Macao, Ceuta and Melilla.

One fascinating example that demonstrates how many of the issues affecting borderland studies also affect the study of enclaves and exclaves is the case of Kaliningrad.[68] Before the end of the Second World War it was known as the city of Königsberg and was located in the region of Eastern Prussia that belonged to Imperial Germany between 1871 and 1918. It was a multicultural and multi-ethnic space, but was dominated by German culture. In the interwar period, as a result of the Versailles Peace Treaty and the resurfacing of the Polish nation state that had been eradicated from the map of Europe by the imperial alliances of Prussia, the Habsburg and the Romanov empires, Königsberg and parts of Eastern Prussia became a German exclave and a Polish enclave. The National Socialist conquest of Europe reunited Eastern Prussia temporarily with Germany, but the defeat of Germany in the Second World War saw a western shift of Poland and Königsberg, and the area around it, alongside the three Baltic republics, became part of the Soviet Union. It was now renamed Kaliningrad. It was strategically important to the Soviet Union as the only ice-free harbour for the Soviet navy. The Soviet plan for the city and region was to build the new Communist 'city beautiful', in which the German past played no role. After the collapse of the Soviet Union it became a Russian exclave, bordering the Baltic republic of Lithuania and Poland. Many of the conflicts surrounding, for example, smuggling, migration, economic cooperation and a range of substitute conflicts surfaced here during the 1990s. Of particular interest has been the discussion surrounding the identity of the city and the oblast of Kaliningrad. In 2005 the city celebrated 750 years of its history, and one year later, in 2006, it celebrated sixty years of Kaliningrad, highlighting the ambiguities inherent in identity discourses in the city and region.[69] In 2005 the city was presented with several gifts from the surrounding nations, including Poland, Lithuania, Belarus and Germany, and it was intriguing that every nation gave a present, usually a monument, alluding to the significance of the history of Kaliningrad for the history of their respective nation state. In particular, the German past of the city has been rediscovered from the 1990s onwards, and especially intellectual circles in the city have been speaking up in favour of strengthening the cultural pasts of the city that relate to German culture. In response the Russian state has implemented a range of policies in order to strengthen the Russianness of the exclave. In the museum landscape of the city, conflicting messages about the identitarian anchors of Kaliningrad can be observed, but the history politics of the Russian state has highlighted the links of the city and region to Russia. It is funding visits of all schoolchildren in Kaliningrad to Moscow and the 'motherland' of Russia, and the school history curricula teach mainly the local and regional history in relation to Russian history. While inside Kaliningrad, most of the people feel Russian, and while the promotion of tourism in the region has strengthened the ties to Russia, the identitarian discourses still tremble in light of the many layers of the past that are present in the memory politics of the city.[70]

Towards a Comparative History of Borders and Borderlands

The studies on Kaliningrad underline the simple fact that most research on enclaves and exclaves, and on borderlands more generally, focuses on local and regional case studies. The field as a whole would therefore greatly benefit from the development of comparative and global frameworks for the study of borders. Conceptually there is an arsenal of interesting concepts available that could be used in such comparisons. Thus, for example, Michael Hechter's notion of 'internal colonialism' could be very helpful in understanding state policies at the border.[71] In this volume we are aiming to compare European and East Asian experiences at and with borders. In this way we are also aiming to contribute towards the decentring of border studies from its current focus on the Americas and Europe. Thus, we start off with Andrea Komlosy's and Kwangmin Kim's chapter on economic processes of integration in eighteenth and nineteenth-century Habsburg and Chinese borderlands. Shizue Osa and Małgorzata Głowacka-Grajper subsequently discuss the role of tourism in borderlands of Japan and Poland. In the following chapters by Hiroko Matsuda and by Nobuya Hashimoto and Hiromi Komori, the construction of sea and land borders between Taiwan and Japan on the one hand, and between Estonia and Russia on the other, take centre stage. Thereafter, Loretta Kim and Ilaria Porciani discuss the establishment of food classifications in Chinese and Italian borderlands with a view to establishing the importance of food for regional and national identities. The next tandem of chapters, penned by Takehiro Okabe and Takahiro Yamamoto, analyse the importance of the ethnic gaze in the Russian and Soviet borderlands of the west (with Finland) and the east (with Japan). The penultimate two connected chapters by Seonmin Kim and Balázs Szalontai discuss migration and interethnic conflicts in borderlands in Manchuria and Mongolia. The final two chapters by Elena Campbell and Zhao Xin discuss Russia's far northern and far eastern peripheries, both shaped by imperial endeavours from the eighteenth to the twentieth centuries. Overall, these tandem chapters provide intriguing comparative glimpses into themes that have a special relevance for borderlands, and the editors hope that they might encourage future comparative research into European and Asian borderlands.

Stefan Berger is Professor of Social History and Director of the Institute for Social Movements at Ruhr-Universität Bochum. He is also the executive chair of the Foundation History of the Ruhr and an Honorary Professor at Cardiff University in the UK. He has published widely on comparative labour history, the history of deindustrialization, industrial heritage, memory studies, the history of historiography, the history of nationalism and British–German relations. His most recent monograph is: *History and Identity: How Historical Theory Shapes Historical Practice* (Cambridge University Press, 2022).

Notes

1. Wastl-Walter, *The Ashgate Research Companion to Border Studies*; Wilson and Donnan, *A Companion to Border Studies*; Diener and Hagen, *Borders*; Brunet-Jailly, *Border Disputes*; Nicoll and Townsend-Gault, *Holding the Line*; Michaelsen and Johnson, *Border Theory*. There are even handbooks on specific regions, including those of interest to readers of this volume. See, for example, Horstmann, Saxer and Rippa, *Routledge Handbook of Asian Borderlands*.

2. See https://www.qub.ac.uk/research-centres/CentreforInternationalBordersResearch/ (accessed 29 November 2020).

3. See https://www.utep.edu/liberalarts/cibs/ (accessed 29 November 2020).

4. See https://www.ru.nl/nsm/imr/vm/research-centres/nijmegen-centre-border-research/ (accessed 29 November 2020).

5. See http://src-h.slav.hokudai.ac.jp/ubrj/eng/ (accessed 4 December 2020).

6. See https://absborderlands.org/ (accessed 29 November 2020).

7. Newman, 'Borders and Bordering', 171–86.

8. On the everyday of border experiences see also Jones and Johnson, *Placing the Border in Everyday Life*.

9. Paasi, *Territories, Boundaries, Consciousness*.

10. On the materiality of borders, see also Demetriou and Dimova, *The Political Materialities of Borders*.

11. Berger, 'Border Regions, Hybridity, and National Identity', 366–81.

12. Amin, Massey and Thrift, *Decentering the Nation*.

13. Hannam, Sheller and Urry, 'Editorial', 1–22.

14. Agnew, 'The Territorial Trap', 53–80.

15. Krishna, 'Cartographic Anxiety', 507–21.

16. Paasi, 'Bounded Spaces in a "Borderless World"', 213–34.

17. An influential attempt to create a typology of borders can be found in Martinez, *Border People*.

18. Ganster and Lorey, *Borders and Border Politics*.

19. Forlenza and Turner, 'Das Abendland', 6–23.

20. Brettell, *Constructing Borders/Crossing Boundaries*.

21. Auer, 'The Construction of Linguistic Borders', 3–31. See also Watt and Llamas, *Language, Borders and Identity*.

22. Ring, 'Borders and Boundaries', chapter 2.

23. van Vilsteren and Wever, *Borders and Economic Behaviour in Europe*.

24. Herrschel, *Borders in Post-Socialist Europe*, especially chapter 3: 'Multi-Level Bordering: Borders, Scale and the "New Regionalism"', 53–74.

25. Aaron, Altink and Weedon, *Gendering Border Studies*. See also Shekhawat and del Re, *Women and Borders*; Kulawik and Kravchenko, *Borderlands in European Gender Studies*.
26. van Houtum, 'The Geopolitics of Borders and Boundaries', 672–79.
27. Hansen and Papademetriou, *Managing Borders*.
28. Parker and Vaughan-Williams, *Critical Border Studies*.
29. Rumford, *Citizens and Borderwork*.
30. Staudt, *Border Politics in a Global Era*.
31. Wimmer and Glick Schiller, 'Methodological Nationalism and Beyond', 301–34.
32. O'Dowd, 'From a "Borderless World" to a "World of Borders"', 1031–50.
33. Hutchinson, *Nations as Zones of Conflict*.
34. Piper, *Alfred Rosenberg*.
35. Wellings and Gifford, 'The Past in English Euroscepticism', 88–105.
36. Starr and Thomas, 'The Nature of Borders and International Conflict', 123–39.
37. Côté-Boucher, Infantino and Salter, 'Border Security as Practice', 195–208.
38. Donnan and Wilson, *Borderlands*.
39. Bhabha, 'Of Mimicry and Man', 125–33; see also Bhabha, *The Location of Culture*.
40. Omoniyi, 'Borders', 123–34.
41. Baud and van Schendel, 'Toward a Comparative History of Borderlands', 211–42.
42. See already Barth, *Ethnic Groups and Boundaries*.
43. Prescott, *Political Frontiers and Boundaries*.
44. Horstmann and Wadley, *Centering the Margin*.
45. Lorey, *The US-Mexican Border in the Twentieth Century*.
46. Maier, 'Consigning the Twentieth Century to History', 807–31.
47. Paine, *Imperial Rivals*.
48. Photographed by the author during a visit to the museum in the summer of 2018.
49. In the city of Heihe, Chinese consumers can buy Russian products, but there was not a single bridge connecting the city to the Russian city of Blagoveshchensk, on the other side of the Amur river, when I visited the region in 2018.
50. Deleuze and Guattari, *A Thousand Plateaus*.
51. Donnan and Wilson, *Border Approaches*.
52. See, for example, Binicewicz, *Contemporary Identity and Memory*.
53. Smith, 'The Valleys'.
54. Cento Bull and Hansen, 'On Agonistic Memory', 390–404.
55. Cubitt, *History and Memory*.
56. van Houtum and van Naerssen, 'Bordering, Ordering and Othering', 125–36.
57. Calligaro, *Negotiating Europe*.
58. Berezin and Schain, *Europe Without Borders*.
59. Snyder, *Bloodlands*.
60. Kaiser, Krankenhagen and Poehls, *Exhibiting Europe in Museums*.
61. Grundy-Warr and Schofield, 'Reflections on the Relevance of Classic Approaches and Contemporary Priorities', 650–62.
62. Meinhof, *Living (with) Borders*; Kohli and Novak, *Will Europe Work?*
63. Leontidou, 'Exclusion and Difference along the EU Border', 389–407.
64. Brack and Costa, *Euroscepticism within the EU Institutions*.
65. Edler, *Die Integration der südamerikanischen Staaten durch den Mercosur*.
66. Fatemi, *North American Free Trade Agreement*; see also Cunningham and Heyman, 'Introduction', 329–50.
67. Vinokurov, *A Theory of Enclaves*.
68. Berger, *Kaliningrad in Europa*.
69. Berger, 'German Pasts in a Russian City', 196–218.
70. Berger and Holtom, 'Locating Kaliningrad and Königsberg', 15–38.
71. Hechter, *Internal Colonialism*.

Bibliography

Aaron, Jane, Henrice Altink and Chris Weedon (eds). *Gendering Border Studies*. Cardiff: University of Wales Press, 2010.

Agnew, John. 'The Territorial Trap: The Geographical Assumptions of International Relations Theory'. *Review of International Political Economy* 1(1) (1994), 53–80.

Amin, Ash, Doreen Massey and Nigel Thrift. *Decentering the Nation: A Radical Approach to Regional Inequality*. London: Catalyst, 2003.

Auer, Peter. 'The Construction of Linguistic Borders and the Linguistic Construction of Borders', in Markku Filppula, Juhani Klemola, Marjatta Palander, and Esa Pentillä (eds), *Dialects across Borders* (Amsterdam: John Benjamins, 2005), 3–31.

Barth, Fredrik. *Ethnic Groups and Boundaries: The Social Organization of Cultural Difference*. Oslo: Scandinavian University Press, 1969.

Baud, Michiel, and Willem van Schendel. 'Toward a Comparative History of Borderlands'. *Journal of World History* 8(2) (1997), 211–42.

Berezin, Mabel, and Martin Schain (eds). *Europe without Borders: Remapping Territory, Citizenship, and Identity in a Transnational Age*. Baltimore, MD: John Hopkins University Press, 2003.

Berger, Stefan. 'Border Regions, Hybridity, and National Identity: The Cases of Alsace and Masuria', in Q. Edward Wang and Franz L. Fillafer (eds), *The Many Faces of Clio: Cross-Cultural Approaches to Historiography: Essays in Honour of Georg G. Iggers* (Oxford: Berghahn Books, 2007), 366–81.

——— (ed.). *Kaliningrad in Europa: Nachbarschaftliche Perspektiven nach dem Ende des Kalten Krieges*. Wiesbaden: Harrossowitz, 2012.

———. 'German Pasts in a Russian City – Kaliningrad between 1946 and 2006', in Marek Tamm (ed.), *Afterlife of Events: Perspectives on Mnemohistory* (Basingstoke: Palgrave Macmillan, 2015), 196–218.

Berger, Stefan, and Paul Holtom. 'Locating Kaliningrad and Königsberg in Russian and German Collective Identity Discourses and Political Symbolism in the 750th Anniversary Celebrations of 2005'. *Journal of Baltic Studies* 39(1) (2008), 15–38.

Bhabha, Homi. 'Of Mimicry and Man: The Ambivalence of Colonial Discourse'. *Psychoanalysis* 28 (1984), 125–33.

———. *The Location of Culture*. London: Routledge, 1994.

Binicewicz, Aleksandra. *Contemporary Identity and Memory in the Borderlands of Poland and Germany*. Newcastle upon Tyne: Cambridge Scholars, 2017.

Brack, Nathalie, and Olivier Costa (eds). *Euroscepticism within the EU Institutions: Diverging Views of Europe*. London: Routledge, 2012.

Brettell, Caroline B. (ed.). *Constructing Borders/Crossing Boundaries: Race, Ethnicity and Immigration*. Lanham, MD: Lexington Books, 2007.

Brunet-Jailly, Emmanuel (ed.). *Border Disputes: A Global Encyclopedia*, 3 vols. Santa Barbara, CA: ABC Clio, 2012.

Calligaro, Oriane. *Negotiating Europe: EU Promotion of Europeanness since the 1950s*. Basingstoke: Palgrave Macmillan, 2013.

Cento Bull, Anna, and Hans Lauge Hansen. 'On Agonistic Memory'. *Memory Studies* 9(4) (2016), 390–404.

Côté-Boucher, Karine, Frederica Infantino and Mark B. Salter. 'Border Security as Practice: An Agenda for Research'. *Security Dialogue* 45(3) (2015), 195–208.

Cubitt, Geoff. *History and Memory*. Manchester: Manchester University Press, 2007.

Cunningham, Hilary, and Josiah Heyman. 'Introduction: Mobilities and Enclosures at Borders'. *Identities: Global Studies in Culture and Power* 11(3) (2004), 329–50.

Deleuze, Giles, and Felix Guattari. *A Thousand Plateaus: Capitalism and Schizophrenia*. Minneapolis, MN: University of Minnesota Press, 1987.

Demetriou, Olga, and Rozita Dimova (eds). *The Political Materialities of Borders*. Manchester: Manchester University Press, 2019.

Diener, Alexander C., and Joshua Hagen. *Borders. A Very Short Introduction*. Oxford: Oxford University Press, 2012.

Donnan, Hastings, and Thomas M. Wilson (eds). *Border Approaches: Anthropological Perspectives on Frontiers*. Dublin: The Anthropological Society of Ireland, 1994.

────── (eds). *Borderlands: Ethnographic Approaches to Security, Power and Identity*. Lanham, MD: University Press of America, 2010.

Edler, Christoph. *Die Integration der südamerikanischen Staaten durch den Mercosur*. Munich: Herbert Utz, 2012.

Fatemi, Khosrow (ed.). *North American Free Trade Agreement: Opportunities and Challenges*. Basingstoke: Macmillan, 1993.

Forlenza, Rosario, and Bryan S. Turner. 'Das Abendland: The Politics of Europe's Religious Borders'. *Critical Research on Religion* 7(1) (2019), 6–23.

Ganster, Paul, and David E. Lorey (eds). *Borders and Border Politics in a Globalizing World*. Lanham, MD: SR Books, 2005.

Grundy-Warr, Carl Eric Repton and Clive Schofield. 'Reflections on the Relevance of Classic Approaches and Contemporary Priorities in Boundary Studies'. *Geopolitics* 10(4) (2005), 650–62.

Hannam, Kevin, Mimi Sheller and John Urry. 'Editorial: Mobilities, Immobilities, and Moorings'. *Mobilities* 1(1) (2006), 1–22.

Hansen, Randall, and Demetrios G. Papademetriou (eds). *Managing Borders in an Increasingly Borderless World*. Washington DC: Migration Policy Institute, 2013.

Hechter, Michael. *Internal Colonialism: The Celtic Fringe in British National Development, with a New Introduction and a New Appendix*. London: Routledge, 2017 [1975].

Herrschel, Tassilo. *Borders in Post-Socialist Europe: Territory, Scale, Society*. Avebury: Ashgate, 2011.

Horstmann, Alexander, and Reed L. Wadley (eds). *Centering the Margin: Agency and Narrative in Southeast Asian Borderlands*. Oxford: Berghahn Books, 2006.

Horstmann, Alexander, Martin Saxer and Alessandro Rippa (eds). *Routledge Handbook of Asian Borderlands*. London: Routledge, 2018.

Hutchinson, John. *Nations as Zones of Conflict*. London: Sage, 2005.

Jones, Reece, and Corey Johnson (eds). *Placing the Border in Everyday Life*. Farnham: Ashgate, 2014.

Kaiser, Wolfram, Stefan Krankenhagen and Kerstin Poehls. *Exhibiting Europe in Museums: Transnational Networks, Collections, Narratives and Representations*. Oxford: Berghahn Books, 2013.

Kohli, Martin, and Mojca Novak (eds). *Will Europe Work? Integration, Employment and the Social Order*. London: Routledge, 2001.

Krishna, Sankaran. 'Cartographic Anxiety: Mapping the Body Politic in India'. *Alternatives: Global, Local, Political* 19(4) (1994), 507–21.

Kulawik, Teresa, and Zhanna Kravchenko (eds). *Borderlands in European Gender Studies: Beyond the East-West Frontier*. London: Routledge, 2019.

Leontidou, Lila. 'Exclusion and Difference along the EU Border: Social and Cultural Markers, Spatialities and Mappings'. *International Journal of Urban and Regional Research* 29(2) (2005), 389–407.

Lorey, David E. *The US-Mexican Border in the Twentieth Century: A History of Economic and Social Transformation*. Wilmington, DE: SR Books, 1999.

Maier, Charles. 'Consigning the Twentieth Century to History: Alternative Narratives for the Modern Era'. *American Historical Review* 105(3) (2000), 807–31.

Martinez, Oscar J. *Border People: Life and Society in the US-Mexico Borderlands.* Tucson, AZ: University of Arizona Press, 1994.

Meinhof, Ulrike Hanna (ed.). *Living (with) Borders: Identity Discourses on East-West Borders in Europe.* London: Routledge, 2002.

Michaelsen, Scott, and David E. Johnson (eds). *Border Theory: The Limits of Cultural Politics.* Minneapolis, MN: University of Minnesota Press, 1997.

Newman, David. 'Borders and Bordering: Towards an Interdisciplinary Dialogue'. *European Journal of Social Theory* 9(2) (2006), 171–86.

Nicoll, Heather N., and Ian Townsend-Gault (eds). *Holding the Line: Borders in a Global World.* Vancouver: UBC Press, 2005.

O'Dowd, Liam. 'From a "Borderless World" to a "World of Borders": Bringing History Back in'. *Environment and Planning D: Society and Space* 28(6) (2010), 1031–50.

Omoniyi, Tope. 'Borders', in Joshua A. Fishman and Ofelia García (eds), *Handbook of Language and Ethnic Identity, Disciplinary and Regional Perspectives*, vol. 1, 2nd edn (Oxford: Oxford University Press, 2010), 123–34.

Paasi, Anssi. 'Bounded Spaces in a "Borderless World": Border Studies, Power, and the Anatomy of Territory'. *Journal of Power* 2(2) (2009), 213–34.

———. *Territories, Boundaries, Consciousness: The Changing Geographies of the Russian-Finnish Border.* Oxford: Wiley-Blackwell, 1996.

Paine, S. C. M. *Imperial Rivals: China, Russia, and their Disputed Frontier.* Armonk, NY: M. E. Sharpe, 1996.

Parker, Noel, and Nick Vaughan-Williams (eds). *Critical Border Studies: Broadening and Deepening the 'Lines in the Sand' Agenda.* London: Routledge, 2014.

Piper, Ernst. *Alfred Rosenberg: Hitlers Chefideologe.* Berlin: Pantheon, 2005.

Prescott, J. R. V. *Political Frontiers and Boundaries.* London: Routledge, 1987.

Ring, Magnus. 'Borders and Boundaries: Reflections on Conceptual Distinctions of Borders in Sociological Theory', in Anthony Cooper and Søren Tinning (eds), *Debating and Defining Borders: Philosophical and Theoretical Perspectives* (London: Routledge, 2020), chapter 2.

Rumford, Chris (ed.). *Citizens and Borderwork in Contemporary Europe.* London: Routledge, 2009.

Shekhawat, Seema, and Emanuela C. del Re (eds). *Women and Borders: Refugees, Migrants and Communities.* London: I.B. Tauris, 2017.

Smith, Dai. 'The Valleys: Landscape and Mindscape', in Prys Morgan (ed.), *Glamorgan County History: Glamorgan Society 1780–1980* (Cardiff: Cardiff University Press, 1988), chapter 7.

Snyder, Timothy. *Bloodlands: Europe Between Hitler and Stalin.* New York: Basic Books, 2012.

Starr, Harvey, and G. Dale Thomas. 'The Nature of Borders and International Conflict: Revisiting Hypotheses on Territory'. *International Studies Quarterly* 49(1) (2005), 123–39.

Staudt, Kathleen. *Border Politics in a Global Era: Comparative Perspectives.* Lanham, MD: Rowman & Littlefield, 2018.

van Houtum, Henk. 'The Geopolitics of Borders and Boundaries'. *Geopolitics* 10(4) (2005), 672–79.

van Houtum, Henk, and Ton van Naerssen. 'Bordering, Ordering and Othering'. *Tijdschrift voor Economische en Soziale Geografie* 93(2) (2002), 125–36.

van Vilsteren, Gerrit, and Egbert Wever (eds). *Borders and Economic Behaviour in Europe: A Geographical Approach.* Assen: Royal van Gorcum, 2005.

Vinokurov, Evgeny. *A Theory of Enclaves*. Washington, DC: Lexington Books, 2007.
Wastl-Walter, Doris (ed.). *The Ashgate Research Companion to Border Studies*. London: Routledge, 2016.
Watt, Dominic, and Carmen Llamas (eds). *Language, Borders and Identity*. Edinburgh: Edinburgh University Press, 2014.
Wellings, Ben, and Chris Gifford. 'The Past in English Euroscepticism', in Stefan Berger and Caner Tekin (eds), *History and Belonging: Representations of the Past in Contemporary European Politics* (Oxford: Berghahn Books, 2018), 88–105.
Wilson, Thomas M., and Hastings Donnan (eds). *A Companion to Border Studies*. Oxford: Wiley Blackwell, 2012.
Wimmer, Andreas, and Nina Glick Schiller. 'Methodological Nationalism and Beyond: Nation-State Building, Migration, and the Social Sciences'. *Global Networks* 2(4) (2002), 301–34.

Part I

Economic Borders in the Chinese and Habsburg Empires during the Eighteenth and Nineteenth Centuries

Andrea Komlosy and Kwangmin Kim

The chapters by Kwangmin Kim and Andrea Komlosy cover eighteenth and nineteenth-century borderlands in the Chinese and Habsburg empires respectively, but they do so in different ways. Kwangmin Kim examines a specific frontier: southern Xinjiang. This was a desert oasis region, whose indigenous Muslim people provided intermediary functions for transregional trade on the Silk Road. But it had very few major export items of its own for long-distance market, except for the jade stone much sought after in Chinese market. Kim argues that Chinese occupation transformed Xinjiang into its economic periphery, stimulating the region's exports and profiting from its peripheralization within an unequal transregional division of labour. In order to extract the local resources to finance and supply its military stationed in the region, the Qing state guaranteed the Muslim local elites the rights to exploit collective land, resources, and labour force of the local population there. This process in turn contributed to the integration of the area into global capitalist markets by the late nineteenth century. Thus, the Qing empire's military interests and the frontier elites' economic interests complemented each other in transforming Xinjiang into periphery of Chinese metropole, while deepening the economic stratification with the frontier society. It should be mentioned that Kim's chapter only concentrates on the southern part of Xinjiang territory. The northern part of Xinjiang constituted a different political economy. It was a steppe region, whose original tribal population, Zunghar Mongol people, were mostly killed or scattered into other parts of Central Asia by the Qing conquest in the 1750s. It was colonized primarily by the Han Chinese settlers from north-western China after this.

Andrea Komlosy does not concentrate on one single province of the Habsburg Monarchy, but lists all of them, both old hereditary and newly acquired ones. None of the border provinces corresponds to a frontier similar to Xinjiang. Her contribution points out the different role of the border in the case of the western and northern provinces bordering the Holy Roman Empire and its German successor states (and Switzerland) compared to the border regions in the east and south-east. The western and northern regions bordered states that belonged to the "European System" of international law, based upon Western Christianity, while Tsarist Russia and the Ottoman Porte stood apart. Therefore, state borders were rather open and porous for the movement of people and commodities vis-à-vis the west; meanwhile, eastern and south-eastern borders not only marked different zones of political rule, but also completely different landscapes in cultural and socio-economic respects. While the Habsburg hereditary heartlands in the western parts faced integration and administrative centralization efforts in the course of the eighteenth century, the new acquisitions on the eastern and south-eastern borders had a different status, providing military-strategic space against the Russian and Ottoman neighbours and at the same time serving as commodity frontiers and internal peripheries.

For the purpose of comparison, we have to keep in mind the following levels:

1. Comparing Qing China and the Habsburg Monarchy in the eighteenth and nineteenth centuries requires looking into the state orders of the two entities. At first sight, differences prevail between the polities. On the one hand, there was a China-based, multi-ethnic Qing Empire at its height of its political power. The Manchu imperial house of the Qing, originating from Manchuria, held together the various imperial territories in China and Inner Asia (Mongolia, Tibet and Xinjiang) that it conquered from the 1640s to the 1750s more or less successfully. It did so by means of political and cultural persuasion,

appealing to the ruling elite of each region, as well as by providing various material benefits and military protections. At the same time, the Manchu ruling house cautiously limited Chinese migrations into non-Chinese regions. While occasional challenges to Qing power emerged in China and other parts of the empire, including Xinjiang, from the 1800s, the challenges were not strong enough to threaten the imperial unity until the 1842 Opium War. On the other hand, the Habsburg lands formed a conglomerate monarchy. Habsburg princes served as emperors of the loose Holy Roman umbrella-Empire until it was replaced by nation states and nationalizing empires respectively in the time under consideration – the turn of the eighteenth and nineteenth centuries. While the old Holy Roman Empire was overcome, the Habsburg conglomerate took the shape of empire, including enlargements into territories that compensated for the lack of overseas colonies, but conflicted with the aim of imperial homogenization. After 1804–6, the Habsburg Empire remained as much a conglomerate as before, incorporating multiple core regions, as well as frontier and colony-type enlargements, as internal peripheries. In spite of their different size, history, constitution, organization and international position, both empires faced challenges of imperial unity and sovereignty in the course of the nineteenth century and ceased to exist almost at the same moment, in 1911 and in 1918 respectively. Elaborating in-depth comparisons remains a desideratum.

2. Including Western Europe in the comparison can help not only to point out the differences between the Chinese and Western European empires and states, as Kim advocates in his contribution, but also between Western Europe and Central Europe. Central Europe's imperial constitution in the framework of the Holy Roman Empire, with the Habsburg conglomerate as a part that stretched beyond its borders, does not comply with the Western European empires, in particular the Dutch, French and British empires. In many comparative and global history studies, Europe is represented by those Western states and empires, depicted as typically European, that had overseas colonies, while the empires in Central Europe, as well as in Northern and Southern Europe, are classified as being different, particular, not following the general European pattern. In the case of the Habsburg Monarchy it is most obvious that it did not have overseas colonies, but was a continental conglomerate, then transformed into an empire, that possessed internal peripheries, most prominently located in the eastern and south-eastern borderlands. Including the Habsburg case in global comparison challenges findings that are based on Western European empires only. The concept of 'internal

peripheries' could be applicable to the cases of many Chinese borderlands, although Chinese historians have yet to explore the possibility seriously. It follows that such comparisons between China and the Central European empire will lead to some interesting discoveries; they remain another desideratum.

3. Last but not least, we arrive at comparing border regions of the two empires, Qing China and the Habsburg Lands respectively Austria-Hungary. As Kwangmin Kim presents a case study, while Andrea Komlosy an overview of different types of border regions, a comparison must focus those Habsburg regions that do have some similarities with Xinjiang. This applies to Galicia (including Bukovina until 1848) and to Bosnia and Hercegovina.

Galicia

Galicia, acquired upon the occupation and division of Poland-Lithuania among the partition powers of Austria, Prussia and Russia in 1772, 1775 and 1795, was among the biggest Habsburg provinces with regard to space and inhabitants. It was populated by different ethnic and religious groups, mainly Catholic Poles, Greek-Catholic Ukrainians (labelled Ruthenians) and Jews. The strong Polish aristocracy was split between national ambitions opposing Habsburg conquest and rule – finally compromising with Habsburg rule in exchange for political and economic privileges, political representation in central state institutions and regional self-administration. Save Galician Poles' careers in central Habsburg state functions, these privileges are comparable to the co-optation of regional elites in Xinjiang. Until the abolition of serfdom in 1848, Polish landlords were able to compel their subjects to work on manorial agricultural estates producing surplus for export. They were also entitled to oblige their subjects to consume manorial-manufactured products such as beer, tobacco and alcohol.

Upon conquest, the province had a low level of economic development, with only a few export trades. Annexation did not foster industrial development, but focused on an extraction economy based on the manorial estates economy; later, mineral and oil resources were also exploited. At the beginning, military interest prevailed, but it was complemented by interest in rent and resource appropriation in the course of the nineteenth century. Both purposes required the development of railways, connecting the borderland with the core provinces.

Galicia's transit function for transregional trade between the Black Sea and the Baltic Sea was transformed after conquest and integration into the Habsburg customs union. The province served as a selling market for Austrian industrial exports, supplying raw materials to the Habsburg western industrialized provinces. Trade statistics show the rise of raw materials, semi-finished exports and manufactured imports. This is exactly the opposite effect compared to Xinjiang's role: while Xinjiang was integrated into transregional trade (and production) flows, Galicia was disintegrated from transregional trade, obliged to readjust to the framework of the Habsburg customs union, benefitting the western manufacturing regions in the Bohemian and Austrian provinces.

There are a lot of distinctive features that escape comparison; for example, apart from in some mountain regions, a tribal population that was not attached to market relations before annexation did not exist. As Galicia had been part of the Polish-Lithuanian Empire, feudal relations prevailed and were adjusted to the Habsburg administrative system and internal market requirements. Restructuring the regional economy towards cash crop exports impacted labour relations and the labour market. Lacking industrial jobs, Galicia became an important region for seasonal and permanent migration to other parts of Habsburg Austria, Germany, Western Europe and the Americas from the 1880s onwards.

Bosnia and Hercegovina

This small province used to be a part of the Ottoman Empire, therefore comprising a Muslim population, coexisting with Orthodox Serb and Catholic Croat inhabitants. At the beginning there was a strong armed Muslim resistance against occupation, until Muslim elites were won for cooperation. Bosnia and Hercegovina shares with Xinjiang the instrumentalization of local Muslim elites to carry out economic and administrative modernization for the benefit of the occupation force. Under Ottoman rule, this mountain region showed a low level of economic development and a low integration into export markets. Austro-Hungarian governance promoted the development of extractive industries (minerals, wood) delivering raw materials to the Habsburg core.

Among the distinctive features in Bosnia and Hercegovina is the formal Ottoman presence coexisting with a de facto absence, increasing the manoeuvring space for the Austro-Hungarian occupation forces. The local arrangement was the result of an agreement among the European great powers (the Berlin Balkan Conference 1878), empowering the Habsburg ruler to keep balance between Russia and the Porte in reordering South East Europe. It reflects the fact that border changes on the Balkan Peninsula could not be carried out without the – however fragile – consensus of the European Concert.

In the case of Bosnia and Hercegovina, deep cultural gaps existed on several levels: most obviously between the Muslim and the Christian population, and secondly between the Orthodox Serb and the smaller group of Catholic Croat Christians, the latter representing the hegemonic Christianity of the ruling dynasty, which only from the eighteenth century onwards began to tolerate other Christian believers on its lands. By expanding into Bosnia and Hercegovina Habsburg rulers acquired Muslim subjects for the first time. Privileging the Muslim elite produced strong tensions with the Serbian Orthodox population, who felt excluded from the state-building that was taking place in neighbouring Serbia, which had become independent from Ottoman rule in the nineteenth century.

There was a cultural gap in Xinjiang too; however, the geographical pattern between colonizing Han Chinese and Muslim inhabitants of Xinjiang was different. The key difference was the geographical separation between the Han Chinese migrants and the Muslim inhabitants. The former were concentrated in northern Xinjiang, where the majority of the indigenous Mongol population had been expelled and replaced by Han settlers under Qing rule in the eighteenth and nineteenth centuries, in a process reminiscent of ethnic cleansing according to some researchers. On the other hand, the Muslim population was primarily concentrated in the desert oasis districts along the Tarim Basin in southern Xinjiang, located far away from northern Xinjiang (see the map in Kwangmin Kim's article). In southern Xinjiang, the Han Chinese were prohibited from taking up permanent residence as settlers in the Muslim area until the 1830s, except for a small number of the Chinese merchants, who would be staying there temporarily.

The reason was the Qing Empire's policy of separating the indigenous populations of border regions from the Han Chinese colonizers. The Manchu ruling house of the Qing Empire, of non-Chinese origin, had a deep suspicion about the negative impact of the Han Chinese settlers on the security of the non-Chinese regions, believing that the settlers were prone to exploiting indigenous populations and thus inciting ethnic conflicts with the latter. Perhaps the Qing rulers hoped that the geographical separation would prevent the development of a cultural gap similar to that seen in Bosnia and Hercegovina.

However, in spite of the Qing government's discouragement, Chinese migration increased in southern Xinjiang over the nineteenth century, and the tensions between the Muslim population and the Han Chinese settlers grew accordingly. When the Muslim rulers of the neighbouring state of Khoqand began to threaten the south-western oases of Xinjiang in the early nineteenth century, the Han Chinese settlers questioned the local Muslim elites' loyalty to the Qing Empire and raised the possibility of collusion between the oasis Muslims and Khoqand's ruler in a plot to subvert Qing rule in Xinjiang. Yet on balance, the Qing rulers were successful in preventing the cultural gap from developing into major violent conflict between the Han Chinese and the indigenous population until the outbreak of a large-scale local Muslim rebellion against the Qing in Xinjiang in 1864.

In both cases, the tensions between the ruling dynasty and the local population were overshadowed by the empowerment of the local Muslim elites. In southern Xinjiang, where Han Chinese settlers were rich and powerful but few in number, the fault line of social and political conflict developed more along the line of social class among the local Muslims – between the Muslim landlords and the rural population displaced by the former's agricultural development – and the line of politico-religious affiliations between the pro-Qing and anti-Qing Sufi factions, although the cultural tension between Han Chinese and local Muslims also developed. Equally, German-speaking settlers and central state employees were few in number in Bosnia and Hercegovina. Social conflict along the line of class, between landlords and dependent peasants (*kmetovi*), was overshadowed by the cultural difference between Christian Orthodox Serb, Catholic Croat and Muslim populations. After several rebellions were suppressed, the tolerance vis-à-vis the Muslims allowed the Habsburg emperors to underline the multi-ethnic philosophy of their rule. Serbian subjects were more difficult to integrate. Serb Orthodox believers stood against the Catholic identity of the ruling dynasty, while Serbian nationalists considered Habsburg occupation an obstacle to unification as a nation state.

Northern Xinjiang

Xinjiang is a huge area that is composed of two distinctive sub-areas. One is the steppe in the northern half, which used to be populated by tribal Zunghar Mongols. The majority of these people were either killed or scattered into other parts of Central Asia by the Qing conquest in 1754–59. Thus, during the period of Qing rule (1759–1911), northern Xinjiang was sparsely populated. The Qing government encouraged Han Chinese migrations into the region to carry out farming to support the Qing military stationed there. Han Chinese migrants to northern Xinjiang were not former serfs, but free farmers from core Chinese provinces. Some of the Han Chinese colonizers came as soldiers whose major function was to work on the government farm (*tuntian*). Other Chinese settlers came as civilian colonizers on their own.

Does northern Xinjiang's situation show similarities to that of Habsburg borderlands vis-à-vis the Ottoman empire, especially concerning the military border province (*Militärgrenze*) established between the fifteenth and the eighteenth century along the Ottoman border? In spite of the military purpose, the differences prevail. Most importantly, the military border province was not cleared of its indigenous population, but offered refuge for Christian settlers fleeing the Ottoman Empire. As peasant-soldiers, they enjoyed a privileged status and were free from feudal bonds and the local aristocracy. There was no settlement from Habsburg core provinces. Those parts of the military border province that were established in the sixteenth and seventeenth centuries were located in borderlands under Habsburg rule: setting up the province was an administrative act rather than a conquest. In the eastern Transylvanian parts of the province, the territories were won from Ottoman rule in the eighteenth century; the peasant-soldiers were recruited from local Romanian Orthodox people, for whom it meant liberation from serfdom and tolerance for their non-Catholic religion.

However, northern Xinjiang may be similar to the military border province in another sense – once it was integrated into the Chinese Republic in the twentieth century, it was turned into an economic periphery. Oil and other minerals were found in abundance there. It supplied natural resources to both China and Russia. Northern Xinjiang also attracted huge numbers of Han Chinese migrants in the twentieth century, due to the ample availability of uncultivated land.

Southern Xinjiang

On the other hand, the southern half of Xinjiang is composed of desert oases, and was mainly populated by sedentary Muslims. They were composed of city-dwellers and village-dwellers. Importantly, the southern Muslims and the northern tribal people were separated geographically for the most part during the Qing period.

The Qing Empire was sensitive about the possibility of potential interethnic conflict between the oasis Muslims and the Han Chinese migrants. Therefore, the Qing administration discouraged civilian migrations of Han Chinese into southern Xinjiang (while encouraging migration to northern Xinjiang, which was population-scarce). This does not mean that southern Xinjiang was totally devoid of a Chinese population. Chinese merchants (but no farmer-settlers) were allowed to go there.

Some Chinese soldiers were stationed there. Some Han Chinese also sneaked into southern Xinjiang in spite of the discouragement by the government. However, their numbers were small.

Southern Xinjiang shows a lot of similarities with Galicia/Bukovina and Bosnia and Hercegovina. It would be intriguing to make further comparisons.

How Did the Imperial Core Legitimate Foreign Rule in Habsburg and Qing Border Provinces?

Both in Galicia and in Bosnia and Hercegovina we can observe a strong feeling in official and public opinion in the imperial core, justifying conquest, occupation and exploitation with civilizing necessities.

In the Habsburg Empire, arguments that legitimated conquest as a civilizing mission resembled the Orientalizing discourses popular in Western European colonial empires vis-à-vis their colonized populations. According to the contemporary taxonomy that categorized people by their racial qualities, we can speak of a racist discourse, stressing similarities between landed empires' internal peripheries and overseas empires' colonies and their populations. It is worth comparing the discursive approach in Qing China vis-à-vis the Xinjiang population with Orientalizing practices in the Habsburg Monarchy.

In this respect, difference prevails over similarity. Certainly, there was a colonialist discourse with regard to Xinjiang during the Qing period. However, the Qing rarely justified its conquest of Xinjiang as civilizing mission. Rather, the Manchu emperors of the Qing Empire justified the conquest as the continuation of the historical legacy of the rule of the early Chinese empires over the region (in the first century BC to second century AD and the seventh to eighth centuries AD). The implication was that Xinjiang was originally Chinese imperial territory that was somehow lost. Now, the Qing rulers were recovering this long-lost territory. One may wonder whether the Manchu rulers, as non-Chinese rulers, wanted to prove their greatness to the Han Chinese elites, who may have been sceptical about the legitimacy of Manchu rule, by showing that they were able to recover the territory of the great early Chinese empires.

Meanwhile, Han Chinese scholars – the convicts exiled to Xinjiang who returned to China, and the small number of government officials who had access to information about the Qing rule in Xinjiang – also linked Xinjiang with the Chinese past. They painstakingly searched for the historical Chinese names of places in Xinjiang, while paying only scant attention to the people living there and their cultural specificities in their writings. When they took note of the inhabitants' cultural specificities and thus differences with Han Chinese, they did not advocate transforming the native cultures until the last decades of the nineteenth century. In effect, this amounted to a near erasure of the Mongol and Muslim natives from the Han Chinese colonial discourse on Xinjiang, although such an erasure was never complete.

It cannot be denied, however, that Habsburg rulers also stressed historical arguments to legitimize conquest. In the case of Galicia, a medieval duchy that had been under Hungarian rule was to prove legitimacy. In fact, the partition of Poland had other, contemporary, reasons. In the case of Bukovina and Bosnia and Hercegovina, no historical claims could be made and civilizing arguments could hardly hide strategic and economic interests.

Nor did Habsburg rule eradicate the local population from public opinion. Rather, the locals were depicted as colourful but primitive people, necessitating Habsburg governance in order to overcome their situation of 'backwardness'. Images of laziness, idleness, corruption, dirt and lack of education were common features, contrasted with local costumes and customs in newspaper articles and official ethnographic publications. Making these people inhabitants of Austria-Hungary and entitling them to full citizen's rights was depicted as an act of utmost generosity.

One of the major reasons for the difference between the colonial discourses of the Qing and Habsburg empires, we suspect, is that the Han Chinese public was rarely involved in the colonial enterprise. There were no newspapers to spread news about Xinjiang. Travel to Xinjiang by Han Chinese was severely limited. That is to say, the Qing rule over Xinjiang was a military enterprise more or less hidden to the Han Chinese public. Thus, the Qing colonial enterprise was driven more by the political interests of the Manchu emperor and high-ranking Han Chinese government officials. Furthermore, being non-Chinese minority rulers themselves, the Manchu emperors may have been more cautious about using racial discourses to legitimize their colonial rule in Xinjiang.

CHAPTER 1

Xinjiang and the Peripheral Pattern of Economic Development in Qing China

Kwangmin Kim

Introduction

In 1754–59 the Qing Empire of China conquered a vast area in the heart of Central Asia. Naming it Xinjiang ('New Territory'), the Qing Empire integrated it as the westernmost border of China for the first time.[1] The region still remains a border province under the control of the People's Republic of China. What was notable about the period of Qing rule (1759–1911) was the economic expansion of the Muslim oases along the Tarim Basin, located in the southern part of Xinjiang. In 1772, land under cultivation there was recorded as measuring 3.4–3.5 million *mu*, while by 1909 it measured 9.38 million *mu*. During the same period, the oasis population was estimated to have increased more than eightfold, from a population estimate in 1772 of a little under 200,000 to 1,867,000 in 1909.[2]

This chapter explores the pattern of economic expansion in Xinjiang. This pattern of economic expansion combined the horizontal economic integration of the border with the Chinese metropole on the one hand and the intensifying economic stratification of the border society on the other.

The key to the peripheral pattern of expansion was the political arrangements that the Qing state established in order to handle military financing in the border area. Working as revenue contractors for the local Qing military, Muslim landlord magnates of the Xinjiang oasis received access to the government-controlled wastelands and the right to claim the uncompensated labour of oasis villagers. They used these privileges to expand the production of grain, cotton, animals and animal products on their lands. The Qing administration calculated that the measure would help it to secure tax revenue and key logistical supplies from the border society at the lowest cost. In turn, the specific arrangements for military financing on the Xinjiang border provided the native landlords with a high level of built-in profit in the production process, allowing the Xinjiang oases to export staple goods, most importantly raw cotton, to China and Russia in spite of the prohibitive cost of long-distance transportation.

That is to say, the expansion of oasis agriculture occurred hand in hand with, and as a result of, the transformation of Xinjiang into a periphery of the Chinese metropole. While the politically connected Muslim landlords gained economically under Qing rule, they also transformed the oasis economy in a way that served the financial interests of the Qing imperial state and the economic interests of the Chinese metropole. Not only did the oasis supply financial revenue and military logistics to the Qing military stationed on the border, it also provided raw and semi-raw material to be used for handicraft production in the Chinese metropole. This indicates the emergence of a new level of economic integration of Xinjiang with China – predicated upon the growing economic stratification within the new imperial periphery.

This argument challenges current scholarship's understanding of the pattern of Chinese political economy. In a comparative study of Chinese and European political economy from 1500 to 1900, Roy Bin Wong and Jean-Laurent Rosenthal articulate the pattern of Chinese political economy prior to 1850 as an agrarian expansion, stimulated by light taxation and public spending by the Neo-Confucian state, which cared about people's welfare. The imperial scale of the Chinese state was responsible for this development. As united empires operating on the continental scale, the Chinese empires that came after the Mongol rule in the thirteenth and fourteenth centuries, both Chinese Ming and Manchu Qing, were successful in defending themselves from outside threats. Instead, their main concern was to fend off potential domestic challenges coming from landlord elites and the peasantry. In order to achieve their security goal, Chinese rulers consciously limited their fiscal extraction from the population, while spending bureaucratic energy and financial resources on projects to prop up the empire's economic and social infrastructure, such as water control projects and public granary systems.[3]

Wong and Rosenthal are correct in highlighting the imperial scale of China when discussing its pattern of political economy. However, their conceptualization of this is incomplete. Although Wong and Rosenthal define the Chinese scale as an imperial scale, they do not necessarily treat the Chinese space as imperial on the analytical level. They rarely pay attention to the internal differentiation between metropole and various peripheries inherent in imperial space, ignoring the possibility that different sets of political concerns and institutional arrangements were applied to the metropole and peripheries. Instead, the authors treat the space of the Chinese empire as essentially homogenous, and comparable to the space of each European nation state in nature, albeit larger.

This chapter shows that the metropolitan logic of the welfare-conscious Neo-Confucian rulers of late imperial China crumbled at the Xinjiang border. While the Qing rulers may have been benevolent and military financing of secondary importance in the Chinese metropole, the same rulers were extractive and focused on securing military finance in the border area in much the same way as the kings of Western Europe. Due to the pressing need of military provision, the Qing state decided to develop local agriculture and commerce by granting politically connected landholding magnates special economic privileges to land resources and markets. In the Qing administration's policy decisions, military financing was clearly a primary concern over maintaining the welfare of ordinary peasants. The Qing rulers were even willing to support the Muslim landlords' drive for development, even when it hurt the welfare of ordinary subjects in the area.

Qing Military Financing and Muslim Landlords

During its rule in the region from 1759 to 1864, the Qing Empire stationed between five thousand and fifteen thousand troops in strategic locations in southern Xinjiang. The number of Qing soldiers was recorded as 5,657 in 1774 and 8,078 in 1821. In particular, the four western oasis cities of southern Xinjiang – Kashgar, Yengisar (Yangi Hissar), Yarkand and Khotan – in which the military were concentrated had a combined 2,362 soldiers stationed there in 1774. The number increased to seven thousand in 1829 and to fourteen thousand in 1831.[4] In order to support the military the Qing Empire constantly provided financial subsidies to the local administration in Xinjiang. In the late eighteenth and early nineteenth centuries the Qing administration transferred sixty thousand liangs of silver to southern Xinjiang; the silver transfer increased to two hundred thousand liangs after 1828. From 1826 to 1864, local Muslims joined a series of religious resistances led by a family of Sufi holy men (*khoja*) to express their discontent with the Qing's economic extraction and its Muslim landlord allies.[5] In response, the Qing increased the troop numbers and the silver transfer to southern Xinjiang.[6]

In addition to sending silver subsidies from China, the Qing administration also employed many measures to promote local agrarian production. The expansion of local agriculture also increased the total volume of the land tax revenue locally. However, the increase of the tax revenue per se was only of secondary importance. In fact, the new land reclamation was rarely taxed after the initial Qing conquest in 1759. It was not until 1828–29 that the new land entered the tax register.[7] Rather, the primary calculation behind the Qing promotion of land reclamation was that the increased volume of production and trade would help the Qing military secure a constant supply of key logistical goods, such as grain, animals and horses, from the local market at low cost. In other words, the increase of the local agrarian production would help the Qing military in the oases to maximize the value of the silver it received from the metropole.

In particular, the Qing administration relied on a group of Muslim landholding magnates (*begs*) for the promotion of local agricultural production. These landlords, particularly those who had sided with the Qing during the latter's initial conquest of the region, worked as Muslim governors (*hakim*) in the major oasis districts in southern Xinjiang.[8] As the chief revenue contractors, the native governors took charge of three different revenue-related duties: 1) tax collection, 2) purchasing military provisions and 3) management and development of state-controlled resources, including land and mines. Table 1.1 shows the detailed breakdown of the revenue items that a Muslim governor delivered to a local Qing administration.

The most important part of their duties for the purpose of this chapter was the development and management of government-controlled properties, including land and mines. These state-controlled lands and mines had been off limits for the *begs*' private appropriation. However, as the Qing's imperial agent, the *begs* now gained access to them. The Muslim governors excavated copper and saltpetre from the local mines and sent them to the local military administration of the Qing, located in southern Xinjiang. The governors of Khotan and Yarkand, which had jade mines, excavated the entirety of the jade, which was sent to Beijing to be processed at the workshop of the Imperial Household Department.[9]

In the case of land development, the Muslim governors were charged with developing uncultivated wasteland covering the vast area of the oasis districts under the Qing government control. Highlighting state ownership of the area, the Qing administration called this area 'government wasteland' (*guan huangdi*).[10] Another important category of the government-controlled land given to the Muslim governors' management was 'rebel property' (*fanchan*), also listed in Table 1.1. This referred to the land properties confiscated from various local peoples who had resisted the Qing Empire at the time of the initial Qing conquest in 1754–59 and afterwards. The Muslim elites were charged with managing the properties, and were required to pay duties at the rate of 50 per cent of the harvest. However, the Muslim governors often under-reported the numbers and amount of the properties they managed, illegally appropriating the government-controlled land.[11]

In addition, at the time of their appointment as native governors and other lower-rank native officials, the Qing state provided the *begs* a package of land grants – land, cash, seeds and dependent service households (*yanchi*). More specifically, what the *begs* received included the right to designate for their private use a certain amount of the government-controlled wasteland surrounding the rural villages in the oasis according to their rank; capital in the form of cash and seeds to develop the wasteland; and the right to designate groups of people as their dependent service households to work the plots. The dependent households and the agricultural production from the land became exempt from taxes and other duties to the Qing government.[12]

For instance, the governors of the major oasis districts, such as Kashgar, Yarkand, Khotan and Aqsu, were entitled to receive two hundred *batman* of land, one hundred people for their *yanchi*, and thirty thousand wen of local copper coins, *pul*. The lieutenant governors (*ishikagha beg*) of the districts received 150 batman, fifty people, and fifteen thousand wen.[13] The overall size of the land grants was substantial. According to Saguchi Tōru's estimation, the official land grants to the 257 *beg* officials working for the Qing administration in the oasis region amounted to 7,924 *batman* of land (419,970 *mu*) in total. The Qing land grants to the *begs* composed roughly 70 per cent of the private landed property held by Muslims, which Saguchi estimated as six hundred thousand *mu*.[14]

The *begs* were eager and proactive participants in the land development project. In most cases the native officials went on to take control of more wasteland and employed a greater number of rural villagers as service households than the quota granted by the Qing imperial state. Rural villagers often reported illegal occupation of the land and labour to the Qing government in the hope that it would redress the situation. However, the Qing emperors turned a blind eye to these unofficial land developments as long as it was politically expedient. For instance, in 1786, Osman, the governor of Kashgar, a major south-western district of Xinjiang, was accused of illegally occupying 560 *batman* of wastelands and claiming 176 dependent service households from the subdistrict of Yengisar (Yangi Hissar). These numbers exceeded the government quota of seventy *batman* and twenty-five households allowed to a Kashgar governor by the

Table 1.1. Revenue duties of the Muslim governor of Kashgar District, Zuhur al-Din, 1835.

Category	Revenue item	Annual quota	Frequency of payment	Delivered to
1) Tax collection	Tribute	Grape (200 jin); Golden thread satin (2 bolts)	Monthly	
	Tax grain (guanliang)	32,193 shi★ (composed of 26,508 shi of wheat and 5,685 shi of miscellaneous grain)	Annual	Bureau of military provision (liangxiangju)
	Poll tax (alban)	2,660,088 wen	Monthly (221,674 wen each month)	
2) Purchasing military provisions	Cotton cloth	9,625 bolts (composed of white cloth 5,173 bolts and red cloth 4,452 bolts)	Annual	
	Animal hide, etc.	Animal hide (385 bolts); Madder ['Ma-ta-ha-er'] (385 pieces)★★; crude and fine hemp cords (384 strings); cotton cords (2 jin 5 liang); fine hemp cords (22 jin)		
	Horsehide, etc.	horsehide (6 sheets); Madder (6 pieces); crude hemp cords (12 strings); fine (hemp) cords (5 jin); cotton cords (12 liang)		

	Charcoal (for making gunpowder)	No fixed quota		
	Firewood	360,000 jin	Monthly (300 donkey cargoes; 30,000 jin each month)	
				Office of Manchu governor
	Alfalfa (used for grazing)	816,800 jin		
	Wheatgrass, etc.	Wheatgrass (100 cargoes); reeds (100 loads.)	Annual	
3) Management of state-controlled resources	Copper	600 jin	Annual	
	Saltpetre and sulphur	Saltpetre (3,360 jin); sulphur (456 jin)	Monthly (saltpetre [208 jin]; sulphur [38 jin])	
	Rent from 'rebel property'	Watermill (134,128 wen); buildings (856 wen, or 8,856 wen)	Annual	

Source: Wu, *Qingdai Xinjiang xijian zoudu huibian*, 163–64 and 173.

Notes:
* Shi is a unit of weight of grain. Wen is a unit of cash. Jin (catty in English) is a unit of weight. Liang (tael in English) is a unit of weight and silver currency.
** Madder is a dye substance. It was imported to Xinjiang from Fergana region of Khoqand khanate in the nineteenth century. According to a Russian report, 4900 rules worth of it was imported in 1876 (Kouropatkin, *Kashgaria [Eastern or Chinese Turkistan]*, 75).

subdistrict at the time. However, the Qing court decided to not punish the Muslim governor. Instead, it fired the Qing military governor who brought the charges to the attention of the Qing court, blaming his political insensibility.[15]

New Patterns of Overland Long-Distance Trade between Xinjiang and China

Beginning in the late eighteenth century, when Muslim landlords engaged in energetic land development, an increasing amount of cotton and leather from the oases in southern Xinjiang started to appear in long-distance trade markets in northern Xinjiang, China and Russia. This marked the emergence of a new pattern of overland trade in Eurasia. The Xinjiang oases had long been connected to China by the transit or terminal trade of luxury and specialized goods, including silk, tea and rhubarb from China and jade from Xinjiang. Yet the trade of staple goods such as cotton products and leather was unfeasible in long-distance markets due to the prohibitive transportation cost.

This chapter argues that what contributed to the rise of the long-distance trade of staple goods was politics. First, active state intervention contributed to growing cotton exports from southern Xinjiang to northern Xinjiang. The Qing administration had the Muslim governors purchase a portion of the cotton cloth (Chinese: *huibu*, 'Muslim cotton cloth') directly from the local markets in southern Xinjiang's oases, and collected another in lieu of the grain tax payment at the market price fixed by the government (see Table 1.2). The administration then transported it to northern Xinjiang towns and exchanged it for the livestock that was brought by Kazakh caravan merchants, most importantly horses. The Kazakhs consumed a portion of the cotton goods acquired in the market, but some of them eventually ended up in Russian Central Asia and Siberia.[16]

The total amount of the cotton products sent from the two cities to northern Xinjiang ranges from 55,802 to 58,587 bolts of white cotton cloth, although the quota for raw cotton was fixed at 15,000 *jin* in any given year. One notable feature of the trade was its price structure. In Yarkand and Khotan in the south, the 'market price' at which the government purchased the cloth and that the government remitted to the farmers as the price of cotton cloth was twenty-six *wen* of local *pul* cash per bolt in Yarkand (1779, 1784, 1797 and 1822) and twenty-four *wen* per bolt in Khotan (1784, 1792 and 1821). On the other hand, the sale price of the cloth in Tarbagatai was four *qian* of silver in 1792.[17] Calculated at the official exchange rate of one *qian* = five *wen*, the sale price was twenty *wen*. Therefore, the sale price of

Table 1.2. The amount of cotton collected from Yarkand and Khotan and sent to northern Xinjiang (1779, 1784, 1792, 1797, 1821 and 1822).

	1779	1784	1792	1797	1821	1822
Yarkand (white cotton cloth)	26,760 bolts (market price: 0 tänggä* 26 wen per bolt)	26,760 bolts (0 tänggä 26 wen per bolt)		29,545 bolts (0 tänggä 26 wen per bolt)		29,545 bolts (0 tänggä 26 wen per bolt)
Yarkand (raw cotton)	10,000 jin (market price: 1: 0 tänggä 7 wen per jin)	10,000 jin (0 tänggä 7 wen per jin)		10,000 jin (0 tänggä 7 wen per jin)		10,000 jin (tänggä 7 wen per jin)
Khotan (white cotton cloth)		29,042 bolts (market price: 0 tänggä 24 wen per bolt)	29,042 bolts (0 tänggä 24 wen per bolt)		29,042 bolts (0 tänggä 24 wen per bolt)	
Khotan (raw cotton)		5,000 jin (market price: 0 tänggä 7 wen per jin)	5,000 jin (0 tänggä 7 wen per jin)		5,000 jin (0 tänggä 7 wen per jin)	

Source: Zhongguo di 1 lishi dang'anguan and Zhongguo bianjiang shidi yanjiu zhongxin (eds), *Qingdai Xinjiang Manwen dang'an huibian*, vol. 197, 131–33; vol. 207, 226–27; vol. 242, 72–75 and 448–49.

Note:
* Tänggä and wen are units of cash. Jin (catty) is a unit of weight. For a detailed explanation about the conversion rate of tänggä and wen, see endnote 18.

one bolt of cloth in Tarbagatai was 77 per cent and 83 per cent of the purchase price in Khotan and Yarkand respectively.[18]

The purchasing price of one *jin* of raw cotton by the Qing administration in Khotan and Yarkand was seven *wen* (1779, 1784, 1792, 1797, 1821 and 1822). The purchasing price in the south was only 27–29 per cent of the purchasing price of cotton cloth there. Price data for the sale of raw cotton in northern Xinjiang is not available, although this product was sold to the Kazakh merchants. However, if the sale of cloth is any indication, it would not be far-fetched to assume that raw cotton was also sold at a similar or lower price in northern Xinjiang than in southern Xinjiang.

What the data reveals is the remarkable integration of the market in northern and southern Xinjiang, if the elimination of the price difference between the two markets is taken as a sign of market integration. This level of integration was remarkable because it was achieved in spite of the high cost of long-distance transportation between southern and northern Xinjiang. (Today, the distance between Yarkand and Ili – the city of Yining – is 1,261 kilometres by highway.) The main reason for this market integration was forceful government intervention. The Qing needed to maintain the sale price of raw cotton and cloth in northern Xinjiang in order to make the cotton products appealing to the Kazakh nomads who bartered their horses for the latter. The Qing military in Xinjiang needed the horses dearly. The Qing government was even willing to sell the cotton products at a price lower than their purchasing price in southern Xinjiang due to its high demand for the horses. The Qing administration could make the trade work, for it could transport the cotton and cloth without incurring much cost by using the compulsory labour provided by the oasis Muslims and Qing soldiers. In the economic equation of the long-distance cotton trade between southern and northern Xinjiang in both raw cotton and cloth, the political power of the Qing compensated for the disadvantage of physical distance.

However, ironically, it was also state intervention that prevented further market integration between northern and southern Xinjiang through private trade. Some private merchants from southern and northern Xinjiang – Muslims and Kazakhs respectively – ventured into each other's territory and exchanged the Kazakhs' livestock and the oasis cotton in the late eighteenth century. However, the Qing administration soon banned direct private trade, primarily in order to ensure that the horses imported from the Kazakhs remain in northern Xinjiang, where the horses were needed the most for the use of the Qing military and Chinese migrants. Unrestricted private trade would make it difficult for the Qing administration to achieve this goal.[19]

However, a private long-distance trade in raw cotton and cotton textiles emerged on the west–east axis between the Xinjiang oases and China in the nineteenth century. Politics also played a pivotal role in the realization of the private trade, but in a different way. In 1814, Songyun – the highest-ranking Qing commander overseeing the whole of Xinjiang, known as Ili General – proposed taxing the cotton and leather from southern Xinjiang's oases (*nanlu pizhang*) that were being transported to China. These goods were to be taxed at the rate of 30 per cent of the total trade volume at Jiayugaun Pass, a gateway from Xinjiang to China. The revenue made from the new tax would be used to support the oasis Muslims serving at the military postal relay stations located along the major communication routes in Xinjiang, and to defray the expenses of the local Qing administration.[20]

Songyun only indicated that Chinese merchants bought cotton from the cotton farmers in Turfan, an oasis district located at the easternmost part of southern Xinjiang, bordering the Chinese province of Gansu. However, the cotton traded in Turfan included that transported from the western part of southern Xinjiang, including the oasis districts of Yarkand and Kashgar. Evidence shows the constant eastward movement of raw cotton and cloth carried by the native merchants from the western oases. In 1785, for instance, the Qing administration caught a group of Muslim caravan merchants, as they were about to set out for Aqsu, an oasis city between Yarkand in the west and Turfan in the east. They were transporting jade stone, a trade item under a strict government monopoly, to the east on behalf of Chinese smugglers. However, what is notable for the purpose of this chapter is that the caravan was also transporting thirty-two animal loads of raw cotton and cotton cloth.[21] Likewise, in 1788 a Muslim merchant from Aqsu was caught in Kucha while transporting five horses and six animal loads of raw cotton, cotton cloth, shoes and other goods to Turfan.[22] In all likelihood, the raw cotton transported from the western oases was eventually bought by the cotton and leather merchants and shipped to China.[23]

Xinjiang tuzhi (Illustrated Records on Xinjiang; original edition 1911; revised edition 1923) is an early twentieth-century provincial gazetteer that conveys the situation in Xinjiang at the turn of the twentieth century. This text corroborates Songyun's report. It mentions that a group of Chinese merchants called 'Western merchants' (*Xishang*) from Gansu and Ningxia had travelled to Xinjiang previously during the Qing period and purchased animal skins and wool there before transporting them to China. Most likely, the 'Western merchants' refer to the 'West Road traders', who dominated the tea trade and other trades between China and Xinjiang, along with a group of wealthier and politically connected merchants from

Shanxi, Shaanxi, and Zhili, known as 'North Bend traders', during the Qing period. They were a diverse group of merchants coming primarily from Shaanxi and Gansu, but also from as far as Guangdong, Hunan, Jiangsu, Zhejiang and Sichuan provinces.[24] China remained the prime market for the export of Xinjiang's leather in spite of the difficulty of long-distance transportation and the existence of border passes along the way that slowed travel. The situation changed only after the extension of the Russian railway to right outside the Xinjiang border town of Ili. This made Semipalatinsk in Kazakhstan the largest export market for Xinjiang's leather. In all probability, the Russian railway to which the record refers was the Turkestan–Siberia Railway that was extended in 1915 to Semipalatinsk, located close to Ili.[25]

In turn, the expansion of the specialized cultivation of cotton and animal-raising in the oases led to the growth of the trade of another staple good in local and long-distance markets – grain. As the land and labour that was devoted to specialized cultivation and production expanded, some oases needed to import from nearby and from far away. *Tārīkhi Hāmīdī*, a Turkic-language history of eastern Turkestan written at the turn of the twentieth century, mentions that Kashgar imported two thousand loads of grain (*ašliq*) from Yarkand every week. Grain (*gällä*) and fruit (*yäl-yimish*) were abundant in Yarkand. It also mentions the scarcity of the 'products' (*mähsulat*), probably including grain, in Khotan, although fruit was abundant. In the meantime, Aqsu produced good-quality rice (*gürüč*), which it transported to every city.[26]

The Xinjiang oases even imported grain from beyond the Qing border. In 1788 a party of Kirghiz bandits robbed a caravan composed of Central merchants from Andijan passing through the mountains outside Kashgar district on the Qing border with a Central Asian country of Khoqand. This caravan carried thirty-one loads of goods, including fifteen loads of rice. The remaining sixteen loads included hides, cotton cloth and carpets.[27]

The Qing state was never directly involved in the private trade. Yet it is suspected that a different set of political factors were involved in the private trade of cotton goods. A pivotal element in the expansion of the long-distance trade was the specific nature of the *beg* agriculture, namely its low-cost enterprises predicated on free access to underutilized land and unpaid labour. It is plausible that these privileged production conditions provided the native landlords with a large enough built-in profit to offset the cost of long-distance transportation and still make a profit overall.

Perhaps the growth of indigenous cotton production that occurred under this specific structure prepared the region for its ultimate integration into global capitalist production. At the turn of the twentieth century, Xinjiang raw cotton began to supply cotton production in the world market. It started to be exported to Russian market, primarily Russian Central Asia and Siberia, in addition to China.

What is notable is the persistence of the geography of the cotton production established under Qing rule in the preceding century. The area that emerged as the biggest producer for Russian market was none other than Turfan and its vicinity – the area that had previously been identified as the centre of cotton production and trade in southern Xinjiang by Songyun in the early nineteenth century. Annually, Turfan produced three million *jin* of raw cotton, known for its softness and pure white colour, and exported 500,000–600,000 *liang*'s worth of raw cotton annually to Russia, beginning in 1903.[28] Two neighbouring areas, Shanshan County and Yanqi District's Korla village, produced respectively 500,000 *jin* and 30,000 *jin* annually. Yarkand region, now identified as Shache County, produced 280,000 *jin* annually. Yecheng (Qaġiliq), which belongs to this district, produced 130,000 *jin*. Khotan region, identified as Hezhen County, produced 100,000 *jin* annually. In the meantime, another production centre emerged in the Aqsu area. Identified as Wensu Prefecture, it produced 150,000–160,000 *jin* annually. Shule County (Yengišähär District) had similar production numbers.[29]

The Xinjiang oases also exported cotton cloth. Khotan district produced about 170,000 bolts of cotton cloth. It exported a large portion of its production to various places at an average price of three *qian* of silver per bolt. Khotan exported 120,000 bolts of textile to Andijan, which was under Russian control by then. The region also continued to export cotton textiles to the Chinese 'inland' (*neidi*), primarily north-western China (known as Guanlong). The annual amount of exports was roughly 20,000 bolts.[30]

The growth of trade between Xinjiang on the one hand and China and Russia on the other hand in cotton products – raw cotton in particular – indicated the new level of economic integration of this Central Asian border society into the broader economy of Eurasia. Not only did trade in cotton cloth indicate the deeper level of commercial integration of economic life across Eurasia, involving massive numbers of consumers, but the rise and expansion of trade in raw materials such as raw cotton and leather indicated yet another level: integration through the unequal division of labour in production. The raw cotton and leathers needed to be processed in the textile and leather workshops of the north-western provinces of China, such as Gansu and Shaanxi, or in Russian Central Asia, before reaching the final consumers.

Conclusion

Economic expansion was a politically conditioned process on the Xinjiang border. Taking advantage of their political position as revenue contractors for the local Qing military, Muslim landlords of the Xinjiang oasis acquired access to government-controlled wastelands and the right to claim the uncompensated labour of oasis villagers. They used these privileges to expand the production of grain, cotton, animals and animal products on their lands. The Qing administration calculated that the measure would help it to secure tax revenue and key logistical supplies from the border society at the lowest cost. In turn, the specific arrangements for military financing on the Xinjiang border provided the native landlords with a high level of built-in profit in the production process, allowing the Xinjiang oases to export staple goods, most importantly raw cotton, to China and Russia in spite of the prohibitive cost of long-distance transportation.

The pattern of economic expansion in Xinjiang highlights the extractive nature of the Qing empire in this border area. While the politically connected Muslim landlords gained economically under Qing rule, they also transformed Xinjiang's oases into an economic periphery that served the financial and economic interests of the Chinese core. The expanding oasis agriculture provided financial revenue and cheap military supplies to the Qing military stationed in Xinjiang; moreover, it also exported raw and semi-raw material to Chinese and Russian metropole to be used for handicraft production there.

The economic expansion in the Xinjiang border area followed a pattern that differed substantially from that seen in the Chinese metropole. According to Roy Bin Wong, the metropolitan pattern of economic expansion was characterized by the welfare-conscious state deliberately limiting its fiscal extraction from the population while expending bureaucratic energy and financial resources on projects to support the empire's economic and social infrastructure. In so doing, the Qing state may have indirectly subsidized agricultural production in China. However, in the border area of Xinjiang, what helped economic expansion was the revenue-conscious state, which prioritized raising military revenue over any other social concerns in Xinjiang. In order to achieve this goal effectively, the Qing state was willing to protect the native landlord class, which worked as their revenue agent and accumulated substantial wealth. The result was deepening social division and conflict within the oasis society, a development that also weakened the security of Qing rule in the long run.

The overall patterns of Chinese political economy appear very multidimensional if one takes into account the pattern of economic transformation in the border areas that were integrated into the Qing empire in the eighteenth century – areas that constituted more than half of the territory of Qing China. In order to get a fuller picture of the patterns of Chinese economic development since at least the eighteenth century, it may be necessary to find a way to reconcile the two different patterns of economic development in Qing China – metropolitan and peripheral.

Kwangmin Kim teaches Chinese history at the University of Colorado, Boulder, and specializes in the history of borders and transnational relations in China and East Asia. He is the author of *Borderland Capitalism: Turkestan Produce, Qing Silver, and the Birth of an Eastern Market* (Stanford University Press, 2016), and 'Xinjiang Under the Qing', in the *Oxford Research Encyclopedia of Asian History*, ed. David Ludden (Oxford University Press, 2018). Currently, he is conducting research on Chinese hunter-gatherers in Manchuria, 1800–1920.

Notes

1. This work was supported by the National Research Foundation of Korea Grant, funded by the Korean Government (2017S1A6A3A01079727).

2. Kim, *Borderland Capitalism*, 201–2, Appendices A-1 and A-2. The actual extent of land under cultivation was larger. The official number excluded two prominent portions of land holdings in oasis society. One was land belonging to religious facilities, such as mosques, *mazār*s (Sufi shrines), *khanqah*s (Sufi meeting places) or *madrasa*s (Islamic schools), bestowed as religious endowments (*waqf*). Another was land grants to the native officials serving the Qing Empire, which will be discussed later in this chapter.

3. This was in stark contrast to the European pattern, the authors argue, in which constant inter-state military competition led to urban-centred, capital-intensive industrial development and to the competitive overseas expansion from which Europeans extracted labour and raw materials. For the complete exposition of this idea, see Rosenthal and Wong, *Before and Beyond Divergence*. An early iteration of this thesis is presented in Wong, *China Transformed*, especially in chapters 4 and 6.

4. Kim, *Borderland Capitalism*, 50, Table 2.1.

5. Ibid., 90–125.

6. Hori, 'Shindai Shinkyō no kahei seido—Furu (pul) chūzōsei', 581–602; Millward, *Beyond the Pass*, 60–61.

7. Kim, *Borderland Capitalism*, 54–55.

8. For a comprehensive list of these Muslim collaborator families, see ibid., 208–15, Appendix C.

9. Ibid., 59–61.

10. For the use of the term *guan huangdi* in the Qing official record, see Wu, *Qingdai Xinjiang xijian zoudu huibian*, 19–22.

11. Kim, *Borderland Capitalism*, 60–61.

12. Ibid., 58–59.

13. Fuheng et al., *Qinding huangyu*, vol. 30.

14. Saguchi, *Juhachi-jukyu-seiki Higashi Torukisutan shakaishi kenkyu*, 131.

15. Kim, *Borderland Capitalism*, 82–87.
16. Fan, 'Qingdai Jiangnan yu Xinjiang diqu de Sichou maoyi', 163–66. For detailed examination of the Qing–Kazakh trade, also see Lin and Wang, *Qingdai Xibei Minzu Maoyi Shi*, 131–430; Millward, 'The Qing Trade with the Kazakhs in Yili and Tarbagatai, 1759–1852'.
17. Xingzhao, *Ta'erbahatai shiyi*, vol. 4. The price of a horse purchased by the Qing from the Kazakhs was between one *liang* seven *qian* and one *liang* eight *qian*; a cow, between one *liang* six *qian* and one *liang* seven *qian*; and a sheep, three *qian* six *fen*.
18. One *tänggä* was equivalent of fifty *pul* units (*wen*) in local copper currency in Xinjiang during Qing rule. One *liang*, or tael of silver, was equivalent of ten *qian*. The Qing government set the official *pul*/silver exchange rate as 1: one *tänggä* of *pul* is equivalent of one *liang* (tael) of silver, although the exchange rate fluctuated widely during Qing rule. Therefore, the official purchase prices of one bolt of cotton cloth in Khotan and Yarkand – twenty-four *wen* and twenty-six *wen* of *pul* – were roughly 4.8 *qian* and 5.2 *qian* of silver, if calculated on the basis of the official exchange rate. Therefore, the sale price of the cloth in Tarbagatai – four *qian* – was roughly equivalent or lower than the purchase prices. For exchange rates of *tänggä* and *liang*, see Millward, *Beyond the Pass*, 70, Table 3; Perdue, *China Marches West*, 394.
19. Onuma, 'Political Power and Caravan Merchants at the Oasis Towns in Central Asia', 49–50.
20. *Renzong shilu* [Veritable Records of the Qing Dynasty: Renzong (Jiaqing) Emperor], vol. 290, JQ19/5/yiwei (6/22/1814), Edict.
21. *Manwen lufu zouzhe* [Manchu language Memorial Copies from the Grand Council Reference Collection] (hereafter MLZZ), QL50/12/12, The First Historical Archives of China (hereafter FHA) 3099-024/136-0445.
22. MLZZ, QL53/3/9, FHA 3061-012/133-2926. The merchant was also carrying jade stones for Chinese smugglers.
23. This inter-oasis distance is not small. The distance between Yarkand and Aqsu is 460.5 km (286.1 miles) on the present-day highway route. The distance between Aqsu and Turfan is 939.5 km (583.7 miles). This makes the distance between Yarkand and Turfan 1400 km. Rosenthal and Wong define long-distance trade as 'exchanges of goods where buyers lived 2000 km or more from sellers'; *Before and Beyond Divergence*, 70. For a comparison, the distance between Denver, Colorado and Albuquerque, New Mexico is 446.7 miles on the US interstate highway I-25.
24. On the West Road traders and North Bend traders, see Millward, *Beyond the Pass*, 160–62.
25. Wang et al., *Xinjiang tuzhi*, vol. 28, 555.
26. Sayrāmī, *Tārīkhi Hāmīdī*, 639 (Kashgar [Kašġär]); 640, (Yarkand [Yarkänt]); 642 (Khotan [Xotän]); 649 (Aqsu).
27. MLZZ, QL53/2/24, FHA 3181-013/141-0855; FHA 0969-0773.
28. According to Russian investigations, the cotton from Turfan consisted of two kinds. One was native, the same kind grown in Bukhara; the other was American, the quality of which was better compared to the native variety. It is not known when the American type was transplanted to Turfan (Wang et al., *Xinjiang tuzhi*, vol. 28, 543). The price of one hundred *jin* of raw cotton was eighteen to nineteen *liang* of silver. See Xie, *Xinjiang Youji*, 111.
29. Wang et al., *Xinjiang tuzhi*, vol. 28, 543.
30. Wang et al., *Xinjiang tuzhi*, vol. 29, 575. A late nineteenth-century British report also confirmed Xinjiang cotton's integration into Russian and Chinese markets. Forsyth's mission reported that both raw cotton and cotton textiles, primarily from Khotan, Yarkand and Turfan were exported to 'east and west'. In the western direction, the cottons

were exported to Central Asian khanates through Khoqand and to the Russian settlement through Almaty (Vernoe) (Forsyth, *Report of a Mission to Yarkund in 1873*, 479).

Bibliography

Primary Sources

Forsyth, Thomas Douglas. *Report of a Mission to Yarkund in 1873, under Command of Sir T.D. Forsyth, with Historical and Geographical Information Regarding the Possessions of the Ameer of Yarkund*. Calcutta: Printed at the Foreign Department Press, 1875.

Fuheng, Liu Tongxun, and Yu Minzhong. *Qinding huangyu Xiyu tuzhi* [Maps and records of the imperial domain of the western regions], 48 vols, in *Yingyin Wenyuange siku quanshu* [Photoprint edition of the complete works of the four branches of literature stored in Wenyuange Pavilion]. Taipei: Taiwan shangwuyin shuguan, 1983 [1782].

He'ning. *Huijiang tongzhi* [Comprehensive gazetteer of the Muslim domain], 12 vols. Taibei: Wenhai chubanshe, 1966 [1804].

Kouropatkin, Aleksieĭ Nicolaevitch. *Kashgaria [Eastern or Chinese Turkistan]: Historical and Geographical Sketch of the Country, Its Military Strength, Industries and Trade*. Translated by Walter E. Gowan. Calcutta: Thacker, Spink and Co., 1882.

Sayrāmī, Mullā Mūsa. *Tārīkhi Hāmīdī* [History of Hāmīd]. Modern Uyghur edition. Trans. Enver Baytur. Beijing: Millätlär näshriyäti, 1986.

Wang, Shunan, Yuan Dahua and Li Yushu. *Xinjiang tuzhi* [Illustrated records on Xinjiang] (XJTZ), 116 vols. Shanghai: Shanghai guji chubanshe, 2015 [1911; revised edition 1923].

Wu, Fengpei. *Qingdai Xinjiang xijian zoudu huibian: Daoguang chao juan* [Collection of the rarely seen memorials and letters on Xinjiang during the Qing Period: Daoguang Period]. Wulumuqi Shi: Xinjiang renmin chubanshe, 1996.

Xie, Bin. *Xinjiang Youji* [Record of travel in Xinjiang]. Wulumuqi: Xinjiang renmin chubanshe, 2010.

Xingzhao (ed.). *Ta'erbahatai shiyi* [Affairs of Tarbagatai], 4 vols. Taipei: Chengwen chubanshe, 1969 [1805].

Zhongguo di 1 lishi danganguan, and Zhongguo bianjiang shidi yanjiu zhongxin (eds). *Qingdai Xinjiang Manwen dang'an huibian* [Collections of the Manchu language archival materials on the Qing Xinjiang], 283 vols. Xinjiang dangan wenxian congshu, Guilin: Guangxi shifan daxue chubanshe, 2012.

Secondary Sources

Fan, Jinmin. 'Qingdai Jiangnan yu Xinjiang diqu de Sichou maoyi' [The silk trade between Lower Yangzi Delta area and Xinjiang during the Qing period]. *Xibeishi yanjiu* 3 (2005), 155–78.

Fletcher, Joseph. 'Ch'ing Inner Asia c.1800', in John K. Fairbank (ed), *The Cambridge History of China*, vol. 10, pt. 1 (Cambridge: Cambridge University Press, 1978), 35–106.

Hori, Sunao. 'Shindai Shinkyō no kahei seido – Furu (pul) chūzōsei' [The currency system of Xinjiang during the Qing Period – system of minting *Pul* currency]. *Nakashi-ma Satoshi Sensei koki kinen ronshū* 1 (1980), 581–602.

Hua, Li. *Qingdai Xinjiang Nongye Kaifa Shi* [History of the development of agriculture in Xinjiang during the Qing Period]. Ha'erbin: Heilongjiang jiaoyu chubanshe, 1995.

Kim, Kwangmin. *Borderland Capitalism: Turkestan Produce, Qing Silver, and the Birth of an Eastern Market*. Stanford, CA: Stanford University Press, 2016.

Lin, Yongkuang, and Wang Xi. *Qingdai Xibei Minzu Maoyi Shi* [History of the trade of north-western peoples]. Beijing: Zhongyan minzu xueyuan chubanshe, 1991.

Millward, James A. *Beyond the Pass: Economy, Ethnicity, and Empire in Qing Central Asia, 1759–1864*. Stanford, CA: Stanford University Press, 1998.

———. 'The Qing Trade with the Kazakhs in Yili and Tarbagatai, 1759–1852'. *Central and Inner Asian Studies* 7 (1992), 1–42.

Newby, Laura. *The Empire and the Khanate: A Political History of Qing Relations with Khoqand c. 1760–1860*. Leiden: Brill, 2005.

Onuma, Takahiro. 'Political Power and Caravan Merchants at the Oasis Towns in Central Asia: The Case of Altishahr in the 17th and 18th Centuries', in Onuma Takahiro, David Brophy and Shinmen Yasushi (eds), *Xinjiang in the Context of Central Eurasian Transformations* (Tokyo: Toyo Bunko, 2018), 33–57.

Perdue, Peter C. *China Marches West: The Qing Conquest of Central Eurasia*. Cambridge, MA: Belknap Press of Harvard University Press, 2005.

Saguchi, Tōru. *Juhachi-jukyu-seiki Higashi Torukisutan shakaishi kenkyu* [Study on Eastern Turkestan society during the eighteenth and nineteenth century]. Tokyo: Yoshikawa Kobunkan, 1963.

Wong, Roy Bin. *China Transformed: Historical Change and the Limits of European Experience*. Ithaca, NY: Cornell University Press, 1997.

Wong, Roy Bin, and Jean-Laurent Rosenthal. *Before and Beyond Divergence: The Politics of Economic Change in China and Europe*. Cambridge, MA: Harvard University Press, 2011.

CHAPTER 2

Habsburg Borderlands

A Comparative Perspective

ANDREA KOMLOSY

Imperial Expansions: Colonies or Peripheries?

What does it mean to speak of a borderland of an empire? How do borderlands relate to the various types of territories constituting the empire at a given moment in history? Depending upon geographical location, empires tend to be sea-based or land-based. Respectively, overseas expansions of sea-based empires have usually been called colonies, while there is dispute on what to call territorial expansions of land-based empires: internal colonies, internal peripheries, conquered territories or new acquisitions?

The International Encyclopedia of the Social Sciences gave the following definition of 'colonialism' in 1968: 'Rule over an alien people that is separate from and subordinate to the ruling power ... Colonialism has now come to be identified with rule over peoples of different race inhabiting land separated by salt water from the imperial center ... Features of the colonial situation are: domination of an alien minority, asserting racial and cultural superiority over a materially inferior native majority ... A non-christian civilization that lacks machines and is marked by a backward economy ... And the imposition of the first civilization upon the second.'[1] This definition reflects the experience of European overseas empires. It does not consider including regions at the borders of European empires as colonized and does not consider any colonialism that is not Christian.

In his book *Colonialism*, Jürgen Osterhammel suggests a much broader definition: 'Colonialism is a relationship of domination between an indigenous (or forcibly imported) majority and a minority of foreign invaders. The fundamental decisions affecting the lives of the colonized peoples are made and implemented by the colonial rulers in pursuit of interests that are often defined in a distant metropolis. Rejecting cultural compromises with the colonized population, the colonizers are convinced of their own superiority and of their ordained mandate to rule.'[2] This definition suggests looking at the power relations, the motivations and the functions that the incorporated lands fulfil for the colonizer, at how the colonized are perceived and at which arguments are used to legitimate colonization. Whether the borders between the colonizer and the colonized are marked by seas, rivers, mountains or no natural markers at all is of minor importance, and the feeling of cultural superiority does not refer to a specific civilization.

Following Osterhammel's definition, colonialism cannot be reduced to European sea-based empires. Land-based states can equally exercise colonialism. Therefore, the Habsburg Monarchy and the Qing Empire, which did not possess colonies according to the narrow definition, will have to be investigated in terms of whether or not their territorial expansions into neighbouring provinces had a colonial character.

We will also have to deal with the category 'periphery'. According to the core–periphery models that are common in studying regional imbalances in economic development, 'Periphery is a relational term that always includes the relation towards a core or central region. The term is not restricted to hardly accessible, remote regions, or regions situated on the borders of a state. Not every border region is a periphery. We define a region as a periphery when it is stuck in "structural dependency" with a core region.'[3] In other words: the economic and social structures of the dependent region have been deformed into a source of constant transfers of value into the core regions. This definition can fit the narrow and the broad concept of a colony.

While the terms 'colony' and 'periphery' often converge and risk blurring existing differences, the term 'internal periphery' may be a more precise expression to describe a form of dependency that occurs within the boundaries of a state. Hans-Heinrich Nolte proposed using the term to designate a 'region within a society delineated by state boundaries, where conditions are organised to the advantage of people living in another region which we call the center'.[4]

Keeping these definitions in mind will help in differentiating between various types of borderlands of the Habsburg Monarchy, and in comparing them with Qing China. The focus will be the eighteenth and the nineteenth centuries. The following section will discuss the changing character of borderlands in order to provide a conceptual background for the case study of the Habsburg Monarchy.

Varieties of Borderlands

Speaking of borderlands certainly points to those territories that are situated at the fringes of an imperial state. But which notion of borderland is meant? Are borderlands conceived to be:

- Whole lands or provinces, which – for a certain period of time – were annexed to an empire?
- Regions of these provinces that are situated a smaller distance from the state border?

Furthermore, does the notion of borderland also refer to the heartlands, that is, the core provinces and principal hereditary parts of an empire, if they border a neighbouring country?

Borderlands are subject to change along with territorial gains that increase the size of a state, turning former borderlands into interiors. Conversely, territorial losses – for instance, through lost wars, decolonization, secession or declarations of independence – lead to new borders, turning new regions into borderlands.

As a consequence of borderlands' relative position between competing neighbours, a purely regional perspective will not be able to solve the problem of size and extension. On the contrary, border regions by definition require multilateral perception from different sides: from the dominating political and economic centres inside the states to which they belong, from their inhabitants, who identify themselves with the region in question, and from the immediate neighbours on the other side of the border.[5] Borderlands are shaped by their situation at the fringe of one state and its political centre; at the same time, they are shaped by the transborder relations with neighbouring regions, which again influence the relations towards the politically dominating core. Transborder communication may be based on several foundations:

- The borderland may be part of a transborder region comprising territories on both sides of the border, with a common history, common economic integration and common cultural features.
- Having belonged to a political unit now located on the other side of the border impacts the future development of a region after joining another state. The same applies for economic links and cultural

identities. Even if the ties with the former unit are cut, mutual interaction is not immediately stopped, and it may survive long periods of separation, eventually surviving or reappearing as a kind of 'phantom border',[6] even if the physical boundary does not exist any more.
- Often, border regions are characterized by permanent disputes of neighbouring empires concerning which state they belong to, causing armed conflict, changing statehood or partitions, and eventually strengthening the regional identity of the population as being a distinct region in between, giving rise to a transborder identity.
- Not every border region is the product of conquest or secession separating regions that previously formed a political unit. Clear-cut borders, which separate states with their different political, economic and cultural legal systems, may also cause communication: different conditions on the other side may attract smugglers, investors or migrants, giving them access to purchasing, labour or capital markets with different conditions than at home.

The different affiliations of a borderland with the states and societies on both sides impact its functions, too. Serving as a transborder region, it can fulfil common functions for both sides; the functions that it fulfils for one side can also contradict the claims of the other side, causing competition and conflict. Huge borderland territories, especially if they form separate administrative provinces with their own institutions, play a completely different role than do narrower border zones or border towns. In general, borderlands are identified with military-geopolitical, economic, and demographic and sociocultural tasks and purposes in different and changing combinations. Each territorial acquisition at a state border has geopolitical impacts on the size, power and influence of an empire, with direct effects on the military situation, which can be used for defensive purposes, for expansionist purposes or as a buffer zone to isolate conflicting neighbours and neighbouring conflicts. Economically, a borderland can serve as a periphery, delivering the core regions with raw materials and agricultural products, cheap migrant labour or favourable conditions for outsourcing production; it can equally serve as a bridgehead for certain cross-border activities, outgoing as well as incoming ones. It matters whether a borderland is politically dependent on a central government and administration or enjoys self-government. The success of political interference from either side will depend upon the sociocultural and socio-economic integration of the region on each side. It depends on how the imperial core or a competing, neighbouring empire deals with a borderland population that differs from the heartland in ethnic and religious respects. It will also depend on how far the socio-economic system and the level of economic development of borderlands and heartlands differ, and whether or not central governments aim at overcoming these differences and gaps.

Although borderlands are always situated at the geographical fringe of a state, they do not necessarily represent peripheries in the sense of fulfilling dependent functions according to the economic needs of a core, thus preventing the development of the region in its own interests. In many cases, borderlands have undergone peripheralization, but there is no equation between borderland and periphery. Furthermore, economic, political and cultural aspects of borderland peripheralization do not always coincide, giving rise to complex patterns of self-reliant and dependent relations within and across the different spheres of society and state borders.

Borders and borderlands evoke specific politics. Here we do not mean the acquisition of a borderland by whatever means, which is the most obvious form of border politics. Once the territory is incorporated, border politics from the side of the imperial core will shape the relations with the border region as well as with the neighbour (whose border politics have to be considered as well).

- Border politics will shape the border as a zone or as a line; they will decide on methods of fortification and on the permeability of the border for goods, capital and migration; they will set up criteria for the intensity and the selectivity of transborder relations and the means of controls and sanctions. Although measurements aim at the border and will take place at the border, they affect the bilateral relations of the neighbouring states and their international competitiveness beyond the border regions; some have specific regional effects on the borderlands, whether handicapping them or supplying them with special functions.
- Border regions are also affected by the state of internal integration within the empire to which they belong. On a political and administrative level, one has to look at the amount of local and regional autonomy, the contribution of a border region to tax collection and its share of state expenditures and fiscal redistribution. On an economic level, one has to investigate the existence and functioning of internal borders, which affect the circulation of goods, capital and people between the different provinces of an empire. In the case of newly annexed territories, specific strategies of regional integration might be necessary in order to adjust different levels of development or legal traditions and to overcome resistance against conquest or annexation.

The following section is dedicated to sorting the varieties of regions that are considered borderlands in the Habsburg Monarchy. It starts with the general characteristics of the state, before giving a typology of its borderlands.

Habsburg Borderlands: A Typology

A Conglomerate of Lands or an Empire?

In a long-term historical perspective, the territorial composition of the Habsburg Monarchy shows significant variations, with permanent changes in what can be considered 'heartlands' and 'borderlands'; while former heartlands were lost or became bordering regions, former borderlands moved towards a central position, geographically and politically.[7] The formation of an Austrian polity dates back to the Babenberg dynasty (976–1246).[8] Austria cannot be called an empire at that time, because it represented a border province of the Holy Roman Empire – a very loose construction that comprised a large number of independent feudal substates under a common king. In order to claim continuity with the (Western) Roman Empire, coronation took place in Rome, transforming the king into an emperor. The Babenberg and the succeeding Habsburg dynasties were successful in increasing their territories by conquest, succession and marriage treaties, 'collecting' a growing number of lands under their dominion. First in 1273 and then from 1438 onwards, the Habsburg rulers served as Holy Roman Emperors. Only after the separation of the Austrian and Spanish family lines in the early modern period did the scattered Central European Habsburg possessions begin to form a combined territoriality, and the rulers sought diplomatic recognition of their indivisibility. However, they did not form a unity, but a patchwork conglomerate of lands under a common ruler that each enjoyed a certain degree of self-governance, although this was contested between the central ruler and regional aristocratic lords and towns.

At the beginning of the eighteenth century, when Habsburg Austria included the Austrian Netherlands, Lombardy and the former Spanish possessions in Italy, Silesia, Hungary and Transylvania, it extended into the west, north, south and east of the continent. With the loss of Silesia and the Netherlands during the eighteenth century, Habsburg Austria was reduced to its Central European part. Further expansion, as well as commercial connections, were directed eastwards and south-eastwards, that is, into Galicia and Bukovina, Venetia and Dalmatia, and Bosnia and Hercegovina. The Netherlands and Silesia, the borderlands in the west and north, were among the most economically developed regions of the Habsburg Monarchy. After their separation, former heartlands in the interior of the Habsburg complex approached the external borders of the empire: Tyrol in the west and Bohemia and Moravia in the north. The new acquisitions in eastern and south-eastern Europe represented a different type of borderland, conquered or acquired not out of medieval dynastical ambitions and connections, but as a part of empire-like state-building, tending towards the territorial consolidation of the conglomerate as a modern state. However, it was not until the collapse of the Holy Roman Empire that the composite Habsburg lands were declared the Austrian Empire (Österreichisches Kaiserreich) in 1804. Still, unification did not change the composite character of the empire, which maintained a federal character and tolerated the self-governing institutions of the crown-lands in spite of centralizing aspirations.[9]

Hungary enjoyed a special status:[10] the kingdom was officially ruled by a Habsburg according to a succession treaty from 1526. Until 1699 the largest part was under Ottoman domination, however, and when the Habsburgs conquered the country in from 1683 onwards and were confirmed Hungarian kings in 1687, they had to make several concessions to the local aristocracy.

Even before the declaration of empire, a main pillar of eighteenth-century territorial consolidation aimed at the internal integration of the lands and provinces in economic, political and administrative respects.[11] Important steps were the setting up of direct rule and central administration, the abolition of internal customs and tolls, the introduction of a customs union and the transformation of subjects from feudal subordination to a lord to state citizenship. State-building and state centralization provoked strong conflicts with the feudal authorities about who was entitled to exercise political power and juridical rights and to collect revenues and taxes from the subjects, among other things. The central state limited the power of regional rulers by setting up new administrative districts, which were controlled by state authorities. State-building was not only about territorial unification vis-à-vis neighbour states, but also about drawing internal borders between districts and lands. The new territorial delimitations, with their respective internal borders, also served as a means to establish central state authority in the newly acquired provinces.

In order to differentiate types of borderlands, each border province must be checked according to the following criteria:

- Date, motivation for and method of acquisition of province;
- State(s) to which it previously belonged;
- Functions of the province for the political core;
- Functions of the province for the economic core(s);
- Functions of the province in an interstate context (external affiliations, intermediary role, competing external centres, etc.);
- State of internal integration (political, economic, cultural);
- Size and importance of the province for the empire; is the whole province considered a borderland, or is there a narrower border zone,

or a border town with specific functions, such as fortress or military use; duty-free zone or free port; market or place of production for smuggling;
- Transit economy (is it part of a long-distance trade route?); transnational border zone, and so on.

The military-strategic, political and economic functions of regional expansions cannot be separated from one another. Rather, the typology looks for overlaps and intersections between the different features characterizing a specific borderland.

In the nineteenth century the following types of Habsburg borderlands can be observed:[12]

Borderlands vis-à-vis the Ottoman Empire

The borderlands with the Ottoman Empire date back to the sixteenth century, when the latter incorporated vast parts of Hungary (as a *pashalik*) and Transylvania (as a suzerain duchy) into its sphere of influence. A military border zone (*Vojna krajina*, *Militärgrenze* or *Confin*) was established all along the border with the Ottoman Empire by the Habsburg rulers, whose claim to the Hungarian lands resulted from a succession treaty with the Jagellonian dynasty, who ruled Hungary until their last king died in the Battle of Mohács, lost against the Ottomans in 1526. It can be classified as a 'frontier'.[13] The military border was exempted from the local aristocracy's rights; it became a special military province, directly governed from the court (first in Graz, later in Vienna). Its inhabitants, most of them Orthodox settlers fleeing the occupation of their lands by the Ottomans, served as soldiers; they were rewarded for their services with land, which they cultivated for their families' subsistence without being subjected to a feudal lord. When the Ottoman army was driven out of Hungary and Transylvania after the defeat at Vienna in 1683, the military borderland province originally built up in Croatia and Slavonia was enlarged with a Transylvanian section.[14] This section attracted Romanian settlers who had formerly served as serfs on Hungarian estates, now hoping for social advancement and overcoming feudal bonds as peasant-soldiers. At the moment of its maximal extension, the military border province stretched out for 1,800 kilometres and enclosed 49,000 km² and a population of 1.25 million. The provincial status was abolished in 1881, when Serbia and Romania had succeeded the Ottoman Empire as neighbouring states.

The military border province had a purely military function; agriculture served subsistence and was subordinated to military services.[15] After a while, the soldiers were trained to be elite troops, fighting not only against the Ottoman army but on other battlefields as well. This caused further neglect of the regional agriculture. Towns were small, handicrafts and industry hardly developed and military supplies imported into the province. The borderland province was thus economically very backward. Nevertheless, it cannot be regarded an economic periphery, because there were no resources to be withdrawn except military ones. From a military point of view it was a key province, delivering specialists to various battlefields, such that it may be labelled a military centre or a military bridgehead. As a result of its specific location at one of the most contested military fronts of Europe, it does not make sense to apply the terms 'centre' and 'periphery' in their economic meaning. Once the *Vojna krajina* lost its military function and became part of the Hungarian kingdom, however, strategic centrality turned into economic peripherality. The property rights and the ethno-religious orientation of the former warrior-peasants nonetheless guaranteed them a special status within Hungary.

Dalmatia, a former part of Venetia, became part of the Habsburg Monarchy in 1797 and received the status of a separate crown-land after the end of Napoleonic rule in 1815. Although it had a long border with the Ottoman Empire, it was not incorporated into the military border province, but remained a civil province, although it provided ports for the Austrian navy.

Bosnia and Hercegovina represent a special case.[16] The Ottoman province was occupied by Habsburg troops in 1878 and administered as a Habsburg protectorate. Occupation took place with the consent of the Great Powers and of the Ottoman Porte, who agreed on a protectorate status at the Berlin Congress. This compromise allowed maintenance of formal Ottoman dominion, thus preventing Russia from extending its influence in the Balkan peninsula, as well as the partition of the province among the newly arising neighbouring nation states along ethno-religious lines. The incorporation into the Habsburg Monarchy was only partial until the annexation in 1908, which ended the equilibrium of power and paved the way for a military conflict over the Balkan state borders. When the province of Bosnia and Hercegovina was annexed in 1908, it still remained outside of the two sub-imperial entities into which the Austro-Hungarian Empire had been divided since the Dual Settlement of 1867, the imperial Austrian lands (Cisleithania) and the Kingdom of Hungary (Transleithania), united by a common monarch. Bosnia and Hercegovina did not belong to either political part, representing a special entity that deserves the label 'colony'.

Borderlands vis-à-vis the Russian Empire

For a long time, the Austrian and Russian empires did not have a common border. They only became neighbours in the last quarter of the eighteenth century as a result of the partition of the Polish–Lithuanian Empire and the Moldavian Duchy.[17] The Polish Empire was partitioned in 1772, 1775 and 1795 between Prussia, Russia and Austria. The Duchy of Moldavia, which was suzerain to the Ottoman Porte, was partitioned in 1775 between Russia and Austria, which gained Bessarabia and Bukovina, while the rest of Moldavia remained under Ottoman influence.[18] These expansionist advances corresponded with the territorial consolidation of the Prussian, Austrian and Russian empires, which were directed against each other – at the expense of independent states in between, which were transformed into border provinces. At the same time the partition powers were interested in diminishing the Ottoman zone of influence, carefully ensuring that the territorial gains did not change the balance of power in favour of one of them.

Galicia and Bukovina first of all had a military and a geostrategic function. Galicia was a huge province, with 78,500 km^2 and 5.4 million inhabitants in 1869. Bukovina, with 10,500 km^2 and 457,000 inhabitants, was administered as a part of Galicia until it obtained its own provincial government in 1849. The population was predominantly agrarian, with a majority of smallholders producing for subsistence and working on the estates of a small minority of feudal landlords. Handicrafts and industrial production were at a low level. Galicia was at the crossroads of several trans-European east–west and north–south trading routes. When Galicia was annexed in 1772, the question soon arose of whether it should join the Customs Union, which was established in 1775, comprising the Austrian hereditary lands (but not Hungary), Tyrol, the Netherlands and Lombardy.[19] Merchants opposed accession, because the new customs border cut though older trade connections and increased the costs of transit trade; Austrian and Bohemian industrialists argued in favour because of the huge Galician market. A compromise was found, and Galicia joined the Union in 1784, while Brody, Podgórze and Biała were exempted as duty-free merchant towns.[20]

Economic considerations were thus important right from the beginning.[21] Integrating the province into the Customs Union meant opening it to industrial exports from the western provinces, while no major efforts were undertaken to develop industry or civil infrastructure in Galicia. Such endeavours only took place in the second half of the nineteenth century, when Galicia's resources were discovered to be useful for the core provinces. In order to transport salt, coal and oil to the western regions, a railway line was opened in 1847. After the abolition of serfdom, agricultural products, especially wheat, became valuable for export. With some exceptions, such as brewing and distillery, there was no large-scale industrial production. Oil, which gained importance after the development of new drilling techniques, left the region unrefined, while the big refineries were located in the Vienna region and in the seaports of Fiume/Rijeka and Trieste.[22] We may therefore speak of Galicia as an internal periphery supplying the central regions with raw materials, agricultural products and labour, thus in a way offering the colonial functions that overseas colonies fulfilled for the Western European sea powers.[23]

The benefits of the Galician periphery were claimed by other economic powers as well. Competition can be observed in the field of the oil industry, where know-how and investment was Canadian and US-American rather than Austrian. There was also strong competition for Galician labour migrants from the 1880s, when the concentration process in Galician agriculture did not allow the peasants and smallholders to survive without additional earnings as migrant workers. The majority of labour migrants went to Germany, working on a seasonal basis on the estates of the East Elbian farms, or emigrated to the United States of America. Labour was one of the commodities that Galicia as a labour periphery delivered to core regions; however, Austrian regions only received a small share compared to Germany and the United States, the main destination of Galician migrants in the decades before the First World War.

The labour market also demonstrates how economic and cultural relations may mingle. Social stratification in Galicia had an ethnic component, with Poles (the majority in western Galicia) representing the landed aristocracy, and Ukrainians (in Habsburg Austria called Ruthenians; the majority in eastern Galicia) smallholders and landless people working on the estates. Germany was interested in agricultural migrant labour. As the government did not want to increase the number of Poles working in Germany because of its strong anti-Polish sentiments, it therefore preferred Ruthenians to Poles. Special residence restrictions guaranteed that Galician migrants had to return to Habsburg homelands every winter.[24]

Borderlands vis-à-vis the Holy Roman Empire (until 1804/6), German Confederation (1806–66) and German Empire (1871–1918)

As long as (the Central European part of) the Habsburg Monarchy belonged to the Holy Roman Empire and the House of Habsburg held the role of Emperor, borders with neighbouring German states did not matter in many respects.

Being part of the Holy Roman Empire did not prevent the member states from engaging in wars and territorial disputes. Austria was especially affected by the conquest of Silesia, one of the main industrial provinces, by Prussia in 1740, this loss causing the Viennese authorities to initiate administrative and economic reforms. Bohemia and Moravia, core provinces since their dynastical unification in the sixteenth century, now became border provinces, albeit without ever being considered 'borderlands'. Nevertheless, Bohemian and Moravian regions bordering Silesia and Saxony became locations for illegal exports and imports, with merchants and industrial producers on both sides profiting from avoiding customs. Border-generated traffic took place equally between Tyrol-Vorarlberg and Switzerland, or between Lombardy and France.[25]

The formation of the Habsburg Customs Union from 1775 onwards already set up an economic border. After the dissolution of the Holy Roman Empire and the foundation of the Habsburg Empire in 1804/6, borders with German states became more important. When Habsburg Austria did not join the German Customs Union (Deutscher Zollverein) in 1834, the separation deepened.[26] It was solidified when German and Austrian state-building became exclusive and antagonistic projects, resulting in the war of 1866 and the foundation of the German nation state in 1871. The Austrian Empire underwent a process of integration and unification, with state borders serving to mark political and economic unity. The regions on both sides of the border did not show specific imbalances in their economic development; nevertheless, economic integration between the Austrian Monarchy and the other German states was severed, while the border regions' links with other regions in their respective states became stronger. Labour migration again serves as a good example: until the beginning of the nineteenth century, medium and long-distance labour migration to the Vienna metropolitan region and the industrial districts of Lower and Upper Austria originated mainly from southern Germany; after the political separation, workers came from the Bohemian lands, while migration from Germany significantly diminished during the nineteenth century.[27]

Until the turn of the eighteenth and nineteenth centuries, Habsburg Austria also held – scattered – possessions in the western part of the Holy Roman Empire, which can be regarded as dislocated borderlands. These territories were taken over by Napoleonic France or were seized in the process of territorial consolidation of the German states after the end of the Napoleonic Wars (or both). Their loss was compensated by Habsburg territorial acquisitions in eastern and south-eastern Europe, as mentioned above.

Internal Borders

Internal borders played an important role in the Habsburg Monarchy, which consisted of a number of distinctive provinces (lands) with their specific regional traditions, united by a common sovereign. State formation engendered centralization, which was achieved by the administrative, fiscal and legal reforms of the eighteenth century. Centralizing reforms met with resistance from traditional elites – aristocratic as well as bourgeois-urban ones – who were afraid to lose local or regional governance.

Thus, internal borders, in spite of the ongoing administrative and legal attempts to overcome traditional feudal borders, did not disappear. Unifying the state required a new spatial order, attributing distinctive competences to particular administrative territories with regard to travelling, passports, residence issues and migration from one territory to the other.[28] In this process, new administrative territories with new borders were formed. The struggle between central state administration and local elites was thus reflected by different types of borders competing against each other for the control of their subjects. Internal political-administrative borders existed between each crown-land. They were completed by administrative borders on the regional and local level, including ecclesiastical, juridical and fiscal borders. This complicated network of borders covered the whole state territory, but it did not create borderlands. It supplied state administration with the tools to control mobility, migration and access to poor relief.

How did the spatial administrative reforms affect the incorporation of newly acquired border provinces? Both processes corresponded to the same interest of the central government in territorializing state power against internal and external competition. Internal and external consolidations were more directly linked when conquest and annexation raised the question of how to integrate the newly acquired territories into the existing political, administrative and economic structures. Measurements of integration differed widely, as the following examples demonstrate.

In the case of the Customs Union, initiated in 1775 between the hereditary Austrian and Bohemian lands, we can observe the absence of Hungary, Tyrol, the Netherlands and Lombardy. The exclusion of Hungary was due to the refusal of the Hungarian nobility to introduce administrative reforms that would allow central authorities to collect taxes, control the recruitment of soldiers and establish direct state control over subjects.[29] Moreover, this conflict may also be read as a legacy of Hungary's former status as a borderland under Ottoman rule. Ottoman rule not only brought along political suppression and tax collection by an occupying power; it also offered political privileges and freedom of religion to the local aristocracy. When Hungary moved from being an Ottoman to an Austrian borderland, the Hungarian elites were not ready to accept the political-administrative reforms undermining their traditional power; they preferred political autonomy to economic integration. After Habsburg rule was established in 1687/1699, Hungary was excluded from industrial development; it was dedicated to importing industrial commodities from Austria and to delivering agricultural goods to Austria. The unequal exchange went hand in hand with unequal taxation. High tariffs on Hungarian exports were implemented to compensate for the lack of direct central state taxation.

In the case of Tyrol, joining the Customs Union conflicted with its function as a transit region from German to Italian lands. A compromise was only found in 1825, when Tyrol and Lombardy, after years of French occupation, became members of the Customs Union.[30] When Galician merchants asked for the same privilege after the annexation of the province by Habsburg Austria, they were granted a few duty-free trading towns, but had to join the common economic project in spite of their diverging interests in 1784. Although the province became part of the common market, industrial development was not on the agenda, with Galicia serving as a market for industrial exports from the west of the empire, delivering selected raw materials to the Austrian and Bohemian lands.[31]

The different moments of joining the Habsburg Customs Union indicate that centralization and market unification took a long time and met with resistance and obstacles. The Customs Union was only completed in 1851, when the defeat of the Hungarian Revolution (the declaration of independence in 1848) paved the way for overcoming resistance. Subjection to Viennese rule only lasted until the Dual Settlement of 1867, when the common monarch again had to accept Hungarian autonomy, linked to the establishment of a Hungarian parliament and self-governing institutions.[32]

Similarly, it took a long while for a province to enter the common area of conscription (*Konskribierte Länder*) that took shape at the same time as the Customs Union. Members had to accept central recruitment of soldiers, including the institutions and procedures for selection and control.[33] While Galicia did so right after its annexation, Tyrol and Hungary did not join the common area from the beginning. As a consequence their subjects and citizens had to accept travel restrictions and special passport regulations when they wanted to leave their provinces and enter those crown-lands that formed the 'conscription provinces'. In Hungary, conscription came under the control of the Viennese central authorities when the kingdom lost self-governance after the defeat of the 1848 uprising. Military affairs remained under joint Austro-Hungarian administration, after Hungarian state autonomy was restored under the Dual Settlement of 1867.

Comparing Habsburg Borderlands

Borderlands with western and northern neighbours played a different role for the Habsburg state than did borderlands with Eastern and South Eastern Europe.

In the case of the Holy Roman Empire, one can observe a complicated entanglement, and there were several moments of border enforcement before the Austrian Empire took shape as a sovereign state after the former's dissolution in 1806. From these moments onwards, it was realized that being located at a state border increased traffic control here and there and offered jobs in customs services or opportunities for trade or smuggling. But the regions at the borders did not fulfil specific functions because of their location. They were neither defined as border regions nor did their position at state borders impact on their roles as cores or peripheries.

The Kingdom of Hungary, whose crown was claimed by the Habsburg dynasty from 1526, was a composite monarchy itself, and cannot be classified as a borderland. While the largest part of Hungary belonged to the Ottoman Empire between 1526 and 1699, the battle line between the empires was constantly moving backwards and forwards, transforming the front regions into a military border zone. This frontier was given the status of a border province under direct court governance, guaranteeing special privileges to its inhabitants – mainly Christian refugees from regions occupied by the Ottomans, who in return had to serve as peasant-soldiers. In the case of Hungary, the idea of a borderland was restricted to the 'military border province'.

When Galicia and Bukovina were incorporated into the Habsburg Monarchy in the 1770s, the concept of a military border province was not applied, vis-à-vis neither the Ottoman Empire, of which Bukovina had been a part, nor the Russian Empire, which had occupied another part of former Poland-Lithuania, neighbouring Galicia. At the time of conquest, these regions served as buffer zones rather than border provinces; after they had become crown-lands, the perception changed and they were seen as border provinces – regardless of their large size and the distance of most of their parts to the state border.

Bosnia and Hercegovina, which was the last province to shift from Ottoman to Habsburg dominion, may on the one hand be regarded as a borderland. On the other hand, it was not officially incorporated into the Habsburg dual state, remaining part of the Ottoman Empire, which however withdrew from all administrative functions. As a protectorate of Austria-Hungary, Bosnia and Hercegovina represented a borderland region outside of the Habsburg Empire's state territory. It can therefore be characterized a 'colony', albeit one directly bordering the motherland; after annexation in 1908, the provisional status was formalized.

While the western borders, after the disentanglement of the Habsburg Empire from the Holy Roman Empire, corresponded to linear state borders as was characteristic for the modern interstate system, the eastern and south-eastern acquisitions were established as imperial frontiers. While the much older 'military border province' vis-à-vis the Ottoman Empire lost its significance with the ongoing Ottoman defeat until its final abolition in 1881, the acquisitions won in Galicia and Bukovina and in Bosnia and Hercegovina served as new imperial frontiers.

Conquest and occupation respectively followed a military and geostrategic logic. After the consolidation of Habsburg rule, the military installations and the fortification of the border, other functions followed – according to the resources and economic potential of a province. The newly acquired provinces were turned into export regions of agricultural products, raw materials and migrant labour, at the same time representing easily accessible export markets for Austrian and Bohemian-manufactured goods because of the Customs Union. Representing a frontier was not restricted to military-strategic purposes, but went hand in hand with the exploitation of the provinces as commodity frontiers.

Thus, we have to ask about the peripheralizing effects of occupation and the functions that the border provinces fulfilled in the political economy of the empire. All eastern and south-eastern provinces supplied the developed regions in the western and central parts of the empire with products, gained on the grounds of their specialization in natural resources and cheap labour. Transferring these to the industrialized regions created the uneven division of labour characterizing the economic relationship between core and periphery. Realizing this economic function was inseparably interconnected with the geostrategic position of these provinces, which renders a separation of military and economic frontiers difficult. The frontier character also became manifest in the orientalizing discourse from the imperial cores vis-à-vis the new provinces and their non-German populations.[34] Similarly to the colonial discourses in overseas empires, conquest and penetration were legitimated in terms of bringing civilization to an allegedly 'wild' population, associated with a lack of industry and infrastructure and with ethnic and religious difference. The ethnographic and anthropological studies that developed in the course of the nineteenth century clearly reflect the orientalizing approach of the imperial core towards the empire's internal peripheries.

These border regions played a role for the continental empire that was provided by colonial acquisitions for overseas empires. As internal peripheries, they can be perceived as compensations for colonial expansion.

Internal peripheries were not restricted to border regions populated by non-dominant ethnic and religious groups, however. They can equally be found in German or Magyar-speaking regions in interior heartlands, usually located in remote, mountain or agrarian areas, fulfilling a similar function for the core as border regions.[35]

Andrea Komlosy is professor at the Department for Economic and Social History, University of Vienna, Austria, where she is a coordinator of the Global History and Global Studies programme. She has published widely on work and labour, migration, borders and uneven development on regional, European and global scales, with recent publications including *Work: The Last 1000 Years* (Verso, 2018) and *Global Commodity Chains and Labor Relations*, edited with Goran Musić (Brill, 2021).

Notes

1. *International Encyclopedia of the Social Sciences*, 'Colonialism'.
2. Osterhammel, *Colonialism*, 16–17.
3. Senghaas, *Peripherer Kapitalismus*, 27 (translation by the author).
4. Nolte, *Internal Peripheries*, 1.
5. There is a huge volume of literature on borders and border regions. See Diener and Hagen, *Borders*; Komlosy, *Grenzen*.
6. Hirschhausen et al., *Phantomgrenzen*.
7. Komlosy, 'Imperial Cohesion'.
8. For a short history of Austria from the beginning until today, see Vocelka, *Geschichte Österreichs*.
9. Kaps proposes applying the term 'polycentric empire' to the Habsburg Monarchy. See Kaps, 'Internal Differentiation'.
10. For a general overview, see Kontler, *Millennium*.
11. Komlosy, *Grenze*.
12. For an overview, see Komlosy, 'Imperial Cohesion'.
13. Heeresgeschichtliches Museum, *Die österreichische Militärgrenze*; Krajasich, 'Die Militärgrenze'.
14. Göllner, *Die Siebenbürgische Militärgrenze*.
15. Kaser, *Freier Bauer*.
16. Donia, *Islam*; Donia, 'Proximate Colony'; Ruthner, 'Kakaniens kleiner Orient'.
17. Augustynowicz and Kappeler, *Die galizische Grenze*; Maner, *Galizien*.
18. Hofbauer and Roman, *Bukowina*; Mosser, 'Das Habsburgerreich'.
19. Beer, 'Die Zollpolitik'; Kaps, *Ungleiche Entwicklung*; Komlosy, *Grenze*.
20. Kuzmany, *Brody*.
21. Kaps, *Ungleiche Entwicklung*, analysing the whole period of Habsburg rule over Galicia.
22. Frank, *Oil Empire*.
23. Kaps, *Ungleiche Entwicklung*.
24. Olsson, 'Labor Migration'.
25. Saurer, *Straße*.

26. Koch, 'Österreich'.
27. Komlosy, Grenze.
28. Heindl and Saurer, Grenze; Komlosy, Grenze.
29. Kontler, Millennium.
30. Komlosy and Weitensfelder, 'Regionen vergleichen'.
31. Kaps, Ungleiche Entwicklung.
32. Kontler, Millennium.
33. Komlosy, Grenze.
34. The following volumes contain several case studies on orientalizing positions vis-à-vis non-dominant nationalities, applying Osterhammel's criteria of feeling and expressing cultural supremacy regarding the Habsburg case: Feichtinger et al., Habsburg postcolonial; Hárs et al., Zentren; Müller-Funk et al., Kakanien. See also Kaps, Ungleiche Entwicklung; Kaps, 'Orientalism'; Wolff, Inventing Eastern Europe; Wolff, The Idea (for Galicia); Todorova, Imagining the Balkans (for the Balkan regions).
35. Komlosy, 'Innere Peripherien'.

Bibliography

Augustynowicz, Christoph, and Andreas Kappeler (eds). *Die galizische Grenze 1772–1867: Kommunikation oder Isolation?* Vienna: Lit Verlag, 2007.

Beer, Adolf. 'Die Zollpolitik und die Schaffung eines einheitlichen Zollgebietes unter Maria Theresia'. *Mittheilungen des Instituts für oesterreichische Geschichtsforschung* 14(2) (1893), 237–326.

'Colonialism', in William David L. Sills, *International Encyclopedia of the Social Sciences*, vol. 3 (New York: Johnso Alvin, 1968), 1–6.

Diener, Alexander C., and Joshua Hagen. *Borders: A Very Short Introduction*. Oxford: Oxford University Press, 2012.

Doppler, Elisabeth. *Die sozio-ökonomischen Verhältnisse in Galizien in der zweiten Hälfte des 19. Jahrhunderts*. Vienna: Diplomarbeit Univ. Wien, 1991.

Donia, Robert. *Islam under the Double Eagle: The Muslims of Bosnia and Herzegovina, 1878–1918*. New York: Columbia University Press, 1981.

Donia, Robert. 'Proximate Colony: Bosnia-Herzegovina under Austro-Hungarian Rule', in Clemens Ruthner, Reynolds-Cordileone Diana, Reber Ursula and Detrez Raymond (eds), *WechselWirkungen: Austria-Hungary, Bosnia-Herzegovina, and the Western Balkans, 1878–1918* (Frankfurt: Peter Lang, 2015), 67–82.

Feichtiger, Johannes, Ursula Prutsch and Moritz Csáky (eds). *Habsburg postcolonial: Machtstrukturen und kollektives Gedächtnis*. Innsbruck: Studienverlag, 2003.

Frank, Alison. *Oil Empire: Visions of Prosperity in Austrian Galicia*. Cambridge, MA: Harvard University Press, 2005.

Göllner, Carl. *Die Siebenbürgische Militärgrenze: Ein Beitrag zur Sozial- und Wirtschaftsgeschichte 1762–1851*. Munich: Oldenbourg, 1974.

Hárs, Endre, Wolfgang Müller-Funk, Ursula Reber and Clemens Ruthner (eds). *Zentren, Peripherien und kollektive Identitäten in Österreich-Ungarn*. Tübingen-Basel: A. Francke Verlag, 2006.

Heeresgeschichtliches Museum (ed.). *Die k. k. Militärgrenze: Beiträge zu ihrer Geschichte*. Vienna: Österr. Bundesverlag für Unterricht, Wissenschaft und Kunst, 1973.

Heindl, Waltraud, and Edith Saurer (eds). *Grenze und Staat: Paßwesen, Staatsbürgerschaft, Heimatrecht und Fremdengesetzgebung in der österreichischen Monarchie (1750–1867)*. Vienna: Böhlau, 2000.

Hirschhausen, Béatrice von, Hannes Grandits, Claudia Kraft, Dietmar Müller and Thomas Serrier (eds). *Phantomgrenzen: Räume und Akteure in der Zeit neu denken*. Göttingen: Wallstein Verlag, 2015.

Hofbauer, Hannes, and Viorel Roman. *Bukowina, Bessarabien, Moldawien: Vergessenes Land zwischen Westeuropa, Rußland und der Türkei*. Vienna: Promedia, 1997.

Kaps, Klemens. *Ungleiche Entwicklung in Zentraleuropa: Galizien zwischen überregionaler Arbeitsteilung und imperialer Politik (1772–1914)*. Vienna: Böhlau, 2015.

———. 'Orientalism and the Geoculture of the World-System: Discursive Othering, Political Economy and the Cameralist Division of Labor in Habsburg Central Europe (1713–1815)'. *Journal of World-Systems Research* 22(2) (2016), 315–348.

———. 'Internal Differentiation in a Rising European Semi-Periphery: Cameralist Division of Labour and Mercantile Polycentrism: Two Different Models of Political Economy in Eighteenth-Century Habsburg Central Europe'. *Review (Fernand Braudel Center)* 36 (3–4) (2013), 315–50.

Kaser, Karl. *Freier Bauer und Soldat: Die Militarisierung der agrarischen Gesellschaft in der kroatisch-slawonischen Militärgrenze (1535–1881)*. Vienna: Böhlau, 1986.

Koch, Klaus. 'Österreich und der Deutsche Zollverein (1848–1871)', in *Die Habsburgermonarchie 1848–1918, Bd. 6/1: Die Habsburgermonarchie im System der internationalen Beziehungen* (Vienna: Verlag der Österreichischen Akademie der Wissenschaften, 1989), 537–60.

Komlosy, Andrea. *Grenze und ungleiche regionale Entwicklung: Binnenmarkt und Migration in der Habsburgermonarchie*. Vienna: Promedia, 2003.

———. 'Innere Peripherien als Ersatz für Kolonien? Zentrenbildung und Peripherisierung in der Habsburgermonarchie', in Endre Hárs, Wolfgang Müller-Funk, Ursula Reber, and Clemens Ruthner (eds), *Zentren, Peripherien und kollektive Identitäten in Österreich-Ungarn* (Tübingen-Basel: A. Francke Verlag, 2006), 55–78.

———. 'Imperial Cohesion, Nation-Building and Regional Integration in the Habsburg Monarchy', in Stefan Berger and Alexej Miller (eds), *Nationalizing Empires* (Budapest: CEU Press, 2014), 369–427.

———. *Grenzen: Räumliche und soziale Trennlinien im Zeitenlauf*. Vienna: Promedia, 2018.

Komlosy, Andrea, and Hubert Weitensfelder. 'Regionen vergleichen: Am Beispiel Vorarlbergs und des Oberen Waldviertels im 18. und 19. Jahrhundert'. *Geschichte und Region* 6 (1997), 197–240.

Kontler, László. *Millennium in Central Europe: A History of Hungary*. Budapest: Atlanzisz, 1999.

Krajasich, Peter. 'Die Militärgrenze in Kroatien mit besonderer Berücksichtigung der sozialen und wirtschaftlichen Verhältnisse in den Jahren 1754 bis 1807', in *Schriftenreihe des Heeresgeschichtlichen Museums in Wien* (Vienna: Heeresgeschichtliches Museum, 1973).

Kuzmany, Börries. *Brody: Eine galizische Grenzstadt im langen 19. Jahrhundert*. Vienna: Böhlau, 2011.

Maner, Hans-Christian. *Galizien: Eine Grenzregion im Kalkül der Donaumonarchie im 18. und 19. Jahrhundert*. Munich: IKGS Verlag, 2007.

Mosser, Alois. 'Das Habsburgerreich als Wirtschaftsraum unter besonderer Berücksichtigung der östlichen Karpatengebiete', in Ilona Slawinski and Joseph P. Strelka (eds), *Die Bukowina in Vergangenheit und Gegenwart* (Vienna: Lang, 1995), 53–72.

Müller-Funk, Wolfgang, Peter Plener and Clemens Ruthner (eds). *Kakanien revisited: Das Eigene und das Fremde (in) der österreichisch-ungarischen Monarchie*. Tübingen-Basel: A. Francke Verlag, 2002.

Nolte, Hans-Heinrich (ed.). *Internal Peripheries in European History*. Göttingen: Muster-Schmidt, 1991.

Olsson, Lars. 'Labor Migration as a Prelude to World War I'. *International Migration Review* 30 (1996), 875–900.
Osterhammel, Jürgen. *Colonialism: A Theoretical Overview.* Princeton, NJ: Markus Wiener, 2010.
Ruthner, Christian. 'Kakaniens kleiner Orient: Post/Koloniale Lesarten der Peripherie Bosnien-Herzegowinas (1878–1918)', in Endre Hárs et al. (eds), *Zentren, Peripherien und kollektive Identitäten in Österreich-Ungarn* (Tübingen-Basel: A. Francke Verlag, 2006), 255–84.
Saurer, Edith. *Straße, Schmuggel, Lottospiel: Materielle Kultur und Staat in Niederösterreich, Böhmen und Lombardo-Venetien im frühen 19. Jahrhundert.* Göttingen: Vandenhoeck & Ruprecht, 1989.
Senghaas, Dieter. *Peripherer Kapitalismus: Analysen über Abhängigkeit und Unterentwicklung.* Frankfurt: Suhrkamp, 1974.
Todorova, Marija Nikolaeva. *Imagining the Balkans.* New York: Oxford University Press, 1997.
Vocelka, Karl. *Geschichte Österreichs.* Munich: Heyne, 2002.
Wolff, Larry. *Inventing Eastern Europe: The Map of Civilization on the Mind of Enlightenment.* Stanford, CA: Stanford University Press, 1994.
———. *The Idea of Galicia: History and Fantasy in Habsburg Political Culture.* Stanford, CA: Stanford University Press, 2010.

Part II

TOURISM AND BORDERLANDS

Shizue Osa and Małgorzata Głowacka-Grajper

Travelling is often seen as a challenge to established state borders. In tourism studies, researchers emphasize that travelling means crossing political, social and cultural boundaries and define travellers' identities against the background of changing cultural contexts. The places in which the problems of identity and cultural diversity are particularly complex are borderlands. That is why in both these chapters, the authors deal with the issue of tourism in borderlands. However, these borderlands are quite different. In the Polish case, these areas are close to the state borders and have been under Poland's cultural and political influence for centuries. The chapter on Japanese students' travels deals with areas that at the time in question had recently been occupied by Japan and were seen as 'new' areas that required Japanese migration and investment. Therefore, the purpose of compiling these two chapters is not to make systematic comparisons between the situations in Japan and Poland, but to indicate how broad the spectrum is of topics on relations between state borders and travel and tourism. The analyses clearly show that areas close to national borders are spaces of negotiation of power and identity. The power exercised there by the state may have a different character, but it is the state that decides how a given territory is perceived by its citizens – will they be the newly conquered territories that constitute the starting point for the building and expansion of the empire (as in the Japanese case), or areas defined as belonging 'forever' to the state, perceived as the cradle of national culture (as in the Polish case)?

Shizue Osa deals in her chapter with the analysis of written reports of very specific travels – school trips to Manchuria organized by Women's Higher Normal Schools in Tokyo and Nara for educational purposes after the outbreak of the Second Sino-Japanese War in 1937. In the 1930s, massive agrarian migration from the Japanese mainland was organized through state policies, and Japanese immigrants were settled along the borderland between Manchukuo and the Soviet Union, and students from women's schools were also supposed to choose to work there. Osa points at the circumstances of these women's tours and analyses travel writings by students as records of their colonial representation of different, unfamiliar cultures. These travels may be interpreted as a social and cultural strategy of linking the conquered territories on the continent with the Japanese mainland. This strategy was realized by visiting two kinds of places: first, colonial cities connected to the future (to prospective modernization for the sake of Japanese empire) and second, former battlefields connected to the past (to the glory and sacrifice of Japanese soldiers). Nowadays, these 'colonial travels', as well as the history of Japanese occupation on the continent, are silenced in Japanese society and have become an uncomfortable part of national memory.

The memory of former Polish eastern borderlands is also uncomfortable for contemporary Polish society and for the state. These territories were incorporated into the Lithuanian, Belarusian and Ukrainian Soviet Socialist Republics and the memory of their past as a part of the Polish state creates problems for relations between Poland and its eastern neighbours (because it is perceived as a starting point for revisionist claims or a sign of Polish 'colonialism'). Changing state borders also meant displacement of millions of people. Małgorzata Głowacka-Grajper writes on the contemporary memory practices of these people. After the beginning of post-communist sociopolitical transformation, a special kind of travelling emerged in Poland – 'memory tourism' of displaced persons and their families. This tourism is mainly sentimental but can also have the character of an 'imperial gaze' when contact with the traces of Polish material culture leads to nostalgia for the past glory of a great commonwealth (defined almost exclusively as the Polish state). 'Memory tourists' are people who cross not only state but also time boundaries. They travel first of all for personal reasons, but at the same time they feel drawn to the duty to remember and to search for the sources of the collective identities focused around memory of the former Polish eastern borderlands.

Borderland tourism is very diverse, as are the borderlands themselves and people's motivations for travelling. Analyses regarding Poles and

Japanese travelling to the borderlands within the political and cultural influences of their own countries show that personal contact with a given territory is an necessary experience for reflecting on its relationship with national ideology.

CHAPTER 3

Travelling *Jokoshi* Students

Construction of the 'Imperial Gaze' through Colonial Tourism during War

SHIZUE OSA

Introduction: Travelling *Jokoshi* Students

The Japanese military occupation and domination of so-called Manchuria, the north-eastern part of China, became more serious in 1932 and continued until the end of the Second World War. As the development of a total war of aggression against the entire Chinese territory from 1937 increased the strategic significance of Manchuria for Japan, imperialistic violence raged over the Chinese and Korean populations in the region. This included depriving people of their land and suppression of the anti-Manchurian and anti-Japan movements among Chinese citizens. At the same time, massive agrarian migration from the Japanese mainland was organized through state policies, and Japanese immigrants were settled along the borderland between Manchukuo and the Soviet Union.

In the 1990s, *Manchuria under Japanese Dominion* by Shin'ichi Yamamuro[1] became a milestone of the Manchurian studies that were being carried out intensively in Japan. These studies endeavoured to clarify Manchuria's significance for modern Japanese politics. The author depicted the structural features of Japanese domination over Manchuria, in which context the various intentions and interests of different political and military forces competed with each other. He also exposed the actual facts of 'five races under one union (五族協和)' – a notion that Manchukuo propagated as its state ideal – and the real violence against various peoples in this 'idealist' state, using a wide range of different materials in various languages. This work put special emphasis on and exaggerated the 'violence and modernity' of the domination of Manchuria. Since its publication, especially in the 2000s, the development of Chinese–Japanese War Studies has allowed for new perspectives that paid attention to 1937 as the turning point of the age. Additionally, Manchurian studies widened their scope from aspects of political and military history to include cultural ones too. The construction plan for Xīnjīng (Changchun) as a colonial city, Manchurian films, the development of railway networks and other matters attracted scholarly attention as new topics for investigation, and Manchurian tourism studies have also produced many works that question colonial 'leisure and modernity'.[2]

In terms of tourism, this chapter examines school trips to Manchuria that were organized by women's higher normal schools in Tokyo and Nara for educational purposes after the outbreak of the Second Sino-Japanese War in 1937. These schools were the highest educational institutions for women in pre-war Japan, where women's admission into imperial universities was not permitted on principle, and their students were expected to become the female elites of the Japanese Empire. Their experiences in Manchuria reveal the asymmetry between imperial rule over the native peoples in the territory on the one hand and the Japanese on the other. At the same time, they demonstrate the transformation of connotations attached to Manchurian tourism from 'leisure' to 'warfare' and 'instruction', and expose the changing of gender roles for both sexes. These points will contribute to a reconsideration of the Japanese domination of Manchuria as a project for modernity.

Infrastructure was a prerequisite for tourism to allow for visitors' required mobility. Maritime routes and colonial railroads were indispensable for the travelling activities under consideration in this chapter. The question of why anyone travels anywhere confronts us with the necessity of considering the historical prerequisite for the journeys in question. Colonial tourism provokes the question of what was recorded in travellers' writings and what was omitted, because travelling by railway as a modern phenomenon – and the view from train windows, for example – puts barriers between travelling 'bodies' and the objects of their perception. The act of observation in itself invests authority and power in travellers as observers. At the same time, however, 'observation by tourists' is not necessarily a unidirectional process – seeing or being seen – but involves mutual negotiation at that moment. When we consider Mary Pratt's idea of the 'contact zone', what kind of travel writings does 'observation by tourists' produce?

In this chapter, I try to examine the writings of wartime colonial tourism from this perspective.

Figure 3.1 shows travel schedules for 'continental tours' to the Korean peninsula and north-eastern China organized by two women's higher normal schools in Tokyo and Nara during the 1939 summer recess. As mentioned above, Tokyo Women's Higher Normal School (the predecessor of Ochanomizu University, hereafter abbreviated as 'Tokyo Jokoshi') and Nara Women's Higher Normal School (the predecessor of Nara Women's University, hereafter abbreviated as 'Nara Jokoshi') were the highest seats of learning for women in pre-war Japan. Nara Jokoshi made a trip as late as 1940. As for 1941, the tour was cancelled immediately prior to departure in spite of permission from the Ministry of Education, and despite the fact that students had already been informed about their trip, which had been planned in detail.[3] This chapter sheds light on the circumstances of these tours and analyses travel writings by students as records of their colonial representation of different and unfamiliar cultures. Principal questions concern the conditions that enabled highly qualified female students to organize tours to the outskirts of the empire in the midst of the war mobilization and the significance of these tours.

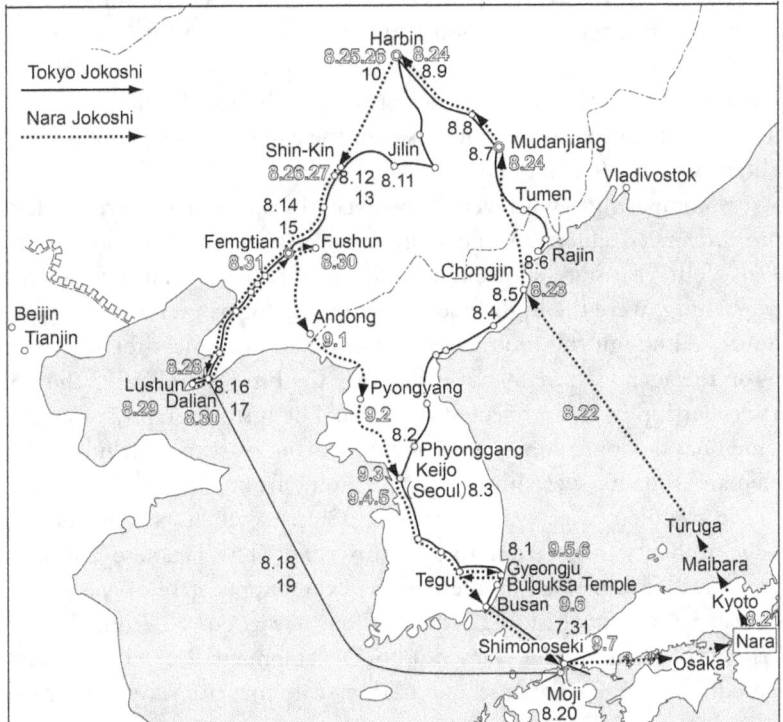

Figure 3.1. Routes of Two Jokoshis' Travel (1939). © Shizue Osa.

The *Jokoshis'* Continental Tours and the Age in Which They Took Place

In July 1937, the Second Sino-Japanese War began with the Japanese army invading the Chinese mainland; the battlefield soon spread throughout China. In the historiography of contemporary Japan, the period between the Manchurian Incident in 1931 and the end of the war in 1945 was traditionally regarded as one coherent age, comprising 'The Fifteen Years War'. Recently, however, 1937 has been recognized as the turning point towards total war and the prerequisite for the Asia-Pacific War that began in December 1941. Even at the outbreak of war in 1941, most troops were deployed to the Chinese mainland.

The major transformation from 1937 was the radical acceleration of wartime mobilization towards total war, and Japanese society changed completely in response to this. Higher educational institutions also underwent a sharp reorientation.

The higher educational system in pre-war Japan, including its colonies, was composed of nine imperial universities at the top and less prestigious state-sponsored professional colleges. The number of students who received opportunities for higher education was very small,[4] and they were entitled to privileged exemption from conscription. From 1937 onward, however, students were used as a wartime labour force (*Gakuto-doin*), and from 1943, exemption from conscription was abolished, mainly for those studying humanities; male students over the age of 20 were mobilized for military services (*Gakuto-shutujin*).

By comparison, with very few exceptions, women were excluded from university education under the pre-war system. Therefore, the two *Jokoshi*, four-year state-sponsored professional colleges mainly for secondary teaching, were the highest seats of learning for women in the Japanese Empire. Although the mobilization of women as soldiers for war efforts was on the agenda in many countries after the First World War,[5] the military leadership in Japan rejected this idea. The historiography of Japanese women has demonstrated that their roles during wartime, including those of female students, were limited to the 'home front'.

Meanwhile, what was north-east China, which was included in *Jokoshi* students' itineraries, like at this time? The Japanese Kwantung Army invaded it in 1931, and established the puppet state of Manchukuo under Japan's control in 1932. From then, it was cut off from the main territory of China. The Manchukuo Development Project was implemented from 1932 onwards, and a large-scale migration operation from the Japanese mainland to the region was initiated as a national policy following the enforcement of Policy Guidelines of the Project in December

1937. Between then and 1945, about two hundred and seventy thousand people migrated there to work in agriculture. Because of a shortage of labourers, even boys aged 15–19 were sent to Manchuria as members of the Volunteer Pioneer Youth Army of Manchuria and Mongolia. This migration policy, which utilized civilians as a shield against border conflicts between Manchukuo and the Soviet Union, produced about eighty thousand casualties.

Thus, north-east China, or Manchuria, to which *Jokoshi* students were headed, was adjacent to the disputed border with the Soviets and was a territory subject to continuing deployment of immigrants by national policy. In fact, destinations of students' tours included villages where pioneer immigrants had settled, and meetings with the boys of the Volunteer Pioneer Youth Army were scheduled in the itineraries.

In light of these trips, it is worthwhile to consider the condition of the railroad, the main means of transport. From 1932, the South Manchuria Railway Company, established in 1906 in the context of the Japanese Empire's national policies, was a driving force for the 'development' of Manchukuo. The company expanded its transport capacity, widening the track gauge and converting to double tracks. The most prominent cases in point were the double-tracking between Dalian and Changchun in 1934 and the operation of the express trains *Nozomi* and *Hikari* between Pusan and Changchun. Along the border with the Soviet Union, the transportation network was expanded between eastern Manchuria and northern Korea through purchase of the North Manchuria Railway (1935) and completion of the Unna Line (*Unggi–Najin*). This initiated a new phase of development in Manchuria and paved the way for a maritime project to connect Tsuruga and Niigata in Japan directly to Chongjin on the north-east coast of the Korean peninsula.

Many studies on Manchurian tourism, particularly in sociology, have concentrated on the role of the tourist industry as a cultural apparatus that developed a strategic enterprise to link the continent with the Japanese mainland and included sightseeing routes around colonial cities and former battlefields, as well as bus tours between cities in Manchuria. According to these studies, the heyday of Manchurian tourism was the early 1930s. Continental tours, including those to Taiwan and the Korean peninsula, organized by secondary and higher schools for boys, have been regarded as the major cases of this kind of group tourism, as their records have been preserved in great quantity. Researchers of tourism, however, have been interested mainly in the private industry and private consumption; only a few studies have investigated the intention of the imperial state, and in particular, the mechanisms that pushed schools to organize these kinds of tours. Although some researchers have also focused on the enthusiasm for battlefield tourism among schools, their conclusion is that it ceased with the restraints imposed on passengers by the railway company at the outbreak of the Second Sino-Japanese War. Certainly, the government and the Ministry of Education did restrict continental tours by male students. However, the examination of tourism from the historical viewpoint of 'wartime' does not lose its significance. Moreover, we need to develop different arguments about school tours from the perspective of a cultural analysis of consumerism, because they were not organized freely. Therefore, our question is how and why school trips by elite female students, who, unlike male students, were not subject to military service, were motivated and organized.

*Jokoshi*s in Wartime and Their Missions

Nara Jokoshi was founded in 1908 as the second national women's higher normal school in Japan. In the 1930s, its regular courses lasted four years and comprised three departments (Humanities, Housework and Science). Each year, approximately thirty students enrolled in each department, studying a common curriculum for the first two years. The school seems to have offered an atmosphere of immersion in learning and research into one's specialist area through elective courses after the third year.[6] For example, in the Humanities Department's twenty-fifth class (enrolled 1933, graduated 1937), students who chose geography as a major learned regional geography and topographic survey methods from Yoshiro Nishida (1884–1953) and Jiro Katabira (1898–1969), while those who chose foreign history attended lectures on Jacob Burckhardt's *The Civilization of the Renaissance in Italy* by Seitaro Okajima (1895–1948).[7] Each instructor was a leading authority in his respective field. Besides the main curriculum, supplementary and preparatory courses were also provided, for instance professional training in childcare.

The presence of 'exchange' students from colonies and China stood out. Thus, the special preparatory courses of 1923 were mainly established for Chinese students. During the forty-three years leading up to 1952, for which school records are extant, 301 students from Qing China, the Republic of China, and Manchukuo, as well as from Taiwan and Korea, enrolled in regular courses, as well as supplementary courses, or audited lectures.

Surveying the courses, we find a strong emphasis on learning about Manchuria, typically in terms of geographical subjects. In the first-year class on 'Japanese Geography' (twenty hours total), taught by Katabira, the twenty-ninth graduating class (enrolled 1937), which went on a tour to Manchuria in 1940, learned about Kyusyu, Taiwan and Korea. Additionally, 'Nature and Culture of Manchukuo' (twenty-four hours total), 'Manchukuo Humanities/Nature of China' (thirty hours total) and 'Chinese Humanities' (twenty hours total) were taught in 'Foreign Geography',[8] in which preparations for the continental tour were obviously an educational aim.

Moreover, the official history of the school referred to the changing atmosphere that the outbreak of the Second Sino-Japanese War brought. On 22 September 1937, the School Council and Commission of Senior Staff discussed measures for deepening students' awareness of current affairs in China, deciding to screen newsreels on the war situation, conduct lectures on Chinese affairs and purchase books and magazines relating to China.[9] Foreign students from China were divided into 'Republic of China students' and 'Manchukuo students' after 1932, and surveillance of the former began.[10] Collective labour service was organized as wartime mobilization (July 1938), and civilian air defence training started in the school in 1939. In the 1930s, the daily dress was *hakama*, Japanese-style trousers, with no restrictions on Western clothes, but from the 1940 academic year, this changed to a uniform of black or navy blue suits, and the alumni association was renamed the 'Patriotic Brigade'.[11]

A problem that persisted throughout the 1930s was a downturn in the employment market. Graduates' memoirs recorded that Science Department graduates of March 1931 had difficulties finding employment as schoolteachers.[12] In terms of posts for graduates, many from the Humanities Department, for example, would work in private girls' high schools in urban centres such as Tokyo. The department with the greatest number of students was the Housework Department. Its increasing numbers of graduates, including foreign students, found work in the overseas territories.

Would students who had received education in the metropole of the empire choose colonial employment of their own volition? Higher schools for men apparently intended to utilize colonial tourism to activate students' jobhunting in the colonies, and we can find some similar attempts among secondary normal schools for women in the early 1930, whatever the awareness among students was. For example, a secondary normal school in Nara conducted tours to Korea in 1931 and 1932. Of two plans, one for a two-week tour to Manchuria and the other a nine-day tour to Korea and Andong, the latter was chosen to reduce costs, and the nine-day tour excluded any destinations north of Seoul, but included stops in Gyeongju and Miyajima (Hiroshima Prefecture) at a cost of 33 yen. Documentation of the intended tour was submitted to the South Manchuria Railway's Korea and Manchuria Information Office in Osaka.

In these documents, the 'realization of harmony between the mainland and Korea' was emphatically stated as the purpose of the tour.[13] Graduates of state-sponsored secondary normal schools, including women, were expected to become educators, conscious of being subjects of the suzerain power.

Taking such circumstances into consideration, Nara Jokoshi, as a higher school for the teaching profession, seemed to be lagging behind regarding tours to the overseas territories. The school principal's moral lecture on New Year's Day, 1939 therefore merits attention: the principal stated that in addition to existing colonies such as 'Korea, Taiwan, and Sakhalin', going forward, students should look for employment in 'Manchuria, China, and Mongolia'. Territorial expansion through war was interpreted as an extension of job opportunities. In January 1939, when more attention came to be focused on these military occupation zones, the plan for a continental tour first appeared on a faculty meeting agenda[14] – eight months before the trip.

The intention expressed during the faculty meeting of 1939 was to position the continental tour as an extension of earlier study tours (from the first graduating class onwards), and to open 'new horizons' for graduates' activities, with reference to the precedent of secondary normal schools for boys in the prefecture already having toured Manchuria.[15] What was perceived as problematic was not the risk of travelling to a war zone and the required safety measures but rather the cost. Previous 'long-term trips' by final-year students were graduation research events that reflected each department's characteristics, and their costs had been borne by students who had saved since their enrolment years. For this reason, the financial burden of approximately 60–100 yen was a concern. At subsequent meetings, the faculty discussed possible ways to cut costs, for instance cancelling the Humanities Department's third-year trip to Ise, where two ancient Shinto shrines were located. Dissenting opinions were presented in June as well, and removing Harbin from the itinerary was also an option.

Though the cost issue was discussed between principals of the Tokyo and Nara *Jokoshi*s, the former negotiated independently for funds with the government and succeeded because of its close connections to governmental agencies, both geographically and personally. According to Tokyo Jokoshi's application to the Director of the Colonization Bureau, titled 'Regarding Assistance for the Manchuria Settlement Inspection (Proposal)', a small group of about twenty persons was proposed, and if a subsidy was granted, students would pay 60 yen, with the subsidy covering 70 yen.[16] The trip, according to recollections of those involved, was a 'voluntary tour' supported by the alumni association (*Jyoran-Kai*), and its plan was formulated by humanities students.[17] By contrast, Nara Jokoshi's continental tour, which departed a month after Tokyo Jokoshi's, lacked any subsidies from the government, and Nara Jokoshi managed to cover expenditures through funds from the alumni association. The reason that Nara Jokoshi dared to carry out tours in the following two years and even attempted to do so in 1941 was the tours' significance for the accomplishment of educational goals.

We should also pay attention to their compulsoriness as school events. As a rule, all students had to participate in the tours, although absence was permitted for health and financial reasons, and only foreign students were allowed to join the tourist groups of other students at their destinations. On the 1940 tour, an increasing number of students declined participation for reasons that were not recorded, and 'persuasion' from teachers was necessary.[18] Even under conditions of warfare, the education programme continued. Archival documents reveal an impetus towards conducting trips against all difficulties.

Meanwhile, the Ministry of Education aimed to turn male students' continental tours, which they undertook during the summer holidays, into labour mobilization, having sent a directive in the name of the vice-minister for the dispatching of 'Patriotic Youth Labour Corps for the Development of Asia' to Manchuria (14 June 1937). In June 1939, the ministry prohibited travel agents from handling students' group tours to the Chinese mainland (northern China, Mengjiang, and south-central China), and it required permission for tours to Manchukuo. Simple excursions to Manchukuo were thereby prohibited, and (nominal) causes of practical training or research were mandatory. In the case of Nara Jokoshi, in 1939, the Ministry of Education instructed the school to change its initial plans for a visit to Tianjin and Beijing in northern China in favour of visiting only Manchukuo. Finally, one month before their departure, the permission (dated 15 July) arrived at Nara Jokoshi,[19] and conditions were imposed to conduct practical training or research, to emphasize discipline of mind and body, and to avoid areas to which male students' 'Patriotic Youth Labour Corps' had been dispatched. We can surmise that while male students were mobilized for labour in Manchuria prior to military service, women were permitted to continue their continental tours: the latter were expected to substitute for elite male students.

Nara Jokoshi succeeded in acquiring permissions from the Ministry of Education three times. The arguments fielded to accomplish this are evident from the extant petition for the third tour, scheduled for May 1941. According to it, while the aim of the previous tour had been to deepen understanding of current affairs and the situations in Korea and Manchukuo among students of the institution for teacher training,[20] the upcoming tour of 1941 would emphasize their job opportunities. A common goal of both tours was raising awareness of the unity of Japan, Manchukuo and China ruled by Wang Jingwei's government. The application stated that an increasing number of students were hoping to find employment in Manchuria as the Manchuria–Mongolia settlement projects proceeded. Consequently, graduates originally from Manchukuo were occupying leading positions in education there, and as their *alma mater*, the faculty needed to visit the area to facilitate understanding between its students from Japan, Manchuria and China.[21] The document also underlined the institute's role as the highest seat of learning for women of the colonial power. This role was reinterpreted in the context of warfare in Manchuria, and put forward in support of the application for the trip.

When we consider male students' experiences and roles in Manchuria, we can discern three periods, in which they were 1) passengers enjoying colonial tourism, 2) members of the wartime labour force and 3) members of the military service or soldiers (from 1943). In this context, it becomes clear that while the *Jokoshis*' tours to Manchuria during the Second Sino-Japanese War were temporally permitted, this permission was tied to the expectation that female students would substitute for male ones in the various roles that the latter had to play in Manchuria besides their role in military service. However, the *Jokoshi* students' writings manifest their independent spirit and uneasiness that went beyond the colonial consciousness and their expected role on 'the home front'. The impact of wartime tourism as a cultural apparatus on their texts will now be examined.

The Imperial Gaze

After Tokyo Jokoshi succeeded in acquiring funding, students gathered at Shimonoseki Station in July 1939 and left for the continent. The group numbered about forty, mainly third-year students from the Humanities Department. According to the printed records,[22] they mainly stayed in hotels. Having crossed the sea by the regular ship route from Shimonoseki to Pusan, they travelled north up the Korean peninsula on the Chosen Railway. Then, heading east from Seoul via Chongjin and Najin, they entered Manchuria. From Mudanjiang, they toured Harbin, Jilin, Changchun, Mukden, Fushun, Lushun and Dalian, and returned from Dalian to Moji in Fukuoka Prefecture. This was the typical Manchurian tour in the late 1930s.

Nara Jokoshi's large group of seventy-two, comprising final-year students and their supervising teachers, departed in August. It entrusted the planning of the itinerary and the arrangements to travel agents and used third-class steamships and trains, as Tokyo Jokoshi had done. The tour through Manchuria mainly comprised sightseeing by bus of predetermined items of interest, such as modern city architecture, natural resources, museums, shrines and battle sites. In Dalian, 'a pretty bus girl' guided students,[23] and in Jilin a horse-and-cart tour was inserted into the plan. Directed to look around the Manchuria–Mongolia Geological Museum in Dalian in fifteen minutes, science students expressed disappointment and anger in their reports. Although they took pride in studying at one of the highest seats of learning, their tour route fell completely within the framework of Manchurian mass tourism in the 1930s. As Nara Jokoshi's itinerary was compressed to fifteen days (24 August to 7 September) to cut costs, students had few opportunities to disembark, even in Manchuria's big cities, and spent most of the tour looking out at their surroundings through the windows of their bus. They had fewer opportunities to inspect local girls' schools and elementary schools than students of Tokyo Jokoshi. Additionally, we find no descriptions of their meetings with colonial officials, which often appeared in male students' travel writings in the 1930s. Instead, there are complaints about terrible meals in lodgings and lunch boxes on trains, containing only fishcakes to go with their rice. Contrastingly, much was written about the strongly perceived hospitality and gifts from parents and alumni associations, both in Korea and Manchuria.

In spite of their similarities, Nara Jokoshi's tours, operating as 'extended travel' for school events, were in some ways distinct from mass tourism. This is apparent in the itinerary, which used a newly opened regular service to North Korea. In 1939, this group headed from Nara Station to the Sea of Japan and via the regular sea route from Tsuruga to Chongjin, connecting with the South Manchurian Railway in northern Korea. After encountering 'Manchuria' at Mudanjiang and touring it in Harbin, Jilin, Changchun, Mukden, Dalian and Lushun, they journeyed down the Korean peninsula through Pyeongyang, Seoul, Gyeongju and Pusan, before crossing to Shimonoseki and returning to Nara. Following that, students began their second semester. Thus, the trip during their first year, after a hurried tour of Manchuria, tacked on visits to places on the Korean peninsula. The sites chosen for visits differed for each department. Students of humanities made contact with the very foremost scholars of mid-twentieth-century knowledge in Korean Studies and Korean archaeology: Akio Koizumi at the Pyeongyang Museum, Kintaro Osaka and Che Nam-zyu at the Gyeongju Museum, and Kyoichi Arimitsu at the *Chosen Sotoku-fu* (Colonial Governorate of Korea) Museum.

Impressions of 'wartime' were reflected in students' records of these trips. Along with strict security near the border, venturing into unfamiliar dark streets and looking for souvenirs was hard work because of nightly blackout regulations and various restrictions.[24] In lodgings and on trains, curtains were drawn for 'air defence' and lights were prohibited (Humanities, 3 September 1939).[25]

By the second trip, in August 1940, the infrastructure had already suffered damage. Teachers accompanying students, on arriving in Harbin, were informed that they could not use any automobiles, as arranged only six weeks prior, due to a shortage of gasoline.[26] Moreover, the destinations specified by the Ministry of Education certainly differed from the usual 'sightseeing' route. They included visits to immigrant settlers' villages and bases belonging to the Volunteer Pioneer Youth Army of Manchuria and Mongolia; Tokyo Jokoshi visited Jilin province's Shikabo–Ohinata Pioneer Group, and Nara Jokoshi visited the Manchuria and Mongolia Pioneers' Cadre Training Centre in Harbin. Because these were far from the railway, teachers and students rode in trucks belonging to the Manchuria Development Agency – certainly not a comfortable trip. Given that the tours were inscribed with specific goals, it is interesting to ask in what ways the war changed the selection of permitted destinations and intended interactions with locals. Obviously, the reason that students of *Jokoshi*s were permitted to visit sites and installations related to military secrets near the border between Manchuria and the Soviet Union was that they were to become female teachers in the future. At the same time, their records reveal how the 'tourist's gaze' affected their attitudes as writers.

The 'Imperial Gaze' Constructed through Tourism

While Tokyo Jokoshi's records were published with photographs bearing titles such as 'Impressions of the Continental Tour 1939' (*Tairiku Shisatsu Ryoko Shokanshu 1939*), Nara Jokoshi's tour records and students' impressions were compiled into an unpublished brochure, 'All Department Fourth Year Manchuria-Korea (Continental) School Trip Reports' (*Kakuka Yongakunen Mansen Shugaku Ryoko Hokokusho*), which was kept as archival material together with records by teachers, correspondence between the school and the Ministry of Education and other agencies, and other documents about educational affairs. As Nara Jokoshi followed a standardized form in records and accounts of long-term study trips, deliberate conformity to it rather than students' individual personalities characterized the brochure. Although teachers expressed concerns about possible security risks inherent in students' straightforward descriptions of their observations,[27] the reports contain no artificial deletions nor redactions due to censorship. This lack of consideration of possible outside readers indicates their status as internal documents not meant for publication.

> I carried in my right hand the trunk in which the smiles that I made on opening it each day for the past month are enclosed. I'm so happy! Considering the time, repaired leather shoes should be tied up tightly ... (Home Economics, 21 August 1939)

> 'Continental Tour' – It was in that last year that we had first said those words. Even though we were longing for the continent, as though half in a dream, after hearing stories from experiences last year, it didn't seem that far away, like somewhere that you could just drop by without a care ... Anyway, let's go and see. (Humanities, 22 August 1940)

All students wore Western clothing in the first year, whereas, in the following years, they had mandatory uniforms. They left records showing their expectations for the school trip. What they considered necessary was not affirmation of their own tastes in amusement, but of their sense of mission as leaders of Japanese society, as well as of their interest in the respective areas of their future professional activities.

> My long-standing dreams of longing for the continent are finally about to be realized. I want to step onto the soil of the continent, see it with my own eyes, and experience its atmosphere to the fullest through these ears. Our desire is to know in more detail about how our ally Manchukuo is developing. (Home Economics, 22 August 1940)

Even though these were students' 'observations' on two-week tours during wartime, descriptions of panoramic landscapes from train windows amplified the fixed relationship between those perceiving and the perceived. The third day, 23 August 1939, was spent travelling between Chongjin and Mudanjiang, without disembarking. Students' descriptions of the few farmers they saw from the train window included observations of unfamiliar cultures steeped in racist ideology: 'they peered at the train with stretched faces'; 'the Koreans are for the most part very docile. It is a nature that a long history of servitude has produced' (Humanities, 23 August 1939). This Orientalist gaze was often inverted, giving rise to expressions of nostalgia towards people on the other side of the window. The scene from the train window was given meaning as follows.

> The farmers who were walking with hoes over their shoulders turned towards us. Tanned a dark brown, they are more like natural objects clinging to the earth than humans. They look as though they have merged with the soil and don't think about anything. We have come too far away from the soil. Perhaps it would be happiness to imitate them a little? (Humanities, 23 August 1939)

The writer who described these 'others,' after passing into Manchurian territory without a border inspection, continued to write her blunt, one-sided representations of the 'others', comparing 'Korean people' and 'Manchurian people.' She also recorded the understandably tense situation as well as information about places through which she travelled: 'Crossing the Tumangang River into Tumen, we underwent customs inspection and security guards boarded the train. ... With the large number of soldiers gathered together, and the blackout restrictions in place, the newly developed territories near the border have a strict atmosphere' (Humanities, 23 August 1939). In addition to tensions in the border area, travellers suffered a lot of minor physical discomforts – fatigue from the long journey, unsanitary lodgings, unpleasant meals and the same lunch box every day – resulting in them falling sick one after another.

The transition from northern Korea to the continent was noted for the change from narrow-gauge to wide-gauge rails, the imposing appearance of taller, wider railway cars and the high platforms of stations. In particular, regardless of the author or the affiliated department, cities of the 'new world' of Manchuria were praised as modern spaces that 'crusading Japanese people' made possible. Among them, Changchung, where urban construction was proceeding according to the planning for Manchuria's imperial capital, was applauded – together with the railway – as a symbol of modernization granted by Imperial Japan; 'Japan' was a recurring subject in all students' narratives. The writer who wrote of 'the huge difference [compared] to ghosts of the old Changchun' was excited by the fact that 'worries about the newly developing Manchukuo' were unfounded, and that 'cries going up from the building works on every street corner make a cheerful sound' (Humanities, 27 August 1939). It is precisely through the imperial gaze that the writer recorded their thoughts.

What, then, did students write about their mission – their preparation for finding employment on the continent? Teachers wrote that students were 'grasping Manchuria as a whole and gaining a deep understanding', developing the impression that Manchuria was 'not far away', and that they would 'happily accept a post in Manchuria if offered' following graduation. However, as far as the records are concerned, it is doubtful that students would have 'happily accepted' the proposal. In 'Summary', a science student acknowledged that 'the progress that the Japanese have made is remarkable', and that 'the main streets of Changchun, Dalian, and Mukden are almost the same as those in towns on the Japanese mainland'. Regarding her own future, however, the student concluded hypothetically, saying, 'if several friends were working there, we would encourage each other' (Science, 1939). There was clear divergence between the student's account and the teacher's observation, in spite of the tour's purpose of touting participation in projects in Manchuria.

In particular, on their half-day visit to the Manchurian and Mongolian Pioneers' Training Centre on the outskirts of Harbin on 25 August, some students, while showing sympathy for the boys in their khaki trousers, gaiters, and service caps, were critical of the projects themselves. While on the one hand, the records read, 'I clearly understood that in order to truly protect and nurture Manchuria, Japanese people have to put down roots in the soil', the students were worried about whether the boys clearly understood that significance, saying, 'seeing a small boy of around 15 standing as a sentry, he looks adorably pathetic'. And the writers doubted 'whether or not they really understand their important mission' (Humanities, 25 August 1940). On the same day, a science student wrote that while she sincerely perceived the boys as 'people to emulate as sacrificial pawns of development', she warned against 'us women sympathizing carelessly', rejecting sentimentality: 'Even if we spend our lives in some poor village on the mainland, as long [as] our sacrifice benefits the Japanese empire's development, then that is fine' (Science, 25 August 1939). The boys themselves were not subjects of observation, but rather 'they are boys – pupils whom we will teach'. The *Jokoshi* students' actual awareness, through a mutually negotiated perspective on the boys, reveals a discourse critical of the Manchuria policy. As for places where they themselves would become 'sacrificial pawns', they suggested 'a poor village on the mainland', as mentioned above, and did not deny a sense of distance from or unfamiliarity with Manchuria. As far as their own future was concerned, few students affirmed the ideology of a 'crusade' completely in their writings.

Regarding a homogenous image of 'the continent', students' accounts of their shared experience of the continental tour show strong sympathy towards war memorials, to which they were introduced by their teachers. Additionally, students' agency towards the war was evoked by battlefield tourism.

Battlefield Tours

The selection of destinations to be visited was essential for the meanings with which tourism in the form described could be charged. The key feature of Manchurian tourism was the inclusion of old battlefields of the Russo-Japanese War, such as Lushun. From the 1920s onward, major travel agencies like the Japan Tourist Bureau published many tourist guides in which events and Shinto (traditional polytheist religion in Japan) rituals for fallen soldiers were recommend for inclusion in student tours. For example, the *Sen-Man-Shi Tabi no Shiori* ('Travel Guide to Korea, Manchuria and

China') combined battlefield tourism and *Shokonsai* (a rite for the consolation of dead souls) into a package. The latter is closely linked to the commemoration of the fallen performed at the Yasukuni Jinja Shrine. At former battlefields, instructions about *Chureitos* (monuments for fallen soldiers) were provided and student groups were entitled to discounts on guides. The construction of *Chureitos* began after the Russo-Japanese War, and originated in the gathering of remains on the battlefield.

Nara Jokoshi very clearly manifested the tendency to recommend visits to battlefields to female students as well. Even though its itinerary was shortened, it visited the same places as Tokyo Jokoshi, and, especially in 1940, visits to battlefields were the fixed final stage of the tour. The whole party got off the bus to visit colonial shrines and memorials for the victims of the war: *Chureitos* and the Patriots' Monument in Harbin, as well as *Chureitos*, the Kuancheng battlefield and the Nanling battlefield memorial in Changchung. Battlefields were indispensable elements of the tour, and teachers' records indicate that awareness of 'our' roles in warfare was deepened thanks to visits to battlefields.

On the 1939 trip, during which students visited Lushun on 29 August, the group followed a route that included sites of fierce Russian–Japanese battles, such as Baiyu Hill, Dongjiguan Fortress, the Shuishiying meeting room and 203 Hill. While impressions of visits to museums showed striking differences regarding knowledge and points of interest between different departments, uniformity among them stands out in accounts of battlefield tours. A highly popular guidebook from the Japan Tourist Bureau conveyed to students the significance of 'this town in battlefields that we Japanese must never forget', and the students referred to 'our tears' shed for 'our soldiers' belongings' at the exhibits (Humanities, 29 August 1939). One humanities student stated that when she was a young girl, she repeatedly listened in breathless suspense to the story of how suicide squads from the Shikoku regiments from Marugame, Matsuyama and Zentsuuji had untiringly dug a tunnel during the attack on Dongjiguan Fortress, a bloody battle during the Russo-Japanese War. The students were overcome with deep emotion when standing by the battlefield. While the 'glory' of the Russo-Japanese War occupied an important position in the 'national' education of the early Showa period, military tourism added more meanings to those sites, enhancing their significance as spaces for national pride. The teachers, who were prominent researchers at the same time, also expressed great enthusiasm. The September 1940 tour placed the visit to Manchuria in the second half of the itinerary. On the tour of Harbin City, the students, having disembarked from the bus to visit *Chureitos* and graves of patriots and heroes, 'all began listening attentively, heads bowed, to a powerful description provided by a veterans' group for the preservation of battlefields, the *Kanton-shu Senchi Hozonkai*'. Meanwhile, one teacher raised the national 'sun-mark' flag, and everyone shed tears (Science, 1 September 1940).

Visits to battle sites, including *Chureito*s and colonial shrines in each city, stirred students' determination not only to foster modernization in the colonies but also to remember past wars and to pass the memory on to the following generations. For example, Mukden *Chureito*, adjacent to Mukden Shrine (which enshrined Amaterasu, a major Shinto deity, and the Meiji Emperor), despite being surrounded by traditional round gravel, gave the impression of 'modernity' by virtue of its hexagonal, pyramidlike shape. Additionally, students listened to an explanation of 'the enshrinement of thirty-five thousand souls at the Battle of Mukden in the Russo-Japanese War'. The previously visited Harbin, Changchung and Dalian were once more recalled as 'lands where heroes rest', and students offered their sincere gratitude to the dead (Science, 31 August 1939). Battlefield tourism effectively created a homogenous, standardized perspective on Manchuria, as illustrated below.

> Many compatriots are sweating for the construction of tomorrow in the great plains of Manchuria. The spirits of our predecessors, who shed their blood to become the foundation of this construction, are sleeping. Until now, 'peace in the East' was just words, but stepping onto Manchurian soil for the first time, seeing Japan and Manchuria working together hand in hand, I felt their great significance keenly. The construction of East Asia is the great mission given to us youth. (Science, 1940)

Here, 'sweating for the construction' in the present is directly connected to the 'blood' shed in the past, and the active significance of 'our' attitude to Manchuria is recognized. In fact, however, those war memorials in colonial cities were not antiquated devices to commemorate battlefields from forty years ago. Some *Chureito*s with repositories for remains that appear frequently in *Jokoshis*' travel writings had only recently been completed: Changchung in November 1934 and Harbin in September 1936. They only just preceded the *Chureito* construction movement that began on the mainland in 1937. Battlefield tourism and visits to these memorials reread militant and violent expansion of imperial territory as the heroic stories of Japanese soldiers, and turned the actual occupied zone along the South Manchurian Railroad, where violent invasion and resistance clashed, into a space where these soldiers' heroism was accomplished. The structure of the itineraries demonstrates the function that tourism served in this regard. Battlefield tourism during wartime completed narrow, self-satisfied national narratives, hiding the military violence of the Japanese Empire and commemorating national heroes in front of students. Presumably, it burdened female elites, who were exempted from military service, with an alternative mission that was in conformity with their gender role in the age of total war, in which the boundary between the real front and the home front was continuously being redrawn.

Conclusion

Reading the details of *Jokoshi* students' writings, we can find a few vague fluctuations through which to glimpse their attitudes towards Manchuria, through the mutual negotiations between 'the observed' and 'observers'. Students, even if only very slightly, evinced scepticism towards current policies in Manchuria. Their reports also reveal a discrepancy between officially mandated missions as future teachers on the continent and their own expectations for the future. Nevertheless, the admiration of the colonial modernization that the Japanese promoted on the continent and particularly the praise of deified 'military heroes' preserved in the official records of *Jokoshi*s showed that the ongoing violent invasion by the Japanese Empire was concealed from students' observations and awareness. Consequently, the students reaffirmed and consolidated perceptions of Manchuria as a space of commemoration of military heroes for the Japanese nation. This was precisely what male students of secondary and higher schools, as members of the gender able to fight, were to internalize through their Manchurian tourism before their female fellow students did the same. Consequently, the very fact that students of *Jokoshi*s, who followed male students and were not burdened with obligatory military service, promptly accepted and appropriated this kind of official narrative through their tourism on the wartime continent is significant. This may convince us that the Japanese Empire succeeded in amending its gender regime in higher education in accordance with the necessity of promoting war efforts. *Jokoshi* students completed their itineraries on the continent having obtained confidence in the role of Manchuria as a space for their nation's heroism, although some awkward feelings remained.

The Japanese from Manchuria, who returned to the Japanese mainland after the end of the empire, in general banished their experiences of imperial rule from public memory after 1945. Even Nara Jokoshi (and its successor institution, Nara Women's University), which had not suffered from air raids and was able to preserve the records of its past, did not refer to its students' Manchurian tourism in its official history. The confidence that female students had internalized through their Manchurian tourism did not leave any traces in official post-war narratives. It is noteworthy that Nara Women's University had prominent historians of modern and contemporary Japan among its faculty, who could have written the history of *Jokoshi* on the basis of abundant internal documents had they wished to do so.

Private memories of events in Manchuria, however, have continued to haunt East Asia. As Shin'ichi Yamamuro emphasized, Manchuria is a site of negative memories not just for Japanese families, who perceive themselves as victims of both Japanese colonial policies and the Soviets' military operations. This is even truer for Chinese and Koreans, who publicly mourn their subjection to Japanese imperialist aggression. New testimonies have sometimes broken the official silence and provoked disputes. Those Japanese women who were offered for sexual services 'voluntarily' by Japanese immigrant communities and were sexually exploited by advancing Soviet soldiers have started a very public memory campaign for remembrance of this issue, which divides opinion in Japan.

Our investigation of *Jokoshi* students' experiences of Manchuria during the Second World War is an attempt to break the Japanese silence on an uncomfortable memory, and to recover a past that will not go away in the present until Japanese society is willing to confront the darkest shadows of that past.

Shizue Osa is Professor in Japan Studies at the Graduate School of Intercultural Studies at Kobe University. Her research interests include the modernization of Japan from gender perspectives, war and post-war memories and cultural studies of Japan. She is the author of *The Occupation Period, Occupied Territory and Memories of the War* (Yushi-sya, 2013, in Japanese) and many other works. Her recent publications include 'Théories de la race et racialisation dans le Japon modern/'Circulations et métamorphoses du racisme et de l'antiracisme', published in *Politika* (2021) and the edited volume *Major Themes of Gender History* (Mineruva-Shobo, 2022, in Japanese).

Notes

1. Shinichi,Yamamuro, *Manchuria under Japanese Dominion*. The Japanese first edition was published in 1993 with the title *A Chimera: The Portrait of Manchukuo*.
2. Gao, Wen, "Posuto Koroniaru na Saikai". Arayama, Masahiko, 'Gaichi/Syokuminchi Turizumu no Kukan."
3. 'The Recollections of the Thirtieth Class, Draduating in December 1941', in Nara Joshi Daigaku Hachijunenshi Henshu Iinkai, *Nara Joshi Daigaku Hachijunenshi*, 314–316. The official document granting permission from the Ministry of Education was dated 24 June 1941 . See *Senman Chiho Shugaku Ryoko Keikakusho*.
4. In her *Otokonoko no Tame no Guntai Gakushuu no Susume*, Rieko Takada shows that among a hundred boys, only one would be admitted to imperial universities and two enter to technical colleges or private universities.

5. Concerning to the total war, women soldiers and their participation in battles, an international conference was held in Wassenaar, the Netherlands, 11–13 June 2014: *Fighting Women: In Asia and Europe during and after World War II*, at the Netherlands Institute for Advanced Study in the Humanities and Social Sciences.

6. Nara Joshi Daigaku Rokujunenshi Henshu Iinkai , *Nara Joshi Daigaku Rokujunenshi*, 79.

7. Shizue Senmatsu, 'Watashi no Zaigaku Jidai [My School Days]', in'*Nara Joshi Daigaku Hachijunenshi*, 306–7.

8. *Nijukyuki Kyouju Yoko Showa Juninen Shigatu Nyuugaku*.

9. Nara Joshi Daigaku Rokujunenshi Henshu Iinkai, *Nara Joshi Daigaku Rokujunenshi*, 97.

10. Ibid.

11. Tae Sunagawa, 'Junigatsu Sotsugyo no Zengo [The Days of Graduation in December]', Nara Joshi Daigaku Hachijunenshi Henshu Iinkai, *Nara Joshi Daigaku Hachijunenshi*, 314.

12. Nara Joshi Daigaku Hachijunenshi Henshu Iinkai, *Nara Joshi Daigaku Hachijunenshi*, 302.

13. *Nara-ken Joshi Shihan Gakko Sanjunenshi* [thirty years of history of Nara Women's Higher Normal School], 1932.

14. Kaigi Jikoroku, Syouwa14 Nen 1 Gatu – 16 Nen 9 Gatu Kaigi Jikoroku.

15. 'Chosen Taiwan Karafuto Manshu Shina ni Shushoku Kibosha [Job applicants in the Korean peninsula, Taiwan, Sakhalin, Manchuria, and China]', in *Sotugyosei Haito ni kansuru Shorui: Showa 15 Nenndo*.

16. A topic of 1939 in Kaigi Jikoroku, Showa14 Nen 1 Gatu – 16 Nen 9 Gatu Kaigi Jikoroku.

17. Kikue Nagai, 'Watashi no Manshu Ryoko [My Trip to Manchuria]', *Bosho Gekkan*, 25 (August 2002).

18. 'Showa Jurokunen Shichigatsu Yoka Kyokan Kaigi [Faculty Meeting of July 8, 1941], Bunka Yonen Shunin Yori Hokoku, [Report by the chief instructor of the fourth grade of humanities department]', *Senman Chiho Shugaku Ryoko Keikakusho*.

19. 31 July, Minister of Education Sadao Araki: Showa 14 Nen 7 gatu 15 Nichi Nara Jokoshi Dai 571 Go Seito Shugaku Ryoko no Ken: Saki Joken ni Yori Kyokasu [15th July 1939: Nara Jokoshi's Petition for Students' Field Trip No.571: Permission and Conditions]. These materials are included in Showa Jugonendo Tairiku Ryoko ni kansuru Shorui: Kyomuka.

20. *Senman Chiho Shugaku Ryoko Keikakusho*.

21. Ibid.

22. Tokyo Jokoshi(ed), *Tairiku Shisatu Ryoko Shokanshu Showa Juyonen*, 274.

23. Ibid., 53.

24. Ibid., 56.

25. 'Kakuka Shigakunen Mancho (Tairiku) Shugaku Ryoko Hokokusho [All Departments Fourth Year Manchuria-Korea (Continental) School Travel Reports]', in Showa Juyonendo Mancho Shugaku Ryokoki (1939) and Showa Jugonendo Mancho Shugaku Ryokoki (1940). Notes for citations from these two materials are embedded in the text body in the form of (Department, Date Month Year) due to the lack of page numbers in the materials.

26. Showa Jugonendo Tairiku Ryoko ni Kansuru Shorui: Kyomuka.

27. Showa Jugonendo Kugatsu Daini Tairiku Ryoko Jisshi Hokoku (Second Continemtal Tour Report, September 1940.

Bibliography

Archival Sources

(Nara Jyoshi-Daigaku, Koshi-Shiryo of Nara Women's University History Archive. All materials in the archive belong to the university)

Kaigi Jikoroku, Syouwa 14 Nen 1 Gatu – 16 Nen 9 Gatu Kaigi Jikoroku, [Record of Meeting Topics, 1939–1942].

Nijukyuki Kyoju Yoko Showa: Juuninen Shigatu Nyugaku [Syllabus for Twenty Nineth Term, April 1937].

Senman Chiho Shugaku Ryoko Keikakusho [Plan for School Travel to Korea and Manchuria, 1941]

Showa Juyonendo Tairiku Ryoko ni kansuru Shorui: Kyomuka [Documents regarding the Continental Tour, 1939, Registrar's Office].

Showa Jugonendo Tairiku Ryoko ni kansuru Shorui: Kyomuka [Documents regarding the Continental Tour, 1940, Registrar's Office].

Showa Juyonendo Mancho Shugaku Ryokoki (Manchuria-Korea School Travel Records, 1939).

Showa Jugonendo Mancho Shugaku Ryokoki (Manchuria-Korea School Travel Records, 1940).

Showa Jugonendo Kugatsu Daini Tairiku Ryoko Jisshi Hokoku (Second Continemtal Tour Report, September 1940).

Sotsugyosei Haito ni kansuru Shorui: Syouwa15 Nenndo, [Documents regarding Graduates, 1940].

Published Sources

Abe, Yasunari. 'Chotsugai to shiteno Ko-Sho-Syuugakuryokou [Review of Higher Commercial School Studies]. Tokyo: *Annual Report of the Hitotsubashi University Library Research Development Office*, 1 (March 2013.3: 23–42 (in Japanese).

Araragi, Shinzo, (ed). *'Mansyu' Imin no Rekishisyakaigaku [Migration and Repatriation: The Rise and Fall of the Japanese.Empire]*, Tokyo: Fujisyuppan, 2008 (in Japanese).

Arayama Masahiko. 'Spatial Range of Tourism for Colonies and Overseas Territories in Modern Japan', *The Historical Geography* 57, no.1 (January 2015), 46–55 (in Japanese).

Awazu, Kenta. *Tsuikoku to Tsuitou no Shukyou Shakaigaku: Senbotsusha Saishi no Seiritu to Henyou [Memory and Commemoration: Sociological Study of the Formation and Transformation of Religious Rituals for Fallen Soldiers]*. Sapporo: Hokkaido University Press, 2017 (in Japanese).

Centre for Gender and Women's Culture in Asia, Nara Women's University (ed). *Nara-KotoJoshi Sihangakko to Asia no Ryugakusei, [Nara Higher Women's Normal School and Foreign Students from Asia]*. Tokyo: Keibunsha, 2016 (in Japanese).

Gao, Wen. 'Posuto Koroniaru na Saikai [Post-Colonial Re-Encounter].' In Aiko Kurasawa et al. (eds), *Teikoku no Senso Keiken, Azia Taiheiyo Senso 4 [War Experiences of the Empire: Asia-Pacific War, vol. 4]* (Tokyo, Iwanami Shoten, 2006), 351–76 (in Japanese).

Hashimoto, Funsouka. *Seareru Kako: Azia to Yoroppa ni okeru Rekishi no Seijika [Conflicted Past Politicization of History in Asia and Europe]*. Tokyo: Iwanami-shoten, 2018 (in Japanese).

Nagai, Kikue. *'Watashi no Manshu Ryoko [My Trip to Manchuria]'*, *Bosho Gekkan*, 25 (August 2002).

Nara Joshi Daigaku Rokujunenshi Henshu Iinkai. *Nara Joshi Daigaku Rokujunenshi*, ['Sixty Years' History of Nara Women's University*], 1970 (in Japanese).

———. *Nara Joshi Daigaku Hachijunenshi*, [*'Eighty Years' History of Nara Women's University*], 1989 (in Japanese)

Nara-ken Joshi Shihan Gakko Sanjunenshi [*Thirty Years of History of Nara Women's Higher Normal School*], 1932 (in Japanese).

Pratt, Marry Louise. *Imperial Eyes: Travel Writing and Transculturation*. London: Routledge, 1992.

Schivelbusch, Wolfgang. *The Railway Journey: The Industrialization of Time and Space in the 19th Century*. Berkeley: University of California Press,1986.

Takada, Rieko. *Otokonoko no Tame no Guntai Gakushuu no Susume* [Recommendations for Military Study for Boys]. Tokyo: Chikuma-shobo, 2008.

Tama, Shinnosuke. *Soryokusenn-Taisei-ka no Nougyo-Imin*,[*Agrarian Immigrants in Manchuria under Total War Regime*]. Tokyo: Yoshikawa Kobunkan, 2016 (in Japanese).

Tokyo-Jyokoshi (ed.). *Tairiku Shisatu Ryoko Shokanshu Showa Juyonen* [*Impressions from the Continental Inspection Tour 1939*], 1940.

Uchida, Tadataka. 'Tokyo-Jokoshi no Manshu Shugaku Ryoko [Travel to Manchuria of Tokyo Higher Women's Normal School]'. *Bulletin of Society for Changing Customs in Contemporary Japan* 33 (2012), 43–60 (in Japanese).

Urry, John. *The Tourist Gaze: Leisure and Travel in Contemporary Societies*. Thousand Oaks, CA: Sage, 1990. [Japanese edition. Trans. Hirokuni Kabuto. Tokyo: Hosei University Press, 1994].

Yamamuro, Shin'ichi. *Manchuria under Japanese Dominion*, trans. J. A. Fogel. Philadelphia, PA: University of Pennsylvania Press, 2006.

Yoshida, Yutaka. *Nihon no Guntai: Heishitachi no Kindaishi* [*Army of Japan: Modern History of Soldiers*]. Tokyo: Iwanami Shoten, 2002 (in Japanese).

Yoshii, Kenichi. *Minami-Mansyu-Tetudo no Syakai-Henyou,* [*The Social Transformation along the South Manchuria Railway*] Tokyo: Chisen Shokan, 2013 (in Japanese).

Wakakuwa, Midori. *Sensou ga Tukuru Jyoseizou,* [*Images of Women Created by War*]. Tokyo: Chikuma-shobo, 2000 (in Japanese).

CHAPTER 4

Borderlands Tourism as a Memory Practice

A Case Study of the 'Kresy' (The Former Polish Eastern Borderlands)

Małgorzata Głowacka-Grajper

The Second World War exerted a fundamental influence on the shape of modern Europe and the rest of the world. In Europe, in most cases, the state borders established after the war have remained intact until today. The war was a time of genocide and mass displacement. Almost the entire community of Jews that lived in Poland before the war permanently disappeared from Polish society.[1] After the war, the borders of many countries changed. The largest of these border changes affected Poland and two of its neighbours – Germany and the republics of the Soviet Union that lay to the east.[2] These border changes led to the displacement of millions of people. Furthermore, new minority groups emerged that comprised people whose country and citizenship had changed while their place of abode remained the same.

The eastern borderlands of pre-war Poland that were lost after the Second World War and incorporated into the Lithuanian, Belarusian and Ukrainian Soviet Socialist Republics are named the 'Kresy' in contemporary Poland. As in the case of the other lost territories in Europe (for example the lost territories of Germany, Hungary, Italy and Finland), the memory of the former eastern borderlands is ambiguous and problematic in Poland. This also creates problems for relations between Poland and its eastern neighbours – Lithuania, Belarus and Ukraine (all independent states since the early 1990s) – which may view Polish memory of the Kresy as a starting point for revisionist claims or a sign of the Polish state's (post) colonial attitude towards them.[3] This memory also maintains an ambiguous position in domestic Polish social discourse. In fact, it is often viewed as marginal and old-fashioned, only applicable to the groups of people displaced from the former eastern borderlands and irrelevant to the problems and challenges facing contemporary Poland. Despite the prevailing social and political conditions, it is well worth examining the many different memory practices and narratives connected with the Kresy. In my view, doing so presents a valuable opportunity to analyse how memory of the borderlands is being shaped in contemporary sociocultural conditions, all the more so as although this has always been a very ethnically diverse area, it is currently being perceived as both the lost homelands of individual people and the lost territory of a nation state.

The History of the 'Kresy' – Local Communities between Shifting Borders

The first union between the Kingdom of Poland and the Grand Duchy of Lithuania was established in 1385. From that time onwards, Poland began to exert greater influence on the territories that currently belong to Lithuania, Latvia, Belarus, Ukraine and Russia. The history of the Polish–Lithuanian Commonwealth is notable for the manner in which periods of splendour were interspersed with periods when the state was riven by internal and external conflicts and struggles.[4] The state finally collapsed in 1795 as a result of being partitioned for a third time by Prussia, Russia and Austria. The Republic of Poland (which became known as the Second Republic of Poland) regained independence in 1918, immediately after the First World War. The Second Republic was a multinational state with minorities constituting 30 per cent of the population.

The territories of the Polish–Lithuanian Commonwealth and Second Republic of Poland were multi-ethnic and multireligious for centuries. It was here that not only the national identity of Poland, but also that of other contemporary European nations, was shaped.[5] Lithuanian, Belarusian and Ukrainian national movements developed in these areas in opposition to the Polish cultural and political projects that had caused many conflicts during the period when the Polish state had been partitioned and after it regained its independence in 1918. At the beginning of its existence, the Second Republic of Poland tried to take into account the demands of minority groups living within its borders relating to education policy and the protection of ethnic and national cultures. Gradually, however, the policy towards minorities became increasingly severe, until the 1930s, when a policy of total assimilation was adopted,[6] which steadily thrust persons of non-Polish nationality to the margins of social life. This led to numerous conflicts and strengthened the opinion held by Lithuanians, Belarusians and Ukrainians that the Polish state posed a threat to their national aspirations.[7]

In 1939, after the outbreak of the First World War, Lithuania found itself in the Soviet zone of influence, and on 21 July 1940, it was incorporated into the USSR as another republic. The following year, mass deportations to the Asian republics of the Soviet Union began. After German troops entered the area following the successful Operation Barbarossa campaign that forced the Soviet army to retreat from the Kresy, the first period of sustained ethnic cleansing began. This was jointly carried out by Lithuanians and Germans and the victims were primarily Jews, but also Poles of non-Jewish origin. Between December 1944 and June 1945, the returning Soviet authorities carried out numerous deportations of persons associated with the Home Army, as well as other people, who were forced to work in the depths of the USSR.[8] The situation of Poles was becoming progressively more difficult and it became increasingly clear to all concerned that the Vilnius region would not be within the borders of the newly established Polish state. As a result, many Poles decided to take advantage of the possibility of going to Poland, which was created by the Polish government and the Lithuanian SSR by the signing of an agreement on 22 September 1944 on the evacuation of citizens of the pre-war Polish state (Poles and Jews, later joined by Tatars and Karaims).[9]

Under the terms of the Molotov–Ribbentrop pact, the western part of Belarus was occupied by the USSR, and its population was subjected to repression analogous to that in the eastern part of the republic. Four mass deportations led to about three hundred and twenty thousand citizens of the Second Republic of Poland being deported deep into the USSR,[10] and a similar number being murdered, imprisoned or incorporated into the Red Army. Repressions – taking the form of executions and deportations – were also brought about by German occupation. After the Belarusian territories were reoccupied by the Red Army, an agreement was reached on the evacuation of the Polish and Jewish population. On 9 September 1944 an agreement was signed with the authorities of the Belarusian SSR.[11]

In the territories of contemporary Ukraine, the tragic climax of the Polish–Ukrainian conflict occurred during the Second World War, culminating in the Volyn Massacre and ethnic cleansing in the provinces of Lviv, Tarnopol and Stanisławów (eastern Lesser Poland), which were conducted in 1943 and 1944 by the troops of the Ukrainian Insurgent Army, other Ukrainian organizations and the local population. Historians estimate that during the massacres, between fifty and sixty thousand were killed in Volyn and between twenty and seventy thousand in Eastern Galicia. Moreover, over three hundred thousand people of Polish nationality fled from the latter area.[12]

Following the decision to change Poland's borders, an 'exchange of populations' began. This action was based on the conviction that only the physical separation of national and ethnic groups in these areas would prevent another bloody conflict. According to official data, over 1.7 million people came to Poland during two evacuations[13] lasting from 1944 to 1948 and from 1955 to 1959: 217,720 from the Lithuanian SSR, 372,683 from the Belarusian SSR, 860,583 from the Ukrainian SSR and 243,775 from Siberia and Central Asia.[14] In 1960 the people displaced from the Kresy represented about 6 per cent of the Polish population, but in the western provinces, where the majority of them arrived,[15] they constituted as much as 30 to 43 per cent of the population.[16] The largest percentage of displaced people declared Polish nationality. Of all the repatriates who came to Poland between 1944 and 1948, Poles made up 94.48 per cent, Jews 4.33 per cent and other ethnicities 1.19 per cent of the total number of evacuated people.[17]

The need to deploy such a large number of people arriving within the new Polish territory led to the concept of 'longitudinal resettlement' being applied, which amounted to repatriates being resettled more or less along the same parallels of latitude as their former homes. It was believed that this solution would make it easier for them to adapt to their new geographical conditions due to similarities between their former and new places of residence in terms of climate and landscape. Moreover, during the first evacuation there were attempts to resettle entire local groups together (e.g. inhabitants of one or more adjacent villages) in order to help them acclimatize to the new situation.[18] As a result of this policy, the majority of people from Ukraine were resettled in southern Poland, primarily in Lower Silesia, but also in Upper Silesia and Lesser Poland. Repatriates from other regions were relocated in similar fashion: people from the Vilnius region found new homes in northern Poland, mainly in Masuria, Western Pomerania and Kuyavia (especially during the second evacuation), and repatriates from Belarus were relocated in the central swathe of Poland, mainly in Lubuskie Province, but also in Pomerania. The evacuation of scientists and academics was carried out on the same basis. People who had worked at institutions located in Ukraine, for example at Lviv Jan Kazimierz University, the National Ossoliński Institute and Lviv Polytechnic National University, were resettled in Wrocław, Kraków,

Gliwice and Gdańsk,[19] and staff from Stefan Batory University in Vilnius were relocated in Toruń.

The repatriates were also diverse in terms of their social backgrounds. They represented every social class, but their internal composition depended both on their region of origin and the local policy applied. The Lithuanian authorities were surprised by the intention of such a large number of people to leave. Fearing that this would result in the depopulation of rural areas and exert a negative impact on the economy, they tried to prevent mass evacuations from those regions. The consequences of that policy are still visible today. The majority of the 171,168 Poles and Jews evacuated from the Lithuanian SSR were members of the intelligentsia (27.65 per cent) or craftsmen (31.18 per cent). By contrast, farmers only amounted to 18.37 per cent of the total number of repatriates. Additionally, during the second evacuation (1955–59), 46,552 Poles left the Lithuanian SSR, and as was the case previously, many of these belonged to the intelligentsia. Ultimately, the Polish minority was deprived of its intellectual elite, and the resulting vacuum has yet to be filled.[20]

In the Belarusian SSR, the most difficult problem was to recognize the nationality of people who inhabited rural areas, because they frequently did not identify with any one nationality. As in the case of Lithuania, this situation resulted in the draining of the already depleted intelligentsia and a low rate of migration among farmers. Altogether, 272,053 people had left the Belarusian SSR by 1947.[21] The second wave of repatriation granted Poland an additional one hundred thousand citizens.

The most people by far came to the Polish People's Republic from the territory that currently belongs to Ukraine. As soon as the Polish and USSR governments signed the evacuation agreement, the majority of Poles, mindful of the recent ethnic clashes in that region, decided to emigrate immediately. By 1947, 784,524 people had come to Poland (the first wave of evacuation).[22] Since memory of the ethnic conflicts between Poles and Ukrainians was still fresh in the minds of the members of the Soviet government, they came to the opinion that these two nations should not have lived together[23] in the first place. The Soviet authorities therefore had no intention of hindering the repatriation process, as they had in other Soviet Socialist Republics. What is more, the USSR conducted its own forced displacements in order to remove the Polish population from Ukrainian territory.[24] Thus, the composition of the repatriates from Ukraine reflected all the social classes more or less equally, though there was a slight predominance of farmers.[25] During the second wave of repatriation, an additional 76,059 Poles and Jews were displaced to Poland.

Not every Pole managed to resettle within Poland's redrawn frontiers. A significant number of them remained in the Soviet Union, but the Polish communities in each of the three republics being considered here – the Lithuanian, Belarusian and Ukrainian SSRs – were faced with a different situation, determined not only by historical factors, but also by Soviet ethnic policy. When all these republics gained independence in the early 1990s, the presence of Polish minorities within their territories became an important issue in the relations between the newly established states and Poland. Moreover, most of the activities undertaken by the 'Kresy NGOs'[26] have generally been devoted to providing assistance to Poles living in Lithuania, Belarus and Ukraine.

The Beginnings of 'Memory Tourism' and Personal Motivations

Although the border changes initially seemed to some to be temporary,[27] they have permanently redrawn the map of Europe. This means that it is not possible for the repatriates to return to the regions from which they originally came. There are several reasons for this. First, political considerations mean that a person cannot settle in a country unless they are a citizen of that country. Secondly, practical economic factors (like the economic situation worsening in the place of origin, lack of familiarity with its official language and difficulties finding gainful employment) need to be taken into account. Finally, emotional identity issues need to be factored in (since over seventy years have elapsed since the end of the war, such people already feel so settled in their current countries of residence, and their places of origin have changed so much, that they do not feel 'at home' in the latter any more). Sociocultural factors are also important, such as the significant changes that have occurred in the repatriates' places of origin and global processes leading to changes in mindset regarding the need to find 'one's place on the Earth'. Moreover, the repatriates still alive today often abandoned their homelands as children or young people only just emerging into adulthood. Their personal memories of their lost homelands, therefore, mainly date from their childhood, while any reminiscences associated with growing up, starting a family and taking care of their progeny's future and professional development are linked in their minds to completely different places. All of the above account for the observable reluctance of these repatriates to return permanently to their places of origin.

However, these places continue to play a very important cultural and identity role. As Steven Grosby notes, territory is fundamentally important for social groups and the individuals of which they are comprised because it is perceived as a structure that is essential for sustaining social life. It serves as both a locus for memories and the reality needed to structure such memories and make them real.[28] Furthermore, when a place is permeated by signs, symbols and meanings, this can reinforce both the identities of people who are able to interpret such signs, symbols and meanings and the narrative of the past functioning in a given reality.[29] This valorization of a territory as a reservoir of meanings fundamental to the identities of persons associated with it (at both individual and group level) provides fertile ground for the development of two types of travelling, which Sabine Marschall defines as 'homesick tourism' and 'roots tourism'.[30] The difference between these two types of 'memory tourism' are as follows: 'Roots tourists are driven by a desire for rootedness and identity; their search for information and remnants of forebears is an attempt at consolidating a specific (sometimes chosen) cultural identity and a sense of belonging. Homesick tourists are driven by longing, memories and emotions; their search for tangible and intangible traces of the personal past, multisensory "containers" of memory, is an attempt at reflecting upon and consolidating the self, which may include coming to terms with unresolved aspects of the personal past or one's own long-fostered nostalgia.'[31] Homesick tourists travel to their places of origin to experience 'contact with the past' (sometimes defined as returning to the past, and at other times as confronting it) and grant their memories or the stories of their loved ones a real, 'material' dimension. These journeys therefore become an important tool for shaping and reinforcing their own identities.

This chapter makes use of interviews conducted with members of the aforementioned Kresy NGOs and people who cooperate with such associations or foundations. This is a unique group of people whose actions are focused on Polish aspects of the territory contained within the former borderlands. Even if this is not their primary area of interest (as many of them are also interested in Lithuanian, Belarusian or Ukrainian culture, or focus on values that transcend culture, such as the natural environment), references to Polishness dominate their narratives of their trips to the former borderlands.

Some repatriates from the borderlands and their descendants used to visit homelands beyond Poland's eastern border during the People's Republic, but most 'memory tourists' only began making such journeys after the sociopolitical transformations of 1989–91. From this time onwards, many different types of this kind of trip to former homelands developed, from solo excursions to pilgrimages, social campaigns of various kinds (such as providing financial assistance to Poles living beyond the eastern border or restoring cemeteries) and organized tours for tourists or school trips.

For people who visited the borderlands before the sociopolitical transformations in the Eastern Bloc began and before the Soviet Union collapsed, the 1990s were most notable for the rising number of such trips and the opportunities they presented. For such people, these trips were not so much about rediscovering these places, but more about the systematic observation of changes occurring in particular places and across entire countries. For some of these visitors, this meant that the nature of these trips changed, because it became possible, for example, to officially organize pilgrimages or deliver aid. Initially, these trips had a 'cultural' dimension (e.g. the delivery of textbooks and other equipment to schools), but they swiftly acquired a financial dimension because the economic situation in the regions beyond Poland's eastern border had deteriorated significantly. The kind of people visiting the east changed, with new categories appearing, such as Polish teachers, clerics, volunteers of various sorts (with the largest group comprising scouts) and researchers representing various academic disciplines, for whom the borderlands opened up fascinating new research fields. The number of tourists also increased (it had been possible to go on excursions to various places within the USSR in Soviet times, but the scope and availability of these trips had been limited).

All these categories of people beginning to visit the east were joined by others with unique motivations stemming from personal identity issues. They may be described as 'memory tourists' because they had personal recollections associated with these lands or regarded their past as crucially important due to their self-identification with particular families or nations.

The motivations of the people who were born in the Kresy and those who are descended from the original repatriates are linked by a common factor: fascination with these lands. However, for the repatriates, this fascination is inextricably bound up with their biographies and is defined as a 'personal attachment'. 'Like a wolf is drawn to a forest, we are drawn to these places. They are what they are, but once you see them, we're saying to ourselves: here's where we used to play', claims an older man currently living in Lesser Poland. Meanwhile, many people from the middle and younger generations claim that their decisions to travel to the borderlands for the first time were triggered by an inner coming of age process. One woman, who is the daughter of a person displaced from an area currently belonging to Ukraine, accounted for her decision to take a first trip to the lands her family originally come from as follows:

> I became an adult. I became an adult and the priest suggested that we take a trip to the Kresy, and I'm a geographer by education, so these lands interested me. This was '92. Yes, '92 or '93 ... we went to Kolomyia. That's the town mum's family come from so I wanted to see it. ... I was shocked and

pleasantly disappointed. Because, first of all, the weather simply has to be good, and it was, so the land was beautiful, and the Carpathian Mountains were beautiful. Apart from that, I struggled to decide what else I wanted to see. Because I was approaching the most important region ... basically, I filled in some of the gaps in the history I'd learned at school. I ticked off Chocim [Khotyn], and Kamieniec Podolski [Kamianets-Podilskyi] and Krzemieniec [Kremenets]. I also came into close contact with certain things they had taught me about using dry facts, and saw them [close up].

As in many cases of people from borderland families being interested in where their ancestors came from, this is the narrative of a person not only familiar with the history of her family, but also with that of the Polish state; in short, a person who is capable of recognizing the significance of the places she is looking at. She also emphasizes that she was 'pleasantly disappointed', which shows that she was not anticipating that the trip would be a positive experience, but rather that by visiting the towns her mother came from, she was performing a 'duty to remember'. However, other people who were interviewed recall the reverse process: a progression from great expectations and an image they had nurtured of a beautiful, pastoral, almost magical land to disappointment at what they saw when they encountered it in person:

> my professors from Stefan Batory University portrayed this land as splendid, so to speak, with a rich Polish cultural life; there was this multiculturality, everything was colourful, beautiful, such rich cultures, customs. But when I was there the first time, when the Soviet Union still existed, I didn't see this, everything had vanished, the churches had been shut down.

This man had been influenced for many years by the stories of his professors from Stefan Batory University in Vilnius, who went on to lecture at the Nicolaus Copernicus University in Toruń after the war. It would appear that as a mature, educated person, he came to realize that after the war and the post-war repatriations, the situation in Vilnius had completely changed and there was never any chance that the kind of life that had existed in the city during the interwar period would have endured in an unchanged form. This demonstrates the power that narratives of the Kresy can exert when created by people with strong emotional and biographical ties with these lands. It also shows how an 'eternally existing' reality unconstrained by the passage of time can be constructed.[32] Being confronted by the 'here and now' reality could therefore be painful. This man is still an active activist who often visits Vilnius and other places in the former borderlands to assist the Poles that live there. However, he lost that vision of Vilnius that had motivated him to seek the opportunity to visit the city. For many people, images shaped by books, films or other people's stories about the atmosphere of the borderland cities, towns and landscapes still serve as the prime motivation to visit the Kresy.

Touristic Motivations – the Materialization of Notions of a National Past

For most tourists, the Kresy are first and foremost an area containing a plethora of allusions to Polish history. They are a kind of reservoir of material remnants of a national past. Such an attitude is exemplified by comments made by an older man, fascinated by the history of the borderlands, whose family do in fact originally come from these lands, but appeared in Central Poland during the second half of the nineteenth century rather than as a result of the repatriation programme after the war:

> Well, that was what they were telling me and what I saw complemented [what I'd learned] and I was pleased to see it. For example, I really yearned to see Kamieniec Podolski [Kamianets-Podilskyi], that really was a kind of yearning for me because [I only knew it] from pictures, from stories, and so on. But when I went to this Kamieniec Podolski, I was struck with awe at the sight of the fortress ... yes, I sat down, took a seat to take it all in, I absorbed it, it brought everything back to me, how everything had been, how this had happened; here – the Polish marketplace, here – the Jewish marketplace, here – the Armenian marketplace; I wandered around like that; even a friend from Lviv said: 'Why are you traipsing around like that?' And I said: 'Because I'm contemplating.' Because I was looking at these buildings, I was sensing how the Polish army was, how those expeditions were, how Sobieski was, and then on to Chocim [Khotyn] ... here, I said, along this road, the Turks paraded to bow or pay homage to Jan III Sobieski. That was how I experienced it and always, when I go, I say 'take your time' when I lead [tours] there, [I say] 'let's look at these walls, let's look at these churches, let's sit down in this and reflect on what went on here.'

What is occurring in this case is a phenomenon similar to that which arises in the case of encounters with witnesses to history – coming into contact with a real place (be it a settlement, building, monument or landscape feature) reveals that what has previously only been read or heard about really does exist. Some of the interviewees opined that the problem is not so much that the education system and press offer little in the way of information about the Kresy, but rather that they are not treated as being connected in any way with the reality affecting Poles living today, and are therefore swiftly forgotten about. Another interviewee (a second-generation repatriate) compares coming into contact with sites operating on the fringes of social consciousness with being struck by lightning, as the impression is so moving and enlightening:

> Because this is a fantastic story, for it's like in these borderland places there is the ambition [to ensure] that at least one or two trips of the kind that were once called sentimental pilgrimages set off every year. Entire generations go there ... But it could well be claimed that every time this fascination, this discovery, as they say, of some grand message that also happens to be historical, strikes like lightning. ... I also think that experiencing Vilnius at first

hand gives one a completely different perspective because even a panorama of the city is captivating, not to mention walking around one or another cemetery; there's that mine there too and that's striking [enough to inspire] the question: 'God, that's ours, isn't it!?'

Nothing, therefore, can replace direct contact with city-symbols of lost lands. Out of all the borderland places, the above interviewee mentions one that has not only become symbolic of Kresy communities, but also of the development of Polish culture in these lands. Trips to the Kresy, and in particular to places with a symbolic meaning, are therefore perceived as an essential element in the shaping of personal national identity, conceived as an intellectual challenge rather than habitual self-identification with a specific group. They are also essential for another reason – the experiences they provide cannot be replaced by any other available means of becoming acquainted with the past, that is, through the education system or the media. However, clearly, for the youngest generation, the mere act of referencing history does not suffice. There is also a genuine need for 'touristic experiences' of another kind. Nevertheless, coming into contact with remnants of Polishness in regions that are not currently within the borders of the Polish state makes a deep impression on any visitor. Such material remnants lodge more deeply in the memory than a verbal narrative. This experience can also have the character of an 'imperial gaze' when contact with the traces of Polish material culture leads to the nostalgia for the past glory of the great commonwealth (defined almost exclusively as the Polish state). However, most often it is the grief connected with the loss of part of the territory of the interwar Polish state rather than empire from past ages. Still, the buildings and monuments of other ethnic groups that have been living in these places for ages are not recalled in the narratives of the tourists; they talk only about those that are associated with Polishness.

The quest for remnants of Polishness also has specific consequences – it causes trips to the former borderlands to frequently assume a religious dimension, as noted by the man repatriated from the Kresy after the war who currently leads tours there:

> Virtually all the agencies do tours to the borderlands. For better or worse, but they still do them. And pilgrimages are like that. I began leading pilgrimages because even … all Poles, whatever kind of trip they're on, look for traces of Polish culture, don't they? So, where can they be found? In churches! They're taken from one church, they're taken to a second one, they're taken to a third one, aren't they? So, over time, such a trip becomes a pilgrimage of this kind.

A similar motif also appears in many of the interviewees' statements: even if the prime motivation is to become better acquainted with places and objects of historical interest and to come into contact with material remnants of history, at some point in the tourist trips, there is nearly always at least one request to meet Poles living in Lithuania, Belarus or Ukraine. The nature of material heritage also determines the form that sightseeing takes – churches always appear on tour schedules. Entering a church also often means meeting a Polish priest or Polish locals. Churches are therefore situated in a space that combines the two ways in which Polishness can endure in these lands – one is of a material type and the other is the human type.

Coming into contact with the 'local population' does not, however, equate to only meeting Poles, as local inhabitants of other nationalities are also encountered. This leads to confrontations between different memory narratives and conflicting visions of the past. Responses to encounters of this type tend to be generation-specific.[33] Members of the youngest generation are more likely to mention a desire to learn about non-Polish cultures in the Kresy. The tourists coming from other age groups display a greater diversity of sentiment. It needs to be taken into account that not all those displaced from the Kresy have decided to return there. Some have been paralysed by fears (either of the journey itself or the local population) triggered by tragic memories, or by the thought of such a confrontation with the existing reality being too traumatic or painful. One of the younger activists perceived this phenomenon among members of her own organization:

> Few people from the Society travel to the Kresy. They want to preserve what they have in their memory, what was very Polish. I don't think it makes sense to look at things as they do. If we wish to preserve this memory, we also need to learn about Ukrainian Lviv [Lwów], just as the Germans do with Polish Wrocław [Breslau] ... I think they'd be happy to return there, only... if it was Polish Lwów, that would be fine, but as long as it's Ukrainian, they don't want to return.

However, those who do decide to undertake a sentimental journey of this nature react in many different ways: disappointment and reluctance to return again in the future; sad resignation manifested in activities associated with the duty to remember (like tending to the graves of their ancestors); a willingness to reconcile themselves to the situation and forge friendly relations with the people who live there now. Such encounters change the attitudes of both parties, namely both former and new inhabitants. This phenomenon was observed by an academic undertaking research on Germans travelling to Polish lands. On the basis of this research, she claims:

> Personal memory relates to collective memory in similar ways that individual tourist experience relates to official images provided by tourism authorities. On the one hand, one must consider how tangible traces of the past,

many of them being tourist attractions, are represented by the local destination marketing effort, and how, guided by ideological frameworks of memory, remembering and forgetting are reflected in heritage conservation, the treatment of iconic symbols and the performance of commemorative rituals and official interpretations of the past in museums. On the other hand, individual visitors and tourists as 'consumers of memory' have their own ways of making sense of these representations and interpretations, as they bring their own personal memories and experiences, influenced by their own societal frames of memory to the site. Tourism as an agent in the promotion of officially sanctioned images and collective memory is hence always compromised by the potentially subversive power of individuals, both among the guests and the hosts.[34]

In the conversations conducted with members of the Kresy NGOs, repeated reference was made to changes occurring in various regions of the former borderlands due to the influence of 'memory tourists'. Some of these changes are of a material nature – for example, monuments and crosses commemorating specific people and events are appearing, cemeteries are being tidied up and churches are being restored and refurbished, while others are even being built. However, many people speak of the 'interpersonal' outcomes of this kind of journey, for example, forging relationships with local residents that ensure that a steady flow of information is maintained and visitors are helped to cope with the painful past and homesickness. The benefits of maintaining such relationships provide another motive for such trips that is grounded in the present moment, rather than being determined by a desire to return to the past.

Sentimental Tourists – the 'Return Journeys' of the First Generation of Repatriates

Kaja Kaźmierska notes, in her analysis of the experiences of Jews making 'return journeys' to the places in Poland in which they either once lived or that are important from the perspective of Holocaust history, that these Jews are full of emotions that relate to both the collective and personal dimensions of such experiences. The dominant trait of journeys of this kind is a sense of suffering. The personal dimension often involves attempts to attain biographical closure in relation to their own experiences and interpretations of their own emotions. However, powerful emotions can also be provoked by their observation of the contemporary reality, in particular the erasure of remnants of the historical Jewish presence in Poland.[35] The 'homesick tourism' trips that repatriates take to the Kresy also contain such elements. Such tourists need to come to terms with their own tragic memories and the emotions that accompany visits to their former homelands. Yet such trips also have a sociocultural dimension, since these tourists are burdened by personal baggage that not only comprises personal experiences, but also their knowledge of history (that often took place in the distant past), literary models, linguistic terms, stereotypes and prejudices, and images of 'the East' and various states that function within Polish society despite these regions being situated beyond Poland's eastern border.

The first sentimental trips that repatriates take to their former homelands often generate powerful emotions. One interviewee recalls that she travelled with her husband to see his family home, which is currently occupied by Russians: 'The way my husband stood there and looked at this house as his tears flowed made me cry immediately too.' Such visits are often painful because they enable the huge changes that have occurred in the Kresy to be experienced at first hand and make visitors aware that the old world they once knew has gone, never to return. Comparing these homes with their current ones often turns out to do more harm than good. All such narratives contain the theme of destruction wreaked by neglect or wilful action. These areas continue to arouse sentiment and it is still possible to find particular places associated with visitors' personal past, but the overwhelming impression is one of depression caused by the poverty and poor land management that is often encountered. One of the outcomes of such depressing images of neglect is that they make any thought of return seem completely irrational. A man displaced from a region in what is now Ukraine thinks that there is no future there for him and others of a similar background: 'There are resentments of a sort, but I went there, but would I want to return there? No. I went there, looked around and I'll tell you what I think. This is poverty of the worst kind ... too many people there are going nowhere.'

Even if such changes are not assessed negatively and transformations are described as the normal course of events, feelings of alienation appear. These surprise some of those making sentimental trips:

> By which I mean very, very strange, even here, I was telling this schoolgirl that I went there; there, I always remember that [there were] also these buildings there, and like a child, I saw everything differently, and I went there, how tiny everything is [there], [here] we have these tower blocks. ... But when I went there and came to the marketplace, the centre, the town hall and it seemed to me that I knew Drohobych well, I remembered everything so well, yet everything is different, completely different.

Although visitors come across familiar places, the towns or villages that these are in already seem alien to them. This was one of the sensations experienced by an older man who originally comes from Vilnius: 'I was definitely at home and not at home. On the streets I felt at home, and in the churches, this was the Wilno [Vilnius] I knew, yet some districts were not familiar at all. That Wilno was no longer mine.' The sense of irreparable loss associated with being displaced is reinforced through coming into contact with the current state of affairs and is described by some visitors as an existential experience:

> After the war, I went there once, I went to my village and I was accompanied by a television crew that was recording how I was taking this journey. And it was such a great experience [testing whether] it was possible to immerse myself in the same river a second time. And I was forced to look at a village that didn't exist any more, there were other houses there by then, other people, another culture, I had to come to terms with non-existence.

Once it has been established that the family home no longer exists, there is no reason to return there again. Such a once-in-a-lifetime trip may therefore be seen as the fulfilment of a duty to remember or the closure of a biographical strand through final confirmation of the extinguishment of a physical correlate, in this case, a family home or local homeland. This does not, of course, mean that the home has been extinguished in the visitor's memory. Such memories live on forever, but the journey has deprived them of their physicality and plausibility. In such situations, visiting the homeland permanently extinguishes any thought of returning. Nevertheless, emotions maintaining links to the past can still be observed in the oldest members of subsequent generations: 'Some sentiment or nostalgia for what had been lost. As if they wanted to live here, but remembered there. Also, the older they were, the stronger the connection ... the more they experienced such a sense of emptiness, of loss. They often used to repeat that it was beautiful here, but more beautiful there.' This nostalgia is strengthened by the repatriates' awareness that they have managed to settle down in a new place and cannot leave it now. They not only often do not have the financial resources that would be required to leave, but also have their careers and families to consider and may not be strong enough psychologically:

> So many people do actually have regrets. They said that was their place, it was there that they left their hearts, they feel that is, that was, their place, that it was beautiful there, that it's most beautiful there, that the air is so different that still, after all these years have passed ... they say, 'yes, we have regrets that we had to leave there, yet we know now that we wouldn't want to return any more. We want to go there, to see it, but our place now is here.

When homesickness for a world that no longer exists is combined with an awareness of how much it has changed, it makes the notion of returning to these lands unrealistic. It is this 'realism' that is presented as the root cause of repatriates thinking of returning to their homelands in purely symbolic or sentimental terms. This realism has two sources –

awareness of their own circumstances and opportunities and awareness of the changes that have occurred in the countries of their childhoods. This awareness is exemplified by the response of a woman displaced from Lviv, who clearly has no intention of entertaining the possibility of returning there:

> Researcher: Why? Why wouldn't you like to return?
>
> Woman: Precisely for that reason, that it is no longer mine ... because you can't spend your whole life indoors, you are surrounded by people, you are surrounded by a system of some kind, you are surrounded by a mentality that is also different, you think differently. No, no, no, that would be completely out of the question. I think I've basically developed since then and am making progress.

Typically, however, when asked which city she was most attached to – Warsaw or Lviv – she pronounced, without a moment's hesitation, that she was more attached to Lviv. Her decision to abandon any thought of returning was therefore caused by reasons that are negative (for example, the impossibility of depriving the place in question of the social world associated with it) rather than positive (being attached to another place). At the same time, her decision to abandon any thought of returning is defined as 'developing' and 'making progress', which is indicative of the closure of a particular biographical period, one in which she perceived herself as a *Lwowianka* (resident of Lviv). This definition of her identity leaves the past intact, so her emotional attitude to the city itself does not change.

Sometimes, despite the intentions of those visiting their former homelands, such trips turn into experiences that ultimately banish any thought of return. They serve as final confirmation of their need to wrest themselves away from their ancestral lands. One of the interviewed activists related how moved he was by the impressions he had taken away from trips to his homeland: 'An impression so [moving] that I would return there on my knees, and I'd like to be there. But I am fully aware that no one wants us there.' He admitted that he had thought about returning there to live, but 'crossing the border is like entering a completely different world ... I'm aware that no one is waiting for us there.'

Such impressions do not translate into complete reluctance to visit the former borderlands. Furthermore, other visitors have a different attitude to taking such trips, as a man who visited his family's ancestral town for the first time in 2006 explained: 'I took a look around there and pronounced that I knew everything then and had no reason to return there any more and from that day onwards, I've been going there three or four times a year.' When people take return trips, therefore, it is a sign that they have reconciled themselves to the situation and the fact that there is no hope of them returning permanently. In such cases, their attitudes to the homeland have evolved from the expectation that a good time will be found to return to the awareness that this is impossible, irrespective of whether or not the family home has changed in appearance.

In his analysis of the experiences of Germans displaced from Lower Silesia and their attempts to reconcile themselves with the loss of their family homes and small homelands, Andrew Demshuk reached the conclusion that two images of their lost homelands prevailed in their minds: 'The basis for each expellee's process of coping with loss came through recognition of the fundamental incompatibility between two images of *Heimat*. While in their minds they generated the *Heimat of memory*, an idealized vision of what they had lost, they also steadily confronted the *Heimat transformed*, their perception of Silesia as it now existed in Poland. The *Heimat of memory* evoked a pristine, timeless, and bygone German homeland that had never really existed.'[36] This researcher notes that nearly all 'sentimental tourists' return with the feeling that they could not live in their former homelands any more:

> homesick tourism became the most intense, and ultimately effective, means of dislodging lingering fantasies about return. By widening the gulf between the *Heimat of memory* and *Heimat transformed* in the minds of most homesick tourists, the emotionally demanding journeys back to Silesia yielded a new point of maturity in the lifelong search for healing from loss. In general, they were already aware before departing that the *Heimat* had transformed with the passage of time; however, nothing could prepare them for the actual experience, which shattered any remaining illusions and forced them to digest the reality that Silesia could never again be what they remembered.[37]

Similar responses accompany the impressions formed by Polish repatriates from the former borderlands when they return there as 'homesick tourists'. However, while this discovery provides German displaced persons with a great sense of relief and brings them closure from their lifetime struggle to cope with the loss of their small homelands, such a reaction is only displayed by some members of the oldest Kresy generation. For the others, this loss is still painful, even as they perceive it as completely irreversible. By contrast, for the younger generations of 'roots tourists', such journeys more often than not mean discovering a new place capable of defining individual identities. Experiencing this place, rather than supplanting the roots they have laid down in their current places of residence in Poland, enables them to create positive ties with the lands of their ancestors, which often run deep, even though such ties are based on returning there repeatedly rather than living there permanently.

It is not only the original repatriates that feel a need to reconcile themselves to the changes that have taken place in the former borderlands, for their descendants also feel such a need. The consequences of this need tend to vary within every generation. While some people try to disassociate themselves from their former homelands (perceiving them as alien and irrelevant to the lives they currently lead), others wish to seek out even the minutest remnants of the life they or their ancestors once led. These two opposite poles of the response spectrum to changes in the former borderlands were contrasted by a man born in the Western Lands who grew up in an atmosphere suffused by family memories from Polesie:

> I ask others the same [and they reply]: 'But what's there for me in Polesie, I'm living my life in my country, what's there for me to visit?' I say: 'At least you'll see your home, your roots, that rock that stood there once, that old tree that's still there, or maybe not, maybe a piece of it is, maybe it's rotted away, but I'm going there to see!'

'Memory tourism' is therefore not an enterprise only suited to the oldest generation. In fact, it is suited to any people who have family connections with these lands, as well as those who are motivated to take such trips by a personal interest in Kresy history and culture (especially when they are perceived in national terms). The primary goal during such trips is to establish international relationships, so this type of tourism can perform an important social role. As Sabine Marschall notes, 'The potential socio-economic benefits of homesick tourism have been mentioned earlier, but its contribution to cross-cultural understanding, illustrated so abundantly by the German-Polish case, turns the homesick tourism phenomenon into a potentially significant instrument of promoting reconciliation in post-conflict societies. The role of memory is crucial in this process as the travellers take home new perspectives on the past and "braided historical narratives" emerge through the transcultural exchange of memories.'[38] Some interviewees begin speaking of 'sentimental tourism' in the Kresy in similar terms, although the predominant motives are still a desire to perform a 'duty to remember' the homeland and ancestors and to maintain contact with the Polish communities still living in regions of the former borderlands today. The paradox of this type of motivation to travel is that even when their goal is to strengthen feelings of connection with lost lands, the most frequent consequence is to make them more aware of the fact that these regions have changed so much that any permanent return is impossible. Sometimes, however, such changes make visitors even more likely to want to maintain contact with the people who live there today and sharpen their interest in these people's culture and history. However, the essential condition for maintaining such relationships is a joint desire to commemorate the past (whether family-related or of a local nature). Furthermore, the need to tend to sites of memory and the new remembrance practices that appear attract new 'memory tourists', some of whom arrive on their own and some in groups. Nevertheless, the relationships and emotions that unite people who were displaced from the former borderlands cannot be recreated in later generations. However, sites containing material remnants of the old world and markers of memory relating to former residents serve as intersection points where the motivations and hierarchies of values inspiring 'borderlands tourism' of various types meet.

Memory Activism and the Narratives of the Former Eastern Borderlands in Contemporary Poland

Societies do not have a 'social memory', as such, conceived as the accumulated personal memories of each of their members. Instead, a society 'remembers' because interpersonal interactions lead to elements being extracted from the past that appear, at specific moments, to be particularly important or valuable for a specific group or individual people (operating in various spheres, such as domestic or international politics, group identity formation, art or tourism). The act of remembering involves adapting the past to the present moment through the performance of social activities. For Jay Winter, such activities form the essence of how collective memory functions: 'Memory performed is at the heart of collective memory. When individuals and groups express or embody or interpret or repeat a script about the past, they galvanize the ties that bind groups together and deposit additional memory traces about the past in their own minds. These renewed and revamped memories frequently vary from and overlay earlier memories, creating a complex palimpsest about the past each of us carries with us.'[39]

Collective memory is a social relationship between people who share a similar vision of the past and, in this sense, build a shared identity. It is therefore always 'someone's' memory. It differs from history, not so much because it lacks objectivity, but because it cannot exist without being transmitted from person to person. Collective memory is 'social' in the sense that it cannot exist until there are people who regard it as being psychologically important enough to pass down from generation to generation (otherwise, it would only be personal memory, which is shaped within a social framework but does not shape collective identities). Furthermore, collective memory is mediated by the process of social transmission, and develops in a space where the interests of its producer (or supplier), seller and consumer intersect.[40] Such transmission processes are of key importance, since they determine whether or not given elements will be incorporated into collective memory.

Memory transmission is made possible by the division of memory labour. Memory activists can assume one of three roles in the social division of memory work, notably – producer, seller or consumer of memory.[41] These roles may be assumed by different people, groups, organizations and institutions situated at various points along the producer–seller–consumer continuum. The relationship between memory activists and the memories they are producing, selling or consuming may be based on personal and emotional bonds, as in the case of the 'eyewitnesses to history' that can be found among the first generation of displaced persons. Their children and grandchildren then become 'guardians of witness testimonies' and play this role by attempting to generalize and transfer their parents' or grandparents' memories to subsequent generations or people outside their families. However, the role of producer can also be assumed by popularizers (either professional or amateur), who not only rely on eyewitness accounts but also on other types of source. Each of these categories of memory activist develops its own method for transmitting past narratives and defines its role differently with respect to other members of the social world of memory and society as a whole. However, their actions are closely interrelated.

If we consider the kinds of social activities performed by people undertaking memory work within the context of the social framework in which memory of the Kresy is currently being communicated, it is possible to identify certain characteristics that define this memory. These characteristics significantly influence how memory of the former borderlands is transmitted and sometimes even greatly impede it. Much of this memory operates by means of mnemonic processes that are not framed by spatial considerations. This is the case because members of this memory community want to communicate memory of places to which they are no longer bound through the performance of habitual daily activities within a specific space. Consequently, this memory, rather than relating to their current place of residence, evokes places that these people have been deprived of and have no plan to return to, at least not permanently. If these places still exist, they do so as collections of material objects (buildings, streets and elements of the natural environment). And yet even these physical elements have been significantly transformed or damaged beyond repair. They no longer exist as a social space, conceived as a space inhabited by a specific group of people. On this understanding, these borderland places have disappeared irretrievably and cannot be reconstructed. Therefore, a situation arises in which the oldest generation of repatriates cannot share their sense of rootedness with successive generations. Moreover, under communism, for many years, this memory could not officially exist, so had to settle for a place on the margins of the collective memory of society as a whole. Sometimes, the local circumstances were different in areas where repatriates constituted a large percentage of the local population or when they came from one locality in the former borderlands, even though they were officially still not able to cultivate their memory or commemorate the events related to their lives in their former homelands. Consequently, memory was primarily transmitted within families and local communities. In many cases, that memory was traumatic because recalling the past was sometimes extremely difficult for psychological reasons. Moreover, the oldest generation could have been afraid of talking about the past with their children and grandchildren because they did not want to 'burden them' with a past that could be problematic or even harmful to younger generations. This situation can result in the formation of 'memory communities', that is, closed communities of people focused on recalling the past who are convinced that people who do not share similar experiences are incapable of understanding them. Members of such communities also believe that they can talk about the past within the confines of their own group without feeling that they would be burdening anyone unnecessarily.

The social world of the memory of the Kresy is permeated by two forms of remembrance of the lost territories. These might aptly be termed 'sentimental memory' and 'ideological memory'. Sentimental memory, which predominates in this social world of memory, is produced by the representatives of the first generation. It focuses on personal recollections and emotions. This memory of the lost small homelands is presented in an idealized form, that of 'a paradise lost'. The old world is viewed as a place full of happiness and harmony, not only in family life but also in the local community. One recurring theme is the problem-free multiculturalism of the territories of this lost paradise, a multiculturalism that was irrevocably destroyed by the war and post-war repatriations. First-generation repatriates have the feeling that their memories and emotions are largely non-transferable and that people who have no similar experiences are therefore unable to understand them. In the case of this type of memory, there is also a sense of victimhood and of injustice that will never be redressed. The world they remember arouses positive emotions, but these are often combined with a sense of having been wronged and the awareness that their small homelands have disappeared forever. This memory is focused on concrete elements, such as individual people, communities and places. The predominant feeling in this type of memory is nostalgic longing for these places, which is not only experienced by people born in the Kresy who remember what it was like to live there before the war, but is also passed on to subsequent generations.

As mentioned above, such sentimental memory can be contrasted with ideological memory of the former borderlands. This operates at a top-down state level and focuses on national ideology. According to this perspective, the loss of the former borderlands is, first and foremost, a loss experienced by Poland as a country rather than one suffered by private individuals. While the conviction runs deep that the Kresy have been lost forever, this does not mean that they should be forgotten. On the contrary, such memory plays a dual role, that of a guarantor asserting that there will be some form of redress in the future and a guardian protecting against the emergence of a 'victimhood identity'. Sentimental memory is portrayed as too passive, as it would appear to emphasize the role of victim, while ideological memory is portrayed as active, as it seeks to gain, at least symbolically, the upper hand over those whose actions led to the loss of the eastern territories. Such memory does nothing to aid the acceptance of the status quo over time but, instead, offers a vehicle for those affected to express their disagreement (in the full knowledge that things cannot be changed). This kind of memory is perceived, above all, as an identity-based form of defence, which also leads to activities being undertaken in the sociopolitical sphere. As such, ideological memory, unlike sentimental memory, is collective and focused on the present and the future rather than attempting to come to terms with the past.

These two types of memory exist in parallel, and the transmission of both types are interdependent. Sentimental memory testifies to the strong bonds many Poles still have with the lost territories. This, in turn, reinforces ideological memory fuelled by witness testimonies (such testimonies build credibility, authenticate the sense of there being a collective moral obligation to honour this memory, and generate emotions). Ideological memory therefore guarantees the preservation of the repatriates' memories by enabling them to transcend a narrow circle of family members and close neighbours.

Conclusion

The preservation and transmission of past narratives of the eastern borderlands of the Second Republic of Poland is greatly facilitated when ways can be found to help the first generation of repatriates cope with the loss of their 'small local homelands'. In the case of this oldest generation, any coping mechanisms are inextricably bound up with their relationship with their places of origin. However, subsequent generations can greatly assist the oldest generation's attempts to cope with their loss by visiting places of importance for their family or national history. Travelling to the former borderlands facilitates reflection on the relationship between the 'homeland of memory', which emerges from the memories of repatriates (and the literature on the subject), and the 'homeland transformed', which currently exists beyond Poland's eastern border. Such trips help the oldest generation to come to terms with the fact that their old world is gone forever, whereas people who are new to the social world of memory of the historical borderlands can become more aware that this world actually used to exist by discovering the remnants of it that have survived until today.

However, memory of the historical borderlands is politically problematic, as it can be seen as revisionist and, as such, dangerous. For this reason, it receives no support from the government, so large-scale transmission of this memory is difficult. Some awareness of these problems is reflected in statements made by activists affiliated with the Kresy NGOs. Moreover, their ideas promoting the transferral of memory stem from their social milieu's awareness of the potential controversy provoked by their memory work. Consequently, they feel that in order to be effective in the modern world, their message must have a primarily moral character. They therefore feel compelled to draw attention to the duty to remember and the need to gain redress for injustices, while continuing to search for the sources of the collective identities focused around memory of the former borderlands.

However, all those involved in the transmission of memory of the former borderlands share the conviction that the world they want to remember has receded into the past, and that there is no way of returning to it. All that can be done is to recognize its importance. Andrei Demshuk came to similar conclusions when describing the feelings of Germans displaced from Lower Silesia after the Second World War:

> Whatever their backgrounds, when expellees imagined the *Heimat of memory*, they knew that it only existed now in the past and in their minds. Aware that the *Heimat of memory* would vanish upon their deaths, they grew obsessed with preserving their heritage in books and in the minds of their indifferent descendants. But time was working against them. ... Countless projects arose to compile the lost *Heimat* for the expellee youth born in the West, but time took its toll, and the *Heimat* film and *Heimat* book simply went out of style. Today, the living traditions formed by Silesian exiles have become artifacts just like the milieus they had once inhabited in Silesia; owing in no small part to the expellees themselves, these exilic *lieux de mémoire* survive in museums, monuments, anniversaries, and attics, where tradition has become history.[42]

Faced with a situation in which the generation of first-hand witnesses is passing away and little interest is being shown in the former eastern borderlands by contemporary Polish society, the activists affiliated with the Kresy NGOs concentrate today on creating a 'memory resource' comprising a collection of narratives, documents, souvenirs and different forms of commemoration of persons, places and events, in the hope that this resource might be used in the future if the social situation or political circumstances become more favourable.

The experience of mass displacement is not unique to Polish history. This phenomenon affected almost all of Central and Eastern Europe and still affects its present shape. Losing a family home and place of origin or being relocated to a completely different place with no opportunity to return to the old world has been experienced by millions of Europeans. This phenomenon has been summarized by Saskia Sassen as follows: 'Uprooted, displaced, migratory people seem to inhabit the shadows of European history, living in the places which they do not belong to.'[43] Despite the gravity of this situation, it is barely visible amid the collective amnesia of millions of other people. Resettlement is a long-standing issue that has been on the margins of collective memory for many years in Poland, as is the case in other countries.[44] Consequently, the current status of the memory of forced resettlements should be regularly re-examined in order to ascertain the extent to which it could cause potential conflicts today. Such an approach has the additional benefit of providing useful information about the extent to which separate communities can come to a mutual understanding of each other's situations.

Małgorzata Głowacka-Grajper is a sociologist and social anthropologist. She works as an associate professor at the Faculty of Sociology at the University of Warsaw. She is also Head of the Department of Social Anthropology and Ethnic and Migration Studies. Her main research interests include issues of contemporary national and ethnic identity, social memory (especially memory activism) and research on the relationship between the local and national dimensions of memory. Her most recent books are *Milieux de mémoire in Late Modernity: Local Communities, Religion and Historical Politics* (2019, with Zuzanna Bogumił) and *The Burden of the Past: History, Memory, and Identity in Contemporary Ukraine* (2020, edited with Anna Wylegała).

Notes

1. Snyder, *Bloodlands*.
2. Reinisch and White, *The Disentanglement of Populations*.
3. Bakuła, 'Kolonialne i postkolonialne aspekty polskiego dyskursu kresoznawczego (zarys problematyki)'.
4. Snyder, *The Reconstruction of Nations*.
5. Ibid.
6. Chałupczak and Browarek, *Mniejszości narodowe w Polsce 1918–1995*.

7. Snyder, *The Reconstruction of Nations*.
8. Siedlecki, *Losy Polaków w ZSRR w latach 1939–1986*; Srebrakowski, *Polacy w Litewskiej SSR 1944–1989*.
9. Czerniakiewicz, *Repatriacja ludności polskiej z ZSRR 1944–1948*.
10. Ciesielski, Hryciuk and Srebrakowski, *Masowe deportacje radzieckie w okresie II wojny światowej*.
11. Czerniakiewicz, *Repatriacja ludności polskiej z ZSRR 1944–1948*.
12. Motyka, *Od rzezi wołyńskiej do akcji 'Wisła'*.
13. 'Evacuation' was the official term used to describe displacement from the former eastern borderlands of the Second Republic of Poland, but in fact, the term 'repatriation' was also used in official and popular discourse. Displaced people were named 'repatriates'. The term 'evacuation' is not used in contemporary discourse on this topic in Poland and the term 'repatriation' is used rarely. The displaced people are most frequently referred to today as the '*Kresowiacy*' (people from the Kresy).
14. Ruchniewicz, *Repatriacja ludności polskiej z ZSRR w latach 1955–1959*, 38, 255.
15. About 80 per cent of repatriates were evacuated to the western part of Poland.
16. Burszta, *Kultura ludowa*, 120.
17. Czerniakiewicz, *Repatriacja ludności polskiej z ZSRR 1944–1948*, 59.
18. Banasiak, *Działalność osadnicza Państwowego Urzędu Repatriacyjnego na Ziemiach Odzyskanych w latach 1945–1947*.
19. Popławski, *Dzieje Politechniki Lwowskiej 1844–1945*; Makarczuk, 'Ewakuacja Polaków ze Lwowa 1944–1946'.
20. Srebrakowski, *Polacy w Litewskiej SSR 1944–1989*.
21. Misztal, 'Wysiedlenia i repatriacja obywateli polskich z ZSRR a wysiedlenia i przesiedlenia Niemców z Polski – próba bilansu', 64.
22. Ibid.
23. At the same time, a similar number of Ukrainians were evacuated from Poland to the USSR.
24. Some Polish citizens were forcibly displaced due to not wanting to leave Lviv because they held out the hope that this town would remain within Poland's borders (Poles were a majority there). However, the Soviet government brought many Russians and Ukrainians to Lviv whom they then registered there, changing the composition of the population in this region. As a result, Poland was not able to raise the ethnic issue during negotiations in the international arena and that region was ultimately incorporated into the USSR. Polish citizens still resisted evacuation but eventually agreed to be repatriated as a consequence of multiple repressions and arrests and the Archbishop of Lviv's decision to leave the city; see Makarczuk, Wiszka 'Ewakuacja Polaków ze Lwowa 1944–1946'.
25. Czerniakiewicz, *Repatriacja ludności polskiej z ZSRR 1944–1948*.
26. The term 'Kresy NGOs' has been used to define those associations and foundations that have set themselves the objective of preserving memory of the former eastern borderlands of the Second Republic or maintaining the Polish character of these territories today (the latter goal may entail undertaking measures intended to preserve what remains of the material heritage of the culture of the First and Second Republics or assisting Poles living in Lithuania, Belarus and Ukraine). The material used in this chapter comes from eighty-five interviews conducted between September 2013 and June 2015 in fourteen Polish cities: Białystok, Bydgoszcz, Bytom, Gdańsk, Kraków, Legnica, Lublin, Olsztyn, Opole, Poznań, Szczecin, Warsaw (and outlying towns and villages), Wrocław (and outlying towns and villages) and Zielona Góra.
27. Wylegała, *Przesiedlenia a pamięć*.
28. Grosby, 'Territoriality'.
29. Truc, 'Memory of Places and Places of Memory'.

30. Marschall, '"Homesick Tourism"', 876–92.
31. Ibid., 880.
32. Ewa Wiegand describes this kind of narrative, which can be found in 'small homelands' literature, as mythologizing and opposed to the linearity of historical time: Wiegand, *Podróż z Kresów do Europy Środkowej*.
33. Homesick tourists and roots tourists are not the only people travelling to the former borderlands. The many other visitors include children on school trips and participants in various themed trips (e.g. for bird enthusiasts), as well as 'ordinary' tourists. Some of the interviewees refer to the arrogant attitude presented by such people towards local inhabitants (in particular, Belarusians and Ukrainians). They judge attitudes of this kind negatively, but also emphasize that they do not encounter them very often. When such topics do appear in conversations about 'sentimental' trips, they always refer to the same issue – complaints about the poor management of land (in cities, on private estates and on farms) taken over from its former owners.
34. Marschall, 'The Role of Tourism in the Production of Cultural Memory', 190.
35. Kaźmierska, 'Między pamięcią zbiorową a biograficzną'.
36. Demshuk, *The Lost German East*, 13.
37. Ibid., 186–87.
38. Marschall, '"Homesick Tourism"', 889.
39. Winter, 'Introduction', 11.
40. Kansteiner, 'Szukanie znaczeń w pamięci'; Kapralski, *Naród z popiołów*.
41. Kapralski, *Naród z popiołów*.
42. Demshuk, *The Lost German East*, 20.
43. Sassen, *Guests and Aliens*, 6.
44. Reinisch and White, *The Disentanglement of Populations*.

Bibliography

Bakuła, Bogusław. 'Kolonialne i postkolonialne aspekty polskiego dyskursu kresoznawczego (zarys problematyki)'. *Teksty Drugie* 6 (2006), 11–33.
Banasiak, Stefan. *Działalność osadnicza Państwowego Urzędu Repatriacyjnego na Ziemiach Odzyskanych w latach 1945–1947*. Poznań: Instytut Zachodni, 1963.
Burszta, Józef. *Kultura ludowa – kultura narodowa*. Warsaw: Ludowa Spółdzielnia Wydawnicza, 1974.
Chałupczak, Henryk, and Tomasz. Browarek. *Mniejszości narodowe w Polsce 1918–1995*. Lublin: UMCS, 1998.
Ciesielski, Stanisław, Grzegorz Hryciuk and Aleksander. Srebrakowski. *Masowe deportacje radzieckie w okresie II wojny światowej*. Wrocław: Instytut Historyczny UWr, 1994.
Czerniakiewicz, Jan. *Repatriacja ludności polskiej z ZSRR 1944–1948*. Warsaw: PWN, 1987.
Demshuk, Andrew. *The Lost German East: Forced Migration and the Politics of Memory, 1945–1970*. New York: Cambridge University Press, 2012.
Grosby, Steven. 'Territoriality: The Transcendental, Primordial Feature of Modern Societies'. *Nations and Nationalism* 1(2) (1995), 143–62.
Kansteiner, Wulf. 'Szukanie znaczeń w pamięci: Metodologiczna krytyka pamięcioznawstwa', in Kornelia Kończal (ed.), *(Kon)teksty pamięci: Antologia* (Warsaw: Narodowe Centrum Kultury, 2014), 225–46.
Kapralski, Sławomir. *Naród z popiołów: Pamięć zagłady a tożsamość Romów*. Warsaw: Scholar, 2014.

Kaźmierska, Kaja. 'Między pamięcią zbiorową a biograficzną: Podróże do miejsc urodzenia izraelskich Żydów', in Andrzej Szpociński (ed.), *Pamięć zbiorowa jako czynnik integracji i źródło konfliktów* (Warsaw: Scholar, 1995), pp. 25–46.
Makarczuk, Stepan, and Emilian Wiszka. 'Ewakuacja Polaków ze Lwowa 1944–1946'. *Klio* 1 (2001), 110–22.
Marschall, Sabine. '"Homesick Tourism": Memory, Identity and (Be)Longing'. *Current Issues in Tourism* 18(9) (2015), 876–92.
———. 'The Role of Tourism in the Production of Cultural Memory: The Case of "Homesick Tourism" in Poland'. *Memory Studies* 9(2) (2016), 187–202.
Misztal, Jan. 'Wysiedlenia i repatriacja obywateli polskich z ZSRR a wysiedlenia i przesiedlenia Niemców z Polski – próba bilansu', in Hubert Orłowski and Andrzej Sakson (eds), *Utracona ojczyzna* (Poznań: Instytut Zachodni, 1997), pp. 45–74.
Motyka, Grzegorz. *Od rzezi wołyńskiej do akcji 'Wisła': Konflikt polsko-ukraiński 1943–1947*. Kraków: Wydawnictwo Literackie, 2011.
Popławski, Zbysław. 1992. *Dzieje Politechniki Lwowskiej 1844–1945*. Wrocław: Zakład Narodowy im. Ossolińskich, 1992.
Reinisch, Jessica, and Elisabeth. White. *The Disentanglement of Populations: Migration, Expulsion and Displacement in Post-War Europe, 1944–9*. London: Palgrave Macmillan, 2011.
Ruchniewicz, Małgorzata. *Repatriacja ludności polskiej z ZSRR w latach 1955–1959*. Warsaw: Fundacja im. Ericha Brosta, 2000.
Sassen, Saskia. *Guests and Aliens*. New York: New Place, 1996.
Siedlecki, Julian. *Losy Polaków w ZSRR w latach 1939–1986*. Wrocław: Agencja Wydaw. Solidarności Walczącej, 1990.
Snyder, Timothy. *The Reconstruction of Nations: Poland, Ukraine, Lithuania, Belarus, 1569–1999*. New Haven, CT: Yale University Press, 2003.
———. *Bloodlands: Europe Between Hitler and Stalin*. New York: Basic Books, 2010.
Srebrakowski, Aleksander. *Polacy w Litewskiej SSR 1944–1989*. Toruń: Wyd. Adam Marszałek, 2001.
Truc, Gérôme. 'Memory of Places and Places of Memory: For a Halbwachsian Socio-Ethnography of Collective Memory'. *International Social Science Journal* 62(203–4) (2011), 147–59.
Wiegand, Ewa. 'Podróż z Kresów do Europy Środkowej', in Krzysztof Trybuś, Jerzy Kałążny and Radosław Okulicz-Kozaryn (eds), *Kresy – dekonstrukcja* (Poznań: Wydawn. Poznańskiego Tow. Przyjaciół, 2007), 37–54.
Winter, Jay. 'Introduction: The Performance of the Past: Memory, History, Identity', in Jay Winter, Karin Tilmans and Frank van Vree (eds), *Performing the Past* (Amsterdam: Amsterdam University Press, 2010), 11–23.
Wylegała, Anna. *Przesiedlenia a pamięć*. Toruń: Wydawnictwo Naukowe UMK, 2014.

Part III

BORDERS AND MIGRATION
A Comparison between Water and Land

Nobuya Hashimoto

Borders are variable, mobile and permeable despite their apparent robustness. The construction and deconstruction of borders and the resulting territorial changes affect the flow of migration and transform the milieus to and from which people move, crossing them with ambitions for the future, anxieties of the present or unavoidable conditions from the past. Repeated border changes bring layers of various meanings and the accumulation of different memories to borderlands and people.

'Crossing the Water Border' by Hiroko Matsuda and 'A Border Town and Migration' by Nobuya Hashimoto and Hiromi Komori reconsider border construction and deconstruction and their meanings for migrants, addressing small, little-known islands (the Yaeyama Islands) between Taiwan and Japan and a small border town (Narva) between Estonia and Russia. While the former discusses the emigration from the Yaeyama Islands to Taiwan under Japanese colonial rule, the latter focuses on the formation of the town of Narva since the medieval era and Russian and Soviet immigration to the town. The juxtaposition of these two points – which are in far-flung locations, distant from each other and under quite different conditions, on the periphery of Pacific and East Asian waters and on the East European Plain respectively – may sound trivial and arbitrary for historical analysis. Nevertheless, the comparison introduces very interesting insights about borders and migration.

As Hiroko Matsuda points out in the introduction of her chapter, border studies in English have paid little attention to water borders, while there are many works on land borders. Comparative studies of water borders and land borders are even more scarce. In contrast, border researchers in Japan discuss water borders and the islands near them far more, because of Japan's geographical conditions and territorial disputes with neighbours regarding the many small islands north and south of the archipelago.[1] In this vein, we have two Parts in this volume that address both water borders and land borders. The first is the Part about 'Borders and Migration' and the other is Takahiro Yamamoto and Takehiro Okabe's Part about the Ainu people in the Kuril Islands (north of Japan) and the Finnic people in the Karelian region between Finland and Russia (Chapters 9 and 10). While the chapters on the Yaeyama Islands and the Kuril Ainu both reflect the strong interests in water borders and the islands in the periphery among Japanese researchers, the remaining two chapters observe the western borderland of Russia/the Soviet Union; the combination of the four chapters should be beneficial for our overall project. As the regions discussed in these chapters are objects of territorial disputes in the past and the present, or are located near them, the nuanced argument here must help readers understand the depths hidden under the surface of the simplified disputes, though the authors dare not refer to them directly.

Both the Yaeyama Islands and Narva have undergone frequent changes of state affiliation due to the alternation of borders and regional state systems, from the premodern era to the twentieth century. During the late fourteenth century, the Yaeyama Islands became a tributary to the Ryûkyû Kingdom, which would later be put under dual control by the Qing dynasty and the Shimazu Domain (the southern part of Kyûshû Island) under the Tokugawa Shogunate within the ambiguous premodern state system in East Asia. Subsequently, the islands were annexed to the modern Japanese state after the Meiji Restoration as the westernmost parts of Okinawa Province in the 1870s, occupied by the United States during and after the Second World War and reversed to Japanese sovereignty in 1972. Meanwhile, the appearance and disappearance of the border have recurred between Taiwan and the Yaeyama Islands due to the colonialist expansion of the Japanese Empire and its fall. On the other hand, Narva was founded under the Danish rule of the northern part of contemporary Estonia in the medieval era, and subsequently the town was subjugated to the Livonian Order, the Swedish Empire in the Baltic and the Russian Empire in that order. Later, whereas Narva had been incorporated into independent Estonia immediately after the Russian Revolution, Estonia itself was, in turn, unjustifiably annexed to the Soviet Union in August 1940, occupied by German troops the subsequent summer and incorporated again into the USSR in 1944. We observe the recurring appearance and disappearance of the border here as well. In the end, Narva became the easternmost border town of Estonia after the country regained independence in August 1991. Despite being very small in size and unknown among the global public, both the Yaeyama Islands and Narva have undergone a long series of geopolitical transformations of regional or global significance that are typical for border zones.

Finally, both chapters pay attention not only to the construction and deconstruction of borders – facilitated by the expansion and collapse of the Russian/Soviet and Japanese Empires, and the accompanying massive population mobility – on the macro level, but also to the personal motives and experiences of individual migrants and their memories on the micro level, despite the different methodologies and priorities of discussion in the two chapters. Matsuda organized her own oral history project among the former migrants from the Yaeyama Islands to colonial Taiwan and cited their own personal narratives, while Nobuya Hashimoto and Hiromi Komori rely on the sociological and anthropological literatures on the formation of Narvian-Russian identity and re-examine them in the light of the town's history. Both chapters clarify the personal motives and reasons for migration under the conditions of colonial and imperial rule in these regions. Though personal experiences and memories were roused, constrained and contextualized through the macro-level framework of colonial and imperial rule, they are not always reduced to the simplified story of colonialist ambitions. What matters here is the relationship between state policies and personal strategies for survival, and its results.

Note

1. Cf. Matsuda, Liminality of the Japanese Empire, 5–8.

Bibliography

Matsuda, Hiroko. *Liminality of the Japanese Empire: Border Crossings from Okinawa to Colonial Taiwan*. Honolulu, HI: University of Hawaii Press, 2019.

CHAPTER 5

Crossing the Water Border

Migrations and the Japanese Imperial Seaway between Taiwan and the Yaeyama Islands

Hiroko Matsuda

Introduction

For the longest time, it was assumed that Japan's national borders had been naturally determined, mostly because the sea delimits the Japanese archipelago. That delineation has been understood as the basic reason for Japan's ethnic homogeneity and cultural integrity. Recently, the assumption of Japanese homogeneity has been questioned, and there is growing interest in the historical construction of Japan's borders.[1]

This chapter reviews the history of the borders of Japan, China and Taiwan. International and national media attention have spotlighted the region since the political dispute over the sovereignty of the Senkaku Islands heated up in the early 2010s. However, despite strong concern regarding the Senkaku Islands' sovereignty, the region's history is not well known to the public. Thus, this chapter reviews this history, focusing on the people of *Yaeyama-gun* (the Yaeyama Archipelago or Yaeyama Islands), which is at the southern end of Okinawa Prefecture.

Arguably, border studies are one of the most rapidly developing areas of scholarship in the humanities and social sciences worldwide. The historical proponents of border studies were legal scholars and political scientists whose main interests were in analysing national governments and political leaders. Current scholars are paying relatively more attention to the lives and social dynamics of the residents of borderlands. However, most of the English-language literature considers land borders and neglects water borders, partly because North American and continental European topics of interest focus on land borders, such as issues surrounding the United States–Mexico border and border controls by the European Union's members. These studies are not useful to many of East Asia's countries because their political borders are on the water, and border crossings inevitably depend on seaways and oceanic transit. Thus, this chapter concerns border crossing via boats and ships and discusses the role of seaways and oceanic transit in the historical constructions and transitions of the Okinawa–Taiwan border.

The Border Islands and the Imperial Seaway

The Yaeyama Archipelago comprises thirty-two islands in the oceanic subtropical climate region, twelve of which were inhabited in 2020. The distance between Ishigaki Island (the most populated island) and Naha (where the Okinawa Prefecture offices are located) is about 411 kilometres.[2] The official 1927 records indicate that the total residential population of the Yaeyama Islands was 34,075, more than half of which (20,858 people) lived on Ishigaki Island.[3]

During the late fourteenth century, the Yaeyama Islands became a tributary of the Ryûkyû Kingdom after the latter suppressed a revolt by the Yaeyama rulers in 1500.[4] By the late sixteenth century, the Ryûkyû Kingdom controlled all of the Ryûkyû Islands, including the Amami, Okinawa, Miyako and Yaeyama archipelagos. The Shimazu Domain, which ruled the southern part of Kyûshû Island, invaded the Ryûkyû Kingdom in 1609, placed it under tight control and ruled its domestic affairs and foreign trade for more than two centuries. Nevertheless, the Ryûkyû Kingdom maintained some autonomy until its formal annexation by Japan in 1879.

The Domain strictly monitored its foreign relations, and there is no evidence that the Yaeyama islanders had regular contact with people in Taiwan or other nearby countries. Sasamori Gisuke visited Yonaguni Island in 1893 and reported that Sakiyama Yôei, a public official on the island, stated that islanders were sometimes castaways in China, but that he had never heard of castaways in Taiwan.[5]

The Yaeyama Islands' foreign relations dramatically changed after they came under Japan's official control in 1879 when the Ryûkyû Kingdom was absorbed into Okinawa Prefecture. Similarly to the rest of Okinawa

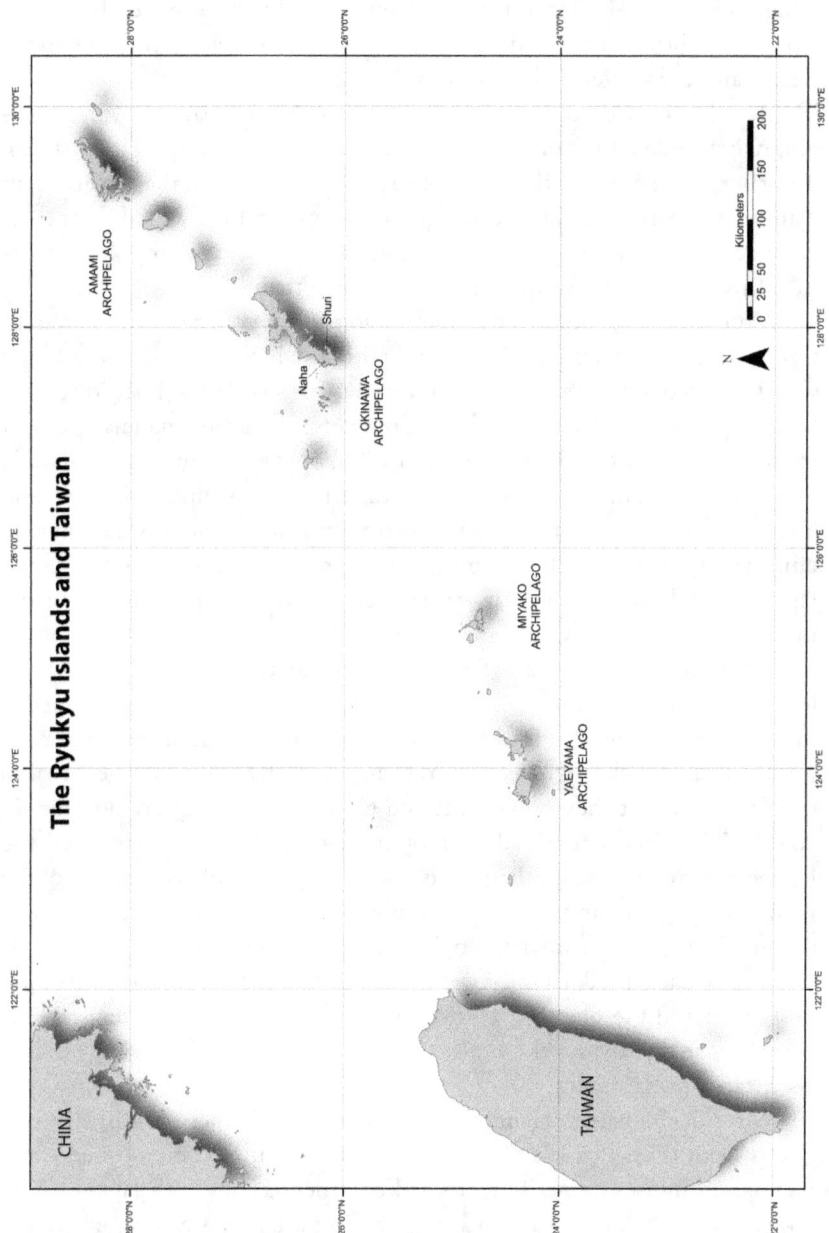

Figure 5.1. The Ryukyu Islands and Taiwan. Map reproduced with the permission of CartoGIS Services, Scholarly Information Services, The Australian National University, CC BY-SA 4.0.

Prefecture, some of the political systems and institutions of the Ryûkyû Kingdom persisted after annexation, but it gradually integrated into the Japanese political, economic and social systems between the late nineteenth and early twentieth centuries.

Another change occurred because of the Sino-Japanese War (1894–95), which ceded Taiwan to Japan and altered the Yaeyama Islands' status. To bring Taiwan under the wing of the Empire of Japan, the government wanted to separate Taiwan from mainland China, which would sever their close economic and social ties, and it aimed to link the metropole to colonial Taiwan by establishing a seaway between them.

Consequently, shortly after the cession in 1895, Japan eliminated all transit between Taiwan and mainland China, which had constituted vital social and economic infrastructural ties between the two. Instead, Osaka Shôsen (the Osaka Merchant Ship Company) received financial support from the Japanese government and, in 1896, opened a transit line between Osaka and Taiwan by way of Kobe, Kagoshima, Ôshima, Okinawa and Yaeyama.[6] In effect, a boundary was drawn and exchange was officially eliminated between China and Taiwan, while a seaway between the Japanese Archipelago and Taiwan created a border crossing between the metropole and the newly acquired colonial territory.

From the perspectives of the Japanese government and the Osaka Merchant Ship Company, the Yaeyama Islands might have seemed a minor port en route to Taiwan, but the opening of the imperial seaway greatly changed the lives of the Yaeyama islanders because the oceanic transit meant that they could visit and trade with the rapidly developing colony. The Yaeyama Islands' remoteness from Okinawa Island and the Japanese mainland meant that it was one of the most isolated regions of the Ryûkyû Kingdom and Japan. It was politically, financially and culturally marginalized, and ordinary people had few opportunities to visit cities and experience modern lifestyles. That changed with the colonization of Taiwan and the opening of the seaway, which gave Yaeyama islanders access to the rapidly developing city of Taipei, in which Japan was making a substantial investment.

Most of the native islanders were small-scale farmers, and the immigrants from Okinawa Island and the Japanese mainland established commercial businesses there. They forged commercial ties with Japanese and Taiwanese in colonial Taiwan using the imperial seaway opened by the Osaka Merchant Ship Company. For example, Yamabishi Shôkai (the Yamabishi Company) was a major timber enterprise on Ishigaki Island, mostly exporting to Taiwan,[7] that was founded by Maeda Sentarô, who immigrated to Taiwan in the 1910s as a farmer from Kagawa Prefecture.[8] The colonial government was promoting infrastructure, such as a railway, and the Taiwanese demand for timber was high. The Yamabishi Shôkai headquarters were in Keelung and there was a Tokyo branch, which provided the timber for these projects. Thus, Japanese mainlanders who immigrated to Taiwan and, from there, to Ishigaki Island, were the key actors in the timber trade between Ishigaki and Keelung.

Yonaguni Island, located at the southern end of the Yaeyama Archipelago, forged particularly close ties with Taiwan. Although Yonaguni Island is only 111 kilometres from Taiwan, it was unique at the time in the sense that ships rarely stopped there, but the islanders frequently visited Taiwan by private motorboat. The residents of the other Yaeyama Islands travelled by ships operated by the oceanic transit companies. Thus, on the one hand, border crossing began with the opening up of imperial transit, whereas, on the other hand, the Yaeyama–Taiwan relationship was constrained by it. Because of its sizeable financial support from the colonial government, the Osaka Merchant Ship Company dominated the seaways between the metropole and colonial Taiwan and contributed to the creation and recreation of imperial space. Because of the colonial government's control over its purse, the company's management, including dates of departure, routing and freight, was significantly controlled by the former.[9]

One ship, operated by the shipping company Kôun Gaisha (the Koun Corporation), regularly travelled between Ishigaki and Naha ports until the Osaka Merchant Ship Company bought it in 1916 when it monopolized the seaways linking Okinawa, Yaeyama and Taiwan.[10] The Osaka Merchant Ship Company faced little competition, and the services were low quality. Local newspapers consistently criticized the numbers and timing of calls, arrival delays and poor customer service for embarking at Ishigaki Island. The *Yaeyama shinpô* (Yaeyama News) reported twenty-two delayed arrivals between 1918 and 1922, which significantly affected Yaeyama residents' lives because they depended on imported necessities.[11] In 1929, a Yaeyama advocacy group petitioned, making five demands: lower fares, improved cabin services, better vessels, more services during busy periods and that the Osaka Merchant Ship Company stop cancelling services.[12]

Consequently, the Yaeyama merchants were increasingly reliant on trade with Taiwan, and island lifestyles and businesses significantly depended on the oceanic transit monopolized by the government-supported transit company. Similarly to many other parts of the world, creating and transforming transit networks depended on the government's long-term economic and industrial strategies. Japan's imperial border shifted between the late nineteenth and early twentieth centuries, but the everyday lives of the Yaeyama islanders were buffeted by the unpredictability of oceanic transit between the metropole and colonial Taiwan.

Colonial Migration via the Imperial Seaway

During the early period, some immigrants from Okinawa Island and the Japanese mainland established successful businesses that relied on oceanic transit to Taiwan, but few of the native farmers benefitted from these enterprises. During the Ryûkyû Kingdom period, the Yaeyama islanders had a self-sufficient economy that was not a money economy, and the use of currency was developed for the islanders only after Japanese began to settle on the islands in the early 1890s to establish sugar cultivation, for which they employed the islanders as labourers.[13] These enterprises on the Yaeyama Islands were almost exclusively worked by immigrants, and the native farmers rarely collaborated with them.

However, opening up the seaways influenced the native Yaeyama farmers, and they experienced major changes after annexation. First, Taiwan introduced modern products and advanced technologies to Yaeyama that significantly changed the people's lives. For example, malaria had been a scourge that for centuries had been considered the biggest obstacle to regional development. But, in the 1920s, the islanders learned of and gained access to the cure developed in Taiwan.[14] In addition, a new rice strain, *Hôrai* rice (*Hôrai* is an alternative name for Taiwan), was brought to Yaeyama. The crop yields of *Hôrai* rice were almost three times those of the traditional rice strain, and it quickly diffused throughout the Yaeyama Islands, dramatically increasing agricultural productivity.

Advances in science and technology tend to first appear in cities, from which they diffuse to rural areas. Historically, the Yaeyama Islands' remote location far from Tokyo and the capital of Okinawa Prefecture meant that they lagged behind in reaping the benefits of scientific and technological advancements. However, the colonization of Taiwan and opening of the imperial seaways increased the likelihood that the Yaeyama islanders would benefit from developments in Taiwan.

Travelling to Taiwan became a part of everyday life. There were many reasons to go to Taiwan. Some people went there to shop, as tourists or to seek medical care. A significant number of islanders immigrated to Taiwan for educational purposes because Yaeyama had no secondary or tertiary schools. Furthermore, many islanders immigrated to Taiwan for work, and some of them permanently settled there with their families. It is well known that large numbers of people emigrated from Okinawa Prefecture to Hawaii, the Americas, the Philippines, Micronesia (South Sea Islands) and the Japanese mainland. These destinations were less common among the Yaeyama islanders, who flowed to Taiwan without needing formal clearance by immigration authorities.

Although when and how many islanders emigrated from Yaeyama to Taiwan is uncertain, the 1920 census recorded that 2,433 Japanese immigrants in Taiwan were registered in Okinawa Prefecture, which included Yaeyama. That number increased more than threefold to 7,442 in 1930, and then it almost doubled to 14,695 by 1940.[15] Immigration or some other governmental authorities documented emigration from the Okinawa Islands to foreign countries, but few documents recorded emigration from Yaeyama to Taiwan. However, anecdotal reports found in many autobiographies and memoirs by Yaeyama islanders frequently mention experiences in colonial Taiwan. For example, Takemoto Seigi, born into a farming family on Ishigaki Island in 1912, explained, 'at that time, the people of Yaeyama used to call Taiwan the "second Tokyo". Tokumori Ine, who was my babysitter, told me "Taiwan is a great place", and encouraged me to migrate to Taiwan.'[16] Shortly after that, he began working as a clerk at a pawnshop in Taipei.

> I departed from Ishigaki Port at 8 o'clock in the morning. Standing on the ramp, I kept watching those who saw me off until they became tiny. We jumped from the ramp to the 700-ton great vessel named the *Daikyû-maru*. I saw Taketomi Island on the left, and the vessel passed by my house and *Kan'non-dô* temple. We were approaching Kohama and Iriomote Islands. I had no acquaintances on board, except my attender *Ine*. First, I was just excited, but I increasingly felt lonely. I was not sure when I would be able to return home. I also thought that I might be in Taiwan forever, and that I would not see my relatives on my home island. I felt like crying, but I tried to cheer up. I was 14 years old at that time.[17]

Takemoto worked at the pawnshop for twelve years and then got a job at a post office in Taipei City. He married his childhood friend from Ishigaki Island, and, later, he went to China. He eventually repatriated from China to Ishigaki Island in September 1946.[18] Takemoto's recollections reveal that it was common in the mid-1920s for Ishigaki islanders to immigrate to colonial Taiwan using family and friend social networks. His memoir indicates that immigration to Taiwan was favourably perceived and recalled after returning home. Takemoto's recollections are not exceptions; in my interviews conducted in 2003 and 2006, all of the people born on Ishigaki Island or Taketomi Island who worked in colonial Taiwan between 1927 and 1946 had immigrated there by relying on family or friends (or both). Many of them mentioned that people had positive opinions of life in Taiwan as 'convenient' and 'modern'.

Immigration from Yaeyama to Taiwan included many women who had recently graduated from primary school or advanced primary school and who moved to Taiwan unaccompanied. For example, Tonoshiro Yoshi, who was born on Ishigaki Island in 1913, first worked in Taiwan as a domestic servant, and later held a job as a bus conductor. For some reason, her biological parents did not raise her, and her extended family members, including her great-grandmother, grandmother, uncle and aunt cared for her as a child. In her autobiography, she recollects her immigration to Taiwan after graduating from the advanced course of primary school.

> It was the year of Showa 2.[19] At that time, it was common for young people to migrate to Taiwan after graduating from primary school. I also nagged my family everyday saying, 'let me go to Taiwan.' I gather they did not want to let me go, but eventually gave their permission in August. I was very excited. My family gave me a new kimono with stripes with a *heko-obi* [heko-band] and *geta* [a pair of wooden clogs] … Partly because my Uncle Shigeo was working at the Taihoku post office, I was not scared at all. I was only worried about leaving behind my family who were getting old.[20]

Soon after she arrived in Taipei, she began work as an apprentice maidservant for a Japanese couple. The husband worked for the Taiwan colonial government. Many female immigrants from the Yaeyama Islands worked as maidservants for Japanese, and, in 1924, a Yaeyama newspaper reported, 'Yaeyama is today known as a source of maidservants.'[21] Other female Japanese immigrated as dependent family members, but female immigrants from Yaeyama worked as maidservants because of the high demand for the latter in colonial Taiwan. Work as a maidservant usually required neither education nor experience, and Japanese customarily employed young women as apprentice maidservants, which was an opportunity for women from Yaeyama.[22]

After Tonoshiro Yoshi returned to her home island, she married in 1934 and became a farmer. After a few years, she returned to Taiwan in 1939 with her husband and three children because 'on our farm income, we could not send our children to school'.[23] This was a rather common experience and people moved back and forth between Yaeyama and Taiwan. Tonoshiro's memoir indicates that it was not just young single adults, but entire families, that immigrated to Taiwan hoping to improve their standards of living.

The End of the Imperial Seaways and Beyond

Japan entered the Second Sino-Japanese War, which was triggered by the Marco Polo Bridge Incident, on 7 July 1937, but even after the Pacific War began in 1941, Okinawans continued to immigrate to Taiwan for educational and financial reasons. In addition, the government anticipated that the Ryûkyû Islands would become a combat zone, and it ordered women, children and elders living on the Miyako and Yaeyama Islands to evacuate to Taiwan. The women, children and elders on Amami-Ôshima, Tokunoshima and Okinawa Island were sent to the Japanese mainland, mainly Kyûshû Island. About three thousand Yaeyama islanders were sent to Taiwan between July 1944 and August 1945.[24] Their situations in Taiwan were different from those of the Yaeyama islanders who had immigrated for educational and financial reasons. Most of the refugees were placed in rural areas far from the established urban Japanese communities. Many of them had no one to rely on in Taiwan, and they were almost completely dependent on government aid and rations. Many refugees starved and contracted tropical diseases in the unfamiliar climate.[25]

In August 1945, Japan accepted the Potsdam Declaration, surrendered, and Taiwan was put under the control of the Republic of China. Nevertheless, the policy of the Nationalist Party of the Republic of China (Kuomintang, KMT) regarding Japanese was not clear for the subsequent few months, even after the Taiwan Province Administrative Office began formally requisitioning the Japanese colonial government at the end of October.

On the Western New Year's Eve 1945, the KMT announced China's official policy regarding the Japanese in Taiwan, which included the seizure of all public and private Japanese properties. It proclaimed that all Japanese, except those designated to remain in Taiwan to maintain administrative and industrial functions, must leave and return to Japan by the end of 1946.[26] The first mass repatriation occurred between March and May 1946, and repatriated almost 90 per cent of the Japanese nationals on Taiwan.[27] Most of the remaining Japanese, including those who had been designated to remain, left Taiwan by early May 1947. A few professionals, such as university professors and highly skilled technicians, were asked to stay until the 1950s.[28]

During this post-war period, the official seaways between Taiwan, Okinawa and the Japanese mainland were controlled by the KMT and the United States, but the Yaeyama islanders continued to travel between islands by personal fishing boat as they had done before the war. My oral history research revealed that most of the Yaeyama return immigrants left Taiwan by pop-pop (steam boiler) boats instead of the official repatriation ships. Some immigrants to Yaeyama described informal repatriations in their memoirs and autobiographies. For example, Ôhama Motoko, who was born in Taiwan in 1925, recalled her emigration from Taiwan by 'black boat', which refers to a privately arranged boat trip, as follows.

> The boat departed from the wharf and the harbour entrance was approaching. I raised my head and saw the land and muttered, 'Good-bye, my homeland, Taiwan. Good-bye, Keelung'. Perhaps, this was my last chance to see Taiwan. I might not come back here again. I got teary. In April 1946, my

younger sister and I repatriated by black boat. There were strict rules about carrying bags in the official repatriation, but we were allowed to bring more by black boat. My parents and another younger sister were going to use an official repatriation ship later.[29]

Ôhama Motoko's father, Shin'ei, was born to a farmer on Ishigaki Island in 1895. In 1923, he immigrated to Taiwan and worked for the Department of Railway in the Japanese colonial government. He married, and Motoko and her two sisters were born in Taiwan. Motoko had never lived on Ishigaki Island, but she was compelled to immigrate to her parents' home island. Although temporary migrations between Yaeyama and Taiwan were popular, this anecdote indicates that some immigrants settled down, married and raised families in Taiwan. The second- or third-generation descendants of these Yaeyama immigrants, such as Ôhama Motoko, were unfamiliar with their parents' homeland, Yaeyama. For many of them, forced migration was not about returning home; it was about leaving home.

Because the United States was occupying the Ryûkyû Islands, the previous money economy and commerce were frozen, and people relied on an informal economy and US rations. The problems related to the population increase on the Yaeyama Islands because of repatriations were exacerbated by shortages of goods when the official ties to Taiwan were cut, because this eliminated the inflow of goods through the strong social and economic ties that existed prior to the war. Before he was repatriated to his home island of Ishigaki, Hazama Rihô, who had graduated from Taiwan Medical College in 1931 and opened a gynaecology clinic in Tainan in 1940, wrote a petition to George H. Kerr, the American Consulate in Taipei, asking for permission to take various medical instruments and medications with him when he left.[30]

> By this time, it is after all settled that I should go back to Yaeyama; therefore I should like very much to request for your special protection so that through you becoming my power, I may be permitted to bring back with me instruments, machinaries, drugs and other materials.

> Yaeyama is a far away off island both from the mainland of Japan and that of Okinawa and is a place where there is not a single gynecological specialist. Therefore, a person with my training, if he should go back without these technical medical instruments, machinaries drugs and other materials, he would not be able to look after the poor Yaeyama villagers nor the women and in that case I will not be at cooperative in the work of constructing a new Okinawa slightly. Hence I will be most sorriest with reluctance. In this respect Yaeyama is entirely different from anywhere in the mainland of Japan where medical instruments, machinaries and etc are easily available. Therefore, I do request that you pass your wise judgement there in and interest yourself particularly in this matter.[31]

Hazama Rihô wrote his letter in Japanese and translated it into English for submission with an itemized list of almost one hundred medical instruments, machines, medicines and other medical paraphernalia, including an electric radiator and electric lamp.[32] His petition clearly reveals the extent to which Yaeyama islanders had materially relied on colonial Taiwan. The fall of the Japanese Empire meant separation from Taiwan, which, in turn, radically changed the Yaeyama islanders' cultural, material and social lives. Hazama Rihô was probably exceptional in his efforts to directly petition the American authorities to help him with these problems. Most repatriated Yaeyama islanders preferred to informally maintain their social and commercial ties with the Taiwanese by secretly continuing to trade with them.[33]

To compensate for the loss of the formal economy and the lack of food and other necessities, smuggling rings emerged throughout the Ryûkyû Islands. Yonaguni Island quickly became the transit centre of the smuggling network. The activities were illegal and under the jurisdiction of law enforcement. The late 1940s and early 1950s were the beginning of the smuggling era in the Okinawa Islands. The police knew that smuggling was the only way that the people on the devastated islands could survive, so they rarely probed far into smuggling activities, and they often ignored them altogether.[34] Then, after the KMT and Ryûkyû governments renewed their formal trade relationship, informal and illegal trade significantly declined.[35]

Nevertheless, some commerce between Taiwan and Yaeyama continued after the informal trades declined. For example, to develop the canned pineapple industry, Yaeyama invited hundreds of Taiwanese labourers to the islands each year of the 1960s, using the pretext of the introduction of technology. Taiwanese labourers were more skilled than the islanders in pineapple canning, and importing their labour greatly contributed to the industry at that time.[36] In addition, shortly after the Ryûkyû Islands were returned to Japan, an Okinawan shipping company, the Arimura Sangyô Corporation, opened up the seaway between Okinawa and Keelung via Miyako Island and Ishigaki Island.[37]

This transit line was closed in 2008, but direct flights between Ishigaki and Taipei airports began regular service in 2013. The improved convenience of transportation has boosted Yaeyama's tourism, and the islands have annually welcomed more than eighty thousand Taiwanese tourists since 2013.[38] Taiwanese tourists accounted for more than 40 per cent of all international tourists to the region in 2019,[39] although no international tourist has been permitted to land on the island during the COVID-19 pandemic. In sum, Taiwan and Yaeyama have continued to maintain their unique and special relationship, and, although Taiwan is no longer a part of everyday life, it is the islanders' closest international neighbour.

Conclusion

People have always crossed political borders on land and by sea. This chapter explains that the operations and controls of oceanic transit are vital to border crossing by sea. The Yaeyama Islands are geographically near Taiwan, but there is no record of exchanges between them during the early modern period. However, we know that people travelled between them after Japan's annexation of Taiwan and opening of the imperial seaway in 1895.

The empire's oceanic transit enabled Yaeyama islanders to trade with Taiwan, which greatly developed their commercial economy and industry and significantly changed their lives. Travelling to Taiwan became an ordinary part of Yaeyama islanders' everyday lives, and many of them immigrated to Taiwan for educational and financial reasons. Some of them settled down and raised families. The Yaeyama economy, society and culture of the early twentieth century was intricately related to Japanese goals for imperial expansion.

Because the imperial seaway was very accessible, few islanders truly understood the gravity of Japanese dominion over Taiwan. Because the imperial oceanic transit was essential to maintaining close ties between Yaeyama and Taiwan, their special relationship swiftly changed with the fall of the Japanese Empire at the end of the Second World War. Yaeyama and Taiwan have clearly maintained a unique and close relationship to date, but it is certainly different from their past relationship.

Hiroko Matsuda is a professor at Kobe Gakuin University, Japan. She received her doctoral degree from the Australian National University. She is the author of *Liminality of the Japanese Empire: Border Crossings from Okinawa to Colonial Taiwan* (University of Hawai'i Press, 2019), and the co-editor of *Rethinking Postwar Okinawa: Beyond American Occupation* (Lexington Books, 2017).

Notes

The Japanese cited texts are translated by the author, unless otherwise noted.

1. See, for example, Batten, *To the Ends of Japan*; Oguma, *A Genealogy of Japanese Self-Images*; Oguma, *The Boundaries of 'the Japanese'*, vol. 1; Oguma, *The Boundaries of 'the Japanese'*, vol. 2.
2. Okinawa-ken, 'Yaeyama chiiki no gaiyô'.
3. Okinawa-ken, *Okinawa-ken tôkeisho*, 39.
4. Kishaba, *Ishigaki chôshi*, 2–3.
5. Sasamori, *Nantô tanken*, vol. 1, 294.
6. Kishaba, *Ishigaki chôshi*, 465; Nomura, *Osaka shôsen*, 77–81.
7. Ishigaki Shishi Henshû Inkai, *Ishigaki shishi, Kakuron-hen*, 588.
8. Miki, '*Yaeyama gasshûkoku*' no keifu, 168–89.
9. Kokaze, *Teikokushugika no Nihon kaiun*, chapter 6.
10. *Ryukyu shinpô*, 23 June 1916.
11. *Yaeyama shinpô*, 21 June 1923.
12. *Sakishima Asahi shimbun*, 23 November 1929.
13. Yaeyama Rekishi Henshû Înkai, *Yaeyama rekishi*, 400–1.
14. Ijima, *Mararia to teikoku*, 85.
15. Taiwan Sôtokufu Kanbô Rinji Kokusei Chôsabu, *Taiwan kokusei chôsa shûkei genpyô*, 826–27; Taiwan Sôtoku Kanbô Rinji Kokusei Chôsabu, *Kokusei chôsa kekkahyô*, 438–39; Taiwan Sôtokufu, *Taiwan tôsei yôran*, 32–33.
16. Takemoto, *Ari no uta*, 29.
17. Ibid., 30–31.
18. Ibid, 119–31.
19. Equal to 1927.
20. Tonoshiro, *Chiruguwâ*, 19.
21. *Yaeyama shinpô*, 21 October 1924.
22. Matsuda, *Liminality of the Japanese Empire*, 62–63.
23. Tonoshiro, *Chiruguwâ*, 28–64.
24. Matsuda, *Taiwan sokai*, chapter 1.
25. Ibid.
26. Ôkurashô, 'Yoroku Nikkyô no tsuioku', 91.
27. Taiwan Sôtokufu Zanmu Seiri Jimusho, 'Jimu hikitsugi hôkokusho', 146–49; Ôkurashô, 'Yoroku Nikkyô no tsuioku', 94–95.
28. Ôkurashô, 'Yoroku Nikkyô no tsuioku', 94–95.
29. Ôhama, 'Dainiji Taiwan hikiage no kiroku', 47.
30. Okinawa, *Gendai Okinawa jimbutsu sanzennin*, 702.
31. Hazama, 'Letter from Dr. Hazama', 155–56. This text is as per the original and not translated by the author.
32. Ibid.
33. Ishihara Masaie, *Kûhaku no Okinawa*, 30.
34. Ibid., 44–47.
35. Ibid., 308–9.
36. Kuninaga et al., *Ishigakijima de Taiwan wo aruku*, 22–23, 52–53.
37. Arimura Sangyô Corporation, 'Genzai made no enkaku'.
38. Okinawa-ken, 'Yaeyama kankô tôkei'.
39. Okinawa-ken, 'Reiwa Gannen (2019-nen) Nenkan gaikyô'.

Bibliography

Arimura Sangyô Corporation. 'Genzai made no enkaku'. Retrieved 20 April 2022 from http://web.archive.org/web/20080116171508/http://www.arimuraline.co.jp/history.html.
Batten, Bruce L. *To the Ends of Japan: Premodern Frontiers, Boundaries, and Interactions*. Honolulu, HI: University of Hawai'i Press, 2003.
Hazama, Rihô. 'Letter from Dr. Hazama', in Committee Members for the Watkins Papers Publication (ed.), *Papers of James T. Watkins IV*, vol. 38 (Okinawa: Ryokuindô shoten, 1994), 155–56.
Îjima, Wataru. *Mararia to teikoku: Shokuminchi igaku to Higashi Ajia no kôiki chitsujo*. Tokyo: Tôkyô Daigaku Shuppankai, 2005.
Ishigaki Shishi Henshû Înkai (ed.). *Ishigaki shishi, Kakuron-hen, Minzoku*, vol. 1. Okinawa: Ishigaki-shi, 1994.
Ishihara, Masaie. *Kûhaku no Okinawa Shakaishi, Senka to mitsubôeki no jidai*. Okinawa: Banseisha, 2000.
Kishaba, Eijun. *Ishigaki chôshi*. Okinawa: Ishigaki-chô, 1935, reprint, Tokyo: Kokusho Kankôkai, 1975.
Kokaze, Hidemasa. *Teikokushugika no Nihon kaiun: Kokusai kyôsô to taigai jiritsu*. Tokyo: Yamakawa Shuppansha, 1995.
Kuninaga, Michiko, et al. (eds). *Ishigakijima de Taiwan wo aruku: Mô hitotsu no Okinawa gaido*. Okinawa: Okinawa Taimususha, 2012.
Matsuda, Hiroko. *Liminality of the Japanese Empire: Border Crossings from Okinawa to Colonial Taiwan*. Honolulu, HI: University of Hawaii Press, 2019.
Matsuda, Yoshitaka. *Taiwan sokai: 'Ryûkyû nanmin' no ichinen jûikkagetsu*. Okinawa: Nanzansha, 2010.
Miki, Takeshi. *'Yaeyama gasshûkoku' no keifu*. Okinawa: Nanzansha, 2010.
Nomura Tokushichi Shôten. *Ôsaka shôsen*. Osaka: Nomura Tokushichi Shôten Chôsabu, 1911.
Oguma, Eiji. *A Genealogy of Japanese Self-Images*. Translated by David Askew. Victoria: Trans Pacific Press, 2002.
———. *The Boundaries of 'the Japanese'*, vol. 1, *Okinawa 1818–1972, Inclusion and Exclusion*. Tranlsated by Leonie R. Stickland. Victoria: Trans Pacific Press, 2014.
———. *The Boundaries of 'the Japanese'*, vol. 2, *Korea, Taiwan and the Ainu 1868–1945*. Victoria: Trans Pacific Press, 2017.
Ôhama, Motoko. 'Dainiji Taiwan hikiage no kiroku: Atarashî shuppatsu', in Ôhama Motoko (ed.), *Chichi no nioi* (Okinawa: Self-published, 1999), 47–54.
Okinawa-ken. *Okinawa-ken tôkeisho*, Shôwa 2-nen, vol. 1. Okinawa: Okinawa-ken, 1929.
———. 'Yaeyama chiiki no gaiyô'. Retrieved 19 April 2022 from https://www.pref.okinawa.jp/site/norin/norin-yaeyama-nosui/keikaku/yaeyamanogaiyou.html.
———. 'Reiwa Gannen (2019-nen) Nenkan gaikyô'. Retrieved 20 April 2022 from https://www.pref.okinawa.jp/site/somu/yaeyama/shinko/documents/documents/documents/gaikyou2019nenkan.pdf.
———. 'Yaeyama kankô tôkei'. Retrieved 20 April 2022 from https://www.pref.okinawa.jp/site/somu/yaeyama/shinko/documents/documents/kankoutantou.html.
Okinawa Taimususha. *Gendai Okinawa jimbutsu sanzennin*. Okinawa: Okinawa Taimususha, 1966.
Ôkurashô Kanrikyoku. 'Yoroku Nikkyô no tsuioku', in Kobayashi Hideo (ed.), *Nihonjin no kaigai katsudô ni kansuru rekishiteki chôsa*, vol. 9 (Tokyo: Ôkurashô Kanrikyoku, 1950), 75–168, reprint, Tokyo: Yumani Shobô, 2000.

Sasamori, Gisuke. *Nantô tanken, vol. 1: Ryûkyû Man'yûki*. Tokyo: privately printed, 1894, reprint, Tokyo: Heibonsha, 1982.
Taiwan Sôtokufu. *Taiwan tôsei yôran, Shôwa 20-nen ban*. Taihoku: Taiwan Sôtokufu, 1945, reprint, Taipei: Chengwen chubanshe, 1985.
Taiwan Sôtoku Kanbô Rinji Kokusei Chôsabu. *Taiwan kokusei chôsa shûkei genpyô. Vol.1, Zentô no bu*. Taihoku: Taiwan Sôtoku Kanbô Rinji Kokusei Chôsabu, 1923.
———. *Kokusei chôsa kekkahyô, Showa 5-nen, Zentô-hen*. Taihoku: Taiwan Sôtoku Kanbô Rinji Kokusei Chôsabu, 1934.
Taiwan Sôtokufu Zanmu Seiri Jimusho. 'Jimu hikitsugi hôkokusho', in Katô Kiyofumi (ed.), *Kaigai hikiage kankei shiryô shûsei*, vol. 31 (Tokyo: Yumani shobô, 2002), 133–76.
Takemoto, Seigi. *Ari no uta: Takemoto Seigi jiden*. Okinawa: Miru Shuppan, 1995.
Tonoshiro, Yoshi. *Chiruguwâ: Omodidasu mamani*. Okinawa: Self-published, 1996.
Yaeyama Rekishi Henshû Inkai (ed.). *Yaeyama rekishi*. Ryukyu: Yaeyama Rekishi Henshû Inkai, 1954.

CHAPTER 6

A Border Town and Migration

The Case of Narva and Russian Speakers in Estonia

NOBUYA HASHIMOTO AND HIROMI KOMORI

Introduction

On a sunny day in July 2000, when a Japanese tourist was strolling along the promenade on the left bank of the river Narva, an aged Russian man coming from the opposite direction abruptly talked to him resentfully about the recent situation in Estonia. The essence of his talk was as follows:

> Indeed, it is we Russians that rebuilt this city [Narva], ravaged and deserted through fierce battles in the Great Patriotic War. None of the original inhabitants remained in this city, when we migrated here. The masters of this city are not Estonians. Rather we Russians should have been … Yet they proclaimed 'independence' in the midst of the confusion, and suddenly drew a border in the middle of this river and built a passport control. It is inconvenient for many of my compatriots to visit Ivangorod, the neighbouring town straightaway over the bridge, although we could have crossed the bridge freely until then. A cursed nuisance!! Even though I myself have Russian citizenship and can cross the border rather easily …

The tourist looked at the beautifully renovated and decorated old castle on the left bank and the ancient, ruined Russian fortress on the opposite side, listening to the old man's boasting and stories of toils. Hermann Castle on the left bank was built in the second half of the thirteenth century and later rebuilt with stone in the early fourteenth century by Danish kings who possessed the northern part of contemporary Estonia. The Ivangorod Fortress across the river was constructed by Ivan III, the Grand Duke of

Moscow, in 1492. It was first used as a bastion against the Livonian Order and later against the Baltic Empire of the Swedes.[1] These two old castles face each other and impress foreign tourists as a symbolic border of the confrontation between Russia and its westward neighbours, or, more generally, between the East and the West, although there is great potential for tourism in the grandiose panorama that they construct with the curves of the river Narva.

Narva is a unique border town in the north-eastern part (Ida-Virumaa) of the Republic of Estonia that is coterminous with the Russian Federation. Its population is composed for the most part of ethnic Russians and Russian speakers who migrated from Russia (RSFSR until the collapse of the USSR) and the other Soviet republics after the Second World War, and their descendants. As a result, Estonians are an absolute minority among Narva's inhabitants. According to data from 1 January 2018, ethnic Russians account for 83 per cent of the entire population of Narva (48,535 among 56,103), while ethnic Estonians constitute only 4 per cent (2,114). The remainder of the population consists of Ukrainians (2 per cent), Belarusians (2 per cent) and other ethnic groups (9 per cent).[2] While only 48 per cent of the population possesses Estonian citizenship more than a quarter-century after Estonia's regaining of independence, 36 per cent of residents are citizens of the neighbouring Russian Federation. Most of the remaining inhabitants (14 per cent) are categorized as 'Välismaalane' or 'Aliens' in the Estonian citizenship legislation,[3] which actually means that they do not have the citizenship of any state (making them stateless persons), although the ratio of the stateless has diminished significantly in the last two decades.

Although the coexistence of the titular nation and minority groups who are titular citizens of neighbouring countries is standard in border areas in general, in the international context and even among ethnic Estonians, the overwhelmingly high ratio of ethnic Russians and Russian citizens in Narva has created the dubious image of a peculiar and potentially secession-oriented 'Russian' town in independent Estonia. It is sometimes referred to as a 'Russian enclave', or, more symbolically, as 'Siberia in Estonia'. Francisco Martinez reported that an Estonian director of the Art Residency in Narva confessed: 'Estonians in Narva are like Estonians in Toronto.'[4] On the occasions when tensions between Russia and its neighbouring countries have run high, especially after the annexation of Crimea into the Russian Federation in 2014, geopolitical apprehension over military pressure from Russia ('counter-action against NATO's feint drillings', in Russia's terms) has strengthened the extremely negative image of Narvians as the 'fifth column'[5] of Russia that might represent Putin's dangerous ambition to annex the Baltic States into the

Russian Federation. It is the demographic similarity between Crimea and Narva that provokes such speculation. Indeed, the resentment that the old man expressed to the tourist on the riverbank exemplifies the sympathy and identification of Russians in Narva towards Russia – particularly towards Ivangorod, Narva's twin town in Russian territory. However, during the six years since the incident in Crimea, there have been no mass movements of Narvians demanding secession from Estonia and annexation into Russia. Nor has there been any evidence of a conspiracy to overturn the Estonian state resonating with Putin's manoeuvres. At present, the border town and its inhabitants seem rather calm and stable, so the notion of a 'fifth column' seems dubious. Several sociological and anthropological studies have clarified Narvians' multiple identities, both as Russian inhabitants of a border town coterminous with Russia and as residents of independent Estonia. This chapter retrospectively provides an overview of the foundation and development of Narva as a 'border town' and traces the formation of the Narvian Russians who migrated there in the town's history and their changing attitudes up to the post-Soviet era. We aim to indicate the complexities of their belonging and identity in the region, and the many factors that have created a multilayered representation of the region's past and present among Russian speakers who migrated to this small border town.

Narva in Formation and Development

At the end of the nineteenth century, a leading Russian encyclopedia offered two hypotheses regarding the foundation of Narva. Based on a German chronicle, it suggested that 'Narva town was founded approximately in 1223 by Danes who obtained the Estonian sea coast and began to disseminate Catholicism there'. On the other hand, it referenced the Novgorod Chronicle's entry of 1256 about the foundation of Narva (Narova).[6] The article also noted that the town was initially founded on the right bank of the river Narva, but moved to the left bank in 1294 after it was burned down by the Novgorodians. A bulky history of Narva published by A. V. Petrov at the beginning of the twentieth century also referred to both 1223 and 1256 as foundation years, although the author held his judgement in suspense, indicating that 'it is not possible to confirm the date of the foundation of Narva town with complete accuracy' based on the references to different descriptions in German and Russian chronicles.[7] Recent historiography has not confirmed the year of its foundation either, instead cautiously suggesting that no documentary records exist to prove the hypothesis that 'Narva's growth as a town and a castle began immediately after the conquest [by Danes] of the Estonian territory in the first half of the thirteenth century'.[8]

Despite its foundational ambiguity, Narva began to develop gradually under Danish rule as a site of transit trade between Novgorodian and Hanseatic merchants. As mentioned earlier, Hermann Castle was built and rebuilt during the thirteenth and fourteenth centuries on the left bank of the river Narva. Although its economic development as a trade centre in the eastern Baltic Sea was hindered due to obstruction from the Hanseatic town of Reval (Tallinn), those conditions changed after the incorporation of Novgorod into Muscovy by the Grand Duke of Moscow, Ivan III, in the second half of the fifteenth century.[9] Ivan III founded the Ivangorod Fortress (1492) opposite Hermann Castle during Muscovy's rivalry with the Livonian Order, which had acquired the northern part of Estonia from the Danes (1346). Thus, the archetypal landscape of the confrontation between the East and West was shaped.

The composition of the population in Narva during these centuries is unknown. The late Professor Sergei Issakov, a historian of Russian culture in Estonia, estimated a population of five to eight hundred, among which the Germans, who ruled the town, made up only one fifth. The remaining *'undeutsche'* in the Estonian source *Süvalep A. Narva ajalugu. I. Taanija orduaeg. 1936* (Narva history, vol. 1. The Age of Danes and Orders, Narva 1936), he speculated, might have referred to Estonians and a small number of Votes (or Vodes), a small Finnic ethnic group that inhabited the region between what is now Saint Petersburg and Narva.[10]

Russian factors in Narva were amplified under successive territorial alternations. At first, Narva was captured by Muscovy in the Livonian War (1558–83). The town was subsequently under Swedish rule from the end of the sixteenth century to the end of the seventeenth. These years were followed by the occupation and return annexation of the town by Peter the Great in the Great Northern War of 1700–21. According to Professor Issakov, the population of Narva increased many times throughout the sixteenth century: six to eight hundred people in the first half of the century multiplied to more than five to seven thousand by the beginning of the 1580s (the last years of the temporary Russian rule in the Livonian War), mostly Russians and Estonians. As Narva became the centre of transit trade with Russia in the seventeenth century, Issakov argues, it became the sole town in contemporary Estonia to have a significant Russian population in addition to German merchants, Swedes and Finns who were soldiers of Swedish garrisons.[11] Russian merchants constructed their community in Ivangorod, which was incorporated into Narva under Swedish rule.[12] Narva was characterized by ethnic diversity during and after the Swedish period, and a German chronicle mentioned that 'in no other place can we hear so many different languages than here; the Swedish, German, Estonian, Polish, Russian and English languages.'[13]

The legal status of Narva and its surroundings after the annexation of Livonian lands into the Russian Empire was particularly unique.[14] Although three provinces (Estland, Livland and Courland) were established in the former Swedish territories, along with the Duchy of Courland, and constituted the *Ostsee* region with special status (*Ostzeiskii osobyi poryadok* in Russian) based on the Swedish administrative system, Narva was administratively separated from the rest of the region and incorporated into the typically Russian province of Saint Petersburg. Nevertheless, Narva had similar privileges to the *Ostsee* provinces in which the Baltic German nobilities maintained their power after the annexation, and the town was placed under the jurisdiction of Estland *Oberlandesgericht* in Reval (Tallinn) with regard to judiciary.[15] As the German nobility were unhappy with Narva's dual jurisdiction of administration and judiciary, despite privileges bestowed on them in the system, they began to campaign for the general incorporation of Narva into the Estland province in the middle of the nineteenth century. Since the Great Reforms that Russian Emperor Alexander II launched in the fields of serfdom, education, the military, the judiciary and local governance to reconstruct the state constitution after the defeat in the Crimean War (1853–56) posed a grave challenge to the ancient interests of the Baltic Germans, the latter were obliged to struggle to defend their interests against the Imperial state and the rising merchants and citizens from the second half of the nineteenth century to the beginning of the twentieth.[16]

The population in Narva and its surroundings, including Ivangorod, increased remarkably in the second half of the nineteenth century and the beginning of the twentieth because of migration from inner Russia and the Estonian villages. As it is difficult to specify and compare the numbers of various periods in the region because of the randomness of sources, we simply adduce a few indicators here. According to the data in 1865, 6,003 people inhabited Narva and its surroundings, and only 366 among them were nobility (probably the Baltic Germans). Another source indicated that among the 5,553 inhabitants of Narva and its surroundings in the 1860s, 3,099 were Orthodox believers (that is, mainly Russians). Finns of the Lutheran congregation constituted 1,829 residents ('Finns' here means speakers of Finnic languages, including Estonian) and 600 were Lutheran Germans.[17] On the other hand, according to the first census of the Russian Empire on 28 January 1897, 7,313 Estonians, 7,287 Russians, 1,000 Germans and 999 individuals of other ethnicities inhabited the town of Narva proper. This census also indicates a total number of 29,883 inhabitants in Narva and its neighbouring townlets of Ivangorod and

Petrov Forshtadt, although the industrial areas administratively affiliated under Estland Province (for example, Kreenholm Island in the river Narva) were excluded from these accounts.[18] If they had been included, the Russian and Estonian population would have been bigger. A dozen years later, in 1910, Narva as a town had 19,742 inhabitants, among which 9,799 were Russians (49.6 per cent) and 7,883 were Estonians (39.9 per cent). In 1913, just before the First World War, Narva consisted of 21,039 citizens, among whom 12,225 were Estonians (58.1 per cent), 7,280 were Russians (34.6 per cent), 523 were Jews (2.49 per cent) and 283 were Poles (1.34 per cent).[19] The ratios of the Russians and the Estonians fluctuated and competed with each other during the second half of the nineteenth century and the beginning of the twentieth. With regard to the ethnic composition of inhabitants, Narva was already a mixed town of Estonians and Russians under the dominion of the German minority as an ancient ruling group, although one Russian bureaucrat pointed out as early as 1857 that 'Narva looks like other Baltic towns only regarding its narrow and devious alleys, and it is Russian in other aspects'. Anton Weiss-Wendt noted that the language of communication in the town in the 1890s was Russian, while the Estonian language spoken in Narva was a kind of jargon that mingled Estonian and Russian.[20]

The significant population growth of Narva in the second half of the nineteenth century was closely related to the rapid industrialization that accelerated the migration of the labour force from Estland, Livland and other Russian provinces. On the other hand, the comparative stagnation of the population in the early twentieth century correlated with the retrogression of industries.

The textile industry was the leading branch of industrial development in Narva. The Kreenholm factory, which harnessed the abundant flow of the river Narva, became the largest textile mill in Europe, employing 1,400 Russians and 3,244 Estonians in 1872, when the second largest worker's strike in the Russian Empire occurred in the factory.[21] Twenty-two years later, the number of Russian workers in the factory rose to 5,295 (2,340 male, 2,673 female, 282 children under the age of 15), while the Estonians made up 72 per cent of the whole workforce.[22] As Reginald E. Zelnik has pointed out, the numerical contrast between Russians and Estonians indicated 'the distribution of status and power at both the factory and regional levels'. 'The most militant strike leaders' were Estonians, and ethnic distinction was also manifested in the workers' home villages and residential patterns. Russians were mainly recruited from the Orthodox villages on the right bank; the Estonians were from Lutheran villages on the left bank. Russians and Estonians were segregated into temporary workers' barracks, and the factory management 'deliberately provided not only for separate housing but also even for separate dining facilities'.[23]

Narva under Wars, Revolution and Independence

Revolutionary and military disturbances in Russia from 1917 to 1920 threw Narva into turmoil. Because the Estonian nationalist movement and the war for independence were inseparably embedded in the final stages of the First World War and the ensuing White Russians' civil war against the Bolsheviks, Narva became the frontline at which various forces clashed, and it was treated as a territorial bargaining chip during the peace negotiations.

Despite the destructive battles on the eastern front of the First World War, the German occupation of the contemporary Estonian territory, including Narva and its surroundings, happened rather late, in the last weeks before the October Revolution. Narva was seized in March 1918, soon after Estonia's declaration of independence. The end of the war in November 1918 did not mean a peaceful construction of the newly independent Estonian state; Narva instead became the focal point for the Estonian War of Independence and the Russian Civil War, in which such varied actors participated as the Allied Powers, the Russian White Army, the Bolsheviks including Estonian communists, and the Estonian nationalists. While the Commune of the Workers of Estonia, regarded 'to be just a step on the road to world revolution',[24] was established in Narva by the Estonian Bolsheviks and the Red Army soon after the defeat of Germany,[25] the commander-in-chief of the White Russian Northwestern Army, General Nikolai Yudenich (Iudenich), who led the assault towards Petrograd, had stationed himself at a base in Narva for a while. The trench along the river Narva was regarded as an 'Estonian Verdun.' Estonian nationalists who aimed to secure independence and to acquire recognition from the international community were obliged to fight along with the Yudenich Army according to demands from the Allies. However, the anti-Bolshevik aims of the White Russians, which presupposed the integrality of the former territory of the empire, contradicted with the Estonian ambition for an independent nation state, and the Estonian general Johan Laidoner therefore stopped supporting the White Russians and opened peace negotiations with the Soviets once the defeat of the Whites was apparent.[26] The peace was beneficial for the newly established Estonian government, which expected the guarantee of security, as well as for Lenin, who aimed for the status of an authentic sovereign state in international relations. Lenin sometimes praised the Estonian non-cooperation with Yudenich from the autumn of 1919.[27]

The Tartu Peace Treaty, concluded on 2 February 1920 between Soviet Russia and the independent Republic of Estonia,[28] was so favourable for the Estonians that they achieved their territorial demand to acquire the strip of land on the right bank of the river Narva, including Ivangorod as well as the Petseri ('Pechory' in Russian) district in southern Estonia. This meant that the issue of the administrative ownership of Narva, outstanding since the second half of the nineteenth century, was eventually resolved through wars and the revolution.[29] However, at the same time, it brought another troublesome problem to the newly independent state. As Kari Alenius pointed out, 'as a result of the treaty, Estonia obtained a new zone on its eastern border with the majority of the population there being Russians with little connection to Estonia'.[30]

The first census of independent Estonia was carried out in December 1922 within the territory defined by the Treaty. It showed the total population of Estonia that year as 1,107,059, among which 26,912 persons inhabited the town of Narva. The population of Petseri district was 60,848.[31] The census also indicated that the total Russian population composed of the original inhabitants of historical Estonia, inhabitants of the newly incorporated eastern borderlands, and refugees or exiles (including former soldiers of the Yudenich Army) was 91,109 (8.2 per cent of the whole population). Among them, 44,000 were inhabitants of historical Estonia, and the others inhabited the Petseri district and both banks of the river Narva. The proportion of Russians in Narva was about one third of the population.[32]

The second census in 1934 indicated a significant decrease in Narva's population, in contrast to the slight increase in the population in Estonia. The number of inhabitants in Narva decreased to 23,515 people (−12 per cent compared to 1922), while the total population rose to 1,126,413 (+1.7 per cent compared to 1922).[33] The demographic decline in Narva was explained by migration to Tallinn or other large towns due to living conditions and the economic situation. Ethnic composition in Narva was rather stable: ethnic Estonians numbered 15,227 (64.8 per cent) and the proportion of Russians was 29.7 per cent (6,986 in number).[34] Narva continued to be characterized by the coexistence of Estonians and Russians, although the ratio had inclined towards Estonian dominance since the 1910s. A local historian pointed out that the demographic alternation from the beginning of the twentieth century was related to the decrease of industrial workers in Narva, especially at the Kreenholm factory.[35] The decline of the Baltic Germans was another feature, just as it was observed in other former *Ostsee* provinces.

The above-mentioned Professor Sergei Issakov, born in Narva in 1931, recollected his home town, characterizing it as a 'town with astonishing unique destiny'[36]:

> Two communities in Narva lived isolated lives from each other, not interacting between themselves so much, nevertheless, there were no particular hostilities and both communities experienced mutual influences at all times. The influences captured all spheres of daily life, culture and even language. It has been long pointed out that the jargon of the Estonians in Narva (especially those who had grown up before the revolution) abounded with borrowings from Russian, not only lexical but also grammatical, syntactic, and phonetical ... In parallel, Estonian and German elements penetrated the language of the local Russians. For example, I have just recollected that my grandparents, commoners from peasant origin, spoke not '*zavtrakat*' ('take breakfast' in Russian) but '*frishtykat*' (from German '*Frühstük*') ... Russian and Estonian elements were remarkable in the language of Narvian Germans, too.[37]

He emphasized that trilingualism was characteristic of Narva, and the Russian, German and Estonian languages were all *kohalik* ('local' in Estonian). He doggedly scrutinized the cultural activities of various genres (literature, theatre, poetry, classical music, song festivals, ballet, dance, fine arts, journalism, architecture, etc.) developed by the Russians in Estonia in parallel with those of the Estonians, and he published numerous works on the theme. The Narvian model of multilingualism and multiculturalism in the interbellum, which guaranteed a respectable status for the Russians and Russian high culture, was not only a formative memory in his childhood, but also the ideal prototype for Issakov, who participated in the political activities and cultural movements of Russian speakers after the collapse of the USSR and fought to establish Estonian-Russian identity.

The Formation of Soviet/Russian Narva

A series of disastrous events in the 1940s destroyed Narva and its population exhaustively: the unjustified incorporation of the Baltic states into the USSR in August 1940, the deportation of the native people to Siberia in June 1941, the German occupation of the Baltic States and the western parts of Soviet Union soon after the outbreak of the German–Soviet War (the 'Great Patriotic War' for the Russians), a string of mass air raids by the Soviet Red Air Forces that ruined almost all the buildings of Narva and the forced evacuation of inhabitants who tagged along with the retreating German army. Obliged to abandon the Narva front, the German Command ordered the population to exit the town, and the evacuation started on 25 January 1944. Therefore, 85 per cent of the inhabitants had left Narva by 1 March.[38] Soon after the end of the Second World War, only two thousand people remained in Narva. Its post-war reconstruction started literally with a blank sheet of paper. As the old man at the beginning of this chapter said in direct terms, it was the Russian immigrants that rebuilt the town from scratch.

The resurgence of the Estonian Soviet Socialist Republic after the German occupation (the 'third occupation' from the Estonian viewpoint and 'liberation' for the Russians) in the post-war era accompanied 'domestic' territorial change. While the former state border between Soviet Russia and the Republic of Estonia drawn by the Tartu Treaty had been transformed into the inner boundary between the two Soviet Socialist Republics at the first annexation of Estonia in August 1940,[39] it moved westwards to the river Narva, and the strip of land on the right bank was incorporated into the RSFSR in 1945. Ivangorod, coupled with Narva since the sixteenth century, was administratively separated from it, and the territory of Narva was narrowed, although these two towns continued to share infrastructure, such as the water network,[40] and in practice maintained unity in daily life. As many scholars have emphasized, 'during the Soviet era, the inter-republican border drawn between two nominally sovereign states did not exist on the ground, Narva-Ivangorod developed as an "international" transborder city, and the population in its reiterative practices eliminated the border from daily life, producing a transnational "space of flows" in the borderlands.'[41]

The population of Narva steadily increased from 1944 to the 1980s. Although most of the initial population vanished at the end of the war, Narva gradually recovered to interbellum numbers; the population approached 30,400 in 1959, despite the fact that former residents who had evacuated to other parts of Estonia were strictly prohibited from returning to their home town. This upward growth continued, reaching 57,900 inhabitants in 1970 and 73,500 in 1980. The number had risen to 82,200 by 1990, one year before the collapse of the USSR.[42] This demographic dynamism was in principle facilitated by migration from Russia and other Soviet republics. A completely new cluster of the population was formed.

The flow of migrants into Narva under the Soviet regime can be divided into three terms, according to their motives, places of origin and other factors:

1) From 1944 to the middle of the 1960s;
2) From the middle of the 1960s to the end of the 1970s;
3) From the end of the 1970s to the end of the 1980s.[43]

During the first half of the first term, there was an urgent need for labour forces to reconstruct the town and facilitate industrial development. The north-eastern region of Estonia that included Narva was granted special status as a target region for intensive investment.[44] Among other things, the demand for workers to build a uranium processing plant had a significant impact on population formation. The dictyonema shale that was to be abundantly mined in the region was uraniferous, and Moscow, aiming to develop nuclear reactors and nuclear weapons to catch up with the advanced technology of the United States, had great expectations for the north-eastern region of Estonia.[45] Although former soldiers and POWs were utilized in the first phase of reconstruction and development, and the forced mobilization of young Estonians was planned in vain, the regime was obliged (and able) to rely on migrant workers from outside Estonia. David Vseviov noted that former residents were prohibited from returning to their home town due to the highly confidential nature of the uranium processing project: 'it was not on the former inhabitants of Narva in the pre-war period, who might be *Kulaks*, spies and exploiters, but on patriots of Leningrad, Novgorod and Pskov oblast who overcame wartime hardships together' that the regime laid expectations.[46] Scholars agree that migrants in the first stage of post-war reconstruction came largely from rural areas of those three oblasts (provinces), although unfortunately there is no accurate numerical data.[47]

As industrialization proceeded during the second term, it became increasingly difficult to secure enough labour forces from the neighbouring provinces. Labour markets extended to more remote regions, including Central Asia, where Narvian enterprises increased their recruitment propaganda. More people migrated into Estonia for personal reasons such as marriage.[48] In conjunction with the factories, vocational schools were opened in response to the growing demand for labour forces, and they also attracted the younger generation from outside Estonia. Interestingly, those students did not remain in Narva after graduation, instead moving to other regions in Estonia, which affected Narva's low migrant settlement rate.

As the third term featured economic stagnation throughout the Soviet Union, employment was no longer the main reason for migration; motivations were further personalized. Most marriages and family reunions took place not between Russians and Estonians, but between the Russians who had migrated earlier and those who remained in their native land, which in turn caused a further increase in the Russian population.

Generally speaking, it is difficult to explain the increase in the Russian population in Estonia, including Narva, through the intentional and vicious policies of the Soviet regime to eliminate the Estonian nation through 'Russification', which were often exaggerated among Estonian nationalists.

Although some nationalist historians in Estonia suggested that industrial development policies in north-eastern Estonia were initiated mainly to provoke the mass migration of Russians into Estonia and to colonialize it,[49] most of the Russian migrants came to Narva without any support from the Soviet state and their motives were instead personal. High standards of living and the portrayal of Estonia as 'a window to the West' were the immediate causes of their migration,[50] even though the policies of Moscow also influenced their choice of life trajectories in some ways.

Narva in Transition and Transformation

The rise of democratic and nationalist movements for sovereignty and independence in Estonia and the two other Baltic countries at the end of the 1980s and the beginning of the 1990s stirred the Russians in Narva. The Supreme Soviet of the Estonian SSR issued the declaration of sovereignty in November 1988, and the ensuing bill of language law that aimed at recovering the equivalent status of the Estonian language disquieted the Russians, who had never considered the necessity of learning the language, enjoying the predominance of Russian not only as the 'international' communicative language within the USSR, but also as a daily communication tool among locals in Narva's monolingual setting. Russian factory workers in Narva started a movement to protest the bill and pro-Soviet Russian activists in Estonia set up organizations (for example, Intermovement and the United Council of Labour Collectives, or OSTK) against the Supreme Soviet of Estonia, in which the democratic People's Front exercised hegemony. The strain between the republic's leadership and local authorities in the north-eastern region, including Narva, increased. The former dissolved the latter and even arrested leaders of pro-Soviet movements, allegedly for supporting the putschists just after the August *coup d'état* in Moscow in 1991.[51] It is noteworthy, nevertheless, that pro-Soviet activists did not receive any support from Yeltsin's government of the RSFSR, as he cooperated with the Baltic leaderships for the sake of common anti-Soviet causes. It was Yeltsin who recognized the independence of the Baltic states on 24 August 1991, prior to any other authorities both inside and outside the Soviet Union except Iceland.[52] Yeltsin also refused Narva's secession from Estonia and its reunification with Russia, which was propagated by local activists. The facets of the confrontation never converged into the simple ethnic model according to which any state would support 'compatriots' who resided in a neighbouring country. This would be a distinct feature of the 'near abroad policies' of Yeltsin's government later in the 1990s.

After the failure of the August coup, three Baltic states succeeded in recovering their independence and were recognized by the international community. The boundary between the Estonian SSR and the RSFSR abruptly changed into a tentative state border, although it is not fixed *de jure* yet, and strict border control was introduced. As the old man said in Narva, the nominal and fictional border between the two Soviet republics on the river Narva suddenly became substantial and functional. Residents of Narva and Ivangorod who had long coexisted in a unified manner in daily life and work were divided into two countries. Even members of the same family were sometimes separated from each other. After the physical border between the neighbouring countries was drawn, the legal 'border' among the population loomed.

Citizenship policies and the relevant legislation of the newly independent Estonia contained controversial elements that created long-standing issues affecting Russian-speaking minorities in the country to this day. While Lithuania, which regained independence along with Estonia and Latvia, adopted the 'zero option' policy and granted citizenship to all who had been citizens of the Lithuanian SSR, Estonia and Latvia granted citizenship only to those who had been citizens of interbellum independent states and their descendants. Due to this political decision, an overwhelming majority of Russian speakers who had migrated to Narva after the Second World War were not granted Estonian citizenship and needed to pass rigorous and deterrent state examination, including official language tests, if they hoped to get it. The available options for Russians in Narva were 1) returning to Russia or other homelands, abandoning a relatively high standard of living, 2) undertaking the examination for Estonian citizenship, 3) acquiring Russian citizenship anew and remaining there as permanent foreign residents or 4) living in Estonia as stateless non-citizens with official registration (they would subsequently be issued 'alien passports'). 'Illegal aliens' also remained, although they were few in number. This resulted in the mass production of stateless non-citizens and Russian citizens: one third of Estonia's total population (approximately five hundred thousand people) did not have Estonian citizenship in 1992. Furthermore, Parliament adopted the Law on Aliens in 1993, which did not guarantee residence permits for stateless people.

Confronted with the difficulties of language, citizenship and residence permits on the one hand, and denied their secessionist ambition by Yeltsin on the other, Russian activists and local elites in north-eastern Estonia resorted to a hard-line policy to establish a high degree of territorial autonomy in the region and forced through referenda for the 'special status' of Narva and Sillamäe in 1993.[53] However, the referenda were ruled unconstitutional by the Supreme Court, and popular support for secessionism among the residents, as researchers have pointed out, was often exaggerated.[54] While the turmoil was appeased after this legal decision, and the president launched a round table for dialogue between the representatives of the minority groups and state officials, the protection of Russian-speaking minorities in Estonia rose up to European and international levels. CSCE (later OSCE) deployed its Mission to Tallinn and opened branch offices in Narva and Jõhvi (the capital of Ida-Virumaa).[55] Other European international organizations also considered the protection of Russian-speaking minorities in Estonia and Latvia as a condition for these countries' accession into those organizations.

Language, statelessness and citizenship were the focal points in this context, and the 'integration' of Russian speakers into Estonian society became an urgent political target concerning its accession to the European Union in 2004, because it was strictly required by *Agenda 2000*, a fundamental document for the eastward enlargement of the EU. Launching the negotiations for accession, the EU set out the 'stability of institutions guaranteeing democracy, the rule of law, human rights, and respect for and protection of minorities' as required political criteria that candidate states should achieve before accession.[56] The EU's requirement of the protection of Russian-speaking 'minorities' was one of the focal points in its Annual Reports that assessed the progress of Estonia and Latvia, and it obliged them to revise their initial citizenship and language policies, as well as the statements of OSCE's High Commissioner of National Minorities. Ironically, the protection of Russian-speaking minorities became a matter of high priority for Estonia and Latvia, which earnestly desired EU membership as a guarantee of state security against Russia. Therefore, they drew up state programmes for the integration of Russian speakers into the national community and implemented measures to achieve this goal despite frequent nationalist counteractions, such as rigidification of language laws and naturalization procedures, as well as school reform schemes to intensify education through the state language. These attempts were severely condemned by the European and international community, and the process of integration proceeded under pressure from the EU, albeit in an uneven manner. In 1999, the University of Tartu Narva College was founded, the only institution of higher education in Estonia to train teachers for schools in which both Estonian and Russian were utilized as languages of instruction. This was a symbolic measure towards the Russian-speaking population in the north-eastern region to protect their rights to language and education and to facilitate their integration into Estonian society.[57]

Meanwhile, Estonian nationalists became increasingly frustrated with the 'tolerant' measures of integration towards Soviet 'occupants' due to pressure from the EU and other international organizations. Their irritation was sometimes exposed in the 'War of Monuments' from the beginning of the 2000s, and it became more apparent after Estonia's accession to the EU was realized in 2004. It appeared that they had been freed from the yoke of accession. Memory conflicts among the population in Estonia culminated in 'Bronze Night' on 26 April 2007,[58] when a political decision just before the general election to relocate a monument to Soviet soldiers in the centre of Tallinn provoked anger and mass violence among the Russians. However, presages of this 'War' also appeared at the beginning of the 2000s in Narva, as will be discussed in the next section. Conflicts of history and memory politics between the Baltic States, Russia and European organizations were the next stage of post-Soviet international politics after the EU's eastward enlargement.[59]

Belonging and Identity of Russian Speakers in Narva

While coming to terms with the crisis in 1993 and other seemingly discriminative measures on the one hand and observing the advancement of integration policies on the other, the Russian speakers in Narva gradually changed their bearings and had to find a way to adapt to their new conditions. The most significant transformation was the decrease in stateless non-citizens after the launch of the integration policies and the simplification of naturalization procedures.

As Table 6.1 indicates, the numbers of non-citizens ('Citizenship Undetermined') in Estonia, Ida-Virumaa and Narva decreased significantly from 2000 to 2011, and continued to decline slowly from 2011 to 2017. The number of stateless people in 2000 was notably smaller than in the initial years of independence and in 1997, when *Agenda 2000* was drafted by the European Commission. As mentioned above, the proportion of the population in Estonia that did not have Estonian citizenship was about one third in 1992. Even in 1997, approximately 330,000 people, 23 per cent of the entire population, remained stateless. In contrast, the proportion of stateless people decreased to 12.4 per cent in 2000, 6.6 per cent in 2011 and 5.9 per cent in 2017. The policy shift under European pressure seems to have accelerated the acquisition of citizenship among the Russian-speaking population. Although considerably higher than the national level, the proportion of stateless in Narva decreased by half: from 33.6 per cent in 2000, to 15.6 per cent in 2011, to 14.9 per cent in 2017. Legal uncertainty among Russian speakers appeared to ease.

This decrease of non-citizens and the increase of the acquisition of citizenship, however, did not directly signify a growing consciousness

Table 6.1. Population in 2000, 2011 and 2017.

Country/County/City		2000			2011			2017		
		Estonia (%)	Ida-Virumaa (%)	Narva (%)	Estonia (%)	Ida-Virumaa (%)	Narva (%)	Estonia (%)	Ida-Virumaa (%)	Narva (%)
Total Population		1,370,052	179,702	68,680	1,294,455	149,172	58,663	1,315,635	143,880	57,130
Ethnicity	Ethnic Estonians	930,219	35,917	3,331	902,547	29,131	3,031	904,639	27,161	2,150
		67.9%	20.0%	4.9%	69.7%	19.5%	5.2%	68.8%	18.9%	3.8%
	Ethnic Russians	351,178	124,961	58,702	326,235	108,208	51,434	330,206	105,177	49,235
		25.6%	69.5%	85.5%	25.2%	72.5%	87.7%	25.1%	73.1%	86.2%
Citizenship	Estonian Citizens	1,095,743	80,540	24,794	1,102,618	80,470	27,259	1,119,146	79,769	28,266
		80.0%	44.8%	36.1%	85.2%	53.9%	46.5%	85.1%	55.4%	49.5%
	Russian Citizens	86,067	34,577	19,836	90,510	42,135	21,771	86,674	39,716	21,527
		6.3%	19.2%	28.9%	7.0%	28.2%	37.1%	6.6%	27.6%	37.7%
	Citizenship Undetermined	170,349	61,921	23,093	85,961	24,994	9,129	77,926	22,053	8,525
		12.4%	34.5%	33.6%	6.6%	16.8%	15.6%	5.9%	15.3%	14.9%

Sources: http://pub.stat.ee/px-web.2001/I_Databas/Population_census/databasetree.as (accessed 4 March 2022). Only the 2017 data is derived from 'Narva in Figures 2016', http://www.narva.ee/en/left_block/narva_in_figures/page:3543 (accessed 4 March 2022).

Note: Total population of Narva in 2017 includes only registered individuals, so there is a small error in this column. Percentages are pro forma.

among Russian speakers of belonging to the Estonian state. According to Table 6.1, those who had Estonian citizenship in Narva were 36.1 per cent in 2000, 46.5 per cent in 2011 and 49.5 per cent in 2017. This indicates a certain degree of success of the integration policy. However, the proportion has never transcended 50 per cent in this border town. In contrast, the proportion in 2000 of those with Russian citizenship was 6.3 per cent in Estonia and 28.9 per cent in Narva. Russian citizens represented 7 per cent of the total population of Estonia and 37.1 per cent of Narva in 2011. A similar tendency was apparent in 2017. Many people continue to identify themselves with the Russian Federation, at least in terms of citizenship. At first glance, it seems that there are two parallel Russian communities of roughly the same size, distinguished by citizenship. This is often cited as evidence of 'Narva as a Russian town'. Yet does this really mean a divided community and identity between pro-Estonian and pro-Russian parties within the Russian-speaking population?

School preference among parents gives us an interesting perspective. The Estonian system of education (basic and secondary) consists of two different types of schools according to the different languages of instruction, inheriting the system of Soviet Estonia that segregated Estonians and Russian speakers spatially as well as linguistically. Although the initial plan of school reforms in independent Estonia aimed at the unification of the dual system, the country was not able to realize this in terms of finance and human resources. Ironically, the deficit guaranteed the right to education in the mother tongue for 'minorities.' Therefore, instead of the dissolution of dualism, the intensification of education in the state language in Russian schools, especially in the upper secondary courses, had long been a policy target and a focal point of ethnopolitics in Estonia. School reform in 2007 that aimed to substantially increase lessons in the Estonian language in upper secondary schools provoked anxiety and opposition among the teachers in Russian schools, who were concerned about their own competence to teach subjects in the Estonian language.[60] In contrast, parents were relatively positive about the reform, even if there were minor protests, as they acknowledged the instrumental significance of acquiring the Estonian language and preferred to enrol their children in pre- and basic Estonian schools. The proportion of pupils in Russian schools began to decrease from the middle of the 1990s, from 31.2 per cent in 1996 to 25.1 per cent in the 2000s.[61] Immersion preschools and classes for Russian-speaking children that were taught only in Estonian gained popularity. A recent report by the Ministry of Education and Research noted that 'for non-Estonians, the instrumental function matters most' and 'more than 70 percent of Russian-speaking respondents agree that Estonian is necessary for living and working in Estonia'.[62]

In Narva, the government opened the experimental Vanalinna Riigikool (Old Town State School) in August 2000, which adopted the immersion programme (*keelekümblus*) and taught first-grade students in Estonian only. It started to teach the Russian language in the second grade, and trilingual education (Estonian, Russian and English) began in the third grade. This indicated the high prestige of the school. This newly opened school gained so much popularity among Russian-speaking parents that an increase in the number of parallel classes was considered.[63] On the other hand, the number of students who entered higher education institutions in Russia from secondary schools in Narva decreased significantly just before Estonia's accession into the EU (6.8 per cent in 2001, 10.1 per cent in 2002, 6.6 per cent in 2003, 2.2 per cent in 2004 and 3.9 per cent in 2005) despite the efforts of the Russian government in the Baltic states (some higher education institutions in the Russian Federation had created a special quota for Russians from Estonia and Latvia). This suggests the rising interest in the 'West' among the younger generation in Narva. Meanwhile, an official at Narva's Department of Education pointed out in an interview in 2005 that positive attitudes among parents towards teaching in Estonian were explicable through Narva's peculiarity that concerns or anxiety over losing one's Russian identity through school education was less common in the monolingual setting of the families and streets than in other parts of Estonia.[64] Although we cannot derive predictive conclusions from these partial episodes, they seem to suggest a complex, fluctuating consciousness among Russian speakers. Regardless of whether they are Estonian citizens, Russian citizens or non-citizens, their strategy for the future has been based on the prerequisite that they will continue to live in Estonia. Those who could not share such sentiments left Narva for Russia in an earlier stage, which caused the initial decrease in population.

Another arena of identity-building was historical memory, including the 'War of Monuments' mentioned in the previous section. The historical memory of Narva is sensitive and multilayered due to its complicated historical trajectory since the medieval era, as we observed in the first half of this chapter. Interbellum Narva was a model for the peaceful coexistence and merging of two cultures (or three cultures, including German) for the late Professor Sergei Issakov, who was born and raised there. He strategically projected this 'blissful' ideal onto both the distant past and the present, and endeavoured to write a 'chronicle' of multicultural concomitance from ancient times.[65] In contrast, an Estonian regional historian whose father was born in Narva reminisced about the historical landscape of the old Swedish and German Narva, inserting many photographs of 'forgotten' buildings and alleys into his book. He quietly condemned its thorough destruction by Soviet air raids and artillery during the Second World War and the Soviet-style post-war 'reconstruction' scheme.[66] Finally, in the nostalgic images cherished among the old Russian generation, Narva was a completely Russian town of their own, reconstructed on deserted ruins by emboldened Soviet and Russian migrants.

Multiple memories stimulated and flustered the historical imaginaries of the residents of Narva at the beginning of the 2000s. The Swedes proposed rebuilding the statue of the Swedish Lion in Narva that had been erected in 1936 thanks to Swedish sponsorship and destroyed by the Soviet artillery in the summer of 1944. The year 2000 was the three hundredth anniversary of the Swedish victory against Peter the Great's Russia at the Battle of Narva at the outset of the Great Northern War, which lasted more than twenty years and in which the Swedes were eventually defeated. Therefore, the monument inevitably provoked complicated feelings among Russian speakers, who held lively memories of another 'Battle of Narva' in 1944 and the 'Great Patriotic War' in general.[67] Notably, the proposition was in line with the official Estonian top-down policies to construct '*Vana Narva* (Old Narva)' ideology and identity, mobilizing the cultural resources from before the Second World War.[68] Russians in Narva soon launched a counteraction to build a statue of Peter the Great, the most popular historical figure among post-Soviet Russians, in the central square named after the tsar. This was not an exceptional event in the 'War of Monuments'. As Siobhan Kattago and Elena Nikiforova have written, there are many disputed *Lieux de mémoire* within and around Narva, where different memories and representations meet, collide, negotiate and coexist: a monument for victims of deportation to Siberia in front of the Narva railway station; the Fraternal Grave; the German military cemetery; a Soviet tank; the Kreenholm factory, etc.[69] There might be minor frictions and troubles as a matter of course: the 9 May celebration of Soviet Victory day, when residents of Narva and visitors from the Russian side gather and march with the black and orange striped ribbons of Saint George on their clothes or in their hands, might provoke unpleasant and, in some cases, more or less angry feelings in most ethnic Estonians.[70] Nevertheless, a serious conflict has never occurred in Narva or Estonia as a whole after 'Bronze Night'.

Conclusion

Despite poisonous and stereotyped representations, such as representations as a 'fifth column', Russian speakers in Narva have more or less been well integrated into Estonia, maintaining their own Russian language community and reconciling themselves with the policies of the central government. Nearly half of them have naturalized themselves to Estonia, and the acquisition of Russian citizenship does not always signify their identification with the Russian state. It embraces such personal causes as kinship with the residents of Ivangorod, avoidance of military service in Estonia, convenience of passing through the border and pension-related advantages. The Vanalinna Riigikool website posts information for pupils and parents in both Russian and Estonian, with Estonian headings,[71] as is found in other schools. The attitudes of Russian speakers seem to depend on the pragmatic consideration of functional adaptation to the situation.

Evidently, the Estonian state has endeavoured to advance integration policies among Russian speakers and obtain their allegiance to Estonia. The '*Vana Narva* (Old Narva)' project and other government measures to transform the town's memory-scape might lead the representation of Soviet Narva to disappear from its landscape and history.[72] On the other hand, the Russian government under Yeltsin's presidency developed 'near abroad policies' in which Russia acknowledged itself as the specific guardian of Russians who remained abroad in former Soviet republics. Moreover, Putin's government recently started developing campaigns for a '*Russkii Mir*/Russian World' to exercise the influence of the Russian language globally, and the cooperation of Narva and Ivangorod is one of its target operations.[73] The project aims to reconstruct the House of Peter the Great, his accommodation in Narva, which was also destroyed in 1944. When the Estonian government invited NATO troops to Narva on 26 February 2015 and celebrated its Independence Day with a military parade under strained conditions after the Crimean crisis of 2014, the Russian Federation reacted with huge military drills in the Pskov region along the Russian border with Estonia and Latvia.[74] This enhanced the stereotyped representation of Narva as an antagonistic front line between the 'West' and the 'East.' Memory and identity manipulations are exercised by both sides, who arbitrarily choose preferred elements from the 'hodge-podge'[75] of the Narvian past and utilize monumental buildings, landscapes and even military forces as their tools. Throughout the decades, exposed by these political and cultural manoeuvres and gnawed at by personal and family issues, the residents of Narva have stumbled into choosing their own citizenship and making their specific Narvian-Russian identity, regardless of any alternative citizenship.

In contrast to incendiary labelling by politicians and journalists, impartial researchers who have observed Narva with respect to the region and its residents agree that a Narvian-Russian identity that is differentiated from the Russians in the neighbouring Russian Federation has been formed, and that the representation of a Russian 'fifth column' is a fiction based on an excessively geopolitical way of thinking. In the early 2000s, David Smith noted that the identity of '"Baltic Russians" distinct from their ethno-national kin in the neighboring RSFSR' was formed in the Soviet era and that Narva developed a particular 'niche' identity at that time.[76] Alena Pfoser reported that the Russians in Narva were utilizing the 'European-ness' or 'Western-ness' of Estonia for their own identity-building, and to assert their 'superiority' over the people in Ivangorod.[77] Although the formation of Estonian-Russian identity was the strategic goal that Professor Sergei Issakov pursued, relying on his childhood memories of peaceful coexistence and prosperous Russian high culture in Narva, his earnest expectation seems to have come true in a different fashion than he supposed; that is, as a response to the competing and antagonistic forces both outside and inside Estonia.

Nobuya Hashimoto is Professor of Russian and Baltic History at Kwansei Gakuin University in Japan. His fields of interest are sociocultural history of education in the Russian Empire, Baltic area studies and history and memory politics in Russia and Central and Eastern European countries. He is the author of *Memory Politics: History Conflicts in Europe* (2016, in Japanese), 'Maneuvering Memories of Dictatorship and Conflicts: The Baltic States, Central and Eastern Europe, and Russia', in Paul Corner and Jie-Hyun Lim (eds), *The Palgrave Handbook of Mass Dictatorship* (2016) and other works. He has edited many books in the fields of comparative social history of education and memory and history politics.

Hiromi Komori is a Professor at Waseda University. She specializes in the modern history of Estonia and her recent research interests include the issues of Russian speaking residents in Estonia and Latvia, historical perception and politics in post-socialist countries. She is the author of *Politics and Historical Perception of Estonia* (2009, in Japanese).

Notes

1. Juske, *Khronika zabytoi Narvy*, 23–24, 115.
2. 'Narva in Figures, 2017'.
3. Välismaalaste seadus (9 December 2009). Välismaalasele rahvusvahelise kaitse andmise seadus (14 December 2005). Article 3 of the former Act prescribes that 'an alien is not an Estonian citizen'.
4. Martinez, *Remains of the Soviet Past in Estonia*, 170.
5. Nikiforova, 'On Victims and Heroes', 434. See Yapici, 'Is Narva the Next?'
6. *Brokgauz i Efron Entsiklopedicheskii Slobal'*. Vol. 40, , 351. See *The Chronicle of Novgorod*, 95.

7. Petrov, *Gorod Narva*, 23.
8. Kivimäe, 'Medieval Narva', 18.
9. Ibid., 24.
10. Issakov, *Put' Dlinnoyu v Tyshachu Let*, 33.
11. Issakov, 'Gorod s udivitel'noi sud'boi', 196.
12. Issakov, *Put' Dlinnoyu v Tyshachu Let*, 50.
13. Issakov, 'Gorod s udivitel'noi sud'boi', 196.
14. On the administrative status of Narva after its incorporation into Russia, see Smolokurov, 'Narvskoe gorodskoe samoupravlenie'.
15. Weiss-Wendt, 'Komu prinadlezhit Narva?', 23.
16. Ibid., 25–35.
17. Petrov, *Gorod Narva*, 461.
18. Smolokurov, 'Narodonaselenie Narvy', 40–42.
19. Ibid., 46.
20. Weiss-Wendt, 'Komu prinadlezhit Narva?', 42–43.
21. Zelnik, 'Russian Workers and Revolution', 623; Zelnik, *Law and Disorder on the Narova River*, 25.
22. Smolokurov, 'Narodonaselenie Narvy', 42.
23. Zelnik, *Law and Disorder on the Narova River*, 6, 26.
24. Brüggemann, 'Defending National Sovereignty Against Two Russias', 24–25.
25. Though Soviet official historiography maintained that the manifesto of the Commune was proclaimed at the old City Hall, it was actually delivered, according to a local Estonian historian, at the Aleksandr Cathedral of the Evangelical Lutheran Church. See, *Khronika zabytoi Narvy*, 132.
26. Cf. Brüggemann, 'Defending National Sovereignty Against Two Russias'.
27. See, for example, Lenin's address at the Eighth All-Russian Conference of the Russian Communist Party (Bolshevik) on the 2–4 December 1919, in *Lenin Polnoe Sobranie Sochinenie*, vol. 39, 339–71.
28. About some important aspects of the treaty, see Medijainen, 'The Tartu Peace Treaty and Permanent Neutrality for Estonia'.
29. Weiss-Wendt, 'Komu prinadlezhit Narva?', 44. Weiss-Wendt wrote that the issue was resolved 'by chance', insofar as there had never been the cultural-historical prerequisite for the incorporation of Narva into Estland Province in the tsarist era.
30. Alenius, 'Dealing with the Russian Population in Estonia', 167.
31. Statistics Estonia, Rahvastik maakondades ja linnades, 1922.
32. Issakov, *Put' Dlinnoyu v Tyshachu let*, 204–5.
33. Statistics Estonia, Rahvastik maakondades ja linnades, 1934.
34. Smolokurov, 'Narodonaselenie Narvy', 49, 52; Issakov, 'Gorod s udivitel'noi sud'boi', 203.
35. Smolokurov, 'Narodonaselenie Narvy', 47.
36. Issakov, 'Gorod s udivitel'noi sud'boi', 195.
37. Ibid., 204.
38. Juske, *Khronika zabytoi Narvy*, 50.
39. On the disappearance of the border and its effect on Estonia, see Mertelsmann, 'The Disappearance of a Border and Incorporation into the USSR'.
40. Cf. Jauhiainen and Pikner, 'Narva–Ivangorod'.
41. Kaiser and Nikiforova, 'The Performativity of Scale', 545. Cf. Pfoser, 'Nested Peripheralisation', 29–30; Brednikova, '"Windows" Project Ad Marginem or a "Divided History" of Divided Cities?', 46–47.
42. 'Narva Arvudes 2012', 7.

43. Vseviov, *Kirde-Eesti urbaanse anomaalia kujunemine ning struktuur pärast teist maailmasõda*, 54.

44. Mertelsmann, 'Die Herausbildung des Sonderstatus der Nordostregion innerhalb der Estnischen SSR', 105–21.

45. In practice the plant was founded in Sillamäe, a close neighbour to Narva, and it began operation at the end of 1948. See Rofer and Kaasik, *Turning a Problem into a Resource*, 5.

46. Vseviov, *Kirde-Eesti urbaanse anomaalia kujunemine ning struktuur pärast teist maailmasõda*, 27.

47. In contrast, the dynamics of migration to and from post-war Kaliningrad, formerly Königsberg in East Prussia, which was reconstructed by Soviet (mainly Russian) migrants, have been scrutinized very extensively by local historians since the period of perestroika. Cf. Kostyashov, *Sekretnaya istoriia Kaliningradskoi oblasti*; Kostyashov, *Povsednevnost' poslevoennoi derevni*.

48. Tammaru, *Venelased Eestis*, 17.

49. Laar, Ott and Endre, *Teine Eesti*, 41–42.

50. Cf. Mertelsmann, 'Die Herausbildung des Sonderstatus der Nordostregion innerhalb der Estnischen SSR', 119.

51. Kolstø, *Russians in the Former Soviet Republics*, 133.

52. Neukirch, 'Russia and the OSCE', 239.

53. Smith, 'Narva Region Within the Estonian Republic', 97–99.

54. Ibid., 105–6.

55. On the OSCE Mission's activities in Estonia, see Heidenhain, 'The Activities of the OSCE'. According to our hearing at the OSCE Mission's Narva office on 12 September 2001, it also engaged in consultations on the personal issues facing Russian speakers, including reunification of separated families in Narva and Ivangorod.

56. European Commission, *Agenda 2000*, 39.

57. See https://www.narva.ut.ee/en/about-college (accessed 4 March 2022).

58. Cf. Brüggemann and Kasekamp, 'The Politics of History and the "War of Monuments" in Estonia'.

59. Cf. Hashimoto, 'Maneuvering Memories of Dictatorship and Conflicts'.

60. *Postimees*, 22 December 2004.

61. Mitte-eestlaste integratsiooni Sihtasutus, Õppekavaarendustöö koolis, 104. According to an interview with a high official of the Ministry of Education and Research conducted by the authors on 30 August 2007, the demographic decrease of the young population in general and the preference for Estonian schools among the Russian-speaking population reinforced the financial difficulty of maintaining Russian schools, and indeed some Russian schools were closed because of the decreasing number of pupils in those years.

62. Ministry of Education and Research, *Summary of the Ministry of Education and Research's Annual Report for 2018*, 17.

63. Interviews with the director, Tatjana Stepanova, and officials of the Department of Education of Narva Town Government were conducted by the authors on 14, 29 and 30 September 2005. In the interview, the director explained the increase of Russian citizens in Narva through the cross-border enrolment in schools in Ivangorod due to low school fees, the convenience of entrance to higher education institutions in Russia and advantages for pensions.

64. Interview with a specialist on foreign language education held on 31 January 2005.

65. See. Issakov, *Ocherki istorii russkoi kul'tury v Estonii*.

66. See, Juske, *Khronika zabytoi Narvy*.

67. See, Burch and Smith, 'Empty Spaces and the Value of Symbols'.
68. Smith and Burch, 'Enacting Identities in the EU-Russia Borderland', 405–6.
69. See, Kattago, 'Commemorating Liberation and Occupation'; Nikiforova, 'On Victims and Heroes'.
70. The ribbon of Saint George is a military symbol of Soviet victory against Fascist Germany, which has been effectively utilized by Putin's government in his history and memory politics. See, Kolstø, 'Symbol of the War – But Which One?'
71. See https://www.nvrk.edu.ee (accessed 4 March 2022).
72. Brednikova, '"Windows" Project Ad Marginem or a "Divided History" of Divided Cities?', 50.
73. See the website of the Russian World Foundation, https://russkiymir.ru/en/fund/decree.php.
74. Freeman et al., 'NATO and Russia Hold Rival Military Exercises on Estonian Border'.
75. Brednikova, '"Windows" Project Ad Marginem or a "Divided History" of Divided Cities?', 59.
76. Smith, 'Narva Region within the Estonian Republic', 91.
77. Pfoser, 'Nested Peripheralisation', 40.

Bibliography

Alenius, Kari. 'Dealing with the Russian Population in Estonia, 1919–1921'. *Ajalooline Ajakiri* 1(2) (2012), 167–82.

Brednikova, Olga. '"Windows" Project Ad Marginem or a "Divided History" of Divided Cities? A Case Study of the Russian-Estonian Borderland', in Tsypylma Darieva and Wolfgang Kaschucba (eds), *Representation on The Margin of Europe: Politics and Identities in the Baltic and South Caucasian States* (Frankfurt/New York: Campus Verlag, 2007) (Russian version is in *Ab Imperio*, No.4, 2004).

Brüggemann, Karsten. 'Defending National Sovereignty against Two Russias: Estonia in the Russian Civil War, 1918–1920'. *Journal of Baltic Studies* 34(1) (2003), 22–51.

Brüggemann, Karsten, and Andres Kasekamp. 'The Politics of History and the "War of Monuments" in Estonia'. *Nationalities Papers* 36(3) (2008), 425–48.

Burch, Stuart, and David J. Smith. 'Empty Spaces and the Value of Symbols: Estonia's "War of Monuments" from Another Angle'. *Europe-Asia Studies* 59(6) (2007), 913–36.

European Commission. *Agenda 2000: For a Stronger and Wider Union: Bulletin of the European Union*. Supplement 5/97, 1997.

Freeman, Colin et al. 'NATO and Russia Hold Rival Military Exercises on Estonian Border'. *The Telegraph*, 25 February 2015, https://www.telegraph.co.uk/news/worldnews/europe/estonia/11435698/Nato-and-Russia-hold-rival-military-exercises-on-Estonian-border.html.Hashimoto, Nobuya. 'Maneuvering Memories of Dictatorship and Conflicts: The Baltic States, Central and Eastern Europe, and Russia', in Paul Corner and Jie-Hyun Lim (eds), *The Palgrave Handbook of Mass Dictatorship* (London: Palgrave Macmillan, 2016).

Heidenhain, Stephan. 'The Activities of the OSCE on Citizenship, Statelessness and Language Issues until 2002 in Estonia and Latvia and their Impact until Now', in Nobuya Hahsimoto et al. (eds), *A Collection of Papers on the History and Today's Situation of Russian-Speaking Population in Estonia and Latvia: From the View Point of the Contemporary History of European Integration and Formation of Multi-Ethnic Society* (Higashi Hiroshima: Hiroshima University, 2005).

Issakov, Sergei G. 'Gorod s udivitel'noi sud'boi'. *Tallinn* 8–9 (1997).
———. *Ocherki istorii russkoi kul'tury v Estonii.* Tallinn: Aleksandra, 2005.
———. *Put' Dlinnoyu v Tyshachu Let: Russkie v Estonii, Istoria Kul'tury.* Tallinn: Chast' Pervaya, 2008.
Jauhiainen, Jussi S., and Tarmo Pikner. 'Narva–Ivangorod: Integrating and Disintegrating Transboundary Water Networks and Infrastructure'. *Journal of Baltic Studies* 40(3) (2009).
Juske, Jaak. *Khronika zabytoi Narvy* [Lood unustanud Narvast/Chronicle of forgotten Narva]. Narva: Hea Lugu, 2015.
Kaiser, Robert, and Elena Nikiforova. 'The Performativity of Scale: The Social Construction of Scale Effects in Narva, Estonia'. *Environment and Planning D: Society and Space* 26 (2008), 537–62.
Kattago, Siobhan. 'Commemorating Liberation and Occupation: War Memorials along the Road to Narva', in Jörg Hackmann and Marko Lehti (eds), *Contested and Shared Places of Memory: History and Politics in North Eastern Europe* (London: Routledge, 2013).
Kivimäe, Jüri. 'Medieval Narva: Featuring a Small Town between East and West', in Karsten Brüggemann (ed.), *Narva und die Ostseeregion/Narva and the Baltic Sea Region* (Narva: Narva Kolledž, 2004).
Kolstø, Pål. *Russians in the Former Soviet Republics.* Bloomington, IN: Indiana University Press, 1995.
———. 'Symbol of the War – But Which One? The St George Ribbon in Russian Nation-Building'. *Slavonic & East European Review* 94(4) (2016), 660–701.
Kostyashov, Yurii V. *Sekretnaya istoriia Kaliningradskoi oblasti: Ocherki 1945–1956 gg.* Kaliningrad: Terra Baltika, 2009.
———. *Povsednevnost' poslevoennoi derevni: Iz istorii pereselencheskikh kolkhozov Kaliningradskoi oblasti 1946–1953 gg.* Moscow: ROSSPEN, 2015.
Laar, Mart, Urmas Ott and Sirje Endre. *Teine Eesti: Eesti iseseivuse taassünd, 1986–1991.* Tallinn: SE & JS, 1996.
Lenin, V. I. *Lenin Polnoe Sobranie Sochinenie (Izdanie Pyatoe)*, vol. 39. Moscow: Politicheskaya Literatury, 1981, 339–71.
Martinez, Francisco. *Remains of the Soviet Past in Estonia: An Anthropology of Forgetting, Repair and Urban Traces.* London: UCL Press, 2018.
Medijainen, Eero. 'The Tartu Peace Treaty and Permanent Neutrality for Estonia', in Eero Medijainen and Olaf Mertelsmann (eds), *Border Changes in 20th Century Europe: Selected Case Studies,* Münster: Lit Verlag, 2010.
Mertelsmann, Olaf. 'Die Herausbildung des Sonderstatus der Nordostregion innerhalb der Estnischen SSR', in Karsten Brüggemann (ed.), *Narva und die Ostseeregion/Narva and the Baltic Sea Region* (Narva: Narva Kolledž, 2004).
———. 'The Disappearance of a Border and Incorporation into the USSR', in Eero Medijainen and Olaf Mertelsmann (eds), *Border Changes in 20th Century Europe: Selected Case Studies,* Münster: Lit Verlag, 2010.
Ministry of Education and Research, Summary of Ministry of Education and Research's Annual Report for 2018, Tartu: Ministry of Education and Research, 2019.
Mitte-eestlaste integratsiooni Sihtasutus, *Õppekavaarendustöö koolis: vahekokkuvõtteid arendustööst ja eestikeelse õppe laiendamisesti,* Tallinn: Mitte eestlaste integratsiooni Sihiasutus, 2004.
'Narva Arvudes 2012/Narva in Figures 2012', Narva, 2012, lk.7, http://web.narva.ee/files/5620.pdf.
'Narva in Figures, 2017'. http://www.narva.ee/en/left_block/narva_in_figures/page:3543.

Neukirch, Claus. 'Russia and the OSCE: The Influence of Interested Third and Disinterested Fourth Parties on the Conflicts in Estonia and Moldova', in Pål Kolstø (ed.), *National Integration and Violent Conflict in Post-Soviet Societies: The Cases of Estonia and Moldova* (Lanham, MD: Rowman & Littlefield, 2003).

Nikiforova, Elena. 'On Victims and Heroes: (Re)Assembling World War II Memory in the Border City of Narva', in Julie Fedor et al. (eds), *War and Memory in Russia, Ukraine and Belarus* (London: Palgrave Macmillan, 2017).

Petrov, A. V. *Gorod Narva: Ego Proshloe i Dostoprimechatel'nosti v Svyazi s Istoriei Uprocheniya russkogo gospodstva nd Baltiiskom Poberedg'e 1223–1900*. Saint Petersburg: Tipografiya Ministerstva Vnutrennykh Del, 1901.

Pfoser, Alena. 'Nested Peripheralisation: Remaking the East–West Border in the Russian–Estonian Borderland'. *East European Politics and Societies* 31(1) (2017), 26–43.

Rofer, Cheryl K., and Tõnis Kaasik (eds). *Turning a Problem into a Resource: Remediation and Waste Management at the Sillamäe Site, Estonia*. Dordrecht: Kluwer Academic Publishers, 1998.

Russian World Foundation, https://russkiymir.ru/en/fund/decree.php.

Smith, David J. 'Narva Region within the Estonian Republic: From Autonomism to Accommodation?' *Regional & Federal Studies* 12(2) (2002), 89–110.

Smith, David J., and Stuart Burch. 'Enacting Identities in the EU-Russia Borderland: An Ethnography of Place and Public Monuments'. *East European Politics and Societies* 26(2) (2012), 400–24.

Smolokurov, A., 'Narvskoe gorodskoe samoupravlenie', in: *Sbornik Narvskogo Muzeya. 1999g.*, Narva:Narve Museum, 1999, 4–23.

———. 'Narodonaselenie Narvy: Demograficheskii obzor istorii roroda', in *Sbornik Narvskogo Muzeya. 2000g.*, Narva: Narva Museum, 2000, 15–65.

Statistics Estonia, Rahvastik maakondades ja linnades, 1922, https://www.stat.ee/et/rahvastik-maakondades-ja-linnades-1922.

Statistics Estonia, Rahvastik maakondades ja linnades, 1934, https://www.stat.ee/et/rahvastik-maakondades-ja-linnades-1934.

Tammaru, Tiit. *Venelased Eestis: Ränne ja kohanemine*. Tallinn: Sisekaitseakadeemia, 1999.

Välismaalaste seadus (9 December 2009). https://www.riigiteataja.ee/akt/119032019083.

Välismaalasele rahvusvahelise kaitse andmise seadus (14 December 2005). https://www.riigiteataja.ee/akt/113032019195.

Vseviov, David. *Kirde-Eesti urbaanse anomaalia kujunemine ning struktuur pärast teist maailmasõda*. Tallinn: Tallinn Pedagogical University, 2002.

Weiss-Wendt, Anton. 'Komu prinadlezhit Narva? K voprosu o territorial'no-administrativnoi prinadlezhnosti goroda 1858–1917 gg.', in I. Belobrovtseva (ed.), *Baltiiskii Arkhiv*, vol. 3 (Tallinn: Avenarius, 1997).

Yapici, Utku. 'Is Narva the Next? The Intra-Regional Limits of Russian Diffusion in Estonia'. *Uluslararası Sosyal Araştırmalar Dergisi/The Journal of International Social Research* 10(54) (2017), 381–92.

Zelnik, Reginald E. *Law and Disorder on the Narova River: The Kreenholm Strike of 1872*. Berkeley, CA: University of California Press, 1995.

———. 'Russian Workers and Revolution', in Dominic Lieven (ed.), *The Cambridge History of Russia: Volume 2, Imperial Russia, 1689–1917* (Cambridge: Cambridge University Press, 2006).

Brokgauz i Efron Entsiklopedicheskii Slobal'. Vol., 40, Saint Petersburg, Brokgauz i Efron, 1890.

The Chronicle of Novgorod, 1016–1471, trans. Robert Michell and Nevill Forbes, with an introduction by C. Raymond Beazley and an account of the text by A. A. Shakhmatov. London: Offices of the Society, 1914.

Part IV

BORDERS AND FOOD CLASSIFICATION

LORETTA KIM AND ILARIA PORCIANI

Chapters 7 and 8 discuss the establishment and maintenance of borders between cultures in two case studies of food classification. Both chapters concentrate on cuisines that are often overlooked in the geographical and social regions where they originate because they are associated with minority populations. The questions raised in these chapters about 'food heritage' in Istria, a peninsula in the Adriatic Sea now divided into the political areas of Croatia, Slovenia and Italy, and the corresponding concept of 'food customs' in north-eastern China shed light on how culturally marginalized groups ensure that their ways of life are sustained, even as their members become more integrated into the mainstream societies of the modern nations in which they exist.

In Chapter 7, Loretta Kim examines how heritage, as embodied in food culture, distinguishes the 'cuisine systems' of Han culinary tradition from those of 'food customs' practised by ethnic minorities in north-eastern China. In the People's Republic of China (PRC), ethnicity was a key marker of collective and individual identity during the 1950s through the 1970s, when extensive state-sponsored research was conducted to classify people into one of fifty-six ethnic groups. Since an ongoing period of economic reform started in the 1980s, ethnicity has mattered less to PRC citizens as gradually more ethnic minority persons have adopted customs associated with the Han ethnic majority. However, ethnicity remains a tool for the PRC state to assert that it is a polyethnic country and that ethnic minorities are still different from the ethnic majority. Kim argues that as borderlands and non-Han peoples have become less (or non-) problematic elements of the modern Chinese nation and its sovereign space, academic conceptions of non-Han cultures in the PRC, which affirm official political doctrine, have become less essentialized and acknowledge the cultural diversity within these cultural groups.

On a very different scale, Ilaria Porciani focuses on other kinds of borderlands in Chapter 8: on the one hand, those which delimit the tiny Istrian peninsula protruding into the north-eastern Mediterranean, and the Italian population living there; on the other, the imaginary borders drawn by Italians living in Istria until the Second World War who experienced forced migration and diaspora after the war. Food has been used and interpreted as an identity marker of this dispersed community. The strong emotional meaning at stake, however, overshadowed the fact that 'Istrian' cuisine was extremely hybrid, and its recipes can hardly be defined as 'Italian'. Porciani argues that the discursive practice of many memory books, as well as of recipe books, has followed the lines of banal nationalism and set aside the constant porosity of the area's cultural borders over time, thus being silent on the gastronomical hybridism fundamental to that area. Moreover, the reconstruction of an *Istrian cuisine* overshadowed other kinds of border: social ones.

CHAPTER 7

The Way We Eat

Evolving Taxonomies of Non-Han Food Customs in North-Eastern China

LORETTA KIM

Introduction

In 2006, the national-level Minority Press in Beijing published the *Annals of Chinese Ethnic Minority Customs* (*Zhongguo shaoshu minzu fengsu zhi*, ZSMF), an 1,892-page reference work.[1] Mao Gongning, the chief editor of this book, belongs to the Zhuang ethnic group, and is a Chinese Communist Party member and senior researcher in the State Ethnic Affairs Commission (SEAC). The text includes one chapter each for all fifty-five officially recognized ethnic minority groups, including the Zhuang.[2] The quantity of information about each group varies, but each chapter includes sections about clothing, food and beverages, architecture, social organization and spiritual beliefs. It is as yet unmatched in length and scope as a comprehensive source of knowledge about the contemporary cultures of the PRC's ethnic minorities. Regarding ethnic minority food customs, the 2001 *Encyclopedia of Chinese Ethnic Minorities' Food Customs* (*Zhongguo shaoshu minzu yinshi wenhua huicui*, ZSYH) provides more detailed descriptions for each group.[3]

The average reader of the ZSMF is likely to believe that all the content is accurate and unproblematic. The editorial group, headed by Mao, does not purport to analyse or interpret any of the subject matter. Presentation of facts is the main and arguably sole objective of the compilation. Most of the details are stated in an ahistorical manner. Some citations for specific sources of evidence provide contextual details about when a particular custom began to be practised. However, there is no systematic attempt to explain the development of most attributes, whether through historical chronology or discrete comparison of contemporary (as of 2006) forms with earlier ones. The reader must accept that the customs, as they are described, comprise the material and intangible cultures of these groups, and assume that most, if not all, members of such groups perform such practices.

From a scholarly view, this kind of text provokes many questions. Most ethnic groups in the contemporary PRC, including the Han, are not concentrated solely in one geographic area and therefore cannot theoretically practise the same material culture wherever they are located because of disparate physical environments and natural resources. Therefore, it is problematic to consider one set of traits as fitting all members of the group. Both the ZSMF and ZSYH contain some references to the existence of subgroups within an ethnically defined population and to the fact that some customs are unique to one or more, but not all, of those subgroups. For example, both publications differentiate between the foods eaten by the ethnic Hui people living in Gansu and Qinghai provinces in north-western China and those of Hui who live in parts of north-eastern China like Liaoning province. Although the disparities within the Hui ethnic group are described, these texts convey very little information about how these Hui subgroups share common traits with other ethnic groups who live around them in these geographically distant areas. The relative dearth of such details about how Hui people have adapted their cultural traits, based not only on where they are located but also who influences them as co-resident members of a local community, results in inaccurate perceptions of how such customs are actually practised.

Adopting approaches to investigating food customs that emphasize both the similarities and differences not only between subgroups of one ethnic group but also between two or more ethnic groups, this chapter explores the meanings and limitations of ethnic classification and cultural taxonomy in modern and contemporary China, as evident in works like the ZSMF and ZSYH, through an analysis of how customs related to food are described as 'food customs' for ethnic minority groups in north-eastern China. The term 'cultural taxonomy' as applied in this chapter adopts some but not all elements of the concept as formulated by Geert Hofstede. From Hofstede's five dimensions of culture, this study investigates individualism versus collectivism and the long-term versus short-term orientation of cultural values and practice.[4] Adopting Hofstede's definition of 'culture' as 'the collective programming of the mind that distinguishes the members of one group or category of people from another',[5] I use the phrase 'cultural taxonomy' to describe the approach of classifying elements of culture within purposefully developed categories. I also note here that north-eastern China is an area that varies in scope by historical period and definition by political, economic, social and cultural criteria. For this research, I use 'north-eastern China' to describe areas corresponding to present-day Liaoning province, Jilin province, Heilongjiang province and the eastern subregions of the Inner Mongolia Autonomous Region.

I argue that as the Chinese state has gained full political control over north-eastern China, which is a political and social borderland, the cultures of ethnic minority populations, which I will refer to as non-Han peoples henceforth, have become *less* essentialized and, like conceptions of the majority Han ethnic group, are construed with greater recognition of internal diversity and place-based differences.[6] Texts like the ZSMF and ZSYH may serve the political objective of promoting the PRC as a polyethnic state, but they are becoming relics of intellectual and popular understandings about ethnicity and an exclusive and static kind of identity that have now given way to perceptions of non-Han groups as populations that are internally diverse due to regional and local differences, like the Han ethnic group. However, non-Han groups are still marginalized by conventional taxonomies such as the 'cuisine system' classification of China's food customs. Moreover, as introduced with the example of the Hui ethnic group above, I believe that food customs are subject to continual change in response to different social and economic circumstances. I therefore adopt the conceptual lens of gastronomical hybridism that Ilaria Porciani introduces and applies to food heritage in Istria in her chapter of this book.

I choose food customs as the trait of taxonomy because many non-Han people today do not express other characteristics that are often associated with ethnicity, such as language, religion and social organization, that distinguish them from Han people. Food customs and clothing remain two ways that non-Han people practise their cultural identities with varying degrees of regularity. Eating and wearing things with ethnic attributes enhances the solidarity among members of an ethnic group and also set them apart as ethnic minorities.[7] As will be discussed in the next section of this chapter, the term 'food customs' refers to a set of ways of preparing and consuming food. Similarly, 'cuisine' will be discussed in the most general sense of foods prepared according to particular methods with ingredients and seasonings that associate them with particular groups of consumers.[8] Connecting food customs and ethnicity with borders determined by geography and culture, the three overarching questions of this analysis are: 1) What is ethnic food in modern and contemporary China?

2) What is ethnic minority food in north-eastern China? and 3) Why are ethnic minority means of producing food considered 'food customs' and not cuisine systems like Han food?

To answer these questions, I examine patterns and comparisons in the evidence about non-Han food customs. To investigate the reasoning for why certain foods are associated with specific groups, this chapter begins in the next section with a discussion of food customs and cuisines as applicable to China broadly, and then an overview of ethnic history and identity in modern China. Then the chapter progresses to two parts about the social and cultural frontiers as reflected in China's food history. The first part explains the general evolution of how knowledge about food customs in north-eastern China, as observed and evaluated from the civilizational heartland, has developed from essentialized concepts that reflect the highly limited scope of information about this frontier borderland to the current recognition – which we may see to some degree in publications like the ZSMF and ZSYH – that non-Han culture evolves just like Han culture. The second part then examines how Han and non-Han food customs are differentiated in the context of north-eastern China through comparison with one another.

Food Customs and Cuisine Systems

Examining the food customs of ethnic minority groups is inherently challenging in ways that Mao's encyclopedia of customs does not reveal or address. The first obstacle to systematic investigation is that most non-Han groups have not maintained recipes that have been transmitted in writing.[9] The lack of recipes compiled in collections ('cookbooks') or embedded in texts of other sorts stems from several factors, including the relatively low rate of literacy until the establishment of public schools and compulsory education in the mid- to late twentieth century. Other reasons for which written recipes cannot serve as a rational way to study food customs are that most non-Han groups in China cook and eat by sensory habit rather than by quantitative prescription and formulaic combination of ingredients. This is also true of the Han ethnic majority, but recipes for Han food have been well documented for much of China's history.

Han culinary culture may be described as 'food customs' but is more frequently referred to in terms of 'cuisine systems'. There is no absolute consensus on what constitutes a 'cuisine system' in Chinese culture, but the conventional understanding is that Han people in each region of China, defined primarily by geographical but also economic and social boundaries, have different tastes and thus prefer to prepare foods using particular ingredients and methods according to the resources available, climate and dietary needs as determined by the precepts of traditional Chinese medicine of their locales.

Eight regional cuisine systems still form the indisputable canon of Chinese culinary tradition, but other cuisines receive lesser acknowledgement in varying degrees.[10] The most fundamental categorization is based on relative directional parameters: north, south, east and west, represented by Lu (Shandong province), Yue (Guangdong province), Huaiyang (central region of Jiangsu province) and Chuan (Sichuan province) as the four great culinary traditions.[11] Expanding to cuisine systems that receive acknowledgement throughout and outside China as the 'modern eight cuisine systems', the list includes the Lu, Yue and Chuan, as well as the Hui (Anhui province), Min (Fujian province), Xiang (Hunan province), Su (a more comprehensive scope of Jiangsu province food than Huaiyang cuisine) and Zhe (Zhejiang province). Conspicuously absent among these categories are borderland regions like Guizhou and Yunnan province, northern and western locales like Tibet, and the three north-eastern Chinese provinces of Liaoning, Heilongjiang and Jilin.

As cookbooks published for both Chinese and non-Chinese audiences show, Chinese cuisine systems or cultural cuisines are subject to varying definitions.[12] A cookbook published in 1976 by the Wei-chuan Foods Corporation based in Taipei is divided into categories by primary ingredient, such as chicken, vegetable and bean curd. Each individual dish is identified by cuisine system, such as the 'Seven-star Appetizer Plate' as 'Sichuan [cuisine]' and 'Stir-fried Chicken Shreds with Bean Sprouts' as 'Peking [cuisine]'.[13] The book also includes recipes that are classified as 'Cantonese [cuisine]', 'Shanghai [cuisine]', 'Hunan [cuisine]' and 'Taiwanese [cuisine]'. These categories differ slightly but meaningfully from the five/eight major cuisine systems introduced previously.

Cuisine system or cultural cuisine also matters in dissimilar ways for cookbooks intended for primarily or exclusively Chinese readers, many of which concentrate on one type of cuisine system as the subject of a whole book. This emphasis on the uniqueness of each cuisine system is different from publications for non-Chinese readers that recognize 'regional' or 'provincial' characteristics but nevertheless use these as subdivisions for comprehensive anthologies of recipes.[14] However, in most cookbooks, non-Han foods are not included, implying that they do not belong to any Chinese cuisine system or cultural cuisine.[15]

References to non-Han foods in documentary records before the twentieth century describe them in simpler terms than for Han food customs and cuisines. Non-Han foods are not appraised in gastronomic ways for the quality of their taste and the culinary skills required to produce them, but are just described by the ingredients they contain and the ways in which these ingredients are combined through basic cooking methods such as roasting, boiling and mixing. They are not evaluated according to sophisticated criteria of 'color, flavor, and taste'.[16] Non-Han foods are furthermore described with less regard for differentiating what is more or less prestigious to consume. The ostensible lack of hierarchical classification may also contribute to the perceptions that non-Han foods do not form proper cultural repertoires like Han cuisine systems.[17]

Although not recognized as cuisine systems by conventional understanding, some non-Han food customs are well known outside of the north-eastern China region. Manchu culture, by virtue of its history as the core culture of the Qing dynasty (1644–1912) imperial elite, has both signature dishes and subdivisions in culinary tradition. Manchu cuisine has its own history, starting with evidence of the Sushen people, who appeared in historical records starting in the sixth century BCE, but its verifiable development took place during the Qing period, along with that of Manchu language, religion and material culture like clothing. Foods such as *sacima* (pastries made of crystal sugar, butter and white flour) and *bobo* (steamed cakes made of various grain flours and bean pastes) are widely known as 'Manchu'. By contrast, relatively few Chinese recognize the Heje ethnonym and even within their home region, Heje cultural characteristics are generally unfamiliar to Han people.[18] Heje people cook a dish known in Heje as *talke* (transliterated in Chinese as *talake'a* or *ta'erka*, and called *sha sheng yu* in Chinese), which is made by mixing raw fish meat with julienned potatoes that have been blanched in hot water, bean sprouts and chives.[19] In Vera Y. N. Hsu and Francis L. K. Hsu's paradigmatic study about food in modern north China, the term 'Manchuria' arises, but there are no specific references to the non-Han peoples or foods of this region. Both well-known groups such as the Manchu or relatively unknown ones like the Heje are absent in this study.[20] Such exclusion reflects how in the Chinese (or Han) imagination, non-Han foods do not belong to any Chinese cuisine system but also do not constitute cuisine systems of their own.[21]

Ethnicity as a Regional, Social and Cultural Identity Marker in Modern China

Distinctions between Han and non-Han cultures continue to exist as popular stereotypes and intellectual conceptions for many reasons, among which is the vast and ostensibly irreparable disparity in the quantities of documented evidence about Han and non-Han groups. Moreover, many extant sources of information about non-Han peoples are texts generated by Han authors who treat non-Han cultural practices first and foremost as subjects to be rationalized rather than as records of lived experiences. In the present, Han attitudes towards non-Han cultures are changing to be more objective and less hierarchical, eschewing received wisdom that Han have always been more civilized than non-Han. However, the truth remains that most non-Han ethnic groups, with some notable exceptions like Mongols, Tibetans and Koreans, have highly limited written historical records. Taking the example of Chinese culinary history, Endymion Wilkinson identified four individuals as China's classical gastronomes: Yuan Mei (1716–97), Su Shi (1037–1101), Ni Zan (1301–74) and Xu Wei (1521–93).[22] All these men would self-identify and be identified according to the social classification schemes of their times as Han. Looking more broadly at the pantheon of contributors to the Chinese epicurean canon, only one person, known as Hu Sihui (life and death years unverified), the author of *Important Principles of Food and Drink* (*Yinshan zhengyao*), was indisputably non-Han.[23]

A profound turning point in the centuries-long division between written texts produced by Han people about non-Han populations and orally transmitted 'insider' knowledge about non-Han cultures, particularly material customs, within their native groups occurred in the midtwentieth century. Coinciding with its measures to consolidate interstate borders and to claim territories that sought autonomy was the PRC government's Ethnic Identification Project that started officially in 1954.[24] To assess the political, economic, social and cultural traits of non-Han groups in various locales, teams of CCP cadres and researchers without official positions conducted social history surveys. These surveys yielded information that is inherently problematic because the investigations were explicitly motivated by political objectives of precise (but ultimately imperfect) ethnic classification and economic development in line with socialist ideology.[25] Despite the bias embedded in the resulting publications, favouring the cadre observers who wrote the survey reports and giving limited voice to the persons studied, these works are useful for understanding what criteria mattered for defining ethnicity and distinguishing ethnic identity from other markers of individual and collective identity. This chapter considers evidence from select social history surveys from the 1950s to the 1990s, as well as earlier texts that represent the governmental perspective, such as officially compiled gazetteers, and evidence from non-official sources, such as private memoirs and texts for a popular readership.

One factor affecting the choice of sources consulted and discussed is that food customs have not always been recorded for these groups, whether by the producers or consumers of the foods. The information documented and remaining in extant records reflects who interacted with or was actively monitored by governments or non-official observers, like travellers. Until the mid-twentieth century, ethnological research was not conducted in a systematic way by state authorities or other institutional bodies. In the twentieth century, such research became part of both official and non-official agendas, but still depended on the interests of the individual or collective record keepers.

In the 1950 and 1960s, when state-sponsored ethnography was intended to be exhaustive, food customs were significantly not mentioned in published survey reports for groups in north-eastern China that are conventionally known as 'advanced'. Social history surveys about Manchus and Mongols did not include as many details about 'food-shelter-clothing-transport', 'material culture' or 'lifestyle' as did those about the Daur, Ewenki, Heje and Orochen groups.[26] Similarly, in a 1959 social history survey about Koreans in Heilongjiang province, no section refers to food customs or other forms of material culture. This survey assesses new modes of governance, economic development, flourishing cultural activities and education, and the advancement of socialism in Korean communities.[27] One explanation would be that the state already had enough evidence on other grounds to confer official recognition to the Manchu, Mongol and Korean groups – not surprisingly all populations with textual records in their own languages and substantial numbers of representatives in political organs. Another reason is that the state could not distinguish among smaller populations, especially those that would use a variety of names to identify themselves. Therefore, it conducted surveys to pinpoint traits that would signify differences among these groups.

All ethnic groups in modern China, including the Han majority, are by principle artificial because they were established as legal categories rather than ones representing fully discrete social and cultural identities.[28] Many of these groups are amalgamations of populations that identify themselves as unique from one another. Many groups in north-eastern China, as in other parts of the PRC, did not receive political recognition but nevertheless claim heritage and cultural differences that set them apart from Han people. Therefore, non-Han populations that are now considered legal ethnic minorities claim traits as one way to aggregate and preserve social and cultural capital.[29] Although these groups do not necessarily agree with the PRC central government's definitions of how they are and how they have been socially classified, many of them accept that they must identify themselves according to such standards, especially when interacting with people who are not of their groups.[30] Establishing and confirming their cultural characteristics also plays the vital function of maintaining social coherence, which is often threatened by the overwhelming benefits of assimilating to a society that places primacy on Han, or more broadly Hua (Chinese), identity.

Both a cause and effect of how fluid social and cultural identities have become in contemporary China has been the fact that the meaning of ethnicity varies for ethnic minorities in the PRC, from those who are socially indistinguishable because they 'look and act Han' to those who are extremely visible as minorities or sociocultural 'Others' because they 'do not look or act Han'.[31] Even those who attempt to be recognized as Han for general social interaction face stereotypes that pose some disadvantages. Food is no exception. As Wu Xu has argued, although Han people are fascinated by the foods, particularly the ingredients, of ethnic minority groups, such foods are frequently regarded as an 'unusual taste' and, even when presented in sanitized forms, such as in 'farmer's joy' restaurants that emphasize the health benefits of consuming locally and organically farmed goods, may be treated as inferior to Han foods.[32] The label of 'ethnic minority food' can also be a factor in (as well as a consequence of) the expectation of lower quality.

North-eastern China is a significant case study for several reasons. The classification of non-Han peoples in north-eastern China, as it has been variably defined in history, as 'borderland populations' affects the region's social and cultural identity to this day. The Sino-Russian border changed several times prior to the twentieth century, and because the interstate border is not a perfect delineation between distinct social and cultural groups, the term 'borderland' applies primarily to the period after treaties that established and modified the border as a tangible boundary. Some scholars have therefore emphasized that north-eastern China should be studied as a region with its own history rather than just as a borderland between two or more states.[33] North-eastern China is also unique because it has not been a politically sensitive region since the 1950s, because there are no ethnic groups that seek greater autonomy or full independence from the PRC central government. However, it is still a place where ethnic diversity is evident. The active and sustained expressions of ethnic differences is interesting because the number of non-Han citizens is relatively small, especially when assessed by ethnic group. Moreover, many people in the region claim heritage from two or more ethnic groups, or by blood quantum calculate their identities in fractions or percentages. Yet even with intermarriage and the consequent standardization of language and material customs in the direction of Han Chinese or 'mainstream' society, non-Han people in north-eastern China generally feel free to identify themselves openly by their ethnic identities, rather than trying to 'pass' or be recognized as Han people.

Table 7.1. 2010 comprehensive official census figures of principal ethnic groups in north-eastern China (all figures refer to the number of persons).

	Heilongjiang	Jilin	Liaoning	Whole Country
Ewenki	2,648	104	448	30,875
Han	36,939,181	25,267,110	37,103,174	1,220,844,520
Heje	3,613	212	154	5,354
Hui	101,749	118,799	245,798	10,586,087
Kyrgyz	1,431	36	125	186,708
Korean	327,806	1,040,167	239,537	1,830,929
Manchu	748,020	866,365	5,336,895	10,387,958
Mongol	125,483	145,039	657,869	5,981,840
Orochen	3,943	111	196	8,659
Russian	312	48	185	15,393
Sibe	7,608	3,113	132,431	190,481

Source: PRC State Council Population Census Office (Guowuyuan renkou pucha bangongshi) and PRC Department of Population and Employment Statistics, National Bureau of Statistics (Guojia tongji ju renkou he jiuye tongji si), *Zhongguo 2010 nian renkou pucha ziliao*, vol. 1, 35–36, 38–39, 45, 48, 50, 52–53.

Non-Han Food Customs in North-Eastern China as Boundaries between Heartland and Borderland

Food customs, like other elements of culture, have been historical markers differentiating the Han-inhabited 'heartland' and non-Han-inhabited 'borderland' in the Chinese space. Prior to the Ming dynasty (1368–1644), there are relatively few texts about the non-Han communities that lived in the area to be known as north-eastern China from the Qing dynasty onward. Chinese-language records describing such groups have a lot of similar content, which may be due to the practice of quoting and thereby transmitting knowledge from precedent works. Starting in the Ming period, texts such as the *Comprehensive Records of the Universe* (*Huanyu tongzhi*) started to describe regions that were both on the geographical and sociocultural margins of the Chinese state with more consideration for knowledge that was acquired through exploration rather than repetition.[34] Ming and Qing-era works like the *Qing Imperial Album of Tributaries* (*Huang Qing zhigong tu*), like earlier texts, reflect a highly limited scope of knowledge, whether because the imperial gaze on 'barbarians' in peripheral places required that such peoples be depicted in particular ways to stress their simple, inferior (to Han) natures, or, as Laura Hostetler argues, because first-hand observation as the source of ethnographical information was a relatively new methodology and many groups were literally observed for the first time.³⁵ The Qing regime brought the Heilongjiang, Jilin and Liaodong areas decisively into its political and economic fold, an arguably unprecedented achievement for a Chinese empire. With those places on its officially commissioned maps and military personnel conducting routine surveys of their inhabitants, the north-east emerged ever more clearly in state-commissioned gazetteers and visiting literati's travelogues alike. We see in the *Qing Imperial Album of Tributaries*, for example, that there were just seven entries about north-eastern groups. The Orochen were described as people who 'raise deer and catch fish', with the implication that they ate those animals.³⁶ For other peoples, like four groups that would eventually all be recognized as 'Heje', the type and specificity of details vary. The Kilen 'catch fish', and the Fiyaka 'fish and hunt'.³⁷ The same text describes the Kiyakara as 'spearing fish and hunting (game) with bow and arrow' and the Heje (the same ethnonym as the contemporary group) as 'fishing [no method indicated] and hunting with bow and arrow'.³⁸ These descriptions of livelihood are simultaneously indirect references to the groups' food customs and more precise explanations than older, vaguer depictions of barbarians as eating too much meat (and not enough grain) and hunting and gathering in a primitive way (rather than engaging in agriculture).

As investigations of society and culture on the regional and local scales became increasingly possible due to adequate resources for documentation, starting in the nineteenth century and continuing into the twentieth, non-Han foods became known by ingredient categories such as the grains, meats, vegetables and fruits they contained. We can think of such classification as related to the inventories of 'native produce' that became important for the economic and social reputations of places. Song Xiaolian (1863–1926), an official who served both the Qing and Republican governments in Heilongjiang, wrote in his investigative report of the Hulun region about its indigenous wildlife, with culinary references. He pointed out which birds were delicious, such as the Argun River teal, mountain hawk-eagle, white-naped crane and sand grouse, and which were formerly sought after as imperial tribute items, such as the hazel grouse.³⁹ Song's record does not mention who ate these birds, but just that they were commonly consumed in the area.

In another example, which is contemporaneous to Song's work, Claude Madrolle (1870–1949) emphasizes the differences among different aboriginal groups by what they eat in his observations:

> The Ghiliak, a fisherman feeding only on fish, curiously dressed in salmon or seal skin, lives in summer in a hut on piles. The Tungus, a hunter, eats the flesh of the strangest animals, fits supple peltry to his body and transports with ease his little conical tent, which is covered in winter with skin and in

summer with birch bark. The Mongol, pastoral, lives chiefly by dairying, milk and its derivatives, even fermented, butter, cheese, koumis and airek, to which he sometimes adds the fleas of his sheep; his loose fitting clothes, high-boots and the whip in his hand, betoken the horseman; his collapsible yourta, whose flaps are kept down by camel-hair ropes and cover a firm trellis-work, is the typical habitation in the steppes when winter is severe. The Chinese, by his ill-chosen dietary but careful cooking, his costume elaborate by the multiplicity of garments, his house religiously planned and decorated, with its solid framework and its carved wood-work, its glazed tiles, paper window panes and khan heating apparatus, brings us face to face with a very rich domesticated life where all the material inventions of an ancient sedentary people have accumulated.[40]

Another lens that was applied in ethnographic literature in the transitional period from empire to republic was what people in the borderland did *not* like to eat, such as Song Xiaolian noting that Mongols do not catch the fish abundantly present in the Argun River.[41] Charles H. Hawes (1867–1943), an English anthropologist, likewise identified some cases of people not taking advantage of their natural environment, which could provide certain food resources, such as Russians eschewing mutton despite having access to flocks of sheep.[42] The subtext of these details is that these (non-Han) borderland people did not follow what Han people would consider the proper utilization of local, abundant resources in their food economies. While contrasting with Ilaria Porciani's evaluation of how Istrian cuisine was borne out of a competition for food resources that pitted peoples and their cuisines against each other, discussion of the 'waste' of indigenous flora and fauna serves as a cultural commentary that elevates the civilized heartland over the borderland.

Food Customs as Boundaries between Han and Non-Han Cultures

From the mid-twentieth century, ethnic identity and culture became predominant classifying markers that have largely supplanted the 'borderland' and 'heartland' lenses. As interstate borders have become indisputable, and successive waves of migration from Shandong and other provinces in the nineteenth and early twentieth centuries have decisively generated a native Han majority population, north-eastern China has become a geographical borderland but a Han-dominated social region. Applying terms that are rooted in Han culture, non-Han food customs in north-eastern China have been described in post-1949 records with food categories such as 'staple foods' and 'supplementary foods'. Within these categories, foods are further classified by type, such as how they are cooked or for what purposes they are consumed. Such analytical arrangements allow for more acknowledgement of both the effects of macro- and micro-changes in food custom, and regional preferences affected by environmental factors. There is also more consciousness about food customs, as in the social and cultural rituals of eating, such as the 'Manchu-Han banquet': this both encompasses foods that are typically prepared for such a meal – which originated from sumptuous repasts at the imperial palace – and also delineates which foods are to be considered 'Manchu' and those that are likewise regarded as 'Han'.[43]

Adaptations to changes in habitat have been reflected in descriptions of food customs since the 1950s. North-eastern China's Indigenous populations, as seen in the *Qing Imperial Album of Tributaries* examples, are known as hunters of game and gatherers of wild (uncultivated) plants. But the conversion of their livelihoods to the simultaneous practices of hunting and agriculture in the nineteenth and twentieth centuries changed their diets, and with more people relying on jobs other than the direct production of food, food customs have become more similar to those of people in other parts of China.

The same principles of culture adapting to the natural environment and human-generated technology is evident for grain-based staples like rice and noodles. Prior to the twenty-first century, Chinese people consumed more noodles in regions where wheat was easier to grow (compared to other grain-bearing plants), and the same held true for Chinese who ate rice because it was the principal crop. Now, Chinese throughout the PRC, irrespective of ethnicity and location, can eat rice and noodles according to what they can afford to purchase, and if their budgets permit them to buy either, their personal tastes. Supermarkets and scientific intervention in the late twentieth and twenty-first centuries have blurred the boundaries between rice and noodle-eating groups as being defined by terrain and climate. Applying the idea that humans have altered the distribution of resources more broadly to all types of food, we can conclude that 'traditional' recipes are only accurate to a point, and are hard to preserve perfectly because both ingredients and their relative availability change.

Another element affecting the evolution of food customs to consider, particularly for north-eastern China, is the inherent ambiguity of identities in a borderland or frontier region because of interaction and acculturation among groups that may have different origins, but live in proximity and in interdependent configurations. There has always been significant mobility across the sociopolitical borders between China, Siberia and the Korean peninsula. Contact through food was crucial for establishing and maintaining cooperative relations between peoples. In one illustrative moment of cultural interaction in the autumn of 1907, the Russian explorer Vladimir Klavdievich Arsen'ev (1872–1930) and his Nanai guide Dersu Uzala (1849–1908) had a conversation about eating whortleberries (of the genus *Vaccinium*). When Arsen'ev ate them happily and in abundance after seeing them, Dersu asked what they were called and said he did not know they were edible.[44] Other vestiges of cross-cultural influence are evident in still-extant food customs, like Ewenki people's claiming of *lieba*, a round bread that betrays its origins with the etymological match of the corresponding word in Russian for bread, *khleb*, as a traditional food.[45]

Since the 1950s, the impact of other cultures on non-Han groups in north-eastern China has been documented primarily in comparisons between these non-Han peoples and a generic 'Han' group. Such assessments can be affirmative, such as that the Hui and the Han in Heilongjiang eat the same kinds of staple foods and vegetables[46] or that Mongols have gradually adopted more elements of a Han diet as part of their routine eating.[47] What aversions or prohibitions remain in non-Han food customs have also been commonly noted, such as the fact that the Hui do not eat horse, mule, donkey or pork, and will not eat game meat,[48] and that the Ewenki cannot eat dog or parts of a bear like the heart and lungs, or even particular fish like the Amur catfish.[49] Value judgements are embedded in comparisons of food habits, such as the observation that the Kyrgyz in Heilongjiang ate meat as their 'staple food' (using the Chinese term *zhushi*, which generally refers to grain-based foods) before having regular and close interaction with the Han. The Han are implicitly credited with the Kyrgyz now eating 'real staple foods' and vegetables, which they did not consume much in the past because 'they did not know about [the vegetables]'.[50]

Conclusion

In this chapter, I have examined two types of borderlands: the social and cultural frontier between north-eastern China, which is regarded as part of China's periphery, and the country's eastern and central regions, which are collectively considered as the country's heartland; and also the one between the Han and non-Han cultures. The former borderland is no longer politically contested but remains a zone in which values and material customs evolve continuously through exposure and mutual influence with non-Chinese cultural communities across state borders. The other kind of borderland is also solidly established in the ways that Han and non-Han peoples identify themselves and distinguish those who are social and cultural Others. PRC law upholds ethnicity as a criterion for political status and the polyethnic composition of China's society as a hallmark trait of the state. However, region has become more significant to many Chinese who claim, or could seek, membership in an ethnic minority group. As Katherine Kaup has argued with the case of the Zhuang in Yunnan and Guangxi provinces, territorial affiliation has been stronger than, or has superseded, ethnic identity as practised on the family or locality levels.[51] In north-eastern China, this phenomenon means that ethnic groups may think of themselves as being 'north-eastern people', and that such an identity may be more meaningful than their separate ethnic identities.

In light of the continuing homogenization of material culture in present-day China, I concur with scholarly precedents that we should think of food as a way of defining regions instead of people, both now and perhaps even in the past.[52] As the shared elements of food custom in this chapter have shown, regional cuisine is a way to promote social and cultural diversity in a non-politically threatening manner. Lindsay J. Whaley has asserted that people of Manchu descent are so integrated into a 'greater Chinese society' that 'Manchu culture' (quotation marks are his) only exists as something 'of historical record', and that 'unique aspects of Manchu society such as arranged marriages and burial practices are no longer employed'.[53] Whaley's observation, although describing the Manchus – now the second-largest ethnic minority in the PRC – suggests that small ethnic groups will have even less incentive to retain cultural characteristics that set them apart from the Han majority and other ethnic minorities in their home regions. Even if certain ethnic groups should cease to exist, an extreme but highly possible vision of the future, their food customs could live on, albeit with increasingly ambiguous awareness of their origins, as habits of the people in a certain region. Whether food remains an ethnic or a regional marker, it is vital to understand the ways in which something so essential has evolved through time and interpretation by one or more human population, and how it should not merely be essentialized.

Solving the question of why non-Han foods are ostensibly excluded from the cuisine-system framework is also a matter of rethinking cultural borders. Since many non-Han food customs have been studied and classified according to criteria that differ from those applied to Han food, such as the characteristics of 'high' and 'low' cuisines or the sophistication of cooking methods, it is possible that non-Han foods will continue to be organized and described separately from Han food.[54] However, if regional cuisine systems are reinterpreted to include non-Han foods and to *recognize* their origins, then the impact of environment and interaction *between* groups on how people create and sustain food customs, rather than social and cultural divisions, will be more evident and reflective of historical and contemporary realities.

Loretta Kim is Associate Professor and Director of the China Studies programme at the School of Modern Languages and Cultures, University of Hong Kong. She is a historian of late imperial and modern China, focusing on the comparative history of borderlands and frontiers, regional identities and histories of China, and Chinese ethnic minority languages and literatures. Her most recent publications include *Ethnic Chrysalis: China's Orochen People and the Legacy of Qing Borderland Administration* (2019) and *The Russian Orthodox Community in Hong Kong: Religion, Ethnicity, and Intercultural Relations* (2021).

Glossary

Groups, Institutions, Places, Text Titles

English	Chinese (Hanyu Pinyin)	Chinese characters
advanced	xianjin	先進
Anhui province	Anhui sheng	安徽省
Amur catfish	nianyu	鮎魚
Annals of Chinese Ethnic Minority Customs	*Zhongguo shaoshu minzu fengsu zhi*	中國少數民族風俗志
Argun River teal	E'erguna he shuiya	額爾古納河水鴨
bobo	bobo	餑餑
borderland populations	bianjiang minzu	邊疆民族
Cantonese cuisine	Guangdong cai	廣東菜
Chuan (Sichuan province)	Chuan	川
Comprehensive Records of the Universe	*Huanyu tongzhi*	寰宇通志
cuisine system	caixi	菜系
Daur ethnic group	Dawo'erzu	達斡爾族
Encyclopedia of Chinese Ethnic Minorities' Food Customs	*Zhongguo shaoshu minzu yinshi wenhua huicui*	中國少數民族飲食文化薈萃
Ethnic Identification Project	minzu shibie gongcheng	民族識別工程

ethnic minority group	shaoshu minzu	少數民族
Ewenki ethnic group	Ewenke zu	鄂溫克族
farmer's joy	nongjiale	農家樂
fascicle	juan	卷
Fiyaka people	Feiyaka	費雅喀
flavour	fengwei	風味
food custom	yinshi xisu	飲食習俗
The Food and Drink System of Yunlin	*Yunlin tang yinshi zhidu ji*	雲林堂飲食製度集
food-shelter-clothing-transport	yinshi-juzhu-fushi-jiaotong	飲食–居住–服飾–交通
Fujian province	Fujian sheng	福建省
Gansu province	Gansu sheng	甘肅省
Guangdong province	Guangdong sheng	廣東省
Guangxi province	Guangxi sheng	廣西省
Guizhou	Guizhou	貴州
Han ethnic group	Hanzu	漢族
hazel grouse	fei long huawei zhenji	飛龍 花尾榛雞
Heilongjiang province	Heilongjiang sheng	黑龍江省
Heje ethnic group	Hezhe zu	赫哲族
Hua (Chinese)	Hua	華
Huaiyang (Jiangsu province)	Huaiyang	淮揚
Hui (Anhui province)	Hui	徽
Hui ethnic group	Huizu	回族
Hulun region	Hulun	呼倫
Hunan cuisine	Hunan cai	湖南菜
Important Principles of Food and Drink	*Yinshan zhengyao*	飲膳正要
Inner Mongolia Autonomous Region	Nei Menggu zizhiqu	內蒙古自治區
Jiangsu province	Jiangsu sheng	江蘇省
Jilin province	Jilin sheng	吉林省
Kazakh ethnic group	Hasake zu	哈薩克族
Kilen people	Qileng	奇楞
Kiyakara people	Qiakala	恰喀拉

Koreans (as an ethnic group in China)	Chaoxian zu	朝鮮族
Kyrgyz ethnic group	Ke'erkezi zu	柯爾克孜族
Liaodong	Liaodong	遼東
Liaoning province	Liaoning sheng	遼寧省
lieba (bread)	lieba	列巴
lifestyle	shenghuo fangshi	生活方式
Lu (Shandong province)	Lu	魯
Manchu ethnic group	Manzu	滿族
Manchu-Han banquet	Man Han quan xi	滿漢全席
material culture	wuzhi wenhua	物質文化
Min (Fujian province)	Min	閩
Minority Press	Minzu chubanshe	民族出版社
Mongol ethnic group	Menggu zu	蒙古族
mountain hawk-eagle	diao ying	雕鷹
native produce	tuchan	土產
North-eastern China	Zhongguo dongbei	中國東北
North-eastern people	Dongbei ren	東北人
Orochen ethnic group	Elunchun zu	鄂倫春族
Peking cuisine	Beiping cai	北平菜
Qing Imperial Album of Tributaries	*Huang Qing zhigong tu*	皇清職貢圖
Qinghai province	Qinghai sheng	青海省
PRC Department of Population and Employment Statistics, National Bureau of Statistics	Guojia tongji ju renkou he jiuye tongji si	國家統計局人口和就業統計司
PRC State Council Population Census Office	Guowuyuan renkou pucha bangongshi	國務院人口普查辦公室
Recipes from the Sui Garden	*Suiyuan shidan*	隨園食單
Regional Ethnic Autonomy Law	Zhonghua Renmin Gongheguo minzu qu zizhi fa	中華人民共和國民族區域自治法
Russians (as an ethnic group in China)	Eluosi zu	俄羅斯族

sacima	saqima	薩其馬
sand grouse	sha ji	沙雞
Seven-star appetizer plate	qi xing zhuan pan	柒星轉盤
Shandong province	Shandong sheng	山東省
Shanghai cuisine	Shanghai cai	上海菜
Sichuan cuisine	Sichuan cai	四川菜
Sichuan province	Sichuan sheng	四川省
social history survey	shehui lishi diaocha	社會歷史調查
staple foods	zhushi	主食
State Ethnic Affairs Commission (SEAC)	Guojia minzu shiwu weiyuanhui	國家民族事務委員會
Stir-fried chicken shreds with bean sprouts	dou ya ji si	豆芽雞絲
Su (Jiangsu province)	Su	蘇
supplementary foods	fushi	副食
Sushen people	Sushen	肅慎
Taiwanese cuisine	Taiwan cai	台灣菜
talke	sha sheng yu talake'a ta'erka	殺生魚 他拉克阿 塔爾卡
Tibet	Xizang	西藏
traditional Chinese medicine	Zhong yi	中醫
unusual taste	yiwei	異味
Wei-chuan Foods Corporation	Weiquan shipin gongsi	味全食品公司
white-naped crane	tu he	土鶴
Xiang (Hunan province)	Xiang	湘
Yuan emperor Renzong	Yuan Renzong	元仁宗
Yue (Guangdong province)	Yue	粵
Yunnan province	Yunnan sheng	雲南省
Zhe (Zhejiang province)	Zhe	浙
Zhejiang province	Zhejiang sheng	浙江省
Zhuang ethnic group	Zhuangzu	壯族

Personal Names

Chinese (Hanyu Pinyin)	Chinese characters
Hu Sihui	忽思慧
Mao Gongning	毛公寧
Ni Zan	倪瓚
Song Xiaolian	宋小濂
Su Shi	蘇軾
Wu Xu	吳旭
Xu Wei	徐渭
Yuan Mei	袁枚

Russian (ALA-LC Romanization)	Russian Cyrillic
Vladimir Klavdievich Arsen'ev	Владимир Клавдиевич Арсеньев
khleb	хлеб
Nanai	Нанай
Dersu Uzala	Дерсу Узала

Notes

1. Mao, *Zhongguo shaoshu minzu fengsu zhi*. Note that Chinese-language sources within the text are cited by the English-language translation of the title, followed by the original Chinese-language title in parentheses, for the convenience of the reader. This order of elements is reversed in the bibliography, and only the Chinese title is used for second and subsequent citations of a source.

2. In post-1949 China, each person may belong to one ethnic group officially, as signified on their identification card. However, an individual may claim more than one identity unofficially to achieve various social and economic purposes.

3. Yan, *Zhongguo shaoshu minzu yinshi wenhua huicui*.

4. Hofstede, *Culture's Consequences*, 28.

5. Ibid., 9.

6. Among works that discuss how the Han ethnic group has developed over millennia as a physically diffuse population with a strong shared identity, while maintaining significant differences in social organization and material culture, are Fei, *The Pattern of Plurality and Unity in the Chinese Nation* (*Zhonghua minzu duoyuan yiti geju*) and Xu, *Snowball* (*Xueqiu*).

7. Stevan Harrell's conception of ethnic consciousness as most fundamentally about 'a sense of relatedness as a people', which is all the more important in the absence or diminishing expression of tangible attributes, manifests in how food customs are the most regular and well-accepted form of ethnic currency. For Harrell's interpretation of ethnic consciousness, see Harrell, 'Introduction', 27–28. I also stress that although 'Han' as an ethnic category is problematic and contested, even as a counterweight to 'ethnic minority', it remains a legal and social identity with great cultural power.

8. For a definition of 'cuisine' most relevant to my research, see Belasco, *Food*, 15–25.

9. I consider an important characteristic of 'ethnicity' in China to be that members of a given ethnic group define themselves by heritage and 'traditions' that originate in time periods predating the memories of currently living persons.

10. For an expository critique of how these cuisine systems, or 'cooking schools', are classified, see Anderson and Anderson, 'Modern China', 353–54.

11. For descriptions of the broad direction-based classification, see Simoons, *Food in China*, 43–60.

12. For a general description of 'cultural cuisine', see Fieldhouse, *Food and Nutrition*, 51–77, and Messer, 'Anthropological Perspectives on Diet', 228. Some scholars have argued that a Chinese 'cuisine system' is a kind of 'cultural cuisine', or a set of certain basic foods, flavourings and modes of processing and consumption. For this argument that *caixi* and cultural cuisine are equivalent terms, see Wu, *Farming, Cooking, and Eating Practices*, 42.

13. See Huang, *Chinese Cuisine*, 1 (seven-star plate) and 169 (chicken shreds with bean sprouts). The term 'cuisine' is in square brackets for the citations in this sentence and in the next sentence because the original references in the text do not specify, but imply, that the regional adjectives refer to the cuisines.

14. See these two relatively early publications in English for general audiences as examples of region or province as characteristics that distinguish different types of Chinese food: Gin, *Regional Cooking of China*, and Lo, *Chinese Provincial Cooking*.

15. For the argument that non-Han foods are excluded from cuisine-systems, see Wu, *Farming, Cooking, and Eating Practices*, 41.

16. Hsu and Hsu, 'Modern China', 316.

17. For the importance of distinctions between foods by social status and consumption value, see Goody, *Cooking, Cuisine, and Class*, 97–153, Ma, *Chinese Dietary Culture (Zhongguo yinshi wenhua)*, 63–65 and Hong, 'The Localization and Globalization of Chinese Cuisine' ('Zhongguo caixi zhi bentuhua yu quanqiu hua'), 265–84.

18. As of the 2010 national census, there were only 5,354 persons in the PRC registered as Heje. See *Tabulation of the 2010 Population Census of the People's Republic of China (Zhongguo 2010 nian renkou puchao ziliao)*.

19. *Social History Survey of the Heje (Hezhe zu shehui lishi diaocha)*, 90, and Zhang, *Relics of Heje Fishing and Hunting Culture (Hezhe zu yulie wenhua yicun)*, 5.

20. Hsu and Hsu, 'Modern China'.

21. There are other ways in which some studies acknowledge the coherence and distinctiveness of some food customs. For example, instead of 'cuisine system', Ma Hongwei uses the term *fengwei* (flavour) to describe Mongol, Uighur, Korean, Tibetan, Manchu and Hui food. See Ma, *Zhongguo yinshi wenhua*, 71–72.

22. See Wilkinson, *Chinese History*, 463. Yuan Mei was the author of *Recipes from the Sui Garden (Suiyuan shidan)* first published in 1792. Ni Zan, who gained acclaim for his artistic talents, compiled the content for a book titled *The Food and Drink System of Yunlin (Yunlin tang yinshi zhidu ji)* during his life.

23. Hu, an imperial court dietician during the Yuan dynasty (1271–1368), was a Mongol. He wrote the three fascicles (*juan*) of *Important Principles of Food and Drink (Yinshan zhengyao)* between 1314 and 1320 for the Yuan emperor Renzong (r. 1311–20).

24. Government policies to gain and strengthen control over borderlands during that time period include negotiating treaties with neighbouring states and the 'liberation' of Tibet, which officially happened between 1950 and 1951 but required significant military intervention afterwards.

25. Regarding the processes of conducting and analysing survey data during the Ethnic Identification Project, see Mullaney, *Coming to Terms with the Nation*.

26. The Sibe are often considered another 'indigenous' group of north-eastern China. While generally regarded as 'non-native' to the region, but with significant presence in modern and contemporary times, are the Hui, Russian, Kyrgyz and Kazakh populations.

27. See *Investigative Report of the Social History of the Chaoxian (Korean) Nationality in Heilongjiang Province* (*Heilongjiang sheng Chaoxian zu shehui lishi diaocha baogao*).

28. Their ethnonyms are similarly imperfect because they do not fully represent historical and current subgroups that identify themselves by other names, and the ancestral groups of these populations that were also known by other terms.

29. I apply the concepts of social and cultural capital as commonly understood according to Pierre Bourdieu's theories of symbolic capital and the intensification of inequality in resource distribution. See Bourdieu, *La distinction*.

30. Such identification standards in the PRC include those codified in laws and policies, like the Regional Ethnic Autonomy Law, most recently revised in 2005, and the requirement that an ethnic identity must be cited on every individual citizen's identity card.

31. The decision-making process and criteria for 'being Han' are similar to what Eurasians in mainland China and Hong Kong faced in the nineteenth and twentieth centuries. Some ethnic minority people in the PRC are able to conform to conventional expectations about physical appearance, political loyalty, lifestyle and blood quantum, and others cannot gain acceptance into Han society or choose not to seek integration.

32. Wu, 'Ethnic Foods as Unprepared Materials', 419–39.

33. Among the countless works about this region as more than a borderland or frontier zone are Janhunen, *Manchuria*, and Yamamuro, *Kimera*.

34. Wang, *Comprehensive Records of the Universe* (*Huanyu tongzhi*).

35. Hostetler, *Qing Colonial Enterprise*, 81.

36. Fuheng, *Qing Imperial Album of Tributaries* (*Huang Qing zhigong tu*), juan (fascicle) 3, 127. Subsequent references to this source are given in 'title, fascicle, page' format.

37. For Kilen, see *Huang Qing zhigong tu* 3, 129, and for Fiyaka, *Huang Qing zhigong tu* 3, 133.

38. For Kiyakara, see *Huang Qing zhigong tu* 3, 135, and for Hezhe, *Huang Qing zhigong tu* 3, 139.

39. The report, entitled *Report of the Frontier Affairs Investigation Conducted in Hulunbuir* (*Hulunbei'er bianwu diaocha baogao shu*), was first published in 1909. This text is paginated in the Chinese style, with each spread consisting of two pages, with the verso as "a" and recto as "b." For the references to birds and whether they are edible, see 23a–b.

40. This book is a travelogue and travel guide with information about hotels and transportation. Madrolle, *Northern China*, 218.

41. Song, *Hulunbei'er bianwu diaocha baogao shu*, 24a.

42. Hawes, *In the Uttermost East*, 74.

43. Zhao, 'The Manchu-Han Banquet and Manchu Culinary Culture' ('Man Han quan xi yu Manzu yinshi wenhua'), 26–30 and 37–41.

44. Arsen'ev, *Dersu the Trapper*, 272. Arsen'ev only recorded some dates in his travelogue, so we can estimate that this encounter with whortleberries occurred sometime in late September or early October of that year.

45. For a description both of how Ewenki prepare and eat *lieba* and of other food words that have been adapted from Russian, see Dumont, 'Declining Evenki "Identities"', 524.

46. *Social History Survey of the Manchu, Korean, Hui, Mongol, and Kyrgyz Ethnic Groups in Heilongjiang* (*Heilongjiang sheng Manzu Chaoxian zu Huizu Menggu zu Ke'erkezi zu shehui lishi*), 76. This source will be referred to in abbreviated form as *Heilongjiang sheng Manzu Chaoxian zu Huizu* in subsequent citations.

47. *Heilongjiang sheng Manzu Chaoxian zu Huizu*, 136.

48. Ibid., 76.

49. Mao, *Zhongguo shaoshu minzu fengsu zhi*, 1568.

50. *Heilongjiang sheng Manzu Chaoxian zu Huizu*, 162.

51. Kaup, 'Regionalism versus Ethnicnationalism', 884.

52. Wu, *Farming, Cooking, and Eating Practices*, 296. Mary Rack has also made the significant argument that groups designated by the central government as 'ethnic minorities' often value their region or place-specific identities over their 'ethnic' ones. She argues that the development of ethnicity is therefore more important than the recognition of specific ethnic identities. See Rack, *Ethnic Distinctions*, 14.

53. Whaley, 'Manchu-Tungusic and Culture Change', 115.

54. Jack Goody described the evolution of culinary cultures in both Asia and Europe as depending on the distribution and permitted consumption of ingredients based on one's social status, with the implication that cuisines lacking complex stratification between 'high' and 'low' are not as developed as those that have such stratification. See Goody, *Cooking, Cuisine, and Class*, 97.

Bibliography

Anderson, Eugene N. [Newton], and Marja L. Anderson. 'Modern China: South', in K. C. Chang 張光直 (ed.), *Food in Chinese Culture* (New Haven, CT: Yale University Press, 1977), 319–82.

Arsen'ev, Vladimir Klavdievich. *Dersu the Trapper*, trans. Malcolm Burr. Kingston, NY: McPherson & Company, 1996.

Belasco, Warren. *Food: The Key Concepts*. Oxford: Berg, 2008.

Bourdieu, Pierre. *La distinction: Critique sociale du jugement*. Paris: Les Éditions de Minuit, 1979.

Dumont, Aurore. 'Declining Evenki "Identities": Playing with Loyalty in Modern and Contemporary China'. *History and Anthropology* 28(4) (2017), 515–30.

Fei, Xiaotong 费孝通. *Zhonghua minzu duoyuan yiti geju* 中华民族多元一体格局 [The pattern of plurality and unity in the Chinese nation]. Beijing: Zhongyang minzu xueyuan chubanshe, 1989.

Fieldhouse, Paul. *Food and Nutrition: Customs and Culture*, 2nd edn. London: Chapman & Hall, 1995.

Gin, Margaret. *Regional Cooking of China*. San Francisco: 101 Productions, 1975.

Goody, Jack, *Cooking, Cuisine, and Class: A Study in Comparative Sociology*, Cambridge: Cambridge University Press, 1982.

Guowuyuan renkou pucha bangongshi 国务院人口普查办公室 [PRC Population Census Office under the State Council] and Guojia tongji ju renkou he jiuye tongji si 国家统计局人口和就业统计司 [PRC Department of Population and Employment Statistics, National Bureau of Statistics] (eds). *Zhongguo 2010 nian renkou pucha ziliao* 中国2010年人口普查资料 [Tabulation of the 2010 population census of the People's Republic of China], 3 vols. Beijing: Zhongguo tongji chubanshe, 2012. Retrieved 7 March 2022 from http://www.stats.gov.cn/tjsj/pcsj/rkpc/6rp/indexch.htm.

Harrell, Stevan. 'Introduction: Civilizing Projects and the Reaction to Them', in Stevan Harrell (ed.), *Cultural Encounters on China's Ethnic Frontiers* (Seattle, WA: University of Washington Press, 1995), 3–36.

Hawes, Charles H. *In the Uttermost East: Being an Account of Investigations among Natives and Russian Convicts of the Island of Sakhalin, with Notes of Travel in Korea, Siberia, and Manchuria*. New York: Charles Scribner and Sons, 1904.

Heilongjiang sheng Manzu Chaoxian zu Huizu Menggu zu Ke'erkezi zu shehui lishi diaocha 黑龙江省满族朝鲜族回族蒙古族柯尔克孜族社会历史调查 [Social history survey of the Manchu, Korean, Hui, Mongol, and Kyrgyz ethnic groups in Heilongjiang]. Ed. 'Minzu wenti wuzhong congshu' Heilongjiang sheng bianji zu 民族问题五种丛书黑龙江省编辑组 ['Five series about ethnic issues' Heilongjiang province editorial board] and 'Zhongguo shaoshu minzu shehui lishi diaocha ziliao congkan' xiuding bianji weiyuanhui 中国少数民族社会历史调查资料丛刊修订编辑委员会 ['China's ethnic minorities social history survey series' revision editorial board]. Beijing: Minzu chubanshe, 2009.

Heilongjiang sheng Chaoxian zu shehui lishi diaocha baogao 黑龙江省朝鲜族社会历史调查报告 [Investigative report of the social history of the Chaoxian (Korean) nationality in Heilongjiang province]. Compiled by Zhongguo kexueyuan minzu yanjiusuo 中国科学院民族研究所[Chinese Academy of Sciences Institute of Ethnology] and Heilongjiang shaoshu minzu shehui lishi diaocha zu 黑龙江少数民族社会历史调查组 [Heilongjiang ethnic minority social history survey group]. Beijing: Zhongguo kexueyuan minzu yanjiusuo and Heilongjiang shaoshu minzu shehui lishi diaocha zu, 1959.

Hezhe zu shehui lishi diaocha 赫哲族社会历史调查 [Social history survey of the Heje]. Ed. Minzu wenti wuzhong congshu Heilongjiang sheng bianji zu 民族问题五种丛书黑龙江省编辑组 ['Five series about ethnic issues' Heilongjiang province editorial board]. Mudanjiang: Heilongjiang Chaoxian minzu chubanshe, 1987.

Hofstede, Geert. *Culture's Consequences: Comparing Values, Behaviors, Institutions, and Organizations Across Nations*. Thousand Oaks, CA: Sage, 1981.

Hong, Guangzhu 洪光住. '*Zhongguo caixi zhi bentuhua yu quanqiu hua* 中國菜系之本土化與全球化' [The localization and globalization of Chinese cuisine], in *Anthology of Papers from the 5th symposium on Chinese Dietary Culture/Di wu jie Zhongguo yinshi wenhua xueshu yantaohui lunwen ji* 第五屆中國飲食文化學術研討會論文集] (Taipei: Caituan faren Zhongguo yinshi wenhua jijin hui, 1998), 265–84.

Hostetler, Laura. *Qing Colonial Enterprise: Ethnography and Cartography in Early Modern China*. Chicago: University of Chicago Press, 2001.

Hsu, Vera Y. N 董一男, and Francis L. K. Hsu 許烺光. 'Modern China: North', in K. C. Chang 張光直 (ed.), *Food in Chinese Culture* (New Haven, CT: Yale University Press, 1977), 295–316.

Hu, Sihui 忽思慧. *Yinshan zhengyao* 飲膳正要 [Important principles of food and drink], 3 *juan*. 1314–20.

Huang Qing zhigong tu 皇清職貢圖 [Qing imperial album of tributaries], 9 *juan*. Ed. Fuheng 傅恆 et al. Yangzhou: Guangling shushe [1761–1805] 2008. [References to this source are given by the original fascicle (*juan* 卷) and the page number as ordered by continuous modern pagination for this reprint version].

Huang, Su Huei [Huang, Shuhui 黃淑惠] (ed.). *Chinese Cuisine: Wei-chuan Cooking Book* [*Weiquan shipu*味全食譜], trans. Nina Simonds 席妮娜. Taipei: Wei-chuan Foods Corporation, 1976.

Huanyu tongzhi 寰宇通志 [Comprehensive records of the universe], 119 *juan*. Compiled by Wang Chong [Zhong] 王重 et al. 1456.

Janhunen, Juha. *Manchuria: An Ethnic History*. Helsinki: Finno-Ugric Society, 1996.

Kaup, Katherine Palmer. 'Regionalism versus Ethnicnationalism in the People's Republic of China'. *The China Quarterly* 172 (2002), 863–84.

Lo, Kenneth H. C. *Chinese Provincial Cooking*. London: Elm Tree Books, 1979.

Ma, Hongwei 馬宏偉. *Zhongguo yinshi wenhua* 中國飲食文化 [Chinese dietary culture]. Huhhot: Nei Menggu renmin chubanshe, 1992.

Madrolle, Claude. *Northern China: The Valley of the Blue River, Korea*. Paris: Hachette, 1912.

Mao, Gongning 毛公宁 (ed.). *Zhongguo shaoshu minzu fengsu zhi* 中国少数民族风俗志 [Annals of China's ethnic minority customs]. Beijing: Minzu chubanshe, 2006. [Abbreviated to ZSMF.]

Messer, Ellen. 'Anthropological Perspectives on Diet'. *Annual Review of Anthropology* 13(1984), 205–49.

Mullaney, Thomas S. *Coming to Terms with the Nation: Ethnic Classification in Modern China*. Berkeley, CA: University of California Press, 2011.

Ni, Zan 倪瓚. *Yunlin tang yinshi zhidu ji*雲林堂飲食製度集 [The food and drink system of Yunlin], 6 *juan* plus 1 supplementary *juan*. Ed. Jian Xi 蹇曦. 1461, original period of authorship unknown.

Rack, Mary. *Ethnic Distinctions, Local Meanings: Negotiating Cultural Identities in China*. London: Pluto Press, 2005.

Simoons, Frederick J. *Food in China: A Cultural and Historical Inquiry*. Boca Raton, FL: CRC Press, 1991.

Song, Xiaolian 宋小濂. *Hulunbei'er bianwu diaocha baogao shu* 呼倫貝爾邊務調察報告書 [Report of the frontier affairs investigation conducted in Hulunbuir]. 1 *ce*. 1909. Reprint, Gong Chuhan 宮楚涵 and Qi Xi 齊希 (eds.), *Zhongguo xijian difang shiliao jicheng di san ji* 中國稀見地方史料集成第三集 [Collection of rare local historical materials of China, volume 3] (Beijing: Xueyuan chubanshe, 2014), 459–569.

Whaley, Lindsay J. 'Manchu-Tungusic and Culture Change among Manchu-Tungusic Peoples', in J. E. Terrell (ed.), *Archaeology, Language and History: Essays on Culture and Ethnicity* (Westport, CT: Bergin & Garvey, 2001), 103–24.

Wilkinson, Endymion. *Chinese History: A New Manual*. Cambridge, MA.: Harvard University Press, 2013.

Wu, Xu 吴旭. *Farming, Cooking, and Eating Practices in the Central China Highlands*. Lewiston, NY: Edwin Mellen, 2011.

———. 'Ethnic Foods as Unprepared Materials and as Cuisines in a Culture-based Development Project in Southwest China'. *Asian Ethnology* 75(2) (2016), 419–39.

Xu, Jieshun 徐杰舜. *Xueqiu: Han minzu de renleixue fenxi* 雪球：汉民族的人类学分析 [Snowball: An anthropological analysis of the Han nationality]. Shanghai: Shanghai renmin chubanshe, 1999.

Yamamuro, Shin'ichi 山室 信一. *Kimera: Manshūkoku no shōzō* キメラ：満洲国の肖像 [Chimera: a portrait of Manchukuo]. Tokyo: Chūō Kōronsha, 1993.

Yan, Qixiang 颜其香 (ed.). *Zhongguo shaoshu minzu yinshi wenhua huicui* 中国少数民族饮食文化荟萃 [Encyclopedia of Chinese ethnic minorities' food customs]. Beijing: Shangwu yinshuguan, 2001. [Abbreviated to ZSYH.]

Yuan, Mei 袁枚. *Suiyuan shidan*隨園食單 [Recipes from the Sui Garden], 4 *juan*. 1792.

Zhang, Minjie 张敏杰. *Hezhe zu yulie wenhua yicun* 赫哲族渔猎文化遗存 [Relics of Heje fishing and hunting culture]. Harbin: Heilongjiang renmin chubanshe, 2008.

Zhao, Zhizhong 赵志忠. 'Man Han quan xi yu Manzu yinshi wenhua满汉全席与满族饮食文化' [The Manchu-Han banquet and Manchu culinary culture], in Yan Qixiang 颜其香 (ed.), ZSYH (Beijing: Shangwu yinshuguan, 2001), 1–42.

CHAPTER 8

Imagined Communities and Communities of Practice

Participation, Territory and the Making of Food Heritage in Istria

Ilaria Porciani

Istria: From Hybridism to Hard Borders and Division

In a comprehensive book about European countries' culinary heritage, the chapter devoted to Croatia reaches back to Greek mythology and to the traditions of the many populations that inhabited the north-western Adriatic coast in ancient and medieval times. In this irenic text, myths and legends rub shoulders with descriptions of food whose extraordinary flavour is said to have pleased the mythological and historical travellers. Thus the reader encounters ancestors' elixirs transmitted to brave heroes of the following generations; vegetables whose extraordinary properties were said to restore strength and courage; and aphrodisiac soups. Considering the small area involved – notes author Veliko Barbieri – nowhere in Europe is such a mingling of Central and Southern European, Mediterranean and partly Balkan traditions to be found as in present-day Croatia. Thus an 'identifiable corpus of dishes and techniques ... can convincingly be termed Croatian cuisine', in spite of the presence of two very distinct gastronomic traditions related respectively to the 'central

European and Pannonian region' and the Mediterranean, the latter described as having 'ancient, even archetypal roots'.[1] In fact, this picture focuses precisely on the harmonious coexistence of these traditions. In presenting the background to these foodways, the author is explicit about the arrival of 'new' people in the region in ancient times – as ancient as the eighth century BC. However, he is completely silent about what was almost a population replacement after the Second World War, when Istria became part of Yugoslavia and the Italians living especially on the coast and in the cities were more or less forced to go. Moreover, the author does not say a word about the most critical issue: the complex and painful context of violence and mass murders in Istria at the end of and after the Second World War.

Violence in this area had already been visible in fascist times: the burning of the Narodni Dom (the 'People's house', that is the house of culture) in Fiume, repression of non-Italian languages and the compulsory change of family names had marked the 1920s and 1930s, when Istria was part of the Italian state and its Slavic inhabitants experienced the fascist policy against minorities. Between 1943 and 1946, however, a new, unprecedented wave of violence came from Tito's people. Its victims were not only fascists, as was often claimed. The title of a collection of memoirs about those hard times efficaciously summarizes this issue: *Ci chiamavano fascisti: Eravamo italiani* (*They Called us Fascists: We Were Italians*).[2] Ordinary Italian men and women were in many cases tortured and thrown dead or alive (often tied together with ropes or iron wire in ways that immediately recall the Armenian genocide) into the karstic pits called *foibe*. These killings were so brutal that they themselves have sometimes even been called 'genocide'. The survivors, though not technically speaking expellees, were forced to leave in what has been defined a silent 'exodus'.[3] Nowadays it is probably more correct to consider it a forced migration, tragic and yet not too dissimilar from the many others in those crucial years, in Italy as well as elsewhere: suffice it to think of the India–Pakistan partition or the population replacements in Eastern Europe. The unwanted Italian minority (250,000–300,000 people) had to decamp, leaving behind their homes and possessions: they went through the painful and sometimes almost twenty-year-long experience of circa 110 refugee camps (some of which had been previously built for the Jews, such as Fossoli in Emilia or the Risiera di San Sabba in Trieste). From there, individuals and families from Istria, as well as from Dalmatia and the city of Fiume, were partly and very slowly resettled in many different areas of Italy, from Sardinia and Tuscany to Piedmont and the South; some of them emigrated to the United States, Canada and Australia. Their story, initially silenced because it did not fit into the post-Second World War master narrative of liberation and the

Resistance, has often been discussed in memoirs and is now the topic of a sizable and rich critical and scholarly literature.[4]

Unsurprisingly, the most urgent issue to be discussed was the political public and private violence: the *foibe* have been at the core of a long and very political debate. Only in recent years have the privations and harsh living conditions in the camps started to resurface in people's memories and in oral history interviews after long being submerged and unspoken.[5]

When balance begins to be lost, writes anthropologist Franco La Cecla, cuisine is the first thing to go: instead of fostering coexistence and tolerance, it turns into the first dividing issue.[6] In Thessaloniki, Jewish, Orthodox and Muslim communities lived next to each other. Their food was extremely similar, though they called it by different names: it was in fact almost identical, but for the use of one single spice. When the conditions for peaceful cohabitation disappeared, however, the food of the others suddenly became 'barbarian' and 'inferior'. The same happened in Istanbul at the time of the Greek–Turkish hostilities: at that point Turks stopped buying spices from Rum shops, and their owners, who had previously been treated in a friendly manner, suddenly became enemies.[7] Such a sudden change is prone to happen when a war starts: it has certainly happened many times in the Balkans. Once more, it is La Cecla who reminds us of the fact that in Croatia during the 1990s, that is during the wars in former Yugoslavia, all of a sudden those eating Serbian food started to be regarded as traitors.[8] Fifty years earlier, immediately after the Second World War, food likewise became a dividing issue in Istria, while border areas, which were to some extent porous and inclusive of different people and habits, changed into places marked first by war, and later by the Cold War. Borders, including gastronomic ones, suddenly hardened.

Food is a strong identity marker and a powerful part of shared heritage and memory. Thus it is a crucial part of the *geteilte Geschichte* (a history at once shared and both divisive and divided). This issue has recently been at the centre of a number of contributions related to forced migrations and partitions,[9] as well as nationalism.[10]

This chapter focuses on food. To be sure, it does not discuss food shortages or the lack of essential nutritional elements in times of war and displacement: a very important aspect that was prominent in many narrations immediately after the events. Instead, it focuses on the deep interweaving of food, identity and the memory of the forced migration. Drawing on the literature of displacement and on food as heritage, as well as on sources such as novels, recipe books, oral history documents and kitchen utensils left behind by those who left and later displayed in museums and in one documentary film, it focuses on the way that both the discourse and practice surrounding foodways and recipes that were once part of a divided and yet shared history became a way of othering 'others' and reimagining a cosy and homey lost community.[11] However, as we will see, this is not the only aspect that emerges, and this story suggests that we be more cautious in our approach and pay more attention to nuances.

Banal Nationalism and/or Local (Hybrid) Identity?

This memory construction is also to some extent the result of the invention of a tradition[12] in line with the banal[13] gastronomic nationalism of the long nineteenth century. On the one hand, empires, and especially the Habsburg Empire to which Istria belonged after more than a century of Venetian rule, were absolutely crucial in promoting, facilitating and easing exchanges and transfers. As Catherine Horel has pointed out,[14] and as many contributions now highlight, Istrian cuisine was a dialogue of cultures, a sort of 'quilt' or culinary patchwork where elements from the Venetian tradition mingled with recipes deeply connected to the empire. The Istrian harbour of Pola (now Pula) was not only the headquarters of the Austro-Hungarian military fleet: it was a cosmopolitan place where German-speaking officers and soldiers from Austria mingled with Italians, Greek sailors and merchants in the kind of mixed population that often inhabits cities on the sea. Nearby Fiume (now Rijeka), for a long time a free port and a free city connected to the Magyar part of the empire, had a possibly even more diverse population, including Orthodox and Armenians, Jews and Russians. It was a global marketplace connecting the north-eastern internal areas of the empire with the global dimension of its trade and connections, easily summed up in Lloyds's constant Atlantic journeys. Moreover, contacts with Italian ports – especially Venice, whose marble lion stood and in some cases still stands prominently in many bell towers of coastal towns – were already intense and continuous in the nineteenth century and even before. They became still more intense after the First World War, when this area was assigned to fascist Italy. Civil servants and traders, merchants and tourists, teachers and post office clerks, or simply internal immigrants coming from other Italian areas populated Istria. They imported or strengthened shared eating habits, while the older ones – which one might term 'imperial' – were never dismissed. The hybridity of recipes and cooking in the area appears clear as soon as we discard nationalism from our methodological approach.

Yet a specific 'Istrian' cooking is what many women (and some men) talk about in novels and interviews and in the documentary film *Magna Istria* (2010), a film whose ambiguous title means simultaneously 'Eating Istria' and 'Istria the great'.

This chapter argues that the definition of an *Istrian* cuisine (or cooking, if we intend to respect the division between cuisine intended as 'haute cuisine' and everyday cooking) in geographical terms tends to insist on precise borders, which don't take into account their constant porosity over time and the gastronomical hybridism fundamental to that area. In the process, the reconstruction of an *Istrian cuisine* overshadows and darkens other kinds of border: social ones. The shared memory of the Istrian diaspora overemphasizes a deep divide between Italians and others who eat Slavic dishes.[15] To be sure, rich people and poor people did not eat the same food, nor cooked the same way: this point appears clear from many sources. Thus, the memory of a common food identity across different social strata is misleading. It functions to (re)construct a cohesive cultural and to some extent ethnic community with little or no internal partitions and divides. Such homogeneity would easily be contradicted by the photographic evidence of extremely poor Istrian peasant homes and their fireplaces used for cooking – often not even a kitchen proper, as is seen in serious ethnographic works.[16] These rude images are certainly not similar to the idealized and nostalgic reproduction of 'Istrian' kitchens (in fact, middle-class kitchens) to be seen in our days in exhibitions organized to appeal to holidaymakers, such as in the Rovigno municipal museum: tourists are rarely interested in observing the unpleasant reality of poor people's lives in the nineteenth and early twentieth centuries. Unsurprisingly, since the focus is on communal and shared cooking tradition, the memory of hunger and the diets of poverty tends to be cancelled out. What occupies the centre of the picture in popular imagination is the memory of festive food prepared for special occasions like Easter, Christmas and Carnival. In short, in this case food heritage helps to provide a good basis for the construction of a shared nostalgic memory among different classes and strata, reinforced by its connection with religious festivities, important cohesive elements in the pre-socialist world. The Catholic background comes up in other practices of this specific group, and may here relate to an unconsciously transposed mystical communion.

A Mystical Communion

Food is often the perfect looking glass to reflect nostalgia, as many narratives of migration prove. However, here the context is more complex. The foodscape of the Italians from Istria (maybe more for those who left than for those who stayed) is not simply a culinary narrative, suffused with nostalgia, like those that 'often manage immigrant memories and imagined returns to the "homeland"', as Indian American cultural critics

Ketu H. Katrak[17] and Anita Mannur[18] observe in many novels regarding other diasporas. In our case, remembering the lost flavours and smells and reimagining the cooking of the lost home is a way of synecdochizing a fatherland lost forever, to which there will be no return. It is also a tool to keep things, traditions, experiences, smells and gestures going on in order to perform the existence of a still-living community and to counter the dispersion of its heritage and ultimately of the people. The narrative on Istrian cooking encompasses the shared memory of a dispersed (to some extent 'mystical') community that in reality was extremely diverse in terms of social and cultural background. This community probably started to further coalesce and to be imagined as one compact group once the forced migration had glossed over the perception of previous differences among Istrians in social and cultural terms, emphasizing the common experience of pain and displacement through which all migrants passed, no matter what their social or cultural background was before. This implies a deep divide between the Italians and the others: exiles are all the same, one people, as opposed to the 'others'.

This fault line, however, reaches back to the divide between the 'urban' inhabitants of the coastal cities and towns (mostly of Italian origin) and the rural people of Slavic origins who inhabited the non-urban areas of the peninsula. Food was one of the features that defined the 'otherness' of Croats, Slovenes and other Slavic populations: their rural origin and habits, as opposed to the 'urbanity' of the Italians living in major coastal towns, such as Pola or Fiume, but also smaller centres that were nevertheless perceived as *città* (cities). Thus, the main opposition in the oral history interviews collected by Gloria Nemec is that between citizens (inhabitants of the cities) and country-dwellers, even if the latter lived only a few kilometres away and worked in fields adjacent to the urban landscape. What emerges from Nemec's interviews is that the lower-class Italians – especially the peasants – were extremely poor and in fact much poorer than the Croats and Slovenes, whose fields further away from the city walls were usually more fertile than those on the rocky soil around the cities where the Italians lived.

This civic identity of the Italians, rooted in Roman history and amplified by the discourse of nineteenth-century Italian nationalism in the area, led to a narrative of opposition.

This was not limited to the higher cultural level. At the moment of the painful forced migration, the highest Roman heritage, the Arena, symbol of the city of Pola, was reworked into the status of a relic, cherished and appropriated with no reference to its artistic significance. Heritage – in this case a monumental and archaeological one – turned into part of the mystical body of the nation (as well as of the city). As such, it could and in fact had to be divided up and shared (like the consecrated host transformed during the Holy Mass into Christ's body) in order to be taken away as a physical token of the lost soil. In the last days before leaving Pola, many people (apparently men rather than women) chiselled off small pieces of the well-preserved Roman Arena of Pola and took them away in their pockets. The Arena was for some the symbol of the Roman identity of the area, while legends and children's tales attributed the building of the Arena to giants or fairies, thus only adding to its symbolic power.[19] But the Arena was first of all the symbol of the city, and had literally to be embodied and symbolically taken away as part of the mystical body in the Catholic holy communion. People breaking off little marble pieces of the amphitheatre to take with them into exile can be seen in the dramatic film *Pola: A Dying City*.[20] The same attitude and deep feelings are at the core of the dialectal song translated into English by Pamela Ballinger: 'I want to say goodbye to the little house/where I passed my youth … . Two things I want to take in order to remember/ In a bag a little piece of the [Roman] arena/in a bottle a little of your beautiful sea.'[21] This is not just a saying: water from the sea and the river was actually taken by some migrants, and two little bottles containing it are to be seen in the Roman Fiume Archive and Museum on the Via Laurentina. Ballinger correctly speaks of a mystical communion with the Istrian soil, which is also evident in visual documents of the time and in exiles' memoirs.

I want to push this argument a little further by including food in the mystical communion, an idea strengthened by the discourse on the Istrian 'martyrs'. This mystical community consciously perpetuates itself through breaking bread together. The Istrians form a distinct group by performing their commune identity. Eating the same food, and therefore following a communal set of recipes, which they refer to in their dialect, *Istroveneto*, builds an even closer connection to the place. Cooking 'the Istrian way' is thus perceived as both inherent to all Istrians and as a marker of the imaginary borderline that includes their community, no matter if fragmented, dispersed and in fact existing only in the memory, since those who left are scattered among various Italian cities sometimes remote from each other, while the young generation has naturalized elsewhere. This is a perfect case in point of Benedict Anderson's concept of 'imagined communities'.[22] Food, or its memory, intimately embodies the roots in the *terroir*, locality or nation: we are well aware that local and national identities do not always stand opposed, but may overlap and combine, not only to produce a multiple identity, but in fact to strengthen each other.

Regional or National Cooking? Istrian and German Expellees

For the exiles, there was no reason to immediately connect their gastronomic tradition to Italy: firstly, because their culinary habits were obviously rather hybrid and rooted in the empire; secondly, because highlighting the 'Italian identity' of their cooking might have detracted from their own peculiar identity. Moreover, once they arrived in Italy they were made to feel most unwelcome, and thus cherished even more the memory of their original community.

This attitude is very similar to that of the German *Vertriebene* or expellees. The issue of the specific gastronomic traditions of these communities has in their case too long been under-investigated and has started to resurface only in the last few years, as the voices of women have been more powerfully heard. 'Keeping and protecting has always been the woman's task' ('erhalten und behüten war seit jeher Aufgabe der Frau'), declared one of the East German expellees.[23] However, women often did not have a strong voice in building the German expellees' *Heimatstuben*, nor in the Italian museums of the Istria, Fiume and Julian March diaspora, until very recently. And yet kitchen tools and recipe books figured among the possessions that the displaced families (and probably the women) took with them when they fled, both for practical and for sentimental reasons.

These aspects have started to be taken into consideration in the museum of Istrian, Dalmatian and Fiume civilization in Fiume, with its collection of things left behind in 'Magazzino 18' of the Old Trieste harbour,[24] as well as in museums in Germany.[25] The trend is a recent one: in Hessen, exhibitions organized upon regional criteria have focused on the life of the expellees, displaying furniture and kitchen utensils and now including recipes and recipe books.[26] In Retschow,[27] between 2012 and 2015 a charity cookbook – sold by the thousand as funding for the restoration of the old church – was based on family recipes (which had to be handwritten), mostly from former expellees. However, the Evangelical church that started the scheme also set about collecting recipes from refugees currently living in the area but coming from various parts of the world. In the town of Kaufbeuren (which now has about thirteen thousand inhabitants), former inhabitants of Gablonz have rebuilt 'a town in the town' – a 'New Gablonz' – and many streets have been renamed after those of the city left behind; in the bakery, 'Butterwischl' are still to be to be found, while East German names are still used for sauces widespread throughout the German area (for instance, *Dillsauce* is still called 'Dilldunge').[28] Many of these recipes, from Istria as well as from East Germany, retain their dialect names: they serve to keep a speakers' community together.

Objects and food have a physical consistency that sets in motion processes of personal or group identification. Through the memory that they embody, they help build relations among people and places: relationships that capture and embody the essence of a place.[29]

Until a few years ago, there was no food in the museums of the Istrian, Dalmatian or Julian March diaspora.[30] It is mostly private homes that tend to preserve little private 'things' as part of *Heimatecken* – those private corners of the lost little fatherland'[31] – as they are called in the houses of the German *Vertriebene*: traditional costumes, for example, or knick-knacks or painted dishes. The same thing happened in the houses of the people from Istria. Then these objects started to appear in museums. This did not happen straight away after the displacement, but dates from about ten years ago.

Susannah Eckersley has noted that in museums, 'food has become an affective, emotive medium through which difficult histories can be made more visible, more tangible and more comprehensible to museum visitors – and perhaps also to a politically-sensitive general public – despite the political concerns and at times the controversies surrounding them. In this way, it acts as an *Ersatz* both for direct political statements and for overt positioning by museums and heritage sites, particularly those which operate within a political realm that is not always sympathetic.'[32] As Eckersley shows, this is the case when the aim is mainly to create links among the dispersed community and to reconnect people who have ended up widely separated and even countries apart.

The exhibition held in Haus des Deutschen Ostens (HDO) in Munich – *Kann Spuren vom Heimat enthalten: Essen und Trinken, Identität und Integration der Deutschen des östlichen Europa* (*May Contain Traces of the Fatherland: Eating and Drinking, Identity and Integration of the Germans from Eastern Europe*) – highlighted the fact that many expellees brought with them handwritten family recipes and cookbooks as well as kitchen tools: partly for practical reasons, partly for sentimental ones.[33]

Rethinking the good food from home was also a way of forgetting the terrible situation of the camps, often epitomized by their smell:

> It was an intense smell: acrid, sweet, born from the union of the cafeteria food … and the meals cooked on the small spirals of the electric stove … . It merged with the pungent smell of the mothballs which would protect the only dress one had to wear, a dress or suit which would be put on and off again and again. Its smell would mix with the dense smell, almost a taste, of dirty hair that could not be washed. We rebuilt the missing pieces of a 'self' immersed in the sensations of 'fake' broth, poor food, lack of vitamins, congenital anaemia, poor things to wear, de facto uniforms, paid [for] by ECA, the municipal institutions that assist poor people. We brought with us the cabin of the refugee camp, even when we came out.[34]

Fiume-born writer and Claudio Magris's late wife Marisa Madieri (1938–96), author of *Verde acqua*, wrote of the mix of noises and smells of the camp. Her lines were until a few years ago to be read in the panels of the Padriciano camp: 'the strong, typical, indescribable smell, a mixture of sweetish food and stale soups, cabbage, fried food, sweat and hospital.'[35] The lack of a private family cooking space was remembered as crucial. In memoirs and memories, in pictures and drawings, it reflects a lost commensality, the lost 'home'. Anthropologists as well as historians have shown how important eating together is to the construction of a sense of community, let alone family and a national community.

But Madieri also remembers life stories of the past generations, typical of an imperial area: the same as we find in the people on the move in Elias Canetti's *Die gerettete Zunge*. These stories are present in her own family: the so-called 'grandmother' who married the writer's father after having lived in Banat, Slavonia, Serbia, Hungary and Romania. 'Grandma Anka would take care of Grandfather Gigio. She would speak to him in German, my father's mother tongue, she would prepare for him dishes typical of the Serbian and Hungarian cooking, bringing back to him tastes and smells of paprika, onion, cinnamon, cumin and poppy.'[36]

With these thoughts, Madieri, herself having experienced exile and the camp, testifies to another attitude: the habit, in families whose background was diverse, of mixing culinary experiences that do not abide by the rigid separation of gastronomic cultures. This attitude therefore contradicts the simplistic binary opposition of 'us' and 'the others'.

Food is a living practice that has the task of safeguarding memory across generations. It links the past to the present, and possibly to the future, in a uninterrupted chain that connects various generations of women within the family. After the death of her grandmother, Giuliana Zelco says to her mother: 'Now you will cook the Christmas dinner like the one grandmother used to prepare.'[37] She does not ask. She just makes a statement, which confirms what appears to be a sort of commitment or even a destiny. Food is a way of talking about festivities, of remembering moments when the frugality, if not poverty, of everyday food makes room for exceptional and almost ritual meals: another occasion on which the exceptional helps to construct a shared experience beyond social classes. As Luce Giard writes:

> The everyday work in the kitchens remains a way of unifying matter and memory, life and tenderness, the present moment and the abolished past, inventions and necessity, imagination and tradition – tastes, smells, colours, flavours, shapes, consistencies, actions, gestures, movements, people and things, heat, savourings, spices and condiments ... . Women's gestures and women's voices make the earth livable.[38]

The writer and journalist Annamaria Mori, who is behind the *Magna Istria* film, has often written about her mother, who lived in Rome but used to cross the border and go back to Istria where, in spite of everything, she could find a dish, one of the things – as she writes – that would make her 'incommunicable' to her new neighbours.[39]

Magna Istria: A Cookbook Weaves Together the Threads of a Dispersed Community

The 2010 film script runs as follows: Francesca, a young woman from Turin, granddaughter of Istrian exiles, has lost her grandmother's cookbook, and is desperately looking for the recipe for a special dessert: *il castello di croccante* (a crispy almond sweetmeat castle). Thus, she begins a long trip from one Italian city to another, to ask women from exile families. Predictably, the lost recipe will not be found. In fact, it is an invention, since it is absent from all the documents that I examined, and I imagine that it never existed. And yet it was the perfect pretext to visit people scattered in many far-flung Italian cities. The old trope of the journey is here used in order to connect now dispersed members of what used to be a cohesive community – and what's more, a national community. It is difficult not to think of the well-known book *Le tour de France par deux enfants*, whose aim was to teach Third Republic schoolchildren that the lost Alsace and Lorraine were connected to the main body of the nation. The film starts in the *villaggi giuliano-dalmati*, neighbourhoods built for the people from the Julian March, Istria and Dalmatia from the 1960s onwards, and winds along the peninsula up to today's Croatia and Slovenia. It comes as no surprise to see that Francesca – from one recipe to the next, from one conversation to another and after so many encounters with 'people who left' (*i partiti*) – finally ends up among the 'ones who stayed' (*i rimasti*). However, unlike in the plot of the *Tour de France*, in this case there is no claim to an 'Italian Istria'.

At the end of Francesca's journey, the audience has learned with her about the difficult history of this beautiful peninsula. Food has provided a soft way of breaking silences and approaching traumatic and post-traumatic memory: the war, exodus, *foibe*, treatises, but also life in the camps and nostalgia, or the terror of concentration and punishment camps in Yugoslavia such as Arbe or Goli Otok. The film ends when the main character experiences a sort of reconciliation with the past of the native land. The search for something as simple and innocent as the recipe for a cake has proved to be the right way into the private sphere of so many homes, and to open so many doors. The young, itinerant woman has not experienced the war or life in the camps. She belongs to the new generation that has to come to terms and make peace with the difficult past of her people. She only meets women. The talk as filmed tends to be in kitchens, where the women are cooking. In a way, it is a film about the memory of 'hands'. Hands and gestures, practices and doings keep alive the material culture and help to soothe the bitter nostalgia for a lost land. The director has commented: 'When I was invited to film this story I didn't really know Istria. The idea was to recount it through food. But we needed a story. I thought of the fame of Istrian cooking: I could start something good. I had the opportunity to let various people tell their different stories. I could have given more room to those who stayed but the story started from the ones who left and it was natural to let them speak more.'[40]

The conversations take place in interiors: metaphorically, the main character opens a door and enters the deep realm of private lives and memories. We see women cooking and we hear them talking: it is the voice of the women that is heard. With their performative gestures, they are the ones who keep Istria alive. They cook what they interpret as old Istrian recipes and are conscious of cooking food that is different from what they have met in the various regions where they have ended up: Sicily or Piemonte. And yet their presence there has in turn somehow modified eating habits, or at least the variety of food ingredients. Inquiries in Turin have shown that in the popular local market of Porta Palazzo, the presence of many customers from Istria and their desire for food that reminds them of their origins has resulted in a clear demand for a number of ingredients whose presence there would be impossible to understand if not for the existence of this community.

If it is true that women played an important part in banal nineteenth-century nationalism in almost every European country (and beyond) by writing cookbooks built around the national ideal, they have also perpetuated traditions, recipes that passed from mother to daughter again and again. This matrilineal line of (national) belonging is clearly found in this film too.

If the *castello di croccante* is an imaginary recipe, what are the dishes perceived as 'Istrian' in the film? They are the ones often recalled in literary works and memoirs. Poet Biagio Marin, in his *Istrian Elegies*, gives voice to the nostalgia for fresh bread and *orosto d'oradele*. *Gnocchi di susine* are recalled in Regina Cimmino's autobiography;[41] *ermelini siropai* (apricots in sugar) are also present in a number of recipe books. *Brodo bruscolà*, a simple soup made of flour and water cooked with an egg so that the egg produces filaments (*zanzarele*), is also often recalled as a memory of childhood and nurture within the family.[42] Desserts such as *crostoli* or *putizza* are inextricably intertwined with the grandmother or the mother's sweetness and care for the family and especially the children, as in Ester Sardoz Barlessi's memoirs.[43] Giuliana Zelco recalls the sweet pies (*pinze*) signed in the Church on Easter Day.[44]

Cabbage (*verze vapofrig*) or fried cookies (*fritole*) are also omnipresent in such memories.[45] *Amlet rosta*, for all its exotic, mysterious name, is in fact a kind of oven-baked pancake not very different from the Austrian *Palachinken*, while *strucolo de ua* is a kind of *Strudel*, with a black grape filling. *Cuguluf* is the Kugelhupf of Viennese origin, present in various areas of Mitteleuropa. True enough, here it is a poor version, since refined white flour is often replaced with corn flour (in this case, it is called *Cuguluf con afior di granturco*). *Fritole* are apple pancakes: a simple, cheap sweet prepared in many other Italian and European areas. They are often to be found in Venice and along the Adriatic coast. They are also present in popular fairy tales.[46]

Another dish perceived as typically Istrian once the exiles reached the Italian mainland was *schmarn*. It is in actual fact the Austrian or German *Kaiserschmarren* (it is not clear which origin is the real one, and maybe it is not even necessary to look for a precise origin). The cake named *Putizza* is far from being only Istrian: a recipe for it was already present in Katharina Prato's cookbook, published for the first time in Graz in 1892. It probably came from the Austro-Hungarian Empire, and was presented as an example of imperial cuisine at a great ball that took place at Miramare castle in Trieste. However, recent research has also suggested that it may be Slovene in origin. The film *Magna Istria* opts for this second version: the origin of the dessert's name is traced to a Slovene verb that means 'to roll'.

Does this mean that an Istrian cuisine does not exist? Not really. These examples hint rather at the hybrid origins of the peninsula's cooking, so deeply marked by both Venetian and Habsburg influence. Again, the use of dialect is crucial: the fact of eating dishes and calling them by the names used 'before' is a further help in reconstructing a speakers' community.

Istria In and Out: Lidia Bastianich or the Shifting of Istria's Perceptions

We come now to our own day. While Cristina Mantis and Francesca Angeleri were working on *Magna Istria*, on the other side of the Atlantic Ocean, Lidia Bastianich was consolidating her public profile. She was born in Pola in 1947, the daughter of a mechanic and a teacher. Her family fled in 1956, and after two hard years at the Risiera di San Sabba was received in the United States with the status of refugees.[47]

Hers is both a Cold War story and the personal success story of a cook who has gained media visibility (being invited onto Julia Child's show), opened important restaurants in New York, written successful recipe books, been a regular guest on television and staged her own show, *Lidia's Kitchen*, watched by no fewer than fifty million people in the United States. She is owner of six important restaurants in the United States and two wine enterprises in Italy, and co-owner with her son Joe, Mario Batali and Oscar Farinetti, of Eataly New York. Joe Bastianich is an implacable judge on Italy's MasterChef.

Here, however, Lidia Bastianich interests us for the shift that characterized the construction of her public image. From being the herald of Italian cuisine, she also became – especially to the Italian public –the voice of Istrian cooking; from silence about her family experiences in her American books, which tend to present hers as 'family cooking', to a sort of 'coming out' or explicit acknowledgement of her Istrian identity and the story of her region, which is present in her latest interviews though absent from her first books. In *Lidia's Italy in America*, Istria's hybrid cooking is only mentioned *en passant* when quoting recipes that recall the middle European influence. However, these recipes, such as sauerkraut with pork and roast goose with *Mlinzi*, are missing both from collections of recipes and memories of exiles. In Bastianich's books, the hybrid dishes of Istria are presented as a mix of seafood from the Adriatic, Viennese-style veal cutlets in breadcrumbs and beef goulash, *Sachertorte* and *Apfel Strudel*. Bastianich's journey continues through Italian regions: Friuli, 'where comes Montasio cheese to make *fricos*; Padua and Treviso with their 'soups'; Piedmont, with its Barolo-stewed beef; down to Tuscany, Lazio and Sicily with Maremman wild boar, Roman artichokes and *panelle* (a fried chickpea snack). As in popular BBC television series, this syncretistic gastronomic heritage goes along with the presentation of other forms of heritage: monuments and palaces, ruins and frescoes. In short: Italian heritage to enjoy. The commercial orientation of *Lidia's Italy in America* is clear from its blurb: 'There's something for everyone in this rich and satisfying book that will open up new horizons even to the most seasoned lover of Italy.'[48]

Bastianich's discourse, however, has the merit of combining love for 'terroir' with perception of a continuous evolution in cooking.

> The story of Italian American cuisine does not end today, for food culture continues to evolve, and as our methods of transportation improve, the Italian cuisine in America is getting ever closer to the regional contemporary cuisine in Italy. My personal quest since my opening of Felidia Ristorante in 1981 was to bring the regional cuisine of Italy to America. I began cooking the regional cuisine of Friuli-Venezia-Giulia and the little

peninsula of Istria where I hail from, and it soon became clear to me that Italian American cuisine was not what my family was cooking. I did what came naturally ... I cooked what we ate at home. But I needed the traditional Italian products, and life today is much easier now that many authentic Italian ingredients are available in the United States. But at the time when I could not get those ingredients, I managed to invent something new and delicious, just as my fellow Italian immigrants have done since their arrival in this country.[49]

Her perspective on the displacement is also turned towards the future and not towards the traumatic second-generation memory of the past: it focuses on the positive acts of immigrants and the construction of a successful melting pot. Her bestseller *Lidia's Italy in America* (2011) is dedicated to her mother and to Italian immigrants: 'This book is dedicated to all of the immigrants like my mother, Erminia, who left behind their country and families to come to America in search of a new life, in search of opportunity so their families and children could have a life of freedom and a chance at a better life. Their hard work, ingenuity, and courage have helped to make America what she is today.'

She tells the story of her painful experience in the Risiera, and of how the Italian food her family prepared in the United States was a way of immediately reconnecting to the lost country. Food, she said in a recent interview, was a connection to her family's roots, but it also meant experimenting, and looking for new possibilities.[50] Recently, she won the Italian Rovagnati prize. The newspaper *Il Giorno* emphasized the fact – probably for the first time – that the writer and cook 'born in Pola was among the displaced Istrian people who fled from Tito's Yugoslavia, and she received the prize because she was able to turn this great disadvantage into a great opportunity'.[51]

Conclusions

In Istria, like in other cases of forced migration, memories of the food prepared in the kitchen of the lost home is part of the traumatic memory or post-memory of the camps. The delicious lost smells and tastes of family cooking are a soft way of coming to terms with such experiences. They stand opposed to the terrible, anonymous smells of the camps, where all domestic space was denied. Keeping family recipe books, handwritten by grandmothers (and more rarely by grandfathers, as in one example from East German expellees[52]), is a way of establishing an affective relation vertically with former generations, but also horizontally with the other members of the same community who have been separated by their different resettlement destinations. The fact that many ordinary people brought with them cookbooks, recipes and kitchen utensils has a poignant meaning. Unfortunately, comparative work has rarely highlighted this issue. In recent years, however, more attention has been devoted to the issue of food under these circumstances.

By way of conclusion, I would like first to highlight similarities existing in different cases of forced migration, such as the German *Vertriebene* and the Italians from Istria, the Julian March and Dalmatia. But it would probably be possible to extend the comparison to non-European areas, as suggested by the museums of North Koreans forcibly displaced in the Cold War.[53] And a global approach might suggest that we extend the investigation to Indian migration. Secondly, in deconstructing these food memories it seems only right that we take account of social class and diversities between rural and town backgrounds. Thirdly, in spite of the temptation to simplify the foodscape and use food to 'other' the others, the memory of hybrid cooking from the original region persists in some cases and should just be appreciated as such.

Istrian cuisine, one can read in Gottardi's historically oriented recipe book, is nowadays in danger of ossifying. Maybe the right perspective is the one adopted by Bastianich: staying as close as possible to the terroir and remaining as respectful of it as possible, yet not fearing hybridity, but being open to innovation and multivocality. Maybe Istrian food is now becoming as multivocal as the destination of the Italians from Istria is plural.

'Food is so good at triggering dialogue',[54] as a public historian wrote. The ritual 'memory meal'[55] staged in *Magna Istria* is open to reconciliation and hybridism. Rethinking food in forced migrations should also deal with these dynamic contemporary aspects, keeping an eye on comparison and not forgetting the new refugees that Europe is experiencing in our own day.

Ilaria Porciani is Professor of Modern and Contemporary History at the University of Bologna. She has published widely on the history of historiography, the university, nationalism and education. She has worked on public history and the history of history museums. Among her recent publications are *Food Heritage and Nationalism in Europe* (Routledge, 2019). She is presently working on a monograph entitled *Cuisine and Nation: A Global History*.

Notes

1. Barbieri, 'Croatia', 106.
2. See Bernas, *Ci chiamavano fascisti*.
3. On the 'silent' exodus, see Ballinger, *History in Exile*. See also: Ballinger, 'At the Borders of Force'; Ballinger, 'Trieste'; and Ballinger, 'Authentic Hybrids in the Balkan Borderlands'.
4. See Pupo, *Il lungo esodo*; Pupo and Spazzali, *Foibe*; Ventura, *Per una storicizzazione dell'esodo giuliano-dalmata*; Cattaruzza, *L'Italia e il confine orientale*; and Gasparini, Del Zotto and Pocecco, *Esuli in Italia*.
5. See Nemec, *Un paese perfetto*.
6. La Cecla, 'Mangiarsi l'identità', 206.
7. A very good representation of this sudden shift can be found in Tassos Boulmetis's 2004 film *A Touch of Spice* (original title *Kousina Politika*).
8. La Cecla, 'Mangiarsi l'identità', 206.
9. See also Roy, 'Reading Communities and Culinary Communities'.
10. See Porciani, 'Food Heritage and Nationalism'.
11. I have already pointed out this issue in relation to the kitchen tools that 'the ones who left' brought with them. Many of them remained in the Trieste Magazzino 18 and are to be seen in the Trieste museum on Istrian, Dalmatian and Fiume civilization. See Porciani, 'Exilescapes in a Hangar'. See also Porciani, 'Conflicts, Borders and Nationalism'.
12. Hobsbawm and Ranger, *The Invention of Tradition*.
13. On food and banal nationalism, see Porciani, 'Food Heritage and Nationalism', 7–9.
14. See Horel, 'Franz Joseph's Tafelspitz'.
15. It would be worth investigating whether the borderline could in this sense be identified by the presence of the *peka* or *sač* (a pot covered by burning coals traditionally used in the non-coastal areas for cooking sheep). I wish to thank Nicoletta Celli for this suggestion.
16. See Gorlato, 'La casa e il suo territorio' and Forlani, 'La ricerca etnografica del centro di ricerche storiche di Rovigno nell'area Istro-romanza'.
17. See Katrak, 'Food and Belonging'.
18. See Mannur, *Culinary Fictions*.
19. Oretti, *A Caminando che 'l va*, 192, 245.
20. *Pola: Una città che muore* (1947) – see https://www.youtube.com/watch?v=pp-QILLUSwHw (accessed 7 March 2022).
21. Ballinger, *History in Exile*, 195.
22. Anderson, *Imagined Communities*.
23. Connerth, 'Pflege der Volkskunst', 10, quoted in Eisler, *Verwaltete Erinnerung*, 142.
24. See Porciani, 'Exilescapes in a Hangar'.
25. See Eisler, *Verwaltete Erinnerung*; Fendl, 'Mitgenommen'; Fendl, 'In Szene gesetzt'; Fendl and Mohr, *HeimatGeschichten*.
26. See https://www.bkge.de/Heimatsammlungen/Verzeichnis/Ueberregional/Vertriebenen-Heimatstube-Neukirchen.php (accessed 7 March 2022).
27. See https://www.nordkirche.de/nachrichten/nachrichten-detail/nachricht/vertriebene-verraten-fuer-kochbuch-antike-rezepte/; https://www.evangelische-zeitung.de/news-detail-home/nachricht/ein-kochbuch-mit-rezepten-aus-der-verlorenen-heimat.html (accessed 7 March 2022). 'Kirchen-Back-Buch', published in 2012, reached a third edition and sold over five thousand copies.

28. See https://www.sueddeutsche.de/bayern/vertriebene-die-insel-der-sudeten-1.2542662 (accessed 7 March 2022).

29. La Cecla, 'Oggetti domestici in ambienti domestici', 9.

30. I am writing on the basis of notes taken before 2018: therefore, I cannot discuss the new permanent exhibition of the Museo della Civiltà Istriana, Fiumana e Dalmata in Trieste.

31. See Eisler, *Verwaltete Erinnerung*, 127.

32. Eckersley, 'A Place at the Table?', 116.

33. This exhibition was the follow-up to the *Mitgenommen – Heimat in Dingen (Taken with – Fatherland in Things)* exhibition, on display in 2015, which was set up by the same organization. See https://www.youtube.com/watch?v=nHPe4PJVeWU;

https://www.svz.de/regionales/mecklenburg-vorpommern/mecklenburg-magazin/ein-potpourri-aus-verschiedenen-kuechen-id17203951.html (accessed 7 March 2022).

34. Quoted in Porciani, *Exilescapes*, 203 (accessed May 2016). Translated by the author.

35. On display in the Padriciano camp, 2015. Bibliographical indications not given, translation by the author.

36. Madieri, *Verde acqua*, chapter entitled '23 gennaio 1982'.

37. Zelco, *Vento di terra perduta*, 101–6.

38. Giard, 'Doing Cooking', 222.

39. Mori, *Nata in Istria*, 251.

40. Il campo della cultura, 'Magna Istria'.

41. See Cimmino, *Quella terra è la mia terra*.

42. Milani, *L'ovo slosso*, 73–74.

43. See Sardoz Barlessi, *E in mezzo un fiume*.

44. See Zelco, *La vita sdoppiata*.

45. See, among others, Criscione, *La donna in Istria e in Dalmazia*, 135–36.

46. Oretti, *A caminando che 'l va*, 79.

47. Rosano, *Natale con Lidia Bastianich*.

48. Ibid.

49. Matticchio Bastianich and Bastianich Manuali, *Lidia's Italy in America*, vi.

50. Minardi, 'Lidia Bastianich'.

51. 'Il premio Rovagnati è arrivato oltre Oceano', *Il Giorno*, 4 December 2018.

52. See *Die Kartoffel, der Mangel steht hier Pathe*. https://sfvv.e-fork.net/sites/default/files/Rezeptbuch_Weihnachtskarte_sfvv_4.pdf (accessed 7 March 2022).

53. See Kim, 'A Korean Community'.

54. See Steinberg, 'What We Talk about When We Talk about Food', 83.

55. Macdonald, *Memorylands*, 7.

Bibliography

Anderson, Benedict. *Imagined Communities: Reflections on the Origin and Spread of Nationalism*. New York: Verso, 1983.

Ballinger, Pamela. *History in Exile: Memory and Identity at the Border of the Balkans*. Princeton, NJ: Princeton University Press, 2003.

———. 'Authentic Hybrids in the Balkan Borderlands'. *Current Anthropology* 45(1) (2004), 31–59.

———. 'Trieste: The City as Displaced Persons Camp'. *Jahrbücher für Geschichte und Kultur Südosteuropas* 8 (2008), 153–74.

———. 'At the Borders of Force: Violence, Refugees and the Reconfiguration of the Yugoslav and Italian States'. *Past and Present* 210(6) (2011), 158–76.
Barbieri, Veliko. 'Croatia: From Myth to Authenticity', in D. Goldstein and K. Merkle (eds), *Culinary Cultures of Europe: Identity, Diversity and Dialogue* (Strasbourg: Council of Europe, 2005), 103–18.
Bernas, Jan. *Ci chiamavano fascisti. Eravamo italiani. Istriani, Fiumani e Dalmati: Storie di esuli e di rimasti*. Preface by W. Veltroni. Milan: Mursia, 2010.
Cattaruzza, Marina. *L'Italia e il confine orientale:1866–2006*. Bologna: Il Mulino, 2007.
Cimmino, Raffaele. *Quella terra è la mia terra. Istria: memoria di un esodo*. Padua: Il Prato, 1999.
Criscione, Giusy (ed.). *La donna in Istria e in Dalmazia nelle immagini e nelle storie*. Rome: Associazione nazionale giuliano-dalmata, 2008.
Eckersley, Susannah. 'A Place at the Table? Food in Museums as an "*Ersatz* Politics of Difficulty"', in I. Porciani (ed.), *Food Heritage and Nationalism* (London: Routledge, 2019), 98–121.
Eisler, Cornelia. *Verwaltete Erinnerung – symbolische Politik: Die Heimatsammlungen der deutschen Flüchtlinge, Vertriebenen und Aussiedler*. Munich: De Gruyter Oldenbourg, 2015.
Fendl, Elisabeth. 'Mitgenommen: Das Gepäck der Heimatvertriebenen'. *Jahrbuch für ostdeutsche Volkskunde* 36 (1993), 229–43.
———. 'In Szene gesetzt: Populäre Darstellungen von Flucht und Vertreibung', in E. Fendl (ed.), *Zur Ästhetik des Verlusts: Bilder von Heimat, Flucht und Vertreibung* (Münster: Waxmann, 2010), 45–69.
Fendl, Elisabeth, and Karen Mohr. *HeimatGeschichten: Aus der Sammlungen des Sudetendeutschen Museums*. Munich: Volk Verlag, 2018.
Forlani, Anita. 'La ricerca etnografica del centro di ricerche storiche di Rovigno nell'area Istro-romanza, con particolare riguardo al territorio di Dignano: Risultati e problemi'. *Zgodovinske vzporednice slovenske in hraske etnologije* 3 (1987), 53–61.
Gasparini, Alberto, Maura Del Zotto and Antonella Pococco. *Esuli in Italia: Ricordi, valori, futuro per le generazioni di esuli dall'Istria-Dalmazia-Quarnaro*. Gorizia: ISIG, Istituto di sociologia internazionale/ANVGD, Associazione nazionale Venezia Giulia e Dalmazia, 2008.
Giard, Luce. 'Doing Cooking', in Michel De Certeau, Luce Giard and Pierre Mayol (eds), *The Practice of Everyday Life*, vol. II, *Living and Cooking* (Minneapolis, MN: The University of Minnesota Press, 1998), 149–252.
Gorlato, Laura. 'La casa e il suo territorio', in *Dignano e la sua gente* (Trieste: Lint, 1975), 179–87.
Gottardi, Francesco. *Come mangiavamo a Fiume nell'Imperial Regia cucina asburgica e nelle zone limitrofe della Venezia Giulia*. Trieste: Coordinamento Adriatico, 2019.
Hobsbawm, Eric J., and Terence Ranger (eds). *The Invention of Tradition*. Cambridge: Cambridge University Press, 1983.
Horel, Catherine. 'Franz Joseph's Tafelspitz: Austro-Hungarian Cooking as an Imperial Project', in Ilaria Porciani (ed.), *Food Heritage and Nationalism* (London: Routledge, 2019), 138–54.
Il campo della cultura. 'Magna Istria: Tra gusto e memoria'. Retrieved 7 March 2022 from http://www.campodellacultura.it/conoscere/approfondimenti/magna-istria-tra-gusto-e-memoria/.
Katrak, Ketu H. 'Food and Belonging: At home in "Alien-Kitchens"', in Arlene Voski Avakian (ed.), *Through the Kitchen Window: Women Explore the Intimate Meaning of Food and Cooking* (Boston: Beacon Press, 1997), 263–75.
Kim, Go. 'A Korean Community of International Diaspora: The Identities of Wollam'ins in Sokcho, South Korea'. *Development and Society* 30(1) (2001), 27–50.

La Cecla, Franco. 'Oggetti domestici in ambienti domestici', in Franco La Cecla, *Vita affettiva degli oggetti* (Bologna: Eleuthera, 1998), 9–13.

———. 'Mangiarsi l'identità', in Roberto Alessandrini and Michelina Borsari (eds), *Condotte alimentari e pasti rituali nella definizione dell'identità religiosa* (Bologna: Banca Popolare dell'Emilia Romagna, 1999), 200–19.

Macdonald, Sharon. *Memorylands: Heritage and Identity in Europe Today*. London: Routledge, 2013.

Madieri, Marisa. *Verde acqua*. Turin: Einaudi, 1987.

Mannur, A. *Culinary Fictions: Food in South Asian Diasporic Culture*. Philadelphia, PA: Temple University Press, 2010.

Matticchio Bastianich, Lidia, and Tanya Bastianich Manuali. *Lidia's Italy in America: A Cookbook*. Westminster: Knopf Doubleday, 2011.

Minardi, Sabina. 'Lidia Bastianich: "La mia cucina, un ponte tra culture e generazioni"'. *L'Espresso*, 18 August 2017. Retrieved 7 March 2022 from http://espresso.repubblica.it/visioni/societa/2017/08/18/news/lidia-bastianich-la-mia-cucina-ponte-tra-culture-1.308142.

Milani, Nelida. *L'ovo slosso*. Rijeka: Edit, 1994.

Mori, Anna Maria. *Nata in Istria*. Milan: RCS Libri, 2006.

Nemec, Gloria. *Un paese perfetto. Storia e memoria di una comunità in esilio: Grisignana d'Istria 1930–1960*. Gorizia: Istituto Regionale per la Cultura Istriana/Libreria Editrice Goriziana, 1998.

Oretti, Laura. *A Caminando che 'l va ... Repertorio della narrativa di tradizione orale delle comunità italiane in Istria*. Trieste: Edizioni Italo Svevo, 1994.

Porciani, Ilaria. 'Conflicts, Borders and Nationalism: The Fiume Archive-Museum in Rome', in Dominique Poulot, José Maria Lanzarote Guiral, Felicity Bodenstein (eds), *National Museums and the Negotiation of Difficult Pasts* (Lingköping: Lingköping University Electronic Press, 2012), 37–59.

———. 'Exilescapes in a Hangar – Exilescapes in a Camp: Period Rooms from the Lost Nation', in S. Costa, D. Poulot and M. Volait (eds), *The Period Rooms* (Bologna: BUP, 2017), 199–206.

———. 'Food Heritage and Nationalism', in I. Porciani (ed.), *Food Heritage and Nationalism* (London: Routledge, 2019), 3–32.

Pupo, Raoul. *Il lungo esodo. Istria: le persecuzioni, le foibe, l'esilio*. Milan: BUR storia, 2006.

Pupo, Raoul, and Roberto Spazzali. *Foibe*. Milan: Bruno Mondadori, 2003.

Rosano, Liliana. 'Natale con Lidia Bastianich: Un'intervista'. *Gambero Rosso*, 25 December 2014. Retrieved 7 March 2022 from https://www.gamberorosso.it/notizie/articoli-food/natale-con-lidia-bastianich-un-intervista/.

Roy, Parama. 'Reading Communities and Culinary Communities: The Gastropoetics of the South Asian Diaspora'. *Positions: East Asia Cultures Critique* 10(2) (2002), 471–502.

Sardoz Barlessi, Ester. *E in mezzo un fiume: Racconti*. Introduction by N. Milani Kuljac. Rijeka: Edit, 1997.

Steinberg, Adam. 'What We Talk about When We Talk about Food: Using Food to Teach History at the Tenement Museum'. *The Public Historian* 34(2) (2012), 79–89.

Ventura, Angelo (ed.). *Per una storicizzazione dell'esodo giuliano-dalmata*. Padua: CLEUP, 2005.

Zelco, Giuliana. *La vita sdoppiata* (1982), in *Un volto per sognare. Poesie scelte 1950–1986*. Trieste: Comune di Trieste, 1988.

———. *Vento di terra perduta o la vita sdoppiata*. Trieste: Edizioni Italo Svevo, 1993.

Part V

GAZING AT AND DEFINING PEOPLE IN THE BORDERLAND

TAKAHIRO YAMAMOTO AND TAKEHIRO OKABE

The two chapters in this section deal with borderlands of the Russian Empire and the Soviet Union. Okabe's chapter describes the history of Finnish and Russian/Soviet visions of unifying Finnic-speaking peoples by addressing the Soviet–Finnish controversy over the *Kalevala*, a Finnish and Soviet national epic and symbol. From the mid-nineteenth century, Finnish intellectual elites were engaged not only in making the Finnish nation but also in imagining a unified Finnic family by supporting and enlightening their kindred peoples, such as Karelians and Estonians. This pan-Finnic vision, through the Russian Revolution and the Finnish Civil War, contributed to an expansionist and irredentist Greater Finland claiming Soviet Karelia and helping Estonia's independence. While Finnish communists brought this pan-Finnic ideology to Soviet Karelia, Russian and Soviet Karelian elites challenged this vision with an emerging Soviet Karelian identity, distinguished from Finnish but tied with Russian. Though Finnish elements were physically removed in the late 1930s, Soviet Karelia again saw Finnish–Karelian kinship with the establishment of the Karelo-Finnish Republic after the Soviet–Finnish War (Winter War). After Finland finally abandoned the Greater Finland policy in 1944, the Soviets selectively utilized the pan-Finnic vision to integrate Soviet Finns, Karelians and Estonians, whom they 'liberated', into the

Soviet family of peoples. Okabe's chapter shows this shift in the centre of pan-Finnism from Finland to the Soviet Union, which was crystalized in two centenary jubilees of the *Kalevala* in 1935 and 1949. At the same time, the *Kalevala* controversy demonstrates how both Finnish and Soviet visions shared paternalistic attitudes towards Finnic peoples.

Yamamoto's chapter, moving to the other end of the Eurasian continent, explores the history of the thorny interactions between the Japanese and the Kuril Ainu, an Indigenous group who lived in the Kuril Islands on the north-western rim of the Pacific from at least the end of the seventeenth century, and whose cultural lineages became largely invisible by the mid-twentieth century. The focus is on the representation of the Kuril Ainu in Japanese discourse in the late nineteenth century, the crucial moment in Japan's assimilation policy towards them, and in the present. After the Japanese government forced the hitherto itinerant Kuril Ainu to settle on Shikotan Island in 1884, the Indigenous group struggled to adapt to the new environment. Amid the shortage of food, widespread disease and the loss of economic ties with the Russian far east, they negotiated with the Japanese officials to improve their living conditions. By analysing various official and private sources, with an emphasis on photographs of the community's chief throughout his life, this chapter argues that the colonial gaze of the Japanese affects almost all the sources relating to the Kuril Ainu from the late nineteenth and early twentieth centuries, reminding the reader of the particular angles that influence how we understand this story. The narratives formed through Orthodox Christian sources could serve as a starting point to counterbalance the official Japanese context, though their narrative was produced with the inclination to present an idealized picture of the Kuril Ainu.

Methodologically, the two chapters employ different types of sources: Okabe's chapter investigates academic discussions of the *Kalevala*'s poetry and its language, which are heavily burdened with political and ideological pressure. Yamamoto's chapter depicts how the Kuril Ainu were represented in the photographs taken by the Japanese and other foreigners, in travel writings and in church gazettes. This methodological contrast and the geographical distance notwithstanding, both chapters develop a common analytical angle on how intellectuals and scholars, and sometimes even ordinary individuals, placed their gaze on peoples in the borderland as a reflection of the political context within which they lived. The two chapters confirm the role of academics in nation-building and the social and discursive formation of borderlands. They also highlight the varied ways in which the peoples of the borderland attempted to influence the narrative emanating from the centre of political power and economic and cultural dominance.

CHAPTER 9

The Japanese Gaze and the Memory of the Kuril Ainu

TAKAHIRO YAMAMOTO

How are people at the margins of political power and the edge of a territorial sovereign state represented in a nation state's historical narratives? When they receive attention from contemporary observers and later historians, what factors affect the ways in which they are represented and remembered? What does the memory of these marginalized people reveal about how people in the political centre understand their borderland? This chapter addresses these questions by looking at the history of the interactions between the Japanese and the Kuril Ainu, an Indigenous group who have lived in the Kuril Islands on the north-western rim of the Pacific since at least the end of the seventeenth century, and whose cultural lineages became largely invisible by the mid-twentieth century.[1]

The Kuril Ainu subsisted primarily through hunting and trading seals, sea otters and foxes, as well as fishing, but they also engaged in agriculture on a limited scale. Men and women moved across the island chain during the hunting season, leaving both the elderly and children in *kotan-ba*, or permanent settlements, in three different locations across the archipelago.[2] Their population decreased gradually, dropping from around 250 or 300 at the beginning of the eighteenth century to about 160 at the beginning of the nineteenth, and to fewer than 100 in the 1820s. From 1830 to 1867, the Russian American Company, a state-backed consortium of merchants engaged in fur animal hunting in Russian America, served as the sole agent for fur trades with the Kuril Ainu.[3] Beginning in the late eighteenth century, the Kuril Ainu were effectively included in the Kamchatka parish of the Russian Orthodox Church, whose chaplains converted the Indigenous population and performed religious services during annual visits to the northernmost Shumushu Island, where a church had been built.[4] Thus, the Kuril Ainu came to experience a strong cultural and religious influence from Russia, not unlike the Indigenous peoples in Siberia.[5]

The conventional narrative on the Kuril Ainu describes their 'deculturation' and disappearance in the late nineteenth and early twentieth centuries, attributing this to Japan's assimilation policy following its territorial claim of the entire archipelago in 1875. David Howell has noted that accounts of their condition in the early twentieth century 'convey their feelings of impotence and indeed apathy about their situation, leaving little doubt that a cultural crisis had overcome them'.[6] The Japanese assimilation policies entailed, most fundamentally, the local peoples' relocation from the Kuril Islands to Shikotan Island, off the eastern coast of Hokkaido, in July 1884, and a ban on their return to the northern Kurils, cutting them off from their previous economic activities. Assimilation also involved the imposition of agriculture on Shikotan; the adoption of Japanese names beginning in 1911; and education at a Japanese primary school in the nearby town of Nemuro. Struggling to adapt to an agricultural working life and suffering from diseases such as flu and pneumonia, the Kuril Ainu became dependent on aid from the government and other interested parties, most notably the Orthodox Church, but also Higashi Honganji, a Buddhist temple headquartered in Kyoto, as well as Japanese activists interested in the security of the northern frontier.

The historical memory about the Kuril Ainu therefore focuses heavily on cultural loss, economic decline and dependence on the Japanese as a result of assimilation policies that made other paths impossible to pursue. Yet one should also note that the contemporary imperative of territorial sovereignty has served to frame the historical memory of these past experiences. This tendency is especially pertinent with regard to the southern Kuril Islands and the adjacent islets, as they have been a subject of diplomatic disputes between the Soviet Union (and later Russia) and Japan since the end of the Second World War. Soviet soldiers occupied the Kuril Islands starting in August 1945, after the Soviets' entry into the war against imperial Japan. The archipelago remained under Soviet rule after the end of the Allied Forces' occupation, and the Japanese government has maintained that the status of the islands south of the 1875 border – Etorofu, Kunashiri, Shikotan and Habomai Islets – is a unsolved question.[7] Because this territorial dispute is linked with the talks over a Russo-Japanese peace treaty, which has not been concluded to date, these four islands are discussed almost exclusively through the prism of Russo-Japanese relations.⁸ Such an understanding, however, risks overlooking the fact that Indigenous peoples had established their lives and cultures here before the arrival of either the Russians or the Japanese. The memory of the Kuril Ainu is a venue in which the framing of the borderland as part of this bilateral relationship has defined the story to be told about the Indigenous residents. In order to arrive at a deeper understanding of the history of the Kuril Ainu, the Japanese gaze upon them and its influence on their memory, we must take a close look at the available sources.

This chapter focuses on the life of a man named Konkamakuru (1837?–1903), also known as Yakov Strozev,⁹ and Japanese perceptions of him. Konkamakuru was born in 1837 or 1838 on Paramushir Island, located in the middle of the Kuril archipelago.¹⁰ He was a long-time chief of his highly mobile community. Konkamakuru married twice and had at least four children.¹¹ After the 1875 Russo-Japanese territorial agreement, the Kuril Ainu were given three years to decide whether to stay in the archipelago and accept becoming Japanese subjects or to leave the islands and move to Russia. The majority of the Kuril Ainu chose the first option, but their connection with the rest of Japan remained minimal; the only visitors were government officials who arrived in a steamer every one to two years. In contrast, between 1875 and 1884, the locals maintained connections with Russian merchants based in Petropavlovsk.¹² But in July 1884, under pressure from the Japanese government, Konkamakuru and 96 Kuril Ainu – at that time, the entire population of the archipelago – permanently migrated to Shikotan Island. Most of them died without being able to see their homeland again. The relocation withered the islanders' ties with Russians, as well as with North American sailors coming from Alaska, San Francisco and beyond, placing them in deeper and almost exclusive contact with the Japanese.

Shikotan Island comprised approximately 255 square kilometres, roughly the same size as Malta. But the climate was nothing like the Mediterranean: it was covered with snow from December to April. As there was a flat grassland, Japanese officials thought the place would be suited for agriculture and raising livestock; however, the Kuril Ainu lacked experience with either. After relocation, the Kuril Ainu retained their Orthodox Christian faith, exemplified by a church built by Konkamakuru in 1887.¹³

Writers tackling the history of Indigenous peoples face a perennial challenge concerning sources, and this chapter is no exception. Konkamakuru's own words are rarely recorded in primary sources, partly because the documents up to 1886 were destroyed in a fire in Konkamakuru's house in that year, according to Saitō Tōkichi, an Orthodox Christian evangelist who worked in Shikotan between 1906 and 1907.[14] Besides, there was an almost palpable motivation on the part of contemporary writers to spin the story in their favour.[15] The remainder of this chapter focuses on two approaches to revisiting the historical memory of the Kuril Ainu. One is to analyse photographs of Konkamakuru and his fellow villagers. The other involves reconstructing the Kuril Ainu's past through sources from the Orthodox Church, contrasting this with the narrative based on Japanese government sources and exploring how contemporary Orthodox Christians in Japan remember the Kuril Ainu within the context of their religious community. The core argument is that the colonial gaze of the Japanese affects almost all the sources relating to the Kuril Ainu from the late nineteenth and early twentieth centuries, challenging us to be aware of the particular angles that might influence how we understand this story. The narratives formed through the Orthodox Christian sources could serve as a starting point to counterbalance the official Japanese context, bearing in mind that the Orthodox Christian portrayal demonstrates a preference to paint the Kuril Ainu in an explicitly positive light.

The Japanese Gaze upon Konkamakuru

Japanese officials in the late nineteenth century employed photographs to display power relations between themselves and the Indigenous peoples in newly acquired territories. The postures, clothes and interactions depicted in photographs can have powerful symbolic associations.[16] In this vein, the Japanese attitude towards the Kuril Ainu may be observed through their photographs.

The first known photograph of Konkamakuru was taken in 1882 (Figure 9.1), when his community was taken on board a hunting vessel and moved from one island to another. The photographer is unknown. While Konkamakuru, at the bottom left, shows little emotion, the facial expressions of others suggest that at least some of the Kuril Ainu did not interpret the photo-taking as an exercise of power onto themselves.

Figure 9.1. Kuril Ainu hunters on a hunting ship, *c*.1882. Konkamakuru is the man on the left in the front row. Snow, *In Forbidden Seas*, between 14 and 15. The photograph has no dates, but the detail of their likely voyage on a hunting vessel is recorded in 'Meiji 16 nen Chishimakoku dojin higai'.

This casual photographic appearance of the Kuril Ainu proved to be a rarity. In 1886, Konkamakuru (second from the right) and his brother Kepurian Strozev (left), who was the chief of the Kuril Ainu at the time, travelled from Shikotan to Hakodate to present their handicrafts at a municipal industrial exhibition (Figure 9.2).[17] This photograph, taken during their stay, belonged to the collection of Kojima Kuratarō (second from the left), a Russian-language interpreter who worked for Hakodate Prefecture.

The position of the subjects can be read as an expression of power relations: the Japanese, who had control over the lives of the Kuril Ainu through policy directives and material and financial allowances, sit on chairs as they make the Ainu men squat on the carpet.[18] Each individual's appearance also conveys the sense of differentiation. Although Konkamakuru and his brother are dressed in Western attire, their roughly chopped forelocks are distinctively different from the Japanese officers' combed hair. Kojima, who had known Konkamakuru and Kepurian since the latter's relocation in July 1884, likely took the picture in order to remember the occasion – the first visit to Hokkaido by the Kuril Ainu who had come under their dominion a few years previously. By capturing the moment in this way, however, he also recorded the Japanese desire to stage themselves in the position of civilizers to whomever might have a chance to view this photograph.

The Japanese gaze upon the Kuril Ainu in Shikotan becomes more apparent when their photographs are juxtaposed with those taken by non-Japanese visitors to the island. Romyn Hitchcock, an American anthropologist who worked at the Smithsonian Museum and held a cross-appointment with Osaka University between 1887 and 1889, spent one day on Shikotan during his tour around Hokkaido in 1888.[19] He took at

Figure 9.2.
Konkamakuru in Hakodate, taken on 24 October 1886. Hakodate City Library, H20-0050.

least seven photographs of the village of the Kuril Ainu, one of which was a group photo (Figure 9.3).

The Kuril Ainu in this photograph appear differently than they do in Japanese photographs with a similar setting. Most of the subjects are dressed in Western-style clothing, and many, including children, put their hands together in front of their bodies and visibly straighten their backs.[20] This point becomes notable when compared to the group photo from the collection of Kataoka Toshikazu, an aide of the Meiji Emperor who explored the northern Kuril Islands in 1891 (Figure 9.4), where such conscious acts of posturing are less observable. A few women do put their hands together, but they do not seem to consciously raise their folded hands above their lap. There is more regimentation in the overall presentation of the subjects before the camera. All those in the front line are sitting on what looks like a long piece of timber, while people in the back stand on top of an object so that they can be visible to the camera. Few people hide behind others, and their bodies are equally exposed to the viewer. In contrast, Figure 9.3 captures less regimentation imposed by the photographer: there is no coordination as to whether one should stand or sit down. Some residents are not clearly visible, instead standing behind others. One woman in the middle holds a guitar, while such showcasing of an additional element is entirely missing from Figure 9.4.

Figure 9.3. The Kuril Ainu in Shikotan, taken on 9 August 1888. Smithsonian Institution, National Anthropology Archive, NAA INV 05290500. Image file provided by Uni Yoshikazu.

The Japanese photographer, overall, managed to impose his vision of order on the village, reflecting the extent of Japanese power within the picture.

In addition to vertical positioning and the use of chairs as expressions of power, the inability to distinguish individuals was a key feature of many colonial photographs. Figure 9.4 conveys the message that the Japanese arrived with the intention of keeping a record not of the Kuril Ainu's individuality, but of their own visit, including their encounter with the Indigenous residents who were receiving material and financial aid from the Japanese government. The very fact that these group photographs were taken indicates the power of Japanese command: the Kuril Ainu were obliged to follow the officials' order to line up, stay still and have their photograph taken, though their identities are masked by the distance and the visual unclarity of the image. The Ainu residents' agency is not considered by the photographer, and the viewer is drawn to align themselves with the photographer's perspective and perceive the Indigenous people as objects.

Another group of people who took an interest in photographing the Ainu at the turn of the century were Japanese anthropologists, whose theories and fieldwork progressed in tandem with Japanese colonial expansion.[21] Their photographs of the Kuril Ainu included close-ups of individuals, as seen in the images by Torii Ryūzō, professor of anthropology at the Tokyo Imperial University, who published a voluminous study of the Kuril Ainu in Japanese (1903) and in French (1919).

Figure 9.4. 'The Chishima Province, Shikotan Island villagers', taken on 15 November 1891. Kataoka Toshikazu Kankei Monjo, reel 2. National Diet Library, Tokyo.

Torii studied Indigenous peoples in the Japanese empire and beyond in the early years of the twentieth century, conducting more than thirty fieldwork trips.[22] He conducted research in the Kuril Islands from May through June of 1899. Figure 9.5, taken in Shumushu in 1884 at the time of the Kuril Ainu's relocation to Shikotan, but later included in Torii's book, has the added purpose of recording their physical character for research.[23] The Ainu were photographed against the same plain background – presumably sitting on the same chair, one after another – in a setting where natural light does not obscure their facial features. In Torii's French publication, the five Kuril Ainu were introduced not by their names but by single letters below their faces. Their physical features mattered and were recorded by taking a close-up from two directions, but the mechanical way in which Torii presented these individuals' images is notable.

Torii's photographs of Konkamakuru (Figure 9.6 and Figure 9.7), taken in 1899 in Shikotan, are slightly different from Figure 9.5. Konkamakuru is sitting outside the church, where the sunlight makes it difficult for the viewer to see his eyes. Among the individual portraits of the Kuril Ainu used in Torii's 1919 publication, this is the only photograph that does not clearly show the subject's eyes.

Torii took multiple portraits of Konkamakuru. Judging from the background, Figure 9.6 and Figure 9.7 were taken at the same location (likely

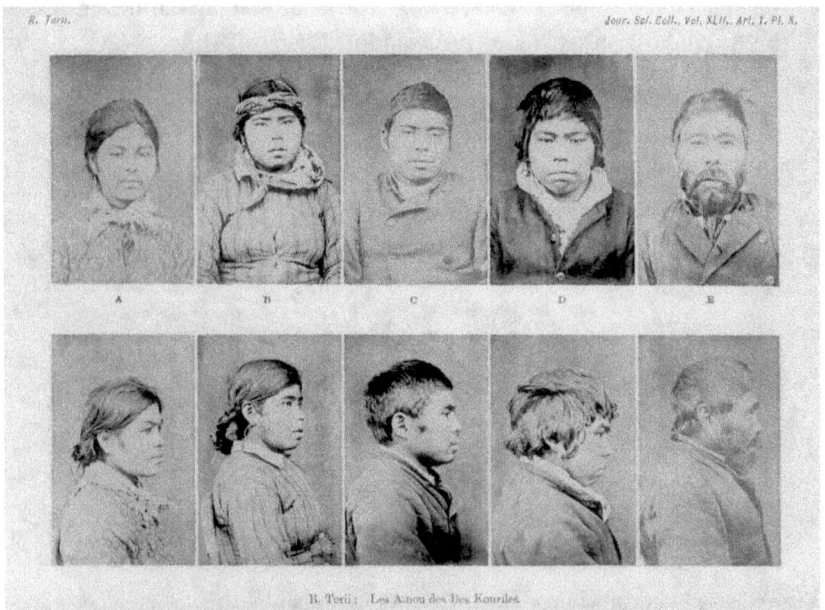

Figure 9.5. Five Kuril Ainu, taken in Shumushu before their relocation to Shikotan, in July 1884. Torii, 'Etudes Archeologiques', here Planche X.

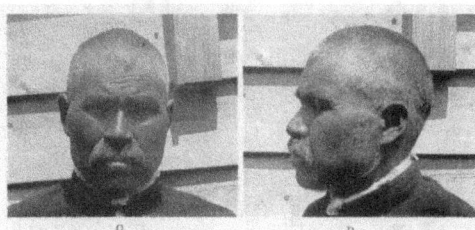

Figure 9.6. 'Jacob, Ainu Chief, Seen from the Front and the Side.' Taken c.1899. Torii, 'Etudes Archeologiques', Planche VI.

Figure 9.7. 'Mr. Yakov Strov, Mayor of the Kuril Ainu.' Taken c.1899. East Asia and Micronesia Old Photographic Images Database 1058, University Museum, University of Tokyo, http://torii.akazawa-project.jp/cms/photo_archive/nakagawa/photo.html (accessed 22 October 2021). The caption on the website inaccurately transcribes Konkamakuru's Russian name: whereas a close Japanese transliteration is *Sutorojefu*, here it reads *Sutorofu*. The spelling of 'Strov' has been chosen by the author to approximate the inaccuracy. The original word used here for 'mayor' is *sonchō*, although this is not completely accurate either. Konkamakuru never held an official position as such; the Japanese officer stationed on the island and given the title *kochō* (lit. 'head of households') was the top figure in the village administration.

outside the church Konkamakuru built). This indicates that after taking Figure 9.7, Torii moved closer to take a close-up of Konkamakuru's face, then told him to look right to capture his head from the side. The background shows that Torii barely moved the camera between these two pictures; it was Konkamakuru who adjusted his posture to accommodate the request. These photographs, considered together, reveal not only Torii's interest in the Kuril Ainu as an anthropologist but also the power hierarchy of which he took advantage. Yet Torii might not have had everything as he wished: though it is impossible to prove or disprove, Konkamakuru's darkened eyes, caused by the location of the photography session, may have been the result of his resistance to moving to a better-lit place.[24] If that is the case, it would demonstrate his attempt to regain agency in the face of Torii's research activity.

After years of requesting the restoration of the Kuril Ainu's earlier ways of life, Konkamakuru was allowed by the Meiji government to go back to the Kuril archipelago at least four times at the end of the nineteenth century.[25] After his stay in Paramushir in 1900, his family was picked up by a ship belonging to the Hokkaido municipal government, the *Musashi*, returning to Shikotan in June of that year. On board, the officers took the group's portrait (Figure 9.8).

Figure 9.8. 'The Party of Shikotan Native Yakov, taken in June 1900.' Hokkaidōchō, *Kita Chishima*, frame 17.

This picture is the first one to depict Konkamakuru with his family members (and two other families). They are mostly dressed in Japanese garments, and the women wear their hair in the Japanese style – a clear departure from the Russian influence observable in Figures 9.3, 9.4 and 9.5. The younger generation, especially the children, by then 'spoke our national language (*hōgo*) well', observed the official report in 1901.[26] Konkamakuru sits in the centre, dressed in what looks like a Western-style double-breasted coat and a hat, giving the impression that he is in charge of this group.

The last known photograph of Konkamakuru was taken in Tokyo. From October to November 1900, four months after returning from Paramushir, Konkamakuru visited Tokyo for the first and last time. Yokoyama Kendō, a popular writer who specialized in biographies of historical figures, took an interest in Konkamakuru, likely after reading a newspaper article on him. According to Yokoyama, the two men met up several times, including one meal at a beef restaurant in the bustling city centre of Asakusa, followed by a visit to a nearby studio of photographer Ezaki Reiji. Yokoyama published an account of this episode and the photograph (Figure 9.9) in 1935 in a periodical called *Denki* (*Biographies*), quipping that 'a mere look at the picture would not tell you which one of us is a tribe chief (*shūchō*)'.[27]

This picture, which Yokoyama claimed was the only one of Konkamakuru taken on the Japanese mainland and the only one that shows his entire body, presents a clear contrast from his earlier photographs in several respects.[28] The background, their posture and their dress do not emphasize their difference. Crucially, though the picture is not completely clear, Konkamakuru's moustache seems to be gone. If that is the case, it means that he decided to shave it off after his return from his stay in the Kuril Islands. This may indicate his attempt – either voluntary

Figure 9.9. 'Shakotan Island Chief Strozev Yakov and the Author (taken on October 19, 1900).' Yokoyama, 'Matsuura Takeshirō'. Konkamakuru sits on the chair.

or imposed – at assimilating into Japanese society, distancing himself from the typical trope of 'hairy barbarian' that was used against the Ainu as a sign of their lack of civilizational advance.[29] Yokoyama later recalled:

> He uses fluent Japanese and makes jokes. Fluent in several languages such as English, French, German, and Russian, he moved around various countries' consulates serving as an interpreter for *kochō* [Kasuga Shōjirō, the head of Shakotan village]. He can write only in Russian and Japanese *katakana* but is proficient in six languages. He says that his native Ainu is the worst.[30]

Here, too, Yokoyama's description is far from the derogatory light in which the Ainu people were typically portrayed, both in the late nineteenth century and at the time of his writing in the early 1930s. Yokoyama extols Konkamakuru's good qualities:

> Yakov, as an Ainu person, is a great man, exceptional since ancient times [of Ainu people] [*Ainu jin to shite korai mare ni miru ketsubutsu*]. [He is] the man who receives special mention in the history of northern defence in the Meiji era. In the book called *Kataoka Jijū Hoppō Tankenki*, only this man among the Ainu is mentioned by name.[31]

Thus, three decades after his death, the memory of Konkamakuru emerged with a positive spin. Yet this does not mean that the Japanese colonial gaze on the Ainu was completely gone. Rather, the image of Konkamakuru gains the position of an exception: someone who, despite his Ainu background, managed to emulate the alleged departure of the Japanese from the backward Asia in an advance towards civilized ways.[32] What Yokoyama conveniently neglected, too, was the fact that Japanese defence of the north was at the same time an assault on the lives of the Kuril Ainu, the community of which Konkamakuru was a chief. Yokoyama thus simultaneously acknowledged and wrote off his past as an Ainu, placing him in the lineage of brave *Japanese* on the northern frontier who served the empire. In order to be a great man, in other words, Konkamakuru had to be separated from the other Ainu and placed in a Japanese context.

Furthermore, Yokoyama's explanation of the reason for Konkamakuru's visit may not be entirely accurate. He claimed that Konkamakuru came from Shikotan to observe the imperial pageant and sell sea otter pelts. But in fact, he had travelled to Tokyo with three other men: Gunji Shigetada, a retired navy official and the head of a patriotic society called Hōkō Gikai; Kasuga Shōjirō, the village chief of Shikotan; and Itō Tainin, a Higashi Honganji monk of Sekitoku Temple in Tokyo's Ushigome ward who had visited Shikotan. The party met with Suematsu Kenchō, the interior minister, and called for the opening of a regular shipping route between the Kurils and Nemuro on eastern Hokkaido. They came to Tokyo because the Hokkaido municipal government had rebuffed this plea, arguing that the existing annual aid of 1,500 yen and another 2,000 yen from Higashi Honganji should be sufficient to support the locals.[33] Konkamakuru's point, with which Gunji agreed, was that the Ainu would be much more productive if allowed to hunt and fish among such islands as Shumushu and Paramushir, and therefore could easily sustain their lives if allowed to return.[34]

The absence of parity between the Japanese and the Ainu is obvious, even with Yokoyama's extolment of Konkamakuru. In Yokoyama's article in *Denki*, Konkamakuru's episode comprises one section of a biography of Matsuura Takeshirō, a Japanese explorer and the person who coined the name Hokkaido for the island previously called Ezo. The article was sandwiched between essays on Mogami Tokunai and Torii Gonnosuke, who both explored Ezo and Karafuto islands during the Tokugawa shogunate's rule. Burying Konkamakuru deep inside this praise for Japanese pioneer spirits, Yokoyama conveniently omitted the fact that the Japanese domination was one of the major causes of the Kuril Ainu's predicament, which had brought Konkamakuru to Tokyo in search of their return to the homeland.

Konkamakuru, therefore, continued to be an object of Japan's political agenda throughout his adult life and even posthumously. The way in which the photographs were and are being used after Konkamakuru's death also speaks to the fundamental asymmetry that remains intact: by analysing the colonial domination and deculturation exerted on the Kuril Ainu, viewers' focus cannot fully reach the Kuril Ainu themselves. Japanese narratives have talked about a Japanese national history using the Kuril Ainu as evidence.

This asymmetry is difficult to overcome. What may be done, at the very least, is to provide a study on an alternative use of the memory of the Kuril Ainu. For that purpose, a case study can be found in the Orthodox Church.

Simple, Honest and Pious: Orthodox Christians' Memory of the Kuril Ainu

It did not take long for Konkamakuru and the other Kuril Ainu to realize that their new life in Shikotan was going to be extremely difficult. Cut off from their traditional hunting grounds, they had to cultivate farms and grow potatoes, white radishes, turnips, wheat, buckwheat and other crops, most of which were unfamiliar to them. Moreover, the island's climate, warmer and more humid than that of their home archipelago, was not the best match for their housing. Diseases and malnutrition claimed forty-seven lives in the first five years.[35] The government, though it ultimately failed to make the Kuril Ainu self-sufficient, tried to do so by providing them with cash and various materials including rice, salt, clothing, building materials for homes, tools for agriculture and livestock.[36] This official assistance was supplemented by sustained engagement from the Orthodox Christian Church in Japan.

From its inception, the Orthodox Church in Japan had a clear focus on the northern part of the country. In late 1859, the first Orthodox Church chaplain, Vasily Makhov, arrived at Hakodate, on the southern tip of what is today called Hokkaido. Makhov joined Iosif Goshkevich, who had just begun to serve as Russia's consul general following Hakodate's opening to foreign trade in 1858. The church attached to the consulate opened in 1860, providing religious services to both Russian and Japanese residents in Hakodate.[37] Some took advantage of this opportunity to study Russian. These Russian-trained students became the base from which the earliest generation of Japanese priests, such as Sawabe Takuma, was recruited.[38]

The Japanese Orthodox priests began to contact the Kuril Ainu in 1885, when Komatsu Tōzō, an itinerant priest serving eastern Hokkaido, met several Kuril Ainu schoolchildren in Nemuro. These children had travelled from Shikotan to Nemuro within a month of their relocation from the Kuril Islands.[39] On 22 May 1885, Komatsu and Sawabe, now an evangelist, boarded the same ship as the Ainu children bound for Shikotan. Upon landing, Uribitoaino (Lavrenti Strozev), one of the children, immediately informed Konkamakuru of the priests' arrival – the first visit of its kind in fifteen years.[40] Konkamakuru was initially sceptical because Komatsu was dressed in Japanese clothes. But as Sawabe reported, showing the Kuril Ainu a letter confirming their priesthood written by Nikolai Kasatkin, who headed the Orthodox Church in Tokyo, dispelled the suspicion and soon all were overjoyed to receive the two. From Konkamakuru's home, the visiting priests performed baptisms, held prayer services, performed the rites of Penance and Holy Communion, and performed thirty-four Chrismations and eleven marriages.[41]

This first encounter of the Kuril Ainu on Shikotan with the Japanese Orthodox Christians was recalled by Uribitoaino in 1906 and published in *Seikyō Shinpō*, the local periodical of the Orthodox Church. From this beginning, the Orthodox Christian community became more involved in the lives of the Kuril Ainu on Shikotan. The priests' visit became an annual event, and beginning in 1894, an evangelist was in permanent residence on the island. After the first visit, Komatsu reported the plight of the Kuril Ainu to Nikolai, which resulted in a wave of donations in money and in kind from Orthodox Christians across the country.[42]

Such broad support from the members of the religious community set the tone for the contemporary portrayal and the memory of the Kuril

Ainu as struggling but honest and pious people, and of Konkamakuru as a dedicated leader. For instance, when Komatsu distributed the donated goods when he returned to Shikotan, the Kuril Ainu reportedly said that he should decide how to distribute the resources; they would gladly accept whatever was given as God's gift.[43] Sakurai Senjirō, a Nemuro-based priest who visited Shikotan in September 1894, deemed Konkamakuru and the older generation of Ainu to be 'flawless as Christians'.[44] Archimandrite Sergius Stragorodsky, who visited Shikotan from Tokyo on 13 August 1898, was duly impressed by this 'truly lovely people' with their 'child-like simplicity'.[45] He recalled in his memoir that 'it was inspiring and touching to see this prayer' of the Kuril Ainu, who 'stood in perfect manners, looking at the Icon, earnestly crossing themselves'.[46] Exactly one year later, Nikolai visited the island from Tokyo; he celebrated the way that the Kuril Ainu maintained their faith despite their isolation from 1870 and 1885:

> Among them there is no theft, lie, fraud or hostility. All there is are such Christian characteristics as truth, honesty, love and humbleness. They are dressed simply and shabbily at home or work, but when they come to church, all of them make themselves tidy and wear the best clothes. Because everyone, young and old, comes to the church, all the village's houses become empty.[47]

A marked difference between the Japanese official narrative and the Orthodox Christian one is the view of the influence of the Japanese residents on the Kuril Ainu. Whereas the former portrays the Japanese on Shikotan as providers of vital material support, the latter takes note of the negative influence exerted by the Japanese. Sakurai worried in 1894 that:

> the younger ones, who are the majority, are miserable in their minds and deeds, and performing ugly things. They are even turning crafty. This is probably because many mainlanders are coming to the island for fishery, enticing these simple-hearted men, and disturbing their character... .[48]

By portraying the Japanese influence as having a degrading effect on the Kuril Ainu's character, this depiction serves to stress to the reader the high standard that had previously existed among the Kuril Ainu community. Accuracy of these individual anecdotes aside, they highlight what the Orthodox Christian community outside Shikotan wanted to remember about this people. At the time it may have served to depoliticize the works of the Russian Orthodox Church, which, especially among the Indigenous peoples within the empire, served as a driver of Russification.[49]

Many stories of proselytization to the Kuril Ainu on Shikotan were reprinted in the newsletter of the Hakodate Orthodox Church in a column on the topic published from 2013 through 2015, noting to contemporary members that their predecessors engaged with the Kuril Ainu not as a domineering force, but as compassionate peers who valued their piety. Yet in this way, the representation of the Kuril Ainu serves as a parable, presenting an aspect of what the Church sees as the ideal moral character. An excerpt from Sawabe's 1885 report was reprinted in 2014:

> ... what they endured last year is, without being put in words, a sermon more powerful than words. What sermon is it, what example is it, [it is] an example of piety, a sermon of mercy. The teaching of piety is what [we] receive from them, the act of mercy is what we sent to them. ... [50]

Thus the memory of the Kuril Ainu among Orthodox Christians today has come to serve a markedly different function from their memory in the national history of nineteenth-century development and modernization in Japan. No longer a mirror image for the Japanese government to use as a contrast when portraying its own nation as civilized, the simple, humble and pious Kuril Ainu set a moral example to follow. They are not forgotten; their memory is kept alive by assigning them a new role for Orthodox Christians, because the Kuril Ainu's faith, which allegedly survived without contact with the church for years and stayed alive even after their move to Shikotan, is beyond any doubt.

Conclusion: Looking beyond the Gaze

Konkamakuru died in Shikotan in 1903. The Japanese government's discriminatory policies towards the Ainu persisted, forming the ideological backbone of the allegedly multi-ethnic Japanese nation throughout the early twentieth century.[51] Meanwhile, the Kuril Ainu on Shikotan continued to struggle for survival; they never managed to end the downward population trend. Seasonal visits to the Kuril Islands continued until 1909 (with an interruption in 1904 due to the Russo-Japanese War), but permanent repatriation never materialized. Once the official aid was cut in 1932, the Ainu had to survive mainly through collecting and selling kelp on the island's shore. Increasingly, they intermarried with the Japanese.[52] By the time Soviet troops vandalized the church built by Konkamakuru, only a handful of people remained on the island to evacuate to Hokkaido.[53]

It is a difficult and elusive endeavour to identify people carrying on the culture of the Kuril Ainu today.[54] Yet the historical narrative of the Orthodox Church community in Japan keeps the memory of the Kuril Ainu alive. For them, the Kuril Ainu's fate paradoxically added force to their message: this was a people who lived frugally, maintained faith in times of hardship and demonstrated praiseworthy moral character. Decoupled from the diplomatic cul-de-sac between two states, the

Japanese Orthodox Christian community came to find a model for living in the Kuril Ainu.

What has not been resurrected in this turn, however, is the Kuril Ainu's own Indigenous culture and their agency. Emphasizing the Christian character of the Kuril Ainu could lead to the further forgetting of their own Indigenous culture, which they appear to have maintained in parallel with their Orthodox Christian faith. In 1891, Okamoto Kansuke, a retired officer and a devout advocate for Japan's northern defence since the 1868 Meiji Restoration, went alone to investigate eastern Hokkaido, Shikotan and the southern part of the Kuril Islands, hoping to form a patriotic society and spark development in the abandoned archipelago.[55] During his week-long stay on Shikotan in May 1891, Okamoto spent a great deal of time speaking to Konkamakuru at his house, attempting to learn more about the natural resources, topography and geography of the Kuril Islands. Konkamakuru and others who met with him provided considerable information on the resources on and around each island. Okamoto's account shows that the Ainu's knowledge of the Kuril Islands was extremely detailed and extensive. They listed what could be obtained on each island, including fur animals like sea otters, seals, foxes and bears; fish including salmon, cod and trout; vegetables like potatoes, radishes and turnips; good timber for shipbuilding; and edible wild plants.

On one such occasion on 24 May 1891, Okamoto visited Konkamakuru at 10 a.m.[56] Konkamakuru and others made themselves available to Okamoto and continued the conversation. After taking meticulous notes about the Kuril Islands' natural, geographical and ecological conditions, Okamoto offered Konkamakuru and other Kuril Ainu the liquor he had brought from Nemuro. Later, he reported that 'Everyone got drunk and showed they were very happy'.[57] One of them sang, another played a guitar and both men and women stood up and danced in what they described as a 'Russian way'. One old man performed a different dance, which Okamoto thought was 'completely the Ezo style'.[58]

Okamoto returned to Konkamakuru's home a few more times, dining and drinking with him and building a degree of emotional bonding, at least to Okamoto's mind. His knowledge of the Ainu language seems to have helped him gain the villagers' confidence.[59] For instance, an unnamed Ainu confided that they wanted to go back to the Kuril Islands but did not dare say so.[60] Before his departure, Konkamakuru gave Okamoto a guitar, 'probably because I enjoyed watching their dance', Okamoto noted.[61]

This description of drinking and dancing Kuril Ainu who possessed an extremely broad knowledge of the environment of their homeland complicates both the mostly condescending official Japanese gaze and the Orthodox Christian rendition of them as sober, simple, pious, almost saintly people. Yet this is all it does: it complicates but does not alter the power relations in the formation of narratives. The attention always goes from the metropole to the borderland.

The only thing historians can do in such a situation is to make the maximum use of the available sources. What was attempted in this chapter via the cross-examination of photographs was one tiny step in that direction. Though not conclusive, such efforts may create the possibility of a new interpretation by using what is already visible, such as a photograph's location or a shaven face. Accumulating these small possibilities seems to be the only way forward in salvaging the voices of the borderland from the depth of colonialism, national history and historical memory.

The long conversation with an Ainu-speaking Japanese visitor and the ensuing drinking and dancing jubilations at Konkamakuru's house includes one such tiny opening: 24 May 1891 was a Sunday.[62] The Kuril Ainu residents may have decided to forgo their religious routine for a rare chance to enjoy themselves with plenty of drink and merriment. After the festivities ended, the Kuril Ainu thanked Okamoto, 'because there is no fun [here]'. Okamoto replied in Ainu: 'Your fun is my fun, this is the treat'. Everybody understood, looked at each other and cried – or so Okamoto claimed.[63] There is no way to confirm.

Takahiro Yamamoto (PhD in international history, LSE) is an assistant professor of cultural economic history at the Heidelberg Centre for Transcultural Studies at Ruprecht-Karls-Universität Heidelberg (Germany). Previously he was a Japan Society for the Promotion of Science Research Fellow at the University of Tokyo and a teaching fellow at NYU Shanghai. His monograph *Demarcating Japan: Imperialism, Islanders, and Mobility, 1855–1884* is forthcoming from the Harvard University Asia Center. His edited volume *Documenting Mobility in the Japanese Empire and Beyond* is forthcoming from Palgrave Macmillan. His articles have discussed issues around modern Japan's border history, cross-border mobility and personal identification.

Notes

1. After the Second World War and the Soviet occupation of Shikotan Island, the Kuril Ainu moved to Hokkaido. There, the cultural traces of their offspring became impossible to discern, due to deaths and intermarriages. Malgorzata, *Chishima Ainu No Kiseki*, 174.
2. Sasaki, 'Chishima Ainu No Dentō Bunka', 40.
3. Torii, *Chishima Ainu*, 87.
4. Hokkaidōchō, *Kita Chishima*, 101.

5. Accounts from the early nineteenth century suggest that the Kuril Ainu took care to show their adherence to the Orthodox faith in the presence of Russians. Malgorzata, *Chishima Ainu no Kiseki*, 37.

6. Howell, *Geographies of Identity*, 190–91.

7. Hasegawa, *The Northern Territories*; Kimura, *The Kurillian Knot*.

8. Togo, 'The Inside Story'; Stephan, *The Kuril Islands*.

9. For this chapter, I use Ainu names wherever possible. The spelling is based on Torii, *Chishima Ainu*.

10. Some sources have indicated that Konkamakuru was born on Rashowa Island, but in an 1884 interview with a Japanese official, he is recorded as stating that he was born on Paramushir Island. See 'Chishima Junkō Nikki'.

11. *Kushiro Seikyōkai Hyakunenshi* gives the name of Konkamakuru's wife as Akurina, who passed away between May 1885 and September 1886, while the report of the Japanese navy officers who transported his family in 1900 notes his wife's name as Baragē. See 'Hokkaido mitsuryō keibi gunkan Tenryū haken narabini hōkokusho' vol.7. For the number of children, see Torii, *Chishima Ainu*, 95, where it records Konkamakuru's son and 'the third daughter'.

12. Malgorzata, *Chishima Ainu No Kiseki*, 84–95.

13. S. Y., 'Seikyō Dendō (2)', 10. Another source notes that the church was built in 1894 (Hokkaidōchō, *Kita Chishima*, 101), but given that Komatsu seems to have brought the tools to Shikotan in 1886 (Kushiro seikyōkai hyakunenshi iinkai, 'Kushiro Seikyōkai Hyakunen No Ayumi'), it is likely that the former is accurate.

14. Saitō, *Feodoru Saitō*, 106–7. On the duration of Saitō's stay in Shikotan, see ibid., 49.

15. For a rare oral history of the Ainu from Sakhalin, see Yamabe, *Ainu Monogatari*.

16. Sand, 'Tropical Furniture'. One can also find a similarly careful reading of paintings as sources in Timothy Brook's *Vermeer's Hat*.

17. Kepurian's Ainu name is not known from the sources.

18. For an analysis of similarly staged photographs, see, for instance, Sand, 'Tropical Furniture', 107–8.

19. Hitchcock, *Ainu Jin*, 248.

20. For Hitchcock's photograph collection, now stored at the Smithsonian Institution, see Uni, 'Romin Hicchikokku'.

21. For the anthropologists' role in constructing a modern nation and an empire, see Oguma, *Tan'itsu minzoku*, 73–86.

22. 'Torii Ryūzō to sono sekai'.

23. The pictures were taken not by Torii but a member of the 1884 mission to Shumushu that brought the Kuril Ainu to Shikotan; however, they were publicized to an international audience through their inclusion in Torii's publication.

24. Other close-up portraits clearly show the eyes of the depicted individuals. See Torii, 'Etudes Archeologiques'.

25. Hokkaidōchō, *Kita Chishima*; 'Hokkaido mitsuryō keibi gunkan Tenryū haken narabini hōkokusho' vol. 3. The seasonal repatriation scheme took place every year from 1897 until 1909. Malgorzata, *Chishima Ainu no Kiseki*, 164. Malgorzata argues that the scheme was driven not by the Ainu's request but by the government's desire to raise profits from their hunting.

26. 'Hokkaido mitsuryō keibi gunkan Tenryū haken narabini hōkokusho', vol. 3.

27. Yokoyama, 'Matsuura Takeshirō', 70.

28. Yokoyama's confusion of the name of the village (Shakotan) and the name of the island (Shikotan) shows that he was unaware of Figure 9.8 and Figure 9.2, both of which show Konkamakuru's entire body.

29. This can be contrasted to the event in the late eighteenth century in southwestern Hokkaido, when a local Ainu grew a beard and hair for the new-year visit to the Japanese lord of Matsumae, 'so he might look properly Ainu' to the Japanese eyes. David Howell argues that the supposed rediscovery of Ainu roots through the act rather stemmed from Japanese cultural appropriation of Ainu practice. Howell, *Geography of Identity*, 119–20. On the historical significance of shaved facial hair as a sign of the Kuril Ainu's alleged assimilation into Japanese culture, see ibid., 145–46; Godefroy, 'The Road from Ainu Barbarian'.

30. Yokoyama, 'Matsuura Takeshirō', 70–71.

31. Ibid., 70.

32. Tanaka, *Japan's Orient*; Eskildsen, 'Of Civilization and Savages'; Suzuki, *Civilization and Empire*.

33. *Asahi Shinbun*, 25 December 1900.

34. *Asahi Shinbun*, 8 November 1900.

35. Torii, *Chishima Ainu*, 102.

36. Malgorzata, *Chishima Ainu no Kiseki*, 116–21.

37. Hakodate Harisutosu Seikyōkaishi Henshū Iinkai, *Hakodate Harisutosu*.

38. Hakodate Shishi Hensanshitu, *Hakodate shishi. Tsūsetsu hen, Dai 1-kan*, 700.

39. Malgorzata, *Chishima Ainu no Kiseki*, 139.

40. The last visit by a Russian priest while the Kuril Ainu resided in the Kuril Islands took place in 1870. Saitō, *Feodoru Saitō*, 111.

41. S. Y., 'Seikyō Dendō (5)', 9–10.

42. S. Y., 'Seikyō Dendō (6)', 12.

43. Ibid.

44. Kushiro seikyōkai hyakunenshi iinkai, *Kushiro seikyōkai*.

45. Ibid.

46. Stragorodsky, *Hokkaidō Junkaiki*, quoted in S. Y., 'Seikyō Dendō (4)', 5.

47. Yamazaki, 'Seikyō Dendō (1)', 5.

48. Kushiro seikyōkai hyakunenshi iinkai, *Kushiro seikyōkai*.

49. On the close links between the Russian empire's expansion and the Orthodox Church, see, for instance, Kan, 'Russian Orthodox Missionaries'; Miller, 'The Romanov Empire'.

50. S. Y., 'Seikyō Dendō (6)', 12.

51. Oguma, *Tan'itsu minzoku*.

52. Akizuki, *Chishima Rettō*, 231.

53. Baba, *Hoppō Minzoku no Tabi*, 24.

54. Ōya and Tōmine, 'Kojima Kuratarō'.

55. Fumoto, 'Meiji chūki no Chishima', 91–92; Akizuki, *Chishima Rettō*, 237–38. Okamoto had resigned from a post in Karafuto (Sakhalin) in 1870 due to a disagreement with the government leadership over policy directions.

56. Arima, 'Okamoto Ian', 88.

57. Ibid., 90.

58. Ibid.

59. Ibid., 92.

60. Ibid., 95.

61. Ibid., 96.

62. This point is made on the assumption that the Kuril Ainu followed the Gregorian calendar used by the Japanese government for their religious events.

63. Arima, 'Okamoto Ian', 92.

Bibliography

Archival Sources

Hokkaido University Library Northern Studies Collection (Japan)
CHI-915-Ha *Chishimashu Kankeisho*, 'Chishima Junkō Nikki'
Betsu-Chishima351.2 'Meiji 16 nen Chishimakoku dojin higai ikken shorui'
Japan Center for Asian Historical Records, National Archive of Japan (JACAR)
C06091317100 'Hokkaido mitsuryō keibi gunkan Tenryū haken narabini hōkokusho', vol. 3.
C06091317500 'Hokkaido mitsuryō keibi gunkan Tenryū haken narabini hōkokusho', vol. 7.
Smithsonian Institution, National Anthropology Archive (USA)
NAA INV 05290500
National Diet Library (Japan)
Kataoka Toshikazu Kankei Monjo, reel 2
University Museum, University of Tokyo
East Asia and Micronesia Old Photographic Images Database 1058
http://torii.akazawa-project.jp/cms/photo_archive/nakagawa/photo.html (accessed 22 October 2021).

Newspapers

Asahi Shimbun

Published Sources

Akizuki, Toshiyuki. *Chishima Rettō o Meguru Nihon to Roshia*. Sapporo: Hokkaidō Daigaku Shuppankai, 2014.
Arima, Takuya. 'Okamoto Ian "Chishima Nisshi" Honkoku'. *Gengo Bunka Kenkyū* 17 (2009), 63–198.
Baba, Osamu. *Hoppō Minzoku No Tabi*. Sapporo: Hokkaido Shuppan Kikaku Sentā, 1979.
Brook, Timothy. *Vermeer's Hat: The Seventeenth Century and the Dawn of the Global World*. New York: Bloomsbury Press, 2008.
Eskildsen, Robert. 'Of Civilization and Savages: The Mimetic Imperialism of Japan's 1874 Expedition to Taiwan.' *American Historical Review* 107 (2) (2002): 388–418.
Fumoto, Shinichi. 'Meiji Chūki No Chishima Kaihatsu Ni Tsuite: Kaigun Taii Gunji Shigetada No Shumushu Tō Ijū Wo Chūshin Ni'. *Niigata Daigaku Kyōiku Ningen Kagakubu Kiyō Jinbun Shakai Kagakuhen* 10 (2) (2008), 91–99.
Godefroy, Noémi. 'The Road from Ainu Barbarian to Japanese Primitive: A Brief Summary of Japanese-Ainu Relations in a Historical Perspective', *Proceedings from the 3rd Consortium for Asian and African Studies: 'Making a Difference: Representing/Constructing the Other in Asian/African Media, Cinema, and Languages*, 2012, 201–12.
Hakodate Harisutosu Seikyōkaishi Henshū Iinkai (ed.). *Hakodate Harisutosu Seikyōkaishi*. Hakodate: Hakodate Harisutosu Seikyōkai, 2011.
Hakodate Shishi Hensanshitsu (ed.). *Hakodate shishi. Tsūsetsu hen, Dai 1-kan*. Hakodate: Hakodate-shi, 1990.
Hasegawa, Tsuyoshi. *The Northern Territories Dispute and Russo-Japanese Relations*. Berkeley, CA: University of California, International and Area Studies, 1998.
Hitchcock, Romyn. *Ainu Jin to Sono Bunka: Meiji Chūki No Ainu No Mura Kara*, trans. Yasuo Kitagamae. Tokyo: Rokkō Shuppan, 1985.
Hokkaidōchō. *Kita Chishima Chōsa Hōbun*. Sapporo: Hokumon Kappansho, 1901.

Howell, David. *Geographies of Identity in Nineteenth-Century Japan*. Berkeley, CA: University of California Press, 2005.
Kan, Sergey. 'Russian Orthodox Missionaries at Home and Abroad: The Case of Siberian and Alaskan Indigenous Peoples', in Robert P. Geraci and Michael Khodarkovsky (eds), *Of Religion and Empire: Missions, Conversion, and Tolerance in Tsarist Russia* (Ithaca, NY: Cornell University Press, 2001), 173–200.
Kimura, Hiroshi. *The Kurillian Knot: A History of Japanese-Russian Border Negotiations*, trans. Mark Ealey. Stanford, CA: Stanford University Press, 2008.
Kushiro seikyōkai hyakunenshi iinkai. 'Kushiro Seikyōkai Hyakunen No Ayumi'. 1992. Retrieved 8 March 2022 from http://www.orthodox-jp.com/kushiro/bef/history.htm.
Malgorzata, Zajac. *Chishima Ainu No Kiseki*. Urayasu, Chiba: Sōfūkan, 2009.
Miller, Alexey. 'The Romanov Empire and the Russian Nation', in Alexey Miller and Stefan Berger (eds), *Nationalizing Empires* (Budapest: Central European University Press, 2014), 309–68.
Oguma, Eiji. *Tan'itsu minzoku shinwa no kigen: 'Nihonjin' no jigazō no keifu*. Tokyo: Shin'yō sha, 1995.
Ōya, Kyōsuke, and Ryōta Tōmine. 'Kojima Kuratarō No Ihin Ni Miru Sono Ashiato: Kuriru Ainu No Kyōsei Ijū to Hokkaidō Bussan Kyōshinkai'. *Hakodate Nichiro Kōryūshi Kenkyūkai Kaihō*, 7 December 2013. Retrieved 8 March 2022 from http://hakodate-russia.com/main/letter/35-06.html.
Saitō, Tōkichi. *Feodoru Saitō Tōkichi Jiden*, ed. Masao Saitō. Tokyo: Seikōkai Shuppan, 1989.
Sand, Jordan. 'Tropical Furniture and Bodily Comportment in Colonial Asia'. *Positions* 21(1) (2013), 95–132.
Sasaki, Tōru. 'Chishima Ainu No Dentō Bunka to Bunka Henka Ni Tsuite'. *Shōwa Joshi Daigaku Kokusai Bunka Kenkyūjo Kiyō* 2 (1996), 37–44.
Snow, Henry James. *In Forbidden Seas: Recollections of Sea-Otter Hunting in the Kurils*. London: E. Arnold, 1910.
Stephan, John J. *The Kuril Islands: Russo-Japanese Frontier in the Pacific*. Oxford: Clarendon Press, 1974.
Stragorodsky, Sergius. *Shōin Serugii Hokkaidō Junkaiki*, trans. Yōko Miyata. Tokyo: Kirishitan Bunka Kenkyūkai, 1972.
Suzuki, Shogo. *Civilization and Empire: China and Japan's Encounter with European International Society*. London: Routledge, 2009.
S. Y. 'Chishima Rettō No Seikyō Dendō (2)'. *Hakodate Harisutosu Seikyōkai Kaihō* 33 (2012), 10–11.
———. 'Chishima Rettō No Seikyō Dendō (4)'. *Hakodate Harisutosu Seikyōkai Kaihō* 35 (2014), 5.
———. 'Chishima Rettō No Seikyō Dendō (5)'. *Hakodate Harisutosu Seikyōkai Kaihō* 36 (2014), 9–10.
———. 'Chishima Rettō No Seikyō Dendō (6)'. *Hakodate Harisutosu Seikyōkai Kaihō* 37 (2014), 11–12.
Tanaka, Stefan. *Japan's Orient: Rendering Pasts into History*. Berkeley, CA: University of California Press, 1993.
Torii, Ryūzō. *Chishima Ainu*. Tokyo: Yoshikawa Hanshichi, 1903.
———. 'Etudes Archeologiques et Ethnologiques: Les Ainou Des Iles Kouriles'. *Journal of the College of Science, Imperial University of Tokyo* 42 (1919), 1–337.
'Torii Ryūzō to Sono Sekai'. Retrieved 8 March 2022 from http://torii.akazawa-project.jp/cms/index.html.
Togo, Kazuhiko. 'The Inside Story of the Negotiations on the Northern Territories: Five Lost Windows of Opportunity'. *Japan Forum* 23(1) (2011), 123–45.

Uni, Yoshikazu. 'Romin Hicchikokku Ga 1888 Nen Ni Satsuei Shita Hokkaido to Shikotan Tō No Shashin to Ryotei'. *Hokkaidō Minzokugaku* 11 (2015), 57–74.

Yamabe, Yasunosuke. *Ainu Monogatari*, ed. Kyōsuke Kindaichi. Tokyo: Hakubunkan, 1913.

Yamazaki. 'Chishima Rettō No Seikyō Dendō (1)'. *Hakodate Harisutosu Seikyōkai Kaihō* 32 (2013), 4–5.

Yokoyama, Kendō. 'Matsuura Takeshirō No Kenkyū Ni Tsuite'. *Denki* 2(8) (1935), 69–78.

CHAPTER 10

From Finnic to Soviet Family

Finnic Kinship and Borders in the Soviet–Finnish Controversy over the Kalevala from the Mid-Nineteenth Century to the 1940s

TAKEHIRO OKABE

On 28 February (the Day of *Kalevala*) 2019, *Helsingin Sanomat*, a major Finnish newspaper, published a news piece about the collected *Kalevala*-related poems in the original Karelian language (with Russian translation) recently published by Russian brothers who believe that Finns stole the *Kalevala* from Karelians, and that this 'injustice' has to be 'redressed'. The piece also included a short comment by Lotte Tarkka, professor of folkloristics at Helsinki University, who refutes this 'puzzling claim' from Russia by saying that the *Kalevala* materials cannot be exclusively categorized as either Finnish or Karelian culture, because they belong to the entirety of 'Finnic culture', and the *Kalevala* is a 'European epic'.[1] On the same day, an internet journal from Petrozavodsk, the capital of the Republic of Karelia in the Russian Federation, featured the centennial jubilee of the *Kalevala*, which was held in Petrozavodsk in 1949. The journal obviously aimed to remind Russian readers of how seriously Russian Karelia has been engaged in the *Kalevala* by explaining in detail the jubilee, which has hardly been a public topic even in Russian Karelia.[2] This story of Russian–Finnish confrontation over the *Kalevala* is not new: indeed, it has deep roots in the history of the two countries, but interestingly has not been remembered for decades.

This chapter addresses the impact of Russian and Soviet–Finnish border changes on the controversy over the *Kalevala*, specifically the influence on the political and scholarly discourse about family-like relationships among the kindred Finnic peoples, both in Finland and in Russia and the Soviet Union. The *Kalevala* has been discussed mainly within Finnish national historiography, despite the fierce Soviet–Finnish dispute over its geographic and ethnic origins and over Finnish–Karelian kinship. Previous studies have addressed the relationship between the *Kalevala* and Finnish nationalist ideology (concerning 'Greater Finland') and, accordingly, have considered 1944 the end of Greater Finland and the *Kalevala* as its symbol.[3] Likewise, the Estonian–Finnish relationship is an important component of the Finnic family because of the similarities of their languages and national epics, the *Kalevala* and the *Kalevipoeg*, which have been integrated into the nationalist interpretation of Finnish–Estonian kinship.[4] However, these studies have ignored what the Russians/Soviets stated about the *Kalevala* and the Finnic family especially after the Second World War, when Estonia was Sovietized and Finland became a 'friendly' neighbour. In contrast, Soviet/Russian historiography only includes a few minor studies on this topic, although the Soviets claimed the *Kalevala* as their own, and recent investigations have actively discussed nationality issues.[5] Understandably, Soviet propaganda trumpeted the idea that the Soviet Union crushed the Greater Finland idea by liberating Soviet Karelia from Finnish occupation. Nevertheless, the Stalinist-period confrontation over the *Kalevala* was not 'useful' for the post-Stalinist Soviet–Finnish friendship; thus, the Russian/Soviet story of the *Kalevala* controversy has rarely been revisited.

This historiographical and memory gap makes it difficult to understand the differences, similarities and continuity of Finnish and Soviet nationalist ideologies for integrating Finnic nationalities, such as Karelians. This makes it difficult to understand how similarly Finnish and Russian/Soviet elites gazed at the Finnic nationalities who were expected to conduct themselves within a supranational hierarchy. This chapter fills this gap by showing the shift from the Finland-centred notion of the Finnic family group that emerged in the nineteenth century, through its radicalization during the interwar period, to the Soviet family of nations in the late 1940s.

The *Kalevala* and the Emergence of Pan-Finnism within the Russian Empire

The *Kalevala* has played a decisive role in building Finnish national identity since the nineteenth century. The primary goal for mainly Swedish-speaking students and elites of the Grand Duchy of Finland was to create the Finnish nation by establishing a common written language, as well as a national literary work with its own heroic past. With this aim in mind, they collected folklore and various dialects spoken elsewhere in the Grand Duchy and beyond. This resulted in the *Kalevala* (the first edition was the *Old Kalevala* in 1835, with the complete edition of the *New Kalevala* following in 1849), published by the native Finnish-speaking intellectual Elias Lönnrot (1802–84). The *Kalevala* offered the emerging Finnish nation its own national literature and epic written in Finnish through the story of a national 'golden' age, with the ancestors and heroes as great as those in other prominent European nations.[6] Fennophile intellectuals and students used the *Kalevala* to compete with pro-Swedish elites who underrated the 'barbarian' Finnish language and culture, and to integrate various Finnish tribes (called *heimo*) and their dialects into the Finnish nation and language.[7]

Despite the well-defined border with Russia, Finnish nation-building went alongside the dream to cooperate with, help and include small kindred Finnic groups outside the Grand Duchy in the Finnic family. In the nineteenth century, Finnish scholars discovered other Finno-Ugric languages in the regions of Volga and Siberia; Finnic folklore, including that related to the *Kalevala*, spread throughout areas where people spoke Baltic Finnic languages in Ingria, Estonia and Karelia. Lönnrot gathered folklore materials (epic poetry) essential to the *Kalevala* on the Russian side of Karelia (White Sea Karelia), where local Karelian singers were still performing the epic poems. Karelia – an important source of inspiration for both scholars and artists who visited it – came to occupy an integral part of the Finnish national imagination, landscape and culture. Since the White Sea Karelians spoke a language very close to Finnish, they attracted those Finnish intellectuals who found in them and their poems what the Finns had lost: untainted purity and primordiality to be salvaged by recording folklore, and savageness and immaturity to be erased by civilization.[8]

To a lesser extent than in the Finnish–Karelian case, the *Kalevala* also occupied a significant place in Finnish–Estonian brotherhood. The *Kalevala*, with Lönnrot as a model, motivated Estophile Baltic Germans and the first generation of native Estonian intellectuals – among them, Friedrich Kreutzwald (1803–82) – to create the *Kalevipoeg*. Due to strict censorship in Estonia, this popular Estonian-language version of the epic was published in Finland in 1862.[9] In addition to similarities between the two epics in terms of language and the names of heroes and places, a metaphor known as 'the bridge of Finland' (*Soome sild*) appeared in the epic that denoted Finnish–Estonian brotherhood.[10] This brotherhood was an unequal relationship in that Estonians expected their 'older brother' Finns to help their 'little brother[s]' modernize and liberate themselves from Baltic German rule. The history of making the *Kalevipoeg* is often considered a good example of this uneven kinship; Lönnrot and the *Kalevala* led Kreutzwald to put together the *Kalevipoeg*. In fact, it is debated whether Kreutzwald truly read the *Kalevala* and unknown what the two talked about when they met in 1844.[11] Nevertheless, the Finnish–Estonian brotherhood was deeply integrated into the Finnish national imagination.

How then did Russians view the *Kalevala* and Finnic peoples within the Russian Empire? The proponents of pan-Slavism believed that 'small' Finnic peoples had developed their own culture, such as the *Kalevala*, 'thanks to' Russian rule and would peacefully merge into the coming pan-Slavic community in the future.[12] Since Russia lacked specialists familiar with Finnish culture, it could not offer a counterargument against leading Finnish scholars until the 1903 article by Russian orientologist Vladimir Gordlevsky (1876–1956). He pointed out that Karelians in Russian Karelia were different from Finns because they had been Orthodox Christians and coexisted peacefully with Russians for centuries.[13] With the escalation of the struggle against Finnish nationalists after the 1905 Revolution aiming to win Karelians' hearts, Russian nationalists came to emphasize the 'Russian characters' of Karelians and warn of the 'pan-Finnic' threat from Finland.[14] However, during the Empire's reign, the *Kalevala* had still not been heavily politicized, since Russian elites had no idea what Finnish nationalists aimed for with the epic and the idea of 'pan-Finnism'.

The *Kalevala* for Finland, Greater Finland and Finnish–Estonian Brotherhood

The Russian Revolution not only gave Finns and Estonians an opportunity to form their own independent states, but also ignited the Greater Finland ideology among Finnish nationalists and expansionists, who urged in favour of 'saving' Karelians by claiming the territories they lived in and supporting Estonian independence. Already during the short but bloody Civil War, the Finns conducted the so-called 'Tribe Wars' (*Heimosodat*), whereby Finnish volunteers performed military expeditions with militant Russian Karelians between 1918 and 1922 to annex parts of Russian Karelia.[15] Likewise, starting in December 1918, about 3,800 Finnish volunteers headed for Tallinn to help their 'little brothers' fight against the Bolsheviks.[16] For the Bolsheviks, Greater Finland was now a real threat, but also a useful – if risky – tool with which to mobilize the Soviet Finnic population to support Soviet power, and to export the socialist revolution to 'White' Finland by placing Red Finns (who fled Finland after the Civil War) in leadership positions in Soviet Karelia.

In Finland, the *Kalevala* became a symbol of the new independent state and a strong tool for those who sought 'pure Finnishness' (*Aitosuomalaisuus*), which further accelerated the 'Finnization' of peoples and spaces where the Swedish-speaking minority had previously been 'unreasonably' well treated.[17] The Day of the *Kalevala* was propagated to promote the *Kalevala*'s popularity and to compete with the Day of Runeberg, a symbol of Swedishness in Finland.[18] In addition, through cultural societies and organizations such as the Kalevala Society (*Kalevalaseura*) and the Union of Finnishness (*Suomalaisuuden liitto*), those who supported 'pure Finnishness' spread information on Karelia and the *Kalevala* to schools, workplaces and local cultural groups, and encouraged the people to 'Finnize' their non-Finnish names.[19] Furthermore, the *Kalevala* was expected to cover the deep division that the Civil War left by performing the unity of the Finnish nation, with the Soviet Union and Russians as *Others*. Consequently, the Karelian-speaking population was forced to comply with the pressure of 'Finnization'; their efforts to create a common written language were futile because leading intellectuals and activists rejected the project, seeing Karelian only as a dialect, and a separate Karelian language as a Russian plot.[20]

At the same time, the *Kalevala* symbolized Finnish irredentism towards Soviet Karelia for those who felt betrayed after the Soviet–Finnish Peace Treaty of 1920, which finally gave up Greater Finland. As the 'older brother', they were determined to help the Karelian and Ingrian Finnish 'tribes' fleeing the Russian Civil War by establishing various organizations, such as the Academic Karelia Society (*Akateeminen Karjala-Seura*, AKS), which soon drew students and activists who supported the dream of Greater Finland.[21] In addition to Russophobia and anti-communism, Soviet collectivization and the deportation of Ingrian Finns in the early 1930s caused anger and protest among those students and activists.[22] These radical nationalists split into several fractions and fascist groups, fragmented due to disorientation and inner struggle, and lost political influence after the abortive rebellion in the early 1930s, while Greater Finland was becoming even more unrealistic as the Soviet–Finnish relationship and the Finnish economy stabilized and the relationship with Sweden improved.[23] Nonetheless, these organizations and their members continued to remind citizens of their 'brothers' under Bolshevik/Russian oppression and urged them to be ready to support the latter.

The sense of brotherhood with Estonians entered a new phase after the upheaval of independence and wars. Tartu University invited Finnish scholars to help 'Estonize' the university by eliminating its German and Russian features. Among other forces, Finnish humanities (archaeology, ethnology, folklore studies and linguistics) greatly helped to establish the field's subdisciplines, scholarly societies and museums in Estonia; they trained and influenced young Estonian scholars, and some of these Estonians earned their doctoral degrees in Helsinki.[24] Moreover, Tartu and Helsinki intellectuals and students formed the Finnish–Estonian Students Club to strengthen their alliance and to transform their grassroots 'tribe work' (*heimotyö*) into a mass movement.[25] While the official Finnish–Estonian relationship continued to cool down, Estonian national and collective identity was, in a sense, constructed by knowledge crossing the 'bridge of Finland'.[26]

However, a discrepancy gradually emerged between the rhetoric of brotherhood and the development of Finish–Estonian relationships. For Finnish political and military leaders, starting in the 1930s, most important was neutral Scandinavian orientation; thus, they did not want Estonia to become involved in Finnish diplomatic and security policy.[27] Despite the fact that the sense of brotherhood was mainly secured by scholarly and cultural elites, the Estonians now found the Finns' arrogance and superiority to be increasingly unbearable. As Sirje Olesk summarized, Finnish nationalists supporting the ideology of Greater Finland were too militaristic, anti-Russian and anti-socialist for the Estonians to sympathize with their pan-Finnic hierarchy. Furthermore, these Finns criticized Estonians for forcing Ingrian Finns in Estonia to be Estonian, which Estonians saw as interfering in their internal affairs. Thus, the Finnish side had to reframe its attitude towards Estonians by removing far-right elements from Finnish–Estonian relationships in the late 1930s.[28]

Finnish *Kalevala* studies had to answer to both the nation state and the idea of Greater Finland. Kaarle Krohn (1863–1933) gained worldwide fame for his folklore methodology, determining the *Kalevala* poetry's geographic origins by utilizing an enormous amount of *Kalevala*-related folklore materials, including Estonian ones.[29] According to Krohn, the epic poems first appeared in south-west Finland and north-west Estonia. They were created by the ancestors of the Finnish and partially Estonian peoples, and later 'migrated' eastward into Ingria and northward into Russian Karelia. Krohn showed that the *Kalevala* and Karelians belonged to Finland and the Finnish nation, with a Western influence (Scandinavian and Christian). He and his followers insisted that the *Kalevala* told the heroic deeds of 'our' ancestors and that its heroes were historical figures who had really existed before Sweden brought Finland into its domain.[30] These works justified the *Kalevala* poems' Finnish origins and the hierarchical relationship between Finns and Karelians (Finns created the *Kalevala* poems, while Karelians merely received and preserved them), and excluded the Slavic influence on the poems.

The *Old Kalevala* centennial jubilee in February 1935 was a good occasion to underscore not only national unity and the moral and cultural strength required to defend it, but also the unity of all Finnic peoples. The idea of Greater Finland was not emphasized, because the official ceremony carefully avoided anti-Soviet/Russian and anti-Swedish discourse so as not to provoke the Soviet Union and split the nation. However, Finnish media and nationalists loudly complained that the official ceremony 'ignored' Karelians and other kindred Finnic groups under Bolshevik/Russian 'oppression', and called for their salvation.[31] A speech given by theologian Uno Harva, a fellow of Krohn, in June 1935 at the *Kalevala* song festival in Sortavala – a border city and historic place for Greater Finland – conveys the relationship between the *Kalevala*, the Finnish nation and (Russian and Finnish) Karelia:

> The *Kalevala* and Karelia are inseparable from each other. ... When the greatest national jubilee of the centenary year of the *Kalevala* is now organized here, on the shores of Lake Ladoga, in the midst of the Karelian tribe, this means that great poem singers of the Karelian tribe have done a wonderful thing for Finnish education and culture. ... We are grateful to them, above all, for they have sung to awaken the Finnish national spirit from national dormancy ... Long Live Karelia! Long Live Our Fathers' Land![32]

Likewise, that same year, August Annist (1899–1972), a leading Fennophile Estonian and translator of the *Kalevala*, stressed the oneness of all Finnic peoples under the *Kalevala*, which encouraged the Estonians to have and be proud of the *Kalevipoeg*. In his piece, published in a Finnish journal, Annist called for the spiritual and cultural unity of all Finnic peoples, especially Finns and Estonians, who, according to Krohn, had jointly created the *Kalevala* poems in ancient times. Worrying about the radicalism of geopolitical Greater Finland and deteriorating Finnish–Estonian relationships, but accepting Finnic hierarchy, Annist advocated for more egalitarian, cultural solidarity among Finnic peoples, with the *Kalevala* as a shared cultural legacy: 'The *Kalevala* is not only *Greater Finnish* [*suursuomalainen*] but also *Common Finnic* [*yhteissuomalainen*], *monumentum aere perennius* of the spirit and culture, not only of ancient Finland and ancient Karelia, but also of ancient Estonia.'[33]

From Class to Nationality: The 'Red' *Kalevala* and Finno-Ugric Studies in the Soviet Union

While condemning the 'adventurist' idea of Greater Finland, the Soviets likewise manipulated this ideology to mobilize Soviet Finns and Karelians, and to use Soviet Karelia as a showcase towards Finland. The Soviet nationality policy of 'indigenization' (*korenizatsiia*) was an opportunity for the Red Finns to dream of a 'Socialist Finland' with united Karelia by exporting the socialist revolution to Finland. Stressing class identity and proletarian internationalism, the Red Finns promoted Finnish language to 'modernize and enlighten' Karelians in the Karelian Autonomous Soviet Socialist Republic. Like Finnish nationalists in Finland, they saw the ethno-linguistic kinship among Finnic peoples as natural and believed that Karelians would merge with the Red Finns, with Finnish as the common language and the *Kalevala* as the (Red) Finnish epic.[34]

Russians and Southern (Olonets) Karelians fiercely opposed this 'Finnization' policy. For the Russians, Russian Karelia was a rich source of *bylina* (Russian heroic epic poems) and Russian territory, where Russians and Karelians had 'peacefully' coexisted for centuries. It was simply unacceptable to Russians that a small number of Red Finns occupied the governing positions in the local party and industrial organizations. Soviet Karelians, especially southern dialect speakers, saw Finns as foreigners, and nationally conscious Karelians, like Viktor Evseev (1910–86), a Karelian folklorist from Olonets who went to Leningrad University to study Finnic languages, demanded the creation of a common Karelian language.[35] For these active Karelians, the *Kalevala* poems had been stolen by the Finns and had to be reclaimed by the Karelians themselves. Notwithstanding these discontents, the Soviet leadership allowed the Red Finns to continue their policy as far as it contributed to modernization of Soviet Karelia and propaganda directed towards Finland.

The *Old Kalevala* centennial jubilee of 1935 in Petrozavodsk took place in the midst of political and scholarly change in Soviet Karelia. The Soviet leadership was shifting its emphasis in identity politics from class to nationality, began to use Russian nationalism and language as a tool for integration, and came to consider the Red Finns an inner threat.[36] During the jubilee, the Red Finns condemned the 'White' *Kalevala* jubilee in Helsinki for rallying 'Finnish, Estonian and German bourgeois-fascists' and utilizing the *Kalevala* to promote Greater Finland.[37] Contrary to Kaarle Krohn, the Red Finns insisted that the birthplace of the *Kalevala* poetry was Soviet Karelia, where Karelian singers were still performing it. Furthermore, as the poetry spread across Finland through the *Kalevala*, a socialist revolution from Soviet Karelia would take place in Finland.[38] However, this was the last chance to advocate for 'Red' *Kalevala*, since Moscow purged the Red Finns in Soviet Karelia after the jubilee, and in the end arrested and shot almost all prominent Red Finns, accusing them of being 'enemies of the people' and 'Finnish spies' in the late 1930s.[39]

Furthermore, newly emerging Soviet Finno-Ugric studies gradually challenged both the Red Finns and bourgeois Finnish scholarship.

Soviet linguists – above all Nikolai Marr and his supporters – attacked the concepts of linguistic kinship and proto-language as racist and fascist. Likewise, Soviet ethnology criticized Finnish and Estonian folklorists for wrongly seeking the 'origin' of epic poems.[40] Stressing class differences between Finns and Karelians, Dmitry Bubrikh (1890–1949), a professor at Leningrad University, criticized the Red Finns for forcing the Karelians to use Finnish. He even denied the relationship between the Karelians and the *Kalevala* because, introducing Kaarle Krohn's theory, the *Kalevala* poems had appeared in south-west Finland as a type of Swedish–Finnish aristocrat production under feudalism.[41] Furthermore, Bubrikh argued that the Karelian language (in this case Olonets Karelian) was now close to Russian as a result of a long historical process and social transformation, thus casting doubt upon Finnish–Karelian kinship.[42] To make matters more confusing, Evseev criticized both the Red Finns and Bubrikh by emphasizing southern Karelian folklore's role in the *Kalevala* poetry, and maintained that the *Kalevala* belonged to Soviet Karelia and Karelians, whose language was different from Finnish.[43]

Although in an unorganized manner, these Soviet scholars tried to remove the Karelians from the pan-Finnic hierarchy and push them closer to being seen as members of the Soviet Union and 'historical friends' of the Russians. Indeed, Bubrikh was assigned to create a common Karelian written language with the Cyrillic alphabet after Finnish was banned in 1937 and the *Kalevala* became the epic of the Karelian people.

Border Changes and Controversy after the Second World War

The Second World War radically changed not only the Soviet–Finnish border but also the Soviet attitude towards the boundaries among Finnic peoples. Stalin established the Karelo-Finnish Soviet Socialist Republic (K-FSSR) soon after the so-called Winter War (1939–40), through which the Soviets gained parts of Finnish Karelia, including the cities of Sortavala and Vyborg/Viipuri, and rehabilitated Finnish, thereby restoring Karelian–Finnish kinship to prepare for the possible emergence of a socialist Finland.[44] The *Kalevala* was now called the epic of the Karelo-Finnish people. In contrast, the Winter War demonstrated to Finns that the Soviet/Russian threat was real, and the Soviet Union unlawfully snatched important parts of Finnish Karelia, which caused more than four hundred thousand people to become evacuees.[45] At the same time, the Winter War temporarily but powerfully blurred domestic divisions and bred fear, anger and a desire to get back the lost territory among the people. This led to the Finnish occupation of Soviet Karelia after Germany's attack against the Soviet Union. Both nationalists and intellectuals practised Greater Finland ideology, using the *Kalevala* to justify their occupation of Soviet Karelia and to educate people in Finnish (about thirty-nine thousand Karelians and people of other Finnic nationalities were under occupation).[46] Furthermore, AKS activists provided support to more than four thousand Estonians fleeing the Nazi occupation and Soviet reoccupation, and arranged for around sixty-three thousand Ingrian Finnish refugees to be received from the occupied Leningrad area.[47] In contrast, the Soviets remained silent about their own Karelo-Finnish kinship during the war.

Therefore, the Soviets had to decide what to do about pan-Finnism after the Second World War, especially during the *New Kalevala* centennial jubilee in 1949. They hoped to show that the war had marked a shift in the centre of the Finnic world from Finland to the Soviet Union. This was true given the situation in Finland. After the armistice in 1944, Finland quickly lost any interest in Greater Finland and was occupied with its own survival as an independent state.[48] Leftist intellectuals and communists criticized the nationalists and Kaarle Krohn's pupils' 'abuse' of the *Kalevala* for Greater Finland, arguing that the *Kalevala* did not reflect the national past. Instead, they reclaimed the 'democratic' *Kalevala* as the literary creation of Elias Lönnrot. In this manner, they came to idolize Lönnrot – rather than the *Kalevala* itself – as a fresh symbol of national unity and post-war Soviet–Finnish friendship, and the 1949 *Kalevala* jubilee in Helsinki organized by the Finnish government also accepted this discourse. Feeling isolated between the two blocs of the Cold War confrontation, as then President Paasikivi mentioned in his remarks at the event, the Finnish nation had to endure post-war hardships alone, 'like Elias Lönnrot' in the making of the *Kalevala*, forgetting its 'little brothers'.[49]

It was thus the Soviet Union that could unify the 'kindred peoples of Finland' and manipulate Finnic kinship, because the post-war Soviet–Finnish borderland was relatively stabilized and peaceful. Stalin decided not to deport the Karelians that had been under Finnish occupation, and not to dissolve the K-FSSR, which was still useful as a diplomatic card against Finland. Furthermore, Stalin wanted to keep Finland's socio-economic structure intact, because Finland had generally avoided the destruction of its economy and loyally paid reparations to the Soviet Union. In particular, the Soviet–Finnish Treaty of 1948 satisfied Stalin's security concerns regarding Soviet–Finnish borderlands; moreover, he publicly admitted that Finland was now a friend of the Soviet Union.[50] In short, the Soviet leadership wanted to maintain the status quo, but also wished to secure some 'cards' with which to put pressure on the Finns.

This led the K-FSSR to find a balance between Russian–Karelian friendship and Karelian–Finnish kinship for the Soviet *New Kalevala* centennial jubilee. Immediately after the occupation ended, the party launched a massive propaganda campaign about Russian–Karelian friendship. Proud of having endured the harsh trial of war, Karelians were furious with the fact that they had to send their children to national schools, where the language of instruction was Finnish, meaningless for their children's future careers.[51] Indeed, to celebrate the *Kalevala* posed a great risk of being considered Greater Finland, given that the ongoing anti-Western campaign was targeting non-Russian national symbols and interactions among non-Russian peoples.[52]

Preparation for the jubilee and its scholarly session therefore went ahead secretly, sponsored by Otto Kuusinen, an old Finnish communist and chairman of the Presidium of the Supreme Soviet of the K-FSSR. To avoid putting Karelian–Finnish kinship forward, Kuusinen instructed the session speakers to stress the *Kalevala* poetry's geographical origins, as Finnish nationalists and Red Finns had a decade before to meet the ideological demands of the time. Kuusinen advised Evseev, one of the speakers, in April 1948: 'In this paper, you are expected to put forward the idea that the motherland of the *Kalevala* is the territory of our Soviet Karelia.'[53] In addition, Kuusinen depicted the *Kalevala* as the epic of the peace-loving, hard-working Karelo-Finnish people; he portrayed the *Kalevala*'s heroes as hunters, fishermen and blacksmiths of a pre-feudal society, the ancestors of the Karelo-Finnish people. To deny explicitly Finns' role as older brothers, Kuusinen primarily hailed the Karelian singers who created and were still creating the *Kalevala* poetry. The jubilee did not fail to praise the Communist Party, the paternal leader Stalin and the 'oldest brother' Russians, without which the poems of the Karelian people would not have reached a wider audience.[54]

Conforming to this Soviet hierarchical order, Kuusinen led the session speakers to implicitly insist that Karelian–Finnish friendship was based on kinship, and that support by the Russian 'older brother' was an essential factor for the birth of the *Kalevala* poems to secure Soviet Finns' position in Soviet Karelia. To meet this goal, Kuusinen made Bubrikh recant his mid-1930s denial of Karelian–Finnish kinship and of the relationship between the *Kalevala* and the Karelian people. In his short apology, Bubrikh admitted that it had been 'a grave mistake' to accept Kaarle Krohn's theory and to reject the kinship between Finns and Karelians, whom he found to be 'close relatives' after conducting thorough research.[55] Furthermore, the jubilee thanked Lönnrot as a 'progressive Finnish democrat' who 'learned' the poems by the 'creative' Karelian singers and completed the *Kalevala* before the poems went into oblivion.[56]

While accepting Kuusinen's demand for political reasons, both Petrozavodsk and Leningrad philologists were motivated to claim the *Kalevala* and the *Kalevipoeg* as Soviet national epics and to challenge Kaarle Krohn. The preliminary meeting of the jubilee session in June 1947 proposed comparing the *Kalevala* with Slavic, Turkic and Mongolic epics to show how they had developed within the Soviet Union. Leningrad philologist Viktor Zhirmunsky encouraged Elmar Päss, an Estonian folklorist, to ask Estonian philologists to join the session, because if the *Kalevala* jubilee included the University of Tartu, he said, 'This will be very important, new evidence of the Stalinist friendship of our Union'.[57] Reporting on this meeting, the Tallinn newspaper Õhtuleht justified Estonians' participation with the logic of Finnish–Estonian brotherhood, reminding Estonian readers that Lönnrot and the *Kalevala* had motivated Kreutzwald to create the *Kalevipoeg*.[58]

This tacit Soviet Finnic kinship was highlighted by the presence of the Estonians at the jubilee. Discussing the role of the *Kalevala* in the making of the *Kalevipoeg*, Tartu folklorist Eduard Laugaste carefully stressed their differences – rather than similarities – claiming that the *Kalevipoeg* reflects the Estonian people's struggle against the rule of 'foreign' Baltic Germans, and that Kreutzwald created the epic with the help of progressive Baltic German, Estonian and Russian intellectuals.[59] However, when asked by the session's audience about the similarities between the names of the two epics, Laugaste admitted, 'This is the result of mutual influence. The Estonian names appeared under the influence of the Karelo-Finnish names. These words have the same origins. *Kaleva* is the hero. *Kalevipoeg* is the son of the hero of the *Kalevala*.'[60] Despite cautious phrasing, the greeting from Anton Vaarandi, deputy chairman of the Council of Ministers of the Estonian Soviet Socialist Republic, showed that the pre-Second World War Finnish–Estonian brotherhood and the *Kalevipoeg* were integrated into the Soviet family through the *Kalevala*:

> The Estonian people are especially indebted to the *Kalevala*. This is because we have the *Kalevipoeg*, close to your epic in its origins and content. This is because the *Kalevala*, published in Estonia more than 50 years ago, became one of the most popular books among our people. People, animals, birds, fish and all of nature – even the sun and the moon – were completely enchanted by *Väinämöinen* playing the *kantele* [a traditional Finnish and Karelian plucked string instrument]. *Vanemuine*, in the Estonian people's creation, was such a master of music and the father of songs.[61]

The treatment of the jubilee in Estonia more explicitly reveals this Finnic interaction. While Russian-language newspapers in Estonia said little about the jubilee, Estonian-language media actively propagated it.[62] Furthermore, Tartu University organized lectures on the *Kalevala* and a two-day scholarly session in April 1949 to discuss the two Finnic epics.[63] As Heldur Niit, then a Tartu University student, recalled, for Estonian students studying Finnic languages and culture, the jubilee was the first occasion to speak with native Finnish speakers from Petrozavodsk.[64] It is important to note that the jubilee and its preparation went side by side with Moscow's plan to implement collectivization and mass deportation in Estonia; after the jubilee, the attack against intellectuals started both in Soviet Karelia and Estonia.[65] Considering this, the Soviet authorities utilized the jubilee to tie the Estonian people to the Karelo-Finnish people, to entrench them firmly within the Soviet multinational community in order to stabilize the Soviet–Finnish borderland.

In this manner, the jubilee's organizers declared that the *Kalevala* and the Karelo-Finnish people were now members of the Soviet family of nations. The guest speech by the Armenian writer Amayak Siras illustrates this:

> We, the descendants of David of Sassoun [the hero of the Armenian national epic], took six days and nights to arrive at the shores of Lake Onega, and are here to congratulate the descendants of *Väinämöinen*. [Applause] ... Our cultural, all-people's anniversaries show that working peoples in the East and the West are living with a common interest. The *Kalevala* enters the treasury of world culture. *Väinämöinen* is as close to the heart of the Armenian people as the beloved David of Sassoun.[66]

Conclusion

This chapter has described the shift of pan-Finnism from Finland to the Soviet Union, paying attention to the controversy over the *Kalevala* influenced by border changes. From the beginning, the pan-Finnic vision went beyond the borders. This family-like vision, forming a hierarchy among the Finnic people, became quite explosive, galvanizing many Finns after the Russian Revolution, and was exported to Soviet Karelia by the Red Finns, supported by Moscow. This notion of the Finnic family, with an expansionist vision of Greater Finland, mobilized Finnish nationalists to help their 'brothers and relatives', but at the same time caused conflicts among them. For many Russians and anti-Finnish Karelians, it was difficult to understand both Red and White pan-Finnic visions, and humiliating to see the Red Finns occupying leading positions and trying to 'civilize' the Karelians. In the mid-1930s, however, Russian and Karelian national identities strengthened, and Karelian–Finnish kinship was rejected. The Second World War marked a decisive shift at the centre of the Finnic world. Finland became isolated and had to forget its 'tribes'.

To claim the Soviet (neither Red nor White) *Kalevala*, the Soviets had to rearrange the pan-Finnic hierarchy according to the Soviet family-like order of nations. Soviet Finnic nationalities were allowed to enjoy the pan-Finnic vision, but only if they also accepted Soviet ideology and the superiority of the Communist Party, Russian centrality and the cult of Stalin.

In both the Soviet and Finnish Finnic orders, the Karelians were tied to the 'more developed' Finnish language and culture. To a much lesser extent, the Estonians were expected to show gratitude to their Finnish brothers. The differences between these two worlds were apparent. However, one can see the similarity (or perhaps 'collusion') between the Finnish nationalist and Soviet national ideologies in utilizing hierarchy among the broader Finnic family. To acknowledge this tacitly shared paternalistic gaze on Finnic nationalities was ill-suited for post-Second World War Soviet–Finnish friendship, especially after the death of Stalin. Therefore, the Soviet–Finnish story of the *Kalevala* controversy was to be forgotten; however, after the collapse of the Soviet Union, it came back as a 'puzzling' topic.

Acknowledgements

I am grateful to the editors for their valuable comments on my presentation at the Sapporo Conference 'Border History' at Hokkaido University in 2017 and on draft versions of this chapter. This research was supported by the Finnish Cultural Foundation and the Japan Student Services Organization.

Takehiro Okabe is a PhD candidate at the University of Helsinki and completing his doctoral dissertation titled 'Taming Greater Finland: Pan-Finnism, the Soviet-Finnish Kalevala Controversy and the Karelo-Finnish Soviet Republic, 1940–1956'. His research interests are Russian/Soviet borderland policies, nationalities policies and the Finno-Ugric scholarship and peoples in Eurasia.

Notes

1. *Helsingin Sanomat*, 28 February 2019, https://www.hs.fi/kulttuuri/art-2000006016911.html?fbclid=IwAR0DIRfIIXabFS7_hdw8O7IvvYUxYiZCNyMROPk9mNDy__sA9oJQWzvKpJs (accessed 23 May 2019).

2. *Internet-zhurnal Litsei*, 28 February 2019, https://gazeta-licey.ru/culture/75779-borba-za-kalevalu?fbclid=IwAR1PRaiNk7se7p93RjCIEZZ6njZETf-LVwI_E0PrmgDlzHJq8O9GXDLbhMU (accessed 23 May 2019).

3. A classic study is Wilson, *Folklore and Nationalism*. Recent studies have also stressed close relationships between *Kalevala* scholarship, intellectuals and the Greater Finland concept. For example, see Knuuttila, 'Sankariaika suomalaisessa kansanrunoudentutkimuksessa 1930-luvulla', 101–29; Wilson, 'Sata vuotta Kalevalan juhlintaa', 224–39; Näre and Kirves, *Luvattu maa*. On the Finnish and Russian memory politics of the Second World War, see Jokisipilä, *Sodan totuudet*.

4. For example, see Roiko-Jokela, *Virallista politiikkaa*; Salokannel, *Sielunsilta*; Olesk, *Kultuurisild üle Soome lahe*; Rausmaa, *Tuglaksen tuli palaa*.

5. On the Russian and Soviet *Kalevala*, see Vihavainen, 'Kaksi Kalevalan satavuotisjuhlintaa', 487–91; Prushinskaia, 'Karjalais', 63–67; Okabe, 'Negotiating Elias Lönnrot', 129–49. On the Soviet nationalities policy, see, for example, Martin, *The Affirmative Action Empire*; Hirsch, *Empire of Nations*; Smith, *Red Nations*.

6. On the making of the *Kalevala* and how Karelia attracted Finns, see Sihvo, *Karjalan kuva*; Wilson, *Folklore and Nationalism*, chapter 1; Laaksonen, 'Elias Lönnrot runojen jäljillä', 272–95.

7. Klinge, *Ylioppilaskunnan historia III*, 94–95.

8. On the relationship between modernity and folklore and folklore singers in nineteenth-century Europe, see Bauman and Briggs, *Voices of Modernity*, chapters 5 and 6.

9. Metste and Laak, *Kreutzwald*; Zetterberg, *Suomen sillan kulkijoita*, 148–67.

10. In the *Kalevipoeg*, the hero Kalevipoeg went to Finland to rescue his kidnapped mother Linda. Afterwards, he cut down a big oak tree (an important symbol in Finnish and Estonian mythology) to build a bridge between the two countries. Hasselblatt, *Kalevipoeg Studies*, 18.

11. On their meeting in Võru, where Kreutzwald lived, see Zetterberg, *Suomen sillan kukijoita*, 112–14. For details on Kreutzwald's attitude towards Finnish folklore and mythology, see Olesk, 'Vironkielinen Kalevala', 234.

12. Danilevsky, *Rossiia i Evropa*, 22–23.

13. Gordlevsky, 'Pamiati Eliasa Lenruta', 79–108.

14. Vitukhnovskaia, *Rossiiskaia Kareliia i karely v imperskoi politike Rossii*, chapter 7.

15. Vahtola, *Suomi suureksi*.

16. This number is from Zetterberg, *Viro ja Suomi 1917–1920*, 197.

17. Uino, 'Kielitaistelu ja "uusi suomalaisuusliike" 1918–1939', 177–249.

18. Sihvo, 'Kalevalan päivä', 94–102 and Lönnqvist, 'Runebergin päivä', 89–93.

19. On the interwar activity of both organizations, see Kalleinen, *Kansallisen tieteen ja taiteen puolesta*, 30–76 and Tala, *Vuosisata suomalaisuuden puolesta*, especially Jussi Niinistö's article, 11–53.

20. Sarhimaa, *Vaietut ja vaiennetut*, 96–110.

21. Alapuro, *Akateeminen Karjala-Seura*; Virtanen, *Fennomanian perilliset*, 135–43; Silvennoinen, 'Kumpujen yöhön', 16–67.

22. Alapuro, *Akateeminen Karjala-Seura*, 133.

23. Silvennoinen, Tikka and Roselius, *Suomalaiset fasistit*, chapters 6, 8 and 9.

24. Rui, *Ulkomaiset tiedemiehet Tarton yliopistossa ja virolaisten opintomatkat ulkomaille 1919–1940*, 85–112.

25. Sepp, 'Kultuurisild või kaitseliin?', 168–225.
26. Rui, 'Vankan tammen kaksi haaraa', 380.
27. Leskinen, *Vaiettu Suomen silta*, 316–42.
28. Olesk, 'Uus põlvkond hõimutöös', 42–44; Alenius, 'Veljeskansojen kahdet kasvot', 24–26; Rui, 'Vankan tammen kaksi haaraa', 391–92.
29. In addition to his research in Estonia, Kaarle Krohn came to know the very first generation of Estonian folklorists and trained many talented Finnish and Estonian folklorists. Tartu University awarded him an honorary doctorate in 1930. On Krohn's geographic-historical method of folklore studies, see Wilson, *Folklore and Nationalism*, 68–90. On the interaction between Finnish and Estonian folklorists, see Ilomäki, 'Eesti ja Soome rahvaluulealasd teaduskontaktid kahe maailmasõja vahel', 71–109.
30. Wilson, *Folklore and Nationalism*, 103–8; Fewster, *Visions of Past Glory*, 365–67.
31. For example, Väinö Salminen (1880–1947), professor of folkloristics at Helsinki University after Kaarle Krohn, attacked the official jubilee for its failure to refer to Karelia and Ingria and these regions' poet-singers. Kalleinen, *Kansallisen tieteen ja taiteen puolesta*, 73–75; Wilson, *Folklore and Nationalism*, 90–102.
32. Harva, 'Kalevala ja suomalainen kansallishenki', 229–30.
33. Annist, 'Kalevala ja Viro', 19–25. On Annist's notion of united Finnic people, see Sepp, 'Kultuurisild või kaitseliin?', 164–68.
34. On the nationality policy in interwar Soviet Karelia, see Kangaspuro, *Neuvosto–Karjalan taistelu itsehallinnosta*, 66–147; Sallamaa, 'Kalevala Marxin valossa ja varjossa', 252–69.
35. Savvateev, 'Fol'klorist V. Ia. Evseev', 5–6.
36. Martin, 'Modernization or Neo-Traditionalism?', 161–82; Brandenberger, *National Bolshevism*, chapter 3; Kangaspuro, *Neuvosto–Karjalan taistelu itsehallinnosta*, 260–319.
37. National Archive of Republic of Karelia, f. p-3, op. 3, d. 358, l. 3 (instructions to local party propagandists).
38. Ibid., l. 1.
39. On the repression of Finns in Soviet Karelia, see Takala, 'Natsional'nye operatsii OGPU/NKVD v Karelii', 161–206; Takala, 'The Great Purge', 144–57.
40. Pal'vadre, 'Burzhuaznaia finskaia etnografiia i politika finliandskogo fashizma', 39–43.
41. Bubrikh, 'Iz istorii Kalevaly', xi–xii.
42. Bubrikh, *Karely i karel'skii iazyk*, 5, 8, 12, 18.
43. Evseev, 'K voprosu o proiskhozhdenii run Kalevaly', 198–203.
44. Kilin, 'Karjalais–suomalainen sosialistinen neuvostotasavalta', 195–202; Hyytiä, *Karjalais–Suomalainen Neuvostotasavalta*, 20–38.
45. Raninen-Siiskonen, *Vieraana omalla maalla*, 15.
46. On the Finnish occupation of Soviet Karelia and the *Kalevala*, see Wilson, *Folklore and Nationalism*, 181–94; Laine, *Suur-Suomen Kahdet Kasvot*; Laine, 'Tiedemiesten Suur-Suomi', 91–202; Verigin, *Kareliia v gody voennykh ispytannii*; Verigin, *Predateli ili zhertvy voiny*. The number is from Laine, 'Karelo-Finskaia Sovetskaia Sotsialisticheskaia Respublika i finny', 232.
47. The number of Estonian refugees is from Roiko-Jokela, 'Heimotyötä ja virolaissympatioita', 246, 255. The number of Ingrian refugees is from the National Archive of Finland, http://www.narc.fi/Arkistolaitos/inkerilaissiirtolaiset/tilastot.html (accessed 23 May 2019).
48. Kirves, 'Pyhä ja kirottu sota', 321–73.
49. For details on the post-war Soviet–Finnish controversy, see Okabe, 'Negotiating Elias Lönnrot'.

50. Stalin's speech at the reception for the Finnish delegation after the conclusion of the treaty, published in *Bol'shevik* 7 (1948), 1–2. On Stalin's attitude towards Finland, see Rentola, *Stalin ja Suomen kohtalo*.

51. Zakharova, 'À la recherche des cadres nationaux', 216–17; Hyytiä, *Karjalais– Suomalainen Neuvostotasavalta*, 121–25.

52. For example, the six hundredth anniversary of the Buryat–Mongolian epic, the *Geser*, was finally cancelled in February 1949 due to its anti-people, anti-Russian character and its suspected pan-Mongolism. Okabe, 'Kalevala ja Geser Stalinin Neuvostoliitossa', 17–27. In addition, the concept of Finno-Ugric kinship again became the target of ideological campaigns: for example, Chevoksarov, 'Nekotorye voprosy izucheniia finno-ugorskikh narodov v SSSR', 176–85.

53. Research Archive of the Karelian Research Centre of the Russian Academy of Sciences (NA KarNTs RAN), f. 1, op. 4, d. 73, l. 59.

54. Kuusinen's opening words and presentation at the jubilee session can be found in Kuusinen, 'Doklad', 1–4.

55. Bubrikh, 'Ob moei odnoi gruboi oshibke', 122. On the negotiation between Kuusinen and Bubrikh before the jubilee, see Chistov, 'Vospominaniia o moem pervom direktore', 89–97.

56. Kuusinen, 'Doklad', 1–4.

57. NA KarNTs RAN, f. 1, op. 4, d. 55, l. 61.

58. Õhtuleht, 9 August 1947.

59. Rahvusarhiiv, f. r-2345, nim. 3, s. 3, ll. 1–14.

60. NA KarNTs RAN, f. 1, op. 4, d. 115, l. 71.

61. NA KarNTs RAN, f. 1, op. 4, d. 115, l. 104.

62. The Russian-language newspaper *Sovetskaia Estonia* (24 and 25 February 1949) does not mention the special relationship between the *Kalevala* and the *Kalevipoeg*. The Estonian-language newspapers did refer to this: *Säde*, 3 March 1949; *Sirp ja vasar*, 26 February 1949; *Edasi*, 24 and 26 February and 1949. Nigol Andresen, deputy chairman of the Estonian Council of Ministers, wrote an article about the Karelo-Finnish epic and pointed out that the similarity between the two epics was not yet well known. Andresen, '"Kalevala" mälestuspäevade puhul', 354.

63. *Sirp ja vasar*, 19 April 1949.

64. Salokannel, *Sielunsilta*, 43–44.

65. In Soviet Karelia, the Second Karelo-Finnish Party Congress, held in April 1949, attacked the philologists of the Republic: *Leninskoe Znamia*, 26 April 1949. On Estonia, see Laas, *Teadus diktatuuri kütkeis*, 250–54, 305–8. On the March 1949 mass deportation in Estonia, see Saueauk, *Propaganda ja terror*, 296–313.

66. NA KarNTs RAN, f. 1. op. 4, d. 115, ll. 82, 84.

Bibliography

Aarnipuu, Petja (ed.). *Kalevala maailmalla: Kalevalan käännösten kulttuurihistoria*. Helsinki: Suomalaisen Kirjallisuuden Seura [SKS], 2012.

Alapuro, Risto. *Akateeminen Karjala-Seura: ylioppilasliike ja kansa 1920– ja 1930–luvulla*. Helsinki: WSOY, 1973.

Alenius, Kari. 'Veljeskansojen kahdet kasvot: Naapurimaa-kuva', in Heikki Roiko-Jokela (ed.), *Virallista politiikkaa: Epävirallista kanssakäymistä: Suomen ja Viron suhteiden käännekohtia 1860–1991* (Jyväskylä: Atena, 1997), 13–30.

Andresen, Nigol. '"Kalevala" mälestuspäevade puhul'. *Looming* 3 (1949), 352–58.

Annist, August. 'Kalevala ja Viro'. *Suomalainen Suomi* 1 (1935), 19–25.
Bauman, Richard, and Charles L. Briggs. *Voices of Modernity: Language Ideologies and the Politics of Inequality*. Cambridge: Cambridge University Press, 2003.
Brandenberger, David. *National Bolshevism: Stalinist Mass Culture and the Formation of Modern Russian National Identity, 1931–1956*. Cambridge, MA: Harvard University Press, 2002.
Bubrikh, Dmitry. *Karely i karel'skii iazyk*. Moscow: Izd. Mosoblispolkoma, 1932.
———. 'Iz istorii Kalevaly', in Bubrikh, Dmitrii (ed.), *Kalevala: Finskii narodnyi epos* (Moscow: Academia, 1933), ix–xx.
———. 'Ob moei odnoi gruboi oshibke'. *Na rubezhe* 2 (1949), 121–22.
Cadiot, Juliette, Dominique Arel and Larissa Zakharova (eds). *Cacophonies d'empire: Le gouvernement des langues dans l'empire russe et l'Union soviétique* (Paris: CNRS Editions, 2010).
Chevoksarov, Nikolai. 'Nekotorye voprosy izucheniia finno-ugorskikh narodov v SSSR'. *Sovetskaia Etnografiia* 3 (1948), 176–85.
Chistov, Kiril. 'Vospominaniia o moem pervom direktore', in Georgii Kert (ed.), *D. V. Bubrikh: k 100-letiiu so dnia rozhdeniia* (Saint Petersburg: S-Peterburgskoe otdelenie 'Nauka', 1992), 89–97.
Danilevsky, Nikolai. *Rossiia i Evropa: Vzgliad na kul'turnye i politicheskie otnosheniia slavianskogo mira k germane-romanskomy. Izdanie shestoe*. Saint Petersburg: Izd. SPb universiteta, 1995.
Evseev, Viktor. 'K voprosu o proiskhozhdenii run Kalevaly'. *Zvezda* 3 (1935), 198–203.
Fewster, Derek. *Visions of Past Glory: Nationalism and the Construction of Early Finnish History*. Helsinki: Finnish Literature Society, 2006.
Gordlevsky, Vladimir. 'Pamiati Eliasa Lenruta'. *Russkaia mysl'* 5 (1903), 79–108.
Harva, Uno. 'Kalevala ja suomalainen kansallishenki'. *Kalevalaseuran vuosikirja* 16 (1936), 218–30.
Hasselblatt, Cornelius. *Kalevipoeg Studies: The Creation and Reception of an Epic*. Helsinki: SKS, 2016.
Hirsch, Francine. *Empire of Nations: Ethnographic Knowledge and the Making of the Soviet Union*. Ithaca, NY: Cornell University Press, 2005.
Hoffmann, David L., and Yanni Kotsonis (eds). *Russian Modernity: Politics, Knowledge, Practices*. London: Palgrave Macmillan, 2000.
Hyytiä, Osmo. *Karjalais–Suomalainen Neuvostotasavalta, 1940–1956: Kansallinen tasavalta?* Helsinki: SKS, 1999.
Hämynen, Tapio (ed.). *Kahden Karjalan välillä, kahden Riikin riitamaalla*. Joensuu: Joensuun yliopiston humanistinen tiedekunta, 1994.
Ilomäki, Henni. 'Eesti ja Soome rahvaluulealasd teaduskontaktid kahe maailmasõja vahel', in Sirje Olesk (ed.), *Kultuurisild üle Soome lahe: Eesti–Soome akadeemilised ja kultuurisuhted 1918–1944* (Tartu: Eesti Kirjandusmuuseum, 2005), 71–109.
Jokisipilä, Markku (ed.). *Sodan totuudet: Yksi suomalainen vastaa 5.7 ryssää*. Jyväskylä: Ajatus kirjat, 2007.
Kalleinen, Kristiina. *Kansallisen tieteen ja taiteen puolesta: Kalevalaseura 1911–2011*. Helsinki: SKS and Kalevalaseura, 2011.
Kangaspuro, Markku. *Neuvosto–Karjalan taistelu itsehallinnosta: Nationalismi ja suomalaiset punaiset Neuvostoliiton vallankäytössä 1920–1939*. Helsinki: SKS, 2000.
Karkama, Pertti, and Hanne Koivisto (eds). *Ajan paineessa: Kirjoituksia 1930-luvun suomalaisesta aatemaailmasta*. Helsinki: SKS, 1999.
Kert, Georgii (ed.). *D. V. Bubrikh: K 100-letiiu so dnia rozhdeniia*. Saint Petersburg: S-Peterburgskoe otdelenie 'Nauka', 1992.

Kilin, Iurii. 'Karjalais–suomalainen sosialistinen neuvostotasavalta', in Tapio Hämynen (ed.), *Kahden Karjalan välillä, kahden Riikin riitamaalla* (Joensuu: Joensuun yliopiston humanistinen tiedekunta, 1994), 195–202.

Kirves, Jenni. 'Pyhä ja kirottu sota: Suur-Suomi-aatteen uho ja tuho aikalaisten kokemana', in Sari Näre and Jenni Kirves (eds), *Luvattu maa* (Helsinki: Johnny Kniga, 2014), 321–79.

Klinge, Matti. *Ylioppilaskunnan historia III: K.P.T.: stä jääkäreihin*. Helsinki: Gaudeamus, 1978.

Knuuttila, Seppo. 'Sankariaika suomalaisessa kansanrunoudentutkimuksessa 1930-luvulla', in Pertti Karkama and Hanne Koivisto (eds), *Ajan paineessa: Kirjoituksia 1930–luvun suomalaisesta aatemaailmasta* (Helsinki: SKS, 1999), 101–29.

Knuuttila, Seppo, Pekka Laaksonen and Ulla Piela (eds). *Kalevalan kulttuurihistoria*. Helsinki: SKS, 2008.

Koistinen, Tero, Piret Kruuspere, Erkki Sevänen and Risto Turunen (eds). *Kaksi tietä nykyisyyteen: Tutkimuksia kirjallisuuden, kansallisuuden ja kansallisten liikkeiden suhteista Suomessa ja Virossa*. Helsinki: SKS, 1999.

Kuusinen, Otto. 'Doklad', in *Trudy iubileinoi nauchnoi sessii posviashchennoi 100-letiiu polnogo izdaniia 'Kalevaly'* (Petrozavodsk: Karelo–Finnskoe Gosudarstvennoe izdacheristvo, 1950), 1–4.

Laaksonen, Pekka. 'Elias Lönnrot runojen jäljillä', in Seppo Knuuttila, Pekka Laaksonen and Ulla Piela (eds), *Kalevalan kulttuurihistoria* (Helsinki: SKS, 2008), 272–95.

Laas, Jaan. *Teadus diktatuuri kütkeis*. Tallinn: Argo, 2010.

Laine, Antti. *Suur-Suomen kahdet kasvot: Itä-Karjalan siviiliväestön asema suomalaisessa miehityshallinnossa 1941–1944*. Helsinki: Otava, 1982.

———. 'Tiedemiesten Suur-Suomi: Itä-Karjalan tutkimus jatkosodan vuosina'. *Historiallinen Arkisto* 102 (1993), 91–202.

———. 'Karelo-Finskaia Sovetskaia Sotsialisticheskaia Respublika i finny', in Timo Vihavainen and Irina Takala (eds), *V sem'e edinoi: Natsional'naia politika partii bol'shevikov i ee osushchestvlenie na severo-zapade Rossii v 1920–1950-e gody* (Petrozavodsk: Izd. PetrGU, 1998), 223–50.

Leskinen, Jari. *Vaiettu Suomen silta: Suomen ja Viron salainen sotilaallinen yhteistoiminta Neuvostoliiton varalta vuosina 1930–1939*. Helsinki: Suomen Historiallinen Seura, 1997.

Lönnqvist, Bo. 'Runebergin päivä' in Urpo Vento (ed.), *Juhlakirja: Suomalaiset merkkipäivät* (Helsinki: SKS, 1979), 89–93.

Martin, Terry. 'Modernization or Neo-Traditionalism? Ascribed Nationality and Soviet Primordialism', in David L. Hoffmann and Yanni Kotsonis (eds), *Russian Modernity: Politics, Knowledge, Practices* (London: Palgrave Macmillan, 2000), 161–82.

———. *The Affirmative Action Empire: Nations and Nationalism in the Soviet Union, 1923–1939*. Ithaca, NY: Cornell University Press, 2001.

Metste, Kristi, and Marin Laak. *Kreutzwald. Missioon. Tegelikkus*. Tartu: Eesti Kirjandusmuuseum, 2003.

Näre, Sari, and Jenni Kirves (eds). *Luvattu maa: Suur-Suomen unelma ja unohdus*. Helsinki: Johnny Kniga, 2014.

Niinistö, Jussi. 'Suomalaisuuden Liiton vaiheita 1906–2006'. in Tala, Heikki (ed.). *Vuosisata suomalaisuuden puolesta: Suomalaisuuden Liitto 1906–2006*. (Helsinki: Suomalaisuuden liitto, 2006), 11–96.

Okabe, Takehiro. 'Negotiating Elias Lönnrot: Shared Soviet–Finnish National Symbol Articulated and Blurred, 1945–1952'. *Nordic Historical Review/Revue d'Historire Nordique* 19 (2014), 129–49.

———. 'Kalevala ja Geser Stalinin Neuvostoliitossa'. *Idäntutkimus* 4 (2015), 17–27.

Olesk, Sirje (ed.). *Kultuurisild üle Soome lahe: Eesti–Soome akadeemilised ja kultuurisuhted 1918–1944*. Tartu: Eesti Kirjandusmuuseum, 2005.

———. 'Uus põlvkond hõimutöös', in Sirje Olesk (ed.), *Kultuurisild üle Soome lahe: Eesti– Soome akadeemilised ja kultuurisuhted 1918–1944* (Tartu: Eesti Kirjandusmuuseum, 2005), 39–52.

———. 'Vironkielinen Kalevala: August Annistin elämä ja työ', in Petja Aarnipuu (ed.), *Kalevala maailmalla: Kalevalan käännösten kulttuurihistoria* (Helsinki: SKS, 2012), 233–43.

Pal'vadre, M. Iu. 'Burzhuaznaia finskaia etnografiia i politika finliandskogo fashizma'. *Sovetskaia Etnografiia* 1–2 (1931), 39–43.

Prushinskaia, Natalia. 'Karjalais–suomalainen eepos 1930–40 luvulla Neuvostollitossa'. *Carelia* 2 (1996), 63–67.

Raninen-Siiskonen, Tarja. *Vieraana omalla maalla: Tutkimus karjalaisen siirtoväen muistelukerronnasta*. Helsinki: SKS, 1999.

Rausmaa, Heikki. *Tuglaksen tuli palaa: Tuglas-seuran ja suomalais–virolaisten suhteiden historiaa*. Helsinki: SKS, 2007.

Rentola, Kimmo. *Stalin ja Suomen kohtalo*. Helsinki: Otava, 2016.

Roiko-Jokela, Heikki, and Heikki Seppänen (eds). *Etelän tien kulkija – Vilho Helanen (1899–1952)*. Jyväskylä: Atena, 1997.

Roiko-Jokela, Heikki. 'Heimotyötä ja virolaissympatioita', in Heikki Roiko-Jokela and Heikki Seppänen (eds), *Etelän tien kulkija – Vilho Helanen (1899–1952)* (Jyväskylä: Atena, 1997), 206–60.

———. (ed.). *Virallista politiikkaa: Epävirallista kanssakäymistä: Suomen ja Viron suhteiden käännekohtia 1860–1991*. Jyväskylä: Atena, 1997.

Rui, Timo. '"Vankan tammen kaksi haaraa": Suomen ja Viron kulttuurisuhteiden historiaa', in Tero Koistinen, Piret Kruuspere, Erkki Sevänen and Risto Turunen (eds), *Kaksi tietä nykyisyyteen: Tutkimuksia kirjallisuuden, kansalaisuuden ja kansallisten liikkeiden suhteista Suomessa ja Virossa* (Helsinki: SKS, 1999), 373–93.

———. *Ulkomaiset tiedemiehet Tarton yliopistossa ja virolaisten opintomatkat ulkomaille 1919– 1940*. Joensuu: Joensuun yliopistopaino, 2001.

Sallamaa, Kari. 'Kalevala Marxin valossa ja varjossa', in Seppo Knuuttila, Pekka Laaksonen and Ulla Piela (eds), *Kalevalan kulttuurihistoria* (Helsinki: SKS, 2008), 252–69.

Salokannel, Juhani. *Sielunsilta: Suomen ja Viron kirjallisia suhteita 1944–1988*. Helsinki: SKS, 1998.

Sarhimaa, Anneli. *Vaietut ja vaiennetut: Karjalankieliset karjalaiset Suomessa*. Helsinki: SKS, 2017.

Saueauk, Meelis. *Propaganda ja terror: Nõukogude julgeolekuorganid ja Eestimaa Kommunistlik Parteri Eesti sovetiseerimisel 1944–1953*. Tallinn: SE&JS, 2015.

Savvateev, Iu. A. 'Fol'klorist V. Ia. Evseev: k-100 letiu so dnia rozhdeniia', in *U istokov karel'skoi fol'kloristiki* (Petozavodsk: KarNTs RAN, 2010), 5–20.

Sepp, Helena. 'Kultuurisild või kaitseliin? Üks vaatenurk Soome–Eesti: üliõpilassuhete arengule 1920–1930 aastatel', in Sirje Olesk (ed.), *Kultuurisild üle Soome lahe: Eesti– Soome akadeemilised ja kultuurisuhted 1918–1944* (Tartu: Eesti Kirjandusmuuseum, 2005), 133–247.

Sihvo, Hannes. *Karjalan kuva: Karelianismin taustaa ja vaiheita autonomian aikana*. Helsinki: SKS, 1973.

———. 'Kalevalan päivä', in Urpo Vento (ed.), *Juhlakirja: Suomalaiset merkkipäivät* (Helsinki: SKS, 1979), 94–102.

Silvennoinen, Oula. 'Kumpujen yöhön – eli kuinka historiallinen muisti vääristyi', in Sari Näre and Jenni Kirves (eds), *Luvattu maa* (Helsinki: Johnny Kniga, 2014), 16–67.

Silvennoinen, Oula, Marko Tikka and Aapo Roselius. *Suomalaiset fasistit: Mustan sarastuksen airuet.* Helsinki: WSOY, 2016.
Smith, Jeremy. *Red Nations: The Nationalities Experience in and after the USSR.* Cambridge: Cambridge University Press, 2013.
Takala, Irina. 'Natsional'nye operatsii OGPU/NKVD v Karelii', in Timo Vihavainen and Irina Takala (eds), *V sem'e edinoi: Natsional'naia politika partii bol'shevikov i ee osushchestvlenie na severo-zapade Rossii v 1920–1950-e gody* (Petrozavodsk: Izd. PetrGU, 1998), 161–206.
———. 'The Great Purge'. *Journal of Finnish Studies* 15 (1 and 2) (2011), 144–57.
Tala, Heikki (ed.). *Vuosisata suomalaisuuden puolesta: Suomalaisuuden Liitto 1906–2006.* Helsinki: Suomalaisuuden liitto, 2006.
Tommila, Päiviö, and Maritta Pohls (eds). *Herää Suomi: Suomalaisuusliikkeen historia.* Kuopio: Kustannuskiila, 1989.
Trudy iubileinoi nauchnoi sessii posviashchennoi 100–letiiu polnogo izdaniia 'Kalevaly'. Petrozavodsk: Karelo-Finnskoe gosudarstvennoe izdacheristvo, 1950.
Uino, Ari. 'Kielitaistelu ja "uusi suomalaisuusliike" 1918–1939', in Päiviö Tommila and Maritta Pohls (eds), *Herää Suomi: Suomalaisuusliikkeen historia* (Kuopio: Kustannuskiila, 1989), 177–249.
Vahtola, Jouko. *'Suomi suureksi – Viena vapaaksi': Valkoisen Suomen pyrkimykset Itä-Karjalan valtaamiseksi vuonna 1918.* Rovaniemi: Pohjois-Suomen historiallinen yhdistys, 1988.
Vento, Urpo (ed.). *Juhlakirja: Suomalaiset merkkipäivät.* Helsinki: SKS, 1979.
Verigin, Sergei. *Kareliia v gody voennykh ispytannii.* Petrozavodsk: Izd. PetrGU, 2009.
———. *Predateli ili zhertvy voiny: Kollaboratsionizm v Karelii v gody vtoroi mirovoi voiny 1939–1945 gg.* Petrozavodsk: Izd. PetrGU, 2012.
Vihavainen, Timo. 'Kaksi Kalevalan satavuotisjuhlintaa'. *Kanava* 7 (1983), 487–91.
Vihavainen, Timo, and Irina Takala (eds). *V sem'e edinoi: Natsional'naia politika partii bol'shevikov i ee osushchestvlenie na severo-zapade Rossii v 1920–1950-e gody.* Petrozavodsk: Izd. PetrGU, 1998.
Virtanen, Martti. *Fennomanian perilliset: Poliittiset traditiot ja sukupolvien dynamiikka.* Helsinki: SKS, 2001.
Vitukhnovskaia, Marina. *Rossiiskaia Kareliia i karely v imperskoi politike Rossii, 1905–1917.* Saint Petersburg: Norma, 2006.
Wilson, William A. *Folklore and Nationalism in Modern Finland.* Bloomington, IN: Indiana University Press, 1976.
———. 'Sata vuotta Kalevalan juhlintaa', in Seppo Knuuttila, Pekka Laaksonen and Ulla Piela (eds), *Kalevalan kulttuurihistoria* (Helsinki: SKS, 2008), 224–39.
Zakharova, Larissa. 'À la recherche des cadres nationaux: La langue d'instruction en Carélie en tant qu'instrument de discrimination positive (1945–1964)', in Juliette Cadiot, Dominique Arel and Larissa Zakharova (eds), *Cacophonies d'empire: Le gouvernement des langues dans l'empire russe et l'Union soviétique* (Paris: CNRS Editions, 2010), 205–27.
Zetterberg, Seppo. *Suomen sillan kulkijoita: Yhteyksiä yli Suomenlahden 1800–luvulla.* Helsinki: Siltala, 2015.
———. *Viro ja Suomi 1917–1920.* Helsinki: Docendo, 2018.

Part VI

MIGRATION AND INTERETHNIC CONFLICT AT CHINA'S EDGE

SEONMIN KIM AND BALÁZS SZALONTAI

The two chapters in this section examine China's northern and northeastern borderlands in two different but indirectly connected historical periods. Seonmin Kim's chapter examines migration trends, interethnic relations and boundary management in Manchuria's Yalu River area – that is, the borderlands of the Qing Empire and Chosŏn Korea – in the nineteenth century, while Balázs Szalontai's chapter describes how the changing dynamism of Sino-Mongolian relations influenced the Mongolian Communist leadership's policies towards the country's ethnic Chinese community from 1960 to 1984. At first sight, these two historical situations might appear to be distant from each other, both geographically and chronologically, but a closer look can reveal various illuminating parallels between them – parallels that may be traced back to the fact that both Manchuria and Outer Mongolia occupied a special position in the Qing Empire.

In the heyday of the Qing dynasty, the Manchu rulers strictly prohibited Han Chinese civilians from permanently settling either in Manchuria (the sacred birthplace of the imperial court) or in Outer Mongolia (where loyal Mongol nobles were given the status of 'privileged subjects'). As long as the Qing administration remained firmly in control at home and managed to keep its northern neighbour – Imperial Russia – at bay, the authorities were largely able to enforce these restrictions, and saw little need to revoke them. By the nineteenth century, however, the system of closed areas started to break down under the combined pressures of commercialization, spontaneous migration and Russian expansion. In southern Manchuria, commercial timber logging attracted a growing number of Han Chinese and Korean migrants, while in Outer Mongolia, the emergence of Chinese trade centres was equally stimulated by a growing Mongolian demand for Chinese tea, tobacco, silk and cotton, and by Chinese demand for Mongolian livestock and wool. As Kim points out, initially both the Qing and the Chosŏn authorities tried to prevent the influx of illegal Chinese and Korean immigrants into Manchuria, but by the 1860s, they were compelled to realize that their futile coercive measures merely provoked resistance instead of solving the problem. Kim also quotes a Qing military governor who keenly understood that a sparsely populated border region would offer a tempting target for Russian encroachments, whereas the presence of Chinese settlers might enable Beijing to reinforce its control over the areas threatened by Tsarist expansionism. Motivated by similar considerations, the dynasty's New Policies (1901–12) started to promote the migration of Han Chinese settlers to Outer Mongolia, where the steady growth of Russian commercial influence raised the spectre of political interference.

In many respects, the Chinese and Korean immigrants played an indispensable economic role in their new environment. Kim stresses that in southern Manchuria, the large-scale production of timber, ginseng and grain increasingly relied on a labour force of Korean migrants, and the commercial exchanges between illegal loggers and local Chinese farmers were just as essential for the latter as for the former. In Outer Mongolia, where the indigenous population was composed primarily of nomadic herdsmen and Buddhist monks, Chinese merchants, moneylenders, artisans, horticulturalists and farmers constituted, in the words of a foreign diplomat quoted by Szalontai, 'the most diligent stratum of the society'. Yet the influx of immigrants could (and did) generate interethnic tension, too. In the Yalu River area, competition for land and timber triggered violent clashes between Chinese and Korean residents as early as 1870, which in turn became a bilateral foreign relations concern for the Qing and Chosŏn authorities. In Outer Mongolia, popular discontent over the exploitative practices of Chinese merchants erupted in a series of mob riots that started in 1881 and culminated during the revolution of 1911. Once Mongolia gained its independence from China, the situation of the local Chinese residents became extremely precarious, since both the

Mongolian authorities and ordinary Mongols regarded them as pawns of the Chinese government, but China could not give them effective protection against the recurrent waves of persecution. As Szalontai notes, the Chinese leaders' attempts to involve the ethnic Chinese community in their own diplomatic manoeuvres just reinforced the suspicions that the Mongolian authorities harboured about this economically useful but politically troublesome minority. In the end, the Mongolian Communist leadership decided to sacrifice economic utility at the altar of political distrust.

CHAPTER 11

Environmental Relations in the Yalu River Region in the Nineteenth Century

Seonmin Kim

Introduction

Traversing the modern day Chinese provinces of Liaoning and Jilin, the area north of the Yalu River region was called 'Outside of the Shengjing Willow Palisade' (*Shengjing dongbianwai*) during the Qing period. South of the river was Chosŏn territory, and during the Chosŏn period the areas around the upper streams of the river were specifically called 'the Four Closed Counties' (*P'yesagun*). Surrounded by numerous valleys and rivers originating in the Changbaishan mountain ranges, the Yalu River region was famous for its rich natural resources and mountain forests. Unlike many other provinces in China proper, which had experienced widespread land clearance and deforestation during the Qing era, the Yalu River region was able to maintain its natural environment because the Qing court restricted civilian access to Manchuria – the sacred birthplace of the Manchu imperial court. It was also located at the boundary with Chosŏn: any intrusion over the boundary with the 'outer dependency' (*waifan*), or crossing the river without state permission, was severely punished. From the outset of the Qing dynasty, settlements and development in the vast region between the Shengjing Willow Palisade and the Yalu and Tumen rivers were prohibited. Without state authorization, civilians – notably Han Chinese farmers – were not allowed to clear land, cut down trees or hunt animals in the Yalu River region.¹

Most studies on the Yalu River region have largely focused on Qing–Chosŏn relations, because the Chosŏn tributary envoy to Beijing had crossed the river, and their people had shared the river, resulting in contact and conflicts for centuries. In particular, the Yalu and Tumen rivers in the nineteenth century have been discussed regarding Han Chinese immigration to Manchuria, Korean migration to the northern side of those rivers and the Qing–Chosŏn boundary investigations of the 1880s.² Unlike these conventional narratives, two recent studies have shed new light on environmental relations in the Yalu River region in the nineteenth century. Kwangmin Kim has explored Korean migration to the north of the river from the perspective of global capitalism in the modern period. He argues that Korean migration was a global phenomenon, a part of structurally interrelated migration movements that took place all across China's borders in the nineteenth century. Since 1861, when the first treaty port in Manchuria, Niuzhuang, opened, southern Manchuria witnessed rapid growth in the commercialization of its local agriculture. The large-scale commercial production of timber, ginseng and grain required an extensive labour force, and eventually Korean migrants became the primary source of this labour. As such, Korean migration to Manchuria was essentially a relocation of agrarian labour.³ Yamamoto Susumu discusses the ways in which the Qing and Chosŏn governments responded to the changing nature of the environment of the Yalu River region. While the Qing authorities had more interest in timber, the Chosŏn court sought to maintain its ginseng taxes. Yamamoto also explains that timber logging and land clearance happened concurrently in this region because large-scale logging required a great number of workers and ready access to food supplies.⁴

The Qing court imposed restrictions on Manchuria and the Yalu River region for the purpose of monopolizing profits from natural resources – ginseng, sable and pearls – and protecting Manchu privileges from the Han Chinese majority. By the nineteenth century, however, ginseng, sable and pearls became scarce due to centuries of 'imperial foraging', as David Bello explains.⁵ The depletion of natural resources in Manchuria corresponded with the influx of Han Chinese farmers in the restricted margins of the empire. From the nineteenth century onward, the Qing prohibition on civilian settlements in the north-east gradually broke down; the growing number of Chinese immigrants effectively invalidated the state's restrictions. By the late nineteenth century, when illegal land clearance and timber logging became widespread in the Yalu River region, the Qing court decided to lift the nominal policy of restrictions and legalize the presence of the immigrants. Concurrently with the Qing court's authorization of settlements and development north of the Yalu River, the Chosŏn court was also forced to address the issue of increasing numbers of settlers in the Four Closed Counties. For the Chosŏn court, urgent development of the southern side of the Yalu River was necessary to defend Korean residents against increasing numbers of Chinese settlers on the opposite side of the river. Under strong pressure from both sides of the Yalu River, the Qing and Chosŏn governments came to legalize settlements and development on both sides of the river.

This chapter explains the ways in which settlements and development in the Yalu River region in the late nineteenth century led to intense competition for natural resources among local residents. Timber loggers, in particular, militarized themselves to protect their paths to mountain forests and resisted local Qing and Chosŏn authorities who attempted to rein in their illegal activities. Most notably, Korean immigrants north of the river joined these armed Chinese timber loggers and raided local Chosŏn offices when their encroachment on mountain forests in Chosŏn territory was stopped by the Chosŏn authorities. By exploring several violent incidents caused by timber logging in the Yalu River region in the 1870s, this chapter explains the interactions between nature and culture that took place across the Qing and Chosŏn boundaries in the late nineteenth century.

Figure 11.1. The Qing–Chosŏn borderland. © Seonmin Kim.

Illegal Settlements and Development in the Yalu River Region

During the Jiaqing emperor's reign (1796–1820), the Qing court repeated its prohibition orders against Han Chinese civilian settlements in the sacred birthplace of the Manchus. However, reports of illegal settlements and land development near the Yalu River continued. In 1800 and 1803, the Jiaqing emperor repeatedly emphasized the significance of the restrictions around the Yalu River: 'The outside of the Fenghuangcheng gate on the Willow Palisade is very close to Chosŏn territory and is therefore of grave importance'; 'Anyone found to have illegally gathered in Gaoligou [at the upper Yalu River] to build huts [wafeng] and cut down trees should be arrested.' However, officials who joined the field investigation outside the Shengjing Willow Palisade recognized that a great number of people were involved in illegal timber logging.[6]

During the Daoguang emperor's reign (1821–50), illegal settlements and development in the Yalu River area continued to increase and the number of settlers was reportedly as many as twenty to thirty thousand. A report from the Shengjing military governor in 1831 indicated that on sixty-eight occasions, local authorities had arrested illegal loggers who were posing as authorized timber merchants, and had confiscated 22,760 pieces of timber. By 1836, large-scale timber logging in the Yalu River area grew to the extent that 'capital providers' (caidong) and 'storage owners' (wazhu) were involved in the business.[7]

By the 1840s, the Qing and Chosŏn governments agreed to engage in regular joint patrolling (tongxun huishao) of the Yalu River region in order to curtail the increasing numbers of illegal settlements along the border. In 1841, Chosŏn soldiers of the Sangt'o garrison in P'yŏng'an province reported that Chinese farmers had built huts and tilled the land opposite their jurisdiction. This was near the Aihe River, 700 li, about 350 kilometres, from the gate of the Willow Palisade. These illegal settlers were also reported to have cultivated sorghum and corn to feed themselves. Qing soldiers burned down their huts and removed them from the area. But people soon gathered in the same location. In 1846, Chosŏn soldiers of the Sangt'o garrison again reported that the numbers of Chinese settlers north of the river continued to increase and that the location of their huts and cleared land was even closer to the Chosŏn territory than before. Qing and Chosŏn soldiers engaged in joint searches for illegal settlements, arresting three hundred people, including two hundred illegal loggers, burning their huts and land and confiscating twelve thousand pieces of timber.[8] Soon after arresting the illegal settlers near the Aihe River, the Shengjing military governor made a proposal for controlling the mountains in the Yalu River region. His proposal included the following: an increase in *karun* (outposts) along the river; annual regular patrols during the spring and autumn; special patrols by imperial envoys every three years; joint patrols with Chosŏn soldiers; reinforcement of gate checking at the Willow Palisade; and increases in the number of soldiers stationed at the mouth of the Yalu River.[9]

During his search for illegal settlements in 1846, the Shengjing military governor sent troops not only to the upper areas of the Yalu River where farmers had tilled the land, but also to the lower reaches of the river where loggers transported timber. The arrested timber loggers confessed that they removed the trees from the forests and transported them by way of the river. They bought food from the farmers who tilled the land along the riverbank. Timber loggers also provided necessities for the farmers; they exchanged timber for items found outside the mountains and brought them to the farmers living in the mountains. As the Shengjing military governor pointed out, 'if illegal loggers are prevented from cutting down trees and selling timber, the source of income for the migrants will also be prevented'.[10] By the 1840s, timber logging and land clearance continued to grow in the Yalu River region.

Qing Opening of the Willow Palisade

By the 1850s, the Qing court's policy of restricting civilian settlements in Manchuria was still imposed, but mainly in vain, by repeating the old rhetoric of the 'place of Manchu origins'. However, local military commanders in the north-east had to find ways to overcome new financial shortfalls, and land was the most abundant and readily available resource at their disposal. Eventually, the Jilin and Heilongjiang authorities began to make a series of proposals to Beijing that the restricted areas should be opened to civilian settlement, and through doing so, money and taxes be collected from the settlers. In 1859, the Jilin military governor proposed the opening of the previously prohibited regions of the Suifen and Ussuri rivers, warning of the possibility that Russian ships might land there. He suggested that 'if [our] people can gather and settle in the region and reap profits from timber logging, hunting, ginseng gathering and fishing in the deep mountains, the Russians will retreat'. The Xianfeng emperor (r. 1850–61) agreed that 'it is beneficial that Chinese subjects live in China's vast land' (*yi Zhongguo zhi kuangtu, ju Zhongguo zhi minren, li zhi suozai*), allowing people to protect themselves and prevent foreign aggressions.[11] The following year, in 1860, the Qing court opened parts of southern Jilin for civilian settlement, a decision largely considered to be the first official lifting of the restriction policy in Qing Manchuria. From the 1860s to the 1880s, many prohibited areas in Jilin and Heilongjiang were gradually opened for settlement and the restrictions on civilian settlers became effectively nominal.[12]

Not surprisingly, the Shengjing authorities were well aware of the need for authorization of development of the Yalu River. In 1863, the Jinzhou garrison lieutenant general informed the Tongzhi emperor (r. 1862–74) of the situation in the area between the Willow Palisade and the Yalu River:

> Because of the vast tracts of land and the deep mountains in this region, thorough investigation and patrols are nearly impossible. Trespassers have long been sneaking into the area, first to hunt and to log, and later to pan for gold and to cultivate land. These days, wanderers from Zhili and Shandong arrive and form gangs, causing trouble. Previously they built huts and tilled the land only in the deep mountains, but now there is no limit to the illegal settlements and they are spreading widely over hundreds of *li*. Patrolling soldiers are few in number and thus unable to stop these criminals. Barring access to the area near the boundary is gradually becoming ineffectual; the land outside the palisade is being reclaimed without any official sanction [by the state].[13]

This report shows that local officials in Shengjing recognized that the prohibition on settlements in the Yalu River region was no longer effective. No matter how much the Qing and Chosŏn authorities tried to restrict access to the area, the vast territory near the Yalu River had gradually filled with illegal farmers intent on securing land for themselves.

The illegal residents in the Yalu River region sought official authorization of land development in the area. Despite their increasing numbers, they were largely beyond any protection from Qing officers and soldiers, thereby exposing them to threats from local criminal elements. The immigrants wanted state protection of their lives and property in exchange for the payment of taxes. As local officials and the illegal residents shared the same interests, that is, the legalization of settlements and land development, demand for the lifting of the prohibition in the Yalu River region continued to grow.

By 1867, these illegal settlers had even approached the Shengjing office and volunteered to pay taxes. This was in light of a precedent set in Jilin, where illegal farmers were already allowed to do so. The Shengjing office responded cautiously to the farmers' willingness to pay taxes, since their settlements in the prohibited area outside the palisade were a serious violation of the Qing restriction policy in the north-east. In addition, the relevant area was located near the boundary with the Chosŏn and therefore required special consideration; it was necessary to check whether the settlements could cause problems with the Chosŏn court.[14] Upon the report from the Shengjing office, the Qing court in Beijing first emphasized that Shengjing was the sacred birthplace of the Qing empire and that several thousand *li* of land and mountains there had always been protected by the palisade. Simultaneously, however, it recognized that there were numerous people living outside the palisade and that these people made their living by cultivating the land and logging timber. The officials were rightly concerned that if the illegal settlers were forced to evacuate the prohibited territory, they would lose their livelihoods and likely end up rebelling. The Qing court thus had to find a solution that would place these settlers under the state's authority, but also protect the prohibited land near the boundary with Chosŏn.[15]

In 1869, the Shengjing military governor investigated the conditions of settlements outside of the Shengjing Willow Palisade, reporting to the emperor that 96,000 *xiang* of land had been cleared and one hundred thousand people were living there.[16] 'In some areas 30–40 per cent of the land was cleared, others even up to 70–80 per cent. Wide tracts of wasteland no longer remain in this region.'[17] Local officials proposed to the emperor that settlements and development in the Yalu River region should be legalized by extending the Willow Palisade towards the east. They were also concerned that without enforcing appropriate regulations related to these residents, disorder in the local communities could result. In the end, the Qing court decided to collect taxes from the settlers on the grounds that 'it is very difficult to relocate the settlers because they have already developed a wide swathe of land'.[18] The Yalu River was finally authorized for settlement and development after centuries of restrictions.

The opening of the north-east and the increase in civilian immigrants required a transformation of the administrative system in Manchuria: the Qing government needed a new institutional structure to handle the increase in civil affairs. In 1875, the Shengjing military governor suggested that the Shengjing government be restructured to match the administrative system of China proper, as a necessary response to ever-increasing numbers of Chinese civilians. The Guangxu emperor (r. 1875–1908) eventually approved this proposal, and the Shengjing military governor was granted authority over all affairs involving garrison troops and civilian settlers. While increasing the power of the military governor, this reform also sought to limit the privileges of banner garrisons and shift more administrative authority into the hands of civil officials. Between 1877 and 1883, Jilin also carried out an overall reorganization of its government through the efforts of the Jilin military governor. Throughout the 1870s and 1880s, new county and prefectural administrative offices for civilian affairs were established in various locations in Shengjing and Jilin. As administrative power was transferred from banner garrisons to civil offices, the primary purpose of the government changed from protecting and nurturing the banner forces to supervising and governing Chinese immigrants.[19]

Chosŏn Opening of the Four Closed Counties

South of the Yalu River was Chosŏn territory, but for centuries Koreans were not allowed to settle and develop the land near the river. In fact, the early Chosŏn court endeavoured to expand northward in the area of the Yalu and Tumen rivers and to control the Jurchens living in the northern region. During the years 1416–43, the Chosŏn established four counties in the region at the upper Yalu River, but this effort was unsuccessful because they were located very close to Jurchen bases and the land, being barren, was not suited to settlement and agriculture. By 1459, the Chosŏn court decided to close the four counties; from that time on, this region of the upper Yalu River came to be known as 'the Four Closed Counties'. The Jurchen rise in Liaodong and the violent beginning of Qing–Chosŏn relations in the early seventeenth century devastated the Chosŏn's northern region, rendering it unstable. Until the late nineteenth century, the Chosŏn court did not allow Korean settlements near the boundary with the Qing.[20]

In the eighteenth century, as Qing–Chosŏn relations became more stable, the movement of people into the region at the upper Yalu River continued to increase. East of the Four Closed Counties, Huju (later Huch'ang) in particular witnessed rapid growth in the number of settlers in the eighteenth century. It was local officials who first raised the issue of the necessity of restoring Chosŏn administrative power in the region. In 1794, the Hamgyŏng governor explained to his king that 'the Huju area has fertile land and is surrounded by rich mountain forests, so it can produce a great amount of food and ginseng. But the vast tracts of land have been left empty and people have not lived there. While barbarians [the Qing] are encroaching in search of ginseng and animals, patrolling by soldiers is ineffective and security at the boundary is weak.' He also pointed out that Huju was strategically important in defence against foreign threats; a Chosŏn administrative office in Huju would be required in order to fight against the 'barbarians' who could possibly claim it as their own territory.[21] In 1796, the Chosŏn court restored a county office in Huju, an initial move in the opening of the Four Closed Counties for development after centuries of restrictions.

During the nineteenth century, an increasing number of people moved into the Four Closed Counties from both sides – Hamgyŏng in the east and P'yŏng'an in the west. Seoul continued to receive reports of land development and timber logging. But Chosŏn court officials were still very cautious about the idea of developing the region near the boundary with the Qing. Those moving into the Yalu River region were all considered 'wanderers' who avoided paying taxes; it was assumed that such migrants would scatter upon being required to pay taxes and that people residing in mountain areas would also harm ginseng production in this region. Most of all, settlements and development near the boundary would result in more contacts with Qing subjects, which in turn might lead to Koreans trespassing into Qing territory. Throughout the Chosŏn period, two different ideas about the Yalu River had been held by court officials: the developmentalists argued that the Four Closed Counties were fertile and important, and therefore should be opened. The restrictionists, meanwhile, insisted that development would simply result in conflict with the Qing at the boundary.[22]

Not unlike the situation outside Shengjing Willow Palisade, state prohibitions did not prevent the movement of people into the Four Closed Counties. In 1818, a report said that in the former ginseng mountains in Kanggye, there were some 490 households tilling the land and logging timber. In fact, Kanggye local officials were reprimanded by the Chosŏn court for collecting taxes from these illegal residents.[23] As the number of settlers and the amount of cleared land continued to increase in the Four Closed Counties, demands for civilian administration by the residents grew as well. Local officials were concerned that 'since state offices are far away, this region has become a base for local bandits and it is impossible to police the area'.[24] The Chosŏn officials' proposals for the authorization of development in the Four Closed Counties were also related to the rapid growth in the number of Qing settlers opposite the Yalu River. The more Chinese farmers settled near the river, the more they made contact and trouble with Koreans. In 1868, the P'yŏng'an special inspector reported frequent contacts between Chinese settlers and Korean residents in the Yalu River region.

> The Yalu River flows through the vast land between [Chosŏn's] Ŭiju and the Four Closed Counties. The Qing side of the river has long been empty and restricted [*konghŏ kŭmji*], but within several decades this off-limits area has been developed by the wanderers [*yumin*] and become a hiding place for bandits. As the Great Country [*sangguk*] permitted houses to be built here last year, many residents came to live by the river; it is not known how many people hide in the mountains and live there. Since they settled near the river, they became familiar with our [Korean] residents, frequently visiting each other and illicitly exchanging food, silk, cotton fabrics, oxen, etc.[25]

As contact between Chinese settlers and Korean residents increased across the Yalu River, the Chosŏn court had to enforce security and order at the boundary. The best solution was to restore the Chosŏn administration office in the Four Closed Counties, which 'had been abandoned for 400 years'. In 1869, new county offices were established at Chasŏng in P'yŏng'an and Huch'ang in Hamgyŏng. The following year, in 1870, the Chosŏn court informed the Qing court that administrative offices in the Four Closed Counties had been restored and that Korean settlements south of the Yalu River were authorized.[26] Both north and south of the Yalu River were now open for development after centuries of restrictions.

Violence in the Yalu River Region

For both the Qing and Chosŏn courts, the development of the Yalu River region was not a domestic issue that mattered only to the local authorities. Since Chinese and Korean residents on both sides of the river sought access to land and mountain forests along the boundary, contact and conflict between local residents, especially when volatile and violent, soon became a bilateral foreign relations concern. Two attacks by Chinese timber loggers on Chosŏn local offices in P'yŏng'an province were initially discussed locally, but they soon became a serious issue under discussion between Beijing and Seoul.

On 15 February 1870, when ten Korean residents of Pyŏktong county crossed the river to cut grass, they ran into illegal settlers living there. These Chinese settlers, in fact, had moved from Shandong about ten years ago and lived at the mouth of the Hun River (the Tunggiya River). The Chinese settlers stopped the Koreans from approaching their huts. The next day, when the Koreans returned, the Chinese settlers stole the ploughs and oxen belonging to the Korean interlopers. Five days later, two to three hundred Koreans crossed the river as a group to reclaim their ploughs and oxen from the Chinese and burn down some seventeen huts in the area. During the conflict, eight Koreans were killed. On 4 March, as many as 370 of the Chinese settlers, armed and riding horses, raided and burned down Chosŏn local offices and civilian houses, as well as making off with their weapons. Two of the attackers were arrested; one of them turned out to be a Korean migrant who had defected from his home village to the northern side of the Yalu River.[27]

Later the Korean residents explained to the Chosŏn officials why they wanted to burn down the Chinese settlers' huts across the river: 'In recent days [the Chinese] cross the boundary to till the land and build huts. They have caused us harm. If we do not punish them, we will not be able to continue living here. We decided to burn down their huts as an act of revenge and prevent them from approaching the river.'[28] The increase in settlements in the Yalu River region led to growing competition over land and natural resources, and resulted in armed attacks, injuries and killings on both sides. This raid proved that the Chosŏn court had correctly anticipated the consequences of development in the Yalu River area: the more people gathered at the boundary, the more trouble took place.

By 1870, some parts of the Yalu River region had opened up, but the rest of the area was still restricted from settlement and development. The illegal residents in the prohibited areas expected neither state administration nor protections by officers and soldiers; they were exposed to violence and exploitation by local bandits. In 1872, a resident outside the Willow Palisade accused regular patrols by Qing soldiers of being patrols in name only: 'When the Qing itinerant officer used to come by, we bribed him and he left us alone. Even if the Qing sends troops [next time], if we pay them off, there probably won't be any trouble'; 'Every year, the itinerant officer comes with soldiers and announces that [he will] expel the bandits. However, has this ever happened? We pay them. It is as if they came here to collect tax.'[29] For the illegal residents living beyond state control, the Yalu River region was 'a lawless place where strongmen are the lord'.[30] In fact, local residents built their own independent community (*hoesang*), which had armed itself and policed the area; they defended themselves from various potential threats, including bandits, robbers and even Qing and Chosŏn soldiers.[31]

As the local community became militarized, largely due to a lack of state control in the Yalu River area, competition for natural resources among Chinese and Korean settlers became increasingly violent. On 2 December 1871, when seventy Chinese timber loggers from Qidaogou, at the upper stream of the Yalu River, entered the mountains at Huch'ang, Chosŏn soldiers evicted the Chinese intruders. A month later, four to five hundred Chinese loggers, armed with rifles and spears, crossed the frozen river to raid Chosŏn in revenge. While they burned down offices and homes, two dozen Chinese attackers were killed or injured. Later, the Chinese loggers occupied a Chosŏn village in Tujidong, opposite the Qing's Malupao, and confronted the Chosŏn forces. When the number of injured topped one hundred and ammunition ran out, two leaders from the community of Chinese settlers sent a letter to the Chosŏn local authorities in Huch'ang, proposing peace. The Chinese leaders stated that 'if our people intrude into your territory and make trouble, you should arrest them to send back to us. We will execute them and prevent future problems.'[32] These violent conflicts at the boundary were later solved, but the Qing emperor who was informed of the incident by the Chosŏn king ordered the Shengjing office to investigate and punish the criminals.

In the summer of 1872, the year after the Chinese settlers' raids on Tujidong, the Chosŏn county magistrate of Huch'ang dispatched three military agents north of the Yalu River to collect information about the areas of Ji'an, Tonghua and the Hun River.[33] According to their subsequent report, there were numerous Korean migrants living at the upper Yalu and Hun rivers who were defecting from Musan, Huch'ang and Kanggye and crossing the river to the north. Some were from the elite class, but the majority of the Korean migrants were poor peasants escaping heavy taxes and starvation. The Korean migrants north of the river were mostly employed by Chinese settlers in agriculture, hunting, panning for gold or ginseng farming. Most notably, some Korean migrants joined the Chinese business of illegal timber logging. The transportation of trees by way of the Hun River to the mouth of the Yalu River was very profitable for local residents.[34]

One of the Korean migrants whom Chosŏn agents from Huch'ang met said that 'every year barbarians [*ho'in*] [the Chinese] have crossed the boundary to log timber, a normal practice that [the Chosŏn authorities] have never prevented before'. However, since the Chosŏn county magistrate of Huch'ang had stopped timber logging in his jurisdiction in the past year, Chinese loggers had clashed with Chosŏn forces. The Korean migrant blamed this on the Huch'ang magistrate: 'Barbarians in this region can profit from agriculture by selling food to the loggers. The timber logging business is hugely profitable, as much as a million *liang* a year, and [the loggers] buy food from the locals. Thus agriculture is also very profitable and many people till the land. However, since last year [the Chosŏn authorities] have banned Chinese loggers and now there is no one to buy our food … [The Chosŏn authorities] should allow the Chinese people to cut down trees again.' After losing several tens of thousands of *liang*, the Chinese loggers were believed to be preparing to engage Chosŏn forces in order to ensure their access to mountain forests at the boundary.[35]

Because timber merchants purchased food from both the Chinese and Korean settlers at the Hun River opposite Huch'ang, the business of logging was very important for both the Chinese settlers and the Korean migrants. 'Without the barbarians, how could we make a living here?' This remark by the aforementioned Korean migrant shows that a great number of Chinese and Koreans shared the natural resources of the Yalu River region, resulting in complicated environmental relations across their territorial boundaries in the late nineteenth century.

Acknowledgements

I would like to thank Professors Jie-Hyun Lim, Nobuya Hashimoto and Stefan Berger for inviting me to the 'Border History' Conference in Sapporo, 2017. My special thanks go to Kwangmin Kim and Loretta Kim for our productive and pleasant discussions during the conference.

Seonmin Kim is Professor of the Research Institute of Korean Studies at Korea University, Seoul, Korea. Her research interests include the Qing Empire, Manchuria, the history of Chinese–Korean relations and environmental history. She has co-translated early Qing documents into Korean, including the Old Manchu Archives and the Veritable Records of the Qing Dynasty for the Nurhaci and Hong Taiji periods. She is the author of the monograph *Ginseng and Borderland: Territorial Boundaries and Political Relations between Qing China and Chosŏn Korea, 1636–1912* (University of California Press, 2017).

Glossary

Place Names

Chinese and Korean	Chinese characters
Aihe	靉河
Chasŏng	慈城
Fenghuangcheng	鳳凰城
Jinzhou	錦州
Gaoligou	高麗溝
Huch'ang	厚昌
Huju	厚州
Kanggye	江界
Malupao	馬鹿泡
Niuzhuang	牛莊
Pyŏktong	碧潼
Qidaogou	七道溝
Sangt'o	上土
Tujidong	杜芝洞
Ŭiju	義州

Miscellaneous

Chinese and Korean	Chinese characters	English
caidong	財東	capital provider
hoesang	會上	community
ho'in	胡人	barbarian
konghŏ kŭmji	空虛禁地	empty and restricted place
P'yesagun	廢四郡	the Four Closed Counties
sangguk	上國	the Great Country
Shengjing dongbianwai	盛京東邊外	Outside of the Shengjing Willow Palisade
tongxun huishao	統巡會哨	regular joint patrolling
wafeng	窩棚	hut
waifan	外藩	outer dependency
wazhu	窩主	storage owner
yi Zhongguo zhi kuangtu, ju Zhongguo zhi minren, li zhi suozai	以中國之曠土, 居中國之民人, 利之所在	'it is beneficial that Chinese subjects live in China's vast land'
yumin	流民	wanderer

Notes

    1. Kim, *Ginseng and Borderland*.
    2. Yang and Sun, *Zhong Chao bianjie shi*; Li, *Cho Ch'ŏng kukkyŏng munje yŏn'gu*; Li, *Han Chung kukkyŏngsa yŏn'gu*; Kim, *1880 nyŏndae Chosŏn-Ch'ŏng kongdong kamgye wa kukkyŏng hoedam ŭi yŏngu*.
    3. Kim, 'Korean Migration in Nineteenth-Century Manchuria'.
    4. Yamamoto, *Daishin teikoku to Chōsen keizai*.
    5. Bello, *Across Forest, Steppe, and Mountain*.
    6. *Qing shilu*, 28: 830–31 (Jiaqing5/3/wuyin); 29: 567 (Jiaqing8/8/guihai).
    7. *Qing shilu*, 35: 132–33 (Daoguang 8/7/renzi); 35: 1185 (Daoguang11/12/dingyou); 37: 290 (Daoguang16/6/yichou).
    8. Pae, *Kugyŏk Tongmun hwigo kanggye saryo*, 331–32, 337–40, 343–50, 351–53, 367–73.
    9. For details of the Qing–Chosŏn joint patrolling, see Ku, '19 segi sŏnggyŏng tongbyŏn oe sanjang'; Akizuki, 'Amnokkang hokugan no tōjun kaishō nitsuite'.
    10. Pae, *Kugyŏk Tongmun hwigo kanggye saryo*, 546–49, 563.
    11. *Qing shilu*, 44: 302–3 (Xianfeng 9/9/jimao).
    12. Lin, *Qingji dongbei yimin shibian*, 78–79; Gao, *Jindai Zhongguo dongbei yimin*, 105–13.
    13. Lin, *Qingji dongbei yimin shibian*, 180–81.
    14. Pae, *Kugyŏk Tongmun hwigo kanggye saryo*, 697–98.
    15. Ibid., 703–4.
    16. 1 *xiang* is equivalent to 15 *mu* or 2.4 acres.

17. Pae, *Kugyŏk Tongmun hwigo kanggye saryo*, 724–25.
18. Zhang, *Qingdai yilai yalujiang liuyue yimin yanjiu*, 59–62.
19. Lee, *The Manchurian Frontier in Ch'ing History*, 119–27; Tsukase, *Manchuria shi kenkyū*, 144–52, 161–68.
20. Yi, *Han'guk manju kwan'gyesa ŭi yŏn'gu*, 68–69.
21. *Chosŏn wangjo sillok*, Chŏngjo18/7/27.
22. Kang, *Chosŏn hugi Hamgyŏngdo wa pukpang yŏngt'o ŭisik*, 169–71; Pae, *Chosŏn hugi kukt'ogwan kwa ch'ŏnhagwan ŭi pyŏnhwa*, 223–25.
23. *Pibyŏnsa tŭngnok*, Sunjo18/2/10.
24. Yi, '1872 nyŏn kangbuk ŭi Chosŏnin sahoe', 294–96.
25. *Ilsŏngnok*, Kojong 5/10/26.
26. Pae, *Kugyŏk Tongmun hwigo kanggye saryo*, 735–36.
27. Pae, *Kugyŏk Tongmun hwigo pŏmwŏl saryo*, 4: 822–23, 827–28.
28. Ibid., 857–58.
29. Ch'oe, *Kangbuk ilgi*, 32–33. English translation quoted in Kim, 'Korean Migration in Nineteenth-Century Manchuria', 28.
30. Ch'oe, *Kangbuk ilgi*, 51.
31. Ibid., 12; Yi, '1872 nyŏn kangbuk ŭi Chosŏnin sahoe', 301–4.
32. Pae, *Kugyŏk Tongmun hwigo kanggye saryo*, 742–44, 749–50.
33. The Korean soldiers departed from Huch'ang on 5 July 1872 and returned on 13 August of the same year.
34. Ch'oe, *Kangbuk ilgi*, 19, 52–54.
35. Ibid., 77–79.

Bibliography

Akizuki, Nozomi 秋月望. 'Amnokkang hokugan no tōjun kaishō ni tsuite' 鴨綠江北岸の統巡會哨について [Joint patrolling on the northern side of the Yalu river]. *Kyūshū Daigaku Tōyōshi ronshū* 11 (1983), 117–37.

Bello, David. *Across Forest, Steppe, and Mountain: Environment, Identity, and Empire in Qing China's Borderlands*. New York: Cambridge University Press, 2016.

Chosŏn wangjo sillok 朝鮮王朝實錄 [Veritable records of the Chosŏn dynasty]. Seoul: Kuksa p'yŏnch'an wiwŏnhoe, 1968.

Ch'oe, Chongbŏm 崔宗範. *Kando kaech'ŏk pisa: Kangbuk ilgi* 間島開拓秘史: 江北日記 [Secret history of the development of Kando: Diary of the north of the Yalu river], trans. Ch'oe Kanghyŏn 최강현. Seoul: Sinsŏng ch'ulp'ansa, 2004.

Ilsŏngnok 日省錄 [Daily Records of the Royal Court and Important Officials]. Seoul: Sŏul taehakkyo Kyujanggak, 1992.

Kang, Sŏkhwa 강석화. *Chosŏn hugi Hamgyŏngdo wa pukpang yŏngt'o ŭisik* 朝鮮後期 咸鏡道와 北方領土意識 [The Hamgyŏng province and concepts of northern territory in the late Chosŏn period]. Seoul: Kyŏngsewŏn, 2000.

Kim, Hyŏngjong 김형종. *1880 nyŏndae Chosŏn-Ch'ŏng kongdong kamgye wa kukkyŏng hoedam ŭi yŏngu* 1880年代 朝鮮一淸 共同勘界와 國境會談의 研究 [A study on the joint investigations of the Korea–Chinese borders in the 1880s]. Seoul: Sŏul taehakkyo ch'ulp'an munhwawŏn, 2018.

Kim, Kwangmin. 'Korean Migration in Nineteenth-Century Manchuria: A Global Theme in Modern Asian History', in Wen-hsin Yeh (ed.), *Mobile Subjects: Boundaries and Identities in the Modern Korean Diaspora* (Berkeley, CA: Institute of East Asian Studies, 2013), 17–37.

Kim, Seonmin. *Ginseng and Borderland: Territorial Boundaries and Political Relations between Qing China and Chosŏn Korea, 1636–1912*. Berkeley, CA: University of California Press, 2017.

Ku, Pŏmjin 구범진. '19 segi sŏnggyŏng tongbyŏnoe sanjang ŭi kwalli wa Cho Ch'ŏng kongdong hoech'o' 19世紀 盛京 東邊外 山場의 管理와 朝淸 公同會哨 [Management of the eastern part of the Shengjing Willow Palisade and Qing-Chosŏn joint patrolling in the nineteenth century]. *Sarim* 32 (2009), 261–300.

Lee, Robert H. G. *The Manchurian Frontier in Ch'ing History*. Cambridge, MA: Harvard University Press, 1970.

Li, Huazi 李花子. *Cho Ch'ŏng kukkyŏng munje yŏn'gu* 朝淸國境問題研究 [A study on the Qing–Chosŏn border]. Seoul: Chipmundang, 2008.

———. *Han Chung kukkyŏngsa yŏn'gu* 韓中國境史研究 [A study on the history of the Korea–Chinese border], Seoul: Hye'an, 2011.

Lin, Shih-hsuan 林士鉉. *Qingji dongbei yimin shibian zhengce zhi yanjiu* 淸季東北移民實邊政策之研究 [Immigration and border protection in the north-east during the late Qing period]. Taipei: Guoli zhengzhi daxue lishi xuexi, 2001.

Gao, Lecai 高樂才. *Jindai Zhongguo dongbei yimin yanjiu* 近代中國東北移民研究 [A study on immigration to the north-east in modern China]. Beijing: Shangwuyin shuguan, 2010.

Pae, Usŏng 배우성. *Chosŏn hugi kukt'ogwan kwa ch'ŏnhagwan ŭi pyŏnhwa* 朝鮮後期 國土觀과 天下觀의 變化 [Changes in the concepts of territory and world during the late Chosŏn period]. Seoul: Ilchisa, 1998.

———. *Kugyŏk Tongmun hwigo kanggye saryo* 國譯 同文彙考 疆界史料 [Korean translation of historical materials about boundaries in *Tongmun Hwigo*]. Seoul: Tongbuga yŏngu chaedan, 2008.

———. *Kugyŏk Tongmun hwigo pŏmwŏl saryo* 國譯 同文彙考 犯越史料 [Korean translation of historical materials about border trespassing in *Tongmun Hwigo*], 4 vols. Seoul: Tongbuga yŏngu chaedan, 2012.

Pibyŏnsa tŭngnok 備邊司謄錄 [Records of the border defence council]. Seoul: Kuksa p'yŏnch'an wiwŏnhoe, 1959.

Qing shilu 淸實錄 [Veritable records of the Qing dynasty]. Beijing: Zhonghua shuju, 1986.

Tsukase, Susumu 塚瀨進. *Manchuria shi kenkyū: Manshū 600nen no shakai henyō* マンチュリア史研究: 滿洲600年の社會變容 [History of Manchuria: Social transformation of Manchuria over 600 years]. Tokyo: Yoshikawa kōbunkan, 2014.

Yamamoto, Susumu 山本進. *Daishin teikoku to Chōsen keizai: Kaihatsu, kahei, shin'yō* 大淸帝國と朝鮮經濟: 開發, 貨幣, 信用 [The Qing empire and Chosŏn economy: Development, currency and credit]. Fukuoka: Kyūshū Daigaku Shuppankai, 2014.

Yang, Zhaoquan 楊昭全, and Sun, Yumei 孫玉梅. *Zhong Chao bianjie shi* 中朝邊界史 [History of China–Korean boundaries]. Changchun: Jilin wenshi chubanshe, 1993.

Yi, Tongjin 이동진. '1872 nyŏn kangbuk ŭi Chosŏnin sahoe' 1872년 '江北'의 朝鮮人 社會 [Korean society in the north of the Yalu river area in the year of 1872]. *Tongbuga yŏksa nonch'ong* 8 (2005), 285–332.

Yi, Inyŏng 이인영. *Han'guk manju kwan'gyesa ŭi yŏn'gu* 韓國滿洲關係史의 研究 [A study of the history of Korea–Manchurian relations]. Seoul: Ŭryu munhwasa, 1954.

Zhang, Zhongyue 張鐘月. *Qingdai yilai yalujiang liuyue yimin yanjiu* 淸代以來鴨綠江流域移民研究 [Immigration to the Yalu river area in the Qing period], PhD dissertation. Changchun: Dongbei shifan daxue, 2015.

CHAPTER 12

Smallfolk in a Clash of Empires

Sino-Mongolian Relations and the Ethnic Chinese Community in the Tsedenbal Era, 1960–84

BALÁZS SZALONTAI

> Being common-born is dangerous, when the great lords play their game of thrones.
> —George R. R. Martin, *A Feast for Crows*

Introduction

Earlier studies on the Chinese residents in Mongolia (and the animosities they encountered) have been focused on three historical periods: the Qing era, when the Chinese trade centres in Outer Mongolia came into existence; the first decades of independent Mongolia, when the administration of the Bogd Khan, and later the Mongolian People's Republic (MPR), attempted to control the activities of Chinese residents by various means; and the post-1990 period, when Chinese economic influence once again became increasingly predominant in Mongolia.[1] In contrast, the era of Yumjaagiin Tsedenbal (1952–84) has received comparatively less attention in this respect. While a number of researchers (e.g. Christopher P. Atwood, Tsedendambyn Batbayar, Franck Billé, Elizabeth E. Green, William R. Heaton, Mendee Jargalsaikhan and Sergey Radchenko) have mentioned the anti-Chinese aspects of Tsedenbal's foreign and domestic policies, their publications did not provide a comprehensive overview of the role that the Chinese permanent and temporary residents played – willingly or unwillingly – in these tumultuous events.

This chapter seeks to fill this gap on the basis of Hungarian archival sources, by placing the ruling Mongolian People's Revolutionary Party (MPRP)'s policies towards Chinese residents into the broader context of Sino-Mongolian relations. In turn, the China–MPR relationship is placed into the framework of Sino-Soviet relations, as the Mongolian party-state, having been under Soviet tutelage ever since its inception, was profoundly affected by any conflict or rapprochement between the two neighbouring Communist empires. At the same time, the chapter's narrative is not confined to the sphere of high-level policymaking. Whenever possible, it shows how the interactions between the Mongolian, Chinese and Soviet party leaders (the 'great lords', to borrow an image from George R. R. Martin's *A Game of Thrones*) affected the life of ordinary Chinese residents – the 'smallfolk', to whom 'it is no matter … if the high lords play their game of thrones, so long as they are left in peace. They never are.'[2]

The origins of Mongolia's ethnic Chinese community may be traced back to the 1750s, when the first Chinese trade centres (*maimaicheng*) were established in Qing-ruled Outer Mongolia – partly to facilitate Sino-Russian trade, partly to purchase livestock and wool for the Chinese market and partly to supply Mongolian customers with tea, tobacco, silk, cotton and other consumer goods that would have been otherwise inaccessible to a population composed mainly of nomadic herdsmen and Buddhist monks.[3] Chinese immigration to Mongolia, initially limited by Qing regulations, underwent a gradual increase. By 1910, the estimated number of Chinese residents had reached 100,000 (70,000 in the capital, 3,000 in Kyakhta, 2,500 in Uliastai and 2,500 in Khovd respectively), of whom the majority were merchants and moneylenders, while the rest were engaged in handicrafts and farming.[4]

While Chinese residents played an indispensable economic role in a society devoid of a native entrepreneurial middle class, their relations with the Mongolian population were far from harmonious. 'Because of the seasonal character of the Mongolian economy, many if not most purchases from the Chinese were transacted on credit at crippling rates of interest', which in turn generated popular discontent.[5] In 1881, 1900, 1905 and particularly during the revolution of 1911, this discontent erupted in the form of 'rabble riots', during which Mongolian laymen and Buddhist monks assaulted Chinese merchants, plundered their warehouses and destroyed their account books.[6] In 1921, the brief rule of Baron Ungern-Sternberg, and then the Soviet-assisted Communist takeover, brought new misfortunes upon the ethnic Chinese community. In the mid-1920s, the number of Chinese residents stood at 23,919 (46.7 per cent of all foreign residents).[7] Nevertheless, 85 per cent of the shops in Mongolia were still owned by Chinese entrepreneurs, and Chinese firms accounted for 60 per cent of total trade turnover – a situation facilitated by the then-amicable relationship between the USSR and the Republic of China.[8]

In 1927–29, the breakdown of Sino-Soviet relations induced the Kremlin to drastically reorient Mongolian trade from China towards the USSR. Following the mass expulsion of Chinese merchants, the Chinese community in Ulaanbaatar decreased to ten thousand in 1934, and the Stalinist purges took a further toll on the community.[9] For instance, the show trial held on 28 November 1933 seems to have been expressly directed against ethnic minorities: many defendants were Buryats, while three (Tang Qiu, Wang Wangtao and Zeng Wangqing) were of Chinese origin.[10] In October 1937, Chinese residents were officially placed into the category of 'No. 1 counter-revolutionary elements'.[11] During the 'Port Arthur case' (1948–49) – which was probably triggered by the earlier border clashes between the MPR and Republican China – the secret police arrested eighty-three Chinese, of whom forty-two were executed.[12]

Thus, the regime's recurrent campaigns against the Chinese minority formed an integral part of the Kremlin's efforts to impose its imperial control over Mongolia. At the same time, the Soviet and MPRP leaders strove hard to present the imposition of Communist rule as a process that fulfilled the long-standing national and social aspirations of the Mongolian population. In this narrative, the Chinese community was cast as the villain of the piece – class enemy and national enemy merged into one, rather than an ethnic minority entitled to Soviet-style collective rights. In a joint Soviet–Mongolian monograph, this view was expressed as follows: 'the rapacious actions of the Chinese traders and usurers ... exhausted Mongolia's economy, held back the development of productive forces, and contributed to the pauperization of the *arat* population.'[13] Accordingly, Mongolian Communist historiography described the anti-Chinese mob riots of the nineteenth century as an anti-feudal, anti-Qing 'arat movement', that is, an essentially progressive phenomenon.[14]

From Simmering Antipathy to Confrontation

The fact that the legitimacy of the Mongolian party-state was forged in direct opposition to China in general, and to the ethnic Chinese community in particular, posed formidable obstacles to the normalization of

Sino-MPR relations and the integration of the Chinese minority into Mongolian society. Still, in the first years of the Tsedenbal era it seemed that the triangular partnership between the USSR, the MPR and the recently established People's Republic of China (PRC) might overcome the legacy of historical conflicts.

In January 1961, the Hungarian Embassy in Ulaanbaatar estimated the total number of permanent foreign residents (mostly Chinese and Russians) at over thirty thousand. For a long time, their legal status had remained wholly unregulated, which considerably handicapped them in court cases. The Hungarian report bluntly stated that this legal limbo reflected 'the hatred that the population felt for them'. Ethnic Chinese in particular were regarded as pawns of the Chinese government, be it the Qing dynasty or Republican China. Still, 'the expulsion of the foreign citizens would have caused great economic damage, since these citizens were engaged in industry, commerce, and agriculture, and thus their activities were indispensable for the Mongolian national economy'. Presumably motivated by such considerations, the authorities had recently issued regulations about their rights and duties, the Hungarian diplomats noted, expressing the view that hostility towards foreign residents was no longer common among ordinary Mongolians: 'The limited animosity that still exists is directed nearly exclusively against the Chinese petty traders.'[15]

This optimistic assessment soon turned out to be erroneous, but at that time it was not wholly unfounded. From 1952 to 1960, the CCP leaders made strenuous efforts to regain the trust of their Mongolian comrades. 'Our ancestors exploited you for three hundred years, oppressed you, they ran up quite a debt, therefore, today we want to repay these debts', Mao Zedong told an MPRP delegation in 1956,[16] when Beijing granted aid worth 160 million roubles to Ulaanbaatar. To alleviate the grave shortage of skilled Mongolian workers, China dispatched a massive contingent of construction workers, miners and technicians to the MPR. At the zenith of Sino-Mongolian cooperation, their number stood at seventeen thousand (counting families).[17] The significance of their contribution may be gauged from the fact that in 1958, Chinese workers constituted 74 per cent of the persons employed in the construction sector, and even the Soviet-financed aid projects were heavily dependent on Chinese labour.[18]

In parallel with its aid projects, the Chinese government set up a ten-year school, a hospital and clubs to cater for the needs of the Chinese permanent residents. These institutions were under the supervision of the Chinese Embassy, rather than the Mongolian government. The enclave-like status of the Chinese community thus stood in a marked contrast with that of the ethnic Kazakhs in Bayan-Ölgii province (who were recognized as a national minority, and whose schools were operated by the Mongolian authorities), but had much in common with that of the Russian permanent residents, whose schools fell under the purview of the Soviet Embassy.[19] In general, Beijing treated Mongolia's Chinese community in the same way as it treated the *hoa kieu* (ethnic Chinese) in North Vietnam – exerting control over their education and enabling them to keep their Chinese citizenship but urging them to abide by the local laws.[20] That is, the CCP leaders strove to create a harmonious triangular relationship between the PRC, the neighbouring Communist party-states and the local Chinese minorities.

Despite Beijing's efforts to manage the affairs of the Chinese minority in the spirit of Sino-Mongolian friendship, Chinese permanent residents remained as vulnerable as ever. In August 1960, the Hungarian Embassy reported that ethnic Chinese agriculturalists, horticulturalists and merchants constituted 'the most diligent stratum of the society', but their diligence was not appreciated either by the MPR authorities (who, having launched a forceful collectivization campaign in 1958, treated the wealthier Chinese as 'kulaks' to be expropriated) or by ordinary Mongolians (who hated them so much that they often destroyed their workshops). Out of desperation, several elderly Chinese committed suicide. Facing this situation, the CCP leaders, anxious as they were to solve the problem without confronting the Mongolian government, adopted the position that those ethnic Chinese who wanted to leave the MPR were free to return to the motherland. The Hungarian diplomats found it 'incomprehensible' that the Mongolian authorities were more eager to get rid of the Chinese entrepreneurs than to harness their skills. For instance, the forceful eviction of Chinese agriculturalists created economic problems, whereupon the government asked Beijing to send new workers.[21]

The MPRP leaders evidently considered the presence of Chinese temporary residents a lesser nuisance than that of the community of permanent residents, but ordinary Mongolian citizens thought otherwise. In July 1959, a North Vietnamese diplomat named Han Ngoc Que told a Hungarian colleague that Chinese workers toiled far more assiduously than their Mongolian counterparts, but their diligence earned only disdain from the latter. Ordinary Mongolians were of the view that the Chinese workers had come to the MPR for selfish reasons, that is, they expected to earn more money there than in impoverished, overpopulated China.[22] Such ethnic animosities were unintentionally aggravated by Beijing's practice of sending only Han Chinese workers to Mongolia. Determined to limit contacts between Inner and Outer Mongolia, the Chinese authorities systematically rejected the applications of those ethnic Mongols who volunteered for work in the MPR.[23]

In the early 1960s, these simmering problems were abruptly brought to the surface by the outbreak of the Sino-Soviet conflict. Sandwiched between the two great Communist empires and economically dependent on both, the MPR was profoundly affected by their increasingly acrimonious dispute. The CCP leaders at first attempted to gain Tsedenbal's loyalty by offering to send additional construction workers. In May–June 1960, Premier Zhou Enlai promised to assist Mongolia to achieve a high level of industrialization, provided that Ulaanbaatar sided with Beijing against Moscow.[24] The MPRP leaders balked at confronting their long-time Soviet patrons, whereupon China switched to various methods of arm-twisting. Designed as an instrument of cooperation, the contingent of Chinese workers became an instrument of pressure.

In this atmosphere, any spontaneous strife between ordinary Chinese and Mongolian citizens was likely to get entangled with the grand diplomatic game played by the two party-states. In turn, the high-level dispute increasingly aggravated the already existing interethnic animosities. In mid-1961, a Mongolian truck driver accidentally hit a Chinese cyclist in front of a shoe factory in Ulaanbaatar. The injured cyclist assaulted the driver, whereupon the Mongolian shoe workers went on strike in a show of solidarity with their compatriot. In turn, the Chinese workers employed at the waterworks and mills held a 'revenge strike', and Beijing recalled a part of its workers from the MPR. In the winter of 1961–62, the Chinese Embassy started to organize strikes 'in the manner of a music conductor', as a Hungarian diplomat put it. For instance, the visit of Soviet cosmonaut Gherman Titov was literally darkened by a strike that crippled the capital's power plants from the day of his arrival right until his departure. Even in Kharkhorin, where relations between the Chinese workers and the local population had been far more cordial than in Ulaanbaatar, the workers abruptly adopted a confrontational attitude. In one particular case, they went so far as to slap a pregnant Mongolian woman. The indignant Mongolians called the police, but when the officers arrived, the Chinese threw themselves on the ground to protest against their intervention. The police, instructed as they were to avoid any clash with the Chinese workers, departed without taking any measures, but the workers went on strike anyway.[25] In 1963, a brawl between Mongolian and Chinese workers claimed the life of a Chinese labourer. By 1964, Beijing recalled the majority of its workers on the grounds that the MPR authorities failed to guarantee their safety.[26]

In parallel with the strikes, Beijing put pressure on Ulaanbaatar by raising territorial demands. In the earlier years of harmony, Sino-Mongolian disagreements over the largely undemarcated border had been kept in check, but now China renewed the dormant dispute with a vengeance. For instance, in November 1961 Chinese border guard units occupied a strip of land 300 kilometres long and 4 kilometres wide, ignoring Mongolian calls to withdraw. In May 1962, the Mongolian chargé d'affaires in Beijing told a Hungarian diplomat that the Chinese authorities' unwillingness to accept the boundary as officially delineated caused many border incidents, as Chinese citizens frequently wandered into areas that the Mongolians regarded as theirs, only to be expelled by the Mongolian border guards.[27]

In the fall of 1962, the CCP leaders, increasingly preoccupied as they were with their border conflict with India, decided to demonstrate their goodwill by settling their disagreements with Mongolia and other neighbouring countries. On 17 November, Chinese–Mongolian boundary negotiations resulted in a preliminary agreement in which China relinquished most of its territorial demands. In late December, Tsedenbal visited Beijing to sign the final agreement.[28] During his talks with Zhou Enlai, the Mongolian leader asked China to supply Ulaanbaatar with more rice, silk and other consumer goods, and to send new workers. Zhou expressed readiness to fulfil the first request but said that the second issue could not be discussed unless the two countries resolved their ideological dispute. As he put it, the Chinese workers had left Mongolia because they were displeased by the ideological stance of the MPRP leadership. Tsedenbal replied that the economic questions should not be linked to the ideological ones, but Zhou insisted that the two issues could not be kept separate. In the end, the discussion became so heated that Zhou accused Tsedenbal of blindly following Khrushchev.[29]

Since the fundamental causes of the Sino-Mongolian dispute remained unresolved, the border treaty of December 1962 did not alleviate Ulaanbaatar's fears of Chinese encroachments. On the contrary, in July 1963 the concerned MPRP leaders decided to request accession to the Warsaw Pact. Their application was blocked by Moscow's Eastern European satellites, whereupon, in December 1965, they asked the Kremlin to station a Soviet military unit in Mongolia as a defence against 'possible sudden attacks'.[30] In January 1966, the USSR duly signed a mutual assistance treaty with the MPR, which in turn generated fears of encirclement in Beijing.[31]

Red Guard Diplomacy

Despite Mongolia's strong need for Chinese assistance and Tsedenbal's evident desire to keep the aid flowing, China could not use its economic clout to influence the political stance of the MPRP leadership. Frustrated by Ulaanbaatar's 'blind loyalty' to the Kremlin, the CCP leaders switched from their initial stop-go tactics to a systematic reduction of aid, but by doing so, they further weakened their economic leverage.

By mid-1966, Sino-Mongolian economic exchanges had plummeted to a near-zero level. Having rejected Mongolia's export goods (horses and leather products) on the pretext that they were affected by livestock diseases, the Chinese government refused to supply the consumer staples to which ordinary Mongolian citizens had been long accustomed, thus creating an acute shortage that Soviet and Eastern European shipments could only partially alleviate. The shrinking group of Chinese construction workers (about four thousand persons) constituted the sole remaining economic link between the two countries. The MPRP leadership suspected that they were disguised soldiers who conducted espionage and propaganda work, but it still wanted to extend their stay as long as possible so as to fully utilize their labour.[32] Anxious to maintain a foothold in the MPR, the Chinese government concurred, but, much to the chagrin of the Mongolian authorities, saw to it that construction work slowed down to a snail's pace.[33]

In October 1966, Soviet Ambassador L. N. Solovyov told a Hungarian diplomat that the Chinese construction workers, strictly controlled as they were by the Mongolian police, did not pose a serious security threat.[34] In contrast, the MPRP leaders were so much concerned about the activities of the Chinese permanent residents (about twenty thousand persons, counting families) that they effectively barred them from employment in the capital. In May–June 1966, many ethnic Chinese left Ulaanbaatar for the countryside, where they were allowed to earn a living. Their involuntary departure soon backfired on the regime in more ways than one. The already scarce supply of vegetables shrunk even further; the labour shortage affecting the construction sector became worse than ever; the Chinese residents, now widely dispersed in the rural areas, could not be monitored as effectively as before, when they had been concentrated in Ulaanbaatar; and the Chinese diplomats found ample opportunities to spread propaganda materials in the provinces on the pretext of visiting the relocated Chinese residents.[35]

Following the outbreak of the Cultural Revolution in May 1966, the Chinese Embassy made strenuous efforts to implant the new ultra-leftist ideas in the minds of the Chinese residents, who in turn were instructed to spread them among the Mongolian population. The diplomats frequently used the Chinese school, the hospital and the worker's clubs for political purposes. For instance, they regularly invited Mongolian citizens to watch the propaganda films shown in the clubs. The Mongolian guests were greeted with ostentatious hospitality, only to be told later that they were expected to participate in Maoist political rituals which were, needless to say, anathema to the MPRP leaders. Predictably, these activities further heightened the regime's distrust of the Chinese minority.[36]

In reality, however, the Chinese residents were by no means of one mind about the Cultural Revolution. Those entrepreneurs who had achieved comfortable living conditions were scared by the Red Guards' violent campaign against the 'old ideas, old culture, old customs and old habits of the exploiting classes'. Many parents bristled at the new, 'revolutionary' regulations that the school administration imposed on their children (such as the obligatory short-cut hairstyle), and the embassy had to step in to overcome their resistance.[37] By early 1967, the Cultural Revolution had wholly disrupted the operation of the school. Instead of studying, pupils chanted and memorized Mao quotations in the schoolyard.[38]

Up to the fall of 1966, the Cultural Revolution remained largely confined to domestic politics, but in December 1966–February 1967, it started to distort Chinese diplomacy, too. Nearly all senior diplomats at Chinese embassies (like Zhang Canming, the Ambassador to Mongolia) were summarily recalled for 're-education'; in Beijing, the Red Guards brought the Soviet Embassy under siege; and Chinese embassies, as well as overseas Chinese communities, were instructed to disseminate 'Mao Zedong Thought' by any means possible, no matter whether the host countries liked it or not.[39] In North Vietnam, Burma, Cambodia and elsewhere, ethnic Chinese communities were caught between the violent activities of their Red Guard organizations and the reprisals of the local authorities.[40]

Facing an increasingly belligerent China, the Mongolian leaders seem to have been more concerned about the threat of internal subversion than about a possible military confrontation. In February 1967, both Solovyov and Shagdarsüren, the head of the Central Committee's International Liaisons Department (ILD), assured the Hungarian diplomats that for the time being, the risk of a Chinese attack was low. The border areas were tranquil, the Chinese border guards being preoccupied with preventing defections to the MPR. A few refugees – both Inner Mongolians and Han Chinese – managed to cross the border, only to be forcibly returned by the Mongolian authorities, who feared that Beijing might use their presence as a pretext for confrontational acts. China was likely to use its construction workers as a fifth column, Shagdarsüren opined. The authorities introduced strict customs inspections to prevent the labourers from bringing weapons into the country, and reconsidered their earlier intention to invite additional workers. By May 1967, the bulk of Chinese workers had left Mongolia; the remaining few hundred persons did little else but perform maintenance and repairs.[41]

Thus, in the spring of 1967 there were far fewer Chinese residents and Chinese construction workers in Ulaanbaatar than two years before, but even this shrinking community could (and did) become a bone of contention between the two antagonistic party-states. In May 1967, the Mongolian authorities expelled three Chinese teachers (Wang Zhiyun, Chen Lu and Zuo Guiyi) on the grounds that they and their students had caused a public disturbance at the office of the Mongolian newspaper *Medee Sonin* (which shared a compound with the Chinese school). On 21 May, a crowd of over two hundred Chinese (including the diplomats of the embassy and the representatives of the Association of Chinese Residents) gathered at the railway station to see the expelled teachers off – in open defiance of the Mongolian authorities, who had attempted to dissuade them from doing so. The Chinese soon provoked a brawl with the police, which resulted in the brief detaining of several diplomats (Ku Shiyong and Jiang Chenzhong, third secretaries; Wang Zhonghua and Zhang Delin, attachés). In response, the PRC's propaganda organs denounced the 'shocking fascist incident' committed by the 'Mongolian revisionist ruling clique'.[42] In Beijing, the expelled teachers were received as heroic 'anti-revisionist fighters' by Vice-Premier Xie Fuzhi and other high-ranking officials.[43]

On 9 August, the Red Guards took revenge on the 'Tsedenbal clique' by assaulting a Mongolian embassy chauffeur named Dash-Onolt (who had closed the ambassador's car door on a Mao picture thrust on him by the Red Guards), setting fire to the car, invading the embassy building and painting anti-Mongolian slogans on the walls.[44] The Foreign Ministry expelled the hapless driver the very next day, demanding that the Mongolian embassy 'at once openly admit its guilt and apologize to the Chinese people'.[45] Shortly afterwards, Beijing downgraded Sino–MPR diplomatic relations to the level of chargés d'affaires.[46]

'Mongolia has degenerated into a colony of the Soviet revisionists', Chinese propaganda charged, 'a base for cheap raw material and a market for dumping surplus goods'.[47] These accusations were by no means groundless, but Beijing's confrontational attitude towards Ulaanbaatar actually aggravated Mongolia's dependence on the USSR. In the face of China's pressure, the Soviet leaders felt obliged to help out their beleaguered satellite. In December 1967, the Hungarian Embassy in Ulaanbaatar reported that Soviet–Mongolian trade negotiations for 1968 had been successfully completed. The USSR undertook to fulfil nearly every Mongolian request, granting Ulaanbaatar a commercial credit worth 200 million roubles for the 1966–70 period and an additional credit worth 400 million for the purchase of Soviet technical equipment.[48] In 1967, Soviet military construction units started to build three large military airfields near Ulaanbaatar, Choibalsan (Dornod province) and Saynshand (East Gobi province) – the same areas where Soviet ground troops were deployed.[49] Both the MPRP leaders and their Soviet overlords remembered all too well how Japan had probed Mongolia's defences at Khalkhin Gol (the easternmost part of Dornod) in 1939.

China Changes Tack

China's heavy-handed attempts to put pressure on Mongolia had thus clearly backfired. The spectre of Chinese border incursions triggered the deployment of Soviet combat troops in south-eastern Mongolia – an area much closer to China's heartland than the disputed sections of the Sino-Soviet boundary on the Ussuri River and in the Pamirs. Now it was Beijing's turn to feel threatened. On 1 September 1967, Kang Sheng, one of the most powerful figures of the Cultural Revolution, declared that 'Previously the enemy surrounded China only in a semicircle, but now the Soviet and Mongolian revisionists are brazenly assisting American and Japanese imperialism, and thus the circle has closed'.[50]

Surprisingly enough, the CCP leaders reacted to these unfavourable developments by slightly softening their stance towards the MPR. In the first three months of 1968, the lower-level diplomats of the Chinese Embassy, having been recalled for 're-education' in 1967, returned to Ulaanbaatar, and adopted a more cooperative attitude than before. The Chinese school, the cultural centre and the hospital functioned in a normal way, and the local ethnic Chinese did not provoke similar incidents to those that had occurred the year before. Sino-Mongolian trade negotiations were conducted in a less tense atmosphere than in 1967. Reflecting the two sides' shared interest in reviving commercial exchanges, the planned volume of trade increased from 0.6 million roubles in 1967 to 6 million roubles in 1968. The Mongolian authorities reciprocated Beijing's gestures by toning down their anti-Chinese propaganda.[51]

It is difficult to ascertain why Beijing switched to a less confrontational attitude towards the MPR at a time when Sino-Soviet relations continued to deteriorate, and Ulaanbaatar's loyalty to Moscow showed no signs of wavering. In the opinion of the Hungarian diplomats, the CCP leaders, aware as they were of Mongolia's economic difficulties (e.g. the acute shortage of consumer goods that resulted from the breakdown of Sino-Mongolian trade), adopted a wait-and-see approach in the hope that they might be able to capitalize on the burgeoning popular discontent.[52] It is also possible that China's softening attitude towards Ulaanbaatar was not just a bilateral phenomenon, but rather constituted a part of a broader diplomatic effort. Notably, in 1968 the Chinese leaders started to make efforts to overcome the international isolation into which the Cultural Revolution had plunged the PRC, and their first initiatives were aimed at reaching reconciliation with Nepal, Burma and Cambodia – that is, those weak and essentially friendly states in China's neighbourhood that had been needlessly alienated by the militant extremism of the Cultural Revolution.[53] Beijing's gestures towards Ulaanbaatar may have been motivated by similar considerations.

Still, these signs of change were too superficial to lead to a genuine rapprochement between the two countries. The Sino-Soviet border clashes of March–September 1969 heightened the Mongolian leadership's fears of a Chinese attack, and accelerated the Soviet military build-up in the MPR.[54] In turn, the Chinese leaders expressed their anger over Ulaanbaatar's pro-Soviet stance by disrupting Mongolia's trade with Japan: 'During 1969 the Chinese harassed international express trains on a number of occasions; they held up Mongolian crews for hours and reportedly locked up for a day a group of Mongolian commissioners who had come to China for a meeting of the Joint Chinese-Mongolian Commission.'[55]

Seeking to defuse the border crisis, on 11 September 1969 Soviet Premier Alexei Kosygin held talks with Zhou Enlai, during which Zhou, among others, complained about the presence of Soviet troops in the MPR. Kosygin was unwilling to discuss this matter, but in other respects the meeting resulted in a certain improvement of Sino-Soviet relations.[56] The border clashes ceased, and China toned down its anti-Soviet propaganda. In July 1970, the two countries agreed to re-establish ambassadorial relations, and in November, they signed a new trade agreement.[57] Drawing inspiration from these developments, in October 1970 Tsedenbal likewise expressed readiness to restore ambassadorial relations with the PRC.[58] The CCP leaders, however, were conspicuously slow to respond. In April 1971, the Hungarian Embassy in Beijing reported that China had already appointed ambassadors to every Soviet bloc country except Mongolia and Czechoslovakia.[59] It was not until June 1971 that the Chinese requested an agrément for the new ambassador, Xu Wenyi. The Mongolian government duly granted the agrément but decided to postpone the appointment of its own ambassador to Beijing until Xu's arrival. The MPRP leaders adopted a wait-and-see attitude to ascertain whether China was sincerely committed to improving its relations with Mongolia.[60]

In fact, China's attitude did undergo a positive change during the first half of 1971. Sino-Mongolian negotiations over the new annual trade agreement started earlier than in the previous years. The planned volume of trade for 1971 stood at 3.1 million roubles, that is, 13 per cent higher than in 1970. The Chinese negotiators satisfied Mongolia's requests for consumer goods even though their own attempts to import horses remained unsuccessful due to price disputes. When the Mongolian officials asked them to deliver the desired goods before the celebrations of the fiftieth anniversary of the MPRP (July 1971), they duly complied, presumably because they wanted to make a favourable impression on Mongolian public opinion.[61]

Just like in 1968, the Mongolian officials reciprocated Beijing's softening attitude by toning down their anti-Chinese propaganda. Soviet Minister-Counsellor A. N. Katerinich told a Hungarian diplomat that Mongolian journalists repeatedly cautioned their junior colleagues against publishing articles sharply critical of China. 'Now you are exposing yourself', they warned the eager novices, 'but what are you going to do if the situation might change?' Paying keen attention to the post-1969 Sino-Soviet rapprochement, the MPRP leaders evidently calculated that a further improvement of relations between the two neighbouring empires would not just enable but also require them to make their peace with Beijing.[62]

Despite these favourable changes, the activities of the Chinese minority remained a bone of contention. Throughout 1971, the Chinese authorities made various attempts to smuggle propaganda materials into the MPR. When the Mongolian security organs detected these operations, the Chinese agents switched to more sophisticated techniques of disguise, and tried to approach the Mongolian population through the institutions of the Chinese community. At that time, the number of ethnic Chinese stood at approximately twelve thousand, of whom nearly nine thousand lived in Ulaanbaatar. Earning their livelihood as artisans, horticulturists and petty traders, they were by no means wealthy. They formed a closely knit community, but their school provided education not only to Chinese pupils but also to the *erliiz* children born from Sino-Mongolian mixed marriages and even to a few Mongolian students. On the instructions of the Chinese Embassy, the staff of the school distributed Mao pins, Mao pictures and Mao booklets among the pupils, asking them to spread them among their friends and relatives. The materials circulating among the students glorified the Cultural Revolution, condemned Moscow's 'neo-colonial policy' in Mongolia and depicted the MPRP leaders as Soviet puppets. In retaliation, the authorities prohibited *erliiz* and Mongolian children from attending the Chinese school. In reality, Chinese propaganda reached only a narrow segment of the Mongolian population, but the all-powerful secret police were still concerned about the 'ideological threat' posed by the Chinese pupils. The Mongolian cadres complained in all earnestness that it was 'difficult' to prevent the Chinese children from distributing Mao pins among their Mongolian friends.[63]

Beware of Chinese Bearing Gifts

Paradoxically, however, the MPRP leaders were no less wary of China's sweet words than of the militant slogans of Maoist propaganda. As long as Beijing's engagement tactics towards Ulaanbaatar were more or less coordinated with the improvement of Sino-Soviet relations, the MPRP leaders had a stake in playing along. If, however, China adopted a harsher attitude towards the USSR than towards the MPR, an enthusiastic Mongolian response to Beijing's overtures would have carried the risk of Soviet disapproval. Under such conditions, the chances of Sino-MPR reconciliation remained fairly limited.

Following the lull of 1970–71, in November 1971 the Mongolian media switched to an openly hostile stance towards China. At first sight, this shift appeared quite inexplicable, since Beijing continued to woo the MPR. In May 1972, the Hungarian Embassy in Ulaanbaatar reported that China had displayed increasing flexibility vis-à-vis Mongolia, particularly in the economic sphere. By offering higher prices than the year before, China managed to persuade the Mongolian officials to sell a few thousand horses, and thus the planned volume of trade for 1972 was expected to be 10 per cent greater than in 1971.[64]

Nevertheless, these gestures were insufficient to overcome the strong distrust the MPRP leaders and their Soviet overlords harboured about China's intentions. On the contrary, they gave rise to suspicions that Beijing's engagement policy was merely a ploy aimed at driving a wedge between Ulaanbaatar and Moscow. As early as the spring of 1971, Soviet Foreign Ministry officials emphatically warned the Eastern European diplomats that the recent improvement of Sino-Soviet relations did not eliminate the threat posed by China's 'policy of differentiation' – a strategy that singled out the USSR for criticism and tried to win over its satellites. In their opinion, China's softening stance positively increased the risk of a satellite country being 'neutralized' by Beijing's blandishments.[65] In this mistrustful atmosphere, the MPRP leaders probably felt it necessary to show that their readiness to accept China's attractive economic offers did not imply a weakening loyalty to the Kremlin.

This dichotomy between China's non-confrontational approach and Mongolia's sharply critical stance continued to persist throughout the 1970s. For instance, during the trade negotiations held in February 1973 the Chinese officials adopted a conspicuously flexible attitude. Among other things, they agreed to hand over the designs of the unfinished aid projects, thus enabling the Mongolian authorities to complete them without Beijing's involvement. Having consulted the Soviet diplomats, the MPRP leaders eagerly took advantage of China's economic concessions, and promised to export as many as fifteen thousand horses, but their political standpoint showed no signs of change.⁶⁶ On the contrary, in September 1973 they revived the charge that Beijing was stirring up the ethnic Chinese community against the MPR authorities, accused the Chinese government of holding aggressive military exercises near the border and so on.⁶⁷ If the Chinese sought to demonstrate that they were perfectly able to come to terms with the MPR or any other Communist country except the Soviet 'social imperialists', Tsedenbal's habitual reaction was to outdo the Kremlin in vilifying Beijing. In November 1974, when Brezhnev visited Ulaanbaatar, the US Embassy in Moscow reported that the Soviet leader 'reiterated Moscow's desire for improved relations with Peking', and 'left the heavy denunciation … to Mongolian party chief Tsedenbal, who laid it on with feeling'.⁶⁸

In effect, the MPRP leaders tried to have their cake and eat it too. On the one hand, they tacitly enjoyed the economic benefits of China's engagement diplomacy; on the other hand, they continued to portray China as a clear and present danger to the MPR so as to wheedle as much aid from the Soviet bloc as possible.⁶⁹ Fortunately for them, the Kremlin also had a stake in presenting Mongolia as a country constantly menaced by an expansionist Chinese empire. Since the faraway Eastern European 'people's democracies' did not feel threatened by China, the Soviets were increasingly concerned about the possibility that their satellites might be 'deceived' by Beijing's 'soft methods'. To dispel any 'illusions' about China's intentions, they kept stressing that the PRC posed a direct security threat to each and every neighbouring state – not only to the USSR but also to Mongolia, Vietnam, Laos, Burma and India – and that Beijing systematically used the overseas Chinese communities as its 'agents' and 'tools'.⁷⁰ At the regularly held 'Interkit' meetings of the Soviet bloc's China experts, the Soviet and Mongolian delegations again and again trotted out the charge that the CCP leaders, motivated as they were by 'Great Han chauvinism', plotted to reincorporate Mongolia into China.⁷¹

Thus, in the 1970s the steady growth of Soviet military and economic aid to Ulaanbaatar was based more on Mongolia's status as a front-line member of the Kremlin's supranational empire than on the actual dynamics of China–MPR relations. But if the Soviet leaders mentally linked Mongolia with their broader imperial designs, so did the Chinese government. In the same way as the CCP's earlier activities among the Chinese communities in Mongolia and North Vietnam had followed a similar pattern, the measures Beijing took in response to the plight of Vietnam's Chinese minority were presented as a policy that, if necessary, could be applied to Mongolia, too.

In 1975–77, Hanoi started pressuring the *hoa kieu* to adopt Vietnamese citizenship, and imposed restrictions on those who retained their Chinese citizenship. By February 1978, these measures triggered a mass exodus of *hoa kieu* to the PRC, whereupon CCP Chairman Hua Guofeng declared that 'China opposed any attempt to compel overseas Chinese to change their citizenship, and that it was duty-bound to protect those who decided to keep Chinese citizenship'.[72] On 7 July, the Chinese Foreign Ministry announced that the PRC would issue special travel documents for those 'homeless persons of Chinese origin' who lacked Chinese passports. This measure was inspired by the flight of the *hoa kieu*, but in late July the Chinese Embassy in Ulaanbaatar issued a similar note with reference to the local ethnic Chinese. Since these documents would not specify the citizenship of the holder, neither the Vietnamese nor the Mongolian government accepted them as valid. On 31 August, the Mongolian Foreign Ministry declared that the new travel documents were incompatible with international regulations.[73]

Predictably, the MPRP leaders responded to Beijing's initiative by launching a new tirade of accusations against the Chinese minority. In October 1978, Deputy Premier Tumenbayariin Ragchaa told a Hungarian delegation that the Chinese residents were preparing to commit acts of assassination and sabotage against the country's high-ranking leaders and important facilities. This charge was so far-fetched that the Hungarian diplomats found it prudent to mention that Ragchaa's claim was not supported by the sources available to the embassy.[74]

In fact, this sceptical comment was just one manifestation of the Hungarian embassy's growing awareness of the credibility gap between the alleged 'Chinese threat' and China's actual conduct. In November–December 1978, Hungarian diplomats visited the provinces of Dornogovi, Dornod and Sükhbaatar, all of which shared long borders with China. They encountered a massive Soviet military presence in the visited areas but few, if any, signs of a war scare. In each of the three provinces, the local party and state officials invariably assured them that the border areas were wholly tranquil, and thus the local Mongolian population felt perfectly safe. The Chinese troops occasionally conducted military manoeuvres, but they never violated Mongolian territory, and the Chinese border guards duly returned the animals that had strayed over the border. The second secretary of Dornod's party committee said that the local ethnic Chinese (about two hundred industrial workers) were not involved in any sort of hostile activities. A Hungarian diplomat pointedly contrasted these fact-based local observations with the central leadership's alarmist claims, and astutely noted that whenever the MPRP leaders asked their Soviet and

Eastern European negotiating partners for credit and aid, they were particularly prone to highlight the 'Chinese threat'.[75]

The Gathering Clouds

In the winter of 1978–79, the supranational dimension of Ulaanbaatar's 'China threat' narrative effectively backfired on the Mongolian leaders. Through the lenses of supranational solidarity, a Chinese action against some other front-line state (like Vietnam) was automatically perceived as a threat to the MPR, too, even if Beijing's attitude towards Ulaanbaatar showed no change for the worse. The most forceful campaign that the Tsedenbal regime ever launched against the country's ethnic Chinese community (1979–83) received its initial stimulus from a crisis that erupted in faraway Indochina, rather than from the Chinese residents' own actions.

On 27 December 1978, the MPRP Politburo discussed the latest Interkit meeting (Havana, December 11–13).[76] At this session, the Soviet bloc countries invited Vietnam to join Interkit, and declared that the recently signed Soviet–Vietnamese treaty was a reliable deterrent against any sort of Chinese aggression. These optimistic expectations were soon proven wrong. In February–March 1979, China retaliated for the Vietnamese invasion of Cambodia (December 1978–January 1979) by launching a 'punitive war' against Hanoi.[77] The Sino-Vietnamese War greatly unnerved the MPRP leaders, all the more so because it revealed China's ability to use military force against a Soviet ally without incurring the retaliation of the imperial hegemon. To reassure Ulaanbaatar, the Kremlin dispatched additional Soviet troops to the MPR for the duration of the war. In the whole country, massive Soviet troop movements were carried out as a demonstration of strength, and Soviet military aircraft repeatedly intruded into Chinese airspace to take photographs. In response, the Chinese military command reinforced the troops deployed along the Mongolian border, and took measures to prevent an advance of enemy forces towards Beijing, but otherwise the situation remained calm.[78]

The Sino-Vietnamese War made a lasting impact on the policies of the MPRP leaders. For one thing, it gave an additional impetus to their ongoing military build-up. In December 1979, the Soviet diplomats informed the Hungarian embassy that in 1979–85, Mongolia's annual military expenditures would be twice as high as in 1976–78.[79] Furthermore, the MPRP leaders, alarmed by the Sino-Vietnamese conflict over the *hoa kieu*, decided to pay even closer attention to the local ethnic Chinese community, whose total number stood at six thousand at that time. In May 1979, B. Dashtseren, the deputy head of the International Liaisons Department, informed the Soviet bloc embassies that the Politburo, having discussed the materials of the newest Interkit meeting (Moscow, 30 March), resolved to take 'intense measures' against the Chinese residents in the MPR.[80] In the fall of that year, Politburo member Sampilyn Jalan-Aajav told a Hungarian delegation that the Chinese Embassy sought to recruit local ethnic Chinese into espionage. He acknowledged that many Chinese residents worked diligently – so diligently, in fact, that some of them even earned medals – but stressed that certain individuals conducted illegal trade.[81]

On 12 November 1979, O. Otgonjargal, the police chief of Ulaanbaatar, told an inquiring Hungarian diplomat that the criminal acts that the capital city's four thousand Chinese residents were prone to committing were gambling, food tampering, bride-purchase and, above all, illegal trade. For instance, they purchased potatoes, vegetables and other scarce goods in large quantities, reselling them at higher prices in those months when shops were empty. Otgonjargal's description thus revealed that the environment that allowed the Chinese 'speculators' and their Mongolian accomplices to thrive was the regime's own shortage economy. The police chief remarked that the MPR authorities preferred to expel, rather than to jail, the arrested Chinese criminals, because this method solved the problem for good.[82]

In November–December 1979, Premier Jambyn Batmönkh visited Vietnam, Laos and Cambodia, concluding treaties of friendship and cooperation with Hanoi and Vientiane and an aid agreement with Phnom Penh. During his negotiations, the Indochinese leaders informed him about Beijing's subversive activities.[83] The information Ulaanbaatar received from these sources may have influenced Tsedenbal's subsequent policies towards the ethnic Chinese community. On 12 November 1980, the Mongolian Foreign Ministry told a Hungarian delegation that the MPR authorities in charge of matters related to the Chinese minority 'studied the experiences of the Vietnamese and Laotian comrades'.[84]

The leadership's plan to take 'intense measures' against the ethnic Chinese community, having germinated at the Politburo meeting held in the spring of 1979, seems to have evolved slowly and gradually. On 13 February 1980, ILD official B. Dashtseren informed the Soviet bloc embassies that the Chinese school in Ulaanbaatar exerted a strong ideological influence on the younger Chinese residents. The disgruntled authorities repeatedly contemplated closing the school, but, as Dashtseren explained, they eventually decided to tolerate its operation 'for the time being'.[85] On 12 May, the Hungarian Embassy reported that the committee in charge of the Chinese minority was planning to close down the school and resettle all Chinese residents from Ulaanbaatar to an uncultivated area in Bulgan, a northern province adjacent to the USSR. These measures were aimed at isolating the ethnic Chinese both from the Chinese Embassy and the Mongolian population, and forcing them to abandon their 'illicit' commercial activities in favour of 'productive' work. The authorities intended to create a vegetable-cultivating state farm for the resettled Chinese, whose area they would not be allowed to leave, whose management was to be dominated by Mongolian officials and whose produces were to be sold to the state. The school to be built in the new settlement would use the standard Mongolian curriculum, and Chinese language would be taught only to such an extent as was common in national minority schools. All construction work except that related to the school was to be financed by the resettled Chinese on the grounds that 'they were awash in money'. Still, the MPRP leaders had not made a final decision yet. In any case, they planned to carry out the resettlement operation only after the sixtieth anniversary of the Mongolian revolution (July 1981).[86]

The nature of this planned resettlement operation indicated that the MPRP cadres did take 'the experiences of the Vietnamese comrades' into consideration. Notably, in the spring of 1979 the Vietnamese authorities forcibly resettled eight thousand ethnic Chinese from Hanoi to the southern 'New Economic Zones' (i.e. uninhabited mountainous forested areas) on suspicion of political unreliability.[87] At the same time, the Mongolian leaders seem to have hoped that this drastic measure would 'solve' those issues over which the government and the Chinese Embassy had been at loggerheads for a long time. The Mongolian government, Deputy Foreign Minister Jambalyn Banzar told the Hungarian Foreign Ministry in May 1980, had tried to coax the Chinese authorities into accepting that the Chinese school be integrated into the Mongolian educational system, but Beijing rebuffed the proposal.[88] In essence, the MPRP leaders wanted a 'solution' that would eliminate the 'enclave' status of the Chinese community without fully integrating them into Mongolian society – that is, a combination of forced assimilation and ethnic discrimination.

Nonetheless, the Mongolian leadership still hesitated to take such a drastic step. In December 1980, Soviet Counsellor E. F. Voronin told a Hungarian colleague that the Central Committee dismissed the resettlement plan 'for the time being', because it was likely to trigger some sort of Chinese retaliation.[89] Ulaanbaatar's caution was well founded. In June 1980, when the Foreign Ministry expelled a Chinese attaché for espionage, the PRC authorities promptly banished a Mongolian diplomat of identical rank. Notably, the actual punitive measures that the MPRP leaders took in the immediate aftermath of the Sino-Vietnamese War – that is, when their threat perceptions presumably reached a peak – were fairly limited in scope. In 1979, the authorities expelled forty-eight Chinese residents and their families for 'illegal activities' (smuggling, gambling and drug trafficking), while in August 1980, six additional residents (with their families included, a total of thirty persons) suffered the same fate.[90]

Eviction, Expulsion, Emigration

In 1982–83, the MPRP leaders did launch their long-contemplated resettlement operation, but by that time the triangular dynamics of Sino-Soviet-Mongolian relations had undergone such a marked change that the plan's original inspiration – that is, the threat perceptions generated by the Sino-Vietnamese War – was no longer valid. On the contrary, their decision to cross the Rubicon seems to have been a reaction to the slow but steady rapprochement between the two great Communist empires – a process that implied that they might no longer be able to justify their incessant requests for Soviet support by citing the 'China threat'.

In fact, the first cracks in the edifice of Soviet–Mongolian cooperation started to appear as early as 1978–80, when Tsedenbal's claims about the 'China threat' still fell on receptive ears in the Kremlin. Paradoxically, it was precisely the massive amount of Soviet economic and military assistance that ultimately generated tension not only between the MPRP leaders and their imperial overlords but also between the Soviet garrisons and the ordinary Mongolian citizens whom they supposedly protected. During a meeting held on 23 August 1978, Brezhnev upbraided Tsedenbal for the inefficient and wasteful use of Soviet aid, and by 1979, Soviet diplomats became increasingly outspoken while informing their Eastern European colleagues about the economic mismanagement they encountered in the MPR. Due to the limited skills and careless attitude of the Mongolian managers and technicians, the Soviet-built factories operated below capacity, and their machines often broke down. Instead of ensuring proper equipment maintenance, the MPRP leaders simply kept pressing the USSR for even more credit and aid.[91] Meanwhile, ordinary Mongolians chafed at the ubiquitous presence and overbearing conduct of the Soviet troops (over a hundred thousand persons, counting families) and the thirty thousand plus technical experts. In 1979, Soviet citizens made up nearly one-tenth of Ulaanbaatar's population. Earning salaries thrice those of their native colleagues and shopping in stores from which Mongolians were barred, the 'fraternal' technical experts were widely disliked. In April 1980, the Hungarian Embassy reported that insults and even assaults on Soviet soldiers and civilians were a 'frequent occurrence'.

Dismayed by these sentiments, a Hungarian diplomat took comfort in the fact that the Mongolian population harboured an even stronger antipathy for the ethnic Chinese community than for the Soviet and Eastern European residents.⁹²

Following Brezhnev's Tashkent speech (24 March 1982), these lingering tensions were compounded by Ulaanbaatar's veiled opposition to Moscow's efforts to mend fences with Beijing. Seeking to exploit China's dissatisfaction with Washington's Taiwan policy, Brezhnev stressed that the USSR recognized the PRC's sovereignty over Taiwan, continued to regard China as a socialist country and 'wanted to develop relations with it in all fields without preconditions'.⁹³ What the MPRP leaders thought about his initiative became clear at the next Interkit meeting (Sofia, 11–12 May 1982). In a glaring contrast with the East German, Polish and Hungarian participants who enthusiastically praised the Tashkent speech, the Mongolian delegate did not mention it at all. On the contrary, he indirectly questioned Brezhnev's approval of the 'one China' principle by pointing out that the Taiwanese population did not desire unification with the PRC.⁹⁴ Some other Mongolian cadres expressed their reservations more explicitly. 'We Mongols lived under Chinese oppression for three hundred years, and thus we know the Chinese very well', the head of Darkhan's party committee told the Hungarian ambassador in late July. 'They are so perfidious that one cannot trust them. The small steps they are now taking towards the socialist countries serve only tactical aims.'⁹⁵

To be sure, certain Mongolian officials were less sceptical about the chances of a Sino-MPR rapprochement, and more eager to seize the practical opportunities offered by China's 'small steps' policy. For example, in June 1982, Chulundorj, a departmental head of the Foreign Ministry, told a Hungarian diplomat that the Mongolian authorities were satisfied with the recently launched joint delineation survey of the Sino-Mongolian border. In October, the two governments took steps to establish telephone and telegraph lines between Ulaanbaatar and Beijing. This route would enable the MPR to communicate with the other Asian countries at a lower cost than via Moscow, Chulundorj explained.⁹⁶

Nonetheless, the Soviets evidently felt that the MPRP leaders were dragging their feet. During a meeting held in August 1982, Brezhnev found it necessary to lecture Tsedenbal about the importance of Sino-Soviet rapprochement. As the Soviet Ambassador in Ulaanbaatar put it, 'Mongolia should be appropriately informed, *since they have often diverged from the joint line of foreign policy*' (emphasis in the original).⁹⁷ On 10 November, the long-ailing Brezhnev passed away, but his successor, Yuri Andropov, proved just as eager to pursue reconciliation with China – and, if necessary, to put pressure on the MPR. The MPRP leaders were strongly concerned about the possibility that Andropov might eventually withdraw the Soviet troops from Mongolia so as to make a concession to the Chinese, who stressed that the Soviet military presence in the MPR constituted one of the main obstacles to Sino-Soviet reconciliation. Adopting an attitude of outward compliance, the Mongolian government instructed the media not to make any critical comment on China, but this was just the lull before the storm.[98]

In June 1982, the MPRP Politburo passed a resolution to 'improve work with the Chinese minority', that is, to gradually resettle the Chinese residents to the country's sparsely populated areas and integrate their school into the Mongolian educational system. This decision to carry out the long-contemplated deportation plan was influenced by the leadership's awareness of its inability to shape the views of the ethnic Chinese community by means of propaganda. The two committees in charge of conducting agitation and ideological work among the Chinese residents, headed by Politburo member Damdingiin Gombojav and Central Committee Secretary Gelegiin Adyaa, could not devise any better method than to instruct Mongolian agitators to pay regular visits to the Chinese families. Since the agitators spoke no Chinese, they were utterly unable to counter the impact of Chinese radio broadcasts. The Chinese residents found it hard to understand the ideological harangues they delivered, and, in all probability, considered their uninvited visits a mere nuisance.[99]

The Politburo resolution was not published, but the Chinese residents soon got wind of the deportation plan. In 1982, three hundred ethnic Chinese expressed their intention to repatriate to the PRC. The authorities did not hinder their departure. On the contrary, they welcomed it on the grounds that the more Chinese left on their own initiative, the better. Worse still, they accelerated the process by putting the deportation plan into practice. In March 1983, the city council of Ulaanbaatar instructed sixty-five 'idle' Chinese families to leave for Selenge province's Baruunbüren district.[100] On 30 May, Deputy Foreign Minister Daramyn Yondon told the Soviet bloc ambassadors that so far, 280 Chinese families (altogether fifteen hundred persons) had been ordered to move to the designated area, but no one was willing to go. Instead, they applied for exit visas, which the Mongolian authorities readily issued. By late May, 113 families (580 to six hundred people, including half of the teaching staff of the Chinese school) had left Mongolia.[101]

The Mongolian authorities sought to justify their forceful measures by accusing the Chinese residents of all sorts of illicit activities. There were three thousand Chinese of working age living in Ulaanbaatar, yet only 289 held permanent jobs, Yondon alleged; about one thousand Chinese residents were casual employees, while the others were engaged in black-marketing, smuggling and gambling. In their efforts to find fault with the Chinese community, the authorities went so far as to prohibit Chinese horticulturists from marketing their vegetables. By using human waste as fertilizer, the Chinese gardeners allegedly promoted the spread of infectious diseases – a charge that the Hungarian Embassy took with a pinch of salt. In reality, the authorities seem to have devised the ban 'to prevent the Chinese from getting rich', a Hungarian diplomat concluded. As another example of discrimination, he mentioned that one of his Mongolian acquaintances had been dissuaded by his superiors from giving a bonus to an exceptionally diligent employee who happened to be an ethnic Chinese. In June 1983, L. Zantav, the chairman of Radio Mongolia, told a Hungarian diplomat that the Chinese residents to be evicted from Ulaanbaatar were by no means all 'idlers' or casual employees. Many of them held permanent jobs, but their political loyalty was questionable, and this was why the leadership wanted to resettle them to Selenge. Facing this hostile atmosphere, even some of the permanently employed Chinese found it advisable to emigrate, much to the chagrin of the authorities who tried to prevent their departure by administrative means.[102]

Predictably, Ulaanbaatar's campaign against the Chinese minority aroused Beijing's indignation, all the more so because the travel expenses of the repatriates had to be covered by the Chinese Embassy. Starting in March 1983, the Chinese government made a series of diplomatic representations against the mistreatment of the Chinese residents, only to be told by the MPR authorities that they just wanted to instil diligence into the resettled individuals.[103] 'Those being expelled ... have been greeted as heroes after entering China', the US Central Intelligence Agency (CIA) reported on 28 May. Still, the CCP leaders seem to have wanted to keep the conflict within manageable limits. 'So far the Chinese have not made a public issue of the matter', the CIA observers pointed out. The repatriates were not allowed to travel to Beijing, nor did the Chinese media mention their plight.[104] In early June, the PRC government eventually delivered a formal protest, but the tone of the note was fairly restrained. 'Beijing wanted to avoid publicizing the issue', the CIA concluded. 'The Chinese believe that the USSR approved the expulsions, but they have not blamed the Soviets.'[105]

In fact, it is somewhat doubtful whether the Kremlin really approved the expulsions. A Hungarian report dated 3 December 1984 stated that 'even the fraternal socialist countries failed to support' Ulaanbaatar's action. The Soviet bloc diplomats expressed the opinion that the ethnic Chinese, extremely skilled as they were in the fields of vegetable cultivation, handicrafts and services, should have been mobilized for work in Ulaanbaatar, rather than evicted from the city.[106] Similarly, the CIA noted that the expulsions were not covered by the Soviet media.[107] On 30 May 1983, when Yondon informed the Soviet bloc ambassadors about the issue, the Hungarian Ambassador asked him if the Mongolian government expected the 'fraternal' countries to give media support to Ulaanbaatar's standpoint. The deputy foreign minister gave an evasive answer, saying that if the MPRP leaders considered it necessary to ask for the support of the Soviet bloc, they would do so.[108] In the end, they never made a formal request of this kind.

The fact that both Beijing and Moscow sought to handle the expulsions in a restrained fashion revealed their shared commitment to Sino-Soviet rapprochement. 'Beijing is trying to foil what it sees as an effort by Ulaan Baatar to create enough friction in Sino-Mongolian relations to justify the retention of Soviet troops in Mongolia', the CIA reported on 4 June 1983.[109] The campaign against the Chinese minority may indeed have been aimed at goading Beijing into some sort of retaliation, which in turn would enable Ulaanbaatar to uphold its 'China threat' narrative, and thus restrain (or forestall) Soviet concessions to the PRC.[110]

Still, it is also possible that the MPRP leaders acted on the assumption that Sino-Soviet reconciliation was an irreversible process to which they would have to adapt sooner or later. In June 1983, Zantav told a Hungarian diplomat that China's demand for the withdrawal of Soviet troops from Mongolia had created some temporary friction in Sino-MPR relations, and the Mongolian authorities had to seize this window of opportunity to get rid of the 'undesirable' Chinese residents. Had they waited until next year, he said, it would not have been possible to carry out the evictions. Presumably he meant that the MPRP leaders wanted to settle this long-festering problem before Sino-Soviet rapprochement reached such a stage that would preclude any drastic action.[111]

Towards a New Era

The process of Sino-Soviet rapprochement, having given a strong stimulus to Tsedenbal's campaign against the Chinese minority, seems to have played a similarly important role in putting an end to it. Judging from the conspicuous absence of Soviet media support, the Kremlin was reluctant to side with Ulaanbaatar against Beijing in this particular matter, and the Mongolian government, dependent as it was on Soviet aid, lacked sufficient leverage to derail Sino-Soviet reconciliation. Chinese officials expressed the opinion that the Soviet leaders eventually found it necessary to pressure Mongolia to refrain from further expulsions.[112]

In August 1983, the MPR authorities did halt the evictions. By that time, as many as two thousand Chinese residents had repatriated or were in the process of repatriation.[113] In December 1984, there were only sixteen hundred Chinese citizens and one thousand Mongolian citizens of Chinese origin in Ulaanbaatar.[114] Still, the issue of the Chinese community continued to trouble the MPRP leaders, not least because their grudging adaptation to the accelerating process of Sino-Soviet rapprochement barely masked their anxieties about Beijing's intentions.

Following the Soviet-engineered replacement of the ageing, sclerotic and increasingly troublesome Tsedenbal (23 August 1984), Sino–MPR relations started to show a perceptible but slow improvement. By the end of the year, the two governments toned down their hostile propaganda, but the Mongolian media still adopted a more critical attitude towards China than the Soviet press. The MPRP leaders keenly understood that it suited their commercial interests to import certain products from China, rather than from other countries, but their politically motivated reluctance to increase their exports to China at the expense of Soviet–Mongolian trade hindered them in seizing the trade opportunities offered by Beijing.[115]

The Chinese Embassy appreciated that in 1984, the Mongolian authorities did not take any coercive measures against the ethnic Chinese community. The Chinese diplomats, on their part, assured their hosts that they maintained contacts solely with those residents who held Chinese citizenship, and refrained from reaching out to those who had acquired Mongolian citizenship. Nevertheless, the MPRP leaders still regarded this shrinking minority as potentially unreliable. Many ethnic Chinese (particularly those persons who had been born in the MPR) applied for Mongolian citizenship, but only some of the applicants were naturalized. The government continued to press for the incorporation of the Chinese school into the Mongolian educational system, and this time the Chinese Embassy showed readiness to comply. Yet the fulfilment of their long-standing demand may not have made the MPRP leaders wholly happy. A Soviet diplomat expressed the view (which was probably shared by many Mongolian cadres) that the enrolment of Chinese pupils in Mongolian schools would generate new problems. So far, the government had effectively barred Chinese students from higher education on the grounds that their school curriculum was incompatible with the Mongolian system, but under the new circumstances, it would no longer be able to prevent their admission to Mongolian universities. In turn, Chinese university graduates would be eligible for government jobs, too – a prospect that the MPRP leaders hardly relished.[116]

In the end, a genuine normalization of Sino-Mongolian relations occurred as late as 1989, when the withdrawal of Soviet troops alleviated

China's security concerns but also compelled Ulaanbaatar to make its peace with Beijing. At that time, Mongolian officials, impressed as they were by Deng Xiaoping's economic reforms, expressed a strong interest in learning from China's experiences. Many ordinary Mongolian citizens also welcomed Sino-Mongolian reconciliation, which, they hoped, would lead to the reappearance of Chinese consumer goods on the market.[117] In the subsequent decades, however, anti-Chinese sentiments re-emerged with a vengeance – a trend interrelated with China's growing economic predominance in Mongolia. For instance, a 2008 opinion survey asked Mongolian citizens which country would be the best partner for Mongolia. Only 3.3 per cent of the respondents chose China, a far lower share than that of Russia (47.8 per cent) and America (13.1 per cent). In Ulaanbaatar, only 21 per cent of respondents held positive attitudes towards Chinese people.[118] In Mongolian media, Chinese construction workers were usually portrayed in an unfavourable light. In 2007, Mongolian nationalist groups forcefully removed those restaurant signs that bore Chinese, Japanese or Korean script, compelling the owners to install new signs in Mongolian.[119]

Conclusion

Caught between the two vast Communist empires, landlocked and aid-dependent Mongolia had little, if any, chance of remaining unaffected by the Sino-Soviet rift. From the early 1960s until the late 1980s, the great lords in Moscow and Beijing regarded this thinly populated but strategically important country as a front-line area to be actively contested, rather than a buffer zone to be left in peace. In their global game of thrones, even the highest-ranking leaders of the Mongolian regime were treated as disposable smallfolk, outward courtesies notwithstanding. In 1960–62, Zhou Enlai bluntly rebuffed Tsedenbal's attempts to obtain economic assistance without political strings attached, and disdainfully reproached him for his 'blind loyalty' to Khrushchev. Twenty years later, it was Brezhnev's turn to lecture Tsedenbal about the necessity of making peace with the very country that the Kremlin had long painted in the worst light possible. Soon afterward, the Mongolian leader suffered the final indignity of being unceremoniously deposed by his Soviet overlords, whom he had loyally served ever since he started his political career forty-five years earlier.

Ordinary Mongolians were buffeted even harder by the clash of the two neighbouring empires. In the early 1960s, Chinese pressure on Ulaanbaatar affected, first and foremost, the living conditions of the average citizen, rather than those of the high-ranking party leaders whom Beijing wanted to punish for their recalcitrance. The disappearance of Chinese consumer goods from the shops created a void that the Soviet bloc countries never managed to fill, and that was so keenly felt by Mongolian customers that in the periods of Sino-MPR rapprochement (such as 1962 and 1971), the Mongolian government promptly asked Beijing to resume its shipments. And when Moscow fulfilled Tsedenbal's incessant requests for aid, an increasingly disgruntled population had to live in the shadow of a Soviet armoured force several times bigger than Mongolia's entire army, and endure the presence of tens of thousands of privileged Soviet experts.

From Ulaanbaatar's perspective, any shift in the triangular dynamics of Sino-Soviet-Mongolian relations could be fraught with danger. A Sino-Soviet confrontation compelled the MPRP leaders to choose between the two hostile empires, and if they sided with the USSR, China was likely to retaliate; a Sino-Soviet reconciliation carried the risk of them being abandoned by their Soviet overlords; and a Chinese policy of selective engagement could arouse Soviet suspicions about Ulaanbaatar's loyalty. Nevertheless, Tsedenbal and his co-leaders were by no means passive objects of this grand game of thrones. Anxious to extract as much aid as possible, they tried to manipulate both Beijing and Moscow. While they readily seized the opportunities offered by China's engagement diplomacy, they did their best to minimize the reciprocal concessions they had to make. In parallel with these efforts, they systematically misinformed their Soviet bloc allies about the threat that China allegedly posed to Mongolia, and in 1982–83, they quietly sabotaged the Kremlin's 'Tashkent policy'.

The Mongolian leaders, smallfolk as they were from the perspective of the Kremlin and Zhongnanhai, treated the shrinking ethnic Chinese community in the manner of domineering high lords. Despite occasional periods of temporary respite, Chinese residents were never left in peace for an extended period of time. If the great lords in Beijing, Moscow and Ulaanbaatar were on a collision course, the Chinese community was invariably singled out for reprisals, but their situation remained precarious even in those years when relations between the neighbouring party-states underwent an improvement. In 1959–60, Beijing's generous and tactful attitude could not dissuade the Mongolian authorities from mistreating the local Chinese entrepreneurs, while in 1982–83, the prospect of Sino-Mongolian rapprochement seems to have directly influenced the Politburo's decision to launch a campaign against the Chinese minority.

Furthermore, it was not only the great lords of the Mongolian party-state who looked askance at the ethnic Chinese community. Ingrained animosity towards the Chinese residents was at least as widespread among

Mongolian commoners as among the party elite – possibly even more so, because the MPRP leaders tried to prolong the stay of the Chinese construction workers even in the face of their obstructive behaviour, whereas ordinary Mongolian citizens were hardly pleased by their presence. Negative stereotypes of Chinese merchants and Chinese construction workers proved extremely persistent: the views that ordinary Mongolians held about them in the 2000s had much in common with the popular attitudes in the 1950s.

Still, the woes of the Chinese smallfolk were not caused solely by Mongolian Sinophobia. The great lords of the Chinese Communist Party also strove to maintain a grip over the Chinese minority, compelling them to adhere to the ultra-leftist directives of the Cultural Revolution and enrolling even their children in Beijing's campaign against 'Soviet revisionism'. In this uphill struggle, every sphere of Sino-MPR interactions – construction work, education, medical treatment and cultural exchanges – was blatantly misused for political purposes. In this way, the CCP leaders exposed the small and vulnerable Chinese community to Ulaanbaatar's reprisals without any prospect of success. And if the Mongolian authorities did mistreat the Chinese residents, Beijing's reactions were shaped by political expediency. The hue and cry that the CCP leaders raised about the 1967 expulsion of three teachers stood in marked contrast with the restrained attitude they displayed in the face of the 1960 repatriation crisis or the 1983 mass evictions.

Caught between hammer and anvil, the Chinese residents experienced a wide range of harassment, from the destruction of their workshops to the imposition of a short-cut hairstyle, and from the uninvited visits of agitators to the prohibition of vegetable cultivation. Yet they were not simply passive victims of the two antagonistic party-states, nor were they of one mind. Many of the construction workers, and some of the permanent residents, actively participated in the clashes provoked by the Chinese Embassy, while other ethnic Chinese had their doubts about the Cultural Revolution, or – seeking to fit into Mongolian society – worked so diligently that their Mongolian superiors felt compelled to acknowledge their outstanding performance. Ultimately, the ethnic Chinese community may have even managed to throw a monkey wrench into Tsedenbal's deportation plan. Notably, the government's original intention was to resettle, rather than to expel, the Chinese residents, but when they refused to move to the designated area, their mass flight triggered an international humanitarian crisis, forcing Beijing – and possibly even Moscow – to intervene on their behalf.

Acknowledgements

The author wishes to thank Christopher P. Atwood, Batsaikhan Ookhnoi, Khishi Enkhbayar, Jun-Hyeok Kwak, Brian R. Myers and Craig Urquhart for their help in preparing this chapter. I am particularly indebted to Dr Atwood for providing me with information about the pre-1921 history of the ethnic Chinese community and assisting me with the transliteration of Chinese names.

Balázs Szalontai is Professor of North Korean Studies at Korea University, Sejong Campus (Republic of Korea). He has done extensive archival research on the domestic and foreign policies of Asian and Eastern European Communist regimes, analysing them from a comparative angle. His publications include *Kim Il Sung in the Khrushchev Era: Soviet-DPRK Relations and the Roots of North Korean Despotism, 1953–1964* (2005), as well as numerous peer-reviewed articles and book chapters on North Korean, South East Asian and Mongolian history.

Notes

1. See, among others, Bao, 'Trade Centres (Maimaicheng) in Mongolia'; Atwood, 'Chinese Merchants and Mongolian Independence'; Billé, *Sinophobia*; Jargalsaikhan, 'Anti-Chinese Attitudes'.
2. Martin, *A Game of Thrones*, 251.
3. Bao, 'Trade Centres (Maimaicheng) in Mongolia', 215–19.
4. Atwood, 'Chinese Merchants and Mongolian Independence', 63.
5. Ewing, 'Ch'ing Policies in Outer Mongolia', 147.
6. Bawden, *The Modern History of Mongolia*, 173–74, 184.
7. Jargalsaikhan, 'Anti-Chinese Attitudes', 28.
8. Bawden, *The Modern History of Mongolia*, 290; Morozova, *Socialist Revolutions in Asia*, 152.
9. Morozova, *Socialist Revolutions in Asia*, 58–65, 95.
10. Rinchin, *Uls Töriin Talaar Khelmegdegsdiin Dursgal Tsagaan Nom*, 26, 95, 106.
11. Morozova, *Socialist Revolutions in Asia*, 97.
12. Sanders, *Historical Dictionary of Mongolia*, 584.
13. Shirendyb, *History of the Mongolian People's Republic*, 205.
14. Ewing, 'Ch'ing Policies in Outer Mongolia', 149.
15. Hungarian Embassy in the Mongolian People's Republic, Report, 31 January 1961, Hungarian National Archives (Magyar Nemzeti Levéltár, MNL), XIX-J-1-j (Top Secret Documents) Mongolia, 1945–64, 5. doboz, 10/a, 002455/1961.
16. 'Memorandum of Conversation between Mao Zedong and the Delegation of the Mongolian People's Revolutionary Party and Comments on the Distribution of the Memorandum of Conversation', 24 September 1956, History and Public Policy Program Digital Archive (Woodrow Wilson Center), *Jianguo Yilai Mao Zedong Wengao*, Vol. 6 (Beijing: Zhongyang wenxian chubanshe, 1992), 213–22. Trans. Sergey Radchenko. Retrieved 10 March 2022 from http://digitalarchive.wilsoncenter.org/document/117696.

17. Batbayar, *Modern Mongolia*, 53–54.
18. Hungarian Embassy in the MPR, 28 June 1958, MNL, XIX-J-1-j Mongolia, 1945–64, 6. doboz, 24/b, 004449/1958.
19. Hungarian Embassy in the MPR, Report, 12 December 1960, MNL, XIX-J-1-k [Administrative Documents], Mongolia 1945–64, 6. doboz, 18/g, 008395/1960; Hungarian Embassy in the MPR, Report, 31 January 1961.
20. Han, 'Spoiled Guests or Dedicated Patriots?', 9–17.
21. Hungarian Embassy in the MPR, Report, 1 August 1960, MNL, XIX-J-1-j Mongolia, 1945–64, 3. doboz, 5/b, 006225/1960.
22. Hungarian Embassy in the MPR, Memorandum, 17 July 1959, MNL, XIX-J-1-j Mongolia, 1945–64, 4. doboz, 5/f, 005082/1059.
23. Hungarian Embassy in the People's Republic of China, Report, 6 June 1962, MNL, XIX-J-1-j Mongolia, 1945–64, 7. doboz, 5/bc, 0047/1962.
24. Hungarian Embassy in the MPR, Report, 13 November 1961, MNL, XIX-J-1-j Mongolia, 1945–64, 7. doboz, 25/a, 008157/1/1961.
25. Hungarian Embassy in the MPR, Report, 19 January 1962, MNL, XIX-J-1-j Mongolia, 1945–64, 3. doboz, 5/bc, 009/RT/1962; Hungarian Embassy in the PRC, Report, 6 June 1962.
26. Radchenko, 'The Soviets' Best Friend in Asia', 14.
27. Hungarian Embassy in the PRC, Report, 6 June 1962.
28. Fravel, *Strong Borders, Secure Nation*, 109–12.
29. Hungarian Embassy in the MPR, Report, 15 January 1963, MNL, XIX-J-1-j Mongolia, 1945–64, 8. doboz, 29/h, 003250/1963.
30. Radchenko, 'Soviet Withdrawal from Mongolia', 186.
31. Hungarian Embassy in the MPR, Report, 21 September 1966, MNL, XIX-J-1-j Mongolia, 1967. 66. doboz, 104, 005022/1/1966.
32. Ibid.
33. Hungarian Embassy in the MPR, Report, 7 October 1966, MNL, XIX-J-1-j Mongolia, 1967. 66. doboz, 104, 005022/1966.
34. Ibid.
35. Hungarian Embassy in the MPR, Report, 21 September 1966.
36. Ibid.
37. Ibid.
38. Hungarian Embassy in the MPR, Report, 26 February 1967, MNL, XIX-J-1-j Mongolia, 1967. 66. doboz, 104, 002101/1967; Hungarian Embassy in the MPR, Memorandum, 4 October 1967, MNL, XIX-J-1-j Mongolia, 1967. 66. doboz, 104, 004427/2/1967.
39. Central Intelligence Agency, 'Mao's Red Guard Diplomacy: 1967', Intelligence Report, 21 June 1968, CIA-RDP85T00875R001000010030-3, in CIA Electronic Reading Room (CERR). Retrieved 10 March 2022 from https://www.cia.gov/library/readingroom/home.
40. Han, 'Spoiled Guests or Dedicated Patriots?', 12–13; Fitzgerald, 'Overseas Chinese Affairs and the Cultural Revolution', 103–26.
41. Hungarian Embassy in the MPR, Report, 26 February 1967; Hungarian Embassy in the MPR, Report, 29 May 1967, MNL, XIX-J-1-j Mongolia, 1967. 66. doboz, 104, 003061/1967.
42. 'Mongolian Revisionists Assault Chinese Nationals in Ulan Bator', 45–47.
43. 'Vice Premier Hsieh Fu-chih Receives Returned Chinese Nationals', 47.
44. CIA, 'Mao's Red Guard Diplomacy'.
45. 'Chinese Foreign Ministry Protests at Mongolian Diplomat's Insult', 29–30.
46. Green, 'China and Mongolia', 1351.

47. 'Mongolian Revisionists Trailing Behind Soviet Revisionist Anti-China Campaign', 35.

48. Hungarian Embassy in the USSR, Report, 16 December 1967, MNL, XIX-J-1-j Mongolia, 1967. 66. doboz, 104, 004428/1/1967.

49. Hungarian Embassy in the MPR, Report, 12 November 1967, MNL, XIX-J-1-j Mongolia, 1967. 66. doboz, 104, 002795/1/1967.

50. Hungarian Embassy in the PRC, Report, 20 September 1967, MNL, XIX-J-1-j China, 1967, 58. doboz, 200, 001187/52/1967.

51. Hungarian Embassy in the MPR, Report, 10 May 1968, MNL, XIX-J-1-j China, 1968, 55. doboz, 78-1, 001991/4/1968.

52. Ibid.

53. Hungarian Foreign Ministry, Memorandum, 28 October 1968, MNL, XIX-J-1-j China, 1968, 55. doboz, 78-1, 001500/2/1968.

54. Batbayar, *Modern Mongolia*, 62–63.

55. Smith, 'Mongolia', 26.

56. Minutes of Conversation between the Romanian Delegation to Ho Chi Minh's Funeral and the Chinese Delegation, 11 September 1969, History and Public Policy Program Digital Archive, Romanian Central National Historical Archives (ANIC), fond RCP CC – Foreign Affairs Department, file 72/1969, f. 35–65. Trans. Madalina Cristoloveanu. Retrieved 10 March 2022 from http://digitalarchive.wilsoncenter.org/document/117761.

57. Garver, 'Chinese Foreign Policy in 1970', 224–30.

58. Cassidy, 'Mongolia', 90.

59. Hungarian Embassy in the PRC, Report, 4 April 1971, MNL, XIX-J-1-j China, 1971, 64. doboz, 78-10, 001175/1/1971.

60. Hungarian Embassy in the MPR, Report, 10 July 1971, MNL, XIX-J-1-j China, 1971, 64. doboz, 78-10, 00569/35/1971.

61. Ibid.

62. Hungarian Embassy in the MPR, Report, 5 May 1972, MNL, XIX-J-1-j China, 1972, 56. doboz, 78-10, 00697/1/1972.

63. Ibid.

64. Ibid.

65. Hungarian Foreign Ministry, Memorandum, 2 April 1971, MNL, XIX-J-1-j China, 1971, 64. doboz, 78-10, 00558/3/1971. On China's policy of differentiation, see Fardella et al., *Sino-European Relations during the Cold War*, 11–13, 435–41.

66. Hungarian Embassy in the MPR, Telegram, 13 February 1973, MNL, XIX-J-1-j China, 1973, 65. doboz, 78-10, 001277/1/1973.

67. Heaton, 'Mongolia – Year of Socialist Competition', 34.

68. US Embassy in Moscow to the Secretary of State, Telegram, 26 November 1974. Subject: 'Brezhnev Speech in Ulan Bator'. NARA, Central Foreign Policy Files 1973–79, Record Group 59. Electronic Telegrams, 1974. Document no. 1974MOSCOW17847. Retrieved 10 March 2022 from https://aad.archives.gov/aad/index.jsp.

69. On Soviet aid to the MPR, see Batbayar, *Modern Mongolia*, 62–67.

70. Andreyev, *Overseas Chinese Bourgeoisie*.

71. 'China after Mao Zedong. On the Characteristics of the Political Line of the Current Chinese Leadership'. Analytical materials discussed at the June 1977 Interkit meeting. MNL, M-KS 288. f., 32/b/1977, 86. őe., 68. On Interkit, see Hershberg et al., 'The Interkit Story'.

72. Ungar, 'The Struggle Over the Chinese Community in Vietnam', 608.

73. Hungarian Embassy in the PRC, Telegram, 5 September 1978, MNL, XIX-J-1-j China, 1978, 78. doboz, 78-3, 004917/1978; Hungarian Embassy in the MPR, Telegram, 15 September 1978, MNL, XIX-J-1-j China, 1978, 79. doboz, 78-9, 005110/1978.

74. Hungarian Embassy in the MPR, Telegram, 1 November 1978, MNL, XIX-J-1-j China, 1978, 78. doboz, 78-1, 005811/1978.

75. Hungarian Embassy in the MPR, Report, 20 November 1978, MNL, XIX-J-1-j Mongolia, 1979, 92. doboz, 104-5, 00528/1979; Hungarian Embassy in the MPR, Report, 14 December 1978, MNL, XIX-J-1-j Mongolia, 1979, 92. doboz, 104-3, 00527/1979; Hungarian Embassy in the MPR, Report, 15 December 1978, MNL, XIX-J-1-j Mongolia, 1979, 92. doboz, 104-5, 00528/2/1979.

76. Hungarian Embassy in the MPR, Telegram, 29 January 1979, MNL, XIX-J-1-j Mongolia, 1979, 92. doboz, 104-2, 00966/1979.

77. Szalontai, 'Solidarity within Limits', 391–93.

78. Hungarian Embassy in the MPR, Report, 18 May 1979, MNL, XIX-J-1-j Vietnam, 1979, 135. doboz, 162-1, 001640/143/1979; Hungarian Embassy in the MPR, Report, 22 September 1979, MNL, XIX-J-1-j Mongolia, 1979, 92. doboz, 104-3, 00527/1/1979.

79. Hungarian Embassy in the MPR, Ciphered Telegram, 22 December 1979, MNL, XIX-J-1-j Mongolia, 1979, 92. doboz, 104-4, 004906/1/1979.

80. Hungarian Embassy in the MPR, Ciphered Telegram, 15 May 1979, MNL, XIX-J-1-j Mongolia, 1979, 92. doboz, 104-2, 003470/1979.

81. Hungarian Embassy in the MPR, Report, 14 November 1979, MNL, XIX-J-1-j Mongolia, 1979, 92. doboz, 104-1, 004524/2/1979.

82. Hungarian Embassy in the MPR, Report, 14 November 1979, MNL, XIX-J-1-j Mongolia, 1979, 92. doboz, 104-4, 005882/1979.

83. Hungarian Embassy in the MPR, Report, 14 January 1980, MNL, XIX-J-1-j Mongolia, 1980, 99. doboz, 130, 001165/1980.

84. Hungarian Embassy in the MPR, Report, 13 November 1980, MNL, XIX-J-1-j Mongolia, 1980, 99. doboz, 104-14, 006078/1/1980.

85. Hungarian Embassy in the MPR, Report, 14 February 1980, MNL, XIX-J-1-j Mongolia, 1980, 99. doboz, 104-20, 002159/1980.

86. Hungarian Embassy in the MPR, Report, 12 May 1980, MNL, XIX-J-1-j Mongolia, 1980, 99. doboz, 104-27, 004218/1980.

87. Hungarian Embassy to Vietnam, Report, 9 May 1979, MNL, XIX-J-1-j Vietnam, 1979, 135. doboz, 162-2, 003318/1979.

88. Hungarian Foreign Ministry, Memorandum, 22 May 1980, MNL, XIX-J-1-j Mongolia, 1980, 99. doboz, 104-14, 002213/8/1980.

89. Hungarian Embassy in the MPR, Report, 26 December 1980, MNL, XIX-J-1-j Mongolia, 1981, 106. doboz, 103, 00674/1981.

90. Hungarian Foreign Ministry, Memorandum, 22 May 1980; Hungarian Embassy in the MPR, Report, 13 November 1980, MNL, XIX-J-1-j Mongolia, 1980, 99. doboz, 104-14, 006078/1/1980.

91. Hungarian Embassy in the MPR, Report, 14 June 1979, MNL, XIX-J-1-j Mongolia, 1979, 92. doboz, 104-1, 0039571979; Hungarian Embassy in the MPR, Letter to Deputy Foreign Minister Vencel Házi, 14 November 1979, MNL, XIX-J-1-j Mongolia, 1979, 92. doboz, 104-1, 005977/1/1979.

92. Hungarian Embassy in the MPR, Letter to Deputy Foreign Minister Vencel Házi, 13 June 1979, MNL, XIX-J-1-j Mongolia, 1979, 92. doboz, 104-1, 005977/1979; Hungarian Embassy in the MPR, Telegram, 29 April 1980, MNL, XIX-J-1-j Mongolia, 1980, 99. doboz, 104-10, 003401/1980. See also Radchenko, 'Soviet Withdrawal from Mongolia', 186–87.

93. Radchenko, *Unwanted Visionaries*, 10–11.
94. Hungarian Socialist Workers' Party International Liaisons Department, Report, May 1982, MNL, M-KS 288. f., 32. cs., 1982, 128.őe., 122–39.
95. Hungarian Embassy in the MPR, Report, 1 August 1982, MNL, XIX-J-1-j Mongolia, 1982, 97. doboz, 147, 005033/1982.
96. Hungarian Embassy in the MPR, Ciphered Telegram, 18 June 1982, MNL, XIX-J-1-j Mongolia, 1982, 97. doboz, 104-1, 004227/1/1982; Hungarian Embassy in the MPR, Report, 19 November 1982, MNL, XIX-J-1-j Mongolia, 1982, 97. doboz, 103, 004227/6/1982.
97. Hungarian Embassy in the MPR, Ciphered Telegram, 1 October 1982, MNL, XIX-J-1-j Mongolia, 1980, 99. doboz, 104-103, 004227/5/1982.
98. Hungarian Embassy in the MPR, Ciphered Telegram, 20 December 1982, MNL, XIX-J-1-j Mongolia, 1982, 97. doboz, 104-103, 006995/1982.
99. Hungarian Embassy in the MPR, Report, 12 May 1983, MNL, XIX-J-1-j Mongolia, 1983, 91. doboz, 104-27, 003686/1983.
100. Ibid.
101. Hungarian Embassy in the MPR, Report, 30 May 1983, MNL, XIX-J-1-j Mongolia, 1983, 91. doboz, 104-27, 003686/1/1983.
102. Hungarian Embassy in the MPR, Report, 12 May 1983; Hungarian Embassy in the MPR, Report, 30 May 1983; Hungarian Embassy in the MPR, Ciphered Telegram, 30 June 1983, MNL, XIX-J-1-j Mongolia, 1983, 91. doboz, 104-27, 003686/5/1983.
103. Hungarian Foreign Ministry, Memorandum, 6 April 1983, MNL, XIX-J-1-j Mongolia, 1983, 91. doboz, 104-146, 001510/2/1983; Hungarian Embassy in the MPR, Report, 30 May 1983.
104. CIA, National Intelligence Daily, 28 May 1983, CIA-RDP85T01094R000300010023-8, in CERR.
105. CIA, National Intelligence Daily, 4 June 1983, CIA-RDP85T01094R000300010043-6, in CERR.
106. Hungarian Embassy in the MPR, Report, 3 December 1984, MNL, XIX-J-1-j Mongolia, 1984, 102. doboz, 10, 001669/4/1984.
107. CIA, National Intelligence Daily, 28 May 1983, CIA-RDP85T01094R000300010023-8.
108. Hungarian Embassy in the MPR, Report, 30 May 1983.
109. CIA, National Intelligence Daily, 4 June 1983.
110. Green, 'China and Mongolia', 1356–57; Heaton, 'Mongolia in 1983', 128–30.
111. Hungarian Embassy in the MPR, Ciphered Telegram, 30 June 1983, MNL, XIX-J-1-j Mongolia, 1983, 91. doboz, 104-27, 003686/5/1983.
112. Heaton, 'Mongolia in 1983', 130.
113. Hungarian Embassy in the MPR, Ciphered Telegram, 9 August 1983, MNL, XIX-J-1-j Mongolia, 1983, 91. doboz, 104-27, 003686/4/1983.
114. Hungarian Embassy in the MPR, Report, 3 December 1984.
115. Ibid.
116. Ibid.
117. Hungarian Embassy in the MPR, Report, 20 February 1989, MNL, XIX-J-1-j Mongolia, 1989, 60. doboz, 104-10, 001492/1989.
118. Jargalsaikhan, 'Anti-Chinese Attitudes', 19–20.
119. Billé, *Sinophobia*, 30, 87.

Bibliography

Andreyev, M. A. *Overseas Chinese Bourgeoisie – a Peking Tool in Southeast Asia*. Moscow: Progress Publishers, 1975.
Atwood, Christopher P. 'Chinese Merchants and Mongolian Independence', in S. Chuluun et al. (eds), *XX Zuuny Mongol: Tüükh, Soyol, Geopolitik, Gadaad Khariltsaany Tulgamdsan Asuudluud* (Ulaanbaatar: Mongol Ulsyn ShUA-iin Tüükh, Arkheologiin Khüreelen, 2017), 62–75.
Bao, Muping. 'Trade Centres (Maimaicheng) in Mongolia, and Their Function in Sino-Russian Trade Networks'. *International Journal of Asian Studies* 2 (2006), 211–37.
Batbayar, Tsedendambyn. *Modern Mongolia: A Concise History*. Ulaanbaatar: Offset Printing, Mongolian Center for Scientific and Technological Information, 2002.
Bawden, Charles R. *The Modern History of Mongolia*. London: Kegan Paul International, 1989.
Billé, Franck. *Sinophobia: Anxiety, Violence, and the Making of Mongolian Identity*. Honolulu, HI: University of Hawai'i Press, 2015.
Cassidy, Robert B. 'Mongolia: At Plan's End'. *Asian Survey* 11(1) (1971), 86–91.
'Chinese Foreign Ministry Protests at Mongolian Diplomat's Insult of Portrait of Chairman Mao', NCNA (English), 10 August 1967, in *Survey of China Mainland Press* No. 4001, US Consulate General in Hong Kong, 15 August 1967, 29–30.
Ewing, Thomas E. 'Ch'ing Policies in Outer Mongolia, 1900–1911'. *Modern Asian Studies* 14(1) (1980), 145–57.
Fardella, Enrico, Christian Ostermann and Charles Kraus (eds). *Sino-European Relations during the Cold War and the Rise of a Multipolar World: A Critical Oral History*. Washington, DC: Woodrow Wilson International Center for Scholars, 2015.
Fitzgerald, Stephen. 'Overseas Chinese Affairs and the Cultural Revolution'. *The China Quarterly* 40 (1969), 103–26.
Fravel, M. Taylor. *Strong Borders, Secure Nation: Cooperation and Conflict in China's Territorial Disputes*. Princeton, NJ: Princeton University Press, 2008.
Garver, John. 'Chinese Foreign Policy in 1970: The Tilt towards the Soviet Union'. *The China Quarterly* 82 (1980), 214–49.
Green, Elizabeth E. 'China and Mongolia: Recurring Trends and Prospects for Change'. *Asian Survey* 26(12) (1986), 1337–63.
Han, Xiaorong. 'Spoiled Guests or Dedicated Patriots? The Chinese in North Vietnam, 1954–1978'. *International Journal of Asian Studies* 6(1) (2009), 1–36.
Heaton, William R. 'Mongolia – Year of Socialist Competition'. *Asian Survey* 14(1) (1974), 30–35.
———. 'Mongolia in 1983: Mixed Signals'. *Asian Survey* 24(1) (1984), 127–33.
Hershberg, James, Sergey Radchenko, Péter Vámos and David Wolff. 'The Interkit Story: A Window into the Final Decades of the Sino-Soviet Relationship'. Cold War International History Project Working Paper #63. Washington, DC: Woodrow Wilson Center Press, 2011.
Jargalsaikhan, Mendee. 'Anti-Chinese Attitudes in Post-Communist Mongolia: The Lingering Negative Schemas of the Past', MA thesis. Vancouver: University of British Columbia, 2011.
Martin, George R.R. *A Game of Thrones: Book One of A Song of Ice and Fire*. New York: Bantam Books, 2016.
'Mongolian Revisionists Assault Chinese Nationals in Ulan Bator', New China News Agency (English), 22 May 1967, in *Survey of China Mainland Press* No. 3947, US Consulate General in Hong Kong, 26 May 1967, 45–47.

'Mongolian Revisionists Trailing Behind Soviet Revisionist Anti-China Campaign', NCNA (English), 18 August 1967, in *Survey of China Mainland Press*, No. 4007, US Consulate General in Hong Kong, 23 August 1967, 34–36.

Morozova, Irina Y. *Socialist Revolutions in Asia: The Social History of Mongolia in the Twentieth Century.* London: Routledge, 2009.

Radchenko, Sergey S. 'The Soviets' Best Friend in Asia: The Mongolian Dimension of the Sino-Soviet Split'. Cold War International History Project Working Paper No. 42. Washington, DC: Woodrow Wilson Center Press/Stanford, CA: Stanford University Press, 2003.

———. 'Soviet Withdrawal from Mongolia, 1986–1992: A Reassessment'. *Journal of Slavic Military Studies* 25 (2012), 183–203.

———. *Unwanted Visionaries: The Soviet Failure in Asia at the End of the Cold War.* Oxford: Oxford University Press, 2014.

Rinchin, M. (ed.). *Uls Töriin Talaar Khelmegdegsdiin Dursgal Tsagaan Nom.* Ulaanbaatar: Tsagaatgakh Ajlyg Udirdan Zokhion Baiguulakh Ulsyn Komiss, 1993.

Sanders, Alan J. K. *Historical Dictionary of Mongolia.* Lanham, MD: The Scarecrow Press, 2010.

Shirendyb, Bazaryn et al. (eds). *History of the Mongolian People's Republic.* Moscow: 'Nauka' Publishing House, 1973.

Smith, Robert A. 'Mongolia: In the Soviet Camp'. *Asian Survey* 10(1) (1970), 25–29.

Szalontai, Balázs. 'Solidarity within Limits: Interkit and the Evolution of the Soviet Bloc's Indochina Policy, 1967–1985'. *Cold War History* 17(4) (2017), 385–403.

Ungar, E. S. 'The Struggle Over the Chinese Community in Vietnam, 1946–1986'. *Pacific Affairs* 60(4) (1987–88), 596–614.

'Vice Premier Hsieh Fu-chih Receives Returned Chinese Nationals Expelled by Mongolian Revisionist Authorities', NCNA (English), 24 May 1967, in *Survey of China Mainland Press* No. 3947, US Consulate General in Hong Kong, 26 May 1967, 47.

Part VII

Geopolitical Rivalries in Russia's Far North and Far East

Elena I. Campbell and Zhao Xin

The struggle over borderlands has been a central issue in Russian history that has contributed both to geopolitical rivalries and international conflict, as well as domestic reforms and state-building.[1] Specific local conditions and the different timings of expansion produced distinct relations between the empire's centre of power and the outlying regions. Yet Russia's various borderlands did not exist in isolation. Developments in one region invariably generated challenges, policies and connections with other borderland areas.

Russia's far northern and far eastern peripheries were coastal fringes of larger imperial regions – the Russian North and Siberia – and were known for their harsh natural conditions and vast expanses. Both borderlands were home to Indigenous peoples who had lived there before the arrival of the imperial state and shared a frontier history with their neighbours: Norway's Finnmark in the north-west and Qing Manchuria in the east.[2] During the imperial era, the far northern and far eastern territories experienced both periods of neglect by the imperial centre and waves of enthusiasm associated with possibilities for economic and strategic gains.

Russia's humiliating defeat in the Crimean War (1853–56) weakened the country's position as a Great Power, challenged its imperial order, demonstrated the vulnerability of the empire's borderlands and in turn, stimulated trends that shaped Russia's engagement with its borderlands during the late imperial era. This period was characterized by state-driven reformism, industrialization and development of new modes of transportation (railroads and steamships), state territorialization, the development of the press and emergence of mass politics, the rise of nationalism, and imperial conquest. It was during this time that educated Russians within and outside the government became increasingly interested in the empire's far northern and far eastern borderlands.

Russia's northward and eastward turns not only happened around the same time, but were also interrelated.[3] Not surprisingly, some educated contemporaries, including writer and ethnographer Sergei Maksimov (1831–1901), scientist Dmitrii Mendeleev (1834–1907), Admiral Stepan Makarov (1834–1907) and Sergei Witte, Minister of Finance from 1892 to 1903, contributed to both turns. Economic, political and strategic considerations encouraged a search for new maritime outlets in the Pacific and on the Murman Coast where Russia could have an open access to the oceans, as well as efforts to revitalize the old port in Arkhangelsk. Witte's railroad projects intended to tie both the Pacific Far East and the Far North of European Russia to the empire's centre, and were crucial to his vision of Russia as a modern imperial power. Evgenii L'vov-Kochetov (a conservative journalist who popularized Witte's plans for the North) presented Russia's northward and eastward turns in the late nineteenth century as a patriotic matter.[4] The railroad network linked Arkhangelsk to Moscow; however, the plans for the railroad to the Murman Coast were not realized until the First World War. The Trans-Siberian Railroad project, through the construction of branches across Manchuria to the Russian coastal city of Vladivostok and the ice-free harbour of Port Arthur (Lüshun) on the Liaodong peninsula, extended empire-building beyond the state border and put Russia on a road to war with Japan.[5] At the same time, the construction of the Trans-Siberian Road raised the question of rail cargo transportation and thus stimulated Russians' interest in the exploration and development of the Northern Sea Route. Russia's disastrous defeat in the war with Japan (1904–5), and then the First World War, increased the strategic importance of the Arctic waters and added urgency to this issue.

To develop and protect its distant borderlands, Russia relied on colonists coming from other imperial regions. For example, the inhabitants of Finland participated in the colonization of both peripheries. In the 1880s, the Russian government hoped to use Pomors for the development of Russian fishing on the coast of the Sea of Japan.[6] Chinese labour was an important factor in the economic development of Russia's Far East, and during the First World War also contributed to Russia's railroad construction in the Far North.[7]

The enthusiasm surrounding the Far East and the Far North also intermingled with anxieties concerning the vulnerability of Russia's distant peripheries and the international rivalry in the Arctic and East Asia. Thus, the consolidation of the country's far northern and far eastern peripheries appeared very much to be important matters of state. In the Far North, despite some voices in Russia critical of the 1826 border agreement and the British and Norwegian fears of Russia's supposed intentions to conquer an ice-free harbour in Finnmark, the international border between Russia and Norway remained stable during the late Tsarist period.[8] In contrast, the Far East became a zone of Russia's expansion and of military conflict.

Prior to the seventeenth century, due to a lack of basic geographical knowledge, Chinese central governments of all dynasties had no sense of the country's borderlands and territories, and even no precise maps or strict geographical demarcations of these borderlands from the neighbouring countries. That is, the traditional geographical understanding was that 'any land in this world belongs to China, anyone in this world is subordinate to China',[9] a presumptuous concept established during the Qing dynasty. At that time, Western missionaries introduced their geographical knowledge and maps into the Qing court. It was Emperor Kangsi who adopted the Jesuits' cartography and mapped the whole country, and defended the borders that were established more clearly in the process. The most drastic and durable conflict with foreigners regarding the newly delineated borderlands was the one with Russia, which marched to the Amur River to secure access to a seaport in 1636. But its advance was interrupted by Kangsi, who presided over the signing of the Treaty of Nerchinsk in 1689, the first formal document to define the border between China and foreign countries. As a result of this treaty, Russians had to withdraw from the Amur area, which was regarded as a homeland by the Manchu, who had just conquered China and established a new dynasty, the Qing. In fact, the Qing government did treat Russia in a humiliating way, all the Russia affairs with China were managed by Lifanyuan (an administration for 'barbarians' business); however, the Qing government provided Russia with the privilege to maintain a language school and missionary posts in Beijing. Far from objecting to this state of affairs, Russia sent trade envoys to Beijing periodically, for lucrative benefits were given to the 'barbarians', who did not care too much about being mistaken for tributaries by the Qing court.

The ambiguous diplomatic relationship between Russia and China persisted well into the 1840s, when Western powers entered southern China by force and established a different kind of treaty diplomacy with

China. This aroused the Russians' envy and they tried their best to dispense of the Nerchinsk agreement with China, in order to gain more favourable conditions.[10] They were repeatedly refused, however, by the Qing government. During the 1850s, the Taiping Rebellion occurred, a serious uprising in South China. Together with the first opium war between 1840 and 1842, the rebellion significantly weakened China. Meanwhile, Britain and France fought China over better trading opportunities and permanent consular rights in Beijing, which further exhausted the main force of the Qing government. Thus, the northern border was undefended and Russia seized the opportunity to annex large territories from China on the left bank of the Amur River in the second half of the nineteenth century. It then continuously extended its power southward to Manchuria. The border crisis in northern China became more and more serious. Under these circumstances, some Chinese scholars, most of whom had official titles, such as Zhang Mu, He Qiutao, Cao Tingjie, Wu Dacheng and others, began to study the borderlands between Russia and China through textual study and field work, and published a series of books on the subject.[11] This established an acute consciousness of borders and helped develop the 'geography of borders' as a subject of academic enquiry, which influenced the central government's policies regarding the northern borders. Eventually, the government allowed a great number of Han Chinese immigrants into Manchuria, something they had until then always avoided, and they developed national industries and constructed the national railways, which caused a fresh round of conflicts with Russia and also involved China in international competition.

Russia's interest in the Amur area was not new and was driven by different motives, including a necessity to deliver supplies to Russia's northeast and to find a convenient sea outlet for eastern Siberia. However, in the 1840s and 1850s, the increased British and American activities in the region on the one hand, and the weakening of China on the other, had stimulated Russia's renewed interest and expansion in the Amur area. This was exacerbated by Russia's worries about Britain's strategy in the region and fears of British expansion into it. Russia's activities in north-east Asia were a frequent subject of British correspondence at the time, and the British saw the expeditions into the region as a first step to gaining better geographical knowledge of it, which would serve them well should there be another war with Russia over territory.[12] Meanwhile, in order to isolate Britain, Russia strove hard to maintain a very good relationship with the US. As a reward, the US dispatched a fleet to support Russia during the Crimean War, and a number of American adventurers travelled to the Amur River in search of potential commercial opportunities with China and Russia. As a result, from the 1850s, the complicated interrelationship between China, Britain, Russia and the US regarding the strategically important Amur River region ignited border conflicts of unprecedented severity.

Notes

1. See Rieber, *The Struggle for the Eurasian Borderlands*.
2. On the frontier society in the Amur River region, see Zatsepine, *Beyond the Amur*.
3. On Russia in the Far East, see Bassin, *Imperial Visions*; Remnev, *Rossiia Dal'nego Vostoka*; Lukoianov, '*Ne Otstat Ot Derzhav*'.
4. L'vov, *Po studenomu moriu*, 2–3.
5. Wcislo, *Tales of Imperial Russia*, 180–85.
6. However, these colonization projects were not very successful. Remnev, *Rossiia Dal'nego Vostoka*, 210.
7. See Saveliev, 'Chinese Labor in the Russian War Effort', 259–82.
8. On different aspects of Russian–Norwegian relations in the North, see Nielsen, (ed.) *Sblizhenie*.
9. *Book of Songs Xiaoya Kitayama*.
10. Jackson, *The Russo-Chinese Borderlands*, 36.
11. Zhang Mu, *Supplement to Russia Affairs*; *A Note of Mongolian Nomadic Life*. He Qiutao, *Shuòfāng bèi chéng (The history of Chinese Northern Parts with Russia)*; Cao Tingjie, *The Defence Summary of Northeast Frontier in China*; *The Summary of Eastern Siberia*; *An Illustrated Book of Eastern Three Provinces*. Wu Dacheng, *A Note on Delineating the boundaries of Jilin*.
12. Whittingham, *Notes on the Late Expedition to Japan and Eastern Siberia*, 84.

Bibliography

Bassin, Mark. *Imperial Visions: Nationalist Imagination and Geographical Expansion in the Russian Far East, 1840–1865*. Cambridge: Cambridge University Press, 1999.
Book of Songs Xiaoya Kitayama. Xian: Three Qin Press, 2018.
Jackson, W. A. Douglas. *The Russo-Chinese Borderlands: Zone of Peaceful Contact or Potential Conflict?* Princeton: Van Nosrand, 1962.
Lukoianov, Igor. '*Ne otstat ot derzhav': Rossiia na Dalnem Vostoke v kontse XIX—nachale XX vv*. Saint Petersburg: Nestor-Istoriia, 2008.
L'vov, Evgenii. *Po studenomu moriu. Poezdka na Sever: Iaroslavl', Vologda, Arkhangel'sk, Murman, Nord-Kap, Trondgeĭm, Stokgol'm, Peterburg*. Moscow: t-vo tip. A.I. Mamontova, 1895.
Nielsen, Jens Petter. (ed.). *Sblizhenie: Rossiia i Norvegiia v 1814–1917 godakh* [translated to Russian from Norwegian]. Moscow: Izdatel'stvo 'Ves' Mir', 2017.
Rieber, Alfred. *The Struggle for the Eurasian Borderlands: From the Rise of Early Modern Empires to the End of the First World War*. Cambridge: Cambridge University Press, 2014.
Remnev, Anatolii. *Rossiia Dal'nego Vostoka: imperskaia geografiia vlasti XIX-nachala XX vekov*. Omsk: Izd. OmGU, 2004.
Saveliev, Igor. 'Chinese Labor in the Russian War Effort', in David Wolfe, Shinji Yokote and Willard Sunderland (eds), *Russia's Great War and Revolution in the Far East:*

Reimagining the Northeast Asian Theater, 1914–22 (Bloomington, IN: Slavica Press, 2018), 259–82.

Wcislo, Francis W. *Tales of Imperial Russia: The Life and Times of Sergei Witte, 1849–1915*. Oxford: Oxford University Press, 2011.

Whittingham, Bernard. *Notes on the Late Expedition to Japan and Eastern Siberia*. London: Longman, Brown, Green, and Longmans, 1856.

Zatsepine, Victor. *Beyond the Amur: Frontier Encounters between China and Russia, 1850–1930*. Vancouver: University of British Columbia Press, 2017.

CHAPTER 13

Russia's Expansions towards the Amur River and Westerners' Corresponding Explorations in Early Modern Times

ZHAO XIN

Nowadays, the Amur River[1] is a boundary river between North China and south-east Russia. It is famous for its long course, with wide basins and multiple tributaries. The total length (if counted from its source, the Argun River) is 5,498 km, with a broad drainage area of 1,843,000 km², making it the tenth-longest river in the world. Originally, the Amur River was a Chinese inland river, which was clarified officially by the Treaty of Nerchinsk in 1689. Going back further, the chronicle of the Amur can be tracked by its different names in different periods, such as 'Feather Water', 'Black Water', 'Weak Water' and 'Black Heng River', according to ancient Chinese documents. It was first referred to as 'Black Dragon River' in the Liao dynasty, 'Huntong River' in the Yuan and Ming dynasties, and again 'Black Dragon River' up to now. In Manchu, the Amur River was called 'sahaliyan ula', meaning 'black water', a synonym of 'Halamulian' in Mongolian. Generally, the Amur River has two sources, one being the Kerulun and Argun Rivers in the south,[2] and the other being the Shilka River, originating from the eastern part of Kent Mount in the north. The southern and northern sources converge at the village of Xiluoguhe, where the Amur River is formed and flows to the east, then turning in a 400 km bend with multi-branched confluences to the south-east – including the largest branch, the Huma River – then flowing further to the south, passing by Blagoveschensk and Heihe, where the Zeya River joins it; the Amur broadens abruptly here and steers to the south-east, then absorbs the Bureya River at the Great Bend; then, with the largest branch, the Sugari River, joining at Tongjiang 250 km away, it turns to the north-east, heading for Khabarovsk,[3] where it takes in the Ussuri River and ultimately flows into the Tartar Strait in front of Sakhalin Island at the Pacific Ocean.

Due to setbacks in expanding towards the Black Sea after the Crimean War, Russia began to turn its eyes to north-east Asia, where it took the Amur River as a conduit to the ice-free ports for which it had longed ever since the seventeenth century. In 1858, the Qing government was forced by Russia to sign the Treaty of Aigun,[4] which stipulated the Amur River, from its starting point at the confluence of its southern and northern sources to its junction with the Ussuri River (3474 km in total), as the new Sino-Russia border line. This transformed the river from an inland Chinese river to an international border river, involved in multinational controversies and cooperation between Russia, America, Britain, China and Japan. Many Westerners were also attracted to explore this new landmark.

The Crimean War and Russia's Expansion into the Amur River

Generally speaking, the world from the mid-nineteenth century to the early twentieth century was dominated by Britain and Russia. The conflicts between the two powers openly and privately determined war and peace in Europe, the Near East and East Asia, and the Amur River became a focus in this world based on Anglo-Russian conflicts too. Looking back, prior to the seventeenth century, Russia was almost a hinterland, with its northern waters frozen all the time,[5] the Baltic Sea in the west occupied by Sweden and the Black Sea in the south controlled by Turkey, while the Amur River that flowed to Okhotsk was an inner river of China. Alarmed by Europe's great geographical discoveries in the sixteenth century, Russia began to look desperately for a gate to the sea, and struggled with the countries mentioned above. Judging from the frequency of war and geographical proximity, Russia concentrated more on the Near East than the Amur River, which was only a minor part of the country. Nevertheless, Russia still dispatched many armed colonial missions to the Amur valley via Siberia. Up to the mid-seventeenth century, Russia had covertly established several colonial garrisons around the Amur River. Such invasions were bound to provoke counter-attacks by the powerful Qing government. As a result, Russia's eastern expansion was stopped by the Treaty of Nerchinsk in 1689, which stipulated the Outer Hingan Range and the Argun River as the Sino-Russian boundary line. Subsequently, Russia had to focus on the north Pacific for its sea access. In 1741, two Russian adventurers, Bering and Chirikof, opened up the sea route from the Kamchatka Peninsula via the Aleutian Islands to America, after which dozens of adventurers and merchants, attracted by the lucrative fur trade in the north Pacific, followed this sea route, developing commercial activity and reclaiming territory therein.[6] Meanwhile, Russia's empress Catherine the Great strove towards the Black Sea and attempted to occupy the Turkey Strait and Constantinople, but was stopped by Britain repeatedly. As a consequence, Russia tried to use its advantages in the north Pacific to diminish the power of Britain's colonies in the Near East. This is the reason that Russia adopted the policy of armed neutrality and endeavoured to weaken Britain's power in the sea during the American War of Independence. As a result of England's loss of most of her North American colonies, Asia and the Pacific became a new source of conflict between the British and the Russian empires.[7] From the 1840s, Russia built up its arbitratorship in suppressing the bourgeois revolution that had broken out in Europe, and took the opportunity to seize the Turkish Straits while the Ottoman Empire was declining, then expanding successfully into the Balkan Peninsula. In 1853, Russia triggered the Crimean War with Turkey, fighting for the right to control the Balkans with Britain, who were allied with France and the Kingdom of Sardinia; Russia's fleets were attacked from many directions, in the Crimean Peninsula, the Black Sea, the Baltic Sea, the Bering Sea, the North Pacific and the White Sea. In July 1854, the allies Britain and France traversed the Pacific to chase the Russian fleet; they broke into the ports of Petropavlovsk twice, but all these battles failed, which ignited warfare in the seas of north-east Asia. Meanwhile, the Russian army had footholds along the Amur River under the control of Muraviev, who had established many garrisons there, such as Malinsk, Nicoloievsk and Petropavlovsk, and commanded the expeditionary force to transport provisions to the Russian fleet via the Amur River during the war.[8]

In contrast, the allies had almost no information about the north-east sea except an article, 'The Latest Acquisition of Russia, the River Amoor',[9] published in January 1855. Britain's chief commander, Charles Elliot, had less knowledge on the Amur River than British citizens, for the British government had gained a detailed map of the Amur River's estuary from Holland's marines,[10] but British officials did not even have the map of Lapérouse. In February 1855, the Anglo-French allied fleet arrived in the north-east Asian sea under the command of General Bruce and

James Stirling, and tried to destroy the Russian garrisons of Okhotsk and Kamchatka.¹¹ However, the main force of the Russian Pacific Fleet in Peteropavlovsk had fled when they heard the news several days previously, and retreated towards Die Castries Bay.¹² In order to pursue the Russian army, the allies split into two branches, one with three warships headed for Ayan, the other led by Gilbert John Brydone Elliot to inspect the Tartary Straits. As expected, Elliot found the Russian fleet's trail in Die Castries Bay in May; however, due to an error of judgement, he let the Russians escape from the northern part of Tartar Bay, which the allies did not know was navigable to the estuary of the Amur River in the heavy fog.¹³ Elliot and Sterling met at Kerrylin Corner, the south end of the Sakhalin Islands, and sailed towards the Okhotsk Sea where they captured a two-master junk. They then returned south, while Elliot proceeded to the Tartary Straits in the north, to occupy Urup,¹⁴ where they claimed their colonizing rights to exert pressure on Russia. In comparison, while the allies held twenty-five warships, Russia had only six;¹⁵ however, despite their overwhelming superiority, the allies failed in pursuing the Russians and had to withdraw due to their ignorance of the topography around the Amur. The war in the north-east Asian sea made the allies lose their confidence, which played a key role in ending the Crimean War and led to the signing of the Paris Peace Treaty, which deprived Russian of its garrison rights on the Black Sea.

On the other hand, the victory around the Amur River led the Russian government and the War Office to unanimously agree to march east and to annex the Amur River, for Maraviev proposed that if Russians could take the Amur River Estuary, they would control Siberia, at least the east of Baikal area very firmly; getting the navigation rights of the Amur would help to develop a dense population and create industrial and agricultural prosperity for Siberia and therefore the state as a whole, and to further establish transport links with Kamchatka to secure Russia's hold on the peninsula and maintain trade with China.¹⁶ In addition, by shipping Russian's textiles along the Amur River to Manchuria, which was far from where the British operated, they could avoid unprofitable competition with them.¹⁷ Thereupon, Russia dispatched its armies as pioneers, then sent geographical explorers as academic support, and transported many immigrants as a back-up force to the Amur River, initiating his 'Amur Age'. On 1 June 1857, Uther Krakow commanded a six hundred-strong infantry battalion headed for the Amur. Maraviev led the other troops (one Cossack infantry brigade and one cavalry regiment) down the Amur River, and established many garrisons along the left bank of the river, and even a small post office. Thereafter, a great number of Russian militants were manoeuvred in succession to the valley of the Amur River.

Meanwhile, the academic study of the Amur River was strengthened by Russian geographical explorers M. M. Peschurof, Permikin and others, who entered the valley to survey the field. Botanist Karl Maximovich also collected 904 species along the Amur River.[18] With the endeavour of these scholars, Russia was able to draw the first and most accurate map of the Amur River,[19] which provided the basic information for its policies and strategies of north-east Asian expansion.

In order to occupy the Amur River and its estuary perpetually, Yefim Putyatin, Russia's plenipotentiary in China, sent missions to China and Japan separately to negotiate with them on boundary delimitation, but in vain. In 1856, Russia moved its Pacific naval port from Petropavlovsk in the Kamchatka Peninsula to Nikolayevsk at the Amur estuary, and established the coastal province. From 1858 to 1860, Russia annexed more than one million Chinese territories from the north of the Amur River to the east of the Ussuri River by the Treaty of Aigun and the Treaty of Peking, then created the Amur province on the left bank of the Amur River.[20] Subsequently, China lost the estuaries of the Amur River and the Tumen River, leading mid- and northern Manchuria to be isolated in the hinterland. Russia's greedy annexation of the coast was not only an extreme reaction to its long-term hinterland status, but also epitomized its Pacific strategy[21] to form a power in North China balanced against Britain in South China. After completing its territory annexation, Russia developed the Amur River valley in haste by strengthening its garrisons and moving many migrants into the area, whom it attracted by all kinds of means, such as providing passports, tax breaks, and liberty for refugees; even hundreds of Germany families were attracted there. According to British statistics, in 1859, there were 7,776 informal Russian soldiers deployed in the Amur River; the local population were around ten thousand people, and formal soldiers were at least nine thousand, making a total of about 14,476 soldiers and officials garrisoned there.[22] In 1859, the news of the discovery of a gold mine upstream on the Amur River spread and more than ten thousand colonists swarmed there in a year.[23] However, most immigrants were natives of Eastern Europe and West Siberia, where farming capabilities were lower, so the provisions for them mainly depended on the cargoes transported from Russia proper via the Amur River. Therefore, Russia established the Amur Company to take charge of the trade around the Amur valley, which Russia treated as its base for expanding its marine powers to the Pacific. By 1860, Russia had nineteen ships (total 5,150 horsepower) with 380 guns, handled by 247 officials and 4,365 sailors and soldiers; these included two frigates, five light cruisers, one dispatch boat, five clippers and six small steamers.[24] Under the encouragement of the Russian government, immigration along the Amur River increased rapidly, and the new cities of Blagoveschensk, Khabarovsk and Ussurisk sprung up one after another.

As mentioned, the allies failed to trace the Russians because they were not familiar with the geographical situation around the Amur River, whose geography Russia exploited to expand in the area continually, even pushing forward into the Pacific. Under these circumstances, Westerners with official and academic backgrounds began to explore the Amur River, the centre of north-east Asia. Being more entangled with geopolitical connections and competition than others, explorers from America and Britain made up the majority of the investigating groups around the Amur River.

America's Cooperation with Russia and Its Ambitious Explorations around the Amur River

America actively advocated Russia's expansion towards the Amur on two grounds: first, it could ease Russia's threat to North America; second, America might be able to enter North China to trade. Russia, meanwhile, thought it was necessary to maintain the harmonious relationship with America given the severe geopolitical landscape it was facing. Originally, expanding into the north Pacific was also a strategic aim in Russia's search for seaports. In 1787, a Russian merchant, Shelikhov, supported Russia to exploit the north Pacific coast of Americas and proposed a lucrative way of trading fur there, which soon attracted many Russian merchants to the area. As a result, Russia's government approved the well-known Russo-America Company to be established on the foundation of the Shelikhov North Company, and conferred on it the privileges of hunting, mining and trading on the north-west coast of America and the Aleutian Islands, and further, the privilege of claiming the new-found land for Russia.[25] Obviously, this was a semi-official business agency, which ran the fur business while carrying out Russia's expansion strategy towards the north Pacific. The company soon seized Alaska, then built Port Ross in San Francisco.[26] As a supply depot, the geographical proximity of Ross Port created many opportunities for exchanges but also caused conflicts between the United States and Russia. However, under the pressure of adverse conditions in Europe, Russia had to adopt a cooperative policy with America, and drew back from the latter gradually. This is another reason for which Russia switched its expansion strategy towards the Amur River, even permitting American fishermen to fish for the abundant gadus around Kamchatka.[27] Thus, Russia and America maintained their friendship in trading without direct conflicts. Such conflicts played a key role in the Crimean War, which left Russia on its own – its old allies Austria and Prussia did not provide any help, and Austria even joined the enemy side. The betrayal of its European friends made Russia cherish its friendship with America more and restrain itself more than ever in North America.

Undoubtedly, America helped Russia penetrate into Manchuria for reasons of self-interest. One was to relieve Russian pressure on North America, and another was to exploit the commercial potential of the Amur. In 1853, de Bodisco, Russia's ambassador in America, wrote a letter to Saint Petersburg, noting that the 'Americans told me it was our best chance to occupy the banks of [the] Amur River for Russo-America[n] trade'.[28] To show its sincerity, America gave maximum support to Russia during the Crimean War, but mainly focused on the Amur: first, it provided technical support. In May 1854, the inventor of the revolver, Samuel Colt, and other weapons experts sent improved weapons to Russia. In September 1855, fifteen American machinists went to Saint Petersburg to help with Moscow's railway construction.[29] Secondly, America provided strategic materials and manpower assistance. Russia ordered ships from America; in 1856, the *America*, made by Americans, was escorted by Americans to the Amur estuary for Russia's garrisons there, while the American navy invited Russian military officials to America to demonstrate Euro-American submarine cables' construction. America even dispatched medical workers for Russia's wounded.[30] Thirdly, it provided Russia's navy with provisions from trading stations along the Amur River and Sakhalin Island, and even shipped provisions to Russia's Pacific fleets directly. In return, Russia cancelled all taxation and customs inspection on America, and allowed it to establish banks in territories occupied by Russia at will.[31]

In fact, America did take advantage of Russia's early expansions around the Amur to penetrate further into Manchuria, so the favours for Russia provided by America during the Crimean War were also aimed at intelligence collecting and academic research for trading later on in the periphery. 'The exploration plan in North Pacific and China', which meant investigating the trading and geographical conditions along China's coast to Russia via the Amur River, was such a threefold exploration (constituting a favour for Russia, a demonstration of American power and an opportunity to collect valuable data), carried out by America during the Crimean War. On 21 June 1853, American captain A. W. Habersham was ordered to lead a fleet to the China Sea[32] that consisted of a single-mast battleship, *Vincenes* (the flagship: 800 tons, 10 guns, about 200 soldiers), the screw ship *John Cook* (550 tons, 3 guns, 70 soldiers), the double-mast warship *Dolphin* (400 tons, 5 guns, 70 soldiers), the schooner *Cooper* (88 tons, 1 gun, 20 soldiers) and the supply ship *John Kennedy* (520 tons, 3 guns, 40 soldiers).³³ The fleet set out from Norfolk, Virginia, passed the Cape of Good Hope, then arrived at Singapore, the Malay Peninsula and Hong Kong. Thereafter the fleet sailed north from Canton Bay after a short stay in Hong Kong. Originally, they planned to go to Peking through the water pass via Fuzhou, Shanghai, and then through the Yellow Sea to the Hai River. But they found it impossible to reach Peking through the water pass. They navigated back to Shanghai, then east to Ryukyu, Japanese Fujieda and so on, and later to Kamchatka, from where they sailed back to Okhotsk, then on to the Amur River. By the time they arrived the Crimean War had reached a stalemate. The American fleet's arrival was a great relief to Russia's navy, for the latter was struggling to subsist on the provisions from California that had been transported by the Russo-America Company. As a Russian official mentioned, 'taking provisions from California is our only hope. As long as the war continues, our whole resources is nothing but berries, fish, and wild animal's meat and some plant roots.'³⁴ After delivering necessities to the Russians, American officials communicated with Russia on the situation in the Far East, then sailed back on 15 September 1855 via the Okhotsk Sea to America proper in 1856. The two-year exploration, which covered four thousand nautical miles, ended successfully. The journey provided much useful data on trading, rectified numerous faults in American maps of the Far East, especially for the Amur area,³⁵ improved nautical knowledge of long-term navigation in dangerous and deep seas, and represented a great and impressive global navigation in the stormiest season.³⁶ Habersham published a book based on his log book, *My Last Cruise, Or, Where We Went and What We Saw: Visits to the Malay and Loo-Choo Islands, the Coasts of China, Formosa, Japan, Kamtschatka, Siberia, and the Mouth of the Amoor River*, which became a bestseller among those with an interest in the Far East after it was published, then republished the following year.

To seize the trading opportunity entailed by Russia's expansion around the Amur River, the most influential American representative, Perry McDonough Collins, made his fantastic journey to the area. He himself was an active agitator for Russia's expansion into north-east Asia, and even deemed Russia's actions therein as seductive as the Great Westward Movement in America. Being fond of adventure, Collins resigned from his position as a lawyer at the age of 30 (in 1843) and went to California to seek his fortune. He read a book, *The Explorations in Northeast Asia* by Ferdinand Von Wrangle, and was so excited when he heard the news that Russians had already settled down along the Amur River, that he thought of 'taking the Amur River as the natural pass of American merchants to the ambiguous deep in the North Asia, and opened a trading and civilized new world'.[37] Collins contemplated exploring the Amur River in person. On the strong recommendation of his friends and the Russian Embassy, Collins was interviewed by President Franklin Pierce, and was nominated the 'American commercial deputy in the Amur River'.[38] On 12 April 1856, Collins set out from New York, and first stopped in Saint Petersburg to meet Muraviev for advice. Muraviev was very appreciative of his brave actions and gave him a passport and some useful information on exploring.[39] Then Collins went to Moscow for training to adapt to the climate, and waited for winter – the best season for travelling by sleigh. On 3 December 1856, Collins left Moscow to traverse Russia's hinterlands, accompanied by his partner, Peyton, and Captain Anakoff, a subordinate of Muraviev. The passport given by Muraviev proved very useful and allowed Collins to travel in convenience; the journey went very smoothly, with many generous favours given to him. On 7 January 1857, Collins reached Russia's strategic town in the Far East, Irkutsk, after thirty-five days of hard travelling in the −50°C cold; he changed horses 210 times and covered 3,545 miles.[40] Soon after, Muraviev arrived and held a welcome banquet for Collins, who expressed his aspirations for Russo-American cooperation in developing the trade around the Amur River, a little known place that was destined to be the most important place on the world map.[41] Collins stayed in Irkutsk for nearly a month to restore himself. Meanwhile he explored the surroundings of the city and the circumstances of trade. In the middle of February, Collins left for Chita, where he surveyed the mine and commercial potential. By the beginning of June, Collins began to sail down the Amur River, where he investigated the local geography and trades in detail up to the Sungari River; then he sailed east to Japan.

In total, Collins explored the Amur River and Siberia for more than a year, and the significant mining resources and colossal commercial potential therein made a strong impression on him. He urged America to enter the Amur: 'America could enter into Japan and Hawaii via Kamchatka to Amur River to trade … Through the combined transportation, America would not be the west part of Russia and Europe, but the east part.'[42] Collins boldly proposed establishing a commercial circle around the Pacific Rim, and gave his first petition to the Russian Chancellor and Muraviev to construct a railway traversing Europe to realize quick transportation, then founded the Amur Railway Company. Above all, he proposed building a railway from Chita to Irkutsk and thought it was most feasible to build the Siberia Railway from where Ural Mountain and Altai Mountain crossed to the source of the Amur River, starting from St. Petersburg to Moscow or from Moscow to Warsaw. Thus, merchandise from Siberia's hinterland would help to create a variety of transportation methods which would enable to reach the Pacific via railway and on the Amur River.[43]

Collins suggested setting up a combined transport network in the Pacific, which could mutually complement the railway, and then to create a telegraph line between western America and the Amur River.[44] Collins also vehemently imagined that Irkutsk would be eastern Russia's – and maybe even northern Asia's – greatest commercial centre after the railway and navigation network had been completed; soon after that, the yearly transaction would surpass 50,000,000 roubles.[45] Later on, Collins finished his book, *Voyage Down the Amoor: With a Land Journey through Siberia, and Incidental Notices of Manchooria, Kamschatka, and Japan*; on its title page, he dedicated the book to his hero, Muraviev. The book was very popular after it was published, and there are at least ten reviews of it published in authoritative journals.[46] It was also reported by mass media that Collins won massive honours, which encouraged him to realize his second exploration on the Amur River for the telegraph line's construction, in turn promoting the cooperation of Russia, America, Britain and Canada.[47]

It is certain that Russia and America established a very good relationship during and after the Crimean War. Ostensibly, America's survey of the Amur River achieved three goals, not only expressing its support of Russia, but extending its commercial strategy to North China and Japan via the Amur, and more importantly, showing its strong military and economic power to the world. As a result, Russia expressed its full support for America, though this was not its intention at all, somewhat for fear of the American navy's virtual power. In essence, the relationship between Russia and America was fragile and reciprocal, just as the two countries' leaders' periodical correspondence, intended 'to cultivate the intimate friendship with each other, transfer my firm and loyal hope to your majesty, looking forward to extend the intimate cooperation infinitely',[48] was very superficial and bureaucratic. Under these favourable circumstances, Russia seized the opportunity to annex Manchuria, where it pretended to develop bilateral trading cooperation with America around the Amur River as a further step. In 1859, Russia and America established the American Amur River's Mercantile Agency. America even dispatched the consul stationed there, but all were ultimately suspended by Russia. Fortunately, the Amur River became the main channel by which America transported goods to Russian colonists and the Russo-America Company,[49] which stimulated America to pay more attention to North China from then on.

The British Response to Russia and America around the Amur River

There are two reasons that Britain concentrated on the north-east Asian sea, where it took the Amur River as its centre. One was its failure around the Amur River during the Crimean War, while Russia pressed its advantages from its earlier expansion in the area, which stimulated Britain to remedy its ignorance and misunderstanding of the Amur quickly. One witness, Captain Whittingham, wrote critically: 'no wonder that the Russians are proud! The war found the professions dedicated to war ready for war; and whether at Sebastopol, or at the extremities of the empire in the East, professional talent and command were found combined ... The enemy has taught us a lesson; I trust that professional bigotry will allow us to benefit by it!'[50] The other reason was Russia's subsequently frequent military manoeuvres and substantial colonial expansion around the Amur, as well as America's active participation, which made Europeans, especially Britain, very nervous, for they feared that Russia's expansion towards Manchuria via the Amur would deprive the British superpower in Peking. On 14 December 1857, the *Morning Chronicle* reprinted a short message from the *North Herald,* confirming that Russia had already assembled a large Army, based on news from China received on 17 October. Putyatin submitted a demand to the Chinese Emperor claiming credit for Russia's involvement. As a consequence, China should be willing to cede the two provinces Jilin and Heilongjiang to Russia, and possibly also give up Shengjing. Russia would in this way link its seashore provinces, because Jilin province shared its western boundaries with Russia and its eastern border was Tartary Bay. The report was accurate and Britain should have paid much more attention to it. However, it was rumoured that China had already refused Russia's demands. Many foreign ships, mainly American, engaged in trade between the west coast of America and the Amur River, but it is still a mystery why English soldiers had not been sent to the region to prevent annexations from Russia.[51]

The report indicates that the British public was very concerned about the business in the Amur valley, and was worried about Britain's tardy actions in north-east Asia, which put great pressure on Britain's government for their ignorance.

However, Britain's secret exploration had started before the public's censure, when the nation realized that it needed to learn lessons from the Crimean War. The British took the Amur and its peripheral waters in north-east Asia as a site to develop their military, topographical and nautical studies due to the area's diversified topography and currents, as a means to train their navy and impede Russia's impetuous expansion. In March

1855, Bernard Whittingham, the Royal engineering commander in Hong Kong, heard the news that Britain's fleet meant to make an expedition to the north-east Asian sea. He eagerly applied to go with the fleet, but was refused on the grounds that he lacked 'any experience in attacking oriental ports of Russia'. But soon afterwards, Whittingham was nominated by General Elliot to be his companion, so his desire was fulfilled. The fleet's main aim was 'to discover Russia's expanding situation in the Northeast, [and] make sure whether the news that Russia's invasion into Chinese northern border and Japan Sea is accurate or not'.[52] The fleet, consisting of one frigate and two corvettes, set off from Hong Kong on 7 April and took six months to complete its survey of the Sea of Japan, Tartary Bay, the Okhotsk Sea, Japan itself, Sakhalin Island and Ayan, where Russian forces garrisoned, especially in Die Castries Bay. Obviously, the fleet mainly focused on searching for Russian fleets and collecting geographical information about north-east Asia, where the British had less knowledge than Russia. Whittingham recorded the circumstances and customs of the places they passed through and edited them into a book, *Notes on the Late Expedition, against the Russian Settlements in Eastern Siberia*. *The Spectator* highly praised the book: 'his interviews with the Japanese authorities, his account of the strolls in the neighbourhood of the port of Hakodadi, his visits to the savage aborigines of Saghalin, and the cruises about the neighbouring waters, veiled for the most part by frequent fogs, caused by the temperature of the water being lower than that of the air, remind one of the older navigators, both in the freshness of the matter and the absence of all artificial attempts at doing more than present that matter clearly.'[53] It continues: 'This volume will not supply what, in spite of the multiplicity of books, is still a desideratum – [a] judicious and critical account of the events connected with the campaign in the Crimean and the assault on Sebastopol, by a competent observer. It is superior to some of the works that have already appeared descriptive of camp life and military events.'[54] Soon afterwards, in June 1856, the British navy sent J. M. Tronson and others to make a detailed survey of the waters of north-east Asia. Tronson recorded in detail the route of the fleet, as well as details about geomorphology, local specialties, towns and much other geographical information; above all, he accurately located Sakhalin, the estuary of the Amur River, and then drew accurate maps of the waters therein.[55]

Compared to the military surveys of Whittingham and Tronson, the exploration carried out by Thomas Witlam Atkinson (a member of the Royal Geographical Society, RGS) seems full of artistry and professionalism. Atkinson was a well-known and talented architect in London. In 1842, he left Britain for Germany to rebuild St Nicholas's Church in Hamburg, and was even welcomed as a guest of the Kaiser. It was this chance that led Atkinson to begin travelling around the world and launched his 'Artist's Journey in Siberia' in 1846. The tsar awarded him the privilege of visiting Russia's territories in Asia. Therefore, he spent seven years traversing southern Siberia, the Kyrgyz Plateau and other places in mid- and north-east Asia, and accumulated ample experience and capabilities in geographical exploration. In 1853, the conflicts in the north-east Asian sea and Russia's expansion towards that area enticed Atkinson to explore the Amur Valley via Mongolia and Russia, from where he started to pursue the source of Kerulen River, then following it down its length. He recorded the plants, water courses, animals, birds, inhabitants and so on, as well as details about trade, which provided the precious data for his two valuable works, *Oriental and Western Siberia* (1858) and *Travels in the Regions of the Upper and Lower Amoor and the Russian Acquisitions on the Confines of India and China* (1860). Generally speaking, in addition to their geographical contributions, the motivation of Atkinson's two works was to provide strategic information for Britain's government, as his words in the preface of the latter work indicate:

> Russian territory has now very nearly approached the possessions of Great Britain in India. To him, the contingency may seem inevitable, of a further stride across the Himalayas to Caltutta; but, even if such intention were entertained, of which there is no proof, ample employment for many years to come will be found for the present enlightened ruler of this colossal empire in the development of the resources of Russia on the vast steppes of Central Asia, in the region of the Amoor, and on the island of Karapta or Saghalien, with its commodious harbors and extensive coalfields, and in the establishment throughout these regions of that civil and military system which will bring it in perfect harmony with Russia on the Dwina, Don, Oural, and Volga.[56]

The abundant and detailed information about the unknown north-east Asia provided by Atkinson provoked dramatic reactions in Westerners. Britain's media noted that Atkinson's work provided an unprecedentedly splendid picture of lesser-known areas of the world.[57] 'Atkinson is the first European who explored Siberia and the Amur River.'[58] In 1858, at the annual conference of the Royal Geographical Society, the society's president highly praised Atkinson's latter book, calling it the most valuable contribution to the understanding of the situation and history of the Amur River and East Empire (China), 'for Russia, after occupied the Amur, his navy could be released from the continent detainment between Baltic and Black sea, and dominated China and Japan, made these areas become more and more integrated step by step'.[59] According to the *North American Review*, Atkinson was instrumental in reporting from Asia.[60]

The honour gained by these pioneers in their explorations and Russia's further expansions in north-east Asia incited more Englishmen to travel to the Amur River. In 1859, Arthur Adams, a naturalist and also a member of the RGS, followed the British fleet to north-east Asia. He sailed in the *Action*, with some military officials – Messrs Kerr, Blackney, Farmer, Bedwell, Lieutenant Bullock, Mr Ellis and others. Before setting off, they managed to obtain a new map of the frontiers of China's seas, drawn by Major W. S. Sherwell, the Vice-Deputy of British India, which roughly marked the approximate positions of each province from Canton to the Bohai Gulf, including some important cities, such as Canton, Shanghai and Peking. The most valuable parts of the map are some statistical lists and reviews; its scale is one inch per twenty-four miles, and it was drawn in 1859 in Calcutta.[61] On the map, the spacious waters and wide territories of North China were marked very ambiguously, which indicates Britain's very limited knowledge of Manchuria. Adams's aim was to offset this weakness, 'to spy out the situation on Russian's occupation in Manchuria, and survey the coastal geography of Northeast Asia'.[62] The fleet went via San Sebastian, the Cape of Good Hope, and then to the East Door, Java; it thereafter passed the Dongsha Islands to Hong Kong and Macao, and sailed upstream of the Yangtze River to the Bohai Gulf (Chili Bay), then traversing the Great Wall, Korea, Victoria Bay (Dalien), and entering into Russian Manchuria (Ussuri and Amur), where the fleet surveyed Russian garrisons and other geographical information. Adams especially collected abundant samples of tobacco, millet, rice and other plants, in addition to all kinds of poultry, fish and animals, which deeply struck him: 'if Russia who had not turned his greedy eyes on Manchuria, we would have never known this fertile land where stored so much ample gold mine, coal and cotton.'[63] Adams completed a diary, *Travels of a Naturalist in Japan and Manchuria*. Given its involvement with military secrets, the book was not published until 1870. Though it seemed a little outdated, Adams's work was still highly recommended in Britain: 'the shrewd and talent traveler provided us totally new and valuable information in Hydrology, topography, meteorology and biology. Our sciolistic knowledge on Manchuria by pirates from disintegrated China was renovated totally.'[64]

During this period, other members of the British military, such as Henry Arthur Tilley and J. W. King, also travelled to the Amur River to gain further intelligence. Tilley's group took a Russian cruiser, *Rynda*, and shuttled back and forth in the Sea of Japan, the Amur River and the north Pacific. Afterwards, Tilley wrote a book based on his survey, *Japan, the Amoor, and the Pacific, with Notices of Other Places, Comprised in a Voyage of Circumnavigation in the Imperial Russian Corvette 'Rynda', in 1858–1860* (1861). Meanwhile, King explored the Sea of Japan, Tartary Bay and the Amur Valley, and then wrote *The China Pilot: Comprising the Coasts of China, Korea, and Manchuria; the Sea of Japan, Gulf of Tartary and Amur, and*

Sea of Okhotsk, which was more popular and was republished three times in a year.

In addition to military missions' investigations, the RGS – the representative body of Western scholars – especially emphasized the use of Russian documents to strengthen the surveillance of Russia's action and studies on the Amur watershed. On 13 December 1858, at the annual conference of the RGS, its president read in translation an article by the Russian adventurers Peschurof and Permikin, *Notes on the Amur River and Its Surroundings*, which included a map of the Amur watershed with detailed records of where Peschurof's party explored, with intelligence on towns, trade, mines, hydrology, biology, topography and geomorphology, and so on.[65] E. G. Ravenstein, a British man of German origin and a member of the RGS who served in the Topography Department of the British War Office for twenty years, was an expert in the drawing and compilation of military maps. Based on his extensive experience, he published a very instructive work, *Russians on Amur, its Discovery, Conquest, and Colonisation*, which collected most of the explorations (and their achievements) of the Amur River and north-east Asia generally since the seventeenth century; the work also recorded the detailed history of Sino-Russian boundaries and provided the most valuable reference for later explorers. Ravenstein adopted the geographical naming system recommended by the RGS to annotate Russian maps, and marked the routes and achievements of Russians who explored the upper and lower Amur River and its waterfront cities, such as Blagoveshchensk, Heihe and Aihun, as well as the Bureya River and Bureya mountains.[66] What Ravenstein did won him the Victoria Medal, awarded by the RGS; he was the first to attain this special prize. Regarding Russian manoeuvres in north-east Asia, Ravenstein suggested:

> the progress of Russia in Asia, her rapid strides in the direction of India, and the acquisition from China of provinces far exceeding the British Islands in extent, cannot fail of being important to a nation with such vast interests at stake in China and the East as England has. In presenting therefore a work on Russian advance on the Amur, within the confines of the Celestial Empire, we feel that we are laying before the public a subject well worthy of their attention. It has been our endeavor to convey a correct idea of the past and present condition of the countries we treat of, their productions, inhabitants, and germs of future development, information of value not only to the geographer, politician, or merchant, but also attractive to that daily-increasing portion of the public who find a pleasure in studying the state and prospects of distant countries.[67]

Obviously, Ravenstein's suggestion was also that of the above-mentioned British explorers. Their counter-reconnaissance and academic exploration around the Amur River was in fact a potential form of defence against Russia's expansion towards Manchuria via the Amur, where it would be bound to threaten Britain's sphere of interests in South China and India; it was thus necessary for Britain to adopt such explorations as a prerequisite to formulating effective defence policies. However, this exploration, tangled with geopolitics and academic pursuits, also brought some side effects, such as Russophobia, which became more and more widespread in England as the explorations proceeded, laying the foundations of the long-lasting 'Great Game' between Britain and Russia from the end of the nineteenth century to the beginning of the twentieth, and demonstrated the new Anglo-Russian intelligence race in many areas.

Conclusion

Russia's activities aimed at relations with America or expansion towards the Amur River were all founded on a good understanding of its own geopolitical environment, evidently based on its early academic surveys. In comparison, Westerners' corresponding explorations, under the leadership of Englishmen and Americans, seemed somewhat reactive, for their actions were only a symmetrical geopolitical strategy of defence, or a precursor to commercial activity; they were, however, acts of active competition. On the other hand, because almost all Western explorers had political or military backgrounds, the explorations, which involved great academic achievements, vividly illustrated the close connections between geopolitics and scientific explorations around the Amur River, which was pushed by those explorers into global focus and deeply influenced the geopolitical situation in north-east Asia and the economic development of the world.

Firstly, the Westerners' explorations retarded Russia's expansion towards the Pacific via the Amur, affecting the political balance of the Far East at this time. Though American exploration around the Amur was mainly oriented to trade, while Britain's was focused on strategic defence against Russia, both nations objectively demonstrated their naval powers, which naturally caused Russia to hesitate. From another perspective, Britain and America's participation in business around the Amur increased the openness of Japan and Manchuria. In 1854, Major General Matthew Calbraith Perry compelled Japan to open two ports for trading with America after hard negotiations. Britain heard this news and immediately followed suit. On 7 September 1854, Commodore James Sterling led a fleet of four warships from the Yangtze River to Japan to negotiate for trade. On 15 October, Sterling signed the Anglo-Japan Agreement,[68] whose main contents stipulated that the British navy was not allowed to enter Nagasaki and other inner Japanese ports, nor to navigate the outer islands and their surroundings, on the condition that other British ships (not designed for war) could utilize and trade in Japan's ports. Nor would British warships be allowed to engage in battle with other countries near Japan's coastal waters. As a consequence, Russian ambassador E. V. Putyatin travelled to Japan to ask for equal treatment, and signed the Russo-Japan Agreement, whose content was almost the same as that of the agreements with Britain and America, which led to parity in the Sea of Japan. Obviously, the opening up of parts of north-east Asia had a far-reaching influence on the British defence system in the region, as British authorities predicted: 'Russia has already taken enough advantages in the coast of Manchuria, Liaodong is doomed to be their preys sooner or later.'[69] Britain's continuous exploration around the Amur River was keeping pace with the Russians' expansions there, and this was also a kind of antagonism against Russia. Meanwhile, Britain tried to develop relations with Japan and America in order to restrain Russia. Thereafter, on the basis of explorations, Britain's navy garrisioned Dairen during the Second Opium War, then opened Port Newchuang, and later occupied Hamilton Island.[70] Obviously, all the Western explorations and British defence strategies effectively decreased the pace of Russia's expansion towards the Pacific via the Amur.

Secondly, the explorations complemented Westerners' geographical knowledge, rectified their misunderstandings of the Amur River and promoted the internationalization of north-east Asian geography. On the whole, most Westerners' explorations on the Amur River belong to the natural geographical adventures of modern times, which contributed much to the common-sense geographical knowledge system in Western countries. These explorations (1) rectified misconceptions regarding the Amur River's source. Previously, European academics widely believed the Onon River to be the source of the Amur River. It was Atkinson who argued that the Kerulun River was its real source[71] and proved this proposition with data from his exploration: 'the watershed of the Kerulun River and Erguna River is more than 1,000 miles, while the watershed of Onon River and Silka River is less than 750 miles.'[72] The explorations (2) overturned the widely accepted argument that Sakhalin Island was a peninsula linked to the mainland downstream of the Amur River in Tartary Bay. In May 1856, Tronson verified that Sakhalin Island was a true island after navigating around it, and oriented it accurately: N54° 24'-45° 54', E141° 40'-44°46', six hundred miles in circumference and more than twenty miles wide at the widest point.[73] This data is quite accurate even by modern standards, which indicates that British explorers' mapping abilities were very advanced. The explorations (3) provided abundant geographical data on the Amur River, broadened Westerners' knowledge and enriched their database of relevant geographical information. They completed the mapping of the Amur River, collected multiple biological samples and gathered various data on geomorphology, hydrology and geology. As a result, the Amur River came to be seen more and more as remarkable in the Western world, and it was evaluated as 'the most valuable river in North Asia, also is the shortest way to link the plateau in Middle Asia and every part in the world, its watershed is between N43°-55°,E110°-141°, which took away all the waters in the desert, and feeds several navigable rivers, made its flow path nearly 2,280 miles to Sakhalin Island.'[74]

Thirdly, the explorations by Westerners promoted economic globalization, which spurred Americans and Russians to conceive the continental railways and the Trans-Siberian Railway, accelerating the process of global integration. Undoubtedly, the Amur River, with its vast watershed, rich natural sources and strategic location, motivated the adventurers' great conceptions of regional development in north-east Asia. Though the ideas of Collins et al. seemed rather fantastic at that time, they did positively influence the grand development plans of Russia and America. For Russia, Collins's argument for the construction of a railway and telegraph lines provided the earliest blueprints for the Trans-Siberian Railway and guided Russia's expansion in trade and adventuring into Eurasia and America. Based on this, the American Western Allied Telegraph Company established a branch company to set up the 'Collins' Continental Telegraph Line' in 1864. In 1865–67, the Russia America Company and the Canada Company completed the hardest part of the Collins Line, opening direct electronic communication between Europe and America, which promoted harmonious relations between America, Canada and Russia. As for America, the concept of intercontinental railway construction also originated from Collins's idea, which promoted the even distribution and effective circulation of resources between the West and the East, and strengthened communications both in economics and culture among different areas. Later on, Collins's conception was also instrumental in forming continentalism, which turned America towards global expansion, leading it to extend towards the western Pacific and even to purchase Alaska from Russia in 1867.[75]

Zhao Xin is Professor in the College of History, Culture and Tourism at Guangxi Normal University and the academic leader of Historical Geography in the same department. She has published more than forty articles on historical geography in modern China, the history of Chinese border relationships with foreign countries in the late Qing period, environmental history, British sinology and other topics.

Notes

1. In China, it is called 'Black Dragon River', or Heilongjiang 黑龍江 in Tuotuo, *Liao History*. Around the thirteenth century, Westerners called it the 'Amur River', which originates from Russian 'Амурская', which in turn originates from Ewenki-language 'Amar', meaning 'great river'. Povoroznyuk, 'The Toponym's Changes and Its Influences'.
2. The upstream of the Argun River, called the Kerulun River.
3. This was a Chinese town called Boli before the Russians' occupation.
4. The original text of the Treaty of Aigun was only in Manchu, Russian and Mongolian; it was translated into Chinese later on. Wang, *The Collection of Sino-Foreign Treaties*, vol. 1, 85–86.
5. In 1584, its first international port, Arkhangelsk near the White Sea, was established, which played an important role in trading with the Dutch and British, but within a very short navigating period each year.
6. Okun, *Russia-America Company*, 4.
7. Ibid., 14.
8. Barsukov, *Muraviev*, vol. 2, 103; Gough, 'The Crimean War in the Pacific', 130–36.
9. 'The Latest Acquisition of Russia, the River Amoor', *Fraser's Magazine*, January 1855.
10. Marx, *Naval, Military, Diplomatic Operations*, 8.
11. Stephan, 'The Crimean War in the Far East', 257–77.
12. Die Castries Bay is located at the estuary of the Amur River, the Tartary Straits, close to Malinsk.
13. Marx, *Naval, Military, Diplomatic Operations*, 8.
14. Stephan, 'The Crimean War in the Far East', 257–77.
15. Gough, 'The Crimean War in the Pacific', 130–36. While Muraviev said that the Russian navy smashed the allies here, and even set up a monument to this battle in front of the square of Petropavlovsk, Russian documents have no detailed records on this incident.
16. Barsukov, *Muraviev*, vol. 2, 45.
17. Ibid., 46.
18. 'The Russians on the Amur', *The Morning Post*, 26 November 1861.
19. Peschurof et al., 'Notes on the River Amúr and the Adjacent Districts'.
20. From 1851 to 1864, China suffered a very serious civil war, the Taiping Rebellion, and the rebels even established their own regime, the Taiping Heavenly Kingdom. This war involved almost all the troops of the Qing government, so the soldiers garrisoned at the north-east boundaries were very few.
21. See Bassin, *Imperial Visions*, 9–18.
22. Ravenstein, *The Russians on the Amur*, 147. According to another letter, written by Muraviev to Putyatin, there were twenty-three thousand soldiers on the frontier of Siberia, Manchuria and Mongolia. Obviously, the Russian data seems more accurate, but a little conservative. To Earl Putiatin, 4 June 1857, No. 1, Zeya Post, Barsukov, *Muraviev*, vol. 2, 152.
23. Gamsa, 'California on the Amur', 236–66.
24. Ravenstein, *The Russians on the Amur*, 157.
25. See Vinkovetskiy, *Russian America*.
26. Kerner, 'Russian Expansion to America', 25.
27. Untelberg: *Coastal Province (1856–1898)*, 17.
28. 'Original Letters in the National Archives', 137–45.
29. Ibid.
30. Ibid.
31. Barsukov. *Muraviev*, vol. 2, 145.

32. Habersham, *My Last Cruise*, 13.
33. Ibid., 13.
34. Ibid., 491.
35. Ibid., 495.
36. Ibid.
37. Collins, *Voyage down the Amoor*, 'Preface'.
38. Ibid.
39. Ibid., 221.
40. Ibid.
41. Ibid., 54.
42. Collins, Extract from Notes, 28 Feb 1857. Congress, 1st session, House Ex. Doc. 98, 63.
43. Collins to Korskoff, 9 March 1857, Congress, 1st session, House Ex. Doc. 98, 382.
44. The telegraph line was designed starting from a point in western America or Canada, travelling via British Colombia, then to Alaska, through the Bering Sea to Siberia, then crossing the Amur River via Irkutsk to the whole of Europe.
45. Collins to Mouravief, 4 April 1857, Congress, 1st session, House Ex. Doc. 98, 388.
46. According to JSTOR.
47. Naske, 'Review', 35.
48. James Buchanan to Emperor Alexander II of Russia, 6158489, National Archives of America.
49. Ravenstein, *The Russians on the Amur*, 139.
50. 'Whittingham's Notes on the Late Expedition to Japan and Eastern Siberia', 137.
51. 'China', *The Morning Chronicle*, 14 December 1857.
52. Whittingham, *Notes on the Late Expedition*, 2.
53. 'Whittingham's Notes on the Late Expedition to Japan and Eastern Siberia', 1440.
54. Ibid.
55. Tronson, *Personal Narrative of a Voyage to Japan*, 144.
56. Atkinson, 'Travels in the Regions of the Upper and Lower Amoor', 2.
57. 'Aktinson's Amoor and Central Asia', *The Spectator*, 25 August 1860.
58. No. 545, BIOGRAPHICAL OR HISTORICAL DATA, Thomas Witlam Atkinson Collection (Record no. 232529), SSC/143, Royle Library. RGS.
59. *The Edinburgh Review* 228 (October 1860), 315; no. 545, BIOGRAPHICAL OR HISTORICAL DATA, Thomas Witlam Atkinson Collection (Record no. 232529), SSC/143, Royle Library. RGS.
60. Atkinson, 'Travels in the Regions of the Upper and Lower Amoor', 586.
61. Adams, *Travels of a Naturalist in Japan and Manchuria*, 167.
62. Ibid., 168.
63. Ibid., 167.
64. The Earl de Grey and Ripon, 'Address to the Royal Geographical Society of London'.
65. Peschurof et al., 'Notes on the River Amúr and the Adjacent Districts'.
66. Ravenstein, *Russians on Amur*, 226.
67. Ibid., 'Preface'.
68. Ad. 1-5629, no. 71, Stirling to Adm., 26 October 1854. This letter is printed in part in P R, 1856, LXI, no. 2014; Ad. 1-5657, Stirling to Sir James Graham, 27 October 1854.
69. Ravenstein, *Russians on Amur*, 154.
70. Swinhoe, *Narrative of the North China Campaign of 1860*, 14.
71. Atkinson, 'Travels in the Regions of the Upper and Lower Amoor', 333.
72. Ibid.

73. Tronson, *Personal Narrative of a Voyage to Japan*, 144.
74. Peschurof et al., 'Notes on the River Amúr and the Adjacent Districts', 376.
75. Vevier, 'The Collins Overland Line and American Continentalism', 237–53.

Bibliography

Adams, Arthur. *Travels of a Naturalist in Japan and Manchuria*. London: Hurst and Blackett, 1870.
Atkinson, Thomas Witlam. *Travels in the Regions of the Upper and Lower Amoor and the Russian Acquisitions on the Confines of India and* China. New York: Harper, 1861.
Bassin, Mark. *Imperial Visions: Nationalist Imagination and Geographical Expansion in the Russian Far East, 1840–1865*. Cambridge: Cambridge University Press, 1999.
Barsukov, Ivan Platonovich. *Muraviev, Earl Amursky*, vol. 2, trans. Foreign Language Department, Heilongjiang University and Philosophy and Sociology Institute in Heilongjiang Province, Peiking: Commercial Press, 1974.
Brougham Loch, Henry. *Personal Narrative of Occurrences During Lord Elgin's Second Embassy to China in 1860*. London, 1900.
Collins, Perry. 'Explorations of the Amoor River'. *Perry Md Harper's New Monthly Magazine*, 1 June 1858.
Collins, Perry. Extract from Notes, 28 February 1857. Congress, 1st session, House Ex.Doc.98, Charles Vevier, 'The Collins Overland Line and American Continentalism', *Pacific Historical Review*; 1 August1959; 28(3), 237–53.
Dvoichenko-Markov, Eufrosina. 'Americans in the Crimean War', *Russian Review* 13(2) (1954).
Fleming, George. *Travel on Horseback in Manchu Tartary: And a Summer's Ride Beyond the Great Wall of China*. London, 1863.
Gamsa, Mark. 'California on the Amur, or the "Zheltuga Republic" in Manchuria (1883–86)'. *The Slavonic and East European Review* 81(2) (2003), 236–66.
Gough, Barry M. 'The Crimean War in the Pacific: British Strategy and Naval Operations'. *Military Affairs* 37(4) (1973), 130–36.
Hall, Philip B. 'Robert Swinhoe (1836–1877), FRS, FZS, FRGS: A Victorian Naturalist in Treaty Port China'. *The Geographical Journal* 153(1) (1987), 37–47.
Habersham, Alexander Wylly. *My Last Cruise, Or, Where We Went and What We Saw: Visits to the Malay and Loo-Choo Islands, the Coasts of China, Formosa, Japan, Kamtschatka, Siberia, and the Mouth of the Amoor River*. Philadelphia: J.B. Lippincott & Co., 1857.
Kerner, Robert. 'Russian Expansion to America: Its Bibliographical Foundations'. *The Papers of the Bibliographical Society of America* 1 (1931), 25.
Lansdell, Henry. *Through Siberia*. London, 1882.
Lloyd, W. V. 'Notes on the Russian Harbours of Possiette, Wladivostock, Nakhodka, and Olga Bay, on the Coast of Manchuria'. *Proceedings of the Royal Geographical Society of London* 11(6) (1866–67), 253–55.
Marx, Francis. *Naval, Military, Diplomatic Operations from 1855 to 1861*. London: Robert Hardwicke, 1861.
Collins, Perry McDonough. *Voyage Down the Amoor: With a Land Journey through Siberia, and Incidental Notices of Manchooria, Kamschatka, and Japan*. New York, 1860.
Michie, A. 'Narrative of a Journey from Tientsin to Moukden in Manchuria in July, 1861'. *Journal of the Royal Geographical Society of London* 33 (1863), 153–66.
Naske, Claus-M. 'Review: Continental Dash: The Russian-American Telegraph by Rosemary Neering'. *The Pacific Northwest Quarterly* 81(1) (1990), 35.

Okon, C. B. *Russia and America Company*. Cambridge, MA: Harvard University Press, 1951.

Peschurof, M. M. et al. 'Notes on the River Amúr and the Adjacent Districts'. *Journal of the Royal Geographical Society of London* 28 (1858), 376–446.

Povoroznyuk, Olga. 'The Toponym's Changes and Its Influences of Amur River', Proceedings of Manchurian Traffic System and Social Vicissitudes since 19th Century, September, 2013.Unpublished paper, in the possession of the editor.

Ravenstein, Ernest George. *The Russians on the Amur, its Discovery, Conquest, and Colonisation*. London, 1861.

Reardon Anderson, James. *Reluctant Pioneers: China's Expansion Northward, 1644–1937*. Stanford, CA: Stanford University Press, 2005.

Stephan, John J. 'The Crimean War in the Far East'. *Modern Asian Studies* 3(3) (1969), 257–77.

Swinhoe, Robert. *Narrative of the North China Campaign of 1860*. London, 1861.

The Earl de Grey and Ripon. 'Address to the Royal Geographical Society of London'. *Proceedings of the Royal Geographical Society of London* 4(4) (1859–60), 117–209.

Tronson, J. M. *Personal Narrative of a Voyage to Japan, Kamtschatka, Siberia, Tartary, and Various Parts of Coast of China in H.M.S. Barracouta*. London, 1859.

Vevier, Charles. 'The Collins Overland Line and American Continentalism'. *Pacific Historical Review* 28(3) (1959), 237–53.

Vinkovetskiy, Ilya. *Russian America: An Overseas Colony of a Continental Empire, 1804–1867*. Oxford: Oxford University Press, 2011.

Wang, Tieya. *The Collection of Sino-Foreign Treaties*, Vol. 1. Peking: Sanlian Bookstore, 1957.

Whittingham, Bernard. *Notes on the Late Expedition, against the Russian Settlements in Eastern Siberia*. London, 1857.

Williamson, Alexander. 'Notes on Manchuria'. *Journal of the Royal Geographical Society of London* 39 (1869), 1–36.

Tuotuo. *Liao History*, Peking: Zhonghua Book Company, 1974.

Untelberg, P. Ch., *Coastal Province (1856–1898)*, trans. Department of Russian, Heilongjiang University, Peking: The Commercial Press, 1980.

CHAPTER 14

'Land of Bounty'

Constructing the Russian North as a National Treasure

Elena I. Campbell

In a recent comparative study of the nationalizing empires of Europe during the long nineteenth century, scholars have convincingly demonstrated the close entanglement of nation state and empire by discussing the nation-building projects that were conceived and implemented at the heart of these empires.[1] Among others, Alexei Miller has provided an insightful contribution to this collaborative study and introduced the Russian case by analysing the Russian nationalistic discourse of territoriality, which he has examined in relation to a range of borderlands in the empire's west, south and east, as well as in some areas beyond the empire's borders.[2] My chapter builds on this scholarship to explore the northern dimension of Russian nationalism during the late tsarist period.

Geographically, Russia is predominantly a northern country with a long coast along the Arctic Ocean. Russia's first imperial zone was established along the White Sea during the mediaeval period and subsequently was incorporated into the Muscovite state, which by the early eighteenth century had transformed into a vast and continuously expanding Eurasian empire with a new centre in Saint Petersburg (founded in 1703). Yet it was after Russia experienced a humiliating defeat in the Crimean War (1853–56) and embarked on a project of state-driven modernization that some educated Russians within and outside the government turned their attention to the northern part of European Russia (called the Russian North), which they began to see as a promising zone of national development and imperial ambition. As a result, the region was conceptualized as a national treasure trove of natural resources. This image served to promote a better incorporation of the North into the nationalizing and modernizing imperial core. The North was perceived as ancient and native, but neglected, Russian territory. Thus, the projects of integration of the North mainly focused on economic development through the creation of a modern transportation network and 'rational exploitation' of the region's supposedly abundant natural endowments. This development (or *ozhivlenie* – 'revitalization' – as contemporaries termed it) was a form of civilizing mission that aimed to develop a higher culture for the benefit of the entire Russian nation.

The Russian nationalistic discourse that developed during the late tsarist period regarding northern natural resources implied that they were integral to national territory, should be used to improve the lives of the Russian people and should be protected from the exploitation of foreigners as a necessary condition for achieving national sovereignty and prosperity. These ideas were related to the politics of industrialization, infrastructure development, colonization and border-making, all of which were expected to serve the national economy. The Russian nationalistic discourse about the North had an imperial dimension as well, since it advocated for expansion and claiming new territories for Russia. Although this discourse was appropriated by different regional and metropolitan actors, both state and non-state, and in some of its variations presented a challenge to the autocratic estate-based order, it did not seek equality and inclusion in imperial politics for all northerners, but rather worked to reconfigure existing imperial hierarchies along different lines.

Claiming and protecting natural resources were particularly acute problems in the distant and sparsely populated polar periphery of the Russian North, especially because it was also a maritime border region administratively included in Arkhangelsk province.[3] The Arctic Ocean, along with its seas and some of its islands, was seen by many Russians as an integral part of the borderland and a valuable reservoir of natural resources. The North's seeming vulnerability to economic penetration and even domination by other European countries (particularly neighbouring Norway) added urgency to the task of better integrating the region into the imperial core.

By investigating the interrelated discourses of nation, environment and development in the North, this chapter seeks to contribute to a better understanding of the northern dimension of Russia's imperial nation-building project, while also revealing the changing views of nature and the tsarist state.

Re-Envisioning the North

In the eleventh–thirteenth centuries, Eastern Slavs pursued their quest for furs to the northern edges of Eurasia and subjugated the coast of the White Sea and the banks of the rivers flowing into it, as well as its Indigenous peoples, to the republic of Novgorod, which traded the furs and other valuable northern commodities with European merchants.[4] Novgorodians also advanced to the east towards the Urals and extended their power in the north-west to the Kola Peninsula. The power of Novgorod in the North was challenged by the Rostov-Suzdal principality and later by Moscow, which at the end of the fifteenth century subjugated Novgorod and its northern possessions. The flow of new settlers to the North continued until the seventeenth century.[5] Orthodox monasteries became important religious, cultural and economic centres. Arkhangelsk (founded in 1584) developed as an important port through which Muscovy conducted trade with Western Europe and (from the end of the seventeenth century) as a centre for Russian shipbuilding. In the eighteenth century it became the administrative centre of the vast Arkhangelsk province.[6] Russia's imperial expansion to the Baltic Sea and Black Sea regions, the Caucasus, Central Asia and the Far East, a preoccupation with the 'Eastern Question', and the railway boom of the 1860s–70s, which did not affect Arkhangelsk province, changed the position and the role of this northern region within the expanding and modernizing empire. The North gradually lost its economic appeal and became marginalized in Russia's imperial plans. With the closure of the Arkhangelsk military port and the naval shipyard in 1862, the European North lost its strategic importance and significance for the Imperial Navy.[7] Similarly to Siberia, it served as a destination for exiles. Orthodox monasteries, especially the prominent Solovetskii Monastery, continued to draw pilgrims from different parts of Russia, yet for many educated Russians in the capitals, the North remained a 'distant' and 'unknown' periphery.

The immense distances and the absence of modern transportation infrastructure in the North presented a challenge for travellers. For example, Sergei Maksimov (1831–1901), a writer who in 1856 was sent to Arkhangelsk province by the Naval Ministry and later published a popular book about the North, described his trip from Saint Petersburg to Arkhangelsk as 'a week of torture'.[8] To travellers who ventured to the area, the region's cold climate and forbidding environment appeared very different from what some perceived as the more familiar and seemingly national landscape of central Russia, characterized by its forests of 'silvery birch trees, spread-out villages with white churches, and fields of yellowing wheat'.[9] Travellers and some locals who wrote for general readers described a 'wild Lapland covered by snow for most of the year', or 'cold Sahara', 'the empty and despondent tundra', 'miserable' and 'inhospitable' Novaya Zemlya and 'the dreadful Arctic Ocean'.[10] The white nights at first appeared strange and unpleasant for some visitors, while the acoustic surroundings were also foreboding, either filled with an oppressive silence or the crashing and monotonous roar of raging rivers.[11] These descriptions were further dramatized by artists who captured images of polar bears and icebergs, underscoring for the large, educated publics of Moscow and Saint Petersburg a vision of the North as an alien, snow-covered land of death and eternal darkness.[12] Although these depictions served different functions, together they conveyed a message that northern nature posed a serious challenge for human survival. Thus, even to some local administrators it was not surprising that Arkhangelsk province, while being the largest in European Russia, was the least populated. As one local official rhetorically asked: 'Who will venture into the jaws of the Pole?'[13]

The harshness of nature seemed to explain the poverty of the scarce local population (both Russian and non-Russian), who to some educated observers appeared to be dominated by their natural surroundings. The population of the vast Arkhangelsk province (the majority of whom were peasants), depending on the location, survived by combining multiple economic activities, including fishing, hunting, cattle breeding and reindeer herding, logging, salt production and trade, as well as migrating for seasonal work beyond the province. While the coastal North was unsuitable for farming, the peasants of the southern districts of Kholmogory and Shenkursk supplemented their income by engaging in husbandry and growing barley, rye and flax. Yet even during good harvest years, inhabitants of Arkhangelsk province relied on grain supply from the Vologda and Viatka regions. The situation worsened during the reoccurring crop failures when the region's population faced a hunger crisis. Although the Russian government provided loans to relieve the famine, the grain supply problem was a chronic issue and the repeated cases of famine in the Arkhangelsk region gave it a reputation as a 'cold and hungry' province.[14] While crop failures due to unfavourable climate conditions were not unusual in northern Russia, the living conditions of some local communities worsened during the Crimean War when the Anglo-French fleet attacked several northern coastal settlements and established a blockade of the White Sea, thus disrupting local fishing and trade.[15] The extreme need of the local lower classes (who were also the main taxpayers) was the subject of official concern, not only because of the sympathy of some officials and government paternalism, but also because it affected the fiscal needs of the state, which faced the persistent problem of collecting tax arrears.

It was, however, the famine in 1867–68, which occurred after the abolishment of serfdom in 1861, that made the material welfare of peasants a key element of Russian politics, and thus caused especially strong public and official reaction, while turning the central government's attention to the problem of popular welfare in the North. In 1868, the government sent an expedition headed by Nikolai Danilevskii (1822–85), an inspector of agriculture and fisheries at the Ministry of State Domains and a naturalist who would also soon become an influential pan-Slavic philosopher and publicist, to investigate the economic conditions and the food supply issue in the North. In his report, Danilevskii evaluated natural conditions in the Russian North as unfavourable overall. In his view, compared to other Russian provinces and neighbouring Norway, Arkhangelsk province had meagre natural resources that were thinly spread across the vast territory, making it difficult for the local population to use them. At the same time, Danilevskii argued that these natural obstacles did not have to lead to inevitable poverty. He did not see an overall decline in the northern economy and instead drew attention to other factors that, in his view, contributed to poverty, notably increases in taxes and the price of grain. He proposed to improve the northerners' living conditions by easing peasant access to timber resources and expanding agriculture through the use of slash-and-burn techniques in some state-owned forests. He also proposed relieving the tax burden, as well as connecting the Northern Dvina River at Kotlas with Viatka province via a railway to improve the delivery of grain to the North and the transportation of northern fish to new domestic markets.[16]

The North also drew the attention of public associations concerned with Russia's economic development, such as the Imperial Free Economic Society and the Society for the Advancement of Trade and Industry. In 1866, at a meeting of the Free Economic Society, Mikhail Sidorov (1823–87), a Siberian entrepreneur and Arkhangelsk native, presented a report that, according to one observer, 'broke the general indifference to the northern region. Everyone started talking about the North.'[17] In this report (published in *Russkii vestnik* by the influential editor Mikhail Katkov), as well as elsewhere, Sidorov sought to debunk the dominant perception of Russia's northern periphery as a cold, barren and hopeless land. He contrasted what he interpreted as the 'perpetual North's poverty' with the region's supposedly bountiful natural resources, including fur, minerals, fish, timber and oil, which had great potential to bring prosperity to the local population and Russia at large.[18] He called for the 'revitalization' of the North, so that northerners would no longer go south to find bread and work. Instead, the southerners would move north to acquire personal wealth.[19] Unlike Danilevskii, who thought that Russians (including northerners) were not seafaring people,[20] Sidorov believed in Russia's great potential to become a maritime power in the North. He also disagreed with Danilevskii's evaluation of northern natural resources and his proposal to expand agriculture by allowing peasants to clear the forests. Sidorov argued that forests should serve the needs of Russian shipbuilding. His vision of northern development focused on fishing, whaling, extraction of mineral resources, trade and shipbuilding, but not on farming.

Sidorov was not alone in his enthusiasm for the North, which was shared by other entrepreneurs, scientists, artists, writers and journalists (both local and from outside the region), as well as by multiple special government committees (in Saint Petersburg and Arkhangelsk) whose work focused on northern economic development. The Romanovs and high-ranking officials also took interest in the North. In 1858, Alexander II (r. 1855–81) visited Arkhangelsk. Later his sons, the grand dukes Aleksei (in 1870) and Vladimir (in 1885 and in 1899), toured the northern periphery. Sergei Witte, Minister of Finance from 1892 to 1903, and rear admiral Alexander Sidensner (1842–after 1917?) had a special interest in the ice-free Murman Coast (the northern coast of the Kola Peninsula), which they visited respectively in 1894 and 1896 when the government was expanding Russia's railroad network, and discussed plans for a new naval base.

While this attention to the North was fuelled by different motivations, the numerous resulting reports were characterized by a striking similarity – most of the texts shared the trope of a 'rational' exploitation of the region's supposedly abundant and untapped natural resources. For example, visitors told of 'huge herds of seals' near Novaya Zemlya, Arctic waters 'teeming with fish' and 'clouds of geese' in the Pechora region.[21] As one Russian traveller and writer summed up, the North was a 'land of bounty'. 'There is plenty of everything – just manage to get it – from the sea, from the air and from the land.'[22] The vision of the North as a reservoir of natural riches awaiting their exploitation was popularized at the 1896 All-Russian Fair of Industry and Art in Nizhnii Novgorod and the 1900 World Exposition in Paris, both of which aimed to demonstrate to the domestic and international audiences Russia's industrial and imperial power. Each exhibition had a special pavilion devoted to the Russian Far North that displayed monumental decorative panels designed by the famous Russian artist Konstantin Korovin (1861–1939) alongside the samples of northern natural riches.[23] The exhibits revealed a vision of Russia whose power was based not only on military might but also on industrial-commercial growth. The supposedly abundant natural riches of the Far North, as well as of other imperial borderlands, such as Siberia and Central Asia, were crucial for this project.[24]

To draw attention to the North, its promoters challenged the popular association of the region with severe cold and unbearable conditions. Some argued that the North was suitable for living and productive economic activities, while others claimed that the northern cold was healthy and developed an entrepreneurial spirit and strength in local Russians. Expanding knowledge about the climate (especially about the role of the Gulf Stream) and diverse geography of the region, as well as the notable periodic relatively warm northern winters, contributed to optimistic views of northern natural conditions.[25] Perhaps even more important was the belief in the power of humans, equipped with scientific knowledge and technology, to dominate natural factors, an idea that underlay optimistic Russian northern visions. Thus, the promoters of the North presented the Russian public and the government with a paradox: the richness in natural resources of a region alongside its scarce population that lived in poverty. The promoters saw the cause of human misery not in the harshness of northern nature, but in what they believed to be existing popular misconceptions about the North as a 'cold and barren land', as well as socio-economic, technological and political factors. The promoters blamed the government for 'forgetting' the North, which, in contrast to other Russian regions in the west and south, was left unaffected by the state's modernization programme and isolated from the imperial core. Some saw this situation as deeply unfair, pointing to the former economic importance of the North for old Muscovy, and especially to the contribution of northern shipbuilding and maritime traditions to the emergence of the new capital of Saint Petersburg and Russia as an imperial power during the reign of Peter the Great.[26]

Nationalistic ideas, which accompanied the modernization process in Russia, played an important role in the growing public and government attention to the North, as well as its reconceptualization in national terms. The burst of historical and ethnographic interest in popular culture in the second half of the nineteenth century, and especially the discovery of the living ancient Russian epic tradition in the North, as well as the growing appreciation for northern wooden architecture as a would-be 'truly Russian' style, contributed to the emergence of the vision of the North as a unique preserve of ancient Russian culture, a perspective that integrated the North into Great Russian culture. At the same time, some collectors of folklore and Russian antiquities in the North also drew attention to the miserable state of the northern Russian peasants, who in public discourse came to be viewed as the guardians of Old Russian culture, thus indicating that the improvement of their lot was a Russian national task.[27]

Ideas about the economic development of the North attracted some Moscow entrepreneurs who sought to develop national industry and decrease the influence of foreign capital in the Russian economy. One of them was Fedor Chizhov (1811–77), a prominent entrepreneur and financier who built the first private Russian railroad, created the Moscow Merchant Bank and Mutual Credit Society and was also a scholar, publicist and Slavophile. The Arkhangelsk–Murmansk steamship company, which he founded in 1875, and his plans for the construction of the northern railroad realized later by his companion Savva Mamontov (1841–1918) were the components of the ambitious patriotic-economic project of the 'revitalization' of the Russian North, rather than pure business ventures.[28] At the same time, the nationalistic image of the northern periphery as Russian land was employed to boost regional development. For example, the tourist guide that promoted travel to the Russian North and was published in 1898 by the Arkhangelsk–Murmansk company advertised the region as a 'treasure trove of Russianness', where one could find houses from the time of the Russian tsar Aleskei Mikhailovich, old Russian wooden churches and traditional Russian garments.[29] Alexander III (r. 1881–94) had a special 'attraction to the Russian North'.[30] Perhaps, his experience (when he was the heir to the throne) of chairing the Committee that provided aid to the northern peasants who suffered from the crop failure in 1867–68 played a role in creating this affection. But it was his nationalistically tinted course combined with Witte's programme of accelerated industrial development, as well as strategic interests, that gave an additional impulse to Russia's turn to the North.[31]

In 1894, more than twenty years after the famine crisis, another terrible disaster in the North occurred. Twenty-five Pomor fishing boats were wrecked in a storm, which again brought government and public attention to the issue of popular welfare in the region. Nationalistic sentiments fuelled a public campaign to help the Pomors (the people of the sea), northern fishermen who were considered 'pioneers of Russian nationality' in the North, 'dear to the heart of the monarch'.[32] A special private committee took the responsibility for managing donations for victims of the disaster and for improving the socio-economic conditions of the Pomor communities. The development of northern fisheries based on scientific knowledge about fishery resources was seen as crucial for this improvement.[33] In relation to these efforts, in 1898 the Murman Scientific Fisheries Expedition was organized with private and government support. Led by zoologist Nikolai Knipovich and then by biologist Leonid Breitfus (1902–8), the expedition conducted studies of northern hydrology and fishery resources.[34]

The images that emphasized the Russianness of the North downplayed the role of Indigenous minority groups.[35] For example, when planning the northern pavilion of the Russian state-sponsored section devoted to the imperial borderlands (which also included Central Asia, Siberia and the Caucasus) at the 1900 World Exposition in Paris, Alexander Engelhardt, the Arkhangelsk governor (1893–1901), who was an energetic promoter of the 'revitalization' of the North and who wrote a book that helped to popularize the concept of the 'Russian North', argued that the pavilion should emphasize the economic potential of the province by featuring its natural resources, including fish, animals, birds and timber, and omit an ethnographic section because for the most part the northern *inorodtsy* had already merged with Russians.[36] According to Engelhardt, the Indigenous minorities were not only destined to eventually assimilate with Russians, but also to share access to their lands and resources, especially in the tundra (the official property of the state, which traditionally claimed the role of protector of Nenets' rights), to anybody who could put them to productive use.[37]

Proponents of the northern 'revitalization' within and outside the government, and from within and outside the region, had different views on how to achieve the desired economic prosperity and better integrate the northern periphery into the imperial core. Many projects were subject to debate within government committees and among broader circles. At the beginning of the twentieth century, the idea to 'revitalize' the North was also appropriated by northern regionalists, represented mainly by local urban intelligentsia, entrepreneurs and tsarist bureaucrats who in 1908 organized the Arkhangelsk Society for the Study of the Russian North. Through their periodical and brochures, as well as public discussions, the Society's members advocated for northern development as a national task and propagandized the image of the North as a reservoir of untapped natural resources, believing that their intensified and rational exploitation would be beneficial for both the region and the entirety of Russia.

Russia's turn to the North involved and was further stimulated by several large infrastructure projects, including regular steamship services in the White and Barents Seas, expansion of telegraph lines to the Kola Peninsula and Pechora district, and the construction of two railroads that connected Arkhangelsk with Moscow via Vologda (in 1898) and the Northern Dvina River at Kotlas with Siberia (in 1899). During the First World War, when Russia lost free access to the Baltic and Black seas, the government in record time constructed and began operating the railroad that connected Petrograd to the new port of Romanov-on-Murman (Murmansk) in order to maintain communication with its allies and transport military cargo.[38]

It was also during the war that another special government conference on the North in Petrograd recognized the 'revitalization' of the northern borderland and the development of 'the Russian land for the Russian people' as a national task.³⁹ In 1916, Alexander Trepov, the Minister of Transportation (1915–16) and the chair of the special conference, proposed to create a Supreme State Committee on the North to oversee the development of the region during and after the war, when, as he expected, the bountiful resources of the North would help restore the Russian economy.⁴⁰ Given the deforestation in the western parts of the empire on the one hand, and the advantageous conditions of the European markets for timber on the other, Trepov placed great hopes in the exploitation of northern forests, which could satisfy domestic demands while also improving Russia's international trade balance. His vision of post-war development also included a large-scale exploitation of northern fishery resources, thus finally putting an end to what he saw as Russia's dependency on Norway.⁴¹ Trepov was not alone in his concerns about the competition with the northern neighbour. Indeed, the Norwegian factor (the comparisons with and anxieties about the perceived threat of economic domination by the neighbouring Norway) played an important role in the conceptualization of the northern borderland as Russian land and the growing support for its 'revitalization' among educated Russians within and outside the government during the late imperial period.

The Russian North versus the Norwegian North

Historians have characterized the relations between the large Russian empire and smaller Norway as 'asymmetrical'. The shared border in the North played a greater role for Norway. At the same time, in the second half of the nineteenth and the early twentieth century, a perceived asymmetry in economic development on both sides of the Russian–Norwegian border also contributed to growing concerns among educated Russians about Russia's power in the Far North and raised questions about how to better develop and incorporate the northern periphery into the imperial core.⁴²

It was Russian consul-general in Christiania (Oslo) Henrik Adolf Mechelin (1850–68), who was among the first to draw government attention to what he perceived as the rapid economic development of Norway's northern province, Finnmark.⁴³ Soon, Norway's example became a frequent reference point in government and public discussions of the Russian North's 'revitalization'. Russian officials and members of educated society who travelled to the Russian North often included Norway in their itineraries and compared the Russian and Norwegian northern territories. For example, Danilevskii focused on the comparison of fishing conditions and practices, Witte and Engelhardt paid special attention to the economic development of Norway's North, Mamontov was particularly interested in railroads in Sweden–Norway and Korovin painted both northern Russian and Norwegian landscapes. Many Russian observers noticed a striking contrast between what they perceived as the 'revitalized' Norwegian North and the 'forgotten' Russian North, especially regarding the part that bordered Norway. The visitors reported comfortable towns, high standards of living and education, developed transport infrastructure, telegraph lines, good governance and respect for civil and religious authorities in northern Norway, a picture that they contrasted with the 'emptiness, darkness and poverty' of the Murman Coast.[44] The observers also pointed out that while Norwegian fisheries grew and came to dominate the Russian market, Russian fish catches in the North declined. Some educated Russian observers came to perceive this contrast between smaller Norway and Russia as deeply upsetting and viewed the development of the Russian North as a matter of maintaining 'Russian dignity'.[45] As Dmitrii Bukharov, Russian consul in Finnmark (1881–85), recalled, 'Nowhere, other than on the Russian–Norwegian border near the church of St Boris and St Gleb, have I encountered such pain to our pride due to the differences between Russia and neighbouring Norway'.[46] At the same time, the striking improvements of the material conditions in northern Norway raised hopes for the possibilities of the economic 'revitalization' of the Russian North.

Some explained the differences in economic development by differences in climate, geography and market conditions. For example, Danilevskii argued that compared to the coast of Finnmark, the natural conditions of the Murman Coast were less favourable for large-scale fishing.[47] Others suggested that compared to Murman, where Russians were 'random' visitors, and even the entire Arkhangelsk province, which was a distant corner of a vast Russian empire, Norway's northern provinces occupied a relatively large part of the country, where 'Norwegians felt at home'.[48] Yet the majority either downplayed these differences or claimed that the natural conditions in northern Norway and Murman were similar; therefore, with the support of the government, Russia could emulate the economic 'revitalization' of northern Norway by borrowing its knowledge and technology.[49] This belief in similarities and the optimistic view of the potential of state-driven modernization affected the visions of 'revitalization' of the Russian North, which included the development of the transportation network, telegraph lines, colonization and technological borrowing. During the 1860s, the Russian government offered privileges to Norwegian colonists on the Murman Coast in the hope that they would introduce 'rational' economic activities and help 'revitalize' the Russian North,[50] while the local authorities encouraged

Pomors to build Norwegian-style fishing boats.[51] The construction of the new church of St Boris and St Gleb in the 1870s and especially the restoration of the Pechenga Monastery a decade later symbolized the Russianness of the empire's northern territory at the border with Norway.[52] With the help of Norwegian expertise, during 1896–99, the new port town of Aleksandrovsk was built.[53] Yet these and other projects that were implemented did not change the general perception that the Russian North was still lagging behind its more developed neighbour. For example, writer Georgii Severtsev-Polilov during his trip in 1913, was especially impressed by the town of Kirkenes in northern Norway, whose growth was fuelled by the development of industrial iron ore mining. He described this town as an 'example of cleanliness and order' and a 'true European town'.[54] At the beginning of the twentieth century, Admiral Sidensner concluded that despite some improvements, 'the entire Kola Peninsula with its Murman Coast was the same desert as Finnmark was a hundred years ago'.[55]

Norway's economic development not only provoked admiration, inspiration and envy among educated Russians interested in northern matters, it also raised anxieties about Russian sovereignty and power in the North. Norwegians appeared as competitors who also (as many in Russia came to see it) exploited Russian natural riches. Thus, the 'revitalization' of the North (especially of its polar periphery) was viewed as a strategy to claim this region and its supposedly abundant natural resources for Russia, and was important not only for economic, but also political reasons.

Protecting Russia's Northern Riches

Anti-foreign rhetoric accompanied Russia's turn to the North. Similar to the anxieties about the American and Japanese incursions into the Russian Far East,[56] patriotic-minded Russians became increasingly concerned about Norwegian, as well as British and German, penetration into the sparsely populated and isolated maritime periphery of the Russian North, a process that came to be perceived as 'a peaceful conquest'.[57] These fears were exacerbated at the beginning of the twentieth century, when Norwegians expanded their commercial fishing and hunting activities in the Arctic, while the development of a modern trawler fleet allowed the Germans and British to begin large-scale exploitation of northern fishing resources. Russian fishermen, merchants, captains, travellers and explorers who ventured to the Far North, as well as local officials, reported British trawlers near Murman and the Kanin Peninsula, as well as Norwegian fishermen and hunters in 'Russian waters' and at Russian Novaya Zemlya.[58] Russian newspapers in Moscow and Saint Petersburg publicized these reports and called for a stop to foreigners 'plundering' Russian natural riches.⁵⁹ The situation was escalated in 1910, when the Russian government learned that the Association of Shipmasters in Tromsø had publicly declared the northern part of Novaya Zemlya no-man's land.⁶⁰ The growing international interest and activity in Spitsbergen (Svalbard), which had the status of no-man's land, raised concerns among the Russian public and some government officials about what they perceived as Russia's 'loss' of Spitsbergen.⁶¹

The 1826 agreement on the Russian–Norwegian border became a subject of public criticism during the late imperial period.⁶² The critics viewed the border as 'unfair' and accused Valerian Galiamin (1794–1855), the Russian official representative at the border negotiations, of 'treason' for 'giving up ancient Russian territories ripe with natural riches'.⁶³ This criticism was a part of a broader nationalistic discourse that emphasized the need for the state to be the true guardian of Russia's national territory and its natural resources, an issue that seemed to be especially pressing in the distant and sparsely populated northern border region. These concerns were further aggravated by Russian–Norwegian negotiations during the last decade of tsarism surrounding the exploitation of the water power resources of the border river of Pasvik. The Norwegian iron ore company A/S Sydvaranger was especially active in seeking access to the 'white coal'. While some within the tsarist administration saw the Norwegian proposal to exploit the waterfalls as an opportunity for the state to profit from the 'wealth that has been wasted' and to 'revive' the 'desolate' area, some nationalistically minded Russians became agitated by what they saw as Norway's aspiration to seize Russia's Murman Coast and the Russian officials' supposed intentions to 'give up the last piece of Russian property on the Russian–Norwegian border'.⁶⁴ The decade-long bureaucratic discussion of the border waterfalls issue did not result in any implemented economic development projects, but it stimulated nationalistic sentiments and calls for including members of broader society (representatives of the State Duma and the inhabitants of the region) in the decision-making concerning national natural resources located on their territory.

The issue of defending the interests of northern Russian fishermen from competition with Norwegians had been on the government's agenda since the 1860s. In the late nineteenth - early twentieth century, a dedicated vessel was employed to patrol the northern Russian waters. Yet the boundaries of Russian territorial waters in the North in terms of fishing limits were not legally defined. The growing foreign fishing and hunting operations in the Arctic waters at the beginning of the twentieth century raised the need to legally establish and expand Russia's northern territorial waters beyond the three mile limit.⁶⁵ As the Arkhangelsk Governor Ivan Sosnovskii (1907–11) put it, the expansion and protection of Russian territorial waters from foreign exploitation was a matter of 'state dignity'.⁶⁶ While often seen by Russians as a rival, Norway, fearlessly defending its maritime domain and national economic interests, also served as an example to emulate.⁶⁷ The officials from the Chief Administration of Land Management and Agriculture, created in 1905 and led by Alexander Krivoshein (1908–15), and the State Duma's Commission on Fisheries had a broader perspective on this issue and connected the protection of northern Russian waters from foreign exploitation with the goal to regulate Russian fisheries, which played an important role in the economic life of Arkhangelsk province. This project was driven by economic considerations as well as the growing concerns about the extinction of some varieties of fish and marine animals, which resulted from what some experts came to see as 'irrational' and 'predatory' fishing and hunting practices. Thus, in the view of the Ministry's officials, the regulation of northern Russian fisheries required a greater involvement of the state in controlling the use of Russia's fishery resources by both foreigners and Russians.⁶⁸

At the same time, as many understood it, neither mere demarcation of the maritime boundaries nor policing alone could effectively protect Russia's interests in the Far North. The government saw colonization of the polar periphery as a possible solution to this problem. Yet the government's 1860s colonization policy of Murman, which relied on Norwegian and Finnish colonists, came under attack. In 1869, the commission on northern development called for a stop to further colonization of the Murman borderland by Norwegians, who, as the commission members saw it, unlike German colonists in the Volga region, maintained close relations with their motherland and subjugated the Russian Kola Peninsula to the economic interests of Norway.⁶⁹ Some critics pointed out that Norwegian colonists did not assimilate with Russians, while also harming the locals by selling them rum.⁷⁰ Others criticized the government for its inattention to Russian interests and emphasized the political role of the northern borderland, which had to be colonized by 'Russian elements'.⁷¹ This issue gained additional urgency in light of the growing colonization on the Norwegian side of the border. The government responded to these criticisms by forming in 1908 a special commission to discuss the 'strengthening of the Russian element' on Murman.⁷² This commission, among several other government initiatives, was undertaken under Minister of Interior and Prime Minister Peter Stolypin (1906–11), who used Russian nationalism to stabilize the country, which was shaken by the 1905 revolution, and consolidate the empire's various borderlands that were claimed as Russia's national territory. State-sponsored colonization was also employed to claim Novaya Zemlya and its natural riches for Russia. But if since the 1870s, the government had relied on Nenets families who were relocated to the archipelago, at the beginning of the twentieth century, the official course on 'strengthening the Russian element' in the borderlands resulted in the government's efforts to support a new Russian colony. This colony, originally consisting of four peasant families, was officially established in 1910 at the Krestovaya Bay. It was named after the grand duchess Olga Nikolaevna and was publicly presented as the 'triumph of the Russian state idea in the Far North'.[73]

While in the nineteenth century the Russian government generally viewed the local Pomor–Norwegian trade, in which Pomors exchanged grain and other goods for Norwegian fish, as an important source of well-being for the northern population,[74] increasingly, in addition to economic concerns,[75] some nationalistically minded Russians came to perceive this trade as an unpatriotic activity. Critics insisted on the need to tax Norwegian fish and strengthen Russian fisheries.[76] Thus, the intensified national use of northern natural resources, along with their protection from foreign exploitation, remained an acute problem during the last decade of tsarist rule.

Conclusion

The state and public discourse concerning the North as Russia's national treasure trove of natural riches reveals important changes in attitudes about nature and state and conceptions of the Russian imperial nation during the last decades of the tsarist era. The natural world took on new value and became increasingly commodified while also being subjected to national claims. Natural resources in the North came to be viewed by some educated Russians within and outside the government as potential engines of national economic development that could reduce poverty, solve the agrarian and financial crisis at the centre and in the northern periphery, and strengthen Russia so that it could compete with other imperial powers. This vision was related to a conceptualization of Russia's future that tied national sovereignty and imperial power not only to military might, but also to industrial growth. To achieve these goals, the nationalistically minded Russians argued that the country's northern natural resources had to be reserved for productive use by the nation. This vision implied the need for a stronger and more active state that would 'rationally' manage the national natural wealth and protect it from foreign exploitation.[77] In addition, 'rational' exploitation required better exploration and evaluation of northern natural riches, based not on anecdotal evidence, but scientific expertise. The tsarist state, which was the main owner of the land and natural resources in Arkhangelsk province, was increasingly criticized for a lack of effective management and even mismanagement of its property (especially of the northern forest resources),[78] while scientists and professional experts sought a greater role for themselves in the state schemes of northern development.[79] As a result, some progress was achieved in understanding fish distribution and the evaluation of northern water energy resources in the North, but the vast forests and mineral deposits remained largely unexplored during the tsarist period. It was during the First World War, when the tsarist government faced the urgent need to mobilize national industry by relying on domestic natural resources, that a special permanent commission was created at the Imperial Academy of Sciences that aimed to lead the 'systematic and comprehensive' exploration of Russia's 'natural productive forces'.[80] The survey of northern natural resources became an important part of the commission's ambitious plan. At the same time, as the example of the Murman Scientific Fisheries expedition demonstrated, the 'rational' development of natural resources privileged modern scientific knowledge over traditional practices of resource use, which were viewed as backward. However, as Julia Lajus has suggested, the scientific results of the expedition without the corresponding technological changes did not help the local fishermen, while the expedition was accused of facilitating the arrival of foreign trawlers who supposedly benefited from the publicized data on northern fishery resources.[81]

The geographic position of the northern periphery as a border region, and especially the nationalization and expansionism of neighbouring Norway and the growing perceived threat of its economic domination in the Arctic, stimulated the development of Russian nationalistic discourse surrounding the North and its natural resources. Yet protecting Russia's northern natural resources, especially in the remote parts of the region, was not an easy task for the tsarist government. The geographic and climatic conditions of the Russian North posed a far greater challenge than some enthusiasts of the North presented. The White Sea was frozen for a long period of time during the year, making it difficult for the Russian coastal population to compete with Norwegians, who followed warm sea corridors and could reach fishing and hunting grounds in the Arctic earlier. No less challenging was organizing and maintaining viable permanent Russian settlements on the Murman Coast and Novaya Zemlya. Unlike the fertile areas of Siberia or the Steppe region, the Russian North did not become a destination for mass Russian colonization, which was predominantly agricultural during the late imperial period.

The political considerations behind the official course on 'strengthening the Russian element' on the distant Kola Peninsula came into conflict with the goal of rapid economic development. Thus, because of the shortage of available Russian capital, the Ministry of Interior had to consider making an exemption in its legislative project that aimed to 'prevent further penetration of foreigners on Murman', by allowing foreigners to lease state land on Murman for the development of wood processing and mining industries at the discretion of the Arkhangelsk governor.[82] During the First World War, due to the problem of recruiting enough Russian workers, prisoners of war and Chinese labourers were employed for the construction of Murman railroad.[83] Some within the government also suggested that while Murman had to be settled by Russians, to alleviate the current shortage of labour, Chinese could also be recruited for the industrial development of the North.[84]

Because of the concern about the possible tensions between Russia and other foreign powers, particularly Britain, the tsarist government did not legally establish and expand Russian fishing zones in the North.[85] The organization of effective naval patrols of Russian waters at high latitudes was another serious challenge. In 1915, Aleksei Zhilinskii (1891–1962), a specialist on northern fisheries, stated that as a result, 'our fisheries are de facto not in our hands and northern coastal waters are not an inalienable property of Russia, but a field for foreign activities', thus indicating that the fishing limit question was also an issue of Russia's territorial integrity and that there was an urgent need for the state to consolidate its northern borderland and its resources.[86]

The project of incorporating the North into the conceptualization of a Russian imperial nation also raised the contentious question of who belonged to the nation in a multi-ethnic and estate-based autocratic state. The tsarist state appropriated the nationalistic discourse by claiming the North as a native Russian land and sought to better incorporate it into the imperial core, but its 'revitalization' projects emphasized the development of a modern transportation network and the potential for intensified resource extraction. At the same time, the peasants who constituted the majority of the population of the North remained outside the modernized imperial structures. One of the most important Great Reforms, the introduction of the institutions of self-government in rural areas (called *zemstvo*), was not extended to Arkhangelsk province. The tsarist officials who opposed the reform justified their position by the remoteness of Arkhangelsk province from the centre and the immense distances within the region, the absence of private landownership and the sparseness and economic and cultural backwardness of the local, predominantly peasant population.[87] Local educated elites used the image of the North as a treasure trove of resources and the nationalistic discourse to advance their region and their position in imperial politics. At the same time, they believed that institutions of self-government were crucial for the 'revitalization' of the North and for the 'rational' use of its natural resources.[88] At the beginning of the twentieth century, when the issue was discussed in the State Duma, the proponents of *zemstvo* in Arkhangelsk province argued for the reform as a way to equalize the inhabitants of the region with the populations of other Russian provinces that had been enjoying a system of self-government. Given the absence of noble landowners (the main element of *zemstvo* administration in Russia) in Arkhangelsk province, they proposed to modify the electoral system and thus challenged the estate-based imperial order.[89] The proponents of *zemstvo* did not anticipate universal suffrage for the northerners. Yet even their modest project met opposition within the highest government circles. As regionalists saw no progress on the *zemstvo* reform in Arkhangelsk province and other northern projects, they came to criticize the 'ruling bureaucracy' for treating the North as the 'stepchild of Russia'.

Finally, Russia's turn to the North included expansionist aspirations that were framed in nationalistic terms. In 1912, in response to the growing British, American and Norwegian mining activities in Spitsbergen and the attention of international diplomacy to the judicial status of the archipelago, the tsarist government sent to Spitsbergen an expedition headed by geologist and ambitious Arctic explorer Vladimir Rusanov (1875–1913) to survey coal-bearing areas and claim Russian interests.[90] After completing the official task, Rusanov pursued his personal mission to explore the Northern Sea Route, but his boat vanished in the icy Arctic waters. Under nationalistic pressure, Russia also became involved in the international race for the North Pole.[91] The deputies of the Duma asked for the government's financial support for the Russian expedition to the Pole, which, they argued, would serve national goals and the universal interests of mankind.[92] Denied government funding, Lieutenant Georgii Sedov (1877–1914) took up the mission to claim the North Pole for Russia and raised private donations with the help of nationalistic newspaper *Novoe Vremia* and the Arkhangelsk Society for the Study of the Russian North, which appealed to the 'national honour and the dignity of the great power'.[93] Sedov's 1912 expedition to the North Pole ended in failure. The same tragic fate befell another ambitious private effort by Lieutenant Georgii Brusilov (1884–1914) to repeat the route of the Swedish polar explorer Adolf Erik Nordenskiöld (1832–1901) from the Atlantic to the Pacific Ocean under the Russian flag, and during this voyage to hunt seals, walruses and polar bears. Russia's successes in the Arctic were achieved by the hydrographic expedition organized by the Imperial

Navy and led by Boris Vil'kitskii. In 1913, the members of this expedition raised the Russian flag on newly discovered land, which was named after Nicholas II (the archipelago Severnaya Zemlya, located north of the Taimyr Peninsula), and later navigated the Northern Sea Route from the east to the west.[94] These failures and successes raised calls for the state and expert community to take a more active role in organizing the 'comprehensive and systematic' national exploration of the Arctic, and stimulated the creation of the Permanent Polar Commission at the Russian Academy of Sciences, which took up this mission.[95] Yet neither the new imperial acquisitions nor the nationalistic fever that accompanied Russia's Arctic ventures helped to boost broad popular support for Nicholas II and his government and unite Russian society, especially when Russia was challenged in its western and southern borderlands by Germany and its allies during the First World War, and the very competence of the tsarist government came into question.

Elena I. Campbell is an Associate Professor of Imperial Russian history at the University of Washington in Seattle and the author of *The Muslim Question and Russian Imperial Governance* (Indiana University Press, 2015). She is currently working on a book project that explores Russia's northward turn during the late tsarist period.

Notes

I am very thankful to William Rosenberg and Willard Sunderland for their helpful feedback on the earlier drafts of this chapter. The research for this chapter was supported in part by the Gerda Henkel Foundation. The author is solely responsible for the content.

1. Berger and Miller, *Nationalizing Empires*, 4.
2. Miller, 'The Romanov Empire and the Russian Nation', 336–47.
3. In the view of contemporaries, the Russian North encompassed the provinces of Vologda, Olonets and Arkhangelsk.
4. Early colonizers of the North also came from Ladoga and the Upper Volga region. See Bernstam, *Pomory*, 20.
5. Ibid., 34–35.
6. On the administrative boundaries of the Arkhangelsk province, see 'Administrativno-territorial'noe delenie' in Kuratov (ed.), *Arkhangelskii* Sever Sever, 28–30.
7. On the history of the port closure, see Ogorodnikov, *Istoriia*, 372–76.
8. Maksimov, *God na Severe*, vol. 1, 175; vol. 2, 148–49, 166. His trip to Kola was even more challenging. See vol. 1, 175.
9. Sergeev, 'S Severa', 1–2.
10. For example, Vereshchagin, *Ocherki*, 35–36, 253, 255–56, 261, 315, 317; Belov, *Opisanie Arkhangelskoi gubernii*, 3,7. Maksimov, *God na severe*, vol. 1, 175; vol. 2, 5, 18.
11. For example, Kharuzina, *Na Severe*, 14, 170.

12. The stern Arctic nature was the main topic of Alexsander Borisov's paintings, including, for example, 'In the Eternal Ice' (1897) and 'The Land of Death' (1903). For an account of his expedition to Novaya Zemlya, see Borisov, *V strane kholoda i smerti*. On Borisov, see Borisov, *Khudozhnik*.

13. Zhilinskii, *Rossiia na Severe*, 22.
14. Mordovtsev, 'Nashi okrainy', 62.
15. On the Crimean War activities in northern Russia, see Davydov and Popov, *Oborona*.
16. Danilevskii, 'O merakh', 503–7, 512–13, 530, 574.
17. Dolinskii, 'O sudostroenii v Severnom krae', 2.
18. Sidorov, 'Sever Rossii', no. 5, 105–6, 108; no. 6, 717–18, 722, 724, 726–27.
19. Sidorov, *Sever Rossii*, xiv.
20. Danilevskii, 'O merakh', 580.
21. RGIA, f. 560, op. 26, d. 91, l. 98; Severtsev, *Po starinnomu 'zamorskomu' puti*, 63; L'vov, *Po studenomu moriu*, 214; Shergin, *Bogatstva Severa*, 125.
22. Eliseev, 'Neskol'ko slov', 50.
23. See *Al'bom uchastnikov*; *Uchastie Rossii*, 46; Kovalevskii, *Vserossiiskaia vystavka*, 175–76. These images of the North reflected a perception of nature as a commodity, as well as an aspiration to 'bring natural riches to life' by turning them into capital. This view did not contradict (and often went hand in hand with) the depictions of northern nature's stark beauty and mystery. For example, artist Alexsander Borisov during his expedition to the Far North pursued a dual goal: to depict the mysterious northern nature and survey the region's natural resources. RGIA, f. 560, op. 26, d. 91, ll. 2–36, 107, 114.
24. *Uchastie Rossii*, 46, 74; Semenov, *Okrainy*.
25. For example, Sidorov, *Sever Rossii*, 92–97; Mordovtsev, 'Nashi okrainy', 83; Zhuravskii, *Bogatstva Severa*, 80–82; Zhuravskii, *Pripoliarnaia Rossiia*. On how Russians perceived and dealt with cold, see Herzberg et al., *The Russian Cold*, especially Julia Herzberg's chapter on the development of meteorology and climatology and Nataliia Rodugina's contribution on the discourse of the Russian press about the 'Siberian frosts'.
26. Dolinskii, 'O sudostroenii', 9–11.
27. For example, Gil'ferding, *Onezhskie byliny*, viii–xi.
28. Polenov, *Ozhivaiushchii Sever*, 46–50; L'vov, *Po studenomu moriu*, 44. On Chizhov, see Simonova, *Fedor Chizhov*, and Owen, *Dilemmas*.
29. Ostrovskii, *Putevoditel'*, 70, 18.
30. Witte, *Vospominaniia*, 391–93.
31. On Witte and his era, see Anan'ich and Ganelin, *Sergei Iul'evich Witte* and Wcislo, *Tales*.
32. Witte, *Vsepoddanneishii doklad*, 4; L'vov, *Po studenomu moriu*, 83; *Otchet o deiatel'nosti*, 4.
33. Lajus, 'Experts on Unknown Waters', 210.
34. Julia Lajus has argued that for Knipovich, the primary goal of the expedition was developing marine science. See ibid., 216–17, 219.
35. According to the 1897 census, the 'Russian element' constituted 85 per cent of the population of Arkhangelsk province. The remaining 15 per cent of *inorodtsy* ('people of different decent', or aliens) included Komi (Zyriane), Karelians, Nenets (Samoedy) and Sami (Lopari). Semenov, *Okrainy Rossii*, 283.
36. GAAO, f. 6, op. 12. d, 76, ll. 15ob. – 17; 61, 64, 71-71 ob., 265 ob.- 269 ob.
37. Engelhardt, *Russkii Sever*, 224-227, 242, 244-245; GAAO, f. 115, op. 11, d. 741, ll. 27 ob.-28 ob. Not all educated Russians shared this view. Some argued that the state should continue protecting traditional Nenets' fishing rights and their use of tundra.

38. On the construction of this railroad, see Nachtigal, *Murmanskaia zheleznaia doroga*.

39. RGIA, f. 1284, op. 190, d. 350b, l. 11.

40. Nicholas II approved Trepov's proposal for the Committee. RGAVMF, f. 23, op. 1, d. 101, ll. 9 ob-10.

41. Ibid., ll. 13 ob.-14 ob.

42. Nielsen and Kari Aga Myklebost, 'Vvedenie' and Nielsen, 'Zakliuchenie i vyvody', in Nielsen (ed.), *Sblizhenie*, 19–20, 359, 367.

43. GAAO, f. 115, op. 1, d. 306, ll. 1–4; f. 1, op. 5, d. 969.

44. For example, Eliseev, 'Neskol'ko slov', 44–46; Bukharov, *Poezdka*, 28–32; L'vov, *Po studenomu moriu*, 172, Witte, *Vsepoddanneishii doklad*, 5–6.

45. Sluchevskii, *Po Severu Rossii*, 301–2: Mets, *O neobkhodimosti*, 12.

46. Bukharov, *Poezdka*, 28–29.

47. Danilevskii, 'O merakh', 593. Instead, Danilevskii saw parallels between the rich Norwegian and Russian Caspian fisheries. He also disagreed with Mechelin and argued that one should compare not the countries, but the ways in which Norwegians and Russians utilized the resources of their northern regions. See *Issledovaniia o sostoianii*, 240–41; Gerard Mineiko (a vice-chairman of the Arkhangelsk Statistical Committee) also supported this view; see GAAO, f. 1, op. 8, t. 2, d. 561, l. 5.

48. L'vov, *Po studenomu moriu*, 211.

49. RGAVMF, f. 410, op. 2, d. 3186, ll. 16–16 ob; Witte, *Vsepoddanneishii doklad*, 3, 5–6; RGAVMF, f. 417, op. 1, d. 1539, l. 11 ob. Sidensner, *Opisanie*, 232, Engelhardt, *Russkii Sever*, 27; Sluchevskii, *Po Severu Rossii*, 305–6; RGIA, f. 1284, op. 190, d. 350b, l. 12ob.

50. On colonization, see Nielsen and Yurchenko, *In the North*.

51. GAAO, f. 1, op. 5, d. 765, ll. 1–53, 139–40.

52. These efforts were a part of a larger campaign for the restoration of Orthodox churches during the late nineteenth and early twentieth century, which aimed at the national consolidation of imperial borderlands. See Miller, 'The Romanov Empire', 314.

53. Nielsen, 'Stroitel'stvo porta v Aleksandrovske', in Nielsen (ed.), *Sblizhenie*, 412–13.

54. Severtsev, *Po starinnomu 'zamorskomu' puti*, 83–84.

55. Sidensner, *Opisanie*, 239.

56. Sluchevskii, *Po Severu Rossii*, 247; L'vov, *Po studenomu moriu*, 117. On Russian concerns about Japanese fishing in Primor'e's waters, see Sokolsky, *Fishing*. On Russian resentment towards foreign whalers, see Jones, 'The Tragedy'.

57. Severtsev, *Po starinnomu 'zamorskomu' puti*, 113; M-skii, 'Mirnoe zavoevanie', 4.

58. For example, M-skii, 'Mirnoe zavoevanie', 4; 'Rybnye hishchniki', 3; GAAO, f. 1, op. 8 t. 2., d. 631, ll. 1–2.

59. 'Severnyi vopros', 1.

60. RGIA, f. 1284, op. 190, d. 289a, ll, 32–33.

61. Nosilov, 'Chto nam nuzhno sdelat' dlia nashego severa', 3; 'Severnyi vopros', 1; GAAO, f. 1, op. 8 t. 2., d. 631, ll. 1–2.

62. On the history of the Russian–Norwegian border demarcation, see Nielsen and Zaikov, 'Norway's Hard and Soft Borders'.

63. For example, Sidorov, 'Sever Rossii', no. 5, 90; Severtsev, *Po starinnomu 'zamorskomu' puti*, 102–13; RGIA, f. 190, op. 8, d. 513, l. 15a. Sidensner argued that accusations against Galiamin were unfounded and that the 'regrettable border' was the result of the general neglect of the Russian North; see his *Opisanie*, 74–83.

64. RGIA, f. 387, op. 12, d. 53889, ll. 43–44, 46–46 ob., 83–93 ob., 191–94; f. 190, op. 8, d. 513, ll. 15 a, 38–38 ob; Sidensner, *Opisanie*, 244.

65. RGIA, f. 1284, op. 190, d. 289a, ll. 13 ob-14. On the Russian policy concerning the issue of territorial waters, see Davydov, *Rossiiskii opyt.*
66. GAAO, f. 115, op. 11, d. 1750, l. 3 ob; RGIA, f. 1284, op. 190, d. 289a, l. 12.
67. Bereznikov, 'Territorial'nye vody Norvegii'; RGAVMF, f.404, op.2, d. 2221, ll.68-69 ob.; GAAO, f. 115, op. 11, d. 1750, ll.13, 16, 26–28. On the territorial waters issue in Norway, see Berg, 'A Norwegian Policy', 7–9.
68. RGIA, f. 1278, op. 6, d. 76, ll. 3–12, 23–27.
69. Danilevskii, 'O merakh', 592; RGIA, f. 1287, op. 7, d. 66, ll. 62 ob.–64.
70. GAAO, f. 1, op. 9, d. 505, l. 67.
71. Shavrov, *Doklad*, 21–22.
72. RGIA, f. 1284, op. 190, d. 289a, ll. 37–38; f. 1284, op. 190, d. 289v., ll. 3-7.
73. Sadovskii, 'O kolonizatsii Novoi Zemli', 18.
74. Danilevskii, 'O merakh', 589–59; GAAO, f. 1, op. 8, t. 2, d. 561, l. 3–8; f. 1, op. 9, d. 520, ll. 20–21ob.
75. Witte, *Vsepoddanneishii doklad*, 6. By the end of the nineteenth century the demand in northern Norway for Russian products brought by the pomors declined, while the pomors paid money for fish caught by Norwegians.
76. RGIA, f. 1405, op. 82, d. 309, ll. 10 ob.-11; RGIA, f. 1284, op. 190, d. 289b, l. 72; GAAO, f. 1, op. 8 t. 2, d. 622, l. 9 ob.; Severtsev, *Po starinnomu*, 159. On the Pomor trade and the debate concerning the proposals to tax the Norwegian fish, see Nielsen, Chapter 18 in Nielsen (ed.), *Sblizhenie*, 518–24.
77. On the changing attitudes towards natural resources in relation to the debate on public property in imperial Russia, see Pravilova, *A Public Empire*, 55–128.
78. I.P.S., *Lesa severa*, 11–13, 43; 'Ot redaktsii', 1–4.
79. See, for example, Mets, *O neobkhodimosti;* Varpakhovskii, *O rybatskikh shkolakh.*
80. Vernadskii, *O blizhaishikh zadachakh.*
81. Lajus, 'Experts on Unknown Waters', 218–19. At the same time, as Lajus has noted, Knipovich's legacy led to the foundation of the Soviet industrial fishing that eventually almost eliminated local users of marine resources. Ibid., 216, 219–20.
82. RGIA, f. 1284, op. 190, d. 289v, ll. 226-228.
83. RGAVMF, f. 23, op. 1, d. 101, l. 11 ob.
84. Ibid., l. 19 ob.
85. RGIA, f. 1278, op. 6, d. 76, l. 58 ob.
86. Zhilinskii, *Promysly severa*, 1, 17.
87. RGIA, f. 1278, op. 2, d. 2331, l. 3 ob. Witte argued that 'self-government did not correspond with autocracy'. See Anan'ich, 'Novyi kurs', 432–35.
88. Kolychev, 'Zemstvo na okrainakh', 5–7; Petrov, 'Raboty', 950.
89. RGIA, f. 1278, op. 2, d. 2331, l. 3 ob., f. 1278, op. 5, d. 827, ll. 1–3.
90. RGIA f. 1284, op. 190, d. 351a, ll. 106, 131-131ob. Russia was also an active participant in international negotiations concerning Spitsbergen and insisted on maintaining its status as *terra nullius* open to access for all powers interested in resource exploitation. On Russia's interests in Spitsbergen, see Karelin, *Rossiiskie delovye interesy.*
91. On the connection between exploration and empire-building, see Sunderland, 'Exploration in Imperial Russia', 139, 142.
92. RGIA, f. 1278, op. 2, d. 2461, l. 2 ob.
93. GAAO, f. 1, op. 8, t.1, d. 2608, l. 49.
94. McCannon, *A History*, 191–92.
95. Breitfus, *Severnye poliarnye ekspeditsii*, 2, 41–44.

Bibliography

Archives in the Russian Federation

RGIA *Rossiiskii gosudarstvennyi istoricheskii arkhiv*
(Russian State Historical Archive, Saint Petersburg)
RGAVMF *Rossiiskii gosudarstvennyi arkhiv voenno-morskogo flota*
(Russian State Naval Archive, Saint Petersburg)
GAAO *Gosudarstvennyi arkhiv Arkhangelskoi oblasti*
(State Archive of the Arkhangelsk Oblast', Arkhangelsk)

Archival and Bibliographical Abbreviations

f. *fond* (collection)
op. *opis'* (inventory)
d. *delo* (file)
l., ll. *list, listy* (page, pages)
t., vol. (volume)
no. (number)
tip. *tipografiia* (press or printing house)

Published Sources

Al'bom uchastnikov Vserossiiskoi Promyshlennoi i Khudozhestvennoi Vystavki v Nizhnem Novgorode 1896 g. Saint Petersburg: tipografiia Ministerstva Putei Soobshcheniia, 1896.

Anan'ich, Boris V. 'Novyi kurs: "Narodnoe samoderzhavie" Aleksandra III i Nikolaia II', in Boris V. Anan'ich, Viktor M. Paneiakh and Rafail Sh. Ganelin (eds), *Vlast' i reformy: Ot samoderzhavnoi k sovetskoi Rossii* (Moscow: Dmitii Bulanin, 1996, 371–454.

Anan'ich, Boris V., and Rafail Sh. Ganelin. *Sergei Iul'evich Witte i ego vremia*. Moscow: Dmitii Bulanin, 1999.

Belov, Vasilii P. *Opisanie Arkhangelskoi gubernii: Dlia narodnykh uchilishch: Rodinovedenie.* Arkhangelsk: tipografiia gubernskogo pravleniia, 1892.

Bereznikov Vladimir A. 'Territorial'nye vody Norvegii'. *Sbornik konsul'skikh donesenii* 5 (1899), 397–400.

Berg, Roald 'A Norwegian Policy for the North before World War I?' *Acta Borealia* 11(1) (1994), 5–18.

Berger, Stefan, and Aleksei Miller (eds). *Nationalizing Empires.* Budapest: Central European University Press, 2015.

Bernstam, Tat'iana A. *Pomory: Formirovanie gruppy i sistema hoziaistva.* Leningrad: Nauka, 1978.

Borisov, Alexander A. *V strane kholoda i smerti: Ekspeditsiia khudozhnika Borisova.* Saint Petersburg: tipografiia I.V. Leont'eva, 1909.

Borisov, Nikolai P. *Khudozhnik vechnykh l'dov: Zhizn' i tvorchestvo A.A. Borisova, 1866–1934.* Leningrad: Khudozhnik RSFSR, 1983.

Breitfus Leonid L. *Severnye poliarnye ekspeditsii 1912 goda i ikh poiski.* Petrgorad: tipografiia Morskogo Ministerstva, 1915.

Bukharov, Dmitrii M. *Poezdka po Laplandii osen'iu 1883 goda* St. Petersburg: tip. Imp. Akademii nauk, 1885.

Danilevskii, N. Ia. 'O merakh k obespecheniiu narodnogo prodovol'stviia na Krainem Severe Rossii 1869', in *Sbornik politicheskikh i ekonomicheskikh statei N. Ia. Danilevskogo* (Saint Petersburg: N. Strakhov, 1890), 501–623.

Davydov, Ruslan A. *Rossiiskii opyt opredeleniia granits territorial'nykh vod i okhrany morskikh resursov v Evro-Arkticheskom regione (1860-e- nachalo 1910-kh godov)*. Arkhangelsk: Pomorskii universitet, 2009.

Davydov, Ruslan A, and Gennadii Popov, *Oborona Russkogo Severa v gody Krymskoi voiny. Khronika sobytii*. Ekaterinburg: UrO RAN, 2005.

Dolinskii, Vasilii L, 'O sudostroenii v Severnom krae i o vozmozhnosti obrazovat' russkii torgovyi flot', in *Besedy o Severe Rossii v 3 Otdelenii Imperatorskogo Vol'nogo ekonomicheskogo obshchestva po dokladam V.L. Dolinskogo, V.N. Latkina i M.K. Sidorova* (Saint Petersburg: tipografiia Tov-va "Obshchestvennaia pol'za," 1867), 2–70.

Eliseev, Alexander V. 'Neskol'ko slov o pomorskom voprose'. *Ekonomicheskii zhurnal* 7 (1886), 41–51.

Engelhardt, Alexander P. *Russkii Sever: Putevye zapiski*. Moscow: OGI, 2009.

Gil'ferding, Alexander F. *Onezhskie byliny, zapisannye Aleksandrom Fedorovichem Gil'ferdingom letom 1871 goda*. Saint Petersburg: tipografiia Akademii nauk, 1873.

Herzberg, Julia, Andreas Renner, and Ingrid Schierle (eds). *The Russian Cold: Histories of Ice, Frost, and Snow*. New York; Oxford: Berghahn, 2021.

Issledovaniia o sostoianii rybolovstva Rossii: Rybnye i zverinye promysly na Belom i Ledovitykh moriakh: Obshchie otchety i predpolozheniia, vol. 6. Saint Petersburg: izdanie Ministerstva gosudarstvennykh imushchestv, 1862.

I.P.S. *Lesa severa*. Arkhangelskoe obshchestvo izucheniia Russkogo Severa. Arkhangelsk: tipo-lit. t.d. 'V. Cherepanova N-ki', 1912.

Jones, Ryan T. 'The Tragedy of Captain Ligov: The Imperial and Soviet Literature of Whaling, 1860–1960', in Nicholas B. Breyfogle (ed.), *Eurasian Environments: Nature and Ecology in Imperial Russian and Soviet History* (Pittsburgh, PA: University of Pittsburgh Press, 2018), 240–62.

Karelin, Vladimir A. *Rossiiskie delovye interesy na arkhipelage Spitsbergen, 1905–1925: Issledovanie pravitel'stvennoi politiki i predprinimatel'skoi initsiativy (na fone otnoshenii s Norvegiei)*. Arkhangelsk: KIRA, 2013.

Kharuzina, Vera N. *Na Severe: Putevye vospominaniia*. Moscow: tip. t-va A. Levinson i K 1890.

Kolychev, Alexander 'Zemstvo na okrainakh: Arkhangelskaia guberniia'. *Izvestiia Arkhangelskogo Obshchestva Izucheniia Russkogo Severa* 9 (1909), 5–14.

Kovalevskii, Vladimir I. (ed.) *Vserossiiskaia vystavka 1896 g. v Nizhnem Novgorode: Putevoditel': Gorod-Yarmarka-Vystavka*. Saint Petersburg: tipografiia A.S. Suvorina, 1896.

Kuratov Anatolii A. (ed.) *Arkhangelskii sever v dokumentakh istorii: (s drevneishikh vremen do 1917 goda): khrestomatiia*. Arkhangelsk: IPP 'Pravda Severa', 2004.

L'vov, Evgenii L. *Po studenomu moriu: Poezdka na Sever*. Moscow: t-vo tip. A.I. Mamontova, 1895.

Lajus, Julia 'Experts on Unknown Waters: Environmental Risk, Fisheries Science, and Local Knowledge in the Russian North', in Nicholas B. Breyfogle (ed.), *Eurasian Environments: Nature and Ecology in Imperial Russian and Soviet History* (Pittsburgh, PA: University of Pittsburgh Press, 2018), 205–20.

McCannon, John *A History of the Arctic Nature, Exploration and Exploitation*. London: Reaktion Books, 2012.

Maksimov, Sergei V. 'God na Severe', in S. V. Maksimov, *Izbrannye proizvedeniia v dvukh tomakh* (Moscow: Khudozh. lit-ra, 1987), vols. 1–2.

Mets, Mikhail F. *O neobkhodimosti nauchno-promyslovogo issledovaniia u beregov Murmana: V Komitet dlia pomoshchi pomoram Russkogo Severa*. Saint Petersburg: tipografiia Isidora Gol'dberga, 1897.

Miller, Aleksei. 'The Romanov Empire and the Russian Nation', in Stefan Berger and A. Miller (eds), *Nationalizing Empires* (Budapest: Central European University Press, 2015), 309–68.
M-skii, A. 'Mirnoe zavoevanie'. *Russkoe slovo* 160 (1910): 4.
Mordovtsev, D. 'Nashi okrainy: Bezliud'e Severa'. *Delo* 1 (1876), 49–87.
Nachtigal, Reinhard *Murmanskaia zheleznaia doroga (1915–1919): Voennaia neobkhodimost' i ekonomicheskie soobrazheniia* [translated from German]. Saint Petersburg: Nestor-Istoriia, 2011.
Nielsen, Jens P. (ed.). *Sblizhenie: Rossiia i Norvegiia v 1814–1917 godakh* [translated from Norwegian]. Moscow: Izdatel'stvo 'Ves´ Mir', 2017.
Nielsen, Jens P. and Aleksei Yurchenko (eds). *In the North My Nest Is Made: Studies in the History of the Murman Colonization, 1860–1940*. Saint Petersburg: European University at Saint Petersburg Press, 2005.
Nielsen, Jens P. and Konstantin Zaikov. 'Norway's Hard and Soft Borders towards Russia', in Kimmo Katajala and Maria Lähteenmäki (eds), *Imagined, Negotiated, Remembered: Constructing European Borders and Borderlands* (Vienna: LIT Verlag, 2012), 67–84.
Nosilov, Konstantin. 'Chto nam nuzhno sdelat' dlia nashego severa'. *Novoe vremia* 12342 (1910): 3.
Ogorodnikov, Stepan. *Istoriia Arkhangelskogo porta*. Saint Petersburg: tipografiia Morskogo Ministerstva, 1875.
Ostrovskii, Dmitrii N. *Putevoditel' po Severu Rossii*. Saint Petersburg: T-vo Arkhang.-Murm. parokhodstva, 1898.
'Ot redaktsii'. *Izvestiia Arkhangelskogo Obshchestva Izucheniia Russkogo Severa* 9 (1909), 1–4.
Otchet o deiatel'nosti S.-Peterburgskogo otdeleniia Obshchestva dlia sodeistviia russkomu torgovomu morekhodstvu s 4 aprelia 1897 goda po den' otkrytiia deistvii "Obshchestva sudokhodstva"- 22 maia 1898 goda. Saint Petersburg, 1898.
Owen, Thomas C. *Dilemmas of Russian Capitalism: Fedor Chizhov and Corporate Enterprise in the Railroad Age*. Cambridge, MA: Harvard University Press, 2005.
Petrov, Mikhail N. 'Raboty 4-i Gosudarstvennoi Dumy v oblasti voprosov russkogo evropeiskogo Severa'. *Izveztiia Arkhangelskogo Obshchestva Izucheniia Russkogo Severa* 21 (1913), 940–50.
Polenov, Aleksei D. *Ozhivaiushchii Sever: Krainii Sever: Chastnyi pavilion obshchestva Moskovsko-Yaroslavsko-Arkhangelskoi zheleznoi dorogi*. Moscow: Tovarishchestvo tipografii A. Mamontova, 1896.
Pravilova, Ekaterina A. *A Public Empire: Property and the Quest for the Common Good in Imperial Russia*. Princeton, NJ: Princeton University Press, 2014.
'Rybnye hishchniki'. Telegrammy, *Novoe Vremia* 12854, 23 December 1911 (5 January 1912): 3.
Sadovskii, B. I. 'O kolonizatsii Novoi Zemli za 1910 god'. *Izvestiia Arkhangelskogo Obshchestva Izucheniia Russkogo Severa* 1 (1912), 17–22.
Semenov, Petr P. (ed.). *Okrainy Rossii. Sibir', Turkestan, Kavkaz i poliarnaia chast' Evropeiskoi Rossii*. Saint Petersburg: tip. AO 'Brockhaus-Efron', 1900.
Sergeev, P. 'S Severa'. *Delo* 4 (1880), 203–22.
'Severnyi vopros'. *Russkaia zemlia*, 10 July 1910: 1.
Severtsev (Polilov), Georgii. T. *Po starinnomu 'zamorskomu' puti i severnym gnezdam: Putevye zametki, vstrechi, itogi, vpechatleniia*. Saint Petersburg: tip. Aleks.-Nev. ob-va trezvosti, 1914.
Shavrov, Nikolai A. *Kolonizatsiia, ejo sovremennoe polozhenie i mery dlia russkogo zaseleniia Murmana*. Saint Petersburg: tipografiia Isidora Gol'dberga, 1898.
Shergin, Ivan A. *Bogatstva Severa (Zyrianskii krai): Putevye zametki, ocherki i rasskazy*. Saint Petersburg: tip. Pervoi Spb. trud. arteli, 1909.

Sidensner, Alexander K. *Opisanie Murmanskogo poberezh'ia*. Saint Petersburg: Tipografiia Morskogo ministerstva, 1909.

Sidorov, Mikhail K. 'Sever Rossii'. *Russkii vestnik* 63(5) (May 1866), 88–124 and (6) (June 1866), 697–741.

———. *Sever Rossii*. Saint Petersburg: v tipogafii Pochtovogo departamenta, 1870.

Simonova, Inna A. *Fedor Chizhov*. Moscow: Molodaia gvardiia, 2002.

Sluchevskii, Konstantin K. *Po severo-zapadu Rossii*, vol. 1: *Po Severu Rossii*. Saint Petersburg: izdanie A.F. Marksa, 1897.

Sokolsky, Mark 'Fishing, Settlement, and Conservation in the Russian Far East, 1860–1940', in Nicholas B. Breyfogle (ed.), *Eurasian Environments: Nature and Ecology in Imperial Russian and Soviet History* (Pittsburgh, PA: University of Pittsburgh Press, 2018), 221–39.

Sunderland, Willard. 'Exploration in Imperial Russia', in Dane Kennedy (ed.), *Reinterpreting Exploration: The West in the World* (Oxford: Oxford University Press, 2014), 135–54.

Uchastie Rossii na vsemirnoi Parizhskoi vystavke 1900 g. Otchet general'nogo komissara Russkogo otdela/ Ministerstvo finansov, Saint Petersburg: tip. I. Gol'dberga, 1901.

Varpakhovskii, Nikolai A. *O Rybatskikh shkolakh dlia nashego Severa: Doklad N.A. Varpakhovskogo*, report given on 15 November 1896. Saint Petersburg: tip. I. Gol'dberga, 1897.

Vereshchagin, Vasilii P. *Ocherki Arkhangelskoi gubernii*. Saint Petersburg: tip. Ia. Treiia, 1849.

Vernadskii Vladimir I. *O blizhaishikh zadachakh Komissii po izucheniiu proizvoditel'nykh sil Rossii*. Petrograd: tipografiia Akademii nauk, 1915.

Wcislo, Francis W. *Tales of Imperial Russia: The Life and Times of Sergei Witte, 1849–1915*. Oxford: Oxford University Press, 2011.

Witte, Sergey. Vsepoddanneishii doklad ministra finansov po voprosu o Murmane. Saint Petersburg: tip. M. Kirshbauma, 1894.

Witte, Sergey Iu. *Vospominaniia (1849–1894)*, vol. 1. Moscow: Izdatel'stvo sotsial'no-ekonomicheskoi literatury, 1960.

Zhilinskii, Aleksei A. *Promysly Severa i territorial'nye vody Ledovitogo okeana*. Petrograd.: Elktropechatnia 'Maiak', 1917.

———. *Rossiia na Severe (k opisaniiu zhizni i deiatel'nosti M.K. Sidorova)*. Arkhangelsk: Komitet po uvekovecheniiu pamiati M.K. Sidorova, 1918.

Zhuravskii, Andrei A. *Pripoliarnaia Rossiia v sviazi s razresheniem obshchegosudarstvennogo agrarnogo i finansovogo krizisa (ekonomicheskie potentsialy severa)*. Arkhangelsk: gubernskaia tipografiia, 1908.

Zhuravskii, Vikentii M. *Bogatstva Severa, Ekonomicheskoe issledovanie*. Nizhnii Novgorod: tipografiia gubernskogo pravleniia, 1875.

Conclusion

The Horizon of Border Studies
US Military Bases as a Network of Exclaves

Shinji Kawana, Keisuke Mori and Minori Takahashi

Prologue

The co-authors of this final chapter have, by mutually complementing each other's expertise in the fields of area studies, sociology and political science, been conducting joint research that looks at US military bases stationed abroad as so-called 'borderlands'.[1] The common points of interest straddling the three fields include various issues generated by military bases, such as the questions of sovereign rights and the exercising of brute force. While striving to expand the geographical and spatial scope of our case studies, we have, by taking into account the history and time of each, situated military bases as entities that possess a physicality that exists in a mutual relationship with individuals and local communities. Overseas bases are US 'exclaves' that are linked in a network. Today there are approximately five hundred of them, while the number of countries that accept them (from here on, 'hosting countries') is estimated to vary between thirty and thirty-seven in any given year.[2] In the domain of global politics, they form, so to speak, a networked space of power, which is based on separated sovereignty and on severed and constructed time.

After summarizing this volume's discussion in the first half of the chapter, we proceed to consider, based on concrete examples, its implications for social sciences in general. Concretely, using the lens of US bases as a network of exclaves, we reassess the meaning and usefulness of this book from the epistemological standpoint of area studies, sociology and political science, fields that in combination constitute border studies.

Provincialization, Place-Space and Constellations

The main interest of this volume has been to position borderline phenomena of both spatial and non-spatial Europe (the West) and Asia (the East) in tandem and compare them in a relational manner. What the book aimed for was to create venues that could potentially facilitate comparisons of border phenomena and could be termed 'relational spaces' or 'relational borderlands'. Thus, the vector of this book is directed at accumulating examples of border phenomena broadly differentiated as belonging to the East or the West, and at the creation of a common forum that would encourage the establishment of correlations between them.

The work in this volume contributes to the development of border studies in at least two aspects, as follows. One is that by incorporating (East) Asia into the analysis, it suggests that border studies, which have so far been characterized by Western-centrism[3] could be *provincialized*. What does 'provincialization' mean here? It means that the theory and models of border studies, which have been perceived as universal, are being put back into the places where they were produced (and where they should be). Regarding provincialization, Eduardo Kohn points to the creation of regional theories to be developed 'once the European theory we once took as universal' has been 'circumscribed'.[4] His argument about provincialization was inspired by Dipesh Chakrabarty's *Provincializing Europe*.[5] What is common to the two is the effort to 'defamiliarize'[6] our minds with the tendency 'to turn the blind eye to the situated context and apply theories as if they were universal'.[7] In this book we inherit their argument, since we believe that border studies have so far relied heavily on border phenomena in Europe and North America and on theories and models based on them, which have been understood as perspectives capable of explaining border phenomena from all over the globe. In these, the trend of interpreting border phenomena, beginning with the oscillation between bordering, rebordering, debordering and transbordering, from the social structural perspective of identity and intersubjectivism became mainstream. However, such postmodernist interpretations cannot effectively explain border phenomena in (East) Asia, where the formation of physical borders and the defining of borders are pressing matters. Needless to say, since the Western and Eastern understandings of borders differ from each other, premises regarding border phenomena cannot be shared. This book, by placing in the same ring Eastern and Western borderlands that constitute Eurasia, presents 'us' with a fine opportunity to become aware of the fact that Western-based border studies, which have prospered while wrapped in a veil of supposed universality, are in fact closely linked to a *specific, Western context* and should, due to this fact, be placed where they originally belong.

To avoid misunderstanding, let us add that in order to make this happen, we did not in any way start with a negation of Western border studies.[8] Rather, as the discussions in the chapters indicate, our effort should be understood as beginning with an attempt to find possibilities for harmonization with Western border studies by looking at various narrators (for example, of Asian origin) and varied cases, materials and data (coming, for example, from Asia). Exactly because we are referring to *harmony*, we do not stop at the kind of *coexistence* that cultural relativism aspires to.[9] What do we mean by this? The historian Minoru Hokari, as a strategic stance that implies a critique of positivist historical science, introduces the case of an old Aborigine named Jimmy, and writes that when Jimmy tells you that a fish flew in the sky, you can believe it really did, in order to make the point that the narration of history should not be monopolized by any specific authority (such as scholars or nations). In a dimension different from the world of scientific knowledge, Hokari has explored the possibility of connecting and harmonizing the understandings of history held by 'I' and 'you'.[10] In his book, in order to make this happen, he sought to direct attention to various phenomena not by excluding previous theories and models that needed to be questioned (entity A), but by unravelling the knowledge to which authority had been assigned, that is, by strategically unlearning it. In his thinking, what was even more important was, when looking at something that is not A (for example, entity B), *not* to try to rescue or pay special respect to B, but rather to place it side by side with entity A (i.e. not to subsume B under A or exclude it from A), and see in what way we can accept it within the framework of academia or a broader public sphere.[11] As multiple groups of phenomena are placed together in the same category, the possibility of concert between them emerges. In that sense, it can be said that one of the contributions of our book is that it carries the potential for a dramatic pluralization of border studies.

That being said, our goal is not to provincialize Western border studies. We should look further and, after temporarily storing away examples of borderlands from different areas, reconnect them in an organic way. This is because, bearing in mind the introspective realization that border studies have not been able to develop sufficiently as a scientific discipline by solely relying on the accumulation of individual cases in the West, we need to amass case studies of diverse border phenomena from around the world, starting with Asia, and extract their similarities from a relational and cross-cultural point of view.

In that sense, too, the present volume is meaningful. Concretely, by trying to understand border phenomena, which tend to be confined to specific countries, areas, ethnic groups and languages, as elements that transcend those areas and interact with one another, we become able to relate to one another Eastern and Western border phenomena – which previously seemed unrelated due to the geographical divide – as converging in some situations (as having commonalities) and diverging in others (as exhibiting differences). This procedure could be described as grouping placial borderlands, in which connectivity to the whole has been limited due to strong ties with particular economic issues, political tendencies, cultural paradoxes and historical legacies, into constellations as spatial elements that possess the meaning of the whole. This image is similar to the one in our argument regarding the network of exclaves composed of military bases, on which we have for a while been conducting joint research.

Of course, this procedure does not negate the placeness of borderlands. As political geography explains, in analyses of space, the uniformity of space created as a result of the existence of humans and their rational actions is assumed, and, along with the trend in academia that started in the 1970s of aspiring to the recovery of humanity, in recent years attention has focused primarily on the approach that looks at uneven, idiosyncratic spaces, that is, places. This indeed resembles the argument regarding provincialization, which is one of the contributions of this volume, because attention to places relativizes (provincializes) the sort of universality that space possesses and puts emphasis on the pluralistic quality of space.

On the other hand, even without resorting to the argument regarding the territorial trap, it is clear that we must again pay attention to the issue of past national discourses concerning borderlands (which are often interpreted as unique) and the power that informs them.[12] Since the second half of the 1960s, borders, whether official or unofficial, physical or symbolic, have come to be seen not simply as an element constituting a larger whole, but as objects of analysis in their own right. Behind this was the appearance of scholars from different fields who were aware of the fact that national borders do not necessarily correspond with the scope of the area in which the power of a state is practically felt. Objections to the world view ordered, shaped and categorized by modern academia became the driving force of border studies. Nonetheless, it was also true that the fixed relationship with the power of nations into which borderlands under their influence were locked continued to function as an element that restricted our episteme. Needless to point out, what lay ahead was the idiosyncrasy of borderlands, that is, the emphasis on placeness. If this understanding is correct, then contemporary border studies, while taking into account the viewpoint of placeness, need to direct attention to the spaceness of borderlands and not become distracted by particular social or cultural contexts. This implies a conscious effort to prevent (uniquely) national discourses from going hand in hand with and adhering to borderlands, as well as work on reconnecting different borderlands in a relational way.

Here, we need to emphasize the structure of this book, which dissolves the dualistic West (Europe) versus East (East Asia) perspective on borderlands by placing between the two several study cases from *Central and East*ern Europe. (East) Asian border phenomena, including both physical space and collective perceptions, perhaps lend themselves more easily to connection and harmonization with Central and Eastern Europe, where history and memories regarding borders often become politicized, than with Western Europe, where interpretations of borders tend to be postmodernist. In this context, the sociological approach is useful, which, while looking at human actions from a micro-level perspective, also endeavours to capture (the shifting of) the structure generated by their interaction.

Space-Time as an Epistemology

Macro-level theories in sociology analyse history and economy or capitalism as going beyond the framework of national analyses and presenting a single, global dynamics. Such a framework was originally formulated in Fernand Braudel's *The Mediterranean and the Mediterranean World*.[13] Later, the world systems theory of Immanuel Wallerstein, Giovanni Arrighi and others who analysed the historical dynamics of capitalism was developed.[14] World systems theory argues that due to the geographical, political, economic and social movement of the accumulation of capital, the planet becomes divided into three categories: the core, semi-periphery and periphery. The theory takes the long-term duration (*longue durée*) of space and time as the object of analysis and sheds light on complex developments that cannot be captured in analyses that are confined to individual countries. It excels in the sense that it brings into focus the global movement of capital and goods that was neglected by the framework of national analysis, and is primarily interested in the core areas, where wealth is most concentrated.

Another lineage that has endeavoured to overcome methodological nationalism and Eurocentrism is the vision presented by the cosmopolitan sociology of Ulrich Beck and the postcolonial sociology of Gurminder K. Bhambra. These attempt to counteract methodological nationalism and Eurocentrism on a more epistemological level than world systems theory, which has a materialistic focus.

Beck's cosmopolitanism starts by grasping the transnational character of global sociological problems, and, as a new means of dealing with them, advocates the importance of designing transnational systems based on cosmopolitanism.[15] It critically examines the global position of advanced European industrial states and offers a perspective that looks at how endorsing human rights, including in the Global South, contributes to the creation of possible international orders.

On the other hand, Bhambra's postcolonial sociology starts from the position that knowledge, in the same way as the accumulation and flow of capital, travels from the core to the periphery, and that, as a consequence of the fact that the organization of knowledge and historization are generated at the core, people at the periphery are not free (this also applies to the West itself). By dismantling Eurocentric myths about the birth of modernity, she reconstructs space-time in the knowledge-sociological tradition of non-Western European areas, not as a relativization of the Western versus non-Western dichotomy or a complete separation of the two, but as a synchronic development. By doing so, she is able to link European modernity with the establishment of colonial states, which occurred parallel with the formation of that modernity, and the problem of race, and thus portray multiple interconnected modernities.[16]

Space-Time in the Comparative Analysis of Governance: Historical Analysis of States

On the other hand, the lineage of the sociology of the history of states, which takes nation states as the main analytic unit, is also important. This comparative perspective emerged in the late 1980s, when sociocentrism in sociology was criticized for neglecting state analysis, which is indispensable for understanding the process of the historical formation of societies. This sociology of history developed mainly within US sociology. Charles Tilly, Theda Skocpol and others took the stage, advocating the need to bring back the state. This intellectual movement sought to uncover historical, causal relationships concerning the birth of nation states in Europe and formulate theories based on them. In parallel, comparative analysis of states came to be conducted, leading to the appearance of the sociology of states, which focused on the causality of the historical roles played by societies and states and the various forms that nation states have, despite their seeming formal uniformity.[17]

However, while the sociology of the history of states has succeeded in establishing the field of international comparison of states and societies, it also inherently possesses the tendency to revert to methodological nationalism. This is likely a source of worry for area studies that form a part of border studies. Furthermore, the sociology of the history of states has tended to disregard borderlands, internal politics and social movements, as well as the practice of governance in non-Western countries, due to its analytical tendency to focus on core areas, that is, Western states and state actors. In this sense it is worth noting that Chapters 11 to 14 of this book, which focus on borders, interethnic conflict and migration, strongly appeal to readers to recognize the need for cross-border analysis by actively dismantling methodological nationalism from the viewpoint of migrants.

Furthermore, as an effort to overcome the limits of the national framework in the historical analysis of states, governmentality studies should be mentioned. The sociology of history and the sociology of states have treated interstate systems dating from after the Westphalia Accord as self-evident. However, governance in modern nation states cannot be explained only in relation to the issue of sovereignty, without understanding its inherent ties with other technologies of rule, such as how the state has managed and directed the human body or regulated economy and human lives by utilizing population statistics. From this perspective, Foucauldian governmentality studies began in the 1990s.[18] They criticize those nation state analyses that centre on sovereignty and, with regard to the chain of governance consisting of sovereignty (rule of law), discipline (rule of body) and regulation (rule of population) – which, historically, emerged in Europe – view the state as a process of constant governmentalizing.[19] Governmentality studies especially address the issue of how liberal rule, which has been neglected in state analysis, is linked to sovereignty and disciplining power in certain spaces and times, not just in West European countries but also in colonial states.[20] Chapters 5 to 8, on tourism, food and memory, reveal the mutual relatedness of tourism, sovereignty and nationalism in that process of governmentalizing in states. Furthermore, Chapters 11 to 14, focused on migration and the Russian Far East, shed light on the process by which states make political use of ethnic groups and populations as a technology of rule. It is through such multilayered decision-making in governance that borders become redefined.

To a Paradigm Shift through Minor Study Objects: Military Bases as Borders and Exclaves

The focus on borders in border studies has the potential to enable analyses of more diverse entities in the world by, on the one hand, bringing into the spotlight the process of the formation of peripheral areas in the context of the accumulation of capital – which is mentioned but not given importance within world systems theory – and on the other by critically overcoming the methodological nationalism that has been regaining strength through comparisons of nation states. Needless to say, borders are very diverse, ranging from material to conceptual.[21] However, the focus on borders, paradoxically, may have the unintended consequence of effecting change in the existing sociological study framework by clearing the path for the discovery of minor phenomena.

For example, among the border-related matters that seem minor at first glance are the gigantic networks formed through amassing and linking. One such example is the network of US base exclaves that appeared after the Second World War. The existing global network of US bases, for which the concept was formulated during the administration of Franklin D. Roosevelt and which also went through the Cold War phase, is a very interesting object for border studies.

The sovereignty of military bases as exclaves is separated from the country that establishes them, and yet, although the extent varies, they function as domains of that country's sovereignty. For example, in the case of the United States, the rights guaranteed by the country's constitution are applied not only to the mainland but also to the territories governed by the US, which is to say, to US citizens in American military bases, too. In the political process of the establishment of bases, that is, the process of the construction of extraterritoriality, an uneven relationship is usually created in which the country establishing a base (usually, a power) enjoys more benefits than the hosting country and the people who live in the community where the base is located. For example, the US almost always concludes a base agreement and a status of forces (SOFA) agreement with host nations.[22] These specify the arbitration procedure in cases of a conflict between the two countries, police and court jurisdiction in the case that US soldiers commit a crime, and which bases or areas can be used by the US military. These agreements are diverse in form and customized in accordance with the situation in the hosting country and the character of its relationship with the US.[23] What is important to note is the clear asymmetry in the limitation of sovereignty. That is, limitations of sovereignty are almost exclusively imposed on the hosting country. In other words, for the hosting country, the acceptance of a foreign military base may incur the interference of a foreign power into the domains in which state autonomy has traditionally been valued, such as policing, court jurisdiction and religion.

Thus, military bases as exclaves are inseparable from the outer domain, that is, nationalism in the hosting country. What is more, the origin of military bases is often tied to past historical wounds and, as such, they can cause strong feelings in the local populace.[24] Nonetheless, the borderness of military bases is created historically as a consequence of political tensions, confrontations and negotiations concerning them between the US and the hosting nations, as well as within the hosting nations. Of course, the meaning and importance attached to borders differs from place to place and changes with time. For example, the meaning of US (NATO) military bases as borders in Europe and US military bases in Japan (especially in Okinawa), where they were established as part of the post-war occupation, is different. US bases in Europe today rarely evolve into political issues.[25] They did cause serious political confrontation in Spain, Portugal, Greece and Turkey during the Cold War, but those problems have abated. Military bases as borders in Europe have, it may be said, already entered a phase in which they are regarded as natural phenomena.

On the other hand, the borderness of military bases in Okinawa, Japan, which are still clearly visible as fixed entities, presents a problem.[26] As Matsuda points out in Chapter 5, Okinawa is a borderland. Historically, the Ryukyu Kingdom (later known as 'Okinawa') was an Asian political and trade contact zone and meeting point, as well as a zone of cultural exchange and transmission. After the so-called 'disposition of the Ryukyus' in 1879, it was incorporated into Japan's peripheral space by the government in Tokyo, which was aiming to solidify its territory as a modern state and implement homogenization. From there on, Japan strengthened the integration and governance of Okinawa, attaching great importance to it as a borderland in terms of state formation, territorial integrity and preparations for possible incursions from abroad. After the Second World War, Okinawa was placed under US rule until 1972, and its character as an island of military bases has not changed even after its return to Japan. Even at present, the US Army, Navy, Air Force and Marines are stationed in Okinawa, and as much as 15 per cent of the island's territory is taken up by American military bases.

In short, Okinawa has historically been Japan's peripheral borderland, which from the Second World War came to comprise American bases, which themselves present borders and exclaves. It is not easy for states to tame such duplicate borderness. Of course, both the Japanese and the US government have attempted to implement policies for fixing or making these borders natural. For example, the Japanese government has awarded grants and implemented public projects and tax relief measures in Okinawa, while the US military has revised the implementation of the status of forces agreement and organized periodic events involving locals.[27] However, the bases in Okinawa are to too great an extent physical and present in everyday life. The naked violence that occasionally emanates from them has kept the local inhabitants aware of their oppressive character and has made naturalness a distant goal.

Contrasting the bases in Europe and Okinawa in this way clearly shows that borderness is relational and compositional, and also reveals the limitations of border studies theories developed in the West (or the difficulty of applying them to Asian areas).

Synchronizing Two Disciplines: Grasping Space

Currently, then, the study of military bases is contained in the study of borders as one of the latter's domains. In fact, in recent years, in base studies too, similarly to the trend in the study of borders, comparative research across different areas and the construction of a framework for comparison have been necessities.[28] Needless to say, political phenomena concerning US military bases transcend individual areas of the world and arise in all kinds of spaces. For that reason, base studies are a field in which the accumulation of knowledge should not simply stop at noting parallels between different areas; what is called for are analyses that cut across different areas. Achieving results in the field of area studies is a must in terms of dealing with political phenomena concerning military bases.

However, that alone will not suffice. Area studies research tends to be inductive and particularistic, which is why the deeper one goes into the area under study, the more the entire picture that lies outside of it becomes difficult to grasp. However, an area is just one part of the picture, and as long as the whole that subsumes that part is not defined, the part itself cannot not be defined. Furthermore, as globalization advances and the interaction between the inside and outside of borders grows, it becomes increasingly difficult to view an area as a closed space even as an expediency. That is why the study of military bases has not been able to produce its own original theory, different from the theory of strategy or the theory of alliances, despite having accumulated numerous case studies over many years.

Soul-searching regarding this is one of the reasons that today there is a movement away from areas studies and back to placing military bases in a general framework and examining, from some sort of theoretical perspective, the historical differences that brought about the discrepancies in their development. We are referring to the attempts at elucidating what kind of spillover effect global issues have on problems concerning individual bases and how, and to what extent, the conditions and reactions there can be reflected back onto the global world.[29]

However, in such attempts, attention should be paid to clarifying as much as possible the similarities and differences between study cases and to extrapolating the logical structure of all logically possible categories, without oversimplifying political developments regarding the actual military bases (exclaves/borders). This is because, in view of the multidimensional nature of military bases, it is, for example, not wise to regard single or multiple factors that influence political confrontations as regular. An account of each factor or each relationship between factors should be given only upon incorporating the analytical results of individual case studies; to think that they can be determined in advance is rather optimistic.

That, however, does not mean that contemplating referential frameworks of thought and methodology is unnecessary. Particularly when considering the problem of military bases, which is a hotly contested topic in the Asian region, researchers should control their personal, tacit presumptions and values as much as possible and avoid putting excessive focus on issues of particular confrontations or partnerships that are only a small portion of the entire problem. These points are suggestive when it comes to thinking about the future developmental potential of general border studies.

Lastly, there is another strain of base research that possesses a similarly rooted problem awareness to the attempt at new border studies presented in this volume. We are referring to the diachronic comparison of bases in a particular country by experts in historical science and history of diplomacy.

Comparative History of Borders: Taking on History and Time

In the Introduction, Berger states the following:

> Finally, to avoid the curse of presentism, historians have been vital in presenting a longer-term perspective on borderlands, their existence and workings in previous times and their longer-term development, including the manifold changes that borders and borderlands have undergone over the course of time.[30]

These words apply surprisingly well to the present state of base studies. In fact, the borders and domainness generated by military bases have their root causes in the historical context, in practical needs and in geopolitical chance. In other words, military bases, while being affected by the strategic environment and chance, as well as the political environment surrounding them, reinforce themselves over time. Even if they begin as very small outposts without a clear goal, under certain circumstances they can grow with time and, as they repeatedly interact with other bases, acquire functions suitable for the environment they are in. In this process, history is both the cause and consequence of the direction of the development of bases.

Furthermore, regardless of their origins, whether they have been acquired as spoils of war (and are vestiges of occupation) or established as part of a security alliance, military bases entail the division of land. This becomes institutionalized as time progresses and, as a consequence, a clear engineering process of border-making becomes almost natural. This is because, sometimes, people who live in the vicinity of bases adapt themselves to the domains defined by such borders and make efforts to strengthen them from within.[31] The borders created during the development of the Amur River area, about which Zhao Xin writes in Chapter 13, however, are not stable as definite spatial partitions. Rather, they are unstable entities buffeted by chance occurrences and policymakers' caprice.

To grasp this uncertainty regarding military bases, an understanding of their historicity as borders, or the mechanism of the self-reinforcement of borders over time, is indispensable. How are bases as borders constructed, reconstructed and deconstructed? That continuous historical process should be captured not as a still but as a moving image. As Komlosy suggests in Chapter 2, artificially made borders create inner and outer domains and generate tensions with the outer domain. For this reason, enemies and military threats that did not exist until then are produced. The thus-created tensions and confrontations, in return, fix and strengthen the borders. This further leads to either the settling of borders (US military bases) as natural or, quite the opposite, generates border tensions (such as in the case of US bases in Okinawa). This long-term process of mutual feedback between the inner and outer domains produced by borders is one of the central topics of research in base studies.

Thus, beyond the horizon of border studies depicted by this volume lie diverse social science disciplines, including base studies.

Shinji Kawana is Associate Professor at the Institute for Liberal Arts, Tokyo Institute of Technology. He studies international security and has written extensively on US overseas bases policy and its history. In recent years, he has focused on the issue of US military bases in Okinawa, Japan. His most recent work is: Shinji Kawana and Minori Takahashi (eds), *Exploring Base Politics: How Host Countries Shape the Network of U.S. Overseas Bases* (Routledge, 2021).

Keisuke Mori is a sociologist and currently lecturer at Senshu University. His research interests include civil society, security issues and social movements. Among his recent joint and individual publications are 'Connections Result in a General Upsurge of Protests' (*Social Movement Studies*, 2020) and 'Domestic Environmental Policy and Status of Forces

Agreement: U.S. Military Presence and New Water Pollution Risk in Germany' (*Exploring Base Politics*, Routledge, 2020).

Minori Takahashi is Associate Professor of Area Studies at Hokkai-Gakuen University, Japan. His research interests include security issues and the development of living and non-living resources in the Arctic. He is currently conducting a joint research project on different aspects of the interaction between humans and nature that takes the Inuit society in Greenland as a case study. His most recent monograph is *Exploring Base Politics: How Host Countries Shape the Network of U.S. Overseas Bases* (Routledge, 2021).

Notes

1. Our main findings have taken shape in Kawana and Takahashi, *Exploring Base Politics*.
2. Vine, *Base Nation*.
3. See the introduction in this volume by Berger, 'Border Experiences', 13.
4. Kohn, *How Forests Think*, chapter 1, section 4, par. 2.
5. Chakrabarty, *Provincializing Europe*.
6. Kohn, *How Forests Think*, par. 16.
7. Ibid., par. 2.
8. Chakrabarty, *Provincializing Europe*, chapter 1, section 4, par. 2.
9. Ibid., par. 3.
10. Hokari, *Radical Oral History*, 27.
11. Ibid., 28.
12. The authors here recall Berger's words from the introduction: 'In all of these bordering processes, spatial and non-spatial alike, questions of *power* are very much to the fore in explaining why some constructions of borders are more successful than others' (italics ours). See Berger, 'Border Experiences', 3.
13. Braudel, *The Mediterranean and the Mediterranean World*, vol.1; Braudel, *The Mediterranean and the Mediterranean World*, vol. 2.
14. Arrighi, *Adam Smith in Beijing*; Arrighi, *The Geometry of Imperialism*; Arrighi, *The Long Twentieth Century*; Arrighi et al., *Anti-Systemic Movements*; Wallerstein et al., *Overcoming Global Inequalities*; Wallerstein, *The Modern World-System I*; Wallerstein, *The Modern World-System 2*; Wallerstein, *World-Systems Analysis*.
15. Beck, *Macht und Gegenmacht im globalen Zeitalter*; Beck, *Risk Society*.
16. Bhambra, *Rethinking Modernity*; Bhambra and Holmwood, *Colonialism and Modern Social Theory*.
17. Evans et al., *Bringing the State Back In*; Tilly et al., *The Formation of National States in Western Europe*.
18. Bröckling et al., *Governmentality*; Dean, *Governmentality*.
19. Foucault, *Security, Territory, Population*; Foucault, *The Birth of Biopolitics*; Foucault, *Society Must Be Defended*.
20. Kalpagam, 'Colonial Governmentality'; Legg, *Spaces of Colonialism*; Walters, *Governmentality*.
21. Wilson and Hastings, 'Borders and Border Studies'.

22. Cooley and Spruyt, *Contracting States*.
23. Woodliffe, *Peacetime Use*.
24. Kirk, *Okinawa and Jeju*.
25. Holmes, *Social Unrest*.
26. Inoue, *Okinawa and the U.S. Military*.
27. Calder, *Embattled Garrisons*.
28. Kawana and Takahashi, *Exploring Base Politics*.
29. Takahashi, *The Influence of Sub-State Actors*.
30. Berger, 'Border Experiences', 7.
31. Fitz-Henry, *US Military Bases and Anti-Military Organizing*.

Bibliography

Arrighi, Giovanni. *The Geometry of Imperialism: The Limits of Hobson's Paradigm*. London: Verso, 1987.
———. *Adam Smith in Beijing: Lineages of the 21st Century*. London: Verso, 2009.
———. *The Long Twentieth Century: Money, Power and the Origins of Our Times*. London: Verso, 2010.
Arrighi, Giovanni, Terence K. Hopkins and Immanuel Wallerstein. *Anti-Systemic Movements*. London: Verso, 2012.
Beck, Ulrich. *Risk Society: Towards a New Modernity*. London: SAGE, 1992.
———. *Macht und Gegenmacht im globalen Zeitalter: Neue weltpolitische Ökonomie*. Frankfurt am Main: Suhrkamp, 2009.
Berger, Stefan. 'Border Experiences in East Asia and Europe: Some Theoretical and Conceptual Thoughts', in Stefan Berger and Nobuya Hashimoto (eds), *Borders in East and West: Transnational and Comparative Perspectives* (New York: Berghahn Books, 2022).
Bhambra, Gurminder K. *Rethinking Modernity: Postcolonialism and the Sociological Imagination*. Basingstoke: Palgrave Macmillan, 2007.
Bhambra, Gurminder K., and John Holmwood. *Colonialism and Modern Social Theory*. Cambridge: Polity Press, 2021.
Braudel, Fernand. *The Mediterranean and the Mediterranean World in the Age of Philip II*, vol. 1. Berkeley, CA: University of California Press, 1996.
———. *The Mediterranean and the Mediterranean World in the Age of Philip II*, vol. 2. Berkeley, CA: University of California Press, 1996.
Bröckling, Ulrich, Susanne Krasmann and Thomas Lemke. *Governmentality: Current Issues and Future Challenges*. New York: Routledge, 2010.
Calder, Kent E. *Embattled Garrisons: Comparative Base Politics and American Globalism*. Princeton, NJ: Princeton University Press, 2007.
Chakrabarty, Dipesh. *Provincializing Europe: Postcolonial Thought and Historical Difference*. Princeton, NJ: Princeton University Press, 2000.
Cooley, Alexander A., and Hendrik Spruyt. *Contracting States: Sovereign Transfers in International Relations*. Princeton, NJ: Princeton University Press, 2009.
Dean, Mitchell M. *Governmentality: Power and Rule in Modern Society*. London: SAGE, 1999.
Evans, Peter B., Dietrich Rueschemeyer and Theda Skocpol (eds). *Bringing the State Back In*. Cambridge: Cambridge University Press.
Fitz-Henry, Erin. *US Military Bases and Anti-Military Organizing: An Ethnography of an Air Force Base in Ecuador*. New York: Palgrave Macmillan, 2015.
Foucault, Michel. *Society Must be Defended*. New York: Picador, 2003.

———. *Security, Territory, Population.* New York: Picador, 2009.
———. *The Birth of Biopolitics.* New York: Picador, 2010.
Hokari, Minoru. *Radical Oral History: The Historical Practices of Aborigines, the Indigenous People of Australia* [in Japanese]. Tokyo: Ochanomizu Shobo, 2005 [2004].
Holmes, Amy Austin. *Social Unrest and American Military Bases in Turkey and Germany since 1945.* Cambridge: Cambridge University Press, 2014.
Inoue, Masamichi S. *Okinawa and the U.S. Military: Identity Making in the Age of Globalization.* New York: Columbia University Press, 2017.
Kalpagam, Uma. 'Colonial Governmentality and the Public Sphere in India'. *Historical Sociology* 14(4) (2002), 418–40.
Kawana, Shinji, and Minori Takahashi (eds). *Exploring Base Politics: How Host Countries Shape the Network of U.S. Overseas Bases.* Abingdon: Routledge, 2021.
Kirk, Donald. *Okinawa and Jeju: Bases of Discontent.* New York: Palgrave Macmillan, 2013.
Kohn, Eduardo. *How Forests Think: Toward an Anthropology Beyond the Human* [Kindle version]. Berkeley, CA: University of California Press, 2013.
Legg, Stephen. *Spaces of Colonialism: Delhi's Urban Governmentalities.* Oxford: Blackwell, 2007.
Takahashi, Minori (ed.). *The Influence of Sub-State Actors on National Security: Using Military Bases to Forge Autonomy.* Dordrecht: Springer, 2019.
Tilly, Charles, Gabriel Ardant, Social Science Research Council (US) and Committee on Comparative Politics. *The Formation of National States in Western Europe.* Princeton, NJ: Princeton University Press, 1975.
Vine, David. *Base Nation: How U.S. Military Bases Abroad Harm America and the World.* New York: Metropolitan Books, Henry Holt and Company, 2015.
Wallerstein, Immanuel, Christopher Chase-Dunn and Christian Suter (eds). *Overcoming Global Inequalities.* London: Routledge, 2016.
Wallerstein, Immanuel. *The Modern World-System I: Capitalist Agriculture and the Origins of the European World-Economy in the Sixteenth Century.* New York: Academic Press, 1975.
———. *The Modern World-System 2: Mercantilism and the Consolidation of the European World Economy, 1600–1750.* New York: Academic Press, 1980.
———. *World-Systems Analysis: An Introduction*, new edn. Durham, NC: Duke University Press, 2004.
Walters, William. *Governmentality: Critical Encounters.* New York: Routledge, 2012.
Wilson, Thomas M., and Hastings Donnan. 'Borders and Border Studies', in Thomas M. Wilson and Hastings Donnan, *A Companion to Border Studies* (Oxford: John Wiley & Sons, 2016), 1–25.
Woodliffe, John. *Peacetime Use of Foreign Military Installations under Modern International Law.* Dordrecht: Martinus Nijhoff, 1992.

Index

Compiled by Domenica Scarpino, Lukas Gerling and Konstantin am Mihr

0–9
203 Hill, 88

A
Aborigine, 375
Aborigines of Saghalin, 336
Academic Karelia Society, 246
Adams, Arthur, 338
Adria, 209
Adriatic Coast, 196, 208
Adriatic Sea, 169
Adyaa Gelegiin, 304
Aihe River, 270
Aihui Historical Museum, 8
Ainu (people), 218–236
Akateeminen Karjala-Seura (AKS), 246, 251
Alaska, 221, 330, 342
Aleksandrovsk, 358
Aleksei, Grand Duke, 352
Alenius, Kari, 149
Aleutian Islands, 327, 330
Alexander II, 146, 352
Alexander III, 354
All-Russian Fair of Industry and Art, 352
Alsace, 2, 206
alumni association (Jyoran-Kai), 80–83

Amami Islands, 128
Amami–Oshima, 135
America, 209–210, 308, 326–327, 330–335, 340–342
America (Battleship), 331
American Amur River's Mercantile Agency, 334
American War of Independence, 327
Americans, 331
Americas, 13
 in literature, 209–210
 Latin, 8
 North, 330–331, 374
 Russian America, 220
 South, 11
Amur/'Amur Age', 328, 332
Amur Railway Company, 333
Anderson, Benedict, 202
Andijan, 42–43
Andong, 79
Andropov, Yuri, 303–304
Angeleri, Francesca, 208
Anhui Province, 175
Annals of Chinese Ethnic Minority Customs (Zhongguo shaoshu minzu fengsu zhi, ZSMF), 171–174
Annist, August, 248
Aqsu, 35, 41–43

390 Index

Arbe, 206
Arctic (Ocean), 320–321, 347–348, 350, 352, 358–359, 362–365
area, 321–322, 384
Argun River, 182, 325, 327
Arimitsu, Kyoichi, 83
Arimura Sangyô Corporation, 137
Arkhangelsk, 320, 348–349, 352–355
  native, 351
  province, 348–351, 357, 360–364
Arkhangelsk–Murmansk steamship company, 354
Arkhangelsk Society for the Study of the Russian North, 355, 346
Armenia(n), 104, 199, 254
genocide, 197
Arrighi, Giovanni, 377
Arsen'ev, Vladimir Klavdievich, 184
Asia/n, 13, 81, 96, 230, 303, 327, 334, 337, 339, 374–377, 381–383
  Asia-Pacific War, 76
  central/inner Asia, 22, 27, 31, 38, 42–43, 98, 152, 342, 349, 352, 355
  East, 1–2, 9, 11, 13, 89, 91, 123–124, 128, 227, 321–122
  North, 332, 334
  North-East, 326–330, 332, 335–342
A/S Sydvaranger, 359
Ašliq, 42
Association of Borderland Studies, 1
Association of Chinese Residents, 292
Association of Shipmasters in Tromsø, 359
Atkinson, Thomas Witlam, 336–337, 341
Atlantic, 199, 208, 346
Atwood, Christopher P., 283
Australia(n), 197
Austria(n), 24–25, 54, 57–65, 96, 199, 208, 331
  Austria-Hungary, 24, 30 (*see also* Habsburg)
  Austrian Empire (Österreichisches Kaiserreich), 55, 57–58, 60, 62–63
  Austrian Netherlands, 54
  Austrian Provinces/Regions, 25, 58, 59
Ayan, 328, 336

B

Babenberg dynasty, 54
Baikal Area, 328
Baiyu Hill, 88
Balkan, 57, 196, 198, 327
  Peninsula, 25, 57, 327
  Berlin-Balkan Conference 1878, 25
Ballinger, Pamela, 202
Baltic, 6, 124, 142, 147, 153
  'Baltic Russians', 162
  German, 6, 144–145, 149, 244, 253
  Republics, 12
  Sea, 24, 145, 326–327, 337, 349, 355
  States, 143, 150, 153–154, 156, 159
Baltic-Finnic Language(s), 244
Banat, 205
Banzar Jambalyn, 301
Barbieri, Veliko, 196
Barents Sea, 355
Bastianich, Joe, 209
Bastianich, Lidia, 208–211
Batali, Mario, 209
Batbayar, Tsedendambyn, 283
Batmönkh Jambyn, 300
Bayan-Ölgii province, 287
Beck, Ulrich, 377–378
Begs (Muslim landholding Magnates), 34–35
Beijing, 34, 81, 171, 264, 268, 271, 273, 276, 321–322
  as political identification of government, 286–310; *also* Peking, 175, 297, 329, 332, 335, 338
Belarus, 12, 96–98, 100–101, 106, 143
Belarusian SSR, 70, 95, 97–100
Bello, David, 268
Bering Sea, 327
Bering, Vitus, 327
Bessarabia, 58
Bhabha, Homi, 7
Bhambra, Gurminder K., 377–378
Biala, 58
Billé, Franck, 283
Black Sea, 24, 326–328, 337, 349, 355
Blagoveschensk, 326, 330
  Blagoveshchensk, 339
Bogd Khan, 283
Bohai Gulf, 338

Bohemia(n), 54, 58–64
   Province(s), 25
Bolshevik(s), 148, 245–248
Bosnia and Hercegovina, 24–30, 54, 57, 63–64
Braudel, Fernand, 377
Brazil, 5
Breitfus, Leonid, 354
Brexit, 6
Brezhnev, Leonid, 297, 302–303, 308
Britain, 6, 322–323, 326–328, 330, 334–341
   British, 6, 14, 322, 327–329, 335–336, 338–342
   British Empire, 23, 327
   British India, 338
Brody, 58
Bronze Night, 156, 160
Brusilov, Georgii, 364
Brussels, 6, 10
Bubrikh, Dmitry, 250, 252
Buddhist, 220, 264, 284
Bukharov, Dimitrii, 357
Bukovina, 24, 29–30, 54, 58, 63–64
Bulgan province, 301
Bull, Anna Cento, 9
Burckhardt, Jacob, 78
Bureya River, 326, 339
   Mountains, 339
Burma, 291, 294, 297
Buryats, 285

C

Caltutta (Calcutta), 337
Cambodia, 291, 294, 299
Canada, 197, 334, 342
   Canadian, 59
Canetti, Elias, 205
Canton, 175, 332, 338
Cao, Tingjie, 322
Cape of Good Hope, 332, 338
Catherine the Great, 327
Caucasus, 349, 355
Center for Inter-American and Border Studies at the University of Texas in El Paso, 1
Center for International Border Research at Queens University in Belfast, 1

Central Commitee's International Liaisons Department (ILD), 300
Centre for Border Research in Nijmwegen, 1
Ceuta, 11
Chakrabarty, Dipesh, 374
Changchun, 74, 77, 82–83, 86
   Changchung, 86, 88–89 (see also Xīnjīng)
Chasŏng, 276
Che, Nam-zyu, 83
Chen, Lu, 292
Chief Administration of Land Management and Agriculture, 360
China, 6, 8, 22–24, 28–29, 31–34, 38, 41–45, 50, 73, 75–76, 78–82, 88, 127–133, 172–179, 183–185, 263–265, 267–268, 271, 273, 284–289, 291 99, 302 10, 321–222, 325–326, 328–332, 334–340
   Chinese Communist Party (CCP), 177, 286–290, 293–294, 297–298, 305, 310
   Imperial, 33
   Ming, 32, 180, 325
   North-eastern, 169, 171–174, 176, 178–80, 182–185
   Northern, 81, 176, 325, 329–330, 334, 338
   North-western, 22, 31, 38, 43, 73, 75–77
   People's Republic of China (PRC), 31, 169–173, 177–179, 183, 185, 286–287, 292, 294, 297–298, 301, 303–306
   Qing, 22–24, 26–45, 50, 78, 124, 172, 176, 180–81, 183, 263–264, 267–278, 283–286, 319, 321–322, 326
   Republic of China, 28, 78–79, 135, 285–286
   Southern, 329
Chirikof, Alexei, 327
Chita, 333
Chizhov, Fedor, 354
Chocim (Khotyn), 103–104
Choibalsan, 292
Chongjin, 77, 82–83, 85
Chosŏn Korea, 263–264, 267–279

Christian(ity), 22, 26–28, 49, 63, 218, 221–222, 231–235, 245, 247
  Christian Europe, 3
  Christiania, 356 (*see also* Oslo)
Chuan, 175, 186. *See also* cuicine systems
Chulundorj, 303
Church of St Boris and St Gleb, 356–357
Cisleithania, 57
Civil War (Finnish), 217, 246
Civil War (Russian), 148
Cold War, 2, 198, 380–381
  Post, xi–xii
Collins, Perry McDonough, 331–334
colonialism, xiii, 11, 13, 49–50, 70, 236
  neo-colonial, 296
Commune of the Workers of Estonia, 148
communist, 8, 12, 70, 148, 171, 217, 252, 255, 263, 265, 284–285, 287–288, 297, 302, 308, 310–311
  state, 8
Confin, 56, 337. *See also* Military Border Zone
Constantinople, 327
cosmonaut, 288
cosmopolitanism, cosmopolitan, 9–10, 199, 377–378
Courland, 147
Crimea, 143–144, 161, 327, 336
Crimean War (1853–56), 146, 319, 326, 328, 331–336, 347, 350
Croatia, 56, 169, 196, 198, 206
cuisine systems, 174–176, 185–186
  Cantonese, 175, 186
Cultural Revolution, 290–291, 310
Czechoslovakia, 294

D

Daily Telegraph, 6
Dairen, 341
Dalian, 77, 82–83, 86, 89
Dalmatia, 54, 57, 197, 203–204, 206, 211
Danilevskii, Nikolai, 351–352, 356–357
Daoguang, 270
Darkhan, 303
Dash-Onolt, 292
Dashtseren B., 303
Daur (people), 178, 186
Davies, Norman, xii

Day of Runeberg, 246
de Bodisco, Alexander, 331
Democracy, x–xii, 155
Demshuk, Andrew, 111, 117
Denmark, Danish, 124, 142, 144
Die Castries Bay, 329
Dongjiguan Fortress, 88
Dongsha Islands, 338
Dornod province, 292, 298
Dornogovi province, 298
Drohobych, 108
Dutch Empire, 23
Dvina River, 351, 355

E

East Elbian, 59
East Gobi province, 292–293. *See also* Saynshand
Eastern Bloc, 102, 251
Eckersley, Susannah, 204
economy, economic, 1, 3–6, 8, 12–13, 21–22, 24–25, 28, 30–33, 40, 43–45, 49–62, 65–66, 99–102, 112, 130–132, 136–138, 145, 149, 152, 169, 173–174, 177–178, 181, 218, 220, 236, 146, 251, 264–265, 283–290, 293–297, 300–302, 308, 319–320, 334, 340, 342, 348–363, 376–377, 379
Elliot, Charles, 327–328
Elliot, Gilbert John Brydone, 328, 336
Emilia, 197
enclaves, 2, 11–13, 143, 286, 301
Encyclopedia of Chinese Ethnic Minorities' Food Customs (*Zhonggu shaoshu minzu yinshi wenhua huicui*, ZSYH), 171–174
Engelhardt, Alexander, 355–356
ethnic(ity), 1, 3–4, 6–8, 10–13, 22, 24, 26–28, 52, 59, 64–65, 96–100, 105, 118, 127, 143, 145–47, 149, 153, 160, 169–174, 176–186, 200, 234, 243, 263–265, 283–288, 290–291, 293, 295, 297–301, 303–305, 307, 309–310, 363, 376, 379
The East, x–xii, 13, 89, 143, 254, 273, 319, 325, 329, 338–339, 342, 374. *See also* East Asia

(Republic of) Estonia(ns), 13, 123–125, 142–162, 217, 243–251, 253–255
   Estonian Soviet Socialist Republic (SSR), 151–154, 158, 243, 253–254
Etorofu Island, 220
Eurasia, 1, 38, 43, 217, 341, 347, 349, 374
Eurasia Unit for Border Research at Hokkaido University in Sapporo, 1
Europe(an), 1–3, 5, 7, 9, 10–13, 22–26, 32–33, 49–50, 54, 57–59, 65, 95–96, 100, 118, 128, 147, 155–56, 162, 196–197, 207–209, 211, 242, 244, 326–327, 330–331, 333, 335, 337, 341–342, 347–349, 356, 358, 374, 377–379, 382
   'Christian Europe', 3
   East(ern), 10, 25, 60, 63, 118, 123, 197, 204, 289–290, 296–297, 299, 302–303, 329, 377
   Europeanization, 10
   European Russia, 320, 347, 350
   European Union, EU, 1–3, 5, 9, 128, 155
   South(ern), 23, 54, 60, 196
   Western, 10, 23, 25, 29, 33, 59, 349, 374, 377–379
Eurocentrism, Eurocentric, xii–xiii, 377–378
Evseev, Viktor, 249–250, 252
Ewenki (people), 178, 184
exclaves, 2, 11–13, 373, 376, 379–381, 383
exclusivism, xi

F
Farinetti, Oscar, 209
Fenghuangcheng Gate, 270
Finland, Finnish, 13, 95, 124, 217–218, 242–255
   Finnish–Estonian Students Club, 247
   Finnish-Karelian, 243–244, 250–254
   Finnmark, 319, 321, 356–358
   Finno-Ugric languages, 244, 248–249
   Grand Duchy of Finland, 243–244
First World War, 59, 76, 96, 147–148, 199, 320–321, 355, 362–363, 365
Fiume *now* Rijeka, 59, 197, 199, 201–203, 205
Fiyaka, 181

Forshtadt, Petrov, 147
France, French, 5, 23, 60, 62, 206, 230, 322, 327
   Anglo-French allied fleet, 327, 350
   Napoleonic France, 60
Franco-German Border, 3
Free Trade Agreement Zones, 5
Friuli, 209
Fujian province, 175
Fujieda, 332
Fukuoka Prefecture, 82
Fushun, 82
Fuzhou, Shanghai, 332

G
Gablonz, 203
Gakuto-doin, 76. *See also* wartime labour force
Gakuto-shutujin, 76. *See also* Military Service(s)
Galiamin, Valerian, 359
Galicia(n), 24–25, 29–30, 54, 58–59, 62–64, 98
Ġällä, 42
Gansu, 41–43, 172
Gaoligou, 270
Gdańsk, 99
Germany, German, xi–xii, xiv, 2, 6, 12, 22, 25, 27, 59–60, 62, 64, 65, 95, 97, 106, 111–112, 117, 125, 144–151, 159–160, 199, 203–205, 208, 211, 230, 244, 246, 249, 251, 253, 303, 329, 336, 339, 358, 360, 365
   East, 2, 203, 210
   German Confederation, 59
   German Customs Union, Deutscher Zollverein, 60
   National Socialist Germany, 6, 12
   West, 2
Ghiliak, 181
Giard, Luce, 205
Gibraltar, 11
Gliwice, 99
Global South, 378
globalization, xi, 4–5, 342, 382
Goli Otok, 206
Gombojav Damdingiin, 304
Gordlevsky, Vladimir, 245
Goshkevich, Iosif, 232

grand duke, 142, 145, 352
Graz, 56, 208
Great Northern War, 145, 160
Great Reforms (of Alexander II), 146, 363
Greece, Greek, 24, 196, 198–199, 381
Green, Elizabeth E., 283
Grosby, Steven, 100
Guangdong, 42, 175
Guangxi province, 185
Guangxu, 273
Guanlong, 43
Guizhou province, 175
Gulf Stream, 353
Gunji, Shigetada, 230–231
Gürüč, 42
Gyeongju, 79, 83

H
Habersham, A. W., 331–332
Habomai Island, 220
Habsburg, xii, 13, 53–57, 59–64, 208
 Empire, 12, 21, 22–23, 29–30, 54–55, 60, 63–64, 199
 Monarchy, 22–23, 50–51, 53–57, 59–60
Habsburg Customs Union, 60, 62
Haihe, 332
Hakama, 79
Hakodate/Hakodadi, 223, 232–233, 336
Hamgyŏng, 274, 276
Hamilton Island, 341
Han Ngoc Que, 287
Han, 22, 26–30, 169–170, 173–177, 179–185, 187–188, 263–264, 267–268, 270, 287, 291, 197, 322
Hanoi, 298–301
Hansen, Hans Lauge, 9
Harbin, 80, 82–84, 87–89
Harva, Uno, 248
Haus des Deutschen Ostens (HDO), 204
Hawaii, 132, 333
Hawes, Charles H., 182
Hazama, Rihô, 136–137
He, Qiutao, 322
Heaton, William R., 283
Hechter. Michael, 13
Heihe, 326, 339
Heilongjiang, 172, 175, 178, 180–181, 184, 187, 271–272, 335

Heimat, 111, 117, 204
 of Memory, 111, 117
 transformed, 111
Heje, 176, 178, 180–181, 187
Helsingin Sanomat, 242
Helsinki, 242, 247, 249, 251, 256
Hessen, 203
Hezhen County, 43
Higashi Honganji, 220, 230–231
Himalaya(s), 337
Hiroshima Prefecture, 79
Hitchcock, Romyn, 223
hoesang, 277, 280
Hofstede, Geert, 172
Hokari, Minoru, 375
Hokkaido *formerly called* Ezo, x, xiv, 1, 220, 223, 228, 230–232, 234–235, 255
Hōkō Gikai, 230
Holy Roman Empire, 23, 59–60, 63
Hong Kong, 11, 186, 332, 336
Horel, Catherine, 199
Hostetler, Laura, 180
House of European History in Brussels, 10
Howell, David, 220
Hsu, Francis L. K., 176
Hsu, Vera Y. N., 176
Hu, Sihui, 177, 190
Hua, Guofeng, 298
Huaiyang, 175, 187
Huch'ang, 274, 276–279
Hui, 172, 175, 187
 people, 172–173, 180, 184, 187
 See also cuisine systems
Huibu, 38
Huju, 274, 279
Huma River, 325
Hun River, 276, 278
Hunan provence, 42, 175, 189
Hungary, Hungarian, 30, 54–58, 61–63, 95, 205, 284, 286–296, 298–303, 305–306
 Kingdom, 57

I
Ida-Virumaa, 156–157
Il Giorno, 210
Ili, 40, 42. *See also* Yining
 General, 42

Imperial, 29, 49, 73, 82, 84, 128, 132, 134, 146
　Imperial Academy of Sciences, 362
　Imperial Free Economic Society, 351
　Imperialism, 236
India, 5, 197, 211, 189, 297, 337–340
Indian-American, 200
Ingria, Ingrian, 244, 246–247, 251
Interdisciplinary Research on the Function of National Histories and Collective Memories for the Democracyin the Globalized Society, NHCM, x
International Monetary Fund, 5
Irkutsk, 333–334
Ise, 80
Ishigaki Island, 128, 130–131, 133, 136–137
Ishikagha beg, 35
Issakov, Sergei, 145, 150, 159, 162
Istanbul, 198
Istria(n), 169–170, 173, 182, 196–204, 206–211
Istroveneto, 202
Italy, Italian, 13, 54, 62, 78, 95, 169–170, 197, 199–203, 206, 208–211
Ito, Tainin, 230
Ivan III, the Grand Duke of Moscow, 142, 145
Ivangorod, 142, 144–146, 149, 151, 154, 161–162
Iwashita, Akihiro, xiv

J
Jagellonian dynasty, 56
Jalan-Aajav Sampilyn, 300
Jan III Sobieski, 104
Japan, Japanese, x–xv, 6, 13, 69–71, 73–79, 82–83, 85–91, 123–124, 127–128, 130–138, 142, 162, 218–225, 227, 229–236, 255, 293–294, 308, 320, 326, 329, 332–334, 336–338, 340–341, 358, 381
　Imperial, Empire, 8, 74, 76–77, 86–87, 89–91, 124–125, 127, 130–131, 137–138, 226, 236, 293
Japanese Orthodox Christian community, 232, 235
Jargalsaikhan, Mendee, 283

Java, 338
Jesuits, 321
Jews, Jewish, 24, 95, 97–99, 104, 107, 147, 197–199
Ji'an, 278
Jiang, Chenzhon, 292
Jiangsu, 42, 175, 187, 189
Jiaqing, 270
Jiayugaun Pass, 42
Jilin provence, 83–84, 173, 180–181, 187, 271–273, 335. See also Liaoning
Jin, 37, 39
Jingwei, Wang, 82
Jinzhou garrison, 272
Johnson, Boris, 6
Jõhvi, 155
Journal of Borderland Studies, 1
Jurchens (people), 274
Jyoran-Kai, 81. See also alumni association

K
Kagawa Prefecture, 130
Kagoshima, 130
Kalevala Society (*Kalevalaseura*), 246
Kalevala, 217–218, 242–255
Kalevipoeg, 243–245, 248, 253
Kaliningrad, 12–13
Kamchatka parish, 221
Kamchatka Peninsula, 327–329, 333
Kamieniec Podolski (Kamianets-Podilskyi), 103–104
Kanggye, 275, 278–279
Kangsi (Chinese Emperor), 321
Kanin Peninsula, 358
Karafuto island, 231. See also Sakhalin (island) and Saghalin
Karaim(s), 97
Karelian(s), 217, 242–255
　Region, 124, 242, 244–254
　Soviet Karelia, 217, 243, 246, 249–254
　White Sea Karelia, 244
Kang, Sheng, 293
Karelo-Finnish Republic, 217, 250–255
Karelo-Finnish Soviet Socialist Republic (K-FSSR), 250, 255
Kasatkin, Nikolai, 232
Kashgar, 33, 35–37, 41–42
Katabira, Jiro, 78

Kataoka, Toshikazu, 224–225
Katerinich, A. N., 295
Katkov, Mikhail, 351
Katrak, Ketu H., 201
Kattago, Siobhan, 160
Kaufbeuren, 203
Kaup, Katherine, 185
Kazakh, 38, 40, 187
Kazakhstan, 42
Kaźmierska, Kaja, 107
Kazuga, Shōjirō, 230
Keelung, 131, 135, 137
Kent Mount, 325
Kerr, George H., 136
Kerrylin Corner, 328
Kerulun River, 325, 341
Khabarovsk, 326, 330
Khalkhin Gol, 293
Kharkhorin, 288
Khishi, Enkhbayar, 311
Khoja, 33
Kholmogory district, 350
Khoqan, 27, 37, 42
Khotan, 33–35, 38–40, 42–43
Khovd, 284
Khrushchev, Nikita, 289, 308, 311
Kilen, 181, 187
Kim, Il Sung, 311
Kim, Kwangmin, 13, 21, 24, 26, 45, 268, 279
King, J. W., 338
Kirghiz, 42
Kirkenes, 358
Kiyakara, 181, 187
Kmetovi, 27
Knipovich, Nikolai, 354
Kobe, 91, 130, 138
Kohn, Eduard, 374
Koizumi, Akio, 83
Kojima, Kuratarō, 223
Kola Peninsula, 349, 352, 355, 358, 360, 363
Kolomyia, 102
Komatsu, Tōzō,, 232, 233, 237
Königsberg, 12, 13. See also Kaliningrad
Konkamakuru, 221–236
Konskribierte Länder
Korea(n), x–xii, xiv, 73–87, 91, 177–188, 263–280, 308, 338
   North, 83, 86, 211

Korla village, 43
Korovin, Konstantin, 352, 357
Kosygin, Alexei, 294
Kotlas, 352, 355
Kôun Gaisha (Koun Corporation), 131
Kraków, 328
Krakow, Uther, 329
Kreenholm Island, 147, 149, 160
Kremlin, 285, 289, 290, 296, 297, 299, 302, 305, 306, 308, 309
Krestovaya Bay, 361
Kresy, 95–117
Kreutzwald, Friedrich, 244, 245, 253
Krivoshein, Alexander, 360
Krohn, Kaarle, 247–253
Krzemieniec (Kremenets), 103
Ku, Shiyon, 292
Kuancheng, 88
Kucha, 41
Kulaks, 152, 287
Kunashiri Island, 220
Kuril Ainu, 124, 218–236
Kuril Islands, 124, 128, 219, 220, 224, 226, 229, 232, 234, 235
Kuusinen, Otto, 252, 253
Kuyavia, 98
Kwak, Jun-Hyeok, 311
Kwantung Army, 76
Kyakhta, 284
Kyoto, 220
Kyrgyz (people), 180, 184, 188
   Plateau, 337
Kyusyu, 79

L

La Cecla, Franco, 198
Laidoner, Johan, 148
Lajus, Julia, 362
Lake Ladoga, 248
Laos, Laotian, 297, 300
Lapland, 350
Latin America(n), 8
Latvia, 96, 154, 155, 159, 161, 162
Laugaste, Eduard, 253
Lazio, 209
Lenin, Vladimir, 148, 152, 249, 250, 251, 253
Leningrad University, 249, 250
Leningrad, 152, 251, 253
Liang, 33, 36, 37, 43, 278

Index

Liao dynasty, 325
Liaodong (peninsula), 188, 274, 320, 341
Liaoning, 172, 173, 175, 180, 188, 267
Lifanyuan, 321
Lim, Jie-Hyun, xii, xiv, 162, 279
Lithuania, 12, 24, 25, 58, 63, 70, 95–101, 106, 154
   Lithuanian SSR, 97–100, 154
L'vov-Kochetov, Evgenii, 320
Livland, 146, 147
Livonian Order, 124, 143, 145
Livonian War, 145
Lombardy, 55, 58, 60–62
Lönnrot, Elias, 244, 245, 251–253
Lorraine, 206
Lu, 175, 188. *See also* cuisine systems
Lubuskie Province, 98
Lushun, 82, 83, 87, 88
Lviv (Lwów), 97, 98, 104, 106, 110
Lviv Jan Kazimierz University, 98
Lviv Polytechnic National University, 98
Lwowianka, 110. *See also* Lviv

M

Macau (Macao), 11, 338
Madieri, Marisa, 205
Madrolle, Claude, 181
Maeda, Sentarô, 131
Magazzino, 18, 203
Magris, Claudio, 205
Magyar, 199
Mähsulat, 42
Makarov, Stepan, 320
Makhov, Vasily, 232
Maksimov, Sergei, 320, 349
Malay Peninsula, 332
Malinsk, 327
Mamontov, Savva, 354, 357
Manchu, 23, 26, 29–30, 32, 176, 178, 183, 185, 263, 267–271, 321, 325
   Manchu imperial house of the Qing, 22
Manchukuo, 70, 73, 74, 76–79, 81, 82, 85, 86
   Manchukuo Development Project, 76
Manchuria, 22, 45, 70–91, 176, 263–273, 279, 319, 320, 322, 328, 329, 331, 334, 335, 338, 340, 341
Manchuria Railway Company, 77
Mannur, Anita, 201

Mantis, Cristina, 208
Mao, Gongning, 171, 190
Mao, Zedong, 286, 291
   Maoist, 291, 296
Marco Polo Bridge Incident, 134
Marin, Biagio, 207
Marr, Nikolai, 250
Marschall, Sabine, 101, 112
Martin, George R. R., 283, 284
Martinez, Francisco, 143
Marugame, 88
Masuria, 98
Matsuda, Hiroko, 13, 123–125, 127, 138, 381
Matsuura, Takeshirō, 229, 231
Matsuyama, 88
Mechelin, Henrik Adolf, 356
Medee Sonin, 292
Mediterranean, 170, 196, 197, 221, 367
Meiji, 222, 224, 228, 229, 230
   Restoration, 124, 235
Melilla, 11
memory, xiv, 5, 9, 13, 14, 70, 89–91, 95, 96, 99–102, 105–107, 109, 112–118, 156, 159, 161, 162, 170, 198–211, 219–236, 243, 379
   ideological memory, 115, 116
   sentimental memory, 115, 116
Mendeleev, Dmitrii, 320
Mengjiang, 81
Mercosur, 5, 11
Mexico, 128
   Mexican-US border, 128
Micronesia (South Sea Islands), 132, 227
Mikhailovich, Aleskei, 354
Military Border Province, 28, 56–57, 63–64
   Military Border Zone, 56, 64
   Militärgrenze, 28, 56
Military Service(s), 56, 76, 78, 81, 83, 90, 161
Miller, Alexei, 347
Min, 175
Ming. *See* China
Miyajima, 79
Miyako (Island), 128, 134, 137
Moji, 82
Moldavia, 58
   Duchy of Moldavia, 58
Molotov–Ribbentrop pact, 97

Mongolia(n), 13, 24, 77, 80, 84, 87, 173, 263–265, 283–310, 325, 337
  Manchuria-Mongolia, 82–83
  Mongolian People's Republic (MPR), 283–297, 299–301, 303–307, 309–310
  Mongolian People's Revolutionary Party (MPRP), 284–291, 293–304, 306–307, 309–310
  Mongols, 27, 177–178, 182, 184, 265, 288, 303
  radio, 304
  Zunghar, 22, 27
Moravia, 54, 60
Mori, Annamaria, 205
Morning Chronicle, 335
Moscow Merchant Bank and Mutual Credit Society, 354
Moscow, 12, 143, 152–154, 249, 254, 288, 293, 296–297, 300, 303, 306, 308–310, 320, 333, 349–350, 353–355, 359
Mudanjiang, 82–83, 85
Mukden, 82–83, 86, 89
Muraviev, 327, 333–334
Murman Coast, 320, 352, 357–359, 362
Murman Scientific Fisheries Expedition, 354, 362
Musan, 278
Muscovy, 145, 349, 353
  Muscovite state, 347
Muslim, 21, 25–27, 30–35, 38, 41, 44
  minority, 198

N

Nagasaki, 341
Naha, 128, 131
Najin, 82
Nanling, 88
Nanlu pizhang, 41
Nara Women's Higher Normal School (Nara Jokoshi), 70, 74–75, 78, 80–84, 88, 90
Nara, 79
Narodni Dom, 197
Narva, Narvian, 123–125, 142–162
National Ossoliński Institute, 98
National Socialist Germany, 6

nationalism, 5–6, 11, 170, 198–199, 201, 207, 249, 320, 347, 360, 377, 379–380
Nationalist Party of the Republic of China (Kuomintang, KMT), 135, 137
nation-state, 5
NATO, 143, 161, 381
Neidi, 43
Nemec, Gloria, 201
Nemuro, 220, 230, 232–233, 235
Nenets, 355, 361
Nepal, 294
New York, 209, 333
Ni, Zan, 177
Nicholas II, 365
Nicolaus Copernicus University in Toruń, 103
Nicoloievsk, 327
Niigata, 77
Niit, Heldur, 254
Nikiforova, Elena, 160
Nikolaevna, Olga, 361
Nikolayevsk, 329
Ningxia, 41
Nishida, Yoshiro, 78
Niuzhuang, 268
Nizhnii Novgorod, 362
Nordenskiöld, A. E., 364
Norfolk, Virginia, 332
North American Free Trade Agreement, 11
North Herald, 355
North Manchuria Railway, 77
North Pole, 364
Northern Sea Route, x, 320, 364–365
Norway, Norwegian, 319, 321, 348, 351, 356–360, 362
Novaia Zemlia/Novaya Zemlya, 350, 352, 358–359, 361–362
Novgorod(ians), 144–145, 152, 349, 352
  Republic of, 349
Novoe Vremia, 364

O

October Revolution, 148
Odanaka, Naoki, xiii
Ōhama, Motoko, 135–36
  Shin'ei, 136

Õhtuleht, 253
Okamoto, Kansuke, 235–236
Okhotsk (Sea), 326, 328, 332, 336, 339
Okinawa, 128–137
   Province, 124
   Prefecture, 127–130, 132–133
Olesk, Sirje, 247
Olonets, 249–250
Onon River, 341
Opium War, 23, 322, 341
orientalism, xiii
orientalizing, 29, 64
Orochen (people), 178, 181
Orthodox Church, 220, 222, 231–234
Osaka Shôsen (Osaka Merchant Ship Company), 130–131
Osaka, 79, 83, 130
Osaka, Kintaro, 83
OSCE (CSCE), 155
Oshima, 130
Oslo, 356
Osman, 35
Osterhammel, Jürgen, 50
Otgonjargal O., 300
Ottoman, 22, 25–26, 28, 55–58, 61, 63–64
   Empire, xiii, 25, 28, 56, 63–64, 327
   Porte, 22, 57–58
Outer Hingan Range, 327
Ozhivlenie (Revitalization), 348, 351, 354–259, 363–264

P

Paasi, Anssi, 2–3
Paasikivi, Juho Kusti, 251
Pacific, 123, 134, 218–219, 320, 326–331, 333–334, 338, 340–342, 364
Padua, 209
Pakistan, 197
Pamirs, 293
Pannonia (n Region), 197
Paramushir Island, 221, 228–229, 231
Paris Peace Treaty, 328
Pashalik, 56
Päss, Elmar, 253
Pasvik river, 359
Patriotic Youth Labour Corps for the Development of Asia, 81

Peace of Westphalia *also* Westphalia Accord, 7, 379
Pechenga Monastery, 358
Pechora region, 352, 355
Peking. *See* Beijing
periphery, 21–22, 28, 32, 44, 50, 52–53, 57, 59, 64, 123–124, 184, 331, 348–349, 351–352, 354–356, 358, 360–362, 377–378
Permanent Polar Commission, 365
Permikin, 329, 339
Perry, Matthew Calbraith, 340
Peschurof, M. M., 329, 339
Peter the Great, 145, 160–161, 353
Petrograd, 148, 355
Petropavlovsk, 221, 327, 329
Petseri, 149
Pfoser, Alena, 162
Philippines, 132
Phnom Penh, 300
Piedmont, 197, 209
Piemonte, 207
Pierce, Franklin, 333
Podgórze, 58
Pola *now* Pula, 199, 201–202, 208, 210
Poland, Polish, xi, xiv, 12–13, 24 30, 59, 69–71, 95–108, 111–113, 116–118, 146, 303
   Poland-Lithuania, 24, 63
   Polesie, 112
   Polish-Lithuanian Commonwealth/ Empire, 25, 58, 96
Politbüro, 299–300, 304
Pomerania, 98
Pomors, 320, 354, 358, 361
Porciani, Ilaria, 13
Port Arthur (Lüshun), 82–83, 87–88, 285, 320
Port Newchuang, 341
Port Ross, 330
Porta Palazzo, 207
Portugal, 381
postcolonial, 7
Prato, Katharina, 208
Pratt, Mary, 74
Prussia(n), 12, 24, 58–59, 96, 331
   Eastern, 12
P'yŏng'an province, 270, 275–276
Pskov, 152, 161

Pusan, 77, 82–83
Putyatin, Yefim, 329, 335, 341
Pyeongyang, 83
Pyŏktong county, 276

Q

Qidaogou, 277
Qing Imperial Album of Tributaries (Huang Qing zhigong tu), 180–181, 183
Qing. *See* China
Qinghai, 172

R

Rachi, Chikara, xii
Radchenko, Sergey, 283
Ragchaa Tumenbayariin, 298
Ravenstein, E. G., 339
Red Army, 97, 148
Red Guard, 289, 291–92
reform(s), 60–61, 146, 155, 158, 169, 273, 308, 319–320, 363–364
religion, religious, xi, 3–4, 7–8, 11, 24, 27–28, 33, 52, 57, 61, 64–65, 87, 96, 105, 118, 173, 176, 182, 200, 220, 222, 232, 236, 349, 380
Retschow, 203
Reval (Tallinn), 145–146
Risiera di San Sabba, 197, 208, 210
river (Black Water, Weak Water, Black Heng River, Black Dragon River, Huntong River), 321–323, 325–342
(River) Valley, 326, 329, 335, 337–338
Romania(n), 28, 56, 205
Romanov, 12, 352, 355
Roosevelt, Franklin D., 380
Rosenberg, Alfred, 6
Rosenthal, Jean-Laurent, 32–33
Rostov-Suzdal principality, 349
Rovigno municipal museum, 200
Royal Geographical Society, RGS, 336, 338–339
Rusanov, Vladimir, 346
Russia(n), xiii, xiv, 6, 8, 12–13, 22, 24–25, 28, 32, 38, 42–44, 57–58, 88, 96, 108, 123–125, 142–162, 182, 184, 199, 217, 220–223, 229–230, 232–233, 235, 242–250, 252–255, 264, 271, 284, 286–287, 308, 319–323, 325–342, 347–365

(Far) North, 319–321, 347–365
Bolshevik/Soviet Russia, 148–153, 160, 217, 220, 242–243, 246, 248, 250, 252, 255, 287
Far East, 218, 319–323, 332–333, 335, 340, 358, 379
Federation, 143–144, 158–159, 161, 242
Imperial, xiii, 57–58, 63, 124–125, 146–147, 217, 243, 245, 264, 320–323, 327, 347, 353, 356–357, 361
Revolution, 148, 217, 245–246, 254
Russian America, 219
Russian Soviet Federative Socialist Republic (RSFSR), 143, 154
Sino-Russian, 179, 326–327
Tsarist, 22, 363
White Army, 148
Russia(n) American Company/Russo-American Company, 219
Russkii Mir/Russian World, 161
Russkii vestnik, 351
Russo-Japanese War, 87–89, 234
Ruthenians, 24, 59. *See also* Ukrainians
Ryûkyû (Kingdom), 124, 128–130, 132, 134, 136–137, 332, 381

S

Saghalin, 336. *See also* Sakhalin
Saguchi, Tōru, 35
Sahara, 350
Said, Edward, xiii
Saint Petersburg, 145–146, 331, 333, 347, 349–350, 352–353, 359
Saitō, Tōkichi, 221
Sakhalin (Island), 80, 326, 328, 331, 336, 341–342
Sakiyama, Yôei, 128
Sakurai, Senjirō, 233
San Francisco, 221, 330
San Marino, 11
San Sebastian, 338
Sangt'o garrison, 270
Sardinia, 197
 Kingdom, 327
Sasamori, Gisuke, 128
Sassen, Saskia, 118
Satsuma Domain, 124
Sawabe, Takuma, 232, 234

Saxony, 60
Saynshand, 292
Sea of Japan, 83, 320, 336, 338, 341
Sebastopol, 335–336
Second World War, xi, 8–9, 12, 73, 91, 95, 97, 117, 124, 138, 143, 151, 154, 160, 170, 197–198, 220, 243, 250–251, 253–255, 380–381
Sedov, Georgii, 364
Seikyō Shinpō, 232
Seitaro, Okajima, 78
Semipalatinsk, 42
Senkaku Islands, 127
Seoul, 79, 82–83, 275–276
Serbia(n), 26–27, 56, 198, 205
Serfdom, Serfs, 24, 27–28, 56, 58, 146, 351
Severnaya Zemlia, 365
Severtsev-Polilov, Georgii, 358
Shaanxi, 42–43
Shache County, 43. *See also* Yarkand
Shagdarsüren Puntsagiin, 291
Shandong province, 175, 182, 272, 276
Shanghai, 175, 332, 338
Shanshan, 43
Shanxi, 42
Shelikhov, 330
   Shelikhov North Company, 330
Shenkursk, 350
Shengjing, 267, 270–74, 278, 335
   Willow Palisade (Shengjing dongbianwai), 267, 270, 273, 275
Sherwell, W. S., 338
Shikotan Island, 218, 220–226, 228–335
Shilka River, 325
Shimazu Domain, 124, 128
Shimonoseki, 82–83
Shinto, 80, 87, 89
Shuishiying meeting room, 88
Shule County (Yengišähär District), 43
Shumushu Island, 220, 226, 231
Siberia, 38, 42–43, 98, 143, 150, 160, 183, 220, 244, 319–320, 322, 326, 328–329, 332–334, 336–337, 342, 349, 351–352, 355, 362
Sichuan, 42, 175
Sidensner, Alexander, 352, 358
Sidorov, Mikhail, 351–352
Silesia, 54, 59–60, 98, 111, 117

Silk Road, 21
Sillamäe, 154
Singapore, 332
Sino-Japanese War, 130
   Second, 70, 74, 76, 78–79, 82, 134
Sino-Mongolian, 263, 283–284, 286–290, 293–295, 303, 306–309
Sinophobia, 310
Sino-Soviet, 284–285, 288, 293–296, 302–304, 306–309
Sino-Vietnamese War, 301–302
Siras, Amayak, 254
Skocpol, Theda, 378
slav(s), slavic, 197, 200, 245, 247, 253, 349, 351
Slavic–Eurasian Research Center, SRC, x, xiv
Slavonia, 56, 205
Slavophile, 354
Slovenia, 169, 206
Smith, David, 162
Society for the Advancement of Trade and Industry, 351
Sofia, 303
Sogang University, xi–xii
Solovetskii Monastery, 349
Solovyov, L.N., 290–291
Song, Xiaolian, 181–182, 190
Songyun, 41, 43
Sortavala, 248, 250
Sosnovskii, Ivan, 360
South America, 11
Soviet (Union), 12, 70, 73, 77, 84, 92, 95, 97, 99–100, 102–103, 123–125, 143–144, 149–156, 158, 160–162, 217–218, 220, 234, 242–243, 245–246, 248–255, 284–285, 287–304, 306–310
   Bloc, 251, 294, 297, 299–300, 304–306, 309
Soviet–Finnish War (Winter War), 217
Soviet–Vietnamese treaty, 299
Spain, Spanish, 54, 381
Stalin, Josif, 250–252, 255
Stanisławów, 97
State Duma, 359–360, 364
   Commission on Fisheries, 360
State Ethnic Affairs Commission (SEAC), 171, 189

status of forces (SOFA), 380
Stefan Batory University in Vilnius, 99, 103
Steppe region, 22, 27, 182, 337, 362
Sterling, James, 328, 341
Spitsbergen (Svalbard), 359, 364
Stolypin, Peter, 360
Stragorodsky, Sergius, 233
Strozev, Kepurian, 223
Su, 175, 189. *See also* cuisine systems
Su, Shi, 177, 190
Suematsu, Kenchō, 230
Sufi, 27, 33
Sugari River, 326
Suifen River, 271
Sükhbaatar province, 298
Sushen people, 176, 198
Sweden, Swedish, 145–146, 159–160, 243–244, 246–248, 250, 326, 357, 364
  Swedish Empire, 124
Switzerland, 22, 60

T

Taimyr Peninsula, 365
Tainan, 136
Taipei, 130, 133–134, 136–137, 175
Taiping Rebellion, 322
Taiwan(ese), 13, 77–80, 123–125, 127–138, 175, 189, 303
Takemoto, Seigi, 133
Taketomi Island, 133
Tallinn, 145–146, 149, 155–156, 245, 253
Tang, Qiu, 285
Tarim Basin, 26, 31
Tarkka, Lotte, 242
Tarnopol, 97
Tartar Strait, 326, 328
Tartu Peace Treaty, 149, 151
Tartu University, 246, 253
Tashkent, 303, 309
Thessaloniki, 198
Thirty Years War, 7
Tianjin, 81
Tibet, Tibetan(s), 22, 175, 177, 189
Tilley, Henry Arthur, 338
Tilly, Charles, 378

Tito, Josip Broz, 197, 210, 288
Titov, Gherman, 288
Tohoku University, xiii
Tokugawa Shogunate, 124, 231
Tokumori Ine, 133
Tokunoshima, 135
Tokyo Jokoshi, 75, 80, 83–84, 88. *See also* Tokyo Women's Higher Normal School
Tokyo Women's Higher Normal School, 75
Tokyo, xiv, 70, 74–75, 79–80, 131–133, 225, 229–233, 236, 381
Tonghua, 278
Tongzhi, 272
Tonoshiro, Yoshi, 133–134
Torii, Gonnosuke, 231
Torii, Ryūzō, 225–228
Toruń, 99, 103
Transleithania, 57
Trans-Siberian Railroad (Railway), 320
Transylvania(n), 28, 54, 56
Treaty of Aigun, 326, 329
Treaty of Nerchinsk, 325, 327
Treaty of Peking, 329
Trepov, Alexander, 356
Treviso, 209
Trieste, 59, 197, 203, 208
Tromsø, 359
Tronson, J. M., 336, 341
Tsedenbal Yumjaagiin, 283, 286, 288, 289, 292, 294, 297, 299, 300, 302, 303, 306–310
Tsuruga, 77, 83
Tujidong, 277–279
Tumen River, 86, 267–268, 274, 329
tundra, 350, 355
Tunggiya River, 276
Tungus, 181
Turfan, 41, 43
Turin, 206–207
Turkestan–Siberia Railway, 42
Turkey, Turkish, 198, 326–327, 381
  Strait, 327
Tuscany, 197, 209
Tyrol, 54, 58, 61–62
  Tyrol-Vorarlberg, 60

U

Ukraine, Ukrainians, 96–100, 102, 106, 108, 118
  Ukrainian SSR, 98
Ukrainian Insurgent Army, 98
Ulaanbaatar, 285–310
Uliastai, 284
Ungern-Sternberg, Baron Roman, 284
Unggi-Najin, 77. *See also* Unna Line
Union of Finnishness (*Suomalaisuuden liitto*), 246
United Council of Labour Collectives (OSTK), 153
United Kingdom (UK), 5, 6. *See also* Britain
United States (of America) (USA), 59, 124, 128, 135, 136, 152, 197, 208, 209, 210, 330, 380
University of Tartu Narva College, 155
University of Washington in Seattle, 365
Unna Line, 77
Ural, 333
Uribitoaino (Lavrenti Strozev), 232
Urquhart, Craig, 311
Urup, 328
US Central Intelligence Agency (CIA), 305, 306
USSR, 97–102, 125, 143, 150, 152, 153, 285, 286, 289, 292, 296, 297, 301–303, 305, 309. *See also* Soviet (Union)
Ussuri River, 293, 326, 329
Ussurisk, 330
Uzala, Dersu, 184, 190

V

Vaarandi, Anton, 253
Vana Narva (Old Narva), 160, 161. *See also* Narva
Vanalinna Riigikool (Old Town State School), 159, 161
Vatican State, 11
Venice, Venetia(n), 54, 57, 199, 206, 208
Versailles Peace Treaty, 12
Viatka province, 350, 351
Vienna, 56, 59, 60, 65
Vientiane, 300
Vietnam, Vietnamese, 297–302
  North, 287, 291, 297

Vil'kitskii, Boris, 364
Vilnius, 97–99, 103, 104, 108–109
Violence, 5, 73, 74, 89, 156, 197, 198, 276, 277, 381
Vladimir, 352
  Gordlevsky, 245
  Klavdievich Arsen'ev, 184, 190
  Rusanov, 364
Vladivostok, 320
Vojna krajina, 56, 57. *See also* Military Border Zone
Volga, 244, 337, 360
Vologda region, 244, 337, 360
Volunteer Pioneer Youth Army (of Manchuria and Mongolia), 84
Volyn Massacre, 97–98
Voronin, E. F., 301
Vseviov, David, 152
Vyborg/Viipuri, 250

W

The West, x, xii–xiv, 112, 143, 153, 254, 342, 374–375, 378. *See also* Europe
Wallerstein, Immanuel, 377
Wang, Wangtao, 285
Wang, Zhiyun, 292
Wang, Zhonghua, 292
War of Monuments, 156, 159–160
War, xi, 2, 4, 7, 9, 12, 70, 74, 76, 79, 82, 88, 91, 95, 124, 130, 134, 145–146, 148, 150, 154, 160, 170, 197, 208, 217, 246, 250–251, 253–255, 299, 301–302, 319, 321, 326–328, 331–332, 339, 347, 350, 380–381
Warsaw Pact, 289
Warsaw, xi, 110, 118, 333
Wartime labour force, 76, 82
Washington, 303, 365
Weiss-Wendt, Anton, 147
Wen, 35–36, 38–40
Wensu Prefecture, 43. *See also* Aqsu
Westphalia Accord, 379. *See also* Peace of Westphalia
Whaley, Lindsay J., 185
Whittingham, Bernard, 335–336
Wilkinson, Endymion, 177
Wilno, 109. *See also* Vilnius
Winter War, 217, 250
Winter, Jay, 113

Witte, Sergei, 320, 352, 354, 356
Wong, Roy Bin, 32, 44
World Exposition, 352, 355
World Trade Organization
Wrangle, Ferdinand Von, 332
Wrocław, 98, 106
Wu, Dacheng, 322
Wu, Xu, 179, 190

X
Xianfeng, 271
Xiang, 175, 189. *See also* cuisine systems
Xie, Fuzhi, 292
Xiluoguhe, 325
Xinjiang, 21–35, 37–45
   Southern, 21, 26, 28–29, 33–34, 38, 40–41
Xinjiang tuzhi, 41
Xīnjīng, 74
Xishang, 41
Xu Weny, 294
Xu, Wei, 177, 190

Y
Yaeyama Islands, 124–125, 127–134, 136
   Yaeyama Archipelago, 127, 131
   Yaeyama-gun, 127
Yalu River Area, 264, 270, 277
Yäl-yimish, 42
Yamabishi Shôkai (Yamabishi Company), 130, 131
Yamamoto, Susumu, 13, 124, 217–219, 236, 268
Yamamuro, Shin'ichi, 73, 91
Yanchi, 35
Yangtze River, 338, 340
Yanqi District, 43
Yarkand, 33, 34, 35, 38–43

Yasukuni Jinja Shrine, 88
Yecheng (Qaġiliq), 43
Yellow Sea, 332, 349
Yeltsin, Boris, 153, 154, 161
Yengisar, Yangi Hissar, 33, 35
Yining, 40
Yokoyama, Kendō, 229, 230, 231
Yonaguni Island, 128, 131, 137
Yondon Daramyn, 304, 306
Yuan Dynasty, 325
Yuan, Mei, 177, 190
Yudenich, Nikolai, 148, 149
Yue, 175, 189. *See also* cuisine systems
Yugoslavia, 197, 198, 206, 210
Yunnan province, 175, 185, 189

Z
Zantav L., 305, 306
Zelco, Giuliana, 205, 208
Zelnik, Reginald E., 147
Zemstvo, 363, 364
Zeng, Wangqing, 285
Zentsuuji, 88
Zeya River, 326
Zhang, Canming, 291
Zhang, Delin, 292
Zhang, Mu, 322
Zhe, 175, 189. *See also* cuisine systems
Zhejiang, 42, 175, 189
Zhili, 42, 272
Zhilinskii, Aleksei, 363
Zhirmunsky, Viktor, 253
Zhongnanhai, 309
Zhou, Enlai, 288, 289, 294, 308
Zhuang, 171, 185, 189
Zunghar Mongol people, 22, 27
Zuo, Guiyi, 292

www.ingramcontent.com/pod-product-compliance
Lightning Source LLC
Chambersburg PA
CBHW072043110526
44590CB00018B/3018